Cavalcade
of the
American
Novel

ABRAHAM LINCOLN: HIS LIFE, WORK, AND CHARACTER (1947)

CAVALCADE OF THE AMERICAN NOVEL (1952)

CAVALCADE OF THE ENGLISH NOVEL (1943)

THE CHIMES, BY CHARLES DICKENS (INTRODUCTION BY E.W.) (1931)

THE COLLECTED TALES OF WALTER DE LA MARE (1950)

THE COLLEGE SURVEY OF ENGLISH LITERATURE (WITH OTHERS) (1942)

THE FIRESIDE BOOK OF CHRISTMAS STORIES (1945)

THE FIRESIDE BOOK OF GHOST STORIES (1947)

THE FIRESIDE BOOK OF ROMANCE (1948)

A FIRESIDE BOOK OF YULETIDE TALES (1948)

GERALDINE FARRAR, AN AUTHORIZED RECORD OF HER CAREER (1929)

A GUIDE TO BERNARD SHAW (1929)

AN INTRODUCTION TO DICKENS (1952)

JENNY LIND (1931)

JOAN OF ARC, AN ANTHOLOGY OF HISTORY AND LITERATURE (1948)

LIFE ON THE MISSISSIPPI, BY MARK TWAIN (INTRODUCTION BY E.W.) (1944)

LILLIAN GISH, AN INTERPRETATION (1927)

THE MAN CHARLES DICKENS, A VICTORIAN PORTRAIT (1929)

MARK TWAIN, THE MAN AND HIS WORK (1935)

MURDER BY GASLIGHT (1949)

SIX NOVELS OF THE SUPERNATURAL (1944)

THE STORY OF JESUS IN THE WORLD'S LITERATURE (1946)

A TALE OF TWO CITIES, BY CHARLES DICKENS (INTRODUCTION BY E.W.) (1950)

UTOPIA AMERICANA (1929)

VALUES IN LITERATURE (1928)

WHEN I WAS A CHILD (1946)

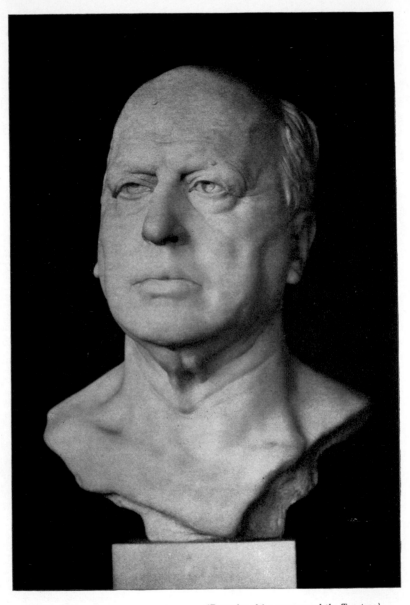

HENRY JAMES

From the Portrait Bust by Francis Derwent Wood, R.A. (1923)
in the Boston Public Library

EDWARD WAGENKNECHT

Cavalcade of the American Novel

FROM THE BIRTH OF THE NATION TO THE MIDDLE OF THE TWENTIETH CENTURY

One would think it a matter of mere common sense, that in order to criticise justly you must put yourself for the time being as nearly as possible at the author's point of sight; form a sympathetic estimate of what he is striving to do, and then you can tell how nearly he attains his purpose.

Harriet Beecher Stowe: *My Wife and I*

HOLT, RINEHART AND WINSTON
New York · Chicago · San Francisco
Toronto · London

The "irrecoverable Past"—there is no such thing! I treat my past as an artist should. It is mine and I visit my vineyard when I will. I prune and tend the vineyard. I make wine from the grapes and in one chalice, in deep moments, know my past's essence.

Michael Forth

PREFACE

Cavalcade of the English Novel was published by Henry Holt and Company in the spring of 1943. Though it displeased the adherents of certain isms and ologies, it enjoyed in general a remarkably favorable press. It has also found widespread and continuous use in American colleges and universities ever since its publication. These circumstances have naturally proved gratifying to the author, and I much regret that my preparation and publication of a baker's dozen of anthologies since 1944 has so long delayed the appearance of this promised companion volume. To the many kind persons who have been solicitously inquiring about the book, and above all to my very patient and co-operative publishers, I can only offer my apologies. I hope that my work is better for the extended reading and living that have gone into it.

The aims and ideals of the new book are substantially those of the earlier volume, and it seems unnecessary to repeat here what I wrote nine years ago. Some changes in the intellectual climate have, to be sure, taken place. In 1943 I thought it necessary to explain why I was not writing sociological criticism and why I did not wish to permit the frame to take the place of the picture. It would be less necessary to labor this point today. But as old heresies die, new heresies are born, and now we have critics who reject historical scholarship altogether and assure us that every work of art contains within itself everything that the reader needs to understand it. I have no more sympathy with this point of view than I have with the attitude of mind against which it came into being as an extreme reaction.

There have also, perhaps, been some changes in me. Though I have exercised as much care in evaluating the achievements of the American novelists as ever I brought to the British novelists, I have found myself even more interested in setting them forth upon their own terms. To enter into another man's experience and think his thoughts after him, to describe his work honestly, and to elucidate its "meaning"—in so far as that meaning can be separated from the form in which he has expressed it—this may not be a more important phase of the critic's function than that which is commonly known as entering a judgment, but I have found it rather more exciting. If it could be done with complete success, it might even obviate the necessity of a formal or explicit evaluation altogether. But in this field even relative success is rare.

I hope that I have given the serious reader of American fiction at least some information on nearly all the novelists of the past about whom he is likely to be concerned. Unfortunately, I cannot say as much for contemporary writers. I have not attempted to rival Professor Harry R. Warfel's immensely useful handbook, *American Novelists of Today* (American Book Company, 1951); had I been so foolish, my book would have grown monstrously not only out of all bounds but also out of all proportions. I have tried to make my choice of contemporary novelists as representative as possible, and I have not felt it necessary to include long lists of names and titles I had no space to consider simply to prove to the reader that I had heard of them. But it will not be safe to conclude either that I have not read— or that I do not value—all the writers whom I have excluded.

The rules governing the bibliography are set forth at the beginning of that section of the work. Perhaps I might have produced a more "original" book if I had read nothing except the works of the novelists themselves. But I happen to believe that originality, like virtue, thrives best when people are not too conscious of it. I have tried to keep my mind upon the presentation of an adequate, fair, and comprehensive view of the various writers considered, and to think as little as possible about the figure I might be cutting. This book is a history of the American novel, not the autobiography of Edward Wagenknecht.

The following persons have very kindly given me the benefit of their critical reading of the sections of my book indicated after their names. To all I express my warmest thanks.

Professor John R. Adams, of San Diego State College (Mrs.

Stowe); Professor George W. Arms, of the University of New Mexico (Howells); Mr. Frederic Babcock, editor of the *Chicago Sunday Tribune Magazine of Books* (Dorothy Canfield, Sinclair Lewis); Miss Sarah J. Bloom (Willa Cather); Professor Herbert Ross Brown, of Bowdoin College (Chapter I); Professor John C. Cooke, of the University of Southern California (Hamlin Garland); Mr. Barton W. Currie (Booth Tarkington); Mr. Bernard DeVoto (Mark Twain); Professor Ernest Earnest, of Temple University (S. Weir Mitchell); Professor Robert H. Elias, of Cornell University (Dreiser); Mr. Irving Howe (Sherwood Anderson); Professor Grant C. Knight, of the University of Kentucky (James Lane Allen, Thomas Nelson Page, F. Hopkinson Smith, John Fox, Jr., Elizabeth Madox Roberts); Miss Joan London (Jack London); Professor Robert Morss Lovett (Robert Herrick); the late Professor F. O. Matthiessen (Henry James); Professor Allen Morris, of The Citadel (Simms); Professor T. M. Pearce, of the University of New Mexico (Mary Austin); Professor Arthur Hobson Quinn, of the University of Pennsylvania (Edith Wharton); Professor Robert E. Spiller, of the University of Pennsylvania (Cooper); Mr. Vincent Starrett (Stephen Crane); Professor Randall Stewart, of Brown University (Hawthorne); Professor Howard P. Vincent, of Illinois Institute of Technology (Melville); Professor Franklin Walker, of Mills College (Frank Norris).

Mr. James Branch Cabell, Mr. Robert Nathan, Mr. August Derleth, and Mrs. Elsie Singmaster Lewars have gone over the sections of the book in which their own work is discussed, and the late Mary Johnston read the article upon which my discussion of her books is based. Mr. Cabell has also read what I have written about Ellen Glasgow and Joseph Hergesheimer.

Professor Gerald Warner Brace, my friend and colleague, himself a novelist, has read all the sections of this book not otherwise assigned in the foregoing tabulation.

E. W.

Boston University
November 1, 1951

CONTENTS

NOTE

For a key to the abbreviations employed in footnotes, etc., see the beginning of the bibliographical section in the back of this book, pages 498 and 499.

CHAPTER I

BROCKDEN BROWN AND THE PIONEERS

> . . . my story was fiction founded on truth—the novel style. . . .
> *Alonzo and Melissa*

1. *The First American Novels*

What was the first American novel? The answer depends upon definitions. Edith F. Wyatt once tried to award priority to Gilbert Imlay's *The Emigrants* (1793) by denying the true novelistic character of its predecessors.[1]

Charlotte Lennox used American scenes and characters in *The Life of Harriot Stuart* (1751), but Charlotte Lennox was an American only by the accident of birth; her literary career belonged to England.[2] That somewhat enigmatic book known as *The Female American; or, The Adventures of Unca Eliza Winkfield* seems to have been regarded as the work of an American when it was published in London in 1767, but it did not appear on this side of the water until 1790. Robert Elias has championed[3] the claims of *Adventures of Alonso* (London, 1775), "by a Native of Maryland, some Years resident in Lisbon," probably Thomas Atwood Digges, but this book was neither published in America nor does it concern an American theme. Ann Eliza Bleecker's Indian story, *The History of Maria Kittle,* though written as early as 1781, did not appear in any form for nearly a decade and between covers not until 1793. And though Miss Loshe calls Hilliard d'Auberteuil's *Miss McRae* (1784) "the first novel both written and published in America," its claim is weakened by the fact that it was written in the French language

---

[1] Edith F. Wyatt, "The First American Novel," *AM,* LXLIV (1929), 466-475; cf. p. 864.

[2] See G. H. Maynadier, *The First American Novelist?* (HUP, 1940).

[3] In "The First American Novel," *AL,* XII (1941), 419-434.

by a Frenchman. More recently, Richard Schlatter went clear back to 1715 to resurrect *The History of the Kingdom of Basaruah,* attributed to Joseph Morgan.[4] As an allegory of the "Covenant" form of Calvinistic theology in terms of the chronicle-history of an imaginary kingdom, this work can hardly be denied the name of fiction but it is far indeed from the mood and method of the novel as commonly considered. All in all, there seems no very cogent objection to the current fashion of choosing as the first American novel *The Power of Sympathy* (Boston, 1789), formerly attributed to Sarah Wentworth Morton, now, conjecturally, to William Hill Brown.

It has been said that a man from Mars, attempting to gauge the interests of the American public in the 1940's from listening to their radio programs, would have come away with the impression that their primary concern was murder. Judged by their fiction, the Founding Fathers might appear primarily devoted to incest, seduction, and suicide. "You ask me when, and how I should like to die. Come to me this night! Bring with thee poison! Bring with thee pistols! and when the clock strikes twelve we'll both become immortal!"[5]

It seems odd that a public so fearful of the malign moral influence of novels should have welcomed such provocative themes. But the Puritan objection to fiction seems to have been based less upon its alleged sensuality than on its untruth. Seven out of the first twenty American novels, as Tremaine McDowell counted them,[6] bear upon the title-page the statement that they were founded upon "fact"; in the 1790's this claim was almost as common as the denial of the same, to ward off lawsuits, has become with us. Yet our ancestors may well have been more honest about the matter than we are, at least if we may judge by *The Power of Sympathy* itself, which was

[4] See Schlatter's introduction to his edition of this work (HUP, 1946). "If *Pilgrim's Progress* is to be reckoned one of the early examples of the English novel, then *The History of the Kingdom of Basaruah* may well be called the first American novel."

[5] John Davis, *The Original Letters of Ferdinand and Isabella* (1798).

[6] "Sensibility in the Eighteenth Century American Novel," *SP*, XXIV (1927), 383-402. See also G. H. Orians, "Censure of Fiction in American Romances and Magazines," *PMLA*, LII (1937), 195-214.

more or less suppressed for its use of a contemporary tragedy in the Boston Apthorp family; by the *Charlotte Temple* (London, 1790; Philadelphia, 1794) of Mrs. Susanna Haswell Rowson (1761-1824); and by *The Coquette* (1797) of Mrs. Hannah Walker Foster (1758-1840), a relative by marriage of its tragic heroine. Charlotte's supposed grave in Trinity Churchyard and Elizabeth Whitman's resting-place at Danvers, Massachusetts, have been brooded over by many sentimentalists. The tragedy of the Whitman girl (who became Eliza Wharton in Mrs. Foster's novel), had already been the subject of a long footnote in *The Power of Sympathy,* and if Charlotte was the girl who was buried in Trinity, there may have been a family connection between the two most famous heroines of early American seduction-romance. Attempts have also been made to identify the villain of *The Coquette* with both Pierrepont Edwards and Aaron Burr.

All these "fallen" women were presented from an oppressively "moral" point of view. As Herbert Brown says,

In fiction which was largely devoted to recitals of attempts to violate the body of the heroine, there is practically no evidence to indicate that the heroine was aware that she possessed a body. Although the effects of physical passion were constantly before the readers of these novels, there is no mention of sexual feeling.[7]

Yet it is impossible to believe that the fetid atmosphere was not savored—and enjoyed. *The Power of Sympathy* is a morbid, nasty book; one of Mrs. Rowson's heroines is nearly violated by her father; and certainly Brockden Brown's imagination was not healthy. It was not quite an accident that fiction did not become really respectable in America until it had been purified by the stalwart manliness of Cooper and Scott.

In the epistolary *Power of Sympathy* the threatened incest follows the usual pattern: Harrington's attempt to wed Harriott Fawcett can only be foiled by revealing the secret that she is his bastard half-sister. Harriott dies of the shock, her lover by suicide—previously announced and discussed—with a copy of *The Sorrows of Werther* beside him. There are two other suicides in this short book, but it was Ophelia's (Fanny Apthorp's) in the subplot, after her seduction

[7] *The Sentimental Novel in America, 1789-1860* (DUP, 1940).

by her brother-in-law, that hit contemporary readers with the strongest impact.

The great master of seduction romance, Samuel Richardson—much the most popular English novelist in Revolutionary America—is written all over *The Power of Sympathy,* and there is good reason to believe that the French heroic romances are here too.[8] Here, too, is Sterne, with all his sensibility but without either his intelligence or his humor.

Charlotte Temple has been the longest-lived of all American[9] novels—R. W. G. Vail has recorded more than 160 editions—the novel which above all others has achieved what Gamaliel Bradford calls "the vast acceptance of those who are wept over at lone midnight by the shop-girl and the serving-maid." It is a much healthier book than *The Power of Sympathy.* Charlotte does not kill herself, and though she dies following the birth of her child, after her lover has deserted her in New York and the wicked Belcourt has tried to inflict upon her a yet deeper wrong, this is more the result of economic want and bitter remorse than a manifestation of the more frenetic aspects of the romantic agony. Pietist and sentimentalist though she was, Mrs. Rowson was as sure as the author of *Tess of the D'Urbervilles* that no girl should be damned for one sin. She herself had endured poverty and deportation. "During her colorful career," writes Mr. Vail, "she was, in turn, governess to the children of the beautiful Duchess of Devonshire, novelist, poet, actress, dramatist, writer of songs, adapter of other men's plays, essayist, editor, teacher, and philanthropist."[10] Such a woman must have

[8] Cf. Thomas P. Haviland, "Preciosité Crosses the Atlantic," *PMLA,* LIX (1944), 131-141, where the influence of the romances is argued also in relation to Brockden Brown. For the English backgrounds of American fiction during this period, the work of Godwin and others, and the definition of "Gothic," "sensibility," etc., see my *Cavalcade of the English Novel,* Chs. IV, VII-IX. For Gothicism, add O. S. Coad, "The Gothic Element in American Literature," *JEGP,* XXIV (1925), 72-93.

[9] Though published first in England, by a writer of English birth, it is, I think, rightly characterized as an American novel in view of its enormous vogue here.

[10] Some aspects of Mrs. Rowson's experiences are reflected more clearly in her other novels than in *Charlotte Temple.* Cf. *Trials of the Human Heart* (1795) and *Reuben and Rachel* (1798), which begins with Columbus and proceeds through ten generations! Vail calls her play, *Slaves in Algiers* (1794)

known the "world" far better than many of the "moderns" who sneer at her, and she must have known something about eighteenth-century morals at first hand, yet she seems to have taken quite in her stride what would have seemed to most of us the not inconsiderable task of finally persuading the good people of Newton, Massachusetts, that an ex-actress was a suitable moral preceptress of youth. She was no Pharisee, and no weakling either; and the compassion she poured into her cheap little book was not the least potent among its preservatives.

Charlotte Temple is full of appeals to women and to critics, exhorting the former not to forsake the path of virtue yet to judge leniently those who do, and pleading with the latter to accept the novel fairly upon its own terms. "I hope, Sir, your prejudices are now removed in regard to the probability of my story? Oh, they are. Well, then, with your leave I will proceed." For so artless a writer, Mrs. Rowson adopts a surprisingly sophisticated time-order, presenting Charlotte's first meeting with Montravers at the very beginning of the book, out of its natural sequence, for emphasis, as George Eliot gave us Gwendolen Harleth at the gaming-tables at the beginning of *Daniel Deronda*. There is more than a touch of eighteenth-century radicalism in the preliminary story of Charlotte's father, where we read that "superfluous wealth" is guilt and that Temple's sisters have all been "legally prostituted to old, decrepit men."

The Coquette has manifested less survival-value than *Charlotte Temple* but it is vastly superior as literature. (Eliza Wharton's story is one of the subjects of the traveling waxworks showman in Longfellow's *Kavanagh*.) The best that can be said of the villain, Peter Sanford, is that he is a not unskillful pastiche of Lovelace, but the complicated character of the girl—so faulty yet essentially so innocent, and so brave a rebel against the conventions of her day—is an achievement of a different order. Considerable skill is shown, too, in Mrs. Foster's approach to her climax and in the finally forceful and sudden presentation of Eliza's "ruin," after long preparation, as

one of the first to use native themes and characters. But in her posthumous sequel to her great success—*Charlotte's Daughter; or, The Three Orphans* (1828)—everybody behaves so beautifully that the story gets smothered in piety and humanitarianism.

a *fait accompli*. Mrs. Rowson had depended upon the conventional feminine "frailty" to motivate Charlotte Temple's fall. Mrs. Foster's way with the willful, pleasure-loving Eliza is different, and there are suggestions of Arnold Bennett's *Clayhanger* in the way in which the same situation is viewed successively from different points of view. Considering its date and the circumstances of its composition, there is little in *The Coquette* for which lovers of American fiction need to apologize.

2. *Revolutionary Potpourri;* Modern Chivalry

Not all sentimental novels were narratives of domestic life. Miss Loshe, the pioneer authority on early American fiction, divided her material under three heads: The Didactic and the Sentimental; The Gothic and the Revolutionary; and Early Historical Novels and Indian Tales. All three overlapped. Enos Hitchcock's *Memoirs of the Bloomsgrove Family* (1790) is an "educational" novel, embellished—*Sanford and Merton*-wise—with many anecdotes; *The Gamesters* (1805), by Caroline M. Warren, is a seduction-suicide tale, with the emphasis, for once, upon a young *man* who goes to the bad. Aside from the works of Charles Brockden Brown, the books which have weathered the years most successfully would seem to be *Modern Chivalry* (1792-1815), by Hugh Henry Brackenridge; *The Emigrants* (1793), by Gilbert Imlay; *The Algerine Captive* (1797), by Royall Tyler; and *Alonzo and Melissa* (1804, 1811), which was written by Isaac Mitchell and then abridged by Daniel Jackson.

The Gothic element may be seen in Mrs. Sally Wood's vast adventure story, *Julia and the Illuminated Baron* (1800), which placed its scene in Revolutionary France and achieved, in its time, a kind of combination of the horrors of the Politburo and the Ku Klux Klan. Gothicism was burlesqued delightfully by Tabitha Tenney in *Female Quixotism* (1801), which performed a service similar to that rendered by Charlotte Lennox in England when she pitted *The Female Quixote* against an earlier heroic romance. Mrs. Tenney reflects the temper of the great eighteenth-century rationalists, but she lies under the common necessity upon satirists to catch the flavor of that which they oppose.

In *Alonzo and Melissa* the "Unfeeling Father" of the subtitle imprisons his girl, to save her from an impoverished lover, in a Gothic castle on Long Island, which had been built by an ancestor for protection against the Indians! "The out buildings were generally in a ruinous situation. The cemetery was the most perfect, as it was built of hewn stone and marble, and had best withstood the ravages of time." Upon arrival, the heroine "flung herself on the bed in a state little inferior to distraction." Throughout the night she suffered from terrifying sights and sounds, all of which are afterwards explained, in Mrs. Radcliffe's manner, as having been produced by a band of smugglers. To restore her at the end to her repentant parent, after the false report of her death, the author used a device similar to Shakespeare's in *Much Ado About Nothing*. For two generations, *Alonzo and Melissa* was read with rapture throughout America; to thousands of story-starved human beings it meant passion, sensibility, even fiction itself. Mark Twain mentions it in *Life on the Mississippi*. Even today, despite all its absurdities, it retains a quaint and innocent charm.[11]

Considering how brief American history had been, the novelists made good use of it. *The Female American* goes back to colonial Virginia, Mrs. Rowson's *Reuben and Rachel* to Columbus. Jeremy Belknap's *The Foresters* (1792) allegorizes the whole English adventure in the new world. The French and Indian War was used in *Maria Kittle* and the Revolution over and over again: in *Amelia; or, The Faithless Baron* (1798); in *Constantius and Pulchera* (1795); in *The Female Review* (1797). Washington's namesake, hero of *The Champions of Freedom* (1812), by Samuel Woodworth, author of the song *The Old Oaken Bucket,* fights in the War of 1812. Some of these "historical novelists" anticipated Brown and Cooper by discovering the American Indian as an effective romantic property. *The First Settlers of Virginia* (1802), by John Davis, is called the first full-fledged Indian story.

More intelligence went into *The Algerine Captives* and *The*

---

[11] Edmund Pearson's amusing essay in *Queer Books* (D, 1928) is not quite fair to *Alonzo and Melissa:* few novels can survive a century without becoming capable of providing amusement by an anthology-like collection of all their most ridiculous passages.

Emigrants. Royall Tyler's novel is not as good as his play, *The Contrast,* but, though it tends to turn into a travel-book in its second half, it never ceases to be readable. The change occurs after the hero, who has unwillingly become involved in the African slave trade, is himself captured by the Barbary pirates (against whose depredations the book directs its propaganda). The blacks whom his skill as ship's surgeon has succored ask God why He put a good black soul into a white body. The book is crammed with social, political, and educational satire of various kinds. Tyler attacks the study of Greek and laments having found in the Harvard museum "the curiosities of all countries but our own." He opposes dueling and glorifies the New England conscience.

The Emigrants pictures an English family in the New World and contrasts two civilizations to America's advantage. It should be accounted unto Gilbert Imlay for righteousness that he realized that America did not stop short at the Alleghenies. "It is impossible for any country to appear to advantage after you have seen the Illinois.' His novel involves an elaborate consideration of domestic problems and argues both for divorce and against it. Imlay himself was not to wait for marriage in his famous "affair" with Mary Wollstonecraft; neither did he consider himself bound without it.

But except for the work of Brockden Brown, the most important early American novel was Brackenridge's *Modern Chivalry.* In many ways it is better than Brown, the work of a distinguished patriot and a distinguished mind. Born in Scotland in 1748 but reared in frontier Pennsylvania, a Princeton classmate of Freneau and James Madison, Brackenridge was teacher, lawyer, and jurist, a Federalist with sympathy for the oppressed, and a Republican who never imagined that a kind heart gains by being combined with a soft head. He served as chaplain in Washington's army, and he wrote heroic dramas on Revolutionary themes. Steeped in the classics, in *Don Quixote,* Rabelais, Montaigne, and the eighteenth-century Augustans, he brought Roman dignity to his backwoods residence, where he lived a long life of distinguished public service, and where he died, at Carlisle, in 1816.

The realism and common sense of *Modern Chivalry* would have delighted the Augustans, though they would not have relished its sprawling form. The first part was published in 1792, but Brackenridge went on adding to it until by 1815 more than 800 pages had been piled up. It is the closest American approach to the picaresque novels of Europe, though it is somewhat overweighted by reflective passages, not all of which are so amusing as the one in which Brackenridge accounts for the races of mankind by assuming that "Adam was a tall, straight-limbed, red-haired man, with a fair complexion . . . and that Eve was a negro woman." The principal characters are Captain Farrago and his stupid, crafty, rascally servant, Teague O'Regan. Some of the scrapes into which O'Regan tumbles involve only personal issues but the most interesting illuminate the faults of the body politic. As politician, preacher, philosopher, actor, and fake Indian treaty maker, he is much in demand, his fellow-countrymen having already developed a fondness for scamps and demagogues which the years have done little to cure. *Modern Chivalry* gives a vivid picture of backwoods America and the eighteenth-century frontier, and nearly every American institution gets a thorough going-over.

3. *The Author of* Wieland

Criticism has dealt somewhat tenderly with Charles Brockden Brown. Ever since Whittier's extravagant praise[12] of the murder scene in *Wieland,* he has been lauded for his intensity, his ability to explore abnormal states of consciousness, and his gift for breathless episode. His lack of unity and his complete failure to master the architectonics of fiction, his interpolated narratives within interpolated narratives (making his novels difficult to follow and impossible to remember), his ineptitude in dialogue, his frantic unmotivated villainies, and his penchant for creating characters who thrust themselves deliberately into adventures which no sane person would embark upon—these things, though admitted, are generally viewed with a charitable eye. He has been claimed as an influence upon both Cooper and Poe; Hawthorne gave him a place in his Hall of Fantasy. He may have influenced Mrs. Shelley's *Frankenstein* and

[12] In his essay "Fanaticism," in Volume IX of his collected *Writings*.

The Last Man.[13] Keats admired him, and Scott, who felt his power without admiring him, borrowed from him the names of two characters in *Guy Mannering.*[14]

Brown was born, of Quaker parentage, in Philadelphia, on January 17, 1771. He had a bookish, sickly boyhood, studied law half-heartedly, and planned grandiose classifications of human knowledge and vast epics on American themes. A friend of Elihu Hubbard Smith, the Connecticut wit, and of William Dunlap, the dramatist, Brown was predisposed toward liberal and radical ideas not only by his Quaker background but by his reading in such varied writers as the English revolutionaries, the French encyclopaedists, and the German romanticists.[15] He published *Wieland* in 1798, *Ormond, Edgar Huntly,* and the first part of *Arthur Mervyn* in 1799. Part II of *Arthur Mervyn* appeared in 1800 and both *Jane Talbot* and *Clara Howard* in 1801. For his livelihood he relied upon business and journalism; he was perhaps the first American professional book-reviewer. In later years he inclined increasingly toward conservative views. He died of tuberculosis on February 22, 1810.

The most obvious inspiration of Brown's fiction is the work of William Godwin, especially *Caleb Williams.* Godwin influenced the consuming curiosity of his characters, his revolt against institutions, his theme of pursuer and pursued, his master-and-man relationships, his use of the villain as patron, and his appetite for independent thinkers as protagonists. Brown did not think of himself, as posterity has often thought of him, as a "Gothic" novelist. Instead, he was in conscious revolt against "puerile superstition and exploded manners, Gothic castles and chimeras," but, except in his last two tame and uncharacteristic novels, where he did seek to substitute "moral causes and daily incidents" of domestic life "in place of the prodigious or the singular," it does not seem to have occurred to him that anything short of sensation could be relied upon to supply

---

[13] Cf. T. W. Higginson in *Carlyle's Laugh and Other Surprises* (HM, 1909); F. C. Prescott, " 'Wieland' and 'Frankenstein,' " *AL,* II (1930), 172-173.

[14] Tremaine McDowell, "Scott on Cooper and Brockden Brown," *MLN,* XLV (1930), 18-20.

[15] On the last-named, see Harry R. Warfel, "CBB's German Sources," *MLQ,* I (1940), 357-365. Warfel argues specifically the influence upon *Wieland* of Tschink's *The Victim of Magical Delusion.*

the "subtilities of reasoning" or the illustrations of "the moral constitution of man" which fiction must embody. For that he needed
"audacious" characters, governed by "powerful motives," and an
action forming a "contexture of facts capable of suspending the
faculties of every soul in curiosity."[16] So he turned to ventriloquism,
insanity, sleep-walking, pestilence, and spontaneous combustion, and
—with sounder instinct—to struggles against Indians and wild beasts
in the American wilderness. He wanted to "excite and baffle curiosity, without shocking belief." Therefore, as Oral Coad has remarked, he went Mrs. Radcliffe one better and explained his wonders
not only naturally but scientifically! In this aspect, he might be called
the ancestor of many purveyors of "science-fiction" in our own day.

The ventriloquist is in *Wieland;* the sleep walker, or, rather,
walkers, are in *Edgar Huntly.* Brown never hesitates to repeat or to
double an effect. He has two panthers also in the wilderness portion
of this book, though he dismisses the second almost before it has been
introduced. The ventriloquist's motives are vaguely and unsatisfac-
torily defined: though his tricks contribute to the mad hero's notion
that God wishes him to make a holocaust of his family, he is not
represented as essentially evil, or, if he is, curiosity is his "only crime."
Welbeck, the financial manipulator of *Arthur Mervyn,* is more
commonplace and therefore more credible; more credible, too, in
some of his aspects, is Ormond of the Illuminati, but he does not
hang together as a consistent character, and the evil past attributed
to him becomes comical at times. Ormond aspires "to nothing more
ardently than to hold the reins of opinion—to exercise absolute power
over the conduct of others"; he "combines the functions of poet and
actor, and his dramas were not fictitious but real"; like Iago, he
enjoys manipulating human lives. Wieland is a more primitive kind
of figure; the modern reader's difficulty here is that it was already
much too late in the day to be able to sympathize with him in his
exaltation, after having made his sacrifice, even though that exaltation is followed by bitter, suicidal remorse, once the truth has been

[16] For a fine study of Brown's literary theory, see Ernest Marchand, "The
Literary Opinions of CBB," *SP,* XXXI (1934), 541-566. There is a very biased
account of Brown's criticism in Bernard Smith, *Forces in American Criticism*
(HB, 1939), pp. 14 ff.

made known.[17] Such characters may be presented sympathetically, perhaps, in ancient literature, composed while child-sacrifice is still held within living memory; in modern times, they belong in the alienist's laboratory.

Nor is this an isolated instance in Brown's pages. In *Edgar Huntly* we are asked to think Clithero's thoughts after him when he attempts to kill his benefactress, Mrs. Lorimer, in order to save her from the bitter grief of learning that her worthless brother has been slain! Wieland's sister, a high-minded Richardsonian heroine, contemplates both murder and suicide; and Constantia Dudley, who was nearly Shelley's favorite heroine,[18] does at last slay Ormond, to save herself from his lustful advances.

Brown's methods of narration, too, are clumsy and unnecessarily involved. Constantia "enjoyed one distant friend, with whom she maintained an uninterrupted correspondence. . . . That friend is the writer of these memoirs." But the friend never develops a characteristic point of view to enrich the narrative, nor does the reader remember that she is the teller of the tale. For all practical purposes, an omniscient author would do quite as good a job.

Yet, with all Brown's shortcomings, American fiction was lucky to have had so richly endowed a writer appear so early. Brown had few models to go by; he was a sick man, and he died young. Whether, under more favorable conditions, he might have developed the sanity of outlook indispensable to a great writer, it would be difficult to say; that he would have achieved a greater technical competence seems unquestionable. What he had nobody could have taught him. His fictions were the brilliant, imperfect productions of a very brief period of his life; at one time he is said to have worked on five stories simultaneously. When life brought him first rate materials, as in the yellow-fever epidemics of 1793 and 1798, he used them with great power, and there is something to be said for his

---

[17] For the real life basis of the story, see Carl Van Doren, "Early American Realism," *Nation*, XCIX (1914), 577-578; James C. Hendrickson, "A Note on 'Wieland,'" *AL*, VIII (1936-1937), 305-306.

[18] Cf. M. T. Solve, "Shelley and the Novels of B," *Fred Newton Scott Anniversary Papers* (UCP, 1929); E. Sickels, "Shelley and CBB," *PMLA*, XLV (1930), 172-173.

Indians.[19] Such experiments as the historical reconstruction of "Thessalonica" or the description of the imaginary kingdom in *Sketches of a History of Carsol* show how fertile his mind was.

With all his unhealthiness, moreover, Brown was capable of nobility of thought and utterance. Having so much more fiction to choose from, the modern reader may not wish to go along with Shelley's high praise of Constantia, yet Shelley is not absurd. Constantia's lack of rancor toward Craig, though he has plunged both her father and herself into blackest poverty, shows Brown's Quaker background at its best, and this high-mindedness can be paralleled elsewhere in his work. "To feel extraordinary indignation at vice," says Arthur Mervyn, "is unjustifiable. To regard the wicked with no emotion but pity, to be active in reclaiming them, in controlling their malevolence, and preventing or repairing the ills which they produce, is the only province of duty."

[19] Cf. Mabel Morris, "CBB and the American Indian," *AL*, XVIII 1946-1947), 244-247.

CHAPTER II

THE NOVEL ESTABLISHED:
THE AGE OF COOPER AND SIMMS

Is it not true, sir, that the romance is the prose epic of modern society, and that we now look to its pages for the most graphic portraitures of men, manners, and events?

REVEREND SAMUEL OSGOOD: *Memorial to Cooper*, 1852

1. *"Whose Name Is with His Country's Woven"*

With Fenimore Cooper the American novel became the novel of the world. Like Scott and Byron, Cooper was as widely read and as influential abroad as he ever was in his own country. He was translated into many languages; Europeans often learned all they knew of America from him. Benjamin West thought of a Mohawk brave when he first beheld the Apollo Belvedere, and Longfellow was reminded of Cooper's Indians by a performance of Corneille in Paris. Schubert enjoyed his novels upon his deathbed, and at home his enemy Thurlow Weed sat up all night to read *The Pathfinder*. Dumas and Balzac were importantly indebted to Cooper, and Thackeray placed Leatherstocking ahead of all Scott's creations. There is even a story by Chekhov in which two Russian boys address each other as "Montezuma Hawkeye" and "my Paleface Brother."

It would be hard to imagine a literary career which developed more curiously than Cooper's. Until he was thirty the writing impulse seems simply not to have been there; then he wrote *Precaution* (1820) because he wished to convince his wife that he could write a better English tea-table novel than the one they were reading.[1] Four years later he produced *The Pilot* on almost equally irrelevant

[1] See George E. Hastings, "How Cooper Became a Novelist," *AL,* XII (1940-1941), 20-51; Susan E. Lyman, " 'I Could Write You a Better Book Than That Myself,' Twenty-Five Unpublished Letters of JFC," *N. Y. Hist. Soc. Bulletin,* XXIX (1945), 213-240.

grounds; this time he was out to create a more authentic sea-tale than Scott's *Pirate*. *Precaution* was admittedly a false start—as James Grossman says, "the American Scott made the mistake of beginning his career as the American Austen"—yet in the larger aspects few great writers have come to their kingdom more unerringly than Cooper. With *The Spy* (1821), *The Pioneers* (1823), and *The Pilot* (1824), he opened up for himself (and for American literature) the three great fictional worlds which he was to possess: history, the forest, and the sea. He had stumbled upon them almost unwittingly; he did not begin to take up a professional attitude toward his work until *Lionel Lincoln* (1825), and *Lionel Lincoln* was a failure. In a sense, much of his fiction stands curiously remote from the main interests of his life. What he really cared for was his work as a publicist, and before he was through he had turned fiction itself into an agency of propaganda. Yet this is not to say that Cooper was a stranger to the things *which make for literature*. Of late years we have been treated to a spate of novels and plays about novelists and playwrights who are engaged in writing novels and plays. Of such unhealthy introversion Cooper was never in any danger. As well as any writer who ever lived he knew that "you can't write writing." And because he knew it he brought American life into American fiction.

James Fenimore Cooper was born at Burlington, New Jersey, on September 15, 1789, of English and Swedish stock, but he grew up at Cooperstown, on the southern shore of Otsego Lake in upper New York, where his father, Judge William Cooper, lived the life of a landed proprietor. After preliminary schooling under an Episcopal clergyman, the boy was sent, at fifteen, to Yale, whence he was expelled for a prank. He sailed before the mast and served in the navy; in 1811 he married Susan De Lancey, daughter of a Loyalist family. ("I loved her like a man and told her of it like a sailor.") In 1822 he commenced a period of residence in New York City, and from 1827 to 1833 he lived in Europe. His later years were dedicated with equal zeal to the production of fiction—eighteen novels in eleven years—and to an unceasing battle against what he regarded as evil influences in American public life. He was a tireless litigant who conducted his own cases and nearly always won; he must be very nearly the only American who won not one but many suits against American newspapers. He died at Cooperstown, on September 14, 1851.

2. The Leatherstocking Tales

The world has placed the novels of which Natty Bumppo (Deerslayer, Hawkeye, Leatherstocking, Long Rifle) is the hero at the head of Cooper's achievement; it was through them that he conquered the world. In the order in which the events narrated fit into the chronology of the hero's life, they are *The Deerslayer* (1841), *The Last of the Mohicans* (1826), *The Pathfinder* (1840), *The Pioneers* (1823), and *The Prairie* (1827). The first gives us Natty in his youth and the next two in his splendid prime; in the last two we see him in age and finally, in *The Prairie,* we watch him die.

The five books have not been cut from the same bolt. The first to be written, *The Pioneers,* has been rightly praised by D. H. Lawrence, in his otherwise rather silly rhapsody about Cooper, for "some of the loveliest, most glamorous pictures in all literature," among them "the raw village street, with woodfires blinking through the unglazed window-chinks on a winter's night" and "the inn, with the rough woodsmen and the drunken Indian John; the church, with its snowy congregation crowding to the fire." For this book is full of Cooper's memories of his boyhood in the curious, cultured frontier that was Cooperstown,[2] and he has invested it with a nostalgic charm. Yet, compared with what was to come, *The Pioneers* was a comparatively unidealized picture of frontier life. The poetic and idealistic side of Natty's character, though not wholly lacking in this book, is certainly underdeveloped. The old man is a bit rude and ill-tempered; he has not yet developed the elevation that was to glorify both his youth in *The Deerslayer* and his extreme old age in *The Prairie.*

The *Mohicans* and *The Deerslayer* have, of course, always been the great favorites, and two books set against similar backgrounds could hardly be more unlike. The *Mohicans* is the great action book, Cooper's prime example of the drama of escape and pursuit which

[2] See Andrew Nelson, "James Cooper and George Croghan," *PQ,* XX (1941), 69-73.

he made his own. *The Deerslayer,* too, has plenty of action, but the freshness of Natty's and of Chingachgook's youth outshines everything else: the book smells of the woods and the promise of a virgin land.

The Pathfinder travels to the Lake Ontario country where Cooper had served in the navy; in this book he may be said to have combined the romance of the forest with the romance of an inland sea. And unhappy as Natty's romance with Mabel Dunham turned out to be, it still helped to deepen the human quality of his portrait. The most thrilling sequence in *The Pathfinder* is the siege of the blockhouse, which involves Cooper's best Indian heroine, Dew-of-June.

There are thrilling scenes again in *The Prairie,* notably the buffalo stampede and the prairie fire; but though our pulses still beat, they beat in the presence of autumn, the going-down of the sun. The nobility of Natty's spirit makes *The Prairie* the most exalted of Cooper's books; but when the squatter Ishmael Bush enters with his family—types of pioneer which other writers were not to discover for many years—it also becomes the most realistic. *The Prairie* is, indeed, a strange combination of disparate elements; for one thing, Cooper has now taken his hero westward toward an undefined region which he himself had not seen, and imaginative rather than authentic is the word for his portrayal of it.[3]

3. Salt Water

The Pilot has the advantage of priority among the great novels of the sea, for it came half a dozen years before Marryat and nearly two decades before Dana and Melville. The main action takes place off the coast of Northumberland, and the leading character is that imperfect hero, John Paul Jones (Mr. Gray), who performs impressively in battle and storm. Nautical authenticity is Cooper's characteristic note in all his novels of the sea, whether he concerns himself with the movements of fleets (*The Two Admirals,* 1842)[4] or with those of a gentleman pirate more sinned against than sinning (*The*

[3] See John T. Flanagan, "The Authenticity of C's 'The Prairie,'" *MLQ,* II (1941), 99-104; E. S. Muszynska-Wallace, "The Sources of 'The Prairie,'" *AL,* XXI (1949), 191-200.

[4] See Richard H. Ballinger, "Origins of JFC's 'The Two Admirals,'" *AL,* XX (1948), 20-30.

Red Rover, 1827), with smuggling in New York harbor during the colonial period (*The Water-Witch,* 1830) or with the doings of a French privateer at Naples in 1798 (*The Wing-and-Wing,* 1842). The plots involve intricate family relationships and mysteries of parentage; there are interminable, indecisive chases; and nobody need be surprised to find the hero taking service in a pirate ship, or a picturesque smuggler casually strolling in and out of a lady's windows. Historical personages are admitted wherever they are needed: Admiral Caraccioli is admiringly depicted—and presented with an imaginary granddaughter—in *The Wing-and-Wing,* while Nelson and Lady Hamilton are deglamourized as mercilessly as Marjorie Bowen has done the job in our own time.[5] Both *The Red Rover* and *The Wing-and-Wing* are exciting narratives, but *The Water-Witch* is dull and long-winded, and its more imaginative scenes quite refuse to blend into the prosaic warp-and-woof of the book.[6]

Cooper never gave up the sea until he relinquished fiction—and life—altogether, not even in his last days when didacticism had claimed him as her own. *Jack Tier* (1848) involves the Mexican War, which Cooper opposed; in *The Sea-Lions* (1849)[7] he audaciously and successfully reached out to possess himself fictionally of the Antarctic, but what he is really interested in is the conversion of his hero to the author's own passionate Trinitarianism. *Ned Myers* (1843) is less a novel than the history of an old shipmate, taken down—or "logged," as Cooper put it—from his narration.

There is one among Cooper's later novels of the sea, however, which does not deserve the neglect that has overtaken it; this is *Afloat and Ashore,* with its continuation, rather than sequel, *Miles Wallingford* (both 1844). It has long been suspected that this book is heavily autobiographical, Miles being a modified portrait of Cooper in his youth and Lucy Hardinge of the girl he loved and

[5] See her life of Lady Hamilton, *Patriotic Lady* (ACC, 1936), also her novel, *The Autobiography of Cornelis Blake* (Cassell, 1934), published under another pseudonym, George R. Preedy.

[6] See William H. Bonner, "Cooper and Captain Kidd," *MLN,* LXI (1946), 21-27.

[7] See W. B. Gates, "C's 'The Sea Lions' and Wilkes' 'Narrative,'" *PMLA,* LXV (1950), 1069-1075.

married. *Afloat and Ashore* opens in 1797 with the running-away to sea of Miles and his finally ne'er-do-well companion, Rupert Hardinge. It has a rambling structure, involving many voyages, both commercial and semi-naval in character, and Cooper brings in almost every conceivable type of adventure by sea and land. There are tempests, wrecks, pirates; there is pearl-diving; and, that nothing may be lacking, there is even a brief encounter with the Indians of the Pacific Northwest. Yet not all of *Afloat and Ashore* is adventure. Some of it is romance—sweet, if timid, romance between the sexes—and charming memories of old New York, later to be recaptured more fully in *Satanstoe*.

The *Miles Wallingford* part is much inferior, at least in its "ashore" portions, which are increasingly concerned with such matters as the "decline" and death of Miles's noble sister Grace, after she has been jilted by Rupert Hardinge; and there is another birth-mystery to be cleared up for the old salt, Moses Marble—he was found on a tombstone—who is reunited with his long-lost mother and who, in his old age, makes a most edifying death, after having been brought by Lucy to accept Christ's mediation for his salvation.

4. *History at Home and Abroad*

History, as we have already seen, was no *terra incognita* to Cooper, but there are a number of works still to consider which, belonging neither to the forest nor to the sea, can only be classified as "historical."

Five of these are American. *The Spy* is probably read today with considerably less interest than *The Deerslayer* and the *Mohicans,* yet it was the book with which both Cooper and American fiction found their way. Harvey Birch is Washington's spy, serving his cause heroically at the cost of personal obloquy, but Washington's own role in the drama as the disguised "Mr. Harper" is frankly incredible. The scene of *Wyandotté* (1843) is once more the interior of New York during the Revolutionary period on a considerably ruder frontier than we visited in *The Pioneers*. Though the book is generally spoken of as having offered, in the central figure of the Indian who "never forgot a favor, or forgave an injury," a more realistic picture of the red man than any contained in the Leatherstocking Tales, this statement surely does not apply to Wyandotté's quite unbelievable conversion and death. Less important is *The Oak Openings* (1848), which concerns Michigan in the War of 1812, and is the fruit of a late visit paid by the author to that region.[8]

There remain the two New England novels: *Lionel Lincoln* (1825) and *The Wept of Wish-ton-Wish* (1829). Cooper did not love New Englanders; neither have they loved him; after Lounsbury's pontifical condemnation, few critics have ventured to say a good word for either of these books.[9] For *The Wept,* which concerns Connecticut in King Philip's War, I have no plea to offer: the book lacks both unity and continuity, nor are the characters ever quite realized. Cooper is evidently here attempting a more psychological interpretation of Indian character than is his wont, but it all seems rather high-flown. *Lionel Lincoln,* however, is another matter. It opens upon a superb picture of Boston on the eve of the Revolution—tense, nervous, brooded over by a sense of momentous impingements—and it goes on to a stirring account of Lexington, Concord, and Bunker Hill. The book is less interesting in its second half, where attention is centered upon an inheritance plot involving ancient guilt, never fused very closely with the historical background. Though Cooper does not probe the tortured and divided mind with the skill of Hawthorne, he still deserves credit for having, as it were, discovered the characteristic theme not only of Hawthorne's fiction but of New England fiction in general. With all its faults, *Lionel Lincoln* achieves a brooding intensity which Cooper was never again to know.

Cooper also produced four historical novels against European backgrounds. *The Bravo* (1831), *The Heidenmauer* (1832), and *The Headsman* (1833) are closely-plotted, heavy-paced historical drama, while the less ideational *Mercedes of Castille* (1840) combines a conventional love story with a leisurely account of Columbus's

[8] See K. R. Oakley, "JFC and 'Oak Openings,'" *Mich. Hist. Mag.,* XVI (1932), 309-320.

[9] A conspicuous exception is George Snell, who devotes to *Lionel Lincoln* the lion's share of the space given to Cooper in *The Shapers of American Fiction.*

first voyage.[10] In the first three he was consciously invading Scott's province "to show how differently a democrat and an aristocrat saw the same thing." These novels are sometimes dismissed as failures (especially by those who have not read them), on the ground that Cooper did not know his European backgrounds well enough to make them live, yet he himself judged *The Bravo* as "perhaps, in spirit, the most American book I ever wrote." Venice in her days of glory, Germany at the Reformation dawn, and Switzerland at the beginning of the eighteenth century—these are Cooper's scenes. Both Venice and Switzerland he sees as false republics; he feared that, in his own country, power was already slipping out of the hands of the people into the hands of the state, and he wrote to warn his countrymen lest they permit themselves to be undone. In *The Heidenmauer* the people are crushed between the church and the Lutheran barons, but Cooper refuses to see the conflict in terms of black-and-white and stands guard instead against selfishness and corruption wherever they appear.[11]

5. *To Save the Nation*

But the novels which lay closest to Cooper's heart were those in which he devoted himself frankly to social criticism.

The earliest were *Homeward Bound* and its sequel, *Home as Found* (both 1838). Edward Effingham, descendant of the Pioneers, returns to his native land after a period of European residence; his resultant disillusionment and his quarrels with his neighbors clearly reflect Cooper's own experiences.[12] *Homeward Bound* started out to be *Home as Found,* but a series of adventures at sea intervened. In the sequel, the polemic is directed with equal vigor against Americans who are blind to American shortcomings and those who

[10] Cf. Donald M. Goodfellow, "The Sources of 'Mercedes of Castille,' " *AL,* XII (1940-1941), 318-328.

[11] On these books, see Emilio Goggio, "The Italy of JFC," *MLJ,* XXIX (1945), 66-71; H. Lüdecke, "JFC and the Democracy of Switzerland," *ES,* XXVII (1946), 33-44; and especially Russell Kirk, "C and the European Puzzle," *CE,* VII (1946), 198-207.

[12] See Ethel R. Outland, "The 'Effingham' Libels on C," *U. of Wis. Studies Lang & Lit.,* No. 28 (1929).

praise every century but this and every country but their own. As in the case of Cooper's personal controversies, one must admit that nearly all the points he makes are valid, but his manner is not often ingratiating.

The Littlepage trilogy is more important. These novels—*Satanstoe, The Chainbearer* (both 1845), and *The Redskins* (1846)—were inspired by the "antirent" controversy in New York state which followed the death of Stephen Van Rensselaer in 1839.[13] All take the form of autobiographical chronicles, covering the period from the middle of the eighteenth century to Cooper's own time, but one generation is skipped between *The Chainbearer* and *The Redskins*.

The finest novel of the group is *Satanstoe,* which is not a propaganda novel but a novel of manners. Here the gracious ways of old New York, recorded for the future lest they should fade from memory, are preserved for posterity as nowhere else in our fiction. The first faint rumblings of the storm are heard in *The Chainbearer,* when Mordaunt Littlepage finds squatters in possession of his land, but it does not really break before *The Redskins.*

Corny's saving Anneke (or her shawl) from a *caged* lion at the beginning of *Satanstoe* seems almost a parody of the heroic rescues in the Leatherstocking Tales, but for this tame beginning Cooper atones in abundance when the sleighs in which both his young couples are traveling down the Hudson get caught in the ice-jam where the river breaks up under the spring rains. This is the most thrilling single scene in all Cooper. And the book as a whole is not only the greatest achievement of his later years but one of the most thoroughly delightful narratives in American fiction.

The Autobiography of a Pocket-Handkerchief (1843)[14] is brief and, as fiction, unimportant, though significant for the study of Cooper's social consciousness. *The Monikins* (1835), *The Crater* (1847), and *The Ways of the Hour* (1850) are each highly-specialized and, in Cooper's roll-call, unique. *The Monikins* is Cooper's *Gulli-*

---

[13] For the historical background, see Robert E. Spiller, *JFC, Representative Selections,* pp. lix ff.; Dorothy Dondore, "The Debt of Two Dyed-in-the-Wool Americans to Mrs. Grant's 'Memoirs': C's 'Satanstoe' and Paulding's 'The Dutchman's Fireside,'" *AL,* XII (1940-1941), 52-58; Granville Hicks, "Landlord C and the Anti-Renters," *Ant R,* V (1945), 95-109.

[14] Ed. G. F. Horner and R. Adams (UNCP, 1949).

ver's Travels, Book IV. For the Monikins are monkeys who believe themselves to have evolved from men. The tail has now become the seat of reason, being better adapted to that purpose than the narrow, crowded human skull, but in Leaplow (the United States) "the law requires . . . that every citizen . . . shall be docked agreeably to a standard measure that is kept in each district." Things are no better in Leaphigh (England), which is cursed with the caste system, nor yet in Leapthrough (France). There are excellent things in *The Monikins,* and it is too bad that Cooper should have attempted to make a full-length novel out of what is essentially *conte drôle* material.[15]

The Crater lies in the unrealistic tradition of the utopia. The scene is a group of volcanic isles in the Pacific; the ideas derive from Lyell's *Principles of Geology* and the economic writings of Henry Charles Carey. A lawyer, four clergymen, and a journalist destroy the society which was being developed upon the Crater according to largely absolutist ideas; at last nature again mercifully assumes control, and the aborted utopia sinks beneath the waves.[16]

Much closer to the interests of most present-day readers is Cooper's last novel, *The Ways of the Hour* (1850), an attack upon the institution of trial by jury. Of course the innocent, though slightly mad, defendant is found guilty of murder the moment before one of her "victims" walks into the courtroom. The mystery itself is well-handled; like Dreiser, in *An American Tragedy,* Cooper attempted a complete study of what goes on during a trial, both in and out of the courtroom. Though it would not be the only candidate to consider, it might be fun to try to make a case for the thesis that *The Ways of the Hour* is the first American "mystery" novel, thus awarding Cooper priority in one more field. Certainly it long antedates *The Leavenworth Case* (1878), by Anna Katharine Green, which is generally called the first American detective novel.[17]

---

[15] See Willi Muller, *"The Monikins" von JFC in ihrem Verhältnis zu "Gulliver's Travels" von J. Swift* (Rostock, K. Hinstorff, 1900).

[16] See Harold H. Scudder, "C's 'The Crater,'" *AL,* XIX (1947-1948), 109-126; W. B. Gates, "C's 'The Crater' and Two Explorers," *AL,* XXIII (1951), 243-246.

[17] Poe's short stories, "The Murders in the Rue Morgue" and "The Mystery of Marie Rogêt," had appeared earlier, at the beginning of the 1840's. *The*

6. *Cooper as Novelist*

Important as Cooper is, his work demands less analysis than that of many of his successors. This does not mean that it is simple. It is not simple. The pigeon-holers always have great difficulty, for example, in deciding whether he was a realist or a romancer. Simms declared rightly of *The Spy* that

It does not lessen the value of such a novel, nor the ideal truth of such a conception, that such a character is not often to be found. It is sufficiently true if it wins our sympathies and commands our respect. This is always the purpose of the ideal, which, if it can effect such results, becomes at once a model and a reality.

Yet much as we admire Harvey Birch, he is not, in the ordinary sense, "idealized." And in this fact lies an important key to the understanding of Cooper's art.

Robert Spiller has said of Cooper that "His personal love of action alone made him interested in the romance of adventure; at heart he was a realist." Yet Spiller also says that "His taste obviously ran to fiction of the romantic type, particularly that depicting action." It was not wholly a matter of taste; milieu and life-experience were important conditioning factors. In the Preface to *The Deerslayer* Cooper vigorously defended his right to conceive both Natty and the Indians romantically. But romance interested him primarily because he was an idealist; the main interests of his life were practical and hard-headed:

. . . our . . . efforts must be limited by an attempt to describe man as God has made him, vulgar and unseemly as he may appear to sublimated faculties. . . . To all those, then, who are tired of the company of their species, we would bluntly insinuate that the sooner they throw aside our pages, and seize upon those of some more highly gifted bard, the sooner they will be in the way of quitting earth, if not of attaining heaven.

Creative though Cooper was in opening up vast new territories for fiction, he was the reverse of creative in technique. He may almost be said to have had no technique; he dutifully imitated the

Ways of the Hour is not mentioned in Howard Haycraft's *Murder for Pleasure; or, The Life and Times of the Detective Story* (ACC, 1941). See E. Wagenknecht, Introduction to *Murder by Gaslight* (Prentice-Hall, 1949).

novels then in vogue.[18] And his most trying aspects for modern readers are generally the result of these imitations.

That he has trying aspects it were vain to deny. He seems more "old-fashioned" than either Hawthorne or Melville. And this is not merely because, as Harry Hansen has said, he had no truck with "the quick, nervous narrative manner" of today. He "took his time. He wrote at ease and fully exhausted his subject. He was listened to with respect." He ought to be easier reading than Hawthorne or Melville, for in the ordinary sense he is less profound. Yet he is not easier reading. Though he employed a plethora of words, he often leaves out the one word necessary to create a vivid picture. Take, for example, the novels which involve escorting a woman from one uncomfortable place where it seems incredible that she could be, through a dangerous wilderness, to another spot which it is impossible to conceive any reason she should desire to reach. Take all the tedious mysteries of birth and parentage. Such things often require as close attention as the meaning of the White Whale. And many contemporary readers do not think they are worth it.

It must also be recognized that the thing Cooper did best of all, and to which he always owed his special vogue—I mean his use of flight and pursuit—can now be done more thrillingly than any writer could ever in the nature of the case be expected to do it, in a new aesthetic medium which has come into the world since Cooper's time. The cinema discovered the chase almost as soon as it discovered itself: to be sure of that, one need only observe the work of two early masters, D. W. Griffith and Mack Sennett. Griffith used the chase seriously, melodramatically, for last-minute rescues; in such great films as *The Birth of a Nation* (1915) and the symphonic *Intolerance* (1916), he achieved almost unbearable tension with it. But it may also be seen in many brief, early Biograph pictures, the experiments through which the technique that flowered in *Intolerance* was being developed. Such are *The Lonely Villa, The Battle, The Battle of Elderbrush Gulch, The Lesser Evil,* and many more. Sennett bur-

---

[18] The most important single influence upon Cooper's novels was inevitably that of Scott, but to describe Cooper as "the American Scott" and drop the matter there is fair to neither writer. Brownell, Lucy L. Hazard, and Erskine have commented illuminatingly upon this matter.

lesqued the chase—and everything else—in the rich tomfoolery of
the Keystone "cops." And once such things had been in the world,
all flight and pursuit upon the printed page was inevitably robbed
of some of its enthralling power.

Fortunately this was not all that Cooper had to offer. It has never
been denied that he did more than even the tobacco trade to define
the character of the Indian in the American mind,[19] but from
Parkman on down the reality of his Indians has been sharply challenged. He has been ably defended by Brownell and Lucy Lockwood Hazard, and more recently by Gregory L. Paine and Albert
Keiser;[20] from where we stand now, he seems to have won that
particular flight. (Yvor Winters has even essayed to refute Parkman
by reference to Parkman's own *Conspiracy of Pontiac!*) It is true
that Cooper had no first-hand knowledge of Indians, but he did
consult the more reliable sources; in glorifying the Delawares against
the Iroquois, he was following the lead of the Moravian missionary,
John Heckewelder (1743-1825), whose Christian charity and gentleness of judgment made a powerful appeal to him. It is often carelessly assumed that all Cooper's Indians are as noble as Uncas and
Chingachgook. They are not; most of them are like Wyandotté or
worse. Chingachgook's own drunkenness, in *The Pioneers,* is also
worth citing in this connection, though Cooper had not, of course,
fully conceived this character when that novel was written.

Cooper's admirers have been somewhat less successful in clearing
him of the objections raised against his women—Lowell called them
"sappy as maples and flat as a prairie"—but even here no blanket
condemnation will do. The absurdly stilted behavior of Eve Effingham and Grace Courtland is certainly trying enough, and the religious solicitude of Ghita in *The Wing-and-Wing* is almost indis-

[19] The Indian, like the cowboy, was one of the early film types. The cowboy has held his place, but "Indian pictures" have nearly faded from the
modern screen. Like Natty Bumppo, the first great cowboy hero of the screen,
Broncho Billy (G. M. Anderson), exemplified the virtue of renunciation.
Beginning in the spring of 1908, Anderson turned out a film a week for
376 weeks. It is interesting, too, to compare the ice-jam in *Satanstoe* with
Griffith's in the film version of *Way Down East* (1920).

[20] See Gregory L. Paine, "The Indians of the Leatherstocking Tales," *SP,*
XXIII (1926), 16-39; Albert Keiser, *The Indian in American Literature* (OUP,
1933).

tinguishable from Elsie Dinsmore's. Surely no modern novelist has surpassed the vulgarity of Cooper's description of Cecilia Howard in *The Pilot:* a "female figure, clad in virgin white," "reclining on the end of a distant couch": "A small hand, which seemed to blush at its own naked beauties, supported her head, imbedded in the volumes of her hair, like the fairest alabaster set in the deepest ebony." Yet Judith Hutter, of *The Deerslayer,* is far from being a stick; so vibrant is she that it is impossible to acquit Natty of priggishness in his rejection of her. Poe warmly praised Maud Meredith of *Wyandotté.* A very different sort of triumph is Ishmael's wife in *The Prairie;* and Maria Edgeworth, an excellent judge of all Irish matters, was much impressed by Betty Flanagan, the filthy sutler of *The Spy.* It is difficult to be quite fair in judging the female characters of novelists who wrote a century ago: *The North American Review* of 1826 censured the women of the *Mohicans* for their unladylike behavior, and many American reviewers were shocked by Cora's Negro blood. Cooper's limitations in this field all sprang from the fact that he was a man's man, a chivalrous gentleman of the old school, who never "knew women" as some men do—or think they do.

But, of course, his great characters are men. It is in Natty Bumppo, Tom Coffin, and a few others—in them and in the great forests they inhabit and the great seas they travel—that Cooper's real glory lies. He added a continent to world fiction, and now that his foolish countrymen have gutted the original, it lives only in his pages as God made it and as Cooper thought His thoughts after Him. It was no accident that Natty should have been one of the first conservationists, denying nobly (but, oh, how mistakenly!) that needless destruction of life is ever the white man's "gift." And though Parkman may have missed on the Indians, he was right about the Cooper landscape:

There is no glow upon his pictures, no warm and varied coloring, no studied contrast of light and shade. Their virtue consists in their fidelity, in the strength with which they impress themselves upon the mind, and the strange tenacity with which they cling to the memory.

For this very reason, Cooper is always free of the pseudo nature-mysticism which is so often the modern surrogate for religion. There are touches of Byronism in Cooper, but there is no Rousseau. If Cooper was anything he was a Christian; I know of no novelist not avowedly a devotional writer who makes a larger use of Christian doctrine. Confronting the Indian, Cooper was inclined to make much the same distinctions that Melville was later to make in the South Seas. Because these men were God's children, God had given them their own "gifts." But theirs were not the white men's "gifts." The Indian's "gifts" please God—in an Indian—but He will not accept them in a white man. For the future belongs to the white man, with all his sins—to civilization, to Christianity. The Indian is doomed. And the romantic glamour with which Cooper has invested him is the by-product of his doom, for the Indian is not responsible for his tragic fate.[21]

Cooper's social and political convictions demand no extended discussion here. They were important *in* but not *for* his novels; he never succeeded in fusing his ideas with his plots.[22] It is the fashion to describe him as an aristocrat; if he was, he was a spiritual aristocrat. His boyhood as the son of the semifeudal squire of Cooperstown no doubt influenced him here, yet he deserted the old Federalist viewpoint of his father and became a Democrat. But equality of rights was the only equalitarianism to which he ever subscribed, and he set his face against demagoguery in all its forms, opposing at every point the tyranny of the majority, or, rather, as it seemed to him,

[21] Dr. Henry Seidel Canby may be right when he argues (*Classic Americans,* HB, 1931) that Cooper's attitude toward the Indians and toward spiritual values in general was importantly influenced by his Quaker background. In Natty's "sense of the immanence of the Creator," his "non-aggression," his "distrust of the intellect," reliance upon the Inner Light, etc., Canby finds "rudimentary Quakerism." "Natty is the best Quaker in American literature." H. H. Hintz echoes Canby in the chapter on Cooper in *The Quaker Influence in American Literature.*

[22] The most elaborate discussion of these matters is in Robert E. Spiller's *FC, Critic of His Times,* but the best place to begin is the same writer's volume of *Representative Selections.* Spiller has also considered Cooper's social criticism in *The American in England* (Ht, 1926) and has brought out new editions of C's *Gleanings in Europe* (OUP, 1928-1930) with valuable introductions. See, further, John F. Ross, "The Social Criticism of FC," *U. of Cal. Publications in English,* III (1933), 17-118; Dorothy Waples, *The Whig Myth of JFC* (YUP, 1938); and H. L. Mencken's introduction to C's *The American Democrat* (K, 1931).

the tyranny of those active, organized minorities who, having gone through the forms of the democratic process, achieve their own selfish ends under the pious fiction that they are representing the people. And if in practice he was generally to be found standing over against the wave of the future, the reason was his dislike of the growing power of merchants and industrialists. All his sympathies were agrarian, and he feared the effects upon manners and freedom alike of a new domination based upon money alone. When he opposed the antirenters, it was not because he had a special attachment to the patroon system; it was rather because he believed in the sanctity of property and contract. Without this, and without a strict adherence to the principle that changes must proceed through legitimate process of law alone, he could see no future for his country. "God help the man whose rights are to be maintained against the masses, when the immediate and dependent nominees of those masses are to sit in judgment!"

Generations of academicians—aided and abetted by two men of genius, Edgar Allan Poe and Mark Twain[23]—have fallen foul of Cooper's style; most of their strictures, though sound enough, are a little pedantic. "He wrote as well as any novelist of his time," said the fastidious Joseph Conrad,[24] and whose praise could any writer desire more? But it is possible that Conrad read him in Polish. The lack of distinction in Cooper's style contributed to his vogue. Unlike writers of marked individuality and distinction, he had nothing to lose in translation; sometimes he even gained. His incurable addiction to the dangling modifier never lessened his skill as a novelist, and when he wrote such sentences as "Remember the heats of July, my daughter; nor venture farther than thou canst retrace before the meridian," he was simply minding his eighteenth-century literary manners. In any case, none of his faults importantly alter the fact that the themes he discovered have kept his descendants occupied clear down to the present hour.

[23] See "C's 'Wyandotté,'" in the Stedman-Woodberry edition of Poe's *Works*, Vol. VII (S, c.1895); Mark Twain, "FC's Literary Offenses," in *In Defense of Harriet Shelley and Other Essays* (H, 1918) and "FC's Further Literary Offenses," *NEQ*, XIX (1946), 291-301. Cf. D. L. Maulsby, "FC and Mark Twain," *Dial*, XXII (1897), 107-109.

[24] *Notes on Life and Letters* (D, 1921).

7. Cooper's Followers and Contemporaries; William Gilmore Simms

Among Cooper's contemporaries, space is available here for a comparatively detailed commentary upon only one: William Gilmore Simms. Some must be recorded as hardly more than names. Some must be omitted altogether. Notes on a number of others will be found in the Appendix.

Some survivals have been due less to intrinsic merit than to the accident of having been written by authors better remembered for other types of literary work. Walt Whitman's temperance story, *Franklin Evans* (1842), was hackwork. And though Edgar Allan Poe's two most extended narratives—*The Narrative of Arthur Gordon Pym, of Nantucket* (1838) and *The Journal of Julius Rodman* (1840)—have touches of that writer's great but erratic genius, they do not show him at his best. *Pym,* which is much the better of the two, is a conglomeration of every conceivable type of sea-horror, with terrifying suggestions of greater, supernatural horrors beyond. Henry Wadsworth Longfellow's *Hyperion* (1839) is a German travelogue, with criticism, legendry, and philosophy superimposed upon it, but Longfellow comes closer to the novel in *Kavanagh* (1849), a New England village idyll. John Lothrop Motley, Mrs. Mowatt, Charles Fenno Hoffman,[25] and Nathaniel Parker Willis also tried their hands at prose fiction among many other things.

More important than any of these is the *Margaret Smith's Journal* (1849), written by John Greenleaf Whittier in the form of a diary kept by an English girl of great heart and liberal temper during a visit to Massachusetts in 1678-1679. It is true that most of the action is crowded into the appendix, but though this "novel" lacks a plot, it has nearly everything else. It shines with the austere beauty of the New England countryside; it preserves a record of rural customs; it is touched with wonder in its references to the legends and superstitions of the region. More significant still, it dramatizes the conflict between humanity and self-righteousness which was so important a

---

[25] Hoffman's *Grayslaer* (1840) was a considerably more oblique and less literal treatment of the Kentucky Tragedy than Simms was to achieve in *Beauchampe.*

part of the New England ordeal. Margaret is not a Quaker, though her brother becomes one through his love for a Quaker girl. But, without ever forcing the note, the Quaker poet manages to touch all the "concerns" in whose connection the Quaker conscience in New England became engaged: slavery, intemperance, persecution for witchcraft, Indian warfare, and religious intolerance. *Margaret Smith's Journal* is one of the minor, neglected classics of American letters.

A much more widely-read book is *Two Years Before the Mast* (1840). Its author, Richard Henry Dana, Jr., was a Boston Brahmin who became a distinguished jurist—the protector of oppressed seamen and runaway slaves. During his sophomore year at Harvard, he suffered a severe attack of measles which left him temporarily unable to use his eyes. To get through the next two years, he shipped in 1834 upon the brig *Pilgrim,* bound from Boston around the Horn to California, on a cruise for a cargo of hides. After his return he wrote his book from the journal he had kept during the voyage and sold the copyright to Harpers for $250.

His aim was "an accurate and authentic narrative" of the life of a common sailor. He even avoided "incorporating into it any impressions but those made upon me by the events as they occurred." Dana had no gift for yarning, to say nothing of a capacity for the psychological subtleties of a Conrad or the cosmic vision of a Melville. It may even be that his book has no proper place in a history of the American novel. But for sheer, straightforward, unmodified narrative power—austere and utterly restrained—it has not often been surpassed.

Among the minor writers of the period who owe such fame as they possess to their fiction alone, the most important is Daniel Pierce Thompson (1795-1868), whose *The Green Mountain Boys* (1839), a story of Ethan Allen and the taking of Ticonderoga has been very widely read.[26] Another novelist of the Revolution, James McHenry, in *The Wilderness; or, Braddock's Times* (1823), achieved at least a variant of the never-ending portraits of Washington in early American fiction when he presented the Great Man as a victim of hopeless love!

[26] See J. E. Flitcroft, *The Novelist of Vermont* (HUP, 1929).

The Cavaliers of Virginia (1834), by William Alexander Caruthers, is an elaborate and romantic historical novel, the work of a Southern moderate, and the pioneering book in a long line of historical romances to come out of the Old Dominion.[27] Much less conciliatory was Nathaniel Beverley Tucker's "Tale of the Future"— the title-page was dated 1856—*The Partisan Leader* (1835), which was written to warn Virginia of impending Northern domination. (It was reissued, opportunely, in 1861.) In 1836 Richard Hildreth brought out *The Slave,* an antislavery novel often credited with having influenced *Uncle Tom's Cabin,* which Howells, despite all its extravagant elements, described many years afterwards as "a powerful piece of realism."[28]

Of a decidedly more flashy character was Theodore Fay's "bestseller," *Norman Leslie* (1835), a murder story, with a wide-ranging social background and a sensational plot. George Lippard's unbelievably lurid book, *The Monks of Monk Hall,* sometimes called *The Quaker City* (1844), serves at least to prove that modern "yellow journalism" did not invent the exposé. Joseph Holt Ingraham, who once told Longfellow that he had written eighty novels for serial publication, twenty of them during a single year,[29] wrote stories about the pirates Lafitte and Captain Kidd that were widely read in their day, but is now best remembered for *The Prince of the House of David* (1855), in which the events leading up to the Crucifixion are related in letters written by a Jewish girl visiting Jerusalem to her father in Egypt. Biblical and classical themes had already appeared in the work of a more scholarly novelist, William Ware, who became the first Unitarian pastor in the city of New York. Ware's best-known novel is *Julian* (1841), a picture of the home life of Jesus, with emphasis upon his human nature.

One of the most prolific of American writers, and the most versatile of antebellum Southern men of letters, William Gilmore Simms

---

27 See Curtis Carroll Davis, "The Virginia 'Knights' and Their Golden Horseshoes: Dr. William A. Caruthers and an American Tradition," *MLQ,* X (1950), 490-507.

28 See Arthur M. Schlesinger, Jr., "The Problem of 'Richard Hildreth,'" *NEQ,* XIII (1940), 223-246.

29 See Warren G. French, "A Lost American Novel," *AL,* XXI (1950), 477-478.

has never received anything like his due. The Civil War stripped him of almost everything he possessed: contacts with Northern publishers, plates for reprinting his books, his library, home, peace of mind, and the way of life he loved. There has never been a really worthy edition of his novels nor is there any adequate study of him.

Simms was born in Charleston on April 17, 1806. His father, a bankrupt merchant, turned to a wandering life in the West and left the boy to be brought up by his grandmother, who filled his head with Southern legendry, much more valuable equipment for the work he was to do than either his apprenticeship to an apothecary or his later legal studies. He read American history hugely, and he knew the Mississippi frontier—with its border ruffians, its Creeks and its Cherokees—at first hand. He wrote poetry, made heroic efforts to give the South a literary magazine, and did an immense amount of work in general literature. He died at Charleston on June 11, 1870.

Simms began his career as fictionist with the brief *Martin Faber* (1833), the study of a criminal and of criminal determinism from the offender's own point of view.[30] The psychology of crime interested him deeply. It appears again in his domestic tragedies: *Confession; or, The Blind Heart* (1841), a study of jealousy suggested by *Othello,* and, more importantly, in *Beauchampe* (1842), the story of a famous Kentucky tragedy of passion, told under the real names of the protagonists.[31] In *Castle Dismal; or, The Bachelor's Christmas* (1844), he studied a noble criminal in a still very readable ghost story.[32]

[30] *Martin Faber* has been interpreted as the literary offspring of Godwin's *Caleb Williams;* see F. H. Deen, *MLN,* LIX (1944), 315-317, and, for a dissenting view, Edward Stone, *MLN,* LXII (1947), 480-483.

[31] No other American crime has inspired so much literature as the Kentucky Tragedy. See Willard Jillson, *Register of the Ky. State Hist. Soc.,* XXXVI (1938), 54-60. Recent years have produced two more novels: Robert Penn Warren, *World Enough and Time* (RH, 1950) and Joseph Shearing, *To Bed at Noon* (Heinemann, 1951). It should be added that Professor Quinn has cleared up the bibliographical puzzle which formerly obscured the relationship between *Beauchampe* and *Charlemont;* see his *American Fiction,* p. 122 ftn.

[32] Simms believed in the supernatural and often makes use of psychic phenomena; cf. the second sight of Harricane Nell, of *Eutaw.* There are a number of ghost stories among his shorter pieces; Poe praised "Grayling" (*The Wigwam and the Cabin,* 1845) as the best ghost story he had ever read.

In the inevitable comparison between Simms and Cooper, the Carolinian's Indians perhaps get more attention than they deserve. This is partly because *The Yemassee* (1835), which deals with an Indian war of 1715 in South Carolina, has proved his most durable, if not his finest, book. The scene in which Matiwan kills her unworthy son Occonestoga, who has been debauched by the white man's fire water, to prevent his being degraded in a tribal ceremony which shall cut him off from his people both here and hereafter, is deservedly famous; but it is not possible to say as much for the old school reader favorite—the scene in which Bess is charmed by a rattlesnake—for Simms was nature-faking here, and he knew it. *The Cassique of Kiawah* (1859) is the only other real Indian novel, but Indians are important in a number of short stories. They are less "different" from white men than they are in Cooper, a method of treatment which makes it somewhat easier for Simms to catch their essential humanity, though perhaps at the sacrifice of a certain quality of picturesqueness.

Simms's most important novels are his stories of the Revolution and his stories of the Mississippi frontier. *Guy Rivers* (1834), which was his first real novel, is a very sensational story of desperadoes in the gold fields of Georgia. *Richard Hurdis* (1838) and *The Border Beagles* (1840) give us similar scoundrels—and the faultless heroes and impeccable heroines who oppose them—in Alabama and Mississippi. Simms derived some of his material for these books from Virgil Stewart, who captured the bandit Murrell. He is by no means exclusively concerned with horrific villainies; he conceives great conceptions and thinks heroic thoughts. But his art is not always equal to the effective presentation of such matters, and he often leaves the impression of sensationalism with pretentiousness unsuccessfully imposed upon it. Yet whatever may be said about the stories in Simms's Border romances, there can be nothing but praise for the picture of the Border itself.

Simms produced seven novels about the end of the Revolution in South Carolina and its aftermath. Three of these—*The Partisan* (1835), *Mellichampe* (1836), and *Katharine Walton* (1851)—compose a trilogy; *Mellichampe* carries on the military action begun in *The Partisan,* but the culmination of the love story between

Katharine and Major Singleton has to wait for the third book. The other four Revolutionary novels are *The Scout,* originally called *The Kinsmen* (1841), *Woodcraft,* originally *The Sword and the Distaff* (1852), *The Forayers* (1855), and *Eutaw* (1856). To these one should perhaps add *Joscelyn* (published serially only, 1867), which concerns the neighboring state of Georgia at the beginning of the struggle.

These works give an excellent picture of the complications engendered by what was essentially a civil war.[33] Mrs. Eveleigh, for example, was enriched, not ruined, because she had friends on both sides. Some of the novels, like *The Partisan,* are concerned essentially with military operations; *Woodcraft,* on the other hand, describes Captain Porgy's adventures on his way home from the war and his struggle to reestablish himself upon his ruined plantation. Porgy's relationship to Sir John Falstaff has occasioned some debate.[34] That there are resemblances in some aspects is evident, but Porgy is, in no sense, a copy; neither is it fair to ignore the other Elizabethan characters who surely made their contribution. Perhaps Simms was fascinated by the Fat Knight's human qualities but repelled by his more sinister aspects; and if Porgy is not quite all of a piece, the explanation may lie in his creator's unwillingness to permit him to appear in an evil light. It is sometimes difficult to reconcile Simms's conception of Porgy as a Southern gentleman with some of his merely ludicrous traits—compare his definition of love as "a fine meat, or delicate vegetable" or his demonstration that it is a man's belly which really does his thinking for him—to say nothing of such outrageous actions as his treatment of the sheriff whom a rascally creditor sends against him. Porgy touches the heart when he refuses to allow the lovely child Dory Bostwick to be forced to testify against her worthless father—or tempted to lie to protect him—but he is merely absurd when he threatens to shoot his slave Tom rather than permit him to belong to somebody else. With all Porgy's faults and virtues, Simms was wise not to permit him to wed

[33] See C. H. Holman, "WGS' Pictures of the Revolution as a Civil Conflict," *Jour. So. Hist.,* XV (1950), 441-462.

[34] See H. M. Jarrell, "Falstaff and Simms's Porgy," *AL,* III (1931), 204-213; C. H. Holman, "Simms and the British Dramatists," *PMLA,* LXV (1950), 346-359.

Mrs. Eveleigh, the rich widow whom he and his cronies rescue from desperadoes on their way home from the war, and who lends him the money to stock his ruined plantation; nor is he allowed to console himself when he turns instead to the accommodating Widow Griffin, whom he had always in a way preferred, for with that lady it was a case of first come first served, and our Porgy had waited too long. All in all, he is surely the prime heroic character of American fiction in the "humours" tradition.

Like Cooper, Simms tried his hand at exotic materials (Spanish in his case): *Pelayo* (1838); *The Damsel of Darien,* which deals with Balboa (1839); *Count Julian* (1845); and *Vasconselos* (1853), in which appears a villainous De Soto. Indeed, Simms was a tireless experimenter. *The Golden Christmas* and *As Good as a Comedy* (both 1852) are tales of aristocratic love and manners in Carolinian and Georgian settings, and in *Marie de Bernière* (1853), he wrote about the Creoles in Louisiana. Even at the very end, in two of the serials which he could not even get published in book form—*Voltimeier* and *The Cub and the Panther* (both 1869)—the tired old man was reaching toward the world of Southern folk ballads out of which not a little distinguished fiction and drama has been created in our own time.

In his Introduction to *The Partisan,* Simms declares that his aim "has been to give a story of events, rather than of persons." After the contemplative Chapter XXXIII, in which he muses over Emily's grave, he returns to action: "The business of life calls for progress rather than repose; for perseverance rather than contemplation." All this is characteristic. For Simms is essentially a story-teller rather than a creator of memorable characters, more essentially a story-teller than Cooper. His temperament was better suited to picaresque materials than Cooper's—for Cooper was too much the moralist to take even an aesthetic delight in a rogue—and there are times when the simplicity and rapidity of his narrative suggest not Cooper but Charles Reade or even *The Family Herald.*

None of this must be taken to indicate that Simms had no interest in his characters or that he did not think—about fiction and about life. It is true that his women have a good deal of the conventional, nineteenth-century, "too-good-to-be-true" quality about them.

Katharine Walton—"one of those high-souled creatures that awe while they attract"—is very grand in her manner, both as a patriot, in her relations with Major Proctor, and again, with her lover, whom she austerely rebukes for pressing the question at what only a novelist with two-thirds of a trilogy ahead of him could possibly have regarded as an unseasonable time. Yet she—and Simms's other heroines —are far from being colorless, and when he forgot his literary manners, he could generally be counted upon to permit them to behave like human beings. As for his thinking, he was not a pretentious writer, and he had no taste for the elaborate formulation of theories concerning his art. Nevertheless it is clear that he had thought about the nature of fiction, about the use of history in fiction, about the difference between historical fiction and factual record, about the distinction between novel and romance and the relationship of both to morals and to life, and it is difficult to find any serious fault with the conclusions he seems to have reached. Nor did he confine his thinking to aesthetic matters. He used Singleton's consumptive sister Emily to expound the pacifist attitude toward war, and while he does not wholly agree with her, there is no doubt that he has considered the problems involved.[35] That he had an appetite for sensation—and even for horror—cannot be denied, but it is easy to make too much of this. It must be admitted that *Beauchampe,* which even some modern critics dislike, has its crudities, but both the husband and the wife have vitality (whatever may be said of the villain), and the intellectual quality of the woman is skillfully suggested. The thing has much of the simplicity of a folk ballad—for the ballads too have ugly things in them—and its melodrama is the kind that lies close to the heart of a people. And Simms's best work is much better than *Beauchampe.*

[35] Harricane Nell, too, is a pacifist of sorts; a more subtle study in the same general field is that of Lance Frampton, of *The Partisan.*

CHAPTER III

THE SOUL'S ROMANCE: HAWTHORNE

> . . . everything, you know, has its spiritual meaning, which to the literal
> meaning is what the soul is to the body. . . .
>
> *Septimius Felton*

1. *Hawthorne's Literary Ideals*

Nathaniel Hawthorne did not consider himself a novelist. He considered himself a romancer. There were times when he thought he liked the novel better than the romance. He had a passion for Trollope, but if his own books had been written by somebody else he hardly thought he could have got through them, or that he would have understood them if he had.

Yet Hawthorne could never have been a Trollope. His temperament, the conditions of his early life, his literary ideals themselves forbade it.

Because Hawthorne was not given to literary allusion he is often given credit for much less reading than he did. Actually, his range was comparatively wide.[1] Of the novelists Scott had much the greatest influence. From Scott, Hawthorne learned how to tell a story, as we may still see plainly by reference to the experimental *Fanshawe,* where virtually every aspect of the Wizard's technique is dutifully imitated.[2] Scott did more than this, for he gave Haw-

---

[1] There have been a number of studies of Hawthorne's reading. The most extensive is Marion L. Kesselring, "H's Reading, 1828-1850," *Bull. N. Y. Public Library,* LIII (1949), 55-71, 121-138, 173-194. See also Jane Lundblad's discussion in her *NH and European Literary Tradition.*

[2] See G. H. Orians, "Scott and H's 'Fanshawe,'" *NEQ,* XI (1938), 388-394; P. E. Burnham, "H's 'Fanshawe' and Bowdoin College," *Essex Inst. Hist. Coll.,* LXXX (1944), 131-138; J. S. Goldstein, "The Literary Source of H's 'Fanshawe,'" *MLN,* LX (1945), 1-8; C. Bode, "H's 'Fanshawe': The Promising of Greatness," *NEQ,* XXIII (1950), 235-242.

thorne (and other young writers) the idea of doing for their own country what he had done for Scotland.[3]

Yet Hawthorne was not permanently or consistently faithful to this ideal, for he soon came to feel that Scott's kind of historical novel had its limitations.[4] He turned to masters who seemed to him better qualified to supply the "more earnest purpose," the "deeper moral," the "closer and homelier truth" that the world now required. These he found in Spenser and Bunyan.[5]

There are great stories all about Hawthorne in the custom house; if the page of life seems dull, he knows well that he must have failed to fathom its deeper meaning. Yet he turns back to the past to find the story of *The Scarlet Letter. The House of the Seven Gables* must not be permitted to "swerve aside from the truth of the human heart," but since it is not a novel but a romance, there can be no objection to the presentation of that truth "under circumstances . . . of the writer's own choosing or creation." *The Blithedale Romance* has an actual autobiographical basis, but the romancer's "present concern with the socialist community is merely to establish a theatre, a little removed from the highway of ordinary travel, where the creatures of his brain may play their phantasmagorical antics, without exposing them to too close a comparison with the actual events of real lives." This "Faery Land," this "license with regard to everyday probability"—so Hawthorne goes on in accents which sound surprisingly like those of Henry James—has long been at the disposal of the European romancer. And "This atmosphere is what the American romancer needs." But the public is not ready for it in "a country where there is no shadow, no antiquity, no mystery, no

[3] See N. F. Doubleday, "H and Literary Nationalism," *AL,* XII (1941), 447-453.

[4] Austin Warren, "H's Reading," *NEQ,* VIII (1930), 480-497, sees *The Scarlet Letter* as Hawthorne's illustration "of the historical novel more deeply conceived [than Scott's], as revelatory of the spirit and philosophy rather than the events and costumes of the past." Cf. Willa Cather's comments on *The Scarlet Letter,* in her essay, "The Novel Démeublé," in *Not Under Forty* (K, 1936).

[5] See Randall Stewart, "H and 'The Faerie Queene,' " *PQ,* XII (1933), 196-206, and in the Introduction to his edition of *The American Notebooks.* For Bunyan, cf. G. P. Lathrop, *A Study of H,* pp. 69-73; W. S. Johnson, *JEGP,* L (1951), 156-166.

picturesque and gloomy wrong, nor anything but a commonplace prosperity, in broad and simple daylight. . . ." So there is a retreat, at last, to the Italy of *The Marble Faun,* frankly "a fanciful story, evolving a thoughtful moral," which "did not purpose attempting a portraiture of Italian manners and character," but which had for its author the advantage of "affording a sort of poetic or fairy precinct, where actualities would not be so terribly insisted upon as they are, and must be, in America."

In developing a story, Hawthorne may begin with an incident or a situation and proceed to interpret its significance, or he may begin with the idea and go on to find an illustration of it in terms of fiction. He never begins with his characters as such, being impelled to write of them as individuals, for their own sake. Even when some actual event or personage takes hold of him, the center of his interest is always in what it "means."

His principal device for developing meaning is the symbol. He records an idea for a story in his notebook, and he adds, significantly: "It might be made emblematical of something." Because Hollingsworth has wounded Zenobia's spirit, he must wound her body literally, when he takes it out of the river. In *The Marble Faun,* Miriam and Donatello find symbols of their guilt in nature, wherever they turn. Hawthorne even saw his own life in terms of symbolism. When Una and Julian shouted and played in the yard while Madame Hawthorne lay dying, her son "seemed to see the whole of human existence at once, standing in the dusty midst of it." Like Wordsworth, he felt "the true unreality of earthly things, made evident by the want of congruity between ourselves and them."

Naturally, then, Hawthorne is greatly tempted by the supernatural. But he is finely restrained in his treatment of it, and a little equivocal, as befits his skeptical temperament (despite all his idealism) and the spirit of the age. Young Goodman Brown thought he saw his fellow-townsmen and his wife at the Devil's Sabbath in the forest, and the sight destroyed him, but the reader must use his own judgment about whether they were really there or not.[6] And this is but one example among many. "I should not be willing to sleep in

[6] See R. H. Fogle, "Ambiguity and Clarity in H's 'Young Goodman Brown,'" *NEQ,* XVIII (1945), 448-465.

that garret," says Hawthorne of a haunted house, "though I do not believe a word of the story."

Yet while all these things are true of Hawthorne, there is a sense in which, stated thus baldly, they misrepresent him. If he did not give us his characters for their own sake, this does not at all mean that he was indifferent to humanity. It was not for nothing that Melville found in his tales "a depth of tenderness, . . . a boundless sympathy with all forms of being, . . . an omnipresent love." Again, though Hawthorne is committed to a search for the meaning of phenomena, he never loses the phenomena themselves in his search. He is always the artist, never the philosopher. The indifference to abstract "ideas" is as evident in his journals as his great gift for minute and particular observation. He realized the danger of losing touch with life, and he used his notebooks as the source of a thousand scenes and characters which he had actually observed.

2. Hawthorne's Life Experience

Hawthorne was born at Salem, Massachusetts, on July 4, 1804. His Quaker- and witch-persecuting ancestors had been in America since 1630; from a malediction pronounced upon one of them, their descendant may have derived the idea of Maule's curse in *The House of the Seven Gables*. But Hawthorne's immediate ancestors followed the sea, and his father died, in 1808, at Surinam, the scene of one of the earliest of English romances, Mrs. Behn's *Oroonoko*.

Like Scott, Hawthorne was partially, though, in his case, temporarily incapacitated in early life, a circumstance which conspired with a long visit, in early adolescence, to his grandfather's house in the forests of Maine to reinforce a tendency toward solitude to which he was already predisposed by his dreamy, thoughtful nature and the secluded circumstances of his mother's life.

After his graduation from Bowdoin College in 1825, he returned to Salem, where he devoted himself obscurely to writing. *Fanshawe,* a brief romance, was published anonymously in 1828, then recalled and destroyed. To *The Token* and other publications he contributed the stories, essays, and sketches afterwards collected in *Twice-Told Tales* (1837, 1842), *Mosses from an Old Manse* (1846), and *The Snow-Image and Other Twice-Told Tales* (1852). In 1836 he edited

S. G. Goodrich's *American Magazine of Useful and Entertaining Knowledge*.[7] For the same publisher, he and his sister wrote or compiled *Peter Parley's Universal History*.[8] *Grandfather's Chair*, stories of New England history retold for children, appeared in 1841-1842. He served in the Custom House at Boston from 1839 to 1841 and at Salem from 1846 to 1849. In 1841 he made an experiment in communal living at the socialistic settlement of Brook Farm. He was married in 1842 to Sophia Peabody of Salem.

Three of Hawthorne's four major works appeared in successive years: *The Scarlet Letter* in 1850, *The House of the Seven Gables* in 1851, *The Blithedale Romance* in 1852. The same period saw his "Gothic" versions of the Greek myths—*A Wonder Book* (1852) and *Tanglewood Tales* (1853)—to say nothing of his campaign *Life of Franklin Pierce* (1852), his friend since college days.

Hawthorne's reward for the life of Pierce was the consular appointment at Liverpool, and the Hawthornes did not return to America until 1860. The factual record of this period lies in *Our Old Home* (1863) and the elaborate series of *English, French,* and *Italian Notebooks;* in art, they produced *The Marble Faun* (1860).

The America to which Hawthorne returned in 1860 was strange and uncongenial to him, and his lack of enthusiasm over the Civil War did not help him. (". . . it will only effect by a horrible convulsion the self-same end that might and would have been brought about by a gradual and peaceful change. Nor am I at all certain that it will effect that end.") As a creative writer, he accomplished little, though he struggled desperately to write a romance about a bloody footstep, a missing heir, and an American claimant to a great English estate. The earliest form of this story, "The Ancestral Footstep," is merely an elaborate series of notes which Hawthorne had written in England and abandoned when he went to work on *The Marble Faun. Doctor Grimshawe's Secret* and *Septimius Felton* (both written between 1861 and 1863), tell each a complete story, though Hawthorne failed to feel sufficiently satisfied with

[7] See Arlin Turner, *H as Editor. Selections from His Writings in "The American Magazine of Useful and Entertaining Knowledge"* (LSUP, 1941).

[8] See Manning Hawthorne, "Nathaniel & Elizabeth Hawthorne, Editors," *Col,* New Graphic Series, III (1939), pp. 47-54.

either to put it into final form. *Septimius,* which has an American Revolutionary setting, subordinates the other themes to the search for the elixir of life. Whether "The Dolliver Romance" would have satisfied him we shall never know, for by the time he came to it sustained composition was quite out of the question, and only the three chapters printed in the *Atlantic* during the last year of his life ever got themselves down on paper.[9]

Hawthorne's once superb health was now permanently shattered. In the spring of 1864, he sought refreshment in a trip under the care of his devoted publisher, William D. Ticknor. But in Philadelphia, Ticknor, who must have had a pretty taste for irony, suddenly died![10] Hawthorne got himself back to Concord somehow, only to be bundled off afresh, this time to the White Mountains with Franklin Pierce. On May 18, Pierce found him dead in his bed in a little hotel at Plymouth, New Hampshire.

3. *The Four Long Romances*

Probably most of the elements of *The Scarlet Letter* appear somewhere in the *Mosses* and the *Tales.* Yet the sustained power of the novel must still have come, when it was first published, as a very great surprise. To be sure, there are fine things among the earlier works. Certainly nothing but admiration remains in the face of such achievements as "Rappaccini's Daughter" and "Ethan Brand." Hellfires glimmer in "Young Goodman Brown." Stories like "The Minister's Black Veil" make an impressive use of symbolic "properties," while "Endicott and the Red Cross" and others vividly dramatize episodes from colonial history. "The Celestial Railroad," that superbly humorous and loving pastiche of *The Pilgrim's*

---

[9] *Septimius Felton* was serialized in the *Atlantic* in 1872; a variant version, under the title, "The Elixir of Life," was printed in part by Julian Hawthorne, in *Lippincott's Magazine,* XLV (1900), 66-76, 224-235, 412-425, 548-561. JH printed *Grimshawe* as a book in 1882; cf. his "A Look into H's Workshop," *Ce,* XXV (1893), 433-448; John A. Kouwenhoven, "H's Notebooks and 'Doctor Grimshawe's Secret,'" *AL,* V (1934), 349-358. The definitive study of this last phase of H's career is now Edward H. Davidson, *H's Last Phase* (YUP, 1949). See also R. Stewart, "H and the Civil War," *SP,* XXXIV (1937), 91-106.

[10] See Leland Schubert, "H and George W. Childs and the Death of Ticknor," *Essex Inst. Hist. Coll.,* LXXXIV (1948), 164-168.

Progress, is a penetrating study of what Hawthorne considered the religious laodiceanism of contemporary Transcendentalists and Unitarians. And certainly we could not easily have spared the delicate parabolism of "The Snow-Image" or "The Great Stone Face."

Only, of course, not all the early work reaches this level. In the sketches, even when a hint of form is thrown out, it is likely to remain undeveloped. Hawthorne can be casual, desultory, even pedagogic in his method; he can be pale and dull. At his worst, he has much feeble and conventional allegory and much that is fanciful rather than truly imaginative, and he had a tiresome weakness for dioramas, processions, and exhibits.

To be sure, some of this casualness carries over into the major works. Not only does the long introductory sketch of "The Custom House" have no real connection with the story of *The Scarlet Letter* but it is hopelessly out of harmony with it. Hawthorne tries to justify it by pretending *à la Defoe* that he found Hester's story in some old papers at the Custom House, but it was too late in the day for anything like that to be either necessary or convincing. Suffering from one of his periodic attacks of admiration for the realists, he even tried to persuade himself that it was "The Custom House" that had made the book successful. At the very close of his career he was pondering similar introductions for "The Ancestral Footstep" and "The Dolliver Romance."

The root conception of *The Scarlet Letter* had already been expressed in the tale of "Endicott and the Red Cross":

There was likewise a young woman, with no mean share of beauty, whose doom it was to wear the letter A on the breast of her gown, in the eyes of all the world and her own children. And even her own children knew what that initial signified. Sporting with her infamy, the lost and desperate creature had embroidered the fatal token in scarlet cloth, with golden thread and the nicest art of needlework; so that the capital A might have been thought to mean Admirable, or anything rather than Adulteress.[11]

11 This was not, however, the beginning of *The Scarlet Letter.* As early as 1838, Hawthorne had been interested in the idea of "a man who does penance in what might appear to lookers-on the most glorious and triumphal circumstance of his life." The ultimate source is probably his early interest in Dr. Johnson's penance at Uttoxeter Market; cf. the sketch of Johnson in his

The adultery is over and done with before the book begins; it is "a triangle after the event," as Herbert Gorman calls it. Here as elsewhere, Hawthorne's interest is not in sin but in the sense of guilt which follows it. Furthermore, as Elizabeth Chandler once pointed out, "The main theme . . . is not the sin of illicit love, but the consequent sins of hypocrisy and revenge, and their effect on the soul."

For this reason, the whole discussion of whether or not Hester "repented" of her sin is rather beside the point. The "love problem," as Woodberry observes, "is never solved. . . ."[12]

Sin, in a sense, creates Hester; it nearly damns Dimmesdale. Yet the clergyman's failing is less hypocrisy than want of courage. And Chillingworth, the wronged husband, turns into a fiend when he dedicates his life to a hideous revenge. "There is one worse than even the polluted priest," cries Dimmesdale. "That old man's revenge has been blacker than my sin. He has violated, in cold blood, the sanctity of a human heart. Thou and I, Hester, never did so!"

Every syllable of that protest throbs with the passionate faith in the sanctity of human personality which was the heart of Hawthorne's religion. Yet when at last the lovers meet again and resolve to cheat fate—perhaps even God—by going away together, Hester is ready to go through with it; it is the weak man who draws back and (acting according to his lights), saves his soul alive. The contrast between the two is not, therefore, maintained with any mechanical consistency, and it is the inconsistency which is the book's glory, for it keeps both alive as human beings, not mere members of a moral equation.

The fourth main character, Pearl, the child of sin, is the one straight allegorical personage in the book, but it may well be that, in the state of knowledge concerning prenatal influences which prevailed in his time, Hawthorne thought her considerably more

"Biographical Stories." And if Hawthorne wrote "The Battle Omen," he had conceived the idea of Dimmesdale's celestial terrors (Ch. XII) as early as 1830. See D. C. Gallup, "Of H's Authorship of 'The Battle Omen,'" *NEQ,* IX (1936), 690-699.

[12] For a fuller, but highly subjective, consideration of some of these problems, see Frederic I. Carpenter, "Scarlet A Minus," *CE,* V (1944), 173-180. Much less useful, because based on a lesser knowledge of Hawthorne's mind, is Philip Rahv's "The Dark Lady of Salem," in *Image and Idea* (ND, 1949).

realistic than she is. He studied her from his own strange and exquisite daughter Una, whom it may be doubted that either he or anybody else ever thoroughly understood. With all her shortcomings, Pearl still serves as a vehicle for some of his most characteristic symbolism.[13]

The Scarlet Letter dispenses with subtlety as only very powerful books can dare to do it. Its exposition, though dramatic, has a classical obviousness; there is no trace of obscurity in any of the characters or relationships.[14] The "operatic" character of the book has been remarked by many critics;[15] it develops itself through a series of tableaux. Certainly it is not an "historical" novel if placed beside the careful, laborious reconstructions of Flaubert or Charles Reade;[16] neither is Hester "real" in the sense in which, say, Emma Bovary is real. To find her parallel one must turn, rather, to older, more imaginative literature. Gorman is right both in finding "something Elizabethan" in *The Scarlet Letter* and in explaining the "air of unreality" which hovers about it as "less the result of a failure to

[13] See Darrel Abel, "H's Pearl: Symbol and Character," *ELH*, XVIII (1951), 50-66.

[14] One does not, of course, imply that *The Scarlet Letter* does not reward repeated reading and study. See, among recent studies, John C. Gerber, "Form and Content in 'The Scarlet Letter,' " *NEQ*, XVII (1944), 25-55; H. H. Waggoner, "NH: The Cemetery, The Prison, and the Rose," *UKCR*, XIV (1948), 175-190; Gordon Roper's Introduction to his edition of *The Scarlet Letter*, etc. (FSY, 1949); M. Cowley, *NYTBR*, Aug. 6, 1950, pp. 1+; John E. Hart, " 'The Scarlet Letter'—One Hundred Years After," *NEQ*, XXIII (1950), 381-395; R. von Abele, " 'The Scarlet Letter,' A Reading," *Accent*, XI (1951), 211-227.

[15] The most elaborate expression of this idea is in Harry Thurston Peck's *Studies in Several Literatures* (DM, 1909). Hawthorne himself said, "I should think it might possibly succeed as an opera, though it would certainly fail as a play." With this, compare William Winter's comments on the play Richard Mansfield produced in 1892 in his *The Life and Art of RM* (Moffat, Yard, 1910), II, 97-106. Walter Damrosch wrote an opera to the libretto of H's son-in-law, G. P. Lathrop, which was produced in Boston in 1896; a more recent effort, Vittorio Giannini's *Das Brandmal*, was heard in Hamburg in 1938. In 1926 Victor Seastrom, the Swedish director, made a film of *The Scarlet Letter* for Metro-Goldwyn-Mayer; Lillian Gish, Lars Hanson, and Henry B. Walthall were in the cast.

[16] See Gustavus Meyers, "H and the Myths about Puritans," *Am. Spectator*, II (1934), 1.

create living personages in a recognizable milieu than . . . the result of a careful aesthetic sensitiveness on Hawthorne's part."

Hawthorne himself preferred *The House of the Seven Gables* to *The Scarlet Letter* because it was a more "natural" book for him to write. He had got less of the devil into his inkpot this time; he seems also to have felt that in dealing with the present day he was coming closer to the real function of the novelist. He was trying

to diffuse thought and imagination through the opaque substance of today, and thus to make it a bright transparency; to spiritualize the burden that began to weigh so heavily; to seek, resolutely, the true and indescribable value that lay hidden in the petty and wearisome incidents, and ordinary characters, with which I was now conversant.

But the present of the *Seven Gables* is a present brooded over by the past. "God," cried old Maule upon the scaffold, just before he was hanged for witchcraft, pointing his finger at Colonel Pyncheon, his persecutor, "God will give him blood to drink!"—and the book was essentially an attempt "to connect a by-gone time with the very present that is flitting away from us."

The piece is played with muted strings throughout, in a minor key; it makes no attempt to reach the depths of pity and terror at which *The Scarlet Letter* was aimed, and there is a delightful strain of humor running through it.

Its great defect is that the story hardly seems worthy of its setting, or, as Henry James puts it, it seems "more like a prologue to a great novel than a great novel itself." Nothing happens for a long time; then, at the close, events rush rapidly by, with some admixture of melodrama, and neither the conventional happy ending nor the *deus ex machina* are scorned. The flight of Clifford and Hepzibah, while their old enemy, Judge Pyncheon, lies dead in the parlor[17] is a tour-de-force, but neither it nor their sudden return advances the action in any way.

[17] Arthur Symons, *Studies in Prose and Verse* (D, 1904) compares this chapter (XVIII) of *The House of the Seven Gables* with Maeterlinck's *Intérieur*. Cf. also Section II of *To the Lighthouse*, by Virginia Woolf. The use of the organ-grinder in the next chapter suggests Katherine Mansfield's "The Daughters of the Late Colonel." Harold Orel has recently studied Chapter XVIII in "The Double Symbol," *AL*, XXIII (1951), 1-6. For an excellent general study of the novel, see Austin Warren, *Rage for Order* (UCP, 1948).

In *The Blithedale Romance,* written the winter he lived in Horace Mann's house in West Newton, Hawthorne tried coming yet closer to common experience, using his own Brook Farm experience (of ten years before) as the setting for a book.[18] But despite the enigmatical, yet haunting, figure of Zenobia, who though not a portrait of Margaret Fuller was certainly influenced by her,[19] the book is not quite successful. The mystery has hardly been so much as superimposed upon the Brook Farm material (to say nothing of having been made a part of it); neither has it been worked out with complete success. Hollingsworth's character was perhaps distorted by Hawthorne's mistrust of reformers, and Zenobia's suicide, though probably consistent in the author's mind with his basic conception of her character, is not adequately prepared for; one is almost tempted to believe that Zenobia had to drown herself so that Hawthorne could take over from his notebook his powerful description of the corpse of Martha Hunt, which, in 1843, he helped recover from the Concord River.[20]

The Marble Faun, Hawthorne's last completed romance, was also his longest and most ambitious. The scene is Italy; the theme (once more), spiritual development through sin and suffering.

Though the background is very rich, Hawthorne inevitably sees Rome as the tourist sees it, not from the point of view of one reared in its tradition, as he had seen his own New England. Since both

[18] See Arlin Turner, "Autobiographical Elements in H's 'The Blithedale Romance,'" *U. of Texas Bull.,* No. 3526, July 8, 1935, pp. 39-62, and the references cited therein; Lina Böhmer, *Brookfarm und H's 'Blithedale Romance'"* (Jena, Gustav Neuenhahn, 1936).

[19] One of the strangest articles in all Hawthorne criticism is Oscar Cargill's "Nemesis and NH," *PMLA,* LII (1937), 848-861, elaborating the theory that H struck at Margaret Fuller to hurt her brother-in-law, Ellery Channing. For this, the death of the writer's sister, in a steamboat accident, on July 27, 1852, was "a most awful punishment," after which Hawthorne "wrote no more fiction for six years, and then was uncertain and ineffective in his work"! This nonsense drew two replies: Austin Warren, *PMLA,* LIV (1939), 615-618; W. P. Randel, *AL,* X (1939), 472-476.

[20] See *American Notebooks,* Stewart's edition, pp. 112-115. This horrible experience haunted Hawthorne's imagination. Comparison of the scene in the novel with the passage in the *Notebooks* shows how closely Hawthorne followed fact, yet what fine restraint and artistic judgment he manifested in omitting the merely repulsive details. It is an excellent illustration of how raw material is transmuted into art.

Kenyon and Hilda are Americans, who view the Eternal City from this same vantage-point, the limitation was less serious than might have been expected, and though Hawthorne takes over many passages from his Italian notebooks without even verbal alteration,[21] I think his material is better assimilated than, say, George Eliot's was in *Romola*. He shows skill, for example, in describing the changing reactions of his characters toward works of art to indicate the developments they undergo in the course of the narrative. Perhaps it was unfortunate, however, that he should have chosen a background in relation to which he was handicapped by his imperfect sympathy with the Roman Catholic Church.[22]

With only a glance from Miriam's eyes to encourage him, Donatello flings the odious persecutor whose hold upon her is never explained[23] from the Tarpeian Rock, and forthwith commences,

[21] See Helen R. Parish, *The Sources of H's "Marble Faun"* (M.A. thesis, Yale, 1929), as cited by Stewart, *American Notebooks*, p. xcii. Other important criticism of *The Marble Faun* includes Elizabeth Peabody, "The Genius of H," *AM*, XXII (1868), 359-374; Austin Phelps, *My Portfolio* (S, 1882); R. H. Fogle, "Simplicity and Complexity in 'The Marble Faun,'" *Tulane Studies in English*, II (1950), 103-120.

[22] Hawthorne may have sympathized more fully with Catholicism than his Puritan prejudices permitted him to realize. This was always the feeling of his younger daughter, Rose, with whom the Roman inoculation was completely successful. Rose Hawthorne Lathrop founded a sisterhood for the relief of the cancerous poor in New York and died Mother Alphonsa, O.S.D. See Katherine Burton, *Sorrow Built a Bridge* (L, 1938); Theodore Maynard, *A Fire Was Lighted* (Bruce, 1848). See, further, Walter V. Gavigan, "H and Rome," *Cath. World*, CXXXV (1932), 555-559; G. P. Voight, "H and the Roman Catholic Church," *NEQ*, XIX (1946), 394-397; C. Wegelin, "Europe in H's Fiction," *ELH*, XIV (1947), 219-245.

[23] Miriam's antecedent mystery, never explained, has occasioned much speculation. Is she guilty, as Turner and Stewart believe, or innocent, as is elaborately argued by Miss Wright? And if she is guilty, what is she guilty of? It seems clear that Hawthorne intended *The Marble Faun* as an oblique study of the Cenci tragedy; see Louis A. Haselmayer, "H and the Cenci," *Neophilologus*, XXVII (1927), 59-65. Paul Elmer More, accordingly, long ago remarked, "for my own part I could never resist the conviction that . . . [Miriam] suffers for the same cause as Shelley's Beatrice Cenci." Stewart goes further: "Her guilt is probably incest. . . . The analogy repeatedly implied between the fate of Miriam and that of Beatrice Cenci would suggest that interpretation. . . . Again, in the following passage in which the model addresses Miriam—'Miriam,—for I forbear to speak another name at which these leaves would shiver above our heads . . .'—the name to be supplied

through suddenly awakened conscience, his tortured development into spiritual maturity. This seems an ideal subject for Hawthorne, and in a way it is. It does not lie within his range, however, to show the pagan, untroubled character of Donatello in his first phase; the contrast, therefore, is less effective than it might have been. Another weakness was pointed out long ago by E. P. Whipple, who observed that Hawthorne's failure to make Miriam's persecutor more than "an allegorical representation of evil" makes it more difficult for us to feel the force of Donatello's sin. We are tempted, instead, to rejoice "in the hero's victory over the Blatant Beast or Giant Despair."

With the New England girl, Hilda (studied from Mrs. Hawthorne), who does not sin, but who feels herself stained by sin when she inadvertently witnesses the crime which involves two of her closest friends, Hawthorne found a character with whom he could not well have failed. The famous chapter in which the young Puritan storms the confessional suggests the possible influence of Charlotte Brontë's *Villette*. He had once planned to have Dimmesdale make such a confession.

The serious difficulty in *The Marble Faun,* however, is not what T. S. Eliot speaks of as "all its Walter Scott-Mysteries of Udolpho upholstery," but rather Hawthorne's unsatisfactory treatment of the element of mystery. He habitually employed what Matthiessen calls "the device of multiple choice," assuming no complete knowledge

would seem to be 'daughter' or, perhaps, 'sister' " (*American Notebooks,* p. xcv). On the other hand, Julian Hawthorne has recorded how it was once suggested to his father that Miriam was Henriette Deluzy-Desportes, and how he replied, "Well, I dare say she was. I knew I had some dim recollection of some crime, but I didn't know what." See Nathalia Wright, "H and the Praslin Murder," *NEQ,* XV (1942), 5-14. Andrew Lang, not cited by Miss Wright, declares maddeningly in *Adventures Among Books* (L, 1905): "I know, now, who Miriam was and who was the haunter of the Catacombs. But perhaps the people are as well without the knowledge of an old and 'ower true tale' that shook a throne." This could refer to the Praslin murder but not to the Cenci tragedy. However, Lang's statement seems over-definite. There is no reason why Hawthorne may not have had both cases in mind, nor is there anything in his novel that would have necessitated his thinking of Henriette (whom he may have met) in any more definite way than his son indicates. If he was thinking of her, then, in a sense, *The Marble Faun* anticipates our two contemporary studies in fiction of the Praslin murder: Joseph Shearing's *Forget-Me-Not* (*The Strange Case of Lucile Cléry,* 1932) and Rachel Field's *All This and Heaven Too* (1938).

of the deeds and minds of his characters but offering the reader a choice between two or more hypotheses. In itself, this method is quite legitimate. Here, however, he carries it to ridiculous extremes, and there has never been a satisfactory reply to the objection raised by the British *Saturday Review* when the book was published, that a "mystery is set before us to unriddle, and at the end the author turns about and asks us what is the good of solving it." Hawthorne seems to have felt that it was rather vulgar of his readers to ask such questions; if any vulgarity is involved, it should be remembered that it was he who raised the question to begin with. The "Conclusion" added in 1860 does not help the novel as a work of art, for it is clearly no part of the fiction but merely a commentary on it.

4. *The Anatomy of Evil*

The problem which has worried Hawthorne's interpreters most is the problem of his solitude. This was much less thoroughgoing than the caricaturists would have it;[24] one gets a very different impression from reading the account of the Salem years in Randall Stewart's fine biography than is derived from many of the older, less well-informed books. Hawthorne was a man who did a man's work in the world. He was poor during most of his life, but he faced every crisis courageously, and when it was necessary to put aside the work of his choice to go out into the world and toil for the support of his family, he never hesitated. At Liverpool, he campaigned for decent treatment of American sailors, visiting prisons, hospitals, lunatic asylums, and other places that must have been very horrible to a man of his temperament. In his opinions on social problems he was far ahead of his time, and there are few points indeed where the liberal of the twentieth century feels impelled to challenge him.[25]

He himself is partly responsible for the popular impression of him as the Hermit of Salem. Perhaps he was not quite fair to himself. Perhaps the difficulty was not only that he indulged in solitude more

[24] So, apparently, was his mother's also; see Manning Hawthorne, *NEQ*, XIV (1941), 388-390, and cf. the same writer's "H's Early Years," *Essex Inst. Hist. Coll.*, LXXXIV (1938), 1-21; "Parental and Family Influences on H," LXXVI (1940), 1-13; and "A Glimpse of H's Boyhood," LXXXIII (1947), 178-184.

[25] See, especially, Lawrence S. Hall, *H, Critic of Society* (YUP, 1944).

than most men do but that he perceived its dangers more clearly. "For the last ten years I have not lived, but only dreamed of living." "If I could only make tables, I should feel myself more of a man." "I'm a doomed man, and over I must go." He knew well that there are special virtues which bloom in solitude, but save that he had preserved "the dew of my youth and the freshness of my heart," it seemed to him that he had acquired few of them. He was no devotee and no scholar; paleness, not profundity, seemed to him characteristic of the work he had done so far.

Few sensitive men can have passed through life without at some time narrowly averting shipwreck; it was Hawthorne's good fortune that Sophia Peabody should have come along to unlock the gate for him when she did. "I used to think I could imagine all passions, all feelings and states of the heart and mind, but how little did I know! Indeed, we are but shadows; we are not endowed with real life; and all that seems most real about us is but the thinnest substance of a dream till the heart be touched."

Hawthorne's earlier interpreters—Lathrop, Woodberry, and Henry James—will have no truck with the notion that writing was for him a cathartic process, that, like D. H. Lawrence, he gave himself to "art for my sake." James reminds us that the "duskiest flowers of his invention sprang straight from the soil of his happiest days," and cites the testimony of the notebooks to prove Hawthorne's "serenity and amenity of mind." With all this Hawthorne himself would have agreed: ". . . when people think I am pouring myself out in a tale or an essay, I am merely telling what is common to human nature, not what is peculiar to myself."

Today, it is difficult to believe that Hawthorne's preoccupation with the theme of the solitary egotist was wholly accidental. Yet his treatment of it shows no abnormality in him. What is the meaning of "Ethan Brand," "Lady Eleanore's Mantle," "The Christmas Banquet"? The unpardonable sin is pride, and moral solitude is the worst—and most blameworthy—fate of all. When a man's intellect develops beyond his moral nature, when it triumphs "over the sense of brotherhood with man and reverence for God," when a woman "seeks to place herself above the sympathies of our common nature," then doom is inevitable. One cannot take refuge from life in a dream of life.[26] One must embrace life, in spite of all its disappointments. "We will not go back. The world can never be dark for us, for we will always love one another."[27] Such is the testimony of the stories Hawthorne wrote at the very time he was supposed to be drifting over the precipice.[28]

Hawthorne's repudiation of pride connects with more important aspects of his thinking. It has always been recognized that he had little sympathy with reformers. He honored their generosity and idealism, but he saw no signs that the millennium would arrive during his lifetime, and he feared the warping effect of a too exclusive devotion to some cause. He could see no sense in casting human vanities into the bonfire unless you were prepared to cast the human heart in after them.[29] As for regenerating that heart, he believed that the only known means was the Christian religion.[30]

Despite all his indifference to churchianity and formal theology, Hawthorne is, therefore, a profoundly Christian writer. All his faith was in the great humanistic-religious tradition; on the matter of pride as the root sin (so obscure to most Protestants), he would have had no difficulty in arranging a meeting of minds with Dante and Aquinas.[31]

Capricious as he felt the world to be [writes Mary E. Coleridge finely], he never speculated as to the Power that made it, as to the end for which it was made, as to the wickedness of everything that runs counter to that end. The world was made by "Providence"; it was made for the expansion and improvement of man; it was marred by sin, and sin is excessively sinful and never can be anything else.[32]

[26] "The Village Uncle."
[27] "The Canterbury Pilgrims."
[28] Cf. Amy L. Reed, "Self-Portraiture in the Work of NH," *SP*, XXIII (1926), 40-54.
[29] "Earth's Holocaust."
[30] Julian Hawthorne, *NH and his Wife*, I, 258.
[31] On this matter, see Harry A. Myers' comments on Hawthorne and Melville in his *Are Men Equal?* (P, 1945).
[32] "The Questionable Shapes of NH," *LA*, CCXLII (1904), 348-353. The most recent, and perhaps the most comprehensive, study of some phases of the matters discussed in the last few paragraphs is Darrel Abel, "The Theme of Isolation in H," *Personalist*, XXXII (1951), 42-59, 182-190.

The easy optimism of contemporary Transcendentalism and Unitarianism struck Hawthorne, therefore, as hopelessly unrealistic.[33] He had none of Emerson's or Thoreau's faith in "nature." Emerson's favorite doctrine of "compensation" he put into the mouth of the half-crazed Clifford Pyncheon on his hapless flight! (For Clifford there had been no compensation.) In other words, though Hawthorne may have lost the theology of his Calvinist ancestors, he still respects their attitude toward life. Like them, he sees the heart of man as desperately wicked; like them, he refuses to become ecstatic over the sight of a man trying to lift himself by his own bootstraps.

In this sense, then, Hawthorne *is* a Puritan, but he is Puritan only in a general way. Saint Augustine—and Saint Paul—discovered the wickedness of the human heart long before Calvin, and the same process of brooding that produced *The Scarlet Letter* lies behind the Greek drama, *Hamlet,* and the novels of Joseph Conrad. Henry James was never more profound than when he saw Hawthorne's way of dealing with his Puritan heritage as the best possible, "for he contrived, by an exquisite process, best known to himself, to transmute this heavy moral burden into the very substance of the imagination. . . ."[34]

Hawthorne's daughter, Mother Alphonsa, remembered in her later life his "religious, . . . Christlike choice of mental companionship (pity) with the greatest of all mourners, those who have sinned. . . ." And Hawthorne himself said of the outcast children of London that "If a single one of those hopeless little ones be lost, the world is lost." Despite his early devotion to *The Newgate Calendar,* Hawthorne must be nearly unique among those who have found a special subject in evil, in his complete lack of interest in the sinful act itself. In "Fancy's Show-Box," he speculates on whether the soul could be stained by evil deeds planned but never carried out, and in *The Marble Faun* Miriam and Donatello feel that their sin has brought them into fellowship with all sinners and made them guilty of all sin. Woodberry calls this "a curious inversion of the doctrine of the communion of the saints," and seems to think of it as something

[33] N. F. Doubleday, "H's Inferno," *CE,* I (1940), 658-670, is important for the understanding of Hawthorne's break with Transcendentalism.
[34] See Barriss Mills, "H and Puritanism," *NEQ,* XXI (1948), 78-102.

peculiar to Puritanism, but Woodberry has evidently forgotten the Epistle to the Romans.

Both *The Scarlet Letter* and *The Marble Faun* touch the daring theme of salvation not through sin but through the suffering which follows sin. Of Hester we are told that

Man had marked this woman's sin by a scarlet letter. . . . God, as a direct consequence of the sin which man thus punished, had given her a lovely child, whose place was on that same dishonored bosom, to connect her parent forever with the race and descent of mortals, and to be finally a blessed soul in heaven!

But Hawthorne avoids the conclusion which many a modern novelist would have drawn. This fact is not justification of Hester's sin; it is merely a striking manifestation of the soul of goodness in things evil; the wrath of man is made to praise the Lord. Elsewhere (in Chapter XIII), he indicates the boldness of Hester's thinking in her imposed spiritual isolation. "The scarlet letter had not done its office"—for Hawthorne did not believe that law can deal with the sins of the soul. But we are never told what Hester's views are. This has sometimes been imputed to timidity on Hawthorne's part. As a matter of fact, it was due to his sound aesthetic instinct. There is no room for an emancipated female's "testimony" in this story.

In *The Marble Faun* the question comes up again. Miriam first puts it to Kenyon. "Was . . . [Donatello's sin] a means of education, bringing a simple and imperfect nature to a point of feeling and intelligence which it could have reached under no other discipline?" And if the answer be yes, then was Adam's fall itself "the destined means by which . . . we are to attain a higher, brighter, and profounder happiness than our lost birthright gave?" Kenyon cannot follow her. "Mortal man has no right to tread on the ground where you now set your feet." Yet he illogically restates her idea, as his own speculation, to Hilda, who is shocked beyond words, as he might have known she would be.

Dorothy Waples thinks that the real subject of *The Marble Faun* is "nature improved by a share of guilt," but that Hawthorne "tempers it to the shorn lambs who may read it."[35] But there is no

[35] "Suggestions for Interpreting 'The Marble Faun,' " *AL*, XIII (1941), 224-239.

more reason for imputing Miriam's heresies to Hawthorne than Hester's.[36] Miss Waples's article recalls John Erskine's rashness, a good many years ago, when he attributed similar notions to Milton. C. A. Moore, E. E. Stoll, Sir Herbert Grierson, and Arthur O. Lovejoy all found themselves unconvinced. Lovejoy shows convincingly that the paradox of the fortunate fall did not begin with Milton, that "it had been embraced by Ambrose, Leo the Great, Gregory the Great, Francis of Sales, and Du Bartas, and had for ten centuries had a place in many missals . . . and it had been put more sharply and boldly by at least two Doctors of the Church . . . than by Milton."[37] None of them had ever interpreted it as a license to sin. The passage in the missal occurs in the Exultet for the Holy Saturday Mass: *"O felix culpa quae talem et tantum meruit habere redemptorem."* Hawthorne gives no sign of familiarity with it.

From other sources, it is clear that Hawthorne did *not* hold Miriam's view. Of Hollingsworth's plan in *The Blithedale Romance* to reform criminals "through an appeal to their higher instincts," Coverdale (Hawthorne's mouthpiece), is frankly scornful. "He ought to have commenced his investigation on the subject by perpetrating some huge sin in his proper person, and examining the condition of his higher instincts afterwards." In *The Scarlet Letter* the author himself declares, "And be the stern and sad truth spoken, that the breach which guilt has once made into the human soul is never, in this mortal state, repaired." While in *The House of the Seven Gables* we read, "It is a truth . . . that no great mistake, whether acted or endured, in our mortal sphere, is ever really set right." Woodberry has attacked Hawthorne at this point as having ignored the Christian Gospel of redemption and anticipated "those ethical views which are the burden of George Eliot's moral genius, and contain scientific pessimism." This statement, however, represents Hawthorne as somewhat sterner than he was. Not even

[36] We know, for example, that Hawthorne did not share Hester's feminism; cf. N. F. Doubleday, *PMLA*, LIV (1939), 825-828.

[37] John Erskine, "The Theme of Death in 'Paradise Lost,'" *PMLA*, XXXII (1917), 573-582; Arthur O. Lovejoy, "Milton and the Paradox of the Fortunate Fall," *ELH*, IV (1937), 161-179.

Dimmesdale's condition, at the close of *The Scarlet Letter,* is represented as hopeless.[38]

Hawthorne's genius had its limitations. His range was deep, not wide, and he lacked fecundity; he had a brief period of important productiveness, but when practical life claimed him, he was compelled, except for his journal, to give up writing altogether. In his later life, his own early works became his principal sources.

His prose is as fine as any we have to show in America, but the eighteenth century still kept her hold upon him. He could write stiffly and formally on occasion, and he never attempted characterization in terms of distinctive speech.

Brownell berated Hawthorne for his weakness in initiative. "In a sense he never meant anything. He drifted." Even Woodberry complains, more gently, that "at every stage [he] was materially aided by his friends in obtaining employment and position." It is somewhat difficult to understand how a man could be expected to appoint himself to the customs or consular service. But the first American who dared to devote himself to the life of the imaginative artist did not lack initiative, nor did the man who sent a sunflower to sorrowing neighbors with the message, "Tell them that the sunflower is a symbol of the sun, and that the sun is a symbol of the glory of God"[39] lack either radiance or courage. Hawthorne's roots went deep into America; his fundamental concern was with the great themes of world art.

[38] Charles Allen Dinsmore, *Atonement in Literature and Life* (HM, 1906) finds a greater measure of reconciliation in *The Scarlet Letter* than in *Adam Bede.* See also his interesting comparison between Hawthorne and Dante.

[39] Bliss Perry, *Park-Street Papers* (HM, 1908), p. 102.

CHAPTER IV

THE AMBIGUITIES OF HERMAN MELVILLE*

> "What are you knitting there, my man?"
> "The knot," was the brief reply, without looking up.
> "So it seems; but what is it for?"
> "For some one else to undo," muttered back the old man.
> *Benito Cereno*

1. *"The Man Who Lived among Cannibals"*

Herman Melville was born in New York, on August 1, 1819, of English mercantile and Dutch patroon stock. A little more than halfway through the forties, he made his bid for fame, with *Typee* and *Omoo,* as the literary discoverer of the South Seas, and seemed slated to go down to posterity as "the man who had lived among cannibals." But when he turned away from what his contemporaries regarded as simple transcripts of exotic adventure to the confusions of *Mardi,* the rich allegorical overtones of *Moby-Dick,* and the tortured, incestuous introversions of *Pierre,* his public deserted him. The last volume of fiction to see print during his lifetime was *The Confidence Man* in 1857; like Hardy, he continued to publish verses, but unlike Hardy, he withdrew himself altogether from the literary world. It was not surprising that when he died, on September 28, 1891, those to whom his name was still familiar should merely have been surprised to learn that he had lived so long.

The extent to which he was, for many years, forgotten has often been overstated; perhaps the unfailing enthusiasm of such readers as William Morris, James Thomson, Edward Carpenter, Robert Louis Stevenson, Sir James Barrie, and John Masefield might even be regarded as compensation for having been dismissed so contemptu-

---

* Under the title "Our Contemporary Herman Melville," portions of this chapter appeared in *The English Journal* and *College English* for March, 1950. Copyright, 1950, by the University of Chicago Press.

ously by Barrett Wendell. The energy of the revival which has taken place since 1919 it would be impossible to overstate. Melville's tragic sense of life has appealed to some of our intelligentsia as much as it repelled the Victorians; he has become, consequently, one of the prime heroes of American literature. Indeed, some of his admirers will not rest until they have crowned him its king-figure.[1]

Contemporary study of Melville was handicapped at the outset by a lack of adequate biographical materials and, in some quarters, by a corresponding lack of good judgment from which we have, indeed, not yet entirely recovered. The reckless guesswork in which some writers have indulged when interpreting such matters as the character of Melville's parents and the author's own friendship with Hawthorne, during his residence at Pittsfield, Massachusetts, can only be described as libel against the helpless dead;[2] surely the parents of any son who seems promising enough ever to have a book written about him must, after examining such effusions, be strongly tempted to strangle their offspring lest they themselves should go down to posterity in the guise of some weird monsters who have crawled out of the Freudian pit. It is to be hoped that the 1951 publication of Jay Leyda's impressive collection of Melville materials (*The Melville Log*) and of Leon Howard's admirable biography, based upon these materials, will tend to discourage further excesses of this kind.

2. *Romances of Experience*

Typee (1846), *Omoo* (1847), *Redburn* (1849), and *White-Jacket* (1850) are generally considered Melville's four autobiographical fictions. Other books also draw upon his life at sea: *Mardi* (1849), which intervened between *Omoo* and *Redburn; Moby-Dick* (1851); "Benito Cereno," the *pièce de resistance* of *The Piazza Tales* (1856); and *Billy Budd*, which was written during the last years of Melville's

---

[1] See O. W. Riegel, "The Anatomy of M's Fame," *AL*, III (1931-1932), 195-203; cf. W. Braswell, *AL*, V (1934), 360-364.

[2] On the Hawthorne matter, see A. H. Starke, *AL*, I (1929-1930), 304-305; Randall Stewart, *SRL*, V (1929), 967; E. K. Brown, *AL*, III (1931), 72-75; Willard Thorp, *HM, Representative Selections,* p. xxxv; F. O. Matthiessen, *American Renaissance,* pp. 488-489. R. S. Forsythe, *AL*, II (1930-1931), 286-289, deals with Mumford's interpretation of *Pierre.*

life but not published until 1924. But these are all fictional treatments of imagined happenings.

No absolute line of demarcation can be drawn between the first four works I have mentioned and the rest of Melville's output. But these early books share a common experiencial background which justifies us in treating them as a group, and they are marked off from most of the later work by their simplicity. It should be noted that Melville did not use his adventures for literature in the order in which life brought them to him. His *first* voyage, as a sailor on a merchantman bound for Liverpool in 1839,[3] he used in his *fourth* book, *Redburn*. His whaling voyage to the South Seas began at New Bedford on January 3, 1841; he left the *Acushnet* for his month among the cannibals in the Marquesas on July 9, 1842 *(Typee)*, whence he escaped in an Australian whaler for Tahiti *(Omoo)*. At Honolulu, on August 17, 1843, he was mustered into the United States Navy *(White-Jacket)*; he was discharged, at Boston, on October 14, 1844. These facts understood, *Typee, Omoo, Redburn,* and *White-Jacket* may be considered in the order of their publication.

Twenty years before Mark Twain visited the Sandwich Islands, more than forty years before Robert Louis Stevenson settled at Samoa, and three-quarters of a century before Frederick O'Brien wrote *White Shadows in the South Seas* and F. W. Murnau came from Germany to make a Polynesian film called *Tabu,* Melville discovered the Pacific paradise, for himself and for the readers of the world.

Typee, A Romance of the South Seas—the main title, which is intended to indicate "man-eaters," and which probably does not, is the name of the tribe with which the author sojourned—*Typee* is generally placed in the Rousseau tradition of the "noble savage." This is not strictly accurate. The book shocked many of Melville's contemporaries by suggesting that the author's relations with Fay-away—who smoked a pipe, ate raw fish, and "for the most part clung to the primitive and summer garb of Eden"—were not wholly platonic.[4] But neither love nor nakedness is necessarily uncivilized.

---

[3] Not 1837, as often stated. See W. H. Gilman, "M's Liverpool Trip," *MLN*, LXI (1946), 543-547.

[4] The essential restraint and chastity of *Typee* is best prefigured in the

Melville did admire wholeheartedly the mental and physical health of the islanders, their excellent dispositions, and their freedom from the vices of civilization, but he saw these things not as the spontaneous productions of "nature," but as the achievements of a social order which they had made, and which was right for them. He is very clear that when the whites and the people of the South Seas come together, the latter do not corrupt but are corrupted. It was on this ground that he threw down the gauntlet by manifesting an imperfect sympathy for the missionaries, who, as he saw it, brought to the South Seas a religion too austere for its people to understand, and who all too often served as an entering wedge for imperialistic aggression. Melville saw "white civilized man" as "the most ferocious animal on the face of the earth"; he even dared suggest that "four or five Marquesan islanders sent to the United States as missionaries might be quite as useful as an equal number of Americans dispatched to the islands in a similar capacity." But this noble indignation never tempted him to believe that a white man might solve his problems by "going native," as we may see by his unfriendly portrait of one Lem Hardy, who had done just that, as well as in his own determination to escape from the Pacific paradise —Fayaway and all—at the earliest possible moment. Cannibals he could regard sympathetically, not because he was a pagan but because he was enough of a Christian to realize that they too were children of God, but cannibalism (and everything that went with it) he could only contemplate with horror. For the young man was already on his way to the breadth and height of insight which were to enable him, a few years later, to take Parkman severely to task for his unhumanitarian attitude toward the Indians:

We are all of us—Anglo-Saxons, Dyaks, and Indians—sprung from one head, and made in one image. And if we regret this brotherhood now, we shall be forced to join hands hereafter. A misfortune is not a

enchanting figure of the nude girl, standing erect with upraised arms in the head of the canoe, with her tappa robe outstretched like a sail. "We American sailors pride ourselves upon our straight clean spars, but a prettier mast than Fayaway was never shipped aboard of any craft." Surely the painter John La Farge was not the only reader whose imagination has been captivated by this scene.

fault; and good luck is not meritorious. The savage is born a savage; and the civilized being but inherits his civilization, nothing more.

Let us not disdain, then, but pity. And wherever we recognize the image of God, let us reverence it, though it hung from the gallows.

Melville was destined to be rescued from the South Seas by an American battleship. His life among the white men on that floating hell, the whole end and object of whose being was organized murder, went far to destroy his faith in his kind. He saved himself, in so far as salvation was possible, by clinging to his memories of the naked, fornicating, heathen, savage cannibals whom he had known in the South Seas! How touching that even in *Moby-Dick* he should have to write that "in the soul of man there lies one insular Tahiti," and that one of Ishmael's closest bonds with life should be through his friendship with Queequeg, who started out to find a better way of life for his people in the West, but who has now been cruelly disillusioned and has ceased his quest. Melville never recovered from his early conditioning. Even in *Billy Budd,* his hero, though a white man, is an illiterate "barbarian."

The continuation of the story in *Omoo,*[5] *A Narrative of Adventures in the South Seas* is less exotic in its materials and more prosaic in its tone. Being confined on suspicion of mutiny is less uplifting and enjoyable than bathing with naked girls, and Melville's description of it is correspondingly less stimulating. But the author's attitude toward his materials has changed also; this time he has got less of the spirit of youth into his book. Nevertheless, Dr. Long Ghost, once a gentleman, is a vivid character in the Smollett tradition, and there are memorable vignettes of Mrs. Bell, the Haughty Youth, and others.

Redburn, His First Voyage, Being the Sailor-Boy Confessions and Reminiscences of the Son of a Gentleman in the Merchant Service has been much abused by many writers, never more unjustly than by Melville himself, who declared that he only wrote it to get money to buy tobacco with. Possibly he resented being obliged to go back to this simpler kind of narrative after the failure of the more ambitious *Mardi.* Masefield's special enthusiasm for *Redburn* helps to atone for some of this injustice.

[5] "a rover, or rather, a person wandering from one island to another. . . ."

The book opens upon vivid, childish memories of old New York, where Redburn's father was an importer, and moves on to a touching picture of the disillusionment of an innocent boy among the rough sailors with whom his lot is cast. As in all of Melville's books, there is much "information," but this is, in general, more successfully transmuted into fiction than in *White-Jacket*. Thus we learn the names and functions of the various ropes as we are made acquainted with Redburn's difficulties in distinguishing them, though it is true that we tend to lose the boy to a certain extent as the voyage proceeds and to focus our attention upon maritime adventure as such. When England is reached, *Redburn* becomes a travel book, and eleven whole chapters are built up on the basis of an old "guide" known as *The Picture of Liverpool*. The closing adventure—the story of the gay young English blade, Harry Bolton, who ruins himself in a gambling hell and then embarks upon the sea—departs from the mood of realistic narration altogether, to take on something of the tone of Disraeli in his more flamboyant episodes, with just a hint of *The Fool of Quality*.

The literary tone of this closing section is not altogether inappropriate however. In his admirable book, *Melville's Early Life and "Redburn"* (1951), William H. Gilman has stressed the aesthetic, as opposed to the experiencial, element in this novel, though without denying that Melville made use in it of his Liverpool voyage. Reinforcing Willard Thorp's earlier observation that "Melville was not telling the story of his life in *Redburn*," and arguing that he did not intend his book to be received as autobiography, Mr. Gilman calls Redburn "a created character" and his creator "a great illusionist, a master of literary legerdemain."[6]

The last of the four books in Melville's first manner, *White-Jacket; or The World in a Man-of-War*, is hardly a novel;[7] it is an account of life on a battleship, notable chiefly for its attacks upon flogging

[6] A briefer critical study of *Redburn* will be found in John J. Gross, "The Rehearsal of Ishmael: M's 'Redburn,'" *VQR*, XXVII (1951), 581-600. Professor Thorp's article is "Redburn's Prosy Old Guidebook," *PMLA*, LIII (1938), 1146-1156.

[7] For a more imaginative interpretation of *White-Jacket*, with heavy stress upon its alleged symbolism, see H. P. Vincent, "'White-Jacket': An Essay in Interpretation," *NEQ*, XXII (1949), 304-315.

and on war itself. The question of flogging had already been raised in *Omoo,* where Melville had contented himself by disapproving of it but admitting that so long as navies themselves were maintained, it was probably necessary. "War being the greatest of evils, all its accessories necessarily partake of the same character; and this is about all that can be said in defence of flogging." In *White-Jacket* he stakes out a more advanced position, showing his fundamental kinship with Hawthorne in his recognition of the inborn dignity of humanity, "which no legislator has a right to violate." "The soul and substance" of the Christian religion he finds in Jesus' doctrine of nonviolence; without that, "Christianity were like any other faith."

Perhaps the most memorable single figure in *White-Jacket* is the surgeon Cadwallader Cuticle, who kills a sailor by an unnecessary operation, first divesting himself "of nearly all inorganic appurtenances." This is comedy in the Swiftian manner. His name and contemporary records combine to attest that this horrible creature came not from Melville's experiences in the navy but from his own imagination and from Smollett.[8]

3. *Romances of Imagination*

Mardi, Moby-Dick, and (save that it is not a story of the sea), *Pierre* (1853) comprise a second group among Melville's fictions. This affinity appears in the metaphysical complexities and allegorical suggestions contained in all three, even if we do not accept Homans's view that all have the same theme.[9]

Mardi represents Melville's first attempt to break away from the simple, direct narratives with which he had begun; it was public demand, and not his own taste, which dictated a return to conventionalities in *Redburn* and *White-Jacket.* But by the time he had produced *Moby-Dick* and *Pierre,* he could no more have gone back

[8] See Livingston Hunt, "HM as a Naval Historian," *Harvard Graduates Magazine,* XXXIX (1930-1931), 22-30; C. R. Anderson, "A reply to HM's 'White-Jacket' by Rear-Admiral Thomas A. Selfridge, Sr.," *AL,* VII (1935), 123-144. See, further, on this book: H. Hayford, "The Sailor-Poet of 'White-Jacket.'" *BPLQ,* III (1951), 221-228; W. L. Heflin, "A Man-of-War Button Divides Two Cousins," *ibid.,* pp. 51-60.

[9] "Is the refusal to be limited to the Penultimate an earthly disease to be suppressed, or a heavenly ideal to be preserved at all costs?"

to his earlier manner than Henry James could have returned to *The American* after *The Wings of the Dove*.[10] I do not mean that Melville had, in the James sense, found himself as a novelist; he never did that. But he must go on in his own orbit or he must be silent.

It should be understood at the outset that the idea that any of these works have allegorical significance rests upon the general impression they produce upon their readers and not upon any specific statement we possess concerning Melville's intent. Melville himself declared that nobody since Adam had "got to the meaning of this great allegory—the world"; why, then, should pygmies like writing men be surprised to find *their* allegories "but ill comprehended"? In *Mardi* he exhorts his readers to "be content with the theology in the grass and the flowers in seed time and harvest." In 1852 he wrote Mrs. Hawthorne about the Whale's story:

I had some vague idea while writing it, that the whole book was susceptible of an allegorical construction, and also that parts of it were— but the specialty of many of the particular subordinates allegories were first revealed to me after reading Mr. Hawthorne's letter [no longer extant, alas!], which, without citing any particular examples, yet intimated the part-and-parcel allegoricalness of the whole.

He went off the deep end, in *Mardi,* in the midst of a narrative which had seemed to augur development, but no radical departure, for the author of *Typee. Mardi* opens not "very far westward from Pitcairn's Island, where the mutineers of the *Bounty* settled." In modern ears this sounds very promising, and the first part of the book richly fulfills the promise in a series of very exciting sea adventures. But when Yillah and her cronies enter there is an important change.

The girl herself is rescued by the hero Taji from an old priest who would have sacrificed her and who is himself killed during the skirmish. For a time, she and Taji live together in perfect bliss; then, abruptly, she disappears, and the rest of the story describes the hero's quest for her, through a series of lands representing various types of human temperament and experience, the nations of the earth, and

[10] He did, to be sure, produce *Israel Potter* afterwards, but this was a special case.

almost everything else in which Herman Melville happened to be interested. Taji and his companions even visit the utopia, Serenia, where all things are regulated in accordance with the teachings of Alma (Christ).[11] The manner of the journey recalls Rabelais; the style is often suggestive of Sir Thomas Browne. But though the ostensible setting remains the South Seas, the ideas involved belong to a much more sophisticated milieu—Melville's own literary and social and political world of New York society.

Yillah herself has been variously interpreted. She is opposed to Hautia, the lady of sensuality and pride, and it seems clear that at least two ideas are involved in her. On one level of meaning, in an anti-ascetic book, she is placed over against both lust and a febrile Platonism; Taji's relationship with her is both physical and spiritual and therefore altogether satisfying. And on another level she is evidently truth, and the value of life itself is bound up with the search for her.[12]

Moby-Dick seems far more coherent than *Mardi*, but its meaning is no less controversial. As fiction, it tells the story of Captain Ahab's attempt to revenge himself upon the Great White Whale that had swallowed his leg. But what *is* Ahab, and what *is* the Whale? The book has been interpreted as a parable of man's struggle against nature, against evil, against "the accidental malice of the universe," and even against God.[13] It is clear that to Ahab the Whale sym-

[11] As Tyrus Hillway has acutely pointed out ("Taji's Quest for Certainty," *AL*, XVIII, 1946, 27-34), Taji's refusal to abide in Serenia does not necessarily imply a rejection of the Christian way either by him or by his creator. The point is simply that Serenia does represent a way of life while Taji is committed to a search for the ultimate truth. See another article of Hillway's, "Taji's Abdication in HM's 'Mardi,'" *AL*, XVI (1944), 204-207, for the interesting suggestion that the "crime" Taji commits at the close is suicide; convinced that Yillah has died, he carries his search for her into the Beyond. Nathalia Wright accepts this suggestion in "The Head and Heart in M's 'Mardi,'" *PMLA*, LXVI (1951), 351-362.

[12] On *Mardi*, see also: J. H. Birss, "A Note on M's 'Mardi,'" *NQ*, CLXII (1932), 104; David Jaffe, "Some Sources of M's 'Mardi,'" *AL*, IX (1937), 56-59; W. Braswell, "M's Use of Seneca," *AL*, XII (1940), 98-104; Gordon Mills, "The Significance of 'Arcturus' in 'Mardi,'" *ibid.*, pp. 158-61; Merrel R. Davis, "The Flower Symbolism in 'Mardi,'" *MLQ*, II (1941), 625-638; M. M. Sealts, "M's Friend Atahalpa," *NQ*, CXCIV (1941), 37-38.

[13] An admirable companion to *Moby-Dick* is M. O. Percival, *A Reading of "Moby-Dick"* (UCP, 1950), which is sound, sensible, and sometimes pro-

bolizes everything malevolent or intransigent in the world and, on occasion at least, everything that runs counter to the will of Ahab. There, for the moment, we must leave it. To the question of the Whale's meaning for Melville, we shall return in another connection.

Moby-Dick may well have begun with "The Town-Ho's Story," now given in Chapter LIV.[14] Melville had read about the actual white whale of his time, Mocha Dick, and he knew about the sinking of the Nantucket whaler *Essex* by a sperm whale in 1820.[15] Newton Arvin has recently suggested that the *Lusiads* of the sixteenth-century Portuguese poet Camoëns may have been known to him, and Howard Vincent has spoken of "The Rime of the Ancient Mariner."[16] Vincent has also shown,[17] however, that Melville's whaling-knowledge was less extensive than has sometimes been assumed. (Lincoln Colcord had already criticized his seamanship.)[18]

found. The most elaborate allegorical interpretation is William S. Gleim, "A Theory of 'Moby-Dick,'" *NEQ*, II (1929), 402-419, which was later expanded in *The Meaning of "Moby-Dick"* (Brick Row Book Shop, 1938). Here the Whale is fate, and every character and incident has its role to play. Percy H. Boynton, *More Contemporary Americans,* sounds, for once, like an unbelievable combination of Transcendentalist and proletarian when he declares that "The ocean is the boundless truth, the land is the threatening reef of human error. The whiteness of the great whale figures for the ghostly mystery of infinitude . . . the symbol of all property and privilege." John Erskine, *The Delight of Great Books* (BM, 1928) finds the Whale "the focus of the story" but not "the main subject of it." The "central theme" is "the sea, and all the vast aspects of nature," and the image of the waters expresses the horror of space. D. H. Lawrence found in the Whale "the deepest blood-being of the white race." But probably Newton Arvin surpasses everybody else on the score of weird imagination when he suggests that, along with much else, both Melville's parents have been embodied in Moby Dick!

[14] Howard P. Vincent, *The Trying-Out of "Moby-Dick"* (HM, 1949), p. 46. This, the most elaborate study of the making of *Moby-Dick,* is indispensable to serious study of Melville. On "The Town-Ho's Story," see also S. Paul, *AL,* XXI (1949), 212-221.

[15] Vincent, *op. cit.,* pp. 166 ff. Cf. R. S. Garnett, "Moby Dick and Mocha Dick," *Blackwood's* CCXXVI (1929), 841-858; Walter Harding, "A Note on the Title 'Moby-Dick,'" *AL,* XXII (1951), 500-501; cf. Sidney Kaplan, "The *Moby Dick* in the Service of the Underground Railroad," *Phylon,* XII (1951), 173-176.

[16] Vincent, *op. cit.,* pp. 210-211.

[17] Vincent, *op. cit.,* pp. 128 ff.

[18] "Notes on 'Moby-Dick,'" *Freeman,* V (1922), 559-562, 585-587.

There is a good deal of "side" in his citation of references; he often gives the impression of having gone to primary sources when he is actually using only a secondary source and employing it somewhat uncritically at that.

In the ordinary sense of the term, *Moby-Dick* is hardly a novel. Melville never mastered the common technique of fiction; he hardly attempted to do so except in *Pierre*. It was upon this ground that contemporary critics condemned the story of the Whale; we accept it today because we believe that the book is great enough to create its own category, at the same time creating the taste by which it is understood.

In the course of his narrative, Melville himself (like another Sterne), glorifies his own apparent lawlessness: "I try all things; I achieve what I can." (He repeats all this in *Pierre:* "I write precisely as I please.") When William Ellery Sedgwick declares that *Moby-Dick* is a "hodge-podge of adventure story, moral drama, mysticism, practical information, diatribe," he is saying, though less admiringly, precisely what Lewis Mumford says when he describes the book as a symphony which employs "every resource of language and thought, fantasy, description, philosophy, natural history, drama, broken rhythms, blank verse, imagery, symbol," etc.[19]

Of plot there is hardly enough to make a good short story; the mood is frequently that of the epic or saga, the method that of the Elizabethan drama.[20] "It is remarkable," writes George C. Homans, "how few pages of the book are used to carry the story forward, remarkable the economy with which Melville widens and widens his canvas while suggesting the lines that pull the composition together."

They pull even through vast chunks of purely factual material—

[19] For the blank verse, see Matthiessen, *op. cit.,* p. 436. N. B. Fagin, "HM and the Interior Monologue," *AL,* VI (1934-1935), 433-434, claims that, in *Moby-Dick,* Chs. XXXVII-XXXIX, Melville used stream-of-consciousness technique before Dujardin.

[20] For the influence of Shakespeare, and especially of *King Lear,* see Raymond G. Hughes, "M and Shakespeare," *Sh. Assn. Bull.,* VII (1932), 103-112; Charles Olson, *Twice a Year,* No. 1 (1938), pp. 165-189, and his book, *Call Me Ishmael* (Reynal & Hitchcock, 1947); also, cf. Matthiessen, *op. cit.,* pp. 423-435.

blocks of unassimilable nonfiction matter which Melville, incredibly, as it appears on first contact, has deliberately thrust between himself and his goal. New readers of Melville are often tempted to tell themselves that the man is a stippler, that an accumulating effect is beyond him. Now, there is much evidence to show that Melville as fictionist was bound to the episodic method. *Moby-Dick* itself is divided into 135 chapters, some of them less than a page in length. Yet it not only has its climax, in Ahab's fatal encounter with the Whale, but when it comes at last, it is one of the most thrilling things in American literature.

The third, and in a sense climactic, book of the group, *Pierre; or, The Ambiguities,* has often gone strangely uncomprehended even during the Melville revival. Some of Melville's discoverers do not take up a much more intelligent attitude toward it than did the contemporary reviewers.[21] This is due partly to the wild character

[21] Carl Van Vechten was an important exception among the critics of the early revival. His "The Later Work of HM," *Excavations* (K, 1926), is a remarkable paper, especially when one remembers that it was first published in 1921. Van Vechten was probably the first to perceive that *Pierre* would have made an excellent subject for Henry James; had it been written latter, by D. H. Lawrence or James Joyce, he declared, its reception would have been very different. Arnold Bennett was also intelligent about *Pierre* (*The Savour of Life,* Do, 1928), and it was appreciated by Thorp, Sedgwick, and Matthiessen. See S. Foster Damon, *Hound & Horn,* II (1929), 107-118; E. L. Grant Watson, *NEQ,* III (1930), 195-234; George C. Homans, *NEQ,* V (1932), 699-720; F. I. Carpenter, *NEQ,* IX (1936), 253-272; Tyrus Hillway, *AL,* XXI (1949), 201-211; G. Giovannini, "M's 'Pierre' and Dante's 'Inferno,'" *PMLA,* LXIV (1949), 70-78—cf. J. C. Matthews, *ibid.,* p. 1238. (Henry Murray's long introduction and notes to his edition of *Pierre,* Hendricks House, 1949, are suggestive but extremely subjective and conjectural.) Echoing a contemporary reviewer, Fitz-James O'Brien, who thought the book might be "a well got-up hoax," W. Braswell, "The Satirical Temper of M's 'Pierre,'" *AL,* VII (1935-1936), 424-438, develops the thesis that Melville, disgustedly through with fiction, wrote the book in a "perversely humorous mood," and flung it contemptuously in the face of the public, intending to wound but not expecting to be taken seriously. This was opposed by Harrison Hayford, "The Significance of M's 'Agatha' Letters," *ELH,* XIII (1946), 299-310, who quotes Melville's letters to Hawthorne and the English publisher Bentley to show not only that Melville intended to go on with fiction but that he expected *Pierre* to be his most popular book, "being a regular romance with a mysterious plot to it, and stirring passions at work, and with all, representing a new and elevated aspect of American life. . . ." The "Agatha" letter itself is printed in *NEQ,* II (1929), 296-307. More recently, Braswell has

of the fable—which is a cross between the Elizabethan tragedy of blood and the Gothic novel[22]—and partly to the tortured quality of the style.

A straightforward, "good" prose style would have been quite inappropriate in such a narrative; Melville's difficulty was that he found at his disposal no such form or tradition as served the Elizabethan dramatists when they faced somewhat similar contingencies. Matthiessen declares that he "was so helplessly open to his emotions that he sometimes could not find language distinguishable from that of the magazine-shocker." If this be true, then for that very reason, this language was not, for Melville, mere jargon. Both Meredith and James were to find a better language for fiction which attempts no realistic picture of common experience, but neither attempted creation under so candescent a light.

The exciting force in Pierre's story is his discovery of his illegitimate half-sister, Isabel, and the necessity immediately laid upon him to care for her, not only as a means of righting her wrong, but because, as Cathy says of Heathcliff, he immediately perceives that she is more himself than he is. To protect his father's memory, he feigns marriage with the girl; he deserts Lucy, his betrothed, and breaks his mother's heart, for that proud, hard, and till now untouched woman has never learned that conventionalities are not to be accepted at their face value. In the city whither he flees with Isabel, Pierre perceives in time both that he cannot support her by his writing, and that they share an incestuous passion for each other. After Lucy, rising above her personal wrongs, has come to live with them and serve them, Pierre is attacked by his cousin, Glen Stanly, once his very emotional friend, now Lucy's suitor; Pierre kills Glen. Lucy dies of shock; Pierre and Isabel swallow poison in prison.

The allegorists have tortured *Pierre* less than either *Mardi* or *Moby-Dick;* those who must have an allegory here find Pierre as

suggested that the early love scenes in *Pierre* were written in the mock-heroic vein, *AL,* XXII (1950), 283-289. In "M's Opinion of 'Pierre,'" *AL,* XXIII (1951), 246-250, Braswell attacks Hayford's interpretation of Melville's letter to Bentley and reaffirms, by implication, his original interpretation.

[22] Newton Arvin has well analyzed the influence of various English novels on *Pierre;* see "M and the Gothic Novel," *NEQ,* XXII (1949), 33-48, and his book on Melville.

Melville's own spiritual being, his father as God, his mother as the World, Lucy as "the simple objective inclination" of his mind, Isabel as the "introspective tendency" of his mind, and Glen Stanly as his public self.[23] The contrast between Lucy and Isabel repeats the pattern already employed in *Mardi,* where Yillah was opposed to Hautia. Unlike Hautia, Isabel is not evil, but hers are the "Songs of Experience" to set over against Lucy's "Songs of Innocence." Isabel does, however, embody the fascination which the tragic side of life held for Melville, and, unlike the ever-virginal Lucy, she embraces the dark, fertile, life-giving qualities of passion. The suggestion of incest, which so unmanned Melville's contemporaries that they were unable to consider the book in any other aspect, may have been intended to suggest introversion and all its dangers, but it also served admirably to indicate the puzzles of moral ambiguity into which Pierre is thrust, and possibly to illuminate the bad judgment which contributes so importantly to his destruction.

4. *Fiction after* Pierre

Melville's next work had no significance for his development as a fictionist, which was, indeed, nearly over. *Israel Potter, His Fifty Years of Exile* (1855) is a delightful, old-fashioned, picaresque adventure story, simple and direct in style. It deals mainly with Israel's experiences in England, contains fine portraits of King George III, Franklin, and John Paul Jones, and includes a thrilling account of the fight between the *Bonhomme Richard* and the *Serapis.* The book was based on a pamphlet account of Potter's career.[24] As the dedication to "His Highness, The Bunker Hill Monument" shows,[25]

[23] See Braswell's summary of allegorical interpretations in "The Satirical Temper of M's 'Pierre.' " Damon, *op. cit.,* points out the parallelism with *Hamlet.*

[24] See R. P. McCutcheon, "The Technique of M's 'Israel Potter,' " *SAQ,* XXVII (1928), 161-174.

[25] The sob-sisters among Melville's critics mark this dedication and that of *Pierre* to Mount Greylock as one more token of the author's loneliness during his later years, his isolation from fructifying contacts with his peers. Unfortunately for the argument, the *Israel Potter* dedication is part of the book's irony—Melville is indignant in his hero's behalf, not his own—while the dedication of *Pierre* must strike the un-Freudian reader as whimsically playful, not despairing, a token of the affection Melville came to feel for the mountain while gazing upon it during the composition of his novel.

Melville intended a protest against the failure of his countrymen to make an honorable place, in his later years, for a hero of the Revolution; but the book is not depressing, for Israel's later struggles are passed over very quickly.

A very different work is "Benito Cereno," a mystery story of the sea whose solution probably no reader has ever guessed before reaching the point at which Melville chooses to reveal it. A beautiful and highly-wrought work of art, and an astonishing anticipation of Conrad, it is perhaps faulty only in that the final resolution of the action is somewhat clumsily made.[26]

The Confidence Man (1857), whose setting is the Mississippi steamboat world which Mark Twain was to make his own, is much less satisfying; Melville himself evidently got tired of it, for it breaks off, for no particular reason, with a half-hearted promise of being some day resumed. Being less intense, it seems less obviously bitter than either *Pierre* or the Ahab portions of *Moby-Dick,* but if Melville has anywhere abandoned faith in human nature, it would seem to be here. The barber's sign "NO TRUST" stands opposed to the deaf-and-dumb stranger's placard "CHARITY NEVER FAILETH," but the barber is right, for the Confidence Man, in his many impersonations, appeals to the better human feelings only to fleece their possessors. The first part of the book contains many vivid scenes and much keen observation, but as the narrative proceeds, the central unifying idea is lost in talk, to be recaptured briefly in the encounter between the barber and the Confidence Man at the close. The treatment of Cairo, Illinois, in this book suggests the influence of *Martin Chuzzlewit*.[27]

[26] See Harold H. Scudder, *PMLA,* XLIII (1928), 502–532; Stanley T. Williams, *VQR,* XXIII (1947), 61–76; Rosalie Feltenstein, *AL,* XIX (1947), 245–255; J. Schiffman, *MLQ,* XI (1950), 317–324; T. B. Haber, *XIX C Fiction,* VI (1951), 146–147.

[27] Richard Chase's special enthusiasm for *The Confidence Man* seems to have stimulated new interest in it, and it is perhaps now due to undergo a certain amount of reinterpretation; see Dan S. Hoffman, "M's 'Story of China Aster,'" *AL,* XXII (1950), 137-149; John W. Shroeder, "Sources and Symbols for M's 'Confidence Man,'" *PMLA,* LXVI (1951), 363-380. Among earlier articles on more specialized aspects, see Egbert Oliver, "M's Goneril and Fanny Kemble," *NEQ,* XVIII (1945), 489-500, and "M's Picture of Emerson and Thoreau in 'The Confidence Man,'" *CE,* VIII (1946), 61-72,

5. Ends and Means

Melville seems never to have formulated a theory of fiction before *The Confidence Man*. What he has to say here[28] is of much interest, but the doctrine comes too late to have exercised any very important influence upon his own production.

He makes two significant points:

(1) He breaks with the naturalistic school by perceiving the clear-cut distinction between literature and life. The mere fact that the reader takes up a book shows that "he is not unwilling to drop real life," to turn, for the moment, to art, for something that life cannot give. A work of fiction is a kind of theater between covers; men go to it, as they go to the theater, for glamour; at the same time, they go to it for truth; from it they expect, in a sense, "more reality than real life itself can show." Art embraces nature, but in art nature is "unfettered, exhilarated, in effect transformed." In life "the proprieties will not allow people to act out themselves with that unreserve permitted to the stage. . . ." "It is with fiction as with religion; it should present another world, and yet one to which we feel the tie."

(2) His second point is not quite consistent with the first, for he anticipated D. H. Lawrence's objection to consistency in characterization. "That fiction, where every character can, by reason of its consistency, be comprehended at a glance, either exhibits but sections of character, making them appear for wholes, or else is very untrue to reality. . . ." Nature produces duck-billed beavers; why may not novelists produce duck-billed characters?

More interesting than this, however, is the matter of his literary method, and this happens to be a point upon which considerable knowledge has been recovered during recent years. Tyrus Hillway has pointed out that nearly one-fourth of *Moby-Dick* is based upon Thomas Beale's *The Natural History of the Sperm Whale* (London, 1839); from such facts as this he draws the conclusion that Melville

with which cf. W. Braswell, "M as Critic of Emerson," *AL*, IX (1937), 317–334. Leon Howard's *HM* has some very interesting critical observations about *The Confidence-Man*.

[28] Chapters XIV, XXXIII.

was "not a literary inventor but an assimilator. He may be said to have recorded rather than devised most of the incidents in his major works."[29] But "recorded" is too strong a word. In his *Melville in the South Seas,* Charles Roberts Anderson has made a very important study of Melville's habit of supplementing his own experience by both reading and imagination. Thus, in *White-Jacket,* the hero's narrow escape from flogging, or rather from the murder and suicide which he says he would have chosen instead—which some of Melville's biographers have accepted not only as an autobiographical transcript but as one of the crucial, conditioning experiences of his life!—now seems never to have occurred, while the thrilling account of the fall from the yards paraphrases a passage in *A Mariner's Sketches,* by Nathaniel Ames (1830).[30] Anderson does not doubt that Melville visited the Marquesas, though his sojourn there was briefer and his experiences less thrilling than has generally been supposed, but he does point out that, in view of the amount of material derived from the writings of others, he might almost have written *Typee* without having gone to the South Seas at all.

Almost, yet perhaps not quite. Melville's reading was part of his experience, and he had the capacity for imaginative realization of experiences which he had never encountered personally. He read creatively, as Chaucer and Shakespeare read, and, like Chaucer especially, he was never more creative than when recharactering his reading. Yet he may well have required some experience in kind to awaken his interest or supply him with a key, and had he himself never visited the Marquesas, the books he read about them might, at least conceivably, have remained dead.

As for the vision of life which Melville used literature to express, I do not believe that we even yet possess the data we should need to expound it fully. This much, however, seems clear: Melville was rediscovered in the futilitarian era, and disillusioned moderns have often used him as a vehicle for the expression of their own dis-

[29] "M's Art: One Aspect," *MLN,* LXII (1947), 477-480.

[30] Anderson lists in his bibliography and summarizes in his notes everything that Melville criticism had achieved by way of illuminating the use Melville made of his reading up to the time his book appeared. For the flogging incident in *White-Jacket,* see also P. S. Procter, Jr., *AL,* XXII (1950), 176-177; cf. K. Huntress, *AL,* XVII (1945), 66-74.

appointment in life. Much Melville criticism, in other words, is merely autobiography.

That Melville himself possessed what we call the tragic sense of life goes, of course, without saying. He was an intensely religious man, and he lived in an age when the traditional interpretations of religion were beginning to be seriously questioned. He was, besides, a passionate democrat, and he perceived the helpless dependence of democracy upon the Christian ideal. Reverence for life was his, and respect for the integrity of personality. Moreover, he knew magnanimity. His blackest villains—Jackson, Claggart—are conceived as even more pitiable than they are loathsome, "for great Sin calls forth more magnanimity than small Virtue."

But none of this kept his mind from being troubled. When he watched gulls and sharks feeding upon a dead whale, he was revolted by the "horrible vulturism of earth." Like Hawthorne, he found Emersonian optimism unconvincing and felt the psychological truth of the doctrine of original sin even while he rejected it as dogma.[31] The difference between the two men was less in "views" than in temperament: Melville was intenser, more impassioned, less patient, and more inclined to bitterness; it is Hawthorne himself who describes his friend's metaphysical struggles, after their meeting, for the last time, at Liverpool, as a "wandering to and fro over . . . [the] deserts [of metaphysical speculation], as dismal and monotonous as the sandhills amid which we were sitting." He added: "He can neither believe, nor be comfortable in his unbelief; and he is too honest and courageous not to try to do one or the other."

Melville found and valued "blackness" in both Hawthorne and Shakespeare. "I love all men who dive." He took his stand for "heart," not "head"; because he would not live in a fool's paradise nor cut himself off from contact with his suffering fellows, he came to feel that sadness was nobler than joy. Even in *Mardi* happiness is "but exemption from great woes—no more. Great Love is sad; and heaven is Love. Sadness makes the silence throughout the realms of space; sadness is universal and eternal." He knew that "The truest

---

[31] See, in this connection, Melville's most significant piece of criticism, his review of Hawthorne's *Mosses*.

of all men was the Man of Sorrows. . . ." But he did not make the sublime affirmation of Faith that life itself is a Divine Comedy.

So far I think we can safely go, but this is a far cry from the view that Melville applauds and identifies himself with Ahab, seeing the power behind the universe as an imbecile jester and flinging blasphemous defiance in the face of life itself. This interpretation is based upon Melville's cryptic statement to Hawthorne: "I have written a wicked book, and feel as spotless as the lamb."[32] Whatever Melville may have thought he meant by this statement, it does not fairly represent his book, for the book is larger than Ahab. It is true, as Vincent says, that "All the way through *Moby-Dick* it is suggested, or hinted, that the Sperm Whale may on occasion be seen as a symbol of the Absolute, or the All." But Vincent also shows how the truth preached by Father Mapple—the necessity of submitting the will of the human individual to the will of God, and of thus achieving reconciliation with life—is the lesson that Ahab never learns, and this is his tragedy.[33] Melville did not wait for the reader to point out that Ahab's dedication of his life to vengeance upon a dumb brute is madness and blasphemy; he was careful to have Starbuck do it for him; and Starbuck, as much as Ahab, is a part of the book and a part of Melville's mind.[34]

[32] This statement is capable of various interpretations. See Charles Olson, *Call Me Ishmael,* and Matthiessen, *American Renaissance,* pp. 448 ff.

[33] Vincent, *op. cit.,* p. 258; pp. 70 ff.

[34] In a paper which I hope he will publish, one of my students, Mr. Charles H. Cook, Jr., has shown that it is Moby Dick the whale, not *Moby-Dick* the novel whose allegorical significance is specifically denied by Melville in Chapter XLV. Melville believed it "impossible for men to comprehend the enigmas of the spiritual universe. The heroes in his tales owe their tragedy to their refusal to recognize the ambiguous nature of good and evil," as expounded in Melville's chapter on "The Whiteness of the Whale." Ahab disregards Melville's warning not to make the whale "a hideous and intolerable allegory." Pierre, similarly, turns Isabel into an allegory. "Every critic who finds a pat symbolic meaning for the whale is another Ahab, committing the same error of projection." Mr. Cook contends that whatever allegory there may be in Melville is "intrinsic with the story and must arise out of the story, not the story out of it." See, further, George C. Homans's discussion of Melville's ways with symbols in "The Dark Angel: The Tragedy of HM," *NEQ,* V (1932), 699-730, and E. E. Stoll's powerful blast against this whole approach: "Symbolism in *Moby-Dick,*" *Journal Hist. Ideas,* XII (1951), 440-465.

Ahab stands aside from all normal human activities and emotions. He rejects not only pleasure[35] and science,[36] but love,[37] fellowship,[38] a decent regard for human needs,[39] and, at last, in Pip, a self-sacrificing devotion worthy of Lear's Fool. He rejects, even, the forbearance of Moby Dick himself, and goes to his doom alone.[40] This does not at all preclude our admiration for his heroism, but we admire him as we admire other titans in literature—Manfred, Prometheus, even Milton's Satan (by whom Professor Pommer believes him to have been influenced)[41]—without feeling called upon to accept their attitude toward the universe or their interpretation of life.

In *Pierre* the issue is less clear, for Pierre is a more sympathetic character. Indeed, an anonymous writer in the *London Times Literary Supplement* once[42] went so far as to declare that in *Pierre* Melville "is trying to show that the completely good man is doomed to complete disaster on earth, and he is trying to show at the same time that this must be so, and that it ought to be so." "In other words, Melville was trying to reveal the central mystery of the Christian religion."

Such a statement deserves careful examination. It is true, as Isabel perceives, that Pierre is (up to a point) one of those "good, harmless

---

[35] Symbolized by his casting his pipe into the sea.

[36] Cf. the breaking of the quadrant.

[37] Seen in his disregard of his young wife and child. It is amusing to recall that by 1925 the Melville renascence had got far enough under way for John Barrymore and Dolores Costello to appear in an elaborate motion-picture version of *Moby-Dick* called *The Sea Beast,* in which Captain Ahab's quest was motivated by love! In 1931, Barrymore used the story again, now under the title *Moby-Dick,* but with lovely woman (this time in the person of Joan Bennett), still the motivating force.

[38] Cf. his brutal and inconsiderate treatment of his crew.

[39] He refuses to turn aside to help the captain of the *Rachel* save his son.

[40] R. E. Watters, "M's 'Sociality,'" *AL,* XVII (1945), 33-49, and "M's 'Isolatoes,'" *PMLA,* LX (1945), 1138-1148, has shown conclusively that, so far from being a Nietzschean superman, Melville, like Hawthorne, "opposed the transcendentalists' approval of solitude and self-reliance by revealing the distortion which accompanied the individual's arrogant separation from his fellows."

[41] See Henry F. Pommer, *Milton and Melville* (U. of Pittsburgh Press, 1950).

[42] July 10, 1924, p. 433.

men" doomed to destruction in a wicked world, "human things placed at cross-purposes in a world of snakes and lightnings, in a world of horrible and inscrutable inhumanities." And he himself reflects, just before his death, that had he been heartless as his mother was heartless, had he "disowned, and spurningly portioned off the girl at Saddle Meadows," he might have been happy on earth and in heaven. When Gandhi was assassinated, Bernard Shaw remarked that the calamity showed how dangerous it was to be good in this world, a remark which was strangely misapprehended by persons incapable of distinguishing between frivolity and truth bitter as death.

Yet even here Melville is clear-sighted. "But Pierre, though charged with the fire of all divineness, his containing thing was made of clay. Ah, muskets the gods have made to carry infinite combustions, and yet made them of clay!" Pierre himself sees more clearly than many of his interpreters. He admits frankly that had Isabel been "a humped, and crippled, hideous girl" who accosted him "in some squalid lane," his response might have been very different. There is a way to hell, as Bunyan had perceived, from the very gates of the Heavenly City, and Pierre finds it out. "Well, be it hell. I will mold a trumpet of the flames, and, with my breath of flame, breathe back my defiance!" A Gandhi does not die thus, to say nothing of a Christ—nor even, for that matter, a Hamlet.

The truth of the matter is that Pierre has, by this time, entered a world that lies beyond good and evil. A terrible compulsive ardor is upon him; a necessary phase of human experience must express itself through him. What he does is wrong; it destroys him and all whose lives are entwined with his, but all such considerations are, in a sense, irrelevant. The dying suicide cries, "Be it hell!" He might cry, too, with a more innocent victim of the world's evil:

> We are not the first
> Who, with best meaning, have incurr'd the worst.

To this I think one need add only that a man cannot believe that the world is false and evil unless he has in his mind an ideal of truth and righteousness which he sets over against it and by which it is condemned. And the man who cherishes such an ideal, though he may die in despair, is not yet a moral nihilist.

Nor—of this much we may be sure—was Herman Melville, who did not die in despair. There are strange—and, as I believe, insoluble —problems in his life. Working over *Moby-Dick,* he cries out, with naïve, boyish enthusiasm, for "Vesuvius' crater as an inkstand," and, again, for "fifty fast-writing youths with an easy style," as if he were about to open a fiction-factory like Dumas'. Yet at the same time he seems to have felt that he had come "to the utmost leaf of the bulb, and that shortly the flower must fall to the mould." Why did he virtually withdraw from the literary life? Many sane and insane reasons have been suggested: He had said what he had to say; he had exhausted his memories, and, being the kind of writer he was, he could do no more; the public had finally demonstrated its unwillingness to buy the only kind of books he was now able or willing to write; he was oppressed by failing health and failing eyesight; he was unhappy with his wife. (For Elizabeth Shaw, like Alan Melville and Maria Gansevoort, has been "smeared.") In the old days, it was even suggested, absurdly, that he had lost his mind.

Melville may have had tragedy in his life: one of his sons ran away from home; another died in circumstances strongly suggesting suicide. But his literary career was not tragic, however disappointing it may have been. He did not kill himself, either physically or spiritually. Like his friend Hawthorne, he went to work to support his family, and his spirit lived on.[43] Whatever may be thought of its quality, *Clarel,* the long poem he published in 1876, is one of his most ambitious works. And if he subsided at last into relative silence, that subsidence may well have had less of despair about it than of a Quaker-like appreciation of the rich, life-giving values of silence. Finally, near the end, came a strange resurrection of fictional power with *Billy Budd, Foretopman. What Befell Him in the Year of the Great Mutiny.*[44]

In *Pierre,*[45] Plotinus Plinlimmon had been permitted to develop

[43] Oscar Wegelin, "HM As I Recall Him," *Col,* N.S. I (1935), 20-24, gives a genially reassuring glimpse of him toward the close of his life.

[44] The definitive edition of this work is now *Melville's "Billy Budd,"* edited by F. Barron Freeman (HUP, 1948).

[45] Book XIV.

his interesting theory about the difference between chronometrical and horological time. According to Plotinus, as "the earthly wisdom of man" is "heavenly folly to God," so "the heavenly wisdom of God" is "earthly folly to man." Christ, it is true, lived by chronometrics alone and remained without folly or sin, but when inferior men attempt this feat, they become involved "in strange *unique* follies and sins, unimagined before." God is not the Lord of this world, or it could not so "give the lie to Him." "A virtuous expediency, then, seems the highest desirable or attainable excellence for the mass of men, and is the only earthly excellence that their Creator intended for them."

Pierre does not live by this view, and there has been much debate as to whether or not his creator accepted it.[46] There can be no doubt, however, that it lies at the heart of *Billy Budd*. For when the sailor, who is virtue, strikes the petty officer who has monstrously slandered him, and accidentally kills the scoundrel, Captain Vere perceives at once that an angel has appeared as agent of the justice of God, yet, because his act is in violation of the Articles of War under which the ship sails, "the angel must hang," and does. He hangs in one of the most richly-charged scenes in American fiction, dies a death full of spiritual significances, dies crying "God bless Captain Vere!" at peace with all men and with life.

Did Melville share that mood of reconciliation? and is *Billy Budd* his *Tempest,* his *Cymbeline,* his *Winter's Tale?* Until recently, this view was not seriously challenged.[47] R. E. Watters finds that *Billy*

[46] In his "Pierre, The Fool of Virtue," *AL,* XXI (1949), 201-211, Tyrus Hillway argues vigorously that Melville rejected the pamphlet, accepting instead Father Mapple's point of view in the famous sermon in *Moby-Dick.*

[47] See E. L. Grant Watson, "M's Testimony of Acceptance," *NEQ,* VI (1933), 319-327; C. R. Anderson, "The Genesis of 'Billy Budd,'" *AL,* XII (1940), 329-341; Charles Weir, Jr., "Malice Reconciled, A Note on M's 'Billy Budd,'" *UTQ,* XIII (1944), 276-285. Skeptical views are expressed by Jacob Schiffman, "M's Final Stage, Irony: A Reexamination of 'Billy Budd' Criticism," *AL,* XXII (1950), 128-136; H. M. Campbell, "The Hanging Scene in M's 'Billy Budd, Foretopman,'" *MLN,* LXVI (1951), 378-381; and, much less convincingly, by Oliver Snyder, *Accent,* XI (1951), 58-60. N. H. Pearson, "'Billy Budd': The King's Yarn," *Am. Q.,* III (1951), 99-114, does not debate the question of reconciliation. The *Billy Budd* play, by Louis O. Coxe and Robert Chapman, is published by PUP, 1951. An opera by Benjamin Britten was produced in London late in 1951; E. M. Forster's libretto for this work has been announced for publication by HB in 1952.

Budd shows "how successfully men *can* impose spiritual value upon a mere physical event—illustrates, in a word, how men may impinge celestial time upon terrestrial time." I do not, myself, find the solution altogether satisfactory. For if the world is going to continue to permit its practical conduct to be governed by the Articles of War, I cannot believe that all its Vere-like perception of spiritual values is going to be able to save it from destruction much longer. When Melville speaks *in propria persona* in *Billy Budd,* his pacifism seems even more uncompromising than in his earlier works.

Long ago, in *Moby-Dick,* he himself had mapped out the stages of mankind's progress "through infancy's unconscious spell, boyhood's thoughtless faith, adolescence' doubt (the common doom), then skepticism, then disbelief, resting at last in manhood's pondering hope of If." In the If-world any doom is possible, but, by the same token, any dream can come true.

CHAPTER V

MRS. STOWE AND SOME CONTEMPORARIES

She belongs to a class whose logic is more of the heart than of the head, and of whom we may expect a strong leaning toward ultraism.

HARRIET BEECHER STOWE: Preface to *The Works of Charlotte Elizabeth Tonna*

1. *"A Damned Mob of Scribbling Women"*

"America is now wholly given over to a damned mob of scribbling women," or so Hawthorne declared angrily in 1855, "and I should have no chance of success while the public taste is occupied with their trash." In the 1850's and '60's the domestic sentimentalists won for themselves about as wide an audience as any American novelists have ever enjoyed; many of their works were dramatized; some of them survived into the twentieth century. Today their books are difficult to obtain and they themselves somewhat snobbishly consigned to the dismal dungeons of "sub-literature." Yet it is impossible to understand nineteenth-century America without understanding them.

The beginnings of such understanding may be achieved if the reader will dig out of old libraries and read such representative novels as *The Wide, Wide World* (1850), by Elizabeth Wetherell, pseud. Susan Warner (1819-1885); *The Lamplighter* (1854), by Maria Cummins (1827-1866); *Ruth Hall* (1855), by Fanny Fern, pseud. Sara P. Willis Parton (1811-1872); *'Lena Rivers* (1856), by Mary J. Holmes (1825-1907); *The Hidden Hand* (1859), by Mrs. E.D.E.N. Southworth (1819-1899); and *St. Elmo* (1866), by Augusta J. Evans Wilson (1835-1909). But it must be remembered that there were many more writers than these and that some of them were immensely prolific; the Street and Smith catalogue once listed ninety-one titles by Mrs. Southworth in ten-cent editions.

Alexander Cowie's recipe for the domestic novel is too good not to quote:

First, take a young and not-too-pretty child about ten years old. Boys are possible, but girls are to be preferred, for the author and the increasing majority of women readers will be more at home in the detail. Make sure that the child is, or shortly will be, an orphan. If the mother is still living, put her to death very gradually, in a scene of much sorrow and little physical suffering, uttering pious hopes and admonitions to the last. The father presumably died years ago under circumstances not well known. Now put the child under the care of a shrewish aunt, who resents being obliged to take care of her dead brother's brat. If it has been impossible to remove the father as suggested above, a reasonably good compromise will be to have him make a second marriage with a frivolous, heartless society woman. In an emergency a cruel housekeeper will do. The child is now unhappy, undernourished, and underprivileged. She is exposed to the taunts of snobbish little rich girls. It is essential that she accidentally overhear unkind comments on her awkward clothes, rustic manners, bad behavior, or even her family honor. Slander may be used freely for spicing the plot. The child's behavior may in fact be actually bad at the beginning. She may "sass" her aunt. She may even shy a stone through a window. But her worst sin is her "pride." Now introduce a young woman living not far away, who embodies all the Christian virtues, especially humility. Let this lady kiss, pray over, and cry with the heroine at intervals of from three to four pages. The lady may or may not be blind; at any rate she has had her sorrows and she is destined to die about two thirds of the way through the book of badly diagnosed tuberculosis. She will die at sunset—without a struggle. She is going home. Tears which have been flowing freely now practically inundate the book. The girl's only remaining friends are an eccentric (Barkis-like) teamster, and a wealthy (Cheeryble-like) merchant who now and then gives her a lollipop. In the meantime she has learned to subdue her pride and to submit graciously to the suffering which is the lot of all mortals in this shabby world. You may end the story here if you will, with the child on the verge of adolescence; but it is preferable to carry on a few years in order that the heroine may be menaced by a proud, handsome, moody, Rochester-like man about thirty who has traveled and sinned (very vaguely) in the Orient. He at first scarcely notices the meek little girl, but her bright spirit and vaguely referred to physical charms finally force him to admit to himself that he must have her. If it weren't for Queen Victoria, he would try to seduce her, but as it is he is reduced to proposing marriage. To his astonishment she refuses. This sends him off darkly on more travels. The girl meanwhile has learned to support herself by teaching, acting as governess, or writing, and she talks rather briskly about independence for women. Let her endure many trials and perform many pious acts. Monotony may be broken by a trip to Saratoga or by the introduction of some physical peril such as a carriage accident, an attack by a mad dog, or a fire. One day the moody man comes back, and finds her sitting in a cemetery. He proposes again and is accepted. Don't be alarmed at this: his pride has been humbled, too, and he is now reformed. He may even become a minister—but he has plenty of money. For her part, the heroine now drops all fantastic notions of female independence, for she realizes that a woman's greatest glory is wifely submission. The acid aunt either dies or experiences a change of heart toward the heroine. In the latter case she may be married off to the neighboring teamster (blacksmith will do). The wealthy merchant turns out to be the heroine's father; he wasn't really lost at sea! Everybody is now happy in a subdued, Christian sort of way.[1]

Thus, as Chaucer would say, "the forme." But it varied notably from writer to writer.

Mary J. Holmes, for example, went out for straight domesticity and decorous romance, but Elizabeth Wetherell and Maria Cummins stressed the religious element. *The Wide, Wide World* is not far from being a tract. The noble clergyman, John Humphreys, is a pious prig, and the kindly farmer Van Brunt, who protects Ellen against her cruel aunt, Miss Fortune, and in the end delivers her from bondage by the simple expedient of himself marrying her oppressor, becomes a Christian through Ellen's influence.

Yet there is much quiet realism in these writers. In Elizabeth Wetherell it often takes the form of authentic pictures of rural customs. In its time her *Queechy* (1852) was often called the great American novel! *The Lamplighter,* by Maria Cummins, has mainly an urban setting, slum life alternating with scenes of "society." Except for the burning ship, Miss Cummins eschewed sensation, though she has the usual mystery of parentage to clear up and separated lovers to reunite. In Miss Patty Pace, with her weird clothes, her perennial youthfulness of spirit, and her formal speech, she created an amusing eccentric. Technically, the most interesting thing in her book is the way she permits her characters to make elaborate

[1] Alexander Cowie, *The Rise of the American Novel,* pp. 413-415. Copyright, 1948, by the American Book Company. Quoted by permission of the publishers.

plans for journeys which never come off, a kind of realism in which she was anticipated by Defoe. All in all, it might, in later days, have made an excellent film-play for Mary Pickford or Margaret O'Brien.

Fanny Fern was a bird of another feather. A popular journalist who, at one period, turned out a story or a sketch every day of her life, she was a good enough businesswoman to pay lip service to the proprieties, but there was no real propriety in her spirit. For one thing, she was too busy paying off scores, especially to her brother, Nathaniel Parker Willis (the Hyacinth of *Ruth Hall*), and to her husband's family, who, as she conceived, had abandoned her shamefully in her widow's need. *Ruth Hall* is clearly autobiographical, with many references to contemporary literary life. Hawthorne exempted Fanny Fern from his condemnation of women writers in general, for a rather strange reason. Fanny Fern, he said, wrote as if the devil were in her:

Generally women write like emasculated men, and are only to be distinguished from male authors by greater feebleness and folly; but when they throw off the restraints of decency, and come before the public stark naked, as it were—then their books are sure to possess character and value.

A friend of Whittier's, and in her later years the mistress of something like a literary salon at her home near Washington, Mrs. Southworth was the Queen of Sensation. Though she enjoyed very wide contacts, she never met a human being who had not read any of her books! She herself inclined to take most stock in *Ishmael* and its sequel *Self-Raised* (1863-1864), but her best heroine is the Lotta-like Capitola of *The Hidden Hand,* who was "as famous as Topsy."

Cap is heiress to a vast estate which has been kept from her by an uncle. (When she was born, her mother's head and right hand were swathed in black crepe!) At one period she lives in New York as a boy—to guard her chastity; to achieve the same end, she later catapults Black Donald (whom John Wilkes Booth portrayed on the stage), down a trap door of unknown origin, more conveniently than convincingly located in her room. She has a fantastic temper and a penchant for recklessly picturesque behavior. Mrs. Southworth herself was a bit complacent about her. "How glad I am to get back to my little Cap," she exclaimed at the beginning of Chapter LX, "for I know very well, reader, just as well as if you had told me, that you have been grumbling for some time for the want of Cap."

But the most gifted writer of this group was the Southern patriot, Augusta J. Evans (after her marriage, in 1868, Augusta Evans Wilson). One of her novels, *Beulah* (1859), gave a name to a Confederate camp near Mobile; another—*Macaria; or, Altars of Sacrifice* (1864)—which had been printed on wallpaper, the only paper stock available, was burned by the federal government for fear that it might have a deleterious effect upon the morale of Union soldiers. But all this was mild compared to the postwar triumph of *St. Elmo*. Children, "plantations in the deep South, steamboats round the bend of great rivers, girls' schools, hotels, various articles of merchandise, and thirteen American towns" were all named St. Elmo; and men wrote the author to describe how they had been "saved" by the book, as its tremendously Byronic hero is saved by the priggish and disgustingly erudite heroine, Edna Earl.[2]

Mrs. Wilson was probably the most allusive novelist who ever lived. Fifteen to twenty allusions per page was nothing for her. She drew them from wide reading in philosophy, mythology, anthropology, and religion, as well as from classical and modern literature, and the fact that she used them with utterly tasteless pedantry does not make her less a phenomenon. Her characters do not converse: they deliver lectures at each other, full of long quotations such as one might expect to encounter in a critical article. Nor is it enough that Edna should have impossible learning and the strength to work all day as a governess and then sit up half the night pursuing a literary career obviously modeled upon Mrs. Wilson's own. She must have all gifts and all accomplishments, singing operatic arias like a professional for her own amusement.

In her love for St. Elmo there is evidently a strong sexual element (since the "respect" she had always believed necessary for love is altogether lacking), but there is no hint that either she or her creator recognized this. Her own sexual desirability may be gauged by the fact that she receives proposals of marriage from four very desirable gentlemen, one of them a British knight. She is poor but she always

[2] See Earnest Elmo Calkins, "St. Elmo; or, Named for a Best Seller," *SRL*, XXI, Dec. 16, 1939, p. 3+.

lands on her feet and in the lap of luxury. She will not have St. Elmo unregenerate, but neither will she relinquish him. The report that he is to wed another she simply refuses to credit: "Though I never look upon his face again, he belongs to me!" In the end, she gets him, conveniently purged of his infamy and a clergyman to boot; and, indeed, this conversion seems less incredible than his earlier transformation (told in retrospect) into a monster upon the revelation of treachery on the part of his sweetheart and his friend. The unparalleled combination of trashy, hyperemotional subject matter and superelegant style has produced in *St. Elmo* a unique hybrid which fascinates while it repels. It is a pious, pretentious, unwholesome book. It may even be a work of genius, if it is possible to have genius without a grain of taste or aesthetic judgment.

Naturally, many of the domestic sentimentalists became interested in the many "causes" that developed during the mid-century years. Aside from abolition itself, the most important of these was the temperance movement, whose laureate was Timothy Shay Arthur (1809-1885). Arthur was a prolific writer, the editor of many periodicals, and a frequent contributor to *Graham's* and *Godey's,* but he is remembered today almost entirely for *Ten Nights in a Bar-Room* (1854), which still lives occasionally in the theater, even though it may have died out in the library. In his attempt to study the evil effects upon a community of the establishment of a tavern, Arthur found a promising theme; it was too bad that he should have ruined his effects by trying to prove too much. He showed his sense of structure by planning a division of material into ten scenes or "nights," but his art was not great enough to permit him to work within such a rigid framework; the attempt was given over, therefore, in favor of a more free-ranging organization, and at last only the title and the now meaningless framework were left. In 1872 Arthur's *Three Years in a Mantrap* attempted a picture of the evils of drink in a large city; two years later, in *Woman to the Rescue,* he celebrated the beginnings of the Woman's Christian Temperance Union.

Juveniles do not properly lie within the range of this history, but it is not possible to ignore them altogether. Martha Farquharson, pseud. Martha F. Finley (1828-1909), won great popular success with the pious *Elsie Dinsmore* (1867), whose further adventures were related in some twenty books, the last published as late as 1907.[3] We might easily spare *Elsie Dinsmore,* but it would be ridiculous to make no mention of the idyll of Concord during its greatest period, the *Little Women* (1868) of Louisa May Alcott (1832-1888).

Little Women is about as close as we have come to creating an American *David Copperfield;* is this fact a sign of the "feminization" of life and letters which some persons are sure has taken place in America? Except for *Tom Sawyer,* it may well be the most beloved American book. It needs—and is susceptible of—little analysis; critics have, therefore, generally neglected it. Collectors, like readers, have been wiser. One night in 1929, Carolyn Wells got A. Edward Newton out of bed in the middle of the night with a telegram in which she asked him whether she should pay the $1,600 she was being asked for a first edition. "Yes," he replied, "and be quick about it."

Miss Alcott lacked neither experience nor training for authorship. As Bronson Alcott's daughter she was born and reared in the atmosphere of plain living and high thinking that the Emerson circle prized. She taught kindergarten under Elizabeth Peabody, and she was not ashamed when the need arose to work as a domestic servant and a seamstress. In dark days she was saved from despair by Theodore Parker. She and her sisters had read and dramatized Dickens passionately, and when, during the Civil War, she went to nurse Union soldiers in Washington hospitals (and to ruin her health), she took Dickens's novels with her to read to them. Like Dickens himself, she might at one time have gone on the stage if an accident had not supervened, for she was no more prig than weakling. Like her own Jo, she began scribbling "rubbish" for bread, in the popular papers, from which she graduated to the *Atlantic* under Lowell's editorship, though his successor, Fields, would have none of her. Her first long story in book form, *Moods* (1865), was a serious adult novel about a matrimonial imbroglio. Henry James, who reviewed it carefully, worried about its morality, and then declared that "With the exception of two or three celebrated names, we know not . . . to whom, in this country, unless to Miss Alcott, we are to look for a novel above the average." She herself was fond

[3] See Janet E. Brown, "The Saga of Elsie Dinsmore: A Study in Nineteenth Century Sensibility," *U. of Buffalo Monographs in English,* No. 4, 1945.

of this book and tried to write in the grown-up manner again in *Work* (1873) and in a very bad piece of pseudo-Hawthorneism called *A Modern Mephistopheles* (1877).

Little Women itself accepts the limitations of the domestic sentimentalists and imposes charm and common sense upon them. It is, as has been said, an idyll, a hymn in praise of family life, not a literal transcription of domestic experiences: "I do think that families are the most beautiful things in all the world!" Nevertheless, it is honest. "Amy teased Jo, and Jo irritated Amy, and semi-occasional explosions occurred, of which both were much ashamed afterwards." Again we are told that "Every one seemed rather out of sorts, and inclined to croak." The Marches are a religious family, but the daughter of a Transcendentalist philosopher could have no truck with bigotry. Tears are shed, but there is no masochistic desire to "kiss the rod"; Mrs. March craves happy, useful lives for her daughters "with as little care and sorrow to try them as God sees fit to send." Beth even dies realistically. "Seldom, except in books, do the dying utter memorable words, see visions, or depart with beatified countenances. . . ."

Louisa Alcott carried on the story of the Marches in *Little Men* (1871), in which Jo and Professor Bhaer apply some of Bronson Alcott's educational theories, and in *Jo's Boys* (1886), but these books are elementary in comparison with her masterpiece. She was variously successful in variously related moods in *An Old-Fashioned Girl* (1870), *Eight Cousins* (1875), *Rose in Bloom* (1876), *Under the Lilacs* (1878), and *Jack and Jill* (1880).

Miss Alcott addressed herself mainly to girls. There is no "boys' writer" really worthy to stand beside her, but some mention should be made of Horatio Alger, Jr. (1834-1899), whose career began in 1867 with *Ragged Dick* and whose vogue lasted until World War I. Alger's hundred or more books are said to have sold 20,000,000 copies.

Alger had no literary gifts save the gift of telling a story. He praised cleanness in body and mind and celebrated the virtues which help a young man to get ahead in the world. When he wrote Lincoln's biography, he called it *Abraham Lincoln, The Backwoods Boy; or, How a Young Railsplitter Became President*. The laureate of the self-made man, Alger appealed to Americans who had been taught to rest their weight upon their own backbone and not to quarter themselves upon the public treasury. Street-life in New York was his special theme—with the old Astor House, before which he loved to open his stories, as the symbol of wealth and success—but he wrote about the West also. Alger had been a clergyman, and sometimes, as in *Phil the Fiddler* (1872), he went in for social consciousness. It was amusing that just as his vogue was running out, so many Americans should have devoured *The Autobiography of Andrew Carnegie* and *The Americanization of Edward Bok* with gusto, all unaware that what they were reading were essentially "Alger books."

Alger's name suggests, in its turn, the dime (and nickel) novels, a subject which has now, at last, been studied adequately.[4] The first dime novels dealt with Indian warfare and the frontier: Beadle's first title was *Malaeska: The Indian Wife of the White Hunter* (1860), whose author was a woman, Ann S. Stephens (1813-1886), "one of the best-known of the New York literati," and a novelist of parts. Edward Ellis, too, wrote Westerns, as did Ned Buntline (pseud. Edward Z. C. Judson) and Prentiss Ingraham, who both specialized in Buffalo Bill, and Edward L. Wheeler, who wrote the Deadwood Dick series. Beginning in the 1880's, John Russell Coryell and Frederick Van Renssalaer Dey produced a different kind of dime novel about the detective Nick Carter, whose adventures are said to fill 1,076 volumes and to have influenced *avant-garde* writers and artists in France. Often printed in similar format during the latter days of the dime novels were some 200 stories by Burt L. Standish (pseud. Gilbert Patten, 1866-1945), about Frank Merriwell, which came considerably closer to the normal experiences of American youth.

It would be a mistake to overestimate the importance of "subliterature." It is even more unfortunate to be snobbish about it. When we consider the conditions under which many of these books were written, the wonder is not that they should lack literary values

[4] See Albert Johannsen's definitive and magnificently illustrated *The House of Beadle and Adams and its Dime and Nickel Novels,* 2 vv. (UOP, 1949). This work comprises history, bibliography, biographies of the authors and extracts from their works.

but that they should have got themselves produced at all. The twenty-odd novels of Marion Harland (pseud. Mary V. H. Terhune, 1830-1922) were merely an incident in her career: she was an authority on domestic science, a newspaper columnist, a lecturer, a world-traveler, and a tireless religious worker. When she was seventy, she suffered an injury to her wrist which made it impossible for her to hold her pen. She learned to type and went on with her work. At eighty-nine she went blind, whereupon she simply took up dictation.

While writing *Retribution*—(a serial work, written, as all my books have been, from week to week, to supply the demands of a weekly paper)—[the speaker is Mrs. Southworth]—I was keeping school and keeping house. The school numbered more than eighty pupils, and I was their sole teacher. At the same time one of my children was confined to his bed with a long and dangerous illness, and I was his nurse. My salary from the school was but two hundred and fifty dollars [per year], and with a family of four to support, it was absolutely necessary to do something else to increase our income. *Retribution* was, therefore, written, and written, too, before and after school hours, at night and in the intervals when the sick was sleeping, or at least free from pain. The great Source of Life gave me vitality enough to do and bear all that was required of me. The school-keeping, the house-keeping, the nursing, and the novelet, all went on,—and not once were my readers disappointed of their chapter.

Miss Alcott allowed Jo to spend an afternoon in the apple tree weeping over *The Wide, Wide World*. It was quite naughty of her to make the boy who sat next to Jo at a lecture an enthusiast for a trashy story by "Mrs. S.L.A.N.G. Northbury."

2. *The Novel as Evangel: Harriet Beecher Stowe*
One of the domestic sentimentalists, Harriet Beecher Stowe, must have separate and more respectful treatment, for her *Uncle Tom's Cabin* (1852) was the most sensational event in the world history of the novel, and it made its author the most famous American woman of her time. Lincoln exaggerated, of course, when he greeted Mrs. Stowe as "the little lady who made this big war." But there is no denying that (though she had intended her book as a pacificator), it had a larger influence upon the war than any other novel had ever

exerted upon so stupendous an event. Translated into thirty-seven languages, it sold by the million. It threw up "Uncle Tom" shops and restaurants clear across Europe and stimulated the sale of the Bible in Paris. Lauded by Heine, George Sand, and others, it encouraged production in many arts, and the Curator of the British Museum was fortunately inspired to begin what developed into an immense collection of "Tomiana." When the *Atlantic Monthly* was founded in 1857, the publisher made its establishment contingent upon Mrs. Stowe's willingness to furnish a serial.[5]

Harriet Beecher was born at Litchfield, Connecticut, on June 14, 1811, the seventh child of the Reverend Lyman Beecher, by his first wife, Roxana Foote. In 1832, when her father became president of Lane Theological Seminary, she moved to Cincinnati, where she lived in the world of McGuffey's *Readers,* one of which was "ghosted" by her sister Catherine. Here she began her half-century career as a writer, and here (in 1836), she married Calvin E. Stowe, a professor in the seminary, already on his way to become the most distinguished Biblical scholar of his time. In 1850 the Stowes moved to Bowdoin College, at Brunswick, Maine, in 1852 to Andover Theological Seminary. After 1864 they lived at Hartford, Connecticut. Mrs. Stowe conducted a column in *The Independent,* beginning in 1852; her "House and Home" papers in the *Atlantic* of the 'sixties pioneered in the "House Beautiful" movement. After her brother, Henry Ward Beecher, became editor of *The Christian Union* (later

[5] Though Mrs. Stowe was in no sense responsible for *Uncle Tom's Cabin* on the stage, and derived no profit from it, the full impact of her work upon the American mind cannot be gauged without some consideration of what became our closest approach to a folk-drama. From 1853 to 1930 the play, generally in George Aiken's dramatization, was never off the boards. "Uncle Tomming" was a recognized branch of the theatrical profession; there were actors who appeared in no other play. Presented in tents and in the finest theaters, it furnished many Americans with practically their only contact with the theater. In 1923 it was made into a musical comedy, *Topsy and Eva,* for the Duncan Sisters, who have since carried the name-characters triumphantly round the world in vaudeville. Aiken's play, revised by A. E. Thomas, may be read in the anthology entitled *S.R.O.,* ed. Bennett Cerf and Van H. Cartmell (D, 1944). The fullest account of the history of *Uncle Tom's Cabin* on the stage is Harry Birdoff, *The World's Greatest Hit—"Uncle Tom's Cabin"* (New York, S. F. Vanni, 1947). See also Barnard Hewitt, *Quar. Journal of Speech.* XXVII (1951), 63-70.

The Outlook), that paper was her medium. She died in Hartford, after a long period of senility, on July 1, 1896.

Mrs. Stowe's ten long fictions divide themselves into three groups: two antislavery novels; four novels of old New England (in which she established the type and the tradition which Mary E. Wilkins Freeman, Sarah Orne Jewett, Alice Brown, and other writers cultivated after her); and three intensely topical "society novels," with their setting in New York. In addition to these, there is one historical novel—*Agnes of Sorrento*.

Mrs. Stowe was a voracious reader. Her childhood discovery of *The Arabian Nights* and Cotton Mather's *Magnalia* she herself described in her last novel, *Poganuc People*. Other early enthusiasms included *Don Quixote* and Sir Walter Scott, all of whose novels she reread, significantly, shortly before she wrote *Uncle Tom's Cabin*.

But she had models nearer home. Of one piece in the third issue of James Hall's *Western Monthly Magazine*, Professor John R. Adams remarks that it "provided a pattern . . . less remote than Scott and Edgeworth, or even Sedgwick and Sigourney."[6] Hall, who gave her a prize for the story she herself published in his columns in April 1834,[7] encouraged a witty realism. Other periodicals for which she wrote were more inclined to be didactic. Adams sees all Mrs. Stowe's work as "the prolonged shadow" of these organs. In view of the "conservative sectarianism and emotional moralizing" of most of her models, he thinks it fortunate that Mrs. Stowe possessed also the "fresher, freer good spirits of the new life of the middle western frontier."

Over *Uncle Tom's Cabin* the critical battle still rages. But there is general agreement on Mrs. Stowe's gifts as a storyteller, her vivid power of invention, her ability to "build" a book. The double plot, as Professor Adams points out,

consists of two journeys, that of escaped slaves to freedom in Canada and that of Tom to martyrdom in the deep South. Tom's adventures fall into three stages, his life in Kentucky with his first owners, his

---

[6] The references are to Catherine Sedgwick's (see Appendix) *A New England Tale* (1822) and to *A Sketch of Connecticut, Forty Years Since* (1824), by Lydia H. Sigourney (1791-1865).

[7] The story was "A New England Sketch," afterwards referred to by Mrs Stowe as "Uncle Lot." It was not, as generally stated, her first story.

sojourn with kindly new masters, and his final torture at the hands of Simon Legree. The first of these sections gives the book its verisimilitude, for Mrs. Stowe had observed the life of Negroes on Kentucky estates. The second section contains most of the humor, in the contrast between the New England spinster, Miss Ophelia, and the wayward slave girl, Topsy. Here also is to be found the most effective discussion of Negro slavery, in the witty and tolerant complaints of Augustine St. Clare. The final section is pure melodrama, intensifying the horror previously suggested in the opening chapters by the frenzied escape of Eliza over the icy Ohio River. Throughout the book, the basic themes of human repression and suffering are described with a vivid awareness that is still appreciable.

But attempts are still made to discredit the novel on the ground that Mrs. Stowe did not know slavery well enough to be able to write about it. This view can be strongly defended. One can well understand the fury of the South when, in her ignorance of the Louisiana laws which specifically prohibited such outrages, Mrs. Stowe showed Uncle Tom whipped to death and a slave girl sold away from her mother. But these are not, strictly speaking, aesthetic considerations. Mrs. Stowe, as Lowell perceived, had the mind of a romancer. Divination, intuition—not scholarship nor exact historical knowledge—are the hallmarks of such a mind. And when we come to characterization, the coarseness and obviousness—in a realistic sense, the glaring unreality—of many of Mrs. Stowe's personages is quite clear, but their tremendous vitality as powerful types of human myth or fantasy is even clearer. The epic-like rhythm of the book has impressed many critics, and Van Wyck Brooks has praised it, in *The Flowering of New England,* for its picture "of an age and a nation." John Erskine admired its breadth of view and charity in the treatment of an unsettled problem, and it is true that Mrs. Stowe had made a determined effort not to indict the South alone. The leading villain is a Vermonter. When the book was published, the first attacks came from the North, and extreme abolitionists objected to its presentation of the patriarchal side of slavery.

Mrs. Stowe showed her own failure to define the true nature of her genius when she attempted to answer her critics by publishing her laboriously accumulated "evidence" in *A Key to "Uncle Tom's Cabin"* (1853); and the confusion crossed the ocean to give Charles

Reade the inspiration for his own method of "documented" fiction.[8]

Much of this material was accumulated after *Uncle Tom's Cabin* had been written, for scientific accuracy was not within the Beecher range. It was not surprising, then, that the author should have used some of it in *Dred: A Tale of the Great Dismal Swamp* (1856). *Dred* is much more literary than its predecessor; pigmentation aside, its hero would have felt quite at home in the world of *Old Mortality*.[9] It should be added that *Uncle Tom's Cabin* itself became a source for *Dred:* Old Tiff is almost Uncle Tom; Harry is nearly George Harris; Tomtit is a mild, masculine Topsy.

But the author's mood is much less conciliatory than it was in her first novel. This time she is out to show the bad influence of slavery not only upon the slaves but also upon their masters. Miscegenation she takes boldly in her stride, for Harry, the faithful steward, is his master's son by a slave woman. She warns the South that there is a day of reckoning coming. In place of the Christian pacifism of Uncle Tom, we now have the Old Testament militarism of Denmark Vesey's son, who takes to the swamps, whence he proposes to strike boldly as the avenger.

In the heroine of *Dred,* Nina Gordon, we get the first striking example of Mrs. Stowe's strange tenderness for the fashionable, frivolous girl. Nina's development, through the love of a wise man and sudden, cruel contact with the world's evil, is beautifully done up to a point. Unfortunately Mrs. Stowe did not know where to stop. A girl of courage and fine humanity did not satisfy her; she had to have a saint; and this is about as convincing as it had been to make Topsy, in her ultimate phase, a missionary to Africa! Worse, having accomplished this, Mrs. Stowe turns about and slays the girl, with typical Victorian sadism, as she had already slain Little Eva and was to slay Mara, of *The Pearl of Orr's Island,* and even the hapless infant at the beginning of *My Wife and I.* And when she killed Nina, she came close to killing the book. Indeed, she never did make up her mind what she was writing about. The novel has been called

[8] See Wayne Burns and E. G. Sutcliffe, " 'Uncle Tom' and Charles Reade," *AL,* XVII (1945-1946), 334-347.

[9] See John H. Nelson, "A Note on the Genesis of Mrs Stowe's 'Dred,' " *U. of Kans. Publ., Humanistic Series,* VI (1940), 59-64.

both *Dred* and *Nina Gordon*. Neither title really "covers." Nobody's problem is actually worked out. Dred dies. Nina dies. Harry escapes. Clayton goes to Canada, to practice emancipation there. Yet with all these faults, *Dred* is still a very absorbing book.

3. Mrs. Stowe: New England and Elsewhere

Among Mrs. Stowe's New England fictions, *Oldtown Folks* (1869),[10] which is based upon her husband's memories of his boyhood in Natick, Massachusetts, is much the finest; at its best, it is quite as good as *Cranford*. *Poganuc People* (1878), Mrs. Stowe's last long story, in which she drew upon her own childhood memories, is *Oldtown Folks* over again, on a less ambitious scale. The stuff of the book is quite as good, but she was getting old and tired by the time she came to it, and it is less completely realized. *The Minister's Wooing* (1859) is the most ambitious project of the group; and *The Pearl of Orr's Island* (1862), in which alone Mrs. Stowe made fictional use of the achievements of Yankee sailors, was apparently an attempt to create a Theocritean idyll of New England.

All Mrs. Stowe's New England novels are set within a comparatively restricted area between Maine and Connecticut and fall between the end of the Revolution and the author's girlhood. The characters are largely fairly humble people. We hear little of the rich merchants and industrialists, the rum-runners, the slave-traders, and the privateers. With the characteristic Beecher horror of accuracy, their creator showed a tendency to throw her stories slightly out of perspective by misdating them, so that they are neither strictly historical nor strictly realistic, but occur in an idealized wonderland, midway between her own experiences and the visions of Cotton Mather.

The Minister's Wooing, which Lowell—no admirer of didactic fiction—judged its author's finest book, suffers today from the difficulty which most modern readers encounter in attempting to sympathize with its central situation. This statement applies alike to Mary Scudder's quixotism in being willing to risk her whole life's happiness rather than ask her freedom of the middle-aged clergy-

---

[10] *Sam Lawson's Oldtown Fireside Stories* (1872), a pendant to *Oldtown Folks,* is an excellent collection of early local color sketches.

man to whom she had pledged herself when she believed her lover to have been lost at sea, and to her agony, as well as his mother's, lest that lover, who was not a "professing" Christian, might have died "unsaved." This religious problem, however, was no fantasy in Mrs. Stowe's time: her sister, Catherine Beecher, had gone through it over her own betrothed, and Harriet herself encountered it when one of her sons was drowned at Dartmouth College.

The minister of the book is the New England theologian, Samuel Hopkins, but it is a mistake to describe the novel as "a long assault on the Puritan faith." It is true that both Mrs. Stowe and her brother Henry Ward Beecher came to repudiate the Calvinistic nightmare in the name of a God of Love. Both brother and sister gave their mature allegiance to a God who loves men in their sins for the purpose of helping them out of them; here they found the true significance of the great doctrine of the Incarnation. This Gospel is movingly preached by Old Candace in *The Minister's Wooing*, when Mrs. Marvyn is on the brink of despair. Yet Mrs. Stowe was Puritan, in spite of all, in every fiber of her being, and it was not, as one writer says, "a harsh but positive gesture" on her part when "she made the black-hearted villain of the piece stem from the family of the great Beecher and Stowe spiritual leader, Jonathan Edwards. . . ." For Aaron Burr *was* the grandson of Jonathan Edwards, and Mrs. Stowe had no idea of using him as a stick to beat his grandfather with. She used him here, and she used him again as Ellery Davenport in *Oldtown Folks,* because he fascinated her, as Byron had fascinated her before him.

This is all incidental so far as the plot of *The Minister's Wooing* is concerned. Incidental too is Burr's affair with Madame de Frontignac, whose coming to a purer way of life through her admiration for the saintly heroine is naïvely handled. Mrs. Stowe's understanding of the French spirit was as narrow as her distrust of it.

Incidental, too, in a way, is the attack on slavery, for Dr. Hopkins imperils his ministerial future by his stand against the trade. What is not incidental is the love story. Essentially *The Minister's Wooing is* a love story, and the author's heart is with love's young dream. Mary cannot ask for freedom, but Hopkins can give it to her, and this is a more powerful sermon than any he has ever preached. The question of whether a Christian girl can wed an unconverted man Mrs. Stowe does not really face, for James comes opportunely into the fold. At the same time, he has made his fortune, in the good old story book fashion, thus illustrating the Puritan habit of making the best of both worlds.

Mara's lover, in *The Pearl of Orr's Island,* is made of less malleable stuff; the poor girl has to die before he glimpses the truth. There is less that needs to be said of this book, which is likely to be the case with an idyll. And at its best, *The Pearl of Orr's Island* is an idyll, as has already been said. It is not always at its best, however; originally the author planned to end the story with the close of its characters' childhood in Chapter XVII, and it would be more of a piece if she had done so.

In *Agnes of Sorrento* (1862) Mrs. Stowe gives us the conventional Italy of nineteenth-century romance, with a heroine as Puritan as Romola is British rationalist. Mrs. Stowe makes a determined effort to be fair to Catholicism, but succeeds only in being condescending: Agnes' soul "was stayed on God and was at peace, as truly as if she had been the veriest Puritan maiden that ever worshipped in a New England meeting-house." The Byronic hero appears again, and love's young dream triumphs once more, though this time the heroine, who had intended herself for the cloister, must first be convinced by her confessor that she has "a vocation unto marriage which should not be denied," and that "Marriage is a sacrament as well as holy orders."

Mrs. Stowe's New York novels were more essay than fiction. She was getting tired of fiction. She saw the world "returning to its second childhood, and running mad for Stories"; herself she was not interested in the story but only in "the things it gives the author a chance to say." Of *Pink and White Tyranny* she declares specifically that it is a parable, not a novel. "We shall tell you in the proper time succinctly just what the moral is, and send you off edified as if you had been hearing a sermon." Such smart, journalistic insouciance turns the devil's weapons against himself.

And that is precisely what Mrs. Stowe was trying to do. The prosperous Episcopalian lady with a winter home in Florida was less austere than she once had been. She had endured—and she was to endure—some terrific blows from life: her son returning from the war a chronic inebriate, to disappear at last on the San Francisco waterfront; a daughter living gaily and carelessly in Cambridge society; her favorite brother, "the greatest preacher since Saint Paul," standing a public trial under accusation of adultery; a half-sister out of her mind; a half-brother a suicide; herself besmirched in the vilest terms ever publicly applied to an American woman for the defense of her dead friend, Lady Byron, which her Puritan conscience had impelled her to make.[11] Through it all she had kept the faith; she had surrendered nothing essential. More than anything else that has been said about her, she would have been grateful for Forrest Wilson's "one of the most consistently Christ-minded women America ever produced." But one must be up to date even in matters of morality. With women like Victoria Woodhull and Tennessee Claflin seductively presenting the claims of immorality and bringing discredit upon the righteous movement for female emancipation, one might still give morality to one's contemporaries, but one had to give it to them, as Harriet says, "hot." This is what she did—in *Pink and White Tyranny* (1871), in *My Wife and I* (1871) and its sequel, *We and Our Neighbors* (1875). And she did it with a clear conscience, remembering that, in *Belinda* and other books, Maria Edgeworth had done much the same thing before her. As literature the results were not important, but they remain a remarkable example of an aging writer's ability to meet the flippant 1870's on their own ground.

My Wife and I gives a picture of contemporary New York journalism, with all its dishonesty and moral humbug. The story is told by Harry Henderson, though scenes which he did not witness are reported and letters he never read are given in full. Through him we get Mrs. Stowe's eminently correct, and completely feminine, views on every conceivable subject of a domestic character.

[11] Incensed by the Countess Guiccioli's memoirs, Mrs. Stowe accused Byron of incest with his half-sister, Mrs. Leigh, in "The True Story of Lady Byron's Life," published in the *Atlantic* in 1869. This was the most sensational magazine article of the nineteenth century, as *Uncle Tom's Cabin* had been the most sensational novel, but the resultant scandal nearly wrecked the magazine. Mrs. Stowe reiterated and enlarged her story in the book, *Lady Byron Vindicated* (1870).

In *Pink and White Tyranny* she portrays a worthless woman as only another woman could have done it. "A woman without magnanimity, without generosity, who has no love, and whom a man loves, is a terrible antagonist." Yet the moral is the indissolubility of marriage. Lillie Ellis makes her husband's home a hell, but there is no redress for him; he has taken her for better or worse. "There is, and must be, good in every one; and gradually the good in him will overcome the evil in her." But Mrs. Stowe was novelist as well as moralist, impatient as she was of fiction at this time. So, like most unwanted (and unworthy) mates in pre-divorce age fiction, Lillie kindly and accommodatingly dies. At the end she is sentimentalized, somewhat after the fashion of David Copperfield's Dora, but much less convincingly, for Dora was a good little thing, with all her faults, while Lillie, as Mrs. Stowe has described her, had not a decent impulse in her.

4. *Mrs. Stowe: The Summing-Up*

Essentially, then, Mrs. Stowe represents the Novel as Evangel. Even *Uncle Tom's Cabin* was more than an antislavery tract. Slavery is used to introduce universal problems: a mother's struggle for her child, the cruelty of the strong and the helplessness of the weak, the terror of all mankind in the face of death. In the Preface she wrote for the French edition, the author defined her purpose as follows:

This story is to show how Jesus Christ, who liveth and was dead, and now is alive and forevermore, has still a mother's love for the poor and lowly, and that no man can sink so low but that Jesus Christ will stoop to take his hand.

May not this be one reason why the novel has so long outlasted the specific institution which it attacked—and helped destroy?

Mrs. Stowe was no bigot and no prude. No bigot could have presented the skeptical St. Clare so sympathetically, or given Clayton, the ideal young hero of *Dred,* so little orthodoxy. No prude could have responded to George Sand and Madame de Staël and George Eliot as Mrs. Stowe did; in an age when it was notoriously improper for a woman to speak out in meeting upon any subject, no prude could have spoken as Mrs. Stowe spoke—of miscegenation, of incest, of every other terrible thing that needed to be spoken of in the name of the Kingdom of God. George Sand called Mrs. Stowe a saint. If she was, she wore her halo at a slightly rakish angle; it was not for nothing that Leonard Bacon said his country was inhabited by "saints, sinners, and Beechers."

The most powerful preachers of the Christian faith in Mrs. Stowe's fiction are two Negro women—Candace, who comforts Mrs. Marvyn when she believes her son lost and damned, and the slave Milly, in *Dred*. Chapter XVI of that novel, which is Milly's account of how it became possible for her to forgive and befriend the heartless mistress who had sold her children, is as powerful a presentation of the Gospel as American literature has achieved. Uncle Tom and Old Tiff *live* the Gospel quite as impressively as these women, but neither expounds it with such power. Of Uncle Tom's pacifism Mrs. Stowe apparently failed to catch all the implications, for she was quite as unchristian during the Civil War as "patriotic" ladies are wont to be in wartime, though it is only fair to add that once the slaughter was over, hers was one of the voices raised for conciliation.

But neither Tom nor Tiff was a woman, and that made a tremendous difference. In Mrs. Stowe's pages, women are the true spiritual guides. She never bowed down to the clergy. She was the daughter, the wife, the mother of a clergyman, and the sister of seven clergymen—she understood that breed only too well. But the insight of a Christian mother—ah! that is the norm by which she tests everything. Of Mary Scudder's wedding she writes, "The fair poetic maiden, the seeress, the saint, has passed into that appointed shrine for women, more holy than cloister, more saintly and pure than church or altar,—*a Christian home.*"

I have said nothing of the best known of all Mrs. Stowe's religionists, Evangeline St. Clare. It is difficult to be fair to Little Eva in this day and age: she belongs to the period of Paul Dombey and Little Nell. But though one may doubt with John Erskine that even Eva could have redeemed Topsy, the distinction Mrs. Stowe is making between the powerlessness of Miss Ophelia, who tried to do her duty by the little imp while fundamentally despising her, and the power of Eva, who loved as Jesus loved, is perfectly sound; neither could one ask for a truer piece of insight on her part than her keen perception of the difference between the New England abolitionist who would free the Negro yet hates to touch him, and the Southerner, who enslaves him, but lives with him, and, in a sense, loves and understands him.

In the Preface to *Oldtown Folks,* the narrator, Horace Holyoke, disdains both teaching and preaching, and presents himself as "the observer and reporter, seeing much, doubting much, questioning much, and believing with all my heart in only a very few things." He has tried to make his mind "as still and passive as a looking-glass or a mountain lake, and then to give . . . merely the images reflected there." In view of the excellence achieved, this pronouncement gives Mrs. Stowe's critics an excellent opportunity to observe how much better a writer she might have been had she everywhere steered clear of didacticism.

Whether she really would have been we shall never know. As she is, she flatters few of our contemporary prejudices, and she pays the price for her refusal. She had the high feminine insight on which she prided herself; she had, too, some of the less attractive traits of femininity. She never mastered the bare mechanics of writing, never got her work in on time; she was never able to give a consistent and coherent account of even the writing of *Uncle Tom's Cabin.* She lived in a world of confusion, fatigue, and cloudy abstraction, and she suffered at times from a Messianic complex. But she had the root of the matter in her, as a writer and as a woman. Her contemporaries paid her no more than her due, and posterity neglects her at its peril.

5. *Two More Contemporaries: Holmes and DeForest*

While Mrs. Stowe and the "damned mob of scribbling women" who were her contemporaries were building their careers, other novels were being published by other writers who had little or nothing in common with them. Two of these writers must be briefly considered here.

In the year the Civil War began, Oliver Wendell Holmes (1809-1894), poet, physician, and "Autocrat of the Breakfast Table," published his famous *Elsie Venner,* a novel which, in his own words, belongs "to that middle region between science and poetry which sensible men, as they are called, are very shy of meddling with."

Though Dr. Holmes's pitiable heroine was by no means the first serpent-woman in literature, she owes little to her predecessors in classical sources or ancient superstitions; instead, she originated "in a psychological conception fertilized by a theological dogma." As a medical man, Holmes did not actually believe that if a pregnant woman were bitten by a rattlesnake, both the appearance and the moral nature of her child might be marked by ophidian characteristics. But he did know that many a human being is born into the world under moral handicaps quite as cruel as Elsie Venner's—and is quite as innocent of all responsibility for them. It was in defense of such unfortunates that he wrote his novel.

Technically the book has grave faults. It is full of unassimilated essay-passages, and the machinery by which the tale is told is as clumsy as it is unnecessary. The avalanche is more meaningless sensationalism than the Hawthornesque symbolism the author seems to have been seeking, and the whole business of the wicked cousin is irrelevant pasteboard melodrama. As for the small town local color, while not uninteresting in itself, it is very annoying because it draws attention away from the tragic theme of the story. But bold thinking and deep feeling redeem *Elsie Venner* from all such shortcomings. We never really see the heroine from the inside; we hardly hear her voice until the very end; yet she never loses her purchase upon the imagination, and it is not too much to say that her death wrings the heart. There was dynamite in this well-bred horror-story by a Boston Brahmin, for it raised the whole question of free will and moral responsibility; but though Holmes hated Calvinistic dogma, he wisely placed his emphasis not upon theological controversy but upon human compassion. The book is a noble plea for the recognition of "moral insanity." Its aim was "to make men charitable and soften legal and theological barbarism."

And it succeeds as art because in spite of all its pseudoscientific fantasy, its human reality is more important than its propaganda. The ophidian side of Elsie's inheritance loosens its hold upon her as she ages beyond the limits of the possible ophidian life-span, but by this time the girl's passion for Bernard Langdon has made her so unhappy that the poison involves "the centers of life in its own decay." Could her teacher have responded to her love, she might have been saved from her cruel inheritance, and her true womanly nature—which, it is clear, is exquisite—freed to take full possession of her. All of which, whether Holmes knew it or not, brings *Elsie Venner* very close to "Beauty and the Beast" and all the other old stories of human beings under evil enchantment who could be saved only by love.[12]

A more important novelist than Holmes was John W. DeForest (1826-1906), perhaps the most unjustly neglected of all American writers. Howells was surely right when he declared in his *Atlantic* review of *Kate Beaumont* (1872) that "we are not so much lacking in an American novelist as in a public to recognize him."

DeForest was New England by birth and breeding, but he knew the South as a social visitor before the war—in which he saw active service—and later as director of the Freedmen's Bureau in Greenville, South Carolina. He also traveled abroad, as far as Syria—whence he derived the material for *Irene the Missionary* (1879).

DeForest essayed various themes—too many, perhaps, for his ultimate fame. He both began and closed his career as an historical novelist: *Witching Times* (1856-1857), which achieved only serial publication,[13] is a rationalistic account of the epidemic at Salem, while *A Lover's Revolt,* with which he broke a long silence in 1898, gives us both patriot and loyalist in Revolutionary Boston. *Seacliff* (1859) and *The Wetherel Affair* (1873) are mystery stories. *Overland* (1871) concerns adventures beyond Santa Fe. *Honest John Vane* and *Playing the Mischief* (both 1875) are studies of political corruption in Washington.

These are not all important books. Though *Irene the Missionary* takes in a political uprising in Syria, it is still a rather dull story, and

---

[12] Holmes wrote two more novels: *The Guardian Angel* (1867) and *A Mortal Antipathy* (1885). Both are much inferior to *Elsie Venner*. In a Ph.D. thesis on Holmes's relation to literary determinism (Boston University, 1951), Arthur Kreisman sees *The Guardian Angel* as a study of normal heredity, *Elsie Venner* as studying accidental heredity, and *A Mortal Antipathy* as concerned with the influence of environment. "In short, the three novels are all parts of one large study dealing with psychological determinism, and handling the problem from every possible point of view." In *A Mortal Antipathy* he finds Holmes anticipating what is now known as the conditioned reflex.

[13] In *Putnam's Magazine,* Volumes VIII, IX, X.

The Bloody Chasm (1881)—which I have not previously mentioned
—has a plot better suited to a "zany" film comedy than to a novel of
the reconstructed South. *Overland,* too, smacks of the films, with its
wicked Spanish villain and the desperado he employs to destroy the
heroine's life, to say nothing of the stalwart, incorruptible young
army officer who guards her through the perilous journey across the
West. DeForest is equally conventional when he relies upon a forged
will to create the mystery in *Seacliff,* employs a shipwreck to bring
the lovers together at the beginning of *Kate Beaumont,* and casts a
Polish count as the murderer in *The Wetherel Affair.*[14] Of the
political novels, *Honest John Vane*—an account of the corruption of
a Congressman—seems, despite Howells's praise, a somewhat slight
thing; more impressive is the history of the fascinating woman
claimant in *Playing the Mischief,* to whom a stupid Congress pays
$100,000 for a barn destroyed in the War of 1812—which had already
been paid for once!

But even when DeForest did not find a subject which called out
all his powers, he still gave his readers much of value. *Overland,* for
example, includes vivid, and, in its day, novel pictures of the great
Southwest. Even in a trifling opus, the characterization is likely to
be well handled. And whether it be economic problems that come up
for incidental consideration, as in *The Wetherel Affair;* or the Negro
question, as in *Miss Ravenel's Conversion;* or the conflict between
religion and science, as in *Playing the Mischief,* the reader never
fails to recognize that he is in the presence of a thoughtful mind.

It is often said that DeForest failed to win popular suffrages
because most of the novel-readers of his time were women, and
women could not forgive him for the way he handled them in his

---

[14] Like Cooper's *The Ways of the Hour,* both *Seacliff* and *The Wetherel
Affair* have been ignored by modern historians of the mystery story. *The
Wetherel Affair*—an absorbing yarn, especially in its first half—differs from
the modern stylized "mystery" in including much more varied material and
in not striving for the same intensity and unity of impression. It does not
have Wilkie Collins's "atmosphere," but it suggests Collins in the author's
matter-of-fact attitude toward his subject and in his use of lovable eccentrics. In *Seacliff* the mystery does not involve murder (though murder is
committed before the end) but a woman's reputation. *Seacliff* represents
about as close an approach to the British country-house novel as can be made
in America.

novels. If this is true, it reflects very adversely upon the honesty and intelligence of our grandmothers. It is true that DeForest has a sizable gallery of female eccentrics, whom he often "tags" amusingly in the Dickens manner.[15] Such are Aunt Maria, the woman's rights enthusiast of *Overland,* and Mrs. Van Leer, of *Seacliff,* with "her low-necked conversation and manner." Many women in fiction have quoted the Scriptures amusingly; the individualizing touch in Ma Treat's quotation (again in *Seacliff*) is that she always adds the number of chapter and verse. Mrs. Dinneford, of *The Wetherel Affair,* is forever quoting Tupper, and Imogene Eleanor, of the same novel, conducts her conversation entirely in terms of romantic clichés borrowed from cheap fiction. Mrs. John Murray, of *Playing the Mischief,* habitually repeats the last words of her husband's just-completed utterance.

Some of these eccentrics of DeForest's are pretty savagely handled. Such are Squire Nancy Appleyard, the "Bloomer" and unbriefed female lawyer of *Playing the Mischief,* and Kate Beaumont's virago-aunt, who finally loses her mind altogether. On the other hand, he was capable of the purely conventional heroine, a bundle of Victorian perfections. Such is Clara, of *Overland;* such is the noble Miss Ledyard, of *Playing the Mischief;* such, surprisingly, since the book which bears her name is one of his two greatest achievements, is Kate Beaumont herself.

Kate's unreality is all the more striking because one cannot but compare her with her sister Nelly, wife of the worthless Bentley Armitage (whom she finally leaves), for Nelly is both entirely real and altogether worthy: she stands with Lillie Ravenel and Josie Murray as one of DeForest's three foremost pieces of feminine characterization. Lillie, the rebel who is converted to the Union cause in the course of the war, is worthy too in the main (though she is certainly silly at times), but contemporary readers may have felt that DeForest had soiled her by marrying her to the essentially worthless Colonel Carter, with his coarse animal glamour, before

[15] DeForest's knowledge of Dickens has been established, but Thackeray, "that pitiless analyst of humanity," was more congenial to his temper. Among other books and writers whom he mentions in his novels are Dante, Shakespeare, *The Arabian Nights,* Bunyan, *Vathek,* and Hawthorne. Like Hawthorne and Melville, he was fascinated by Guido's portrait of Beatrice Cenci.

bringing her in the end to her true love, Captain Colburne. Josie Murray, on the other hand, is a completely unscrupulous woman, a Becky Sharp with no redeeming qualities save her good temper and her technical chastity.[16]

Yet it is perfectly clear that DeForest's unfavorable portraits of women spring merely from his honesty and penetration and not at all from any animus against women as such. As a matter of fact, he handles his men in exactly the same way. We may, he says, well be furious at the hypocrisy of women until we examine the lives of their brothers. "Then, without a further doubt or growl, we concede the purity of womanhood." Edgar Bradford, practically the only incorruptible Congressman of *Playing the Mischief,* has a bad record in love, and the faultless Irene the Missionary cannot get anything better than a weak man who has been unable to resist a dangerous flirtation with a native girl. As a matter of fact, DeForest is as decent in all sexual matters as he is free from prudery; his honesty and his decency are equally apparent in the description of the "cracker ball" in *Kate Beaumont.* He even subscribes to the time-honored idea that men may be "redeemed" through love for a woman: "If any man is clean of the world, it is the lover; if any man is pure in heart, it is the lover. There is no nobler state of mind, with regard at least to merely human nature, than that of a man who loves with his whole being."

In all essential matters, DeForest knew how to interpret life sanely without raising his voice. *Kate Beaumont* is a powerful indictment of dueling precisely because he does not preach about it, and the evils of intemperance are far more impressive in Bentley Armitage's tragedy—perhaps even more so in Kate's father Peyton, who, good as he is at heart, spends his life in an alcoholic fog—than in the whole of *Ten Nights in a Bar-Room.*

But beautifully wrought as *Kate Beaumont* is, Deforest produced an even finer book in *Miss Ravenel's Conversion from Secession to Loyalty* (1867). Colonel Carter has recently been compared to Rhett

---

[16] Mrs. Larue, of *Miss Ravenel's Conversion,* is DeForest's "bad" woman. Though completely honest in his treatment of her, he is careful to keep her generally out of the foreground of the story. He allows both her and her lover, Colonel Carter, some good qualities, and permits us a few glimpses of them through their own self-justifying eyes. In some respects, Mrs. Larue actually has a good influence upon Carter.

Butler in Margaret Mitchell's *Gone With the Wind*. The panoramic sweep of the book suggests *Gone With the Wind* also, though its spirit is very different. Into this novel DeForest poured his own experiences of battle—quite invalidating the familiar claim that Stephen Crane was the first writer to break with the romantic tradition in stories of war—and his wide experience of life and knowledge of character, both north and south. This book alone would suffice to establish DeForest's claim both for historic importance and absolute achievement in the field of the American novel. His work might well be tagged Exhibit A in the museum of American literature to refute the comfortable claim that all good books somehow find the readers they deserve automatically.

CHAPTER VI

"THE LINCOLN OF OUR LITERATURE"*

Hawthorne took me up on the hill behind Wayside, and we had a silence of half an hour together. He said he never saw a perfectly beautiful woman; asked much about the West; and wished he could find some part of America "where the cursed shadow of Europe had not fallen."

W. D. Howells

1. Mark Twain: His Life Experience

Mark Twain was an actor who appeared beneath the proscenium arch of the heavens in many different roles. He was Tom Sawyer (with a touch of Huckleberry Finn); he was Colonel Sellers; he was the Connecticut Yankee; he was Joan of Arc. As Tom Sawyer he spent his youth "drowsing in the sunshine of a summer morning . . . the great Mississippi, the magnificent Mississippi rolling its mile-wide tide along; . . . the dense forest away on the other side"; and many years after, his remembrance of things past made it possible for him to preserve as literature one of the most wonderful aspects of the development of America. As Colonel Sellers, he dreamed mighty dreams of power and glory, dreams of fabulous riches that were to come pouring in upon him, first from the Tennessee land, then from that marvelous typesetting machine of James Paige in which he was to sink a fortune, but always mixing on his palette the colors of fact with the colors of hope until at last, when old age was upon him, he found that he could only remember the things that had never happened. As the Connecticut Yankee, he first vaunted his Americanism against the old culture and the old corruptions of Europe, attacking with leather-lunged frontier laughter everything that the frontier could not understand; then, widening

* Portions of the first section of this chapter have been taken from my book, *Mark Twain, The Man and His Work,* published by the Yale University Press. Copyright, 1935, by Edward Wagenknecht.

his scope, he began to think in broadly human terms, assailing selfishness and corruption everywhere, himself gone "grailing" in behalf of a loftier dream than ever King Arthur knew. Finally, as Joan of Arc, he became the embodiment of the very chivalry and idealism he had sometimes been wont to deride.

Life groomed Samuel Langhorne Clemens for the business of authorship as she has groomed few Americans. Southern by descent, Midwestern by birth and breeding, he opened his eyes in Florida, Monroe County, Missouri, on November 30, 1835. When he was four years old, the family moved to Hannibal, in Marion County, on the west bank of the Mississippi.

Fifteen months after his father's death in 1847, he began five years of work as a printer in Hannibal; then he set out on his own for eastern parts, spending a year in Washington, Philadelphia, and New York. He worked for a time at his brother Orion's printing establishment in Keokuk, Iowa, tarried briefly in Cincinnati, and then left, as he believed, for South America. But a meeting, in New Orleans, with Horace Bixby, changed his plans, and he apprenticed himself instead to "the stupendous task of learning the twelve hundred miles of the Mississippi River between St. Louis and New Orleans—of knowing it as exactly and as unfailingly, even in the dark, as one knows the way to his own features." Within eighteen months he had become one of the best pilots on the river, and he continued at this trade until the Mississippi was closed to peaceful activities by the outbreak of the Civil War in 1861.

With the war itself, Mark Twain's connection was brief and extremely informal.[1] Before the end of 1861 he had left for Nevada with Orion, whom President Lincoln had just appointed governor of the territory. The journey is described in *Roughing It* (1872).

Now Mark Twain enters upon various mining activities, coming into contact with many different aspects of Western life. He had drifted to Aurora, Nevada, and was poor indeed in this world's goods, when the opportunity came, in 1862, to take a place on the staff of the Virginia City *Enterprise*.

[1] See F. W. Lorch, "Mark Twain and the 'Campaign that Failed,' " *AL*, XII (1941), 454-470.

Here he first used the name "Mark Twain," and here he began to build up his West Coast reputation. In those days the journalistic hoax was still his favorite type of humor, and the consequences were not always enjoyable. The results of one affair involved a precipitate retreat to San Francisco, where he found a somewhat uncongenial berth on the *Morning Call.* From San Francisco, too, he found it prudent, in the course of time, to retreat, but this time the circumstances were all to his credit: he had been too outspoken in his criticism of a corrupt police department. As Miss Bellamy remarks, he had early shown "his awareness of the structure of violence in our society and of the crumbling masonry of our human relationships erected on foundations of greed and racial prejudice." For three months he lived in Calaveras County, where, with Jim Gillis, he tried pocket mining on Jackass Hill.

In 1865, Artemus Ward, whom he had met in Virginia City, wrote to ask for a sketch to be included in a new book of humor. Mark Twain sent a story he had heard in California about a jumping frog. Arriving too late to be included in the book, the tale appeared instead in the *Saturday Press,* on November 18, 1865, and "Mark Twain" promptly became a "name" along the Atlantic seaboard.

In 1866 the Sacramento *Union* sent Mark Twain to the Sandwich (Hawaiian) Islands. In December he went east, as he supposed, for a visit. Unexpectedly he lectured at Cooper Union. Still more unexpectedly, he sailed, in June, 1867, on the *Quaker City* Mediterranean steamboat excursion, writing for the *Alta California* the travel letters that soon, revised as *The Innocents Abroad,* were to make him the most famous humorist of his time. It was indeed a momentous voyage, for both his personal and his professional future were decided by it. One day in the Bay of Smyrna, a wealthy young man of Elmira, New York, named Charles Langdon, showed him a miniature reproduction of the face of his sister Olivia. Mark Twain promptly fell in love with that face, and it may almost be said that he never looked at another woman as long as he lived. In July, 1869, *The Innocents Abroad* was published; on February 2, 1870, Samuel L. Clemens and Olivia Langdon were married.

Now Mark Twain plunges into the world of eastern respectability, a social order in which he feels himself an intruder, which in some

of its aspects he scorns, yet which, contradictory as he is, he passionately aspires to fit himself into.[2] His first business venture, an
interest in the Buffalo *Express,* did not turn out well. By the end of
1871 he was settled at Hartford, Connecticut.[3] In 1873, with Charles
Dudley Warner, a Hartford neighbor, he published his first extended
fiction, *The Gilded Age.* In 1876 came *The Adventures of Tom
Sawyer.* A trip to Europe yielded *A Tramp Abroad* in 1880. *The
Prince and the Pauper* followed in 1881, *Life on the Mississippi* in
1883, *The Adventures of Huckleberry Finn* in 1884. In 1889 appeared
an earnest, extended satire, *A Connecticut Yankee in King Arthur's
Court.*

In 1891, sorely harassed by financial difficulties, Mark Twain
closed his Hartford house and moved to Berlin. When the Paige
typesetter and the Charles L. Webster Publishing Company had
alike failed, Mark Twain (like Sir Walter Scott before him), refused
to take advantage of the bankruptcy laws and voluntarily assumed a
debt of some $100,000. In July, 1895, accompanied by Mrs. Clemens
and their second daughter, Clara, he set out across the Pacific for a
lecture tour of the world. His success was all that might have been
hoped for, but just as the crushing burden of debt had been lifted,
Susy, Mark Twain's eldest daughter, whom he so passionately loved,
and who had inherited so much of his own great spirit, died sud-

---

[2] Van Wyck Brooks, *The Ordeal of Mark Twain* (Dutton, 1920, revised
1935), which saw Elmira and the Langdons enlisted in a conspiracy to
destroy the soul of Mark Twain and cause him to surrender his great gift
to the wicked forces of genteel capitalism, misled the literati for a decade,
and though it has been rejected by every special student of the subject, it
still maintains a powerful hold upon persons who prefer brilliant theories
about literature to literature. In 1938, Edgar Lee Masters rehashed it, in the
worst book ever written on the subject, *Mark Twain, A Portrait* (Scribners).
Bernard DeVoto's *Mark Twain's America* was the most elaborate attack on the
Brooks thesis, but see also DeLancey Ferguson, "Huck Finn Aborning,"
Col., N.S. III (1938), 171-180—cf. *AL,* X (1939), 488-491, XI (1939), 218-
219; Ferguson, "The Case for MT's Wife," *UTQ,* IX (1939), 9-21; Max
Eastman, "MT's Elmira," in *Heroes I Have Known* (S&S, 1942).

[3] For a delightful picture of Mark's life in Hartford, his neighbors, and
his milieu, see Kenneth R. Andrews, *Nook Farm, MT's Hartford Circle*
(HUP, 1950). Mr. Andrews is especially good on Joseph H. Twichell, whom
I unintentionally did an injustice in my *MT, The Man and His Work,* though
Mr. Andrews both overstated my position and overlooked my letter of cor-
rection in *SRL,* XVII, Apr. 2, 1938, p. 13.

denly, across the ocean in Hartford, and half the reawakening glory of life died with her.

The books continued, a refuge against despair: *The American Claimant,* his worst long fiction, in 1891; *Tom Sawyer Abroad* and *Pudd'nhead Wilson,* both partial successes, in 1894; then, in 1896, both *Tom Sawyer, Detective* and a long, serious historical novel, "written for love," and published anonymously, the *Personal Recollections of Joan of Arc. Following the Equator,* his last book of travel, and a singularly weary one,[4] came along in 1897 to tell the story of the world tour.

The Clemens family did not return to America until 1900. Three years later, when Mrs. Clemens's health broke, they settled in Florence, where, on June 5, 1904, she died. Desolate without her, her husband and his two remaining daughters came to take up their residence in New York.

Mark Twain was not writing many long pieces these last years of his life, though there are scores of manuscripts among the Mark Twain Papers that he was never able to finish. His "gospel" of determinism, *What Is Man?,* Mrs. Clemens would never permit him to publish. It was privately printed, unsigned, in 1906, but it did not join his collected works until 1917. *The Mysterious Stranger,* his last important work of fiction, had preceded it by a year.

The last books—all brief, and except the second quite unimportant —that Mark Twain himself saw through the press were his attack on *Christian Science* and *Captain Stormfield's Visit to Heaven* in 1907 and *Is Shakespeare Dead?* in 1909. When he was not working, he spent his time playing billiards, or cursing the war lords, or playing with little girls like Elizabeth Wallace and Dorothy Quick.[5] Short pieces were continually coming out, and some of them, like *Eve's Diary,* were gems. He filled the magazines and he filled the public eye. The reporters were always after him; no public occasion was complete without him. A series of academic honors was climaxed in 1907 with a D.C.L. from Oxford. In 1908 he moved to his beauti-

---

[4] Miss Bellamy is the principal admirer of *Following the Equator;* see her *MT as a Literary Artist,* pp. 262-265.

[5] See Elizabeth Wallace, *MT and the Happy Island* (McClurg, 1913); Dorothy Quick, "A Little Girl's MT," *NAR,* CCXL (1935), 342-348, and "My Author's League with MT," *NAR,* CCXLV (1938), 315-329.

ful new house, "Stormfield," at Redding, Connecticut. There, on the day before Christmas in 1909, life struck at him for the last time, when his youngest daughter, Jean, was taken with an epileptic seizure and died instantly in her bath. When spring came, on April 21, 1910, her father followed her, dying, as he had always said he would die, while Halley's Comet, which had ushered him into the world seventy-five years before, again illuminated the heavens.

2. Some Classifications

Mark Twain is so incomparably the dominating personality in American literature, the mightiest figure in our American literary mythology, that one who would write about him as novelist merely must inevitably feel somewhat cabined, cribbed, confined. There is the same difficulty in being dispassionate about him as is in being dispassionate about Lincoln, and when Howells called him "the Lincoln of our literature," he struck out the most telling and illuminating phrase concerning him that has yet been coined. He was the product of the same Midwestern frontier that produced Lincoln; indeed, he himself *was* that frontier in literature as unmistakably as Lincoln was that frontier in world statesmanship.

The fundamental difficulty with people who still imagine that Mark Twain wanted to be Shelley—or Zola—is that they have failed to remember that Mark Twain inherited and fulfilled a tradition: he did not establish one. When he began his work, the frontier already existed as literature, literature of pretty poor quality, much of it, but literature notwithstanding. Mr. DeVoto has described it clearly— fantasy and realism side by side, burlesque and extravaganza closely connected with satire—and Mr. Meine has illustrated its quality in his *Tall Tales of the Southwest*.[6]

The whole thing hangs together beautifully; the picture is one, not many. The frontier humorist was essentially an improviser, a raconteur. At the outset, his art was oral, not written, a literature without letters, and it never wholly lost the insignia of its origin.[7]

[6] Franklin J. Meine, *Tall Tales of the Southwest* (K, 1930). See, also, Walter Blair, *Horse-Sense in American Humor* (UCP, 1942) and his anthology, *Native American Humor, 1800-1900* (ABC, 1937).

[7] In her valuable *MT as a Literary Artist,* Miss Bellamy expresses a certain disagreement with this view, as previously expressed by myself, Con-

The raconteur, like the actor, dramatizes his own personality; and the actor, alone among artists, uses his own body and soul as the instrument upon which he plays. Mark Twain's platform work was no accident, no by-blow; it was an essential expression of his art. Neither is it an accident that, though he wrote one of the very greatest novels in American literature, we should always think of him first and his books afterward. The only thing that could not have been safely prophesied was the vastness and grandeur of the soul he had to express. That was simply a piece of colossal good luck, for America and for the world.

Mr. DeVoto has said that Mark Twain was essentially a novelist. It would surprise him to hear it. He did not consider himself a novelist—"can't write a novel, for I lack the faculty"—and except for the works of W. D. Howells, he did not think he really enjoyed novels. Novelist in the Howells or Henry James sense, he certainly was not, and only in the solitary instance of *The Gilded Age,* written in collaboration, did he even attempt to be.

Yet he importantly enlarged the scope of American fiction. And it is always something of a problem to differentiate between his fiction and his factual writings. There is, for example, a good deal of fiction in his travel narratives, though they can scarcely fall for consideration in a history of the American novel. There might be some question, on the other hand, about such pieces as "The Man That Corrupted Hadleyburg" and "The $30,000 Bequest." Are they novels or short stories? My own working plan for the discussion of Mark Twain's fiction is as follows:

I. FICTION OF THE CONTEMPORARY SCENE. *The Gilded Age,* with its pendant, *The American Claimant.*

II. FICTION OUT OF HANNIBAL. *The Adventures of Tom Sawyer* and *The Adventures of Huckleberry Finn,* with two addenda—*Tom Sawyer Abroad* and *Tom Sawyer, Detective; Pudd'nhead Wilson.*

III. HISTORY AND LEGEND. *The Prince and the Pauper, A Connecticut Yankee in King Arthur's Court, Personal Recollections of Joan of Arc, The Mysterious Stranger.*

stance Rourke, and other writers. But she and I are fundamentally in accord in our attitude toward Mark Twain, and I think I never intended, on this point, to be taken quite so literally as she shows some tendency to take me.

That there is no overlapping here, I do not maintain. There is Mississippi folklore in both *Joan of Arc* and *The Mysterious Stranger,* and Joan's secretary, the Sieur Louis de Conte, sometimes speaks with the voice of Huck and Tom, which is Mark Twain's own voice. There is more of the nineteenth century than of the sixth in *A Connecticut Yankee.* Even as *The Mysterious Stranger* stands, Eseldorf is Hannibal with a medieval coloring, but in the first two (unpublished) versions of the story the coloring is absent; young Satan actually comes to Hannibal and associates with Huck and Tom. On the highest level of his creativity, Mark Twain never left the village where he grew up.

3. *Fiction of the Contemporary Scene*

The American Claimant is too silly to bother with. But *The Gilded Age* is another story. It is not a good novel. Disfigured by crude burlesque in its highest reaches, it lacks unity of both thought and action. It is crowded with undeveloped characters, and the young people are sticks. But nowhere else in our literary history did an American novel become a more important vehicle of social and political criticism.

What Mark Twain threw into *The Gilded Age* was the authentic material of the Tennessee land, which had played such an important part in the dreams and the heartbreak of his own family—that and the mighty figure of Colonel Sellers ("There's millions in it!") with whom the American speculator became part of the literary mythology of the world.[8] Conventional novel-motifs were drawn, with fine impartiality, from the conventional Victorian literature which Mark's collaborator, Charles Dudley Warner, knew so much better than he did, and from life; the fate of the "bad" heroine, Laura Hawkins, whose story turns unconvincingly to melodrama because

[8] A. H. Quinn, *American Fiction,* pp. 246-247, shows reason to believe that Warner too may have contributed importantly to Sellers. For literary influences on *The Gilded Age,* see, further, John W. Chapman, *AM,* CL (1932), 720-721; Edward Wagenknecht, *MT, The Man and His Work,* pp. 36; 270, n. 9; 271, n. 17; E. H. Weatherly, *MLN,* LIX (1944), 310-313. For the contributions of the collaborators and the division of labor between them, cf. Paine's *MT, A Biography,* I, 477, and E. E. Leisy, "MT's Part in 'The Gilded Age,'" *AL,* VIII (1937), 445-447.

the authors were disgusted by the abuse of the insanity plea in murder cases, was taken from a San Francisco trial of current interest.[9] Nor is this the only "topical" note in the book: directly or indirectly, the activities of Fisk, Gould, Rockefeller, and Tweed are all reflected.

And it is merely just that this novel, with all its faults, should have given its name to an age. Precisely because of its faults, it reflects the age more completely. Here are coal, railroads, and steamboating; the real estate boom and the speculative fever of the after-the-war period; unscrupulous banking practices and unscrupulous manipulation of stock. Here are bribery and other forms of political corruption in Washington; the lobby system; the misuse of government bureaus and agencies. Here are snobbery, pseudo-aristocracy, and colossal ignorance and vulgarity in Washington society. Here are philanthropy, education, and religion as the partners and shields of commercial exploitation and political corruption. Here is the new feminist movement, specifically the woman politician and adventuress (Laura) and the professional woman (Ruth Bolton, the young Quaker medical student). Here are crime and punishment and the jury system. Here—please note!—is Mark Twain speaking out on the abuses of his time before many of his contemporaries have learned that (as material for fiction, at least), they exist.

Only one thing is significantly omitted, and that, as Walter Fuller Taylor has pointed out, in the best study of both *The Gilded Age* and *A Connecticut Yankee* as social and economic criticism that has yet been made, is the specific problem of the machine. "For, although capitalistic, . . . [the economy of *The Gilded Age*] is not primarily industrial; the entire novel, notwithstanding the late date of its appearance, is curiously premachine."[10] The ideals of the book are those of simple frontier decency and honesty. For Mark Twain was a child of the Age of Lincoln.

4. *Fiction out of Hannibal*

Mark Twain's masterpieces—*Tom Sawyer* and *Huckleberry Finn*

[9] See Franklin Walker, "An Influence from San Francisco in MT's 'The Gilded Age,' " *AL,* VIII (1936), 63-66.

[10] *The Economic Novel in America* (UNCP, 1942).

—are altogether confined to the world of his youth, and there is nothing in them that he did not understand better than any other writer who has ever lived.

Some years ago, an American publisher asked fifty well-known "critics" to name the ten greatest American books. Thirty-eight out of the forty-two who replied named "Tom Sawyer and Huckleberry Finn" as one of the ten. But these books are two, not one. If they deal with the same life, it is not at all in the same manner or mood.

Huckleberry Finn is by common consent the greater of the two, but this is not because it lacks any of the faults, contradictions, or inconsistencies of its predecessor. Of the two books, *Tom Sawyer* is much the better unified.[11] *Huckleberry* starts uncertainly, achieves magnificence in the great days on the river, the picture of the feud, of the killing of Boggs, and kindred episodes, and then "dies" slowly in the tiresome, long-drawn out account of the "rescue" of Nigger Jim.[12]

It is no closer to "The Novel," then, than *Tom Sawyer* is, in its method, but it comes considerably closer in its point of view. Mark Twain himself was quite accurate when he declared that the earlier

[11] Walter Blair, "On the Structure of 'Tom Sawyer,'" *MP*, XXXVII (1939), 75-88, studies the book against the background of popular literature concerning bad (and good) boys in America, and seeks to explain and to justify the looseness of structure. Professor Blair finds Mark Twain patterning his action in such a way as to show a boy developing toward manhood. There are four lines of action—Tom and Becky, Tom and Muff Potter, the Jackson's Island episode, and the Injun Joe story, leading up to the discovery of the treasure. "Only four of the thirty-five chapters are not in some way connected with the development of at least one" of these themes.

[12] E. V. Lucas, *Visibility Good* (Li, 1931) remarks that when Tom Sawyer enters *Huckleberry Finn* he "has the same depressing effect . . . as Arthur has on *Tom Brown's Schooldays*." DeVoto and others have rightly pointed out that the "rescue" of Nigger Jim, as mere improvisation, naturally suffers by contrast with the superb authenticity of the rest of the book, but that it is masterly of its kind. It is also true to Mark Twain's basic conception of Tom as the literature-bred romanticist who contrasts sharply with the ignorant and realistic Huck. O. H. Moore's "MT and Don Quixote," *PMLA*, XXXVII (1922), 324-346, goes into this aspect of Tom's romanticism and attempts to show indebtedness to Cervantes not only in the two boy books but also in the *Yankee;* cf. E. H. Temple, *Hispania*, XXIV (1924), 269-276. See, further, Quinn, *op. cit.*, p. 248, on possible sources for *Tom Sawyer*, and Bellamy, *op. cit.*, p. 343.

book was "simply a hymn, put into prose form to give it a worldly air." It is "a pastoral poem. . . ." It "transcends realism, transcends its narrative, transcends its characters and becomes mythology." Extremely acute in its minor realisms, it takes in the darker side of village life also, but it presents such things as "phantasy, the insecurity and dread and terror of all boyhood." It is "the supreme American idyll," which preserves, like nothing else in literature, "the since polluted loveliness of a continent."[13]

In Huckleberry Finn's odyssey all this changed. Here is a serious, comprehensive picture of the whole Mississippi frontier, from its scum (Old Man Finn, the "Duke" and the "Dauphin") through its solid backbone of decent citizenry (the Wilks family) to its aristocracy (Colonel Sherburn, the Grangerfords and the Shepherdsons). Here are dueling and slavery. And all this is viewed through the eyes of a young outcast, and described in his (and pre-Civil War Missouri's) backwoods vernacular, a dialectal form of the American language which here and now takes its place as the completely adequate vehicle of great art. "All modern American literature," says Ernest Hemingway, "comes from one book by Mark Twain called *Huckleberry Finn* . . . it's the best book we've had. . . . There was nothing before. There has been nothing as good since."

There are touches of mythology in the river rascals, and there is some "hokum" in the story of the Wilks family, but in the main realism prevails. The "Duke" and the "Dauphin" are colossal figures of fun, but the oils with which their portraits are painted have been liberally mixed with gall, and truth lifts the description of the great

---

[13] The quotations are all from Bernard DeVoto, the last two from *MT's America,* the others from *MT at Work.* DeVoto's critical essays on *Tom Sawyer* and *Huckleberry Finn* in *MT at Work* are valuable. On *Huckleberry Finn,* see, further, John Erskine, *The Delight of Great Books* (BM, 1928); James T. Farrell, *NYTBR,* Dec. 12, 1943, p. 6+; T. S. Eliot's introduction to the edition of *Huckleberry Finn* published by the Cresset Press, 1950; Lionel Trilling, *The Liberal Imagination* (VP, 1950). Most elaborate of all is E. M. Branch's fine study at the close of *The Literary Apprenticeship of MT.* More specialized aspects of the book are considered in *Col,* VI (1931) and N.S. I, No. 2 (1935), pp. 281-295; *S. Folklore Q.,* VIII (1944), 251-275; *MLN,* LXI (1946), 468-469; *AL,* XXI (1949), 108-111. The real importance of *Huckleberry Finn* was understood, upon its publication, by few persons, and certainly not by the author; see A. L. Vogelback, "The Publication and Reception of 'Huckleberry Finn' in America," *AL,* XI (1939), 260-272.

hoax known as *The Royal Nonesuch* as far beyond slapstick as it is
above obscenity.

And it will always be difficult for those who know Huckleberry
to believe that the nihilism of *What Is Man?* represents the real
Mark Twain. For here is Old Man Finn's boy—ignorant, naked,
completely undisciplined outcast of a river town—deliberately risk-
ing hell and defying the universe in heroic obedience to the God
within himself whom, like his creator, he could never long cease to
obey. Huck had not had much training, and most of that had been
wrong; his trouble, like that of many of us, is not merely his ignorance but the number of things he knows "which ain't so." Intel-
lectually he never does get the thing straightened out, but his
instinctive reactions are always right, and there are those who are
more impressed by the evil of slavery in these cool, objective pages
than in *Uncle Tom's Cabin*. Huck's blood runs cold when he hears
Nigger Jim planning the dastardly crime of stealing his own children
away from the man who had bought them and paid his good honest
money for them. But he differs from most of us in that he does not
betray his training to gratify his passions: he betrays it to save his
friend. "All right, then, I'll *go* to hell." The difference between this
and *What Is Man?* is that *What Is Man?* represents Mark Twain's
thinking, which was never in itself very important. This proceeds
from the deeper reaches of his life, where he functioned creatively.

Tom Sawyer Abroad and *Tom Sawyer, Detective* have recently
been defended by eminent critics; it is true that they have fine things
in them, but in the larger aspects they fail. Mark's interest in modern
inventions was one of his more superficial aspects, and he was never
able to use it effectively as an artist; once Tom and Huck have been
carried away from their own country in a balloon, they do not
"belong."[14]

To the two masterpieces, *Pudd'nhead Wilson* is only an addendum, but in one aspect it is an important addendum. It started as a
burlesque, and it still carries the marks of its origin; the "Extraordi-

[14] See DeVoto's essay, "The Symbols of Despair," in *MT at Work,* for
later, uncompleted and unpublished stories about Huck and Tom. For MT's
melancholy idea of bringing them back to Hannibal as broken old men, see
his *Notebook,* p. 212.

nary Twins" themselves are bores, and the whole business of the fingerprinting is not much better. It was Roxy who walked away with the book and made it significant, Roxy that portrait of a slave as sympathetic as it is unsentimental. In Uncle Dan'l, of *The Gilded Age,* Mark Twain had already created what may very well be the first real and real-sounding Negro in American letters. Roxy is a much larger achievement. And though her portrait quite calmly embraces miscegenation with its attendant problems and evils, Mark handled it so matter-of-factly that no word of criticism was ever uttered.

Roxy's own child is as white as her young master, and when she changes the babies in their cradles, no one (save, at last, the fingerprint expert, Pudd'nhead Wilson) is ever the wiser. This is the folklore motive of the Wicked Nurse. But observe the sequel. The "nigger" lives thereafter as a white man and comes to no good, but the white child's fate is more interesting. For the white child becomes a "nigger" in all ways of thought and action, a "nigger" with no drop of Negro blood in his veins!

5. *History and Legend*

Mark Twain's historical tales did not come from the same depths in him as his fiction out of Hannibal, but they were no less characteristic. He had no historic sense, as the scholar uses that term, but he did have a strong feeling for the romance of history, and this was very important to him.

Mark Twain's first extended essay in historical fiction was also his least ambitious. Essentially, *The Prince and the Pauper* is a high-class historical juvenile, one of the very best that have been written. This statement needs qualification only to the extent that Mark Twain's indignation over the inhumanities of Tudor days leads to the inclusion of some passages which it is hard for children to "take," and of which they surely do not grasp all the implications. It was much the genteelest and best-proportioned book he had yet written, and the critical reception was very enthusiastic.[15] He had found the

---

[15] See A. L. Vogelback, " 'The Prince and the Pauper,' A Study in Critical Standards," *AL*, XIV (1942), 48-54. On sources, cf. L. T. Dickinson, *MLN,* LXIV (1949), 103-106.

suggestion for it, but not the plot, in *The Prince and the Page,* by Charlotte M. Yonge, and the historical background was sound and imaginatively handled.

He restrained himself less, and achieved less historical versimilitude, in a much maturer book, *A Connecticut Yankee in King Arthur's Court.* The basic idea was to confront Malory's romanticism with the hard-headedness of a "smart" Yankee, who, accidentally getting transported back into the sixth century—in this aspect the book partially anticipated the many recent novels which have been based on J. W. Dunne's theory of "Serial Time"[16]—should, through his modern technological knowledge, succeed in making himself the "Boss." Mark Twain conceived his hero as "a perfect ignoramus," but this point of view is not maintained; making the puppet his own mouthpiece and the spokesman of modern democratic ideals, the author could hardly have withheld his own knowledge from him. In one aspect, then, the *Yankee* vaunts modernism against the romantic and historic past, but this is only a superficial aspect; those critics who see Mark Twain, in this book, as deserting the problems of his own time to take refuge in the past, and relieving his indignation by blowing off steam on the perfectly "safe" subject of sixth-century England, have not read very carefully.[17]

Yet, in truth, any misunderstanding[18] of the *Yankee* is explicable, for the book is a hodge-podge, ranging from sublimity in the touching picture of the King in the smallpox hut to painful burlesque in the picture of Lancelot and his knights riding to the rescue on high-wheeled bicycles. It is no wonder that three "movies" have been made of it and even a musical comedy. And if Mark Twain's basic conception is degraded in them, he had degraded it before them.

There is no trace of degradation, on the other hand, in the *Personal*

[16] See E. Wagenknecht, *Cavalcade of the English Novel,* p. 464, and, more elaborately, *Six Novels of the Supernatural* (VP, 1944), pp. 776-778.

[17] See, for correction of this error, Howells's contemporary review of the *Yankee,* reprinted in his *My MT.*

[18] See Bellamy, *op. cit.,* pp. 314-315, and the following studies: John B. Hoben, "MT's 'A Connecticut Yankee': A Genetic Study," *AL,* XVIII (1946), 197-218; Robert H. Wilson, "Malory in the 'Connecticut Yankee,'" *UTSE,* XXVII (1948), 185-206.

Recollections of Joan of Arc, the story of "the noble child, the most innocent, the most lovely, the most adorable the ages have produced," as told from the point of view of her page and secretary. The weakness of the book shows in the quotation; Mark Twain's adoration of Joan was lifelong, and he could not resist the temptation to sentimentalize her; even her childhood companions must take up a worshipful attitude toward her. Bernard Shaw called Mark Twain's Joan of Arc "a beautiful and most lady-like Victorian," "skirted to the ground," and while it is easy to retort that she is at least as close to the facts of history as Shaw's own conception, the *tu quoque* does not get us far. It is more to the point to inquire whether it is in order to apply the realistic test to a character who has obviously been conceived as the incarnation of an ideal.

Mark Twain's *Joan of Arc* is not, as he believed, his greatest book, for it carries him, at times, beyond his range, and lacks the complete authenticity of the fiction out of Hannibal; it is derivative, reconstructive, a deliberate contribution to the romantic revival of the 'nineties. But it is a distinguished contribution to that revival and (coming from Mark Twain) a remarkable one; nor must we forget that in those days, before Hewlett and his successors had broken Scott's mold in the historical novel,[19] it was a more original book than it seems today. The limpid beauty of Mark Twain's style is seen at its best in these pages, most touchingly, perhaps, in the Domremy portion; in the great story of the trial, the author succeeds in infusing the closely-followed records with his own distinctive spirit and point of view. Above all, this is a book which must be taken into account by anyone who would understand one whole side of Mark Twain, the Mark Twain who adored Olivia Langdon, and who was capable of a tenderness to match his rages. That Mark Twain was quite as "real" as "the man with a bark on" who came out of the great West.[20]

---

[19] Wagenknecht, *Cavalcade of the English Novel,* pp. 163-166.
[20] Cf. Mentor L. Williams, "MT's Joan of Arc," *Mich. Alumnus Quar. R.,* LIV (1948), 243-250; Bronia Sielewicz, "Joan and MT," in E. Wagenknecht (ed.), *Joan of Arc, An Anthology of History and Literature* (Creative Age Press, 1948); and, on more specialized aspects, Mary A. Wyman, "A Note on MT," *CE,* VII (1946), 438-443; E. H. Long, "Sut Lovingood and MT's 'Joan of Arc,'" *MLN,* LXIV (1949), 37-39.

The Mysterious Stranger, a philosophical romance, goes beyond history to legend. Satan's nephew comes to Eseldorf (Assville, or Donkeyton), in Austria, in 1590, to exhibit his contempt for the human race, to interfere for good or ill with human destiny, and finally to teach the Tom Sawyer-Mark Twain narrator that "Life itself is only a vision, a dream." "It is perfectly horrible," said Mrs. Clemens, when he read it to her—"and perfectly beautiful!" and criticism cannot say much more. In his magnificent essay on "The Symbols of Despair," Mr. DeVoto describes the several versions of *The Mysterious Stranger* in the Mark Twain Papers and connects the book with the great mass of frustrated, aborted manuscripts through which Mark despairingly wrote his way after the calamities of the 'nineties. If he were to go on functioning, he must convince his "trained Presbyterian conscience" that he was not to blame for these sorrows. He exhausted every conceivable excuse, even that offered by his "gospel" of determinism, but none of them would serve. There remained one last possibility. "If everything was a dream, then clearly the accused prisoner must be discharged." He saved himself by detonating the moral universe.

That was the price he paid for peace. It seems a high price. But art is the terms of an armistice signed with fate, and the terms one makes are the terms one can make. At this cost the fallen angel of our literature, the mysterious stranger who seemed only a sojourner in the cramped spaces of our mortal world, saved himself in the end, and came back from the edge of insanity, and found as much peace as any man can find in his last years, and brought his talent into fruition and made it whole again.[21]

There is a subjective element in all this, as Mr. DeVoto himself has pointed out. But the central thesis is not, I think, unreasonable.

One word, however, I must add. It must not be supposed that this terrible fairy tale, in which man's moral sense becomes the source of all evil, is mere nihilism. On the contrary, it contains some of Mark Twain's most prophetic utterances. The moving denunciation of the wars and persecutions of "Christian civilization" and the bitter description in Chapter IX of how a nation can be dragged into war

[21] Bernard DeVoto, *Mark Twain at Work* (Harvard University Press, 1942), p. 130. Copyright, 1942, by the President and Fellows of Harvard College.

—the world has never heeded these things, but if the will to live is still dominant in humanity, the world must heed them in the end. When *The Mysterious Stranger* was published in 1916, Mark Twain's voice spoke from the grave to his America—the only place, as he had pointed out, from which a man may speak with entire frankness—to tell the nation what was in store for her. In six months it had all been fulfilled to the letter. Within twenty-five years, it had all been fulfilled again.[22]

6. *Mark Twain's America*

Mark Twain was volatile as quicksilver, no "philosopher" but a man of genius whose often contradictory perceptions illuminated his world as by flashes of lightning. It is unsafe to try to pin him down in this classification or that; he is wary of classifications, and he slips away. But as time goes on he reminds one more and more often of Bernard Shaw's saying, "My way of joking is to tell the truth. It is the funniest joke in the world."

When one reads what Mark Twain has to say about General Funston after his treacherous capture of Aguinaldo, or about Leopold II, the Butcher of the Congo, "whose personality will surely shame hell itself when he arrives there—which will be soon—let us hope and trust," one is so charmed by the vigor of the expression as to incline to put the whole thing down to whimsical exaggeration. Was it? Is the difference between Mark Twain and those of us who take a more "philosophical" attitude than he did toward such outrages really that we are "better balanced"? Or are we merely less sensitive, less loving, and greatly less good?

Mark Twain in Eruption, the third volume of the autobiography, published in 1940, was particularly rich in this kind of thing. Fifty

[22] For possible sources of *The Mysterious Stranger,* see F. A. G. Cowper, "The Hermit Story, as Used by Voltaire and MT," *In Honor of the Ninetieth Birthday of Charles Frederick Johnson* . . . , edited by Odell Shepard and Arthur Adams (Hartford, Trinity College, 1928), which argues indebtedness to Voltaire's *Zadig* (Ch. XX) and also makes some comparisons with *Faust;* Carroll D. Laverty, "The Genesis of 'The Mysterious Stranger,'" *MTQ.,* VIII, Spring-Summer, 1947, pp. 15-19, which urges among other sources a story of the same title by Jane Taylor which Mark Twain might have read in McGuffey's *Fifth Reader.* For MT's attitude toward war, etc., cf. W. M. Gibson, "MT and Howells: Anti-Imperialists," *NEQ,* XX (1947), 435-470.

years ago Mark Twain saw what "pensions" were doing to our government. (We call it "the bonus.") Fifty years ago, he observed the encroachment of Federal powers upon states' rights, shuddered at the enormous increase in the powers of the White House. (We call it "dictatorship.") "It can pack the Supreme Court with judges friendly to its ambitions," he wrote. Of Roosevelt I he declared that he had "tunneled so many subways under the Constitution that the transportation facilities through that document are only rivaled, not surpassed, by those now enjoyed by the City of New York." When, at the close of his second term—he had only been elected once—T.R. dared to choose his successor, Mark Twain thought that the Republic was dead.

Middleton Murry has pointed out that the problem of unemployment is the crucial problem of democracy: if you cannot find jobs for people, democracy is impossible. So far we have only been able to do it in time of war: we can unify for death but not for life. Mark Twain knew that and says it in his autobiography. Gerald Heard and a dozen others are now perceiving and proclaiming that material prosperity is not progress, that unless our moral development can be brought alongside our technological development, civilization must be destroyed. Mark Twain knew that too and says it in his autobiography.

It was Parrington's opinion that Howells's vision of Mark Twain as "the Lincoln of our literature" had, by his time, come to stand in some need of qualification. Mark Twain was the product of the "frontier centuries, decentralized, leveling, individualistic," but industrialism had now re-plowed the fields and sown them "to a different grain." It is very likely true that if Mark Twain could see what we have made of his America, he would be glad that he is dead. The heart of a perishing America still beats in his pages: here is the Dream That Died, the Hope That Was Cast Away. When the melancholy job of destruction has been completed, we shall have to turn to *Tom Sawyer* and *Huckleberry Finn* to find America. And we shall suck bitter consolation from a much sadder word of Bernard Shaw's than any I have previously quoted, that "only on paper has humanity yet achieved glory, beauty, truth, knowledge, virtue, and abiding love."

CHAPTER VII

THE AMERICAN MIRROR: WILLIAM DEAN HOWELLS

Ah! poor Real Life, which I love, can I make others share the delight I find in thy foolish and insipid face?

Their Wedding Journey

1. *Howells's Life and Career*

The catholicity of William Dean Howells may be adequately judged from the fact that he was for many years the intimate friend and valued adviser of both those great antipodal spirits, Mark Twain and Henry James. Few critics would claim that his own novels revealed a genius comparable to that of either of his friends, but he traveled much closer to the novelistic main stream. Carl Van Doren spoke of him as "an author so prolific during the sixty years between his earliest book and his latest that he amounts almost to a library in himself, as editor and critic so influential that he amounts almost to a literary movement." Few, indeed, among the younger realistic writers of his time, escaped either his influence or his generous, often self-sacrificing, encouragement.

Howells was born, on March 1, 1837, in Belmont County, Ohio, of Welsh, Irish, and German stock, Quaker and Swedenborgian in its religious background. Like Mark Twain, he was a child of the frontier—he even spent one year in a log cabin[1]—but though his formal education was limited, he grew up (under his printer-editor father) in a household intensely devoted to literature; he found the right word for it when he called the best record any man has ever made of his youthful reading enthusiasms *My Literary Passions* (1895). Another autobiographical work, *Literary Friends and Ac-*

[1] Of which he preserved the record, as fact, in *My Year in a Log Cabin* (1893) and which he recreated as fiction in *New Leaf Mills* (1913)

quaintance (1900), no less winningly records his first approach to New England, which was made in the same atmosphere of passionate pilgrimage which Henry James, to whom the East was commonplace because he lived in it, was compelled to reserve for his advance upon Europe.

At three, Howells was removed to Hamilton, the scene of *A Boy's Town* (1890). His formative years were spent in various small towns in Ohio; even as a child he did a man's work in the print-shop; he could never remember when he first learned to set type. He also imposed an heroic program of reading and study upon himself—at one time he was learning five languages—all apparently without interfering unduly with his relish of what are generally considered the more "normal" joys of boyhood. He was reporter and editorial writer while still in his teens; when his father became clerk of the state house of representatives, he wrote correspondence for the Cincinnati *Gazette*. The boy might have had the city editorship at an excellent salary, but he gave it up because he could not stand the fetid atmosphere of police court work.[2] The American consulate at Venice, largely a sinecure, was his reward for a campaign life of Lincoln; here he spent four years in scholarship and literary study, and here, in 1862, he was married to Elinor G. Mead, of Brattleboro, Vermont.

After his return to America, he was employed in New York on

[2] One is not surprised to learn from *Years of My Youth* (1916) that Howells worked himself into a "nervous breakdown," but in view of what seems the complete self-possession of his published work, it is surprising to read that he was tortured with morbid nervous fears. This element in Howells is very dear to those who are deeply distressed by his "repressions": the best study of the matter is E. H. Cady, "The Neuroticism of WDH," *PMLA*, LXI (1946), 229-238. In later life, Howells regretted that he had not seized his early opportunity to learn more about life through newspaper work; actually he could never have endured such work. Some aspects of human experience he simply could not contemplate: he wisely accepted the limitations of his temperament and worked intensively within his range. The mature Howells was, like most men, both optimist and pessimist, but the subject is too large to consider here. His best collection of poems, *Stops of Various Quills* (1895), found both Howells and that great optimist, Howard Pyle, who illustrated it so magnificently, striking some of their deepest notes. For Howells's final testimony to the liveableness of life, see his "Eighty Years and After," *HaM*, CXL (1919), 21-28.

The Nation; from 1866 to 1871 he assisted James T. Fields on *The Atlantic Monthly,* and himself edited the magazine from 1871 to 1881. Toward the end of the 'eighties he left Boston for New York. From 1886 to 1892 he conducted a vigorous campagn against romanticism in the "Editor's Study" of *Harper's Magazine;* he occupied the "Easy Chair" in the same periodical from 1900 until his death. In 1908 he became the first president of the American Academy of Arts and Letters. He died in New York, on May 11, 1920.

2. *His Novels*

Howells's novels are many, and they are not always easy to classify. It is hard to realize that though he brought out more than one hundred books, he did not issue his first work of fiction until he was nearly thirty-five. Poetry was his first love, and from his verses he turned to recording his travels. It was natural, therefore, that his earliest novels—*Their Wedding Journey* (1872) and *A Chance Acquaintance* (1873)—should have been a kind of halfway house between travelogue and fiction.

To the simple type of organization required by the travel-novel, he was capable of returning as late as *Their Silver Wedding Journey* (1899) and *The Kentons* (1902), but he had written almost everything else in between. Four of the early novels—*A Foregone Conclusion* (1875), *The Lady of the Aroostook* (1879), *A Fearful Responsibility* (1881), and *Indian Summer* (1886)—have Italian settings; here Howells comes as close as he ever approached to the early "international novels" of Henry James. All four of these are love stories; so, too, are *A Modern Instance* (1882), which also carries sociological overtones, *April Hopes* (1888), *An Open-Eyed Conspiracy* (1897), *Letters Home* (1903)—Howells's only epistolary novel—and *Miss Bellard's Inspiration* (1905). Naturally, love also plays a large part in many novels generally classified under other headings because of the presence in them of various ideational interests, or grouped together by virtue of their use of some special background or method. Thus *The World of Chance* and *The Coast of Bohemia* (both 1893) and *The Story of a Play* (1898) deal with literary and artistic life, while *The Shadow of a Dream* (1890), *The Son of Royal Langbrith* (1904), and *Fennel and Rue* (1908) are essentially novels of dramatic situation. *Mrs. Farrell* (1921),[3] *The Landlord at Lion's Head* (1897), and *Ragged Lady* (1899), on the other hand, are primarily character-studies.

A large group of Howells's fictions, however, are problem novels of one kind or another. Among these the most definitely sociological are *Annie Kilburn* (1889), *A Hazard of New Fortunes* (1890), *The Quality of Mercy* (1892), and the two utopias—*A Traveler from Altruria* (1894) and *Through the Eye of the Needle* (1907).[4] Allied with these are two other groups. I should call *The Undiscovered Country* (1880), *Doctor Breen's Practice* (1881), *A Woman's Reason* (1883), and the two short pieces about the Shakers—*A Parting and a Meeting* and *The Day of Their Wedding* (both 1896)—novels of ideational conflict; and I should call *The Rise of Silas Lapham* (1885), *The Minister's Charge* (1887), *An Imperative Duty* (1892), and *The Vacation of the Kelwyns* (1920) novels of ethical problem and social dilemma.

This leaves only a few odds and ends. *New Leaf Mills* (1913) and *The Leatherwood God* (1916) are, in a way, historical novels, though from Howells's point of view they were rather an attempt to make fiction out of his memories of youth. He had already reached back to early Ohio for *The Flight of Pony Baker* (1902), but this is an adventure story for boys. If *The Seen and Unseen at Stratford-on-Avon* (1914) is to be included with the novels—it is certainly something more than a short story—it must be classified separately as a fantasy.[5]

3. *The Realistic Ideal*

Howells's range, then, is a contemporary range almost altogether. Geographically his America lies between Ohio and New England.

---

[3] This novel was published posthumously. Under the title *Private Theatricals,* it appeared in *The Atlantic Monthly* in 1875.

[4] The two utopias are more closely connected than the long stretch between their publication dates would seem to indicate. See Kirk and Kirk, *WDH,* p. cxxiii, ftn. 313.

[5] I do not, of course, claim any quality of plenary inspiration in the foregoing classification, whose only purpose is to show the range and variety of Howells's work. In a number of cases, a shift in emphasis would move a book from one category to another.

But this does not mean that he has a narrow range. As Thomas Wentworth Higginson put it, many years ago,

As in England, you may read everything ever written about the Established Church, and yet, after all, if you wish to know what a bishop or a curate is, you must go to Trollope's novels, so, to trace American society in its formative process, you must go to Howells; he alone shows you the essential forces in action.

Howells's practice was often wider and more generous than the theory behind it. Take him literally, in *Criticism and Fiction* (1891) and elsewhere, and you will sometimes find him denying the distinction between literature and life, ignoring the importance of style, ruling the personality of the creator quite out of his creation, and apparently looking forward to the day when art shall be done away with altogether and a scientific factual report enthroned in its place. But when the creative force had him in its grip, he was wiser than when he was giving and taking thwacks in opposition to what seemed to him the shoddy romanticism that must be destroyed before anything like an honest or morally wholesome fiction could have its day.

When Howells was pushed into a corner, he always tried to distinguish between "romance" and "romanticism." He enjoyed, or so he insisted, "the absolutely unreal, the purely fanciful"; what he objected to was "the romantic thing which asks to be accepted with all its fantasticality on the ground of reality; that seems to me hopelessly bad." He even recognized the historic service of romanticism in overthrowing the classical tradition. But romanticism perished "because it came to look for beauty only" and often refused to face the facts of human nature; because it idealized human beings, fell in love with a dream, and then, disillusioned, rejected the real man or woman who had inspired the dream. In a democratic age, the aristocratic spirit seeks its last refuge in the realm of aesthetics; it must be driven thence. "Men are more like than unlike one another; let us make them know one another better, that they may be all humbled and strengthened with a sense of their fraternity."

None of this is logically indefensible. But Howells did not always keep his own distinction sufficiently in mind, and even when he did, it did not always keep him from being unfair to Dickens, to Rostand, or to the best of the historical novelists among his contemporaries.

Howells's self-dedication to the commonplace was, then, deliberate and a matter of conviction. "The novelist who could interpret the common feelings of commonplace people," says Charles Bellingham, "would have the answer to 'the riddle of the painful earth' on his tongue." And the novelist himself takes precisely the same tone, writing to Osgood of *The Minister's Charge*, "I don't believe in heroes and heroines, and willingly avoid the heroic."

What saves all this from being the most dismal kind of levelling down is Howells's own attitude toward it. For the very point that he is making is that the commonplace is meaningful because life itself is meaningful, not merely in exceptional persons under exceptional circumstances but in all human beings all the time. Indeed,

Unless the thing seen reveals to me an intrinsic poetry, and puts on phrases that clothe it pleasantly to the imagination, I do not much care for it; but if it will do this, I do not mind how poor or common or squalid it shows at first glance; it challenges my curiosity and keeps my sympathy.

This is exactly the point that Basil March tries to make in *Their Wedding Journey* when he seeks to convince his bride that Sam Patch, who was drowned leaping the Genesee Falls, is quite as interesting as Leander, who tried to swim the Hellespont. Though in some respects he resembles him in this matter, Howells does not have the tremendous zest of Arnold Bennett in common things, but he does, at times, infuse them with the religious significance of a Wordsworth; the realist, he declares,

finds nothing insignificant; all tells for destiny and character; nothing that God has made is contemptible. . . . He cannot look upon human life and declare this or that thing unworthy of notice, any more than the scientist can declare a fact of the material world beneath the dignity of his inquiry.

With such convictions, it was natural that Howells should have been somewhat suspicious of incident. In 1882 he declared that "The stories were all told long ago; and now we want to know merely what the novelist thinks about persons and situations." But he certainly does not give us that "merely." The "moving accident" was not his "trade," surely; yet he cannot be said to "avoid all manner of dire catastrophes." There is a good deal of "scene" and pageantry in *A Foregone Conclusion;* and in *The Lady of the Aroostook,* Staniford commends his manhood to Lydia, quite in time-honored fashion, by leaping into the sea to save a man who has tumbled overboard. Except in *A Woman's Reason,* where he actually wrecked his hero upon a coral isle, Howells never went quite so far as this in his later novels, yet he uses accident freely—in *Annie Kilburn,* in *Indian Summer,* in *The Minister's Charge.* In *A Hazard of New Fortunes,* both old Lindau and Conrad Dryfoos are killed sensationally in the strike riots, Conrad to the accompaniment of considerable soft music. Conrad's sister Christine, at her parting from Beaton, behaves exactly like one of Charles Reade's viragoes. Mrs. Meredith, of *An Imperative Duty,* may not have intended to commit suicide, but Denton's death from prussic acid, after his mad attempt to "sacrifice" Peace Hughes, in *The World of Chance,* is melodrama in the grand manner. The burning of Silas Lapham's unfinished house, at just the right moment to add to his financial burdens, is daring business for a realist, and there are sensational elements again in the flight and return of the defaulter in *The Quality of Mercy.*

The usual criticism of Howells in this connection is, however, that he was unfaithful to his own creed as a realist because he did not write like Theodore Dreiser. As even so friendly a critic as O. W. Firkins puts it, "The realist in Mr. Howells is an anchorite."

Yet there are passages in Howells that foretell Dreiser: the deterioration of Bartley Hubbard, in *A Modern Instance,* for example, or the frank amorality of Jeff Durgin in *The Landlord at Lion's Head.* ("I didn't make myself, and I guess if the Almighty don't make me go right it's because he don't want me to.") With a different background, Lemuel Barker, of *The Minister's Charge,* might easily have been a Clyde Griffiths. And, as Newton Arvin has remarked, there are a number of financiers who are on the road to Cowperwood.

Much of this criticism of Howells—far more prevalent in the 1920's than today—lacks historical perspective. As we can see by the experience of *Sister Carrie,* no such novels as Dreiser's could have been published in America during any part of Howells's earlier and formative career: Fanny Kemble wished the smallpox on Mrs.

Farrell when she made her serial bow, and the novel in which she appeared had to wait nearly fifty years before it achieved the dignity of covers! Howells faced bravely all the problems involved in what he regarded as an iniquitous social order, but sex simply did not interest him as a writer of fiction. Yet he was quite right when he argued that conditions being what they were in America, imitations of the Russian novel would *not* be realistic over here, and if his unfortunate statement about "the smiling aspects of life" being "the more American" be read for once in its context, it will be perceived that he was not entering a plea for the glossing over of real evils.[6] A careful reading of *My Literary Passions* will make it clear that there was an important neoclassical element in Howells's taste and temperament. The simple equalitarianism of ante-bellum Ohio, with the genteel culture of "the white Mr. Longfellow's" Cambridge somehow blended with it—this was his ideal; and there may still be some question whether twentieth-century America has acquired a better one. One feels a limitation in Howells nevertheless—a lack of passion in something more than sexual matters which is the most serious handicap his books have to overcome in their claim to occupy first rank. Toward the end of his life Howells once admitted to Van Wyck Brooks that he was always perfectly in control of his materials; he never lost himself in his work as Dickens did, or found himself at the mercy of his characters.

Of Howells's technique as a novelist there is comparatively little that need be said. He began with simple travel-narratives; as early as *The Lady of the Aroostook* he had learned how to impose plot upon them. There are passages in his critical writing where he seems almost as severe as James—notably when he berates Thackeray for thrusting himself into his narratives—yet he never withheld his own comments when he had anything to say, and though he sometimes

[6] See E. H. Cady, "A Note on H and 'The Smiling Aspects of Life,' " *AL*, XVII (1945), 175-178; Everett Carter, "WDH's Theory of Critical Realism," *ELH*, XVI (1949), 151-166; Benjamin T. Spencer, "The Smiling Aspects of Life and a National American Literature," *English Institute Essays, 1949* (ColUP, 1950). Carter defends Howells against the charge of prudery in "The Palpitating Divan," *CE*, XI (1950), 423-428. Hamlin Garland's paper on Howells in John Macy's *American Writers on American Literature* puts up a strong defense for the Howells brand of realism.

tells his story from the "point of view" of an observer, he is never rigorous about it. Says Brice Maxwell, of *The Story of a Play*, "I don't know that you are bound to relate things strictly to each other in art, any more than they are related in life." And Howells himself is not far from this when he praises the "free and simple design" of *Don Quixote* and commends the "simplicity" of the Spanish picaresque novelists to American writers. In *A Foregone Conclusion, Ragged Lady*, and *Mrs. Farrell*, he tacks on epilogues, much in the manner of Willa Cather. There is much to say against all these practices, yet they do help Howells to achieve that charming ease in style and manner which, be his matter light or heavy, is one of the never-failing delights of his fiction.[7]

The one feature of Howells's technique that does call for special comment is the rather "homey," Trollopian idiosyncrasy of continually reintroducing characters whom the reader has met in former novels. In the unused preface to *The Story of a Play*, Howells indicated doubt concerning the wisdom of this practice, but his tendency to it remained incorrigible. The Marches, first introduced in *Their Wedding Journey*, reappear again and again, most importantly in *A Hazard of New Fortunes*. Bartley Hubbard, of *A Modern Instance*, interviews Silas Lapham. Sewell and Corey carry over from *The Rise of Silas Lapham* into *The Minister's Charge. Annie Kilburn* contributes Mr. Brandreth to *The World of Chance* and the heroic, alcoholic lawyer, Putney, to *The Quality of Mercy*, whence Brice Maxwell and his wife pass on to *The Story of a Play*. And these are only examples.

4. The Novel and the Meaning of Life

There was a strong ethical element in Howells's fiction: he always thought of his fight for realism as a fight for truth.[8] Like Joseph Conrad, he opposed overt didacticism in novels, yet the value of a work of art always seemed to him dependent upon the soundness of its moral values.

[7] See Mark Twain's eloquent tribute to Howells's style in his essay in *What Is Man?* (H, 1917). H. L. Mencken also writes impressively on this aspect in his otherwise undiscerning paper in *Prejudices,* I (K, 1919).

[8] Cf. Herbert Edwards, "H and the Controversy over Realism in American Fiction," *AL,* III (1931), 237-248.

It seems ironic that the aspect of his "teaching" concerning which Howells perhaps felt most deeply should have turned out, in a sense, the least significant for his writings: I mean his conviction of the iniquity of our economic order.

In 1888 Howells wrote Henry James that "after fifty years of optimistic content with 'civilization' and its ability to come out all right in the end, I now abhor it, and feel that it is coming out all wrong in the end, unless it base itself anew on a real equality." Howells had been interested in social problems from his boyhood, but it took him many years to get his interest in social problems and his interest in literature together. He had begun as an admirer of the neoclassicists, from whom he passed on to Heine, the first writer to make him realize that literature can be made out of the stuff of actual experience. The continental realists carried the work along but it was not until after Tolstoy had replaced Turgenev as his literary ideal that he seemed to himself to have achieved full maturity:

As much as one merely human being can help another I believe that he has helped me; he has not influenced me in aesthetics only, but in ethics, too, so that I can never again see life in the way I saw it before I knew him. . . . Tolstoy gave me heart and hope that the world may yet be made over in the image of Him who died for it, when all Caesar's things shall be finally rendered unto Caesar, and men shall come into their own, into the right to labor and the right to enjoy the fruits of their labor, each one master of himself and servant to every other.[9]

Annie Kilburn, A Hazard of New Fortunes, and the two utopian romances were the leading fruits of this conversion.[10] (The note is

[9] Howells's religious development is an interesting study unfortunately outside the range of this book; see Hannah G. Belcher, "H's Opinions on the Religious Conflicts of his Age as Exhibited in Magazine Articles," *AL,* XV (1943), 262-278. But there are many interesting references in the fiction also. The mystical tendencies encouraged by Swedenborgianism are given freest rein in two volumes of short stories of the supernatural, boldly subtitled "Romances": *Questionable Shapes* (1903) and *Between the Dark and the Daylight* (1908). See his essay on immortality in the symposium, *In After Days* (H, 1910), to which James also contributed. Briefly, after having had his early beliefs disturbed by the science vs. religion controversy, Howells moved in the direction of religious faith and serenity under the leadership of John Fiske.

[10] Tolstoy was by no means the only influence, nor were his views ever accepted uncritically. The best study is the long chapter on Howells in W. F.

forced in *The Quality of Mercy,* where the attempt to impose sociological significance upon the story of a defaulter by blaming society for his fall does not quite come off.) Yet the ethical significance of the awakening was far more important than its aesthetic significance, for Howells was already too old and too firmly-grounded in his own aesthetic method to be able to uproot himself now and embark upon radically new developments. He never knew the American "proletariat," if there is such a thing, and even in the first flush of his enthusiasm he made little attempt to write about it. Though he never joined the party, he continued to call himself a Socialist as long as he lived, but he did not, during his later years, much concern himself with such things as a novelist.[11]

Of much greater importance for Howells's fiction are the attitude which his "realism" caused him to take up toward the treatment of

Taylor, *The Economic Novel in America;* cf. also L. J. Budd, "WDH's Debt to Tolstoy," *Am. Slavic & East European R.,* IX (1950), 292-301. J. W. Getzels does his best to make Marxian influence important in "WDH and Socialism," *Science and Society,* II (1938), 376-386, but without marked success; see further discussion by Conrad Wright, II, 514-517, and George Arms, III (1939), 245-248. Howells read Gronlund, Henry George, Bellamy, etc., but that he read Marx has not been proved; see Kirk and Kirk, *op. cit.,* pp. cxv-cxvi, cxxvi, ftn. 323. A later article by Arms, "The Literary Background of H's Social Criticism," *AL,* XIV (1942), 260-276, demolishes the myth that Boston and the *Atlantic* circle were stultifying influences upon Howells's social thinking.

[11] How did Howells expect the change from a capitalist to a Socialist economy to be made? Some inferences may be drawn from the utopian romances, for Altruria was once capitalist. But he is less specific about what he wants than about what he does not want. He does not want violence; even in *A Hazard of New Fortunes* he is *for* the strikers but *against* the strike. In *Annie Kilburn* Putney calls his clients fools because they use the boycott instead of the much more effective vote. "What do you want to break the laws for, when you can *make* 'em?" Evans, in *The Minister's Charge,* speaks in passing of "the destiny of the future state, which will at once employ and support all its citizens." Howells would probably have considerable sympathy with the peaceful revolution which has taken place during recent years both in Britain and the United States, just as Mark Twain would certainly detest it. Some other aspects of his social and political thinking may here be noted in passing. Almost alone among American writers, he made an outspoken protest against the judicial murder of the Chicago anarchists, following the Haymarket Square riot of 1887. He opposed the Spanish-American War—see W. M. Gibson, *NEQ,* XX (1947), 435-470—but, like Henry James, lost his head over World War I.

romantic love in the novel and his attack upon that aspect of the Puritan morality which glorifies self-sacrifice as necessarily virtuous.

Love itself Howells sees as "the most tremendous of human dramas, the drama that allies human nature with the creative and the immortal on one side, the bestial and the perishable on the other." It is the novelists themselves who are responsible for the life-wrecking errors that have developed around it, for the novelists have presented it "in a monstrous disproportion to the other relations of life." To correct these misapprehensions, it is necessary to realize that love has nothing to do with eternity; it is "a plain, earthly affair, for this trip and train only." Love, in other words, is something quite "natural and mortal, and divine honors, which belong to righteousness alone, ought not to be paid to it."

Howells's gallery of women, especially girls, is very distinguished: this is one of the points at which he may most fittingly be compared to Trollope. How touching are Dan Mavering's failure to feel resentment toward Alice Pasmer when she casts him off, and the real pains which Staniford and his companion take to make Lydia Blood feel safe and comfortable in her somewhat anomalous position as the only woman-passenger on the *Aroostook!* Yet the novelist was often under fire from readers who felt that women in fiction ought to be presented as goddesses to be worshiped rather than as human beings moving in a human world. Such readers resented Howells's reiterated conviction that a young girl possesses little real character, her character being still to be formed through the experiences which life has in store for her, or his comments upon the "keen half-intelligence" which Marcia Hubbard, as a typical devoted wife, brings to her husband's business. Idealism and inexperience make a dangerous combination in Howells. It is the high-minded Alice Pasmer, not her comparatively earthy mother, who puts pain into the world, and Imogene Graham, of *Indian Summer,* makes three people thoroughly wretched when she mistakes her sentimental admiration of Colville for real passion.

More disturbing than this, however, is Howells's insistence that marriage is in itself inevitably a disappointing experience. The Brinkleys, of *April Hopes,* have been thirty years reaching an adjustment, and now they are not sure it was worth the trouble! Silas

Lapham and his wife say terrible things to each other. The Marches, Howells's favorite couple, "often accused each other of being selfish and indifferent." Six months after his wedding, Brice Maxwell admits to himself that despite his "moments of exquisite, of incredible rapture, he had been as little happy as in any half-year he had lived."

Even when, like Dr. Olney of *An Imperative Duty*—who cleaves to his love in spite of the discovery that she has Negro blood in her veins—a Howells character behaves like a romantic hero, it is made clear that he finds only average happiness in his married life. Howells is said to have yielded to advices in giving *A Foregone Conclusion* the happy ending he had not first designed for it, but the wry epilogue would certainly seem to absolve him from any charge of pandering to the appetite for sugar plums. Ferris had long suspected Florida Vervain of bad temper, and he was not mistaken:

People are never equal to the romance of their youth in after life, except by fits, and Ferris especially could not keep himself at what he called the operatic pitch of their brief betrothal and the early days of their marriage.

There are more extended considerations of this matter which are even more devastating. In that small masterpiece, *A Parting and a Meeting,* the lovers, encountering each other again after many years, find that while the man is not sure that he chose wisely when he left his love to enter the Shaker house, the woman, who has known all the satisfactions of love and marriage, has no conviction that she is better off than she would be had she followed his example: in other words, love and religion have proved equally unsatisfying!

Again and again, Howells urges that mating is an extremely hazardous business, that a broken engagement, for example, is nothing to grieve about, the only sad thing being the fact that the engagement was ever made. In *April Hopes* he has devoted a whole novel to this theme, and it ends hopelessly because it ends "happily":

If he had been different she would not have asked him to be frank and open; if she had been different he might have been frank and open. This was the beginning of their married life.

This is terrible, yet Howells is capable of something even worse, and it occurs in that inconsequential "Idyl of Saratoga," *An Open-Eyed Conspiracy:*

"She is very beautiful, and now he is in love with her beautiful girl-hood. But after a while the girlhood will go."
"And the girl will remain," I said.

As Chaucer puts it,

> A wyf wol lasts and in thyn hous endure,
> Wel lenger than thee list, paraventure.

But simply because of its absence of bitterness, of sharp, smart cynicism, Howells's statement is the harder to bear. This is the calm, considered, honest, infinitely regretful judgment of a man of good will upon the most aspiring and most passionately desiderated of human relationships.

Nor is love the only passion which Howells insists upon de-romanticizing: he even dares to lay impious hands upon grief. Un-less we are to give ourselves up to madness or death, we can grieve for our loved ones "only by fits, or impulses." "The house of mourn-ing is decorously darkened to the world, but within itself it is also the house of laughing." Tragedy itself does not fundamentally alter the characters of the people who have been involved in it.

There is comfort here, to be sure. Once one has been reconciled to the fact that "There is no condition of life that is wholly acceptable," one realizes also that there is none "that is not tolerable when once it establishes itself," and that no man will ever be called upon to endure anything that is quite so terrible as the tragic poets had led him to expect that it might be. But this is to take the old heroic passions out of life altogether. The "difficulty" always is "to bring experience to the level of expectation, to match our real emotions in view of any great occasion with the ideal emotions which we have taught our-selves that we ought to feel." Silas Lapham's reward for following the line of financial honesty until it ruins him is to feel like a monster because he has also ruined his ex-partner, the wily Rogers, whom dishonesty on Lapham's part would have saved!

Howells's opposition to the romantic ideal of sacrifice was voiced by Lydia Blood as early as *The Lady of the Aroostook:* "I don't see why anyone should sacrifice himself uselessly." But it is most elaborately argued in *The Rise of Silas Lapham,* where Penelope is finally brought to see that it is right she should wed young Corey even though all the Laphams had mistakenly supposed him to be in love with Irene. "If there's to be any giving up, let it be by the one that shan't make anybody but herself suffer. There's trouble and sorrow enough in the world, without making it on purpose!" Annie Kilburn, Grace Breen, and Rhoda Aldgate all have to learn that human beings are not responsible for the unintended evils which sometimes flow from innocent actions. The elder Mavering is well aware of the weaknesses in his son's character, but he refuses to view them out of perspective: "Harm comes from many things, but evil is of the heart. I wouldn't have you condemn yourself too severely for harm you didn't intend—that's remorse—that's insanity. . . ." Howells applies these principles to love also, thus showing us that his own treatment of it, in his novels, was not dictated by prudishness alone. In *Ragged Lady,* Miss Milray tells Clem that whichever man she wants most is the man it is right for her to have. In *The Minister's Charge,* Sewell, who in an earlier novel had helped put the Laphams right, declares that it would have been better to drive Barker to suicide than to influence him to marry the girl he no longer loves, though she is in broken health, accentuated at least by her passion for him.

5. *How Shall the Reader Choose?*

Which are Howells's best books? *The Lady of the Aroostook* is universally accepted as a delightful trifle with untrifling implications. *A Modern Instance, The Rise of Silas Lapham,* and *Indian Summer* seem the most substantial of the early novels. *A Hazard of New Fortunes* (commemorating Howells's removal to New York) is his widest canvas and represents him best in his sociological aspect. Of the many books of the later years, *The Landlord at Lion's Head, The Kentons,* and *The Son of Royal Langbrith* have been the most admired.

Yet Howells is Howells even in his least significant work, and the reader who is capable of enjoying him at all should not be surprised if he comes up from time to time with even such an uncelebrated work as *An Imperative Duty* or *Fennel and Rue* as ?

favorite. Certainly Howells was never better suited than in the two unpretentious books about the Shakers. And if *The Leatherwood God* does not seem to go very deep, the tender, chronicle-like *New Leaf Mills* does.

Howells is, indeed, a deceptively simple writer. He is not "brilliant," and he does what he does with such surpassing ease that the unwary reader is always in grave danger of supposing that it must be easy to do. He seems to yield all his secrets at first perusal; why, then, do we find it worth while to come back to him again and again?

Indian Summer, for instance, is not an "important" book; it is merely perfect, as a novel by Jane Austen or Trollope, both of whom Howells so greatly admired, can be perfect. In a Florentine setting, a middle-aged man, who has been disappointed in love, encounters his old friend, Mrs. Bowen, now widowed, and her young charge, Imogene Graham. He falls in love with Imogene (though Mrs. Bowen loves him), and the girl fancies that she returns his love. The book traces the increasing strain of the relations between the two— everything which is the breath of life to Imogene is torture to her aging lover—until the final severance of the tie and Colville's sensible union with Mrs. Bowen. Coldly regarded, these people are very foolish, yet, as Howells presents them, the girl's devotion is as touching as the man's dilemma.

Indian Summer is a less "vital," perhaps a less "American" book than *A Modern Instance, The Rise of Silas Lapham,* or *A Hazard of New Fortunes. Silas* is partly a tragedy in the mediaeval sense of the term, the story of a man who encounters misfortune and falls out of his place in the world. But as the man loses his money, he finds himself; his history is the "rise" of Silas Lapham in the sense in which *King Lear* tells of the spiritual rise of that fallen monarch. But with a very important difference: Silas does not die; neither is he altogether a new creature; for though he has vindicated his manhood and performed an heroic action, we find him beginning to brag again before the end in almost the old fashion.

There is tragedy of a different sort in *A Modern Instance,* in which Bartley Hubbard goes at last quite to the bad. But though *A Modern Instance* was a very daring book for its time—a study of divorce and a portrait of a passionate woman whose very loyalty to her husband helps to destroy him—it seems in retrospect to lack inevitability. Howells handled another study of deterioration much better in *The Landlord at Lion's Head,* whose Jeff Durgin is perhaps his most completely realized character, a rascal whom we never fail to understand and, in a way, to accept upon his own terms, and whose punishment, at last, is not to be cast out, in the somewhat melodramatic fashion of poor Bartley Hubbard, but simply to be himself.

Howells himself judged *A Hazard of New Fortunes* "the most vital of my fictions." It is the most ambitious and elaborate at any rate, a comprehensive picture of New York at a very interesting moment in American economic development, and though not completely unified, it manages to present all the problems of the age and all the attitudes that Americans were taking up towards them, from the extreme capitalism of old Dryfoos to the socialism of the German agitator Lindau.[12]

In at least three of his novels—*The Shadow of a Dream, The Son of Royal Langbrith,* and *Fennel and Rue*—Howells lays aside his usual unfolding type of development to employ instead the Jamesian technique of posing a "problem" or setting forth a situation whose probing is the story, and in the first two cases the situation is of such a character as to draw the reader within hailing distance of the mystery which encompasses all human life. Alexander Cowie has compared *The Son of Royal Langbrith* to Melville's *Pierre;* it opens on the picture of a son, in a sense the picture of a community, brooded over by the distorted memory of a dead man, evil in his life, yet revered unjustly in death as a kind of patron saint. *The Shadow of a Dream* draws closer to the hidden side of life, for here the situation is precipitated by a husband's recurrent dream involving suspicion of his wife and his best friend.

In neither case does Howells's development realize the full potentialities of his theme. The first half of *The Shadow of a Dream* does achieve a sinister atmosphere, but this is lost completely in the sequel, where abnormal psychology is forgotten and our attention is centered upon the ethical problem of the wife and the friend when

[12] See George Arms, "H's New York Novel: Comedy and Belief," *NEQ,* XXI (1948), 313-325.

they discover, after the husband's death, that they really do love each other. Once more, Howells takes the common-sense view, opposing sentimentalism and self-torture, as in *Silas Lapham* and so many other books. As an artist and as a man, he chose to live his life in a world of sanity and sunshine.

In spite of all his limitations, however, Howells's achievement was a large one. Though he was timid in sexual matters, he was daring in much else. He possessed large, hitherto disregarded territories for American fiction—it is interesting to remember that at the time of his death he was writing a novel about motion picture people—and his subtlety, his insight into character, his grace, and the charm of his style give his work not merely an historical but a permanent aesthetic value. He increased the dignity of fiction and helped to make it a serious interest for modern men.

CHAPTER VIII

THE AMERICAN AS ARTIST: HENRY JAMES*

It is of course for my reader to say whether or not what I have done *has* meant defeat; yet even if this should be his judgment I fall back on the interest, at the worst, of certain sorts of failure. I shall have brought up from the deep many things probably not to have been arrived at for the benefit of these pages without my particular attempt.

HJ: *Notes of a Son and Brother*

1. *Passionate Pilgrim*

The novelist Henry James was born in New York City, on April 15, 1843, of Scotch-Irish ancestry; son of Henry James, philosopher, theologian, and eminently independent thinker; junior by a year of his brother William, the future psychologist. The founder of the family in America, the novelist's grandfather, William James, had accumulated a sufficient fortune in mercantile pursuits, at Albany, to free his descendants from pressing economic cares, and the elder Henry James was never concerned that life should "pay" for his sons but only that it should be "interesting." "Success" was simply not discussed; the whole emphasis was upon "perceptions."

The family lived, during the children's formative years, all over Europe and up and down the Atlantic seaboard; Henry James's education was wide-ranging but unsystematic. Opportunely incapacitated for the Civil War by a serious injury to his back, he entered the Harvard Law School, where he accumulated impressions, not legal lore. Toward the end of the war, he began his literary career, as a critic for *The North American Review* and *The Nation,* and his first story was accepted not much later.

In 1870, in Cambridge, Massachusetts, he wrote his first apprentice

* Under the title "Our Contemporary Henry James," portions of this chapter appeared in *College English* and *The English Journal* for December 1948. Copyright, 1948, by the University of Chicago Press.

novel, *Watch and Ward* (published in the *Atlantic* in 1871; in book form not until 1878). His first important novel, *Roderick Hudson* (1876), was a study of the deterioration of a young American sculptor abroad. Having shuttled back and forth across the Atlantic and experimented with many types of story, James was by this time convinced that the kind of novels he wanted to write required European background and residence. In 1875 he went to Paris and began *The American* (1877), which, in spite of grave technical defects and a considerable admixture of melodrama, is still a book of great charm and a happy example of his "earlier manner."

James soon discovered, however, that in spite of his sympathy with many French literary ideals, he could not live happily in the Latin moral atmosphere. Toward the close of 1876 he removed to London and embarked upon his first period of important fecundity.

Both *The Europeans* (1878) and *Confidence* (1880) are comparatively unimportant. Like *The American, The Europeans* contrasts trans-Atlantic points of view, but this time the continentals are brought to New England and the conflict presented seems rather trifling.[1] *Confidence* concerns Americans abroad and their misunderstandings in love. *Daisy Miller* (1879) introduced the American "flapper," long before her time, to an absurdly shocked world, and gave James his first and last taste of "popular" success.[2] *Washington Square* (1881) is a brief novel of quiet charm, remarkable for James's ability to make a rather dull girl, of solid moral worth, attractive to the reader. Complete mastery arrived that same year with the long, elaborate, and far-ranging novel called *The Portrait of a Lady,* in which an American girl, heiress of the ages, finds more than glamour behind Europe's glittering façade, and moves on, through suffering, to spiritual maturity.

[1] For a recent study of *The Europeans,* see F. R. Leavis, *Scrutiny,* XV (1948), 178-195.

[2] For recent interesting suggestions concerning the possible sources of *Daisy Miller,* see Katharine Anthony, *Louisa May Alcott,* pp. 178-179; Edgar J. Goodspeed, *AM,* CLIII (1934), 252-253; Viola Dunbar, *PQ,* XXXVII (1948), 184-186—cf. Edward Stone, XXIX (1950), 213-216. On other aspects, see Elizabeth F. Hoxie, "Mrs. Grundy Adopts 'Daisy Miller,'" *NEQ,* XIX (1946), 474-484; Viola Dunbar, "The Revision of 'Daisy Miller,'" *MLN,* LXV (1950), 311-317.

In 1881 and 1882 came the death of James's mother and father—and two trips to America—after which he returned to England and did not see America again for more than twenty years. His next three novels stand, each, somewhat apart.

The Bostonians (1886), a complicated story of reformers and eccentrics—and of a battle between love and "woman's rights" in which feminism goes down and out—seems decidedly earlier than *The Portrait of a Lady;* the other two are transitional works in which James is seen wandering somewhat uneasily between abandoned simplicities and the rich fictional orchestrations of later years. *The Princess Casamassima* (1886) is to him what *Under Western Eyes* and *The Secret Agent* (which were probably influenced by it), are to Joseph Conrad: the hero is a poor, but aspiring, young bookbinder who becomes involved in the anarchist movement.[3] *The Tragic Muse* (1890) observes several aspects of the conflict between art and "the World," but only the vivid, half-Jewish, and quite respectable Miriam Rooth, who develops from a gauche girl to a great actress, vindicates the artist's cause triumphantly.

In the 1890's James's interest in the theater was at its height. It seemed to him that he had mastered "the whole stiff mystery of 'technique,'" "run it to earth," "put it into . . . [his] pocket." Yet he was not destined for success upon the boards.[4] His printed plays are unimpressive, and the stories which are merely transposed plays—"Covering End" (1898) and *The Outcry* (1911)—are not much better, though *The Other House* (1896) holds considerable

---

[3] See Louise Bogan, "HJ on a Revolutionary Theme," *Nation*, CXLVI (1938), 471-474; S. Gorley Putt, "A HJ Jubilee," *CoM*, No. 969 (1946), 187-199, No. 970 (1947), 284-297; and Lionell Trilling's introduction to M's 1948 edition of *The Princess Casamassima*.

[4] All James's plays are now available in *The Complete Plays of HJ*, with an elaborate introduction by Leon Edel (Li, 1949)—cf. Edel, *HJ: Les annes dramatiques* (Paris, Jouve et Cie, 1931). There are interesting comments on James's plays in Bernard Shaw's *Our Theatres in the Nineties*, Vols. XXIII-XXV, Ayot St. Lawrence Edition of Shaw (W. H. Wise, 1931). It seems sad and queerly ironic that since James's death, three plays, made by other dramatists from his novels, should have been very successful: *Berkeley Square,* by John L. Balderston and J. C. Squire (1926), from *The Sense of the Past; The Heiress,* by Ruth and Augustus Goetz (1947), from *Washington Square;* and *The Innocents,* by William Archibald (1950), from "The Turn of the Screw."

interest. Yet James's years in the theater were not wasted, for the method he used in the great novels of his final period was importantly influenced by them.[5]

In 1897 James found at last his perfect setting in the charming eighteenth-century Lamb House, at Rye, in Sussex. That gracious little masterpiece, *The Spoils of Poynton* (1897), ushered in the works written in his famous "later manner." He developed—and experimented with—this manner in three succeeding books. The first of these, *What Maisie Knew* (1897), in which James set himself the phenomenally difficult task of presenting a corrupt society as seen through the eyes of a child, is triumphantly successful. About *The Awkward Age* (1900) and *The Sacred Fount* (1901), there may be more question. The technical skill shown in *The Awkward Age,* which is almost purely dramatic and behavioristic—with no "going behind" any character on the author's part—will always interest special students of the art of fiction, but it is inferior to the great novels which followed because James failed in it to wed technical splendor to any really great or moving theme. And *The Sacred Fount,* a spiritual detective story which arrives nowhere, and which James himself appears not to have regarded highly, impresses most of his admirers as almost a parody of his method.[6] From the wasteland into which he here seemed to be wandering, he turned away to write *The Wings of the Dove* (1902), *The Ambassadors* (1903), and *The Golden Bowl* (1904), which together form a high tableland flooded with light, which cannot be matched in kind in the whole American fiction-terrain.

These works behind him, James felt the need of replenishment, and his thoughts turned to America. He sailed in 1904 and remained for eight months, going as far as San Diego, lecturing for the first time in his life, and gathering new impressions everywhere.

[5] See Elizabeth L. Forbes, *NEQ,* XI (1938), 108-120; Ronald Peacock, *The Poet in the Theatre* (Routledge, 1946); B. M. Levy, " 'The High Bid' and the Forbes-Robertsons," *CE,* VIII (1947), 284-292; Austin Warren, *Rage for Order* (UCP, 1948); Edwin Clark, "HJ and the Actress," *Pac. Spectator,* III (1949), 84-99; Henry Popkin, "The Two Theatres of HJ," *NEQ,* XXIV (1951), 69-83.

[6] The three most detailed studies of *The Sacred Fount* are Wilson Follett, *NYTBR,* Aug. 23, 1926, p. 2+; R. P. Blackmur, *KR,* IV (1942), 328-352; Claire J. Raeth, *ELH,* XVI (1949), 308-324.

Some of these are preserved in *The American Scene* (1907);[7] unfortunately, his American novel, *The Ivory Tower* (1917) was broken off by the war. It got far enough, however, to make it clear that James was growing in power and perception to the end.

After his return to England, his creative work was handicapped in many ways. He took much time to edit and revise his fictions, and to write elaborate prefaces, for the collected New York Edition (1907-1909); he suffered the shock of his brother William's death, which involved another trip to America and inspired him to write his autobiographical works;[8] his own health broke in 1910; and after the outbreak of the war in 1914 all writing became very difficult. He turned from *The Ivory Tower* to the fantastic *Sense of the Past* (1917), but this too was to remain a fragment. In 1915 he identified himself with the embattled country by becoming a British subject. On December 2, he suffered a stroke. With the new year, Lord Bryce brought the Order of Merit to his bedside. He died on February 28, 1916.[9]

[7] Republished by S, 1946, with an introduction by W. H. Auden.

[8] *A Small Boy and Others, Notes of a Son and Brother,* and the fragment *The Middle Years* (S, 1913, 1914, and 1917).

[9] James also wrote much short fiction, collected under various titles: *A Passionate Pilgrim* (1875); *The Madonna of the Future* (1879); *The Author of Beltraffio* (1885); *The Aspern Papers* (1888); *The Lesson of the Master* (1892); *Terminations* (1895); *Embarrassments* (1896); *The Soft Side* (1900); *The Better Sort* (1903); *The Finer Grain* (1910), etc. There are also a number of pieces, like *The Reverberator* (1888) and *In the Cage* (1898), that one does not quite know whether to classify as short stories or novels. A number of volumes of both collected editions of James are devoted to his shorter pieces, and there are several recent anthologies: *Great Short Novels of HJ,* ed. Philip Rahv (Dial Pr., 1944); *Stories of Writers and Artists,* ed. F. O. Matthiessen (ND, 1944); *The Short Stories of HJ,* ed. Clifton Fadiman (RH, 1945); *The American Novels and Short Stories of HJ,* ed. F. O. M. (K, 1947); *Eight Uncollected Tales of HJ,* ed. Edna Kenton (Rutgers U. Pr., 1950), etc. The difficulty of separating James's short fiction from his novels is greater than with most writers, not only because some of his best work went into his shorter pieces, but more because he had no standard length for his fictions, his ideal being to allow the theme such "development" as it required. None of his fictions are short stories in the technical sense. He was also, of course, one of the great masters of the supernatural story; cf. *The Ghostly Tales of HJ,* ed. Leon Edel (Rutgers U. Pr., 1948). Unfortunately, this handsome volume contains a number of stories which cannot properly be classified as supernatural, and the otherwise competent introduction is overloaded with

2. Some Technical Considerations

The important influences upon James's aesthetic were a number of modern French novelists, one Russian (Turgenev), one Briton (George Eliot), and one American (Hawthorne).[10] To the French he owed his knowledge that fiction is an art, not merely story-telling nor the projection of a personality. In his early days, Balzac touched him importantly upon his realistic, George Sand upon his romantic side. But though he never lost his interest in either, as early as 1875 he had passed beyond both: Turgenev, he found, was more "morally interesting."

In the war between realism and romance, James always refused to commit himself to an either-or alternative. If we exclude his ghost stories and such pieces as "The Great Good Place," it is true that never (after such early tales as "De Grey" and "Gabrielle de Bergerac") was James the out-and-out romanticist; never did he quite cut the cable that ties the balloon to the earth. But, by the same token, a candid camera realism was never his note either. William James remarked of *The Bostonians* that "the *datum* seems . . . to belong . . . to the region of fancy, but the treatment to that of the most elaborate realism," and a number of critics have found fairy-tale motives transformed in later and greater books. James himself speaks of *Daisy Miller* as "pure poetry" and admits his "incurable prejudice in favor of grace." Elsewhere, he avows his desire to avoid "excess of the kind of romanticism I don't want." And the narrator of *The Sacred Fount* cries, most suggestively, "I scarce know what odd consciousness I had of roaming at close of day in the grounds of

Freudian jargon. Though James speaks of his ghost stories as "fairy tales," it is clear that they were important to him. There are psychic references, also, in such novels as *The Portrait of a Lady, The Princess Casamassima,* and *The Tragic Muse.* See, further, "HJ's Ghost Stories," *LTLS,* Dec. 22, 1921, pp. 849-850, and the articles on "The Turn of the Screw," noted elsewhere.

[10] Hawthorne's influence has been studied in some detail by Matthiessen, *American Renaissance,* pp. 292-305; by Warren, *Rage for Order;* by Cowie, *The Rise of the American Novel,* pp. 703-704; by Marius Bewley, *Scrutiny,* XVI (1949), 178-195, 301-317. The French influence is fully considered by Cornelia P. Kelley, in her definitive *The Early Development of HJ;* see, also, W. C. D. Pacey, *AL,* XIII (1941), 24-256; Daniel Lerner, "The Influence of Turgenev on HJ," *Slavonic Year Book,* American Series, I (1941), 28-54.

some castle of enchantment. I had positively encountered nothing to compare with this since the days of fairy-tales and of the childish imagination of the impossible."

In his treatment of the relationship between art and morality, James is perhaps not always entirely consistent. He despised didactic fiction and contended valorously for the right of the artist to choose his subject, yet if he himself thought a subject trifling or unclean, he would not handle it at all. For him, art itself was moral, and he sought the morality of a story in its art, just as architecture suggested "difficulties annulled, resources combined, labor, courage, and patience." To James, indeed, subject and treatment were inseparable; to detach one from the other was to obscure the distinction between art and fact and thus remove the subject from critical consideration.

From life he wanted *suggestion*—and that alone. This he would drop "into the deep well of unconscious cerebration," whence, sometimes only after years of apparent neglect and bafflement, the thing would "come." *The Spoils of Poynton* originated in an anecdote told by a lady at a dinner party; James recognized its value at once, and sat in agony, fearing that she would go on to elaborate upon details, thus destroying the usefulness of what she had already given him.

Thus he never forgot the difference between life and art. The one was all "splendid waste," "all inclusion and confusion," the other "all discrimination and selection," a "sublime economy . . . which rescues, which saves." "Things in the real had a way of not balancing; it was all an affair, this fine symmetry, of artificial proportion." It was the "reflected," not the "immediate" view of life which concerned the "painter." Different as their themes were, James and Stevenson were at one, therefore, in believing that it is impossible for art to reproduce life, and that art could only present somebody's impression of life.[11] Art, in other words, is an interpretation of life, a means of imposing pattern and meaning upon the chaos of experience. This is what James means when he cries to the uncomprehending H. G. Wells: "It is art that *makes* life, makes interest, makes importance. . . ."

[11] For Stevenson's theory and practice, see Wagenknecht, *Cavalcade of the English Novel,* pp. 383-384.

He thinks, therefore, and he presents his material in terms of "picture" and "scene"; he "composes" as the painter composes. He was like the man in "Flickerbridge": "it was always his habit to see an occasion, of whatever kind, primarily as a picture."

He despised popular fiction, among other reasons, for its lack of development. He wanted to exhaust his chosen subject, to drain the last drop of significance out of it, and he was frequently in a conflict between the expansive tendency of his themes—spreading out like so many insidious grease spots—and his sense of form, a conflict which could be resolved only through very careful foreshortening.[12] The task of representing processes and developments in time he regarded as the most difficult of all the tasks by which the novelist is confronted, and, by the same token, the most necessary.

James agreed with Turgenev that the novelist should begin with his characters rather than with his plot, with characters conceived "as *disponibles*," as "subject to the chances and complications of existence," and go on from there "to find for them the right relations."[13] This led, in due course, to seeing and presenting his story "through the opportunity and the sensibility of some more or less detached, some not strictly involved, though thoroughly interested and intelligent, witness or reporter, some person who contributes to the case mainly a certain amount of criticism and interpretation of it."[14]

In his early work, James thrust himself into the narrative as naïvely as any novelist ever did: "We trust the reader is not shocked." And again: "Miss Olive Chancellor, it may be confided to the reader, to whom in the course of our history I shall be under the necessity of imparting much occult information. . . ." It is surprising how late such artlessness continues to crop up occasionally in James's work. Yet the tendency toward "point of view" began early: the story of *Roderick Hudson* is reflected in Rowland Mallett's consciousness, that of *The American* in Christopher Newman's. In *What Maisie Knew* and in *The Ambassadors* a single reflector is employed, but

[12] See Morris Roberts, "HJ and the Art of Foreshortening," *RES*, XXII (1946), 207-214.

[13] See the important Preface to *The Portrait of a Lady* in the New York Edition.

[14] See the important Preface to *The Golden Bowl* in the New York Edition.

there are several in *The Wings of the Dove,* and *The Golden Bowl* is divided between "The Prince" and "The Princess."

Some of these reflectors are principal actors rather than detached observers, but James never permits himself the loose fluidity of the old-fashioned biographical novel. He used the *ficelle* or confidant when necessary for clearness. When the method is working well, we get a double drama: the happenings themselves and the observer's reaction to them. James is often reproached for his lack of action. Yet in a sense his novels are all action. Through limiting himself and his reader to the range of the reflecting consciousness, he achieves an intensely dynamic quality, a high degree of intimacy. The omniscient author presumably knows everything in advance. Not so the Jamesian narrator. Like Ralph, in *The Sense of the Past,* James's reader "must grow many of his perceptions and possibilities from moment to moment as they . . . [are] wanted." Thus James makes his novel a self-containing entity, not, like the conventional novel, something manipulated from the outside; hence, too, as L. N. Richardson has remarked, "the reader's attention remains always within the pages."[15]

3. *The Figure in the Carpet*

The first thing which must be understood clearly if James's novels are to be read intelligently is that they were written from the point of view of an observer, not an actor, in the theater of life. He stood on "the rim of the circle," and, as he himself said, "the only form of riot or revel ever known to . . . [him was] that of the visiting mind." Such a temperament may lead its possessor to confront life merely with a claim for exemption; it may, on the other hand, mean rather an uncanny ability to live vicariously, almost selflessly, in others' lives. This is what it meant for James, who, like his own Rowland Mallet, always had "sympathy as an active faculty." But an age which understands the contemplative life so little as our own must necessarily experience great difficulty in comprehending these

[15] For a fuller and more discriminating account of this matter than can be given here, the reader should consult Percy Lubbock's discussion in *The Craft of Fiction* (S, 1921); cf., also, Morris Roberts, "HJ's Final Period," *YR,* XXVII (1947), 60-67.

things. They have, indeed, often quite failed of comprehension, and widespread obfuscations concerning the nature of James's work have been the result.

Setting aside the noncreative sensation of physical pain, it can probably be said that the three intensest forms of experience which human beings can know are sexual intercourse, mystical rapture, and aesthetic creativity. James seems never to have known either the first or the second—though he comes pretty close to having achieved a kind of translation of the latter from the devotional to the aesthetic plane in his rapturous communings with his muse.[16] The third, however, he knew as well as any man who has ever lived.

He is, before all else, the novelist of experience imaginatively apprehended. He wanted to understand life, not merely to fling himself into it, and for understanding a certain detachment is requisite. He embodies, therefore, the principle that experience itself is worthless until it has been adequately interpreted by the mind and its significance assessed.

This is the answer to those who urge that James could not be a great novelist because he never "lived." When he came to write his autobiographical works, he wondered at "the quantity, the intensity of picture recoverable from even the blankest and tenderest state of the little canvas." Like Lambert Strether, of *The Ambassadors,* he knew that "a man might have . . . an amount of experience out of all proportion to his adventures."

There can be no question that James had this. He had it in youth: "Never did a poor fellow have more; never was an ingenuous youth more passionately and yet more patiently eager for what life might bring." And he had it in age, as we may see by reference to his touching and eager protest after H. G. Wells's heartless caricature of him in *Boon:* "Of course for myself I live, live intensely and am fed by life, and my value, whatever it be, is in my own kind of expression of that." In his own way, as Virginia Woolf has remarked,[17] he "lived every second with insatiable gusto."

Perhaps this peculiar intensity shows best in his amazing fecundity.

---

[16] Cf., for example, *Notebooks,* pp. 187, 347-348, and James's notes for *The Sense of the Past,* New York Edition, XXVI, pp. 298, 305.

[17] In her suggestive papers on James in *The Death of the Moth* (HB. 1942).

He was the most prolific novelist of his kind who ever lived. Between 1899 and 1904 he published five novels, including his three elaborate masterpieces—*The Wings of the Dove, The Ambassadors,* and *The Golden Bowl*—two top-flight collections of short stories, and a long biography of W. W. Story—surely a record unmatched, for quantity and quality combined, by any other novelist.

With James observation itself became the intensest possible form of activity. Nothing was taken for granted. Rather it must be "looked at and listened to with absorbed attention, pondered in thought, linked with its associations" and never released "until the remembrance had been crystallized in expression, so that it could be appropriated like a tangible object."[18] This process increased in intensity— and became ever more and more wearing—throughout his life; when, after 1914, he applied it to the harrowing business of the war, it killed him.

In the light of these considerations, the reader ought, I think, to be able to understand that it was something larger than technical preoccupations which drove James to his use of the reflecting consciousness. "I see you as you are," says Ralph Pendrel to Aurora Coyne, "and you don't see me; so that after all I've in a manner the advantage." If it is understanding—"high lucidity"—that you are after, then obviously you must tell your story from the point of view of one who can understand. *The Spoils of Poynton* would not "come," for example, until a Fleda Vetch had been born in the author's imagination to comprehend the significance of what must take place.

All these considerations have been neglected by those who, early and late, have berated James for his residence abroad.[19] He did not, as the man in the street has always believed, love Europe and hate America. Most of his noblest characters are Americans; he was

---

[18] Percy Lubbock, in his Introduction to *The Letters of HJ*.

[19] As notably by Van Wyck Brooks, *The Pilgrimage of HJ* (Du, 1925) and, later, *New England: Indian Summer* (Du, 1940). HJ's own apparent agreement with such writers, in his conversations with Hamlin Garland (*Roadside Meetings*, M, 1930, pp. 454-465) and with Amy Lowell (S. Foster Damon, *Amy Lowell*, HM, 1935, p. 212) may best be interpreted as the expression of a mood of discouragement. James was capable of pessimistic moments, but fundamentally he knew that he had found the way.

conscious of poverty and suffering in Europe long before he wrote
The Princess Casamassima, and he saw the chink in England's
armor long before the armor itself had begun to split. It is quite
true, nevertheless, that he ceased, in a manner, to be an American
without ever quite becoming a European. Only, since he did not
write the kind of fiction which depends upon immersion, or upon
contact with some particular locality, all this is, so far as criticism
is concerned, quite unimportant; if he was detached from America,
he was also detached from business, from politics, and from much
besides. Of course, this is not to say that he paid no price for his
detachment. But it was not due primarily to his European residence.
James would have been detached from the American scene had he
never laid eyes on Europe; however little he may have understood
him in some aspects, William James was quite right when he declared that his brother was never a native of anything except the
James family. And Theodora Bosanquet, his discerning secretary of
later years, went further when she made him, in his own, queer,
secular way, a stranger and pilgrim among men: "He was a citizen
of another world who would never have been at home anywhere on
this earth."

4. *"Historian of Fine Consciences"*

The emphasis upon understanding in the foregoing discussion
might seem to indicate that the writer believes James to have been
a philosophical novelist. But this is exactly what he was not; it is
ironical that so much should have been made of the difficulty of
reading a writer whose books are so innocent of "ideas" and who
was never really "intellectual" except in his attitude toward the art
of fiction. Even in the arts, James's range was narrow. He had a
competent knowledge of painting, and his own work has often been
compared to that of great painters, especially Veronese, Sargent, and
Renoir. But poetry and music meant little to him,[20] and his literary
allusions are conventional. As a critic, he was hardly at home with

[20] He is often spoken of as tone-deaf (cf. his letter to Lady Bell, *Letters,*
II, 233), which seems to me doubtful in view of the use made of musical
figures in his fiction. In 1906 he wrote Conrad: "I read you as I listen to rare
music—with deepest depths of surrender. . . ."

anything except nineteenth- and twentieth-century fiction in French and English.[21] He had a keen sense of the past; this, indeed, is one of his deepest notes. But it is only the recent past which enthralls him—"a palpable, imaginable, *visitable* past." The novel called *The Sense of the Past* is the subtlest monument to this phase of consciousness that has ever been wrought; it is drenched in the same nostalgia that informs the songs of Edward MacDowell. Yet James's essential modernity, his real lack of historic sense, was never better revealed than in the plans he made for the development of this very book. Passionately as he has yearned "to remount the stream of time," Ralph cannot, once he has reached it, be content to remain in the past; and his lovely Nan, "the exquisite, the delicate, the worthy-herself-to-be-modern younger girl," suffers dreadfully because she must be shut out from the future.

Indifferent to "ideas," and uninterested in most of humanity's activities, James thus becomes a novelist of personal relationships. From childhood, his was a human world almost exclusively, and humanity spoke to him as nature speaks to the romantic poet. In *The Question of Our Speech,* he declares bluntly that "all life comes back to the question of our relations with each other."

There are dangers involved in such a concentration, and James did not escape them all. There are unbelievable situations in his books, unthinkable observations and conversations. But he was always saved from the excesses of the narcissists by his objectivity. He is the most objective of all "psychological" novelists, and though he is committed to the consideration of "problems," they are rarely his own problems. This is the classical element in James's art.

James did not feel that either learning or formal philosophy was necessary for the understanding of life, but sensitiveness, or "awareness," was indispensable. The best thing ever said about him is Conrad's description of him as "the historian of fine consciences," but the fineness of his characters is not merely moral. Consequently, they are forever making distinctions which to many readers seem

[21] Daniel Lerner and Oscar Cargill, "HJ at the Grecian Urn," *PMLA,* LXVI (1951), 316-331, have recently protested against the view that HJ lacked classical culture, arguing the influence of the *Antigone* of Sophocles and the *Medea* of Euripides upon *The Bostonians* and *The Other House* respectively.

merely an exercise in hair-splitting; consequently, again, the reader who has really entered into James's world is always tempted to find other novelists crudely underdeveloped in comparison.

Exceptional persons are, by definition, rare; committed as he is to the "superior" case, it is not surprising that James should often seem to stand out of the main stream. And since the logic of the situation often obliged him to set his people free from ordinary domestic and economic cares, so that he—and they—might concentrate upon the spiritual problems which are the primary concern of his fictions, he was obliged to choose many of them from the leisure class. So he has been accused of trifling and of snobbery; neither charge can be sustained. There are many humble, simple souls in his books who are lovingly presented; he refuses to give them the center of his canvas not because he scorns them but simply because they cannot provide him with the material he needs for his subtle and analytic art. In his pages, the world of "society" merely provides a theater for a searching consideration of spiritual realities, a search which he conducts with a sense of values as keen and sound as can be found anywhere in fiction. Thus Milly, in *The Wings of the Dove,* is made fabulously wealthy, not to increase her intrinsic worth—which is beyond price— but merely to accentuate the pathos of her doom; the richer you are, the more, obviously, you have to lose. In *The Princess Casamissima,* James tried to work out Jamesian problems with a "working-man" as protagonist—and was driven to the expedient of having most of the action take place on Sunday!

He wanted to deal with subjects which had "solidity . . . importance, emotional capacity," which were "fine . . . large . . . human . . . natural . . . fundamental . . . passionate." He insisted that a novel must have charm, must inspire even when concerned with a dispiriting subject. When his own seem to lack breadth, his modesty is quite generally the cause. For all his monstrous "development," he was, in his way, an unpretentious writer. He had the idea that any theme is a large theme if it is adequately handled, any subject dignified if treated in a dignified manner, as Maisie, Fleda, and the heroine of *In the Cage* dignify the degraded concerns with which they are doomed to deal: "where a light lamp will carry all the flame I incline to look askance at a heavy."

It is often objected that James's novels cannot embrace vulgarity, being thin, fine-spun, and bloodless. Yet his early tales were steeped in melodrama and violence, and he never lost the power to handle the coarser aspects of life when he chose. If it is vulgarity that you are after, how can you do much better than Kate Croy's dreadful family or that worthy young daughter of the Wife of Bath, the superbly-relished Millicent Henning, of *The Princess Casamassima?* James can always summon a Dickensian vividness when he wants it: Adeney's wife, in "The Private Life," was "all impatience and profile," while Maisie, upon her mother's breast, felt "amid a wilderness of trinkets . . . as if she had suddenly been thrust, with a smash of glass, into a jeweller's shop-front." There is a real "scene" for Drury Lane when Juliana finds the narrator of "The Aspern Papers" rifling her desk, and "thrill" treads upon "thrill" in "The Turn of the Screw."

What people generally mean when they find James deficient in vitality is that he leaves out the fire in the members. Yet it is difficult to see how any novels could well have a more thoroughly sexual basis than the great triumvirate or be set against a more merciless background of sexual corruption than *What Maisie Knew*. It is very dangerous to isolate James's treatment of sex. When Graham Greene accuses him of evasiveness in indicating the nature of the accident which incapacitated him for the Civil War,[22] he forgets not only that we know the injury in question to have been an injury to the back but, more importantly, that literal recording is hardly the characteristic note of any of James's autobiographical writings, and when Bernard Smith objects to his intellectualizing of sex and his lack of interest in copulation as such,[23] one can only point out that James takes up exactly the same attitude toward all other human actions. Deny the legitimacy of an oblique aesthetic method and the whole Jamesian novel-world falls to the ground.

It *is* important, on the other hand, to realize that James is a pre-Freudian novelist. As has often been said, his people "live off the tops of their minds." He is too much committed to the cause of reason to be much interested in the subconscious. Though he has

[22] In *The English Novelists,* ed. Derek Verschoyle (HB, 1936).
[23] *Forces in American Criticism* (HB, 1939), pp. 207-210.

had considerable influence upon the "stream-of-consciousness" novel, he would not have approved of it, among other reasons because, lacking form, it would have seemed to him to lack art also.[24]

5. *The Third Period*

The principal difficulty with James's later books, from the point of view of the average reader, however, is the difficulty of the method and the style. It is important at the outset to establish the fact that there was no quest for mystification on James's part: Philip Guedalla got the thing exactly wrong when he talked about James the First, James the Second, and the Old Pretender. On the contrary, James is committed to clarity up to the hilt, determined to leave nothing to chance, and so eager to explain everything that he becomes obscure through his very anxiety.

[24] The one work of James's which has suffered from Freudian mauling is "The Turn of the Screw," where we are supposed to see the ghosts as subjective, creatures of the governess's sex-starved imagination; see Edna Kenton, "HJ to the Ruminant Reader . . . ," *The Arts*, VI (1924), 245-251, and Edmund Wilson, "The Ambiguity of HJ," in *The Triple Thinkers* (1938). This view, which has about as much critical standing as the aberrations of the Baconians, has occasioned a vast amount of commentary, mostly in refutation: see N. B. Fagin, *MLN*, LVI (1941), 196-202; Mark Van Doren, Allen Tate, and Katharine Anne Porter, in *The New Invitation to Learning*, ed. Van Doren (RH, 1942); R. B. Heilman, *MLN*, LXIII (1947), 433-445; Robert Liddell, *A Treatise on the Novel* (Cape, 1947); A. J. A. Waldock, *MLN*, LXII (1947), 331-334; Heilman, *UKCR*, XIV (1948), 277-289; E. E. Stoll, in "Symbolism in Coleridge," *PMLA*, LXIII (1948), 214-233; Oliver Evans, *PR*, XVI (1949), 175-189; F. X. Roellinger, Jr., *AL*, XX (1949), 401-412, and Glenn A. Reed, pp. 413-423; Carl Van Doren, in his Introduction to the edition of *The Turn of the Screw* published by the Heritage Press, 1949; F. R. Leavis and Marius Bewley, *Scrutiny*, XVII (1950), 115-127, 255-263. James's own statement in his *Notebooks*, pp. 178-179, would now seem to have settled the question against the Freudians; see also E. Wilson, in the revised edition of *The Triple Thinkers* (OUP, 1948). Robert L. Wolff, *AL*, XIII (1941), 6-8, argues unconvincingly the influence upon "The Turn of the Screw" of a picture by T. Griffes, "The Haunted House." James is submitted to the Freudian ordeal in other aspects in a ridiculous article by Saul Rosenzweig, "The Ghost of HJ," *Character and Personality*, XII (1943), 79-100. Another type of recent Jamesian commentator who never would be missed is the one who goes about smelling out homosexual characters in James. This has not been established in any case. Olive Chancellor, of *The Bostonians*, is the most likely candidate, but in view of what James says about her, it is not possible to prove that he had Lesbianism in mind.

This final style has been variously described. William James, who did not like it, called it "the method of narration by interminable elaboration of suggestive reference" and again "complication of innuendo and associative reference on the enormous scale." Mr. Dooley wanted James to " 'pit it right up into Popper's hand." Mrs. Humphry Ward brings out the quality of progression and the excitement involved when she speaks of "this involution, this deliberation in attack, this slowness of approach toward a point which in the end was generally triumphantly rushed."[25]

Several writers have invoked musical parallels: among these, James Huneker actually found "simplification" in James's final manner. What he meant was that James omits much of the framework which most novelists consider necessary. But the omission of these non-creative guideposts, upon which the reader has been brought up to rely, do not contribute to ease in reading: indeed, James's omissions are quite as likely to be troublesome as what may seem to the uninitiated the immense overdevelopment of what he chose to give. His habit of concentrating upon the results which actions exercise upon their actors, rather than upon the actions themselves, was an inevitable concomitant of his quest for "meaning," but Rebecca West was accurate as well as pert when she found James proceeding upon the principle that "if one had a really 'great' scene one ought to leave it out and describe it simply by the full relation of its consequences."

The objective world, in other words, has almost disappeared in James's last novels. He concentrates absolutely upon the subject in hand—refusing himself to relax or to allow the reader to relax—but the resultant intensity is secured at the cost of shifting the action to a plane where the author's own limitations of knowledge and experience do not matter. Arnold Bennett would have given us an exhaustive account of the working of the business in the background of *The Ambassadors,* where James coyly refuses even to name the article that was manufactured. In addition to all this, he has nearly given over the standard novelistic practice of differentiating his

[25] See, also, Owen Wister's excellent analysis, in a letter to S. Weir Mitchell, quoted by Ernest Earnest, S. *Weir Mitchell, Novelist and Physician,* pp. 172-173.

personages through distinctive speech. And this is not because he is trying "to make everybody talk like Henry James" but simply because he is going in for a "surface" as smooth and as finished as that of the great tapestries.[26]

6. Of Good and Evil

The world of James's fiction is not a philosopher's world but it is a world based upon a very definite set of values. James was not formally religious and he did not pretend to be able to explain the mystery of life, but such tales as "The Altar of the Dead" show that he had a deep and abiding sense of the sacred, and he tells us specifically that the origin of the idea for that story could not be isolated for the very reason that the feeling had always been there.

Such a man would obviously subscribe to no unnecessary creedal baggage. So far as doctrine goes, James comes closest to committing himself to faith in immortality.[27] Unlike recent, deterministic novelists, he assumes the freedom of the will. He knew that this could not be demonstrated, but he held that, even were it an illusion, we must cling to it, if for no other reason than because the moral life (and the art of fiction) can only exist upon this postulate. He was not the brother of the great American "pragmatist" for nothing![28]

He is pragmatist, again, on the great question of the livableness of life. He knew that we are placed in a world in which, time and again, the spoils go to the bad, to the impercipient and the undis-

---

[26] There is no space here to consider the very important matter of James's symbolism, especially metaphor, in his later books, a subject worthy of the kind of study that Caroline Spurgeon gave to Shakespeare's imagery. See Matthiessen, *HJ, The Major Phase*; Warren's essay in *Rage for Order*; W. M. Gibson, "Metaphor in the Plot of 'The Ambassadors,'" *NEQ*, XXIV (1951), 291-305. A number of writers, taking their clue from the fact that James developed his later manner only after he had begun to dictate, have made the point that what he developed was essentially an oral style, and that when it is read aloud the difficulties disappear. The most fascinating commentary upon this idea is S. M. Crothers's paper on James in *The Later Years of the Saturday Club*, ed. M. A. DeW. Howe (HM, 1927). Cf., also, W. L. Phelps, *The Advance of the English Novel* (DM, 1915), p. 325.

[27] In his article "Is There a Life After Death?" in *In After Days*, now reprinted in Matthiessen, *The James Family*.

[28] Joseph J. Firebaugh, *VQR*, XXVII (1951), 419-435, studies *The Awkward Age* as exemplifying HJ's pragmatism.

cerning, but he knew too that, even in defeat, their opponents win a dark victory which they alone among all the sons of men can ever know. Fleda Vetch comes to the end empty-handed, but with the spoils of Poynton in ashes, she is the only character in the book who is rich because she alone has ever spiritually possessed anything. James would not have cared much for Samuel Butler's novels, but he would surely have agreed with Butler that the question "Is life worth living?" was a question for an embryo, and not for a man.[29]

Of late years much has been made of James's sense of evil. Graham Greene goes so far as to find it "religious in its intensity" and "the ruling fantasy which drove him to write." This is a bit melodramatic; after all, it was James's father and his brother, not James, who each experienced a "visitation" of supernatural evil.[30] Socialistically-minded critics, on the other hand, have been inclined to exaggerate James's social consciousness, though there is no denying that he was aware of "something in the great world covertly tigerish," and that he saw wide-spreading corruption encrusting civilization itself.

But except in "The Turn of the Screw," evil in James is not something that has crawled out of the Pit. It is something much more dangerous than that. It wears the best clothes and moves in the best society; often it fails to recognize that it is evil at all. With a start, Isabel Archer realizes that she has met it in Madame Merle. Mrs. Gereth, of *The Spoils of Poynton,* has certainly not led a degraded life. But she has "really no perception of anybody's nature," and so she fails. Dante described the damned as those who had lost the good of the understanding. For James, no trouble one may take to understand another human being can be too great; to fail to do this is immorality and failure. And salvation is as difficult in his world as it is in the New Testament.

Much has been made of his interest in manners. But manners for James are merely the outward signs of an inner spiritual grace. So he is wholeheartedly on the side of Daisy Miller, because though she behaves recklessly, she is innocent and decent and means no harm to anybody, and so Gaston Probert, of *The Reverberator,* achieves

---

[29] See, in this connection, James's magnificent letters to Grace Norton, *Letters,* I, 100-102, and to Henry Adams, II, 360-361; also *Notebooks,* pp. 106, 179.
[30] See Matthiessen, *HJ, The Major Phase,* pp. 140-147.

his manhood by cleaving to his love for Francie Dosson, for all her stubborn wilfulness and gaucherie. But there can be no forgiveness, save through repentance and amendment of life, for Jasper, of "The Patagonia," who compromises a girl for selfish pleasure, though he does not even love her; for Kate and Densher, who use Milly's love to further selfish ends; for the Newsomes, who would damn the whole world outside of New England; or for the Wingraves, who would force their son into the army, though every fiber of his body and soul cries out against it.

Love and fidelity were the virtues he admired most—the love that accepts and forgives (and refuses ever to admit defeat); the love that will not claim even a just reward, lest one should seem, even to oneself, to have wrought pure deeds for hope of gain; the forgiveness which reaches out and saves and redeems those who, like Prince Amerigo in *The Golden Bowl,* are redeemable, and which nobly disdains (but does not punish) those who, like Newman's antagonists in *The American,* are not. "When you love in the most abysmal and unutterable way of all," says Maggie Verver—"why then you're beyond everything and nothing can pull you down."

Such love necessarily implies fidelity. And the essential point with regard to James's sexual ethic is not, as has so often been said, that he regarded the sexual act as "wrong," but that he believed that in order to have human dignity, a sexual relationship, once established, must endure. "The great thing is to keep faith," as Fleda tells Owen Gereth. "Where's a man if he doesn't? If he doesn't he may be so cruel."

Fanny Assingham calls Maggie "terrible." She is terrible, as all persons who can "bear anything for love" are terrible. And Milly Theale is even more terrible than Maggie, for Milly dies for her love. Toward Kate and Densher she practices a perfect nonresistance. She turns her face to the wall and gives them the power to kill her; in their last interview, she forgives and blesses her false lover; dying, she leaves him the money which was the whole end and object of his plot against her, puts into his hands and Kate's the very thing they had needed to secure their happiness and to obtain which they had done her to death. And by her very surrender she disarms them completely. "I used to call her, in my stupidity—for want of anything better," says Kate—"a dove. Well she stretched out her wings, and it was to *that* they reached. They cover us." And the result? "We shall never be again as we were."

The Ambassadors may seem to the careless reader less idealistic than either the *Dove* or the *Bowl,* but this is not really true. It is only superficially that *The Ambassadors* can be regarded as an anti-puritan book, for even Madame de Vionnet learns that "the only safe thing is to give." Strether ends as no champion of license; he merely acquires the tolerance, the understanding of alien ways that the good people of Woollett have been unable to learn. Even Chad belongs to Woollett at heart: we know at last that he will not be faithful to his mistress; such men are never free; they merely take moral holidays. But Strether, the detached observer, will be faithful in his fashion, as Stransom alone, in "The Altar of the Dead," was faithful to Kate Creston; and the fact that the relationship which existed between the French gentlewoman and the young American cad was, in the technical sense, illicit merely testifies once more to James's ability to distinguish between the real and the apparent, to his essential superiority to all the stuffy formalism, legalism, and propriety for which he has been so unjustly reproached.

"To be completely great," Henry James wrote in an early review, "a work of art must lift up the heart." His own novels do this in so eminent a degree as to leave him not indeed the greatest novelist who ever wrote the English language but certainly the greatest artist who ever became a novelist. "Here," cries Howells, "you have the work of a great psychologist, who has the imagination of a poet, the wit of a keen humorist, the conscience of an impeccable moralist, the temperament of a philosopher, and the wisdom of a rarely experienced witness of the world. . . ." It ought, one feels, to be enough. A generation after his death, the great expatriate who professed to have no opinions stands foursquare in the great Christian-democratic tradition. The men and women who, at the height of World War II, raided the second-hand shops for his out-of-print books knew what they were doing. For no writer ever raised a braver banner to which all who love freedom may adhere.

CHAPTER IX

NOVELISTS OF THE 'EIGHTIES

There is only one expert who is qualified to examine the souls and the life of a people and make a valuable report—the native novelist. . . . This native specialist is not qualified to begin work until he has been absorbing during twenty-five years. . . . Almost the whole capital of the novelist is the slow accumulation of *un*conscious observation—absorption.

MARK TWAIN: *What Paul Bourget Thinks of Us**

The closer we approach our own time, the larger is the number of novelists who still have a claim upon our attention. In many chapters, therefore, only a few outstanding or representative figures can be considered in the text. By such titles as "Novelists of the 'Eighties," one indicates writers who began their work or consolidated their reputations during the decade in question, though they may, of course, have gone on producing long after it.

1. *The Far-Ranging Novels of Marion Crawford*

Julia Ward Howe's nephew, Francis Marion Crawford (1854-1909), son of the sculptor whose "Liberty" adorns the dome of the Capitol in Washington, was the most versatile and prolific novelist of his day, the author of more than forty novels. His most substantial achievement is the Saracinesca tetralogy,[1] which deals with the life of a great Italian family from 1865 to the 1890's. But he had

---

* From *In Defense of Harriet Shelley and Other Essays,* by Mark Twain. Copyright, 1918, by the Mark Twain Company.

[1] This comprises *Saracinesca* (1887), *Sant' Ilario* (1889), *Don Orsino* (1892), *Corleone* (1896). Many other novels have an Italian setting, and some of these are more or less related to the Saracinesca series. Among these are *Marzio's Crucifix* (1887); *Children of the King* (1892); *Pietro Ghisleri* (1893), *Casa Braccio* (1895), *The Heart of Rome* (1903), *A Lady of Rome* (1906), and *The White Sister* (1909). *A Roman Singer* (1884) is said to describe the career that Crawford himself would have liked to have.

begun, in 1882, with *Mr. Isaacs,* a story of India; and before he finished he had ranged all over Europe, invading Germany for *Greifenstein* (1889) and *A Cigarette-Maker's Romance* (1880), Bohemia for *The Witch of Prague* (1891), and Turkey for *Paul Patoff* (1887). *A Tale of a Lonely Parish* (1886) is the only important novel with an English setting; but in *Katharine Lauderdale* (1894) and *The Ralstons* (1895), he began to study a New York family with the care he had devoted to the Saracinescas, and it is said that only popular indifference aborted his plan to write of them at length.[2]

Nor did he confine himself to the contemporary scene. His best-known historical novels—*Via Crucis* (1898), which is a story about Eleanor of Aquitaine and the Second Crusade, and *In the Palace of the King* (1900), which revolves around Philip II of Spain—keep more or less to the beaten path of historical romance;[3] but *Zoroaster* (1885) goes back to the days of Darius the Persian (with the prophet Daniel thrown in for good measure), and *Khaled* (1891), which is probably the most imaginative of all his works, explores with considerable success the world of *The Arabian Nights.*[4]

Crawford's living was on the same lavish scale as his work. He was a Greek god of a man, the kind of romantic figure who inspires legends. Born in Italy, he was educated in England, in Germany (where he is said to have fought duels as a member of a *Studentenkorps*), and at Rome. His interest in Sanskrit—he mastered, in all, nearly twenty languages—led him in 1879 to India, where he served as editor of a paper published at Allahabad. In his prime he inhabited a villa on the Mediterranean, with a private tower to do

[2] Other American novels are *An American Politician* (1884), *The Three Fates* (1892), which is interesting for its concern with the literary life, and *Marion Darche* (1893).

[3] *Marietta* (1901) and *Stradella* (1909) have Venetian settings; *Arethusa* (1907) involves fourteenth-century Turkey.

[4] In the contemporary fantasy, *With the Immortals* (1888), a wealthy young Englishman, interested in scientific experimentation, creates conditions on the Mediterranean which give visibility and the power of speech to the shades of Caesar, Leonardo, Heine, Dr. Johnson, and other great men. The book is a conversation piece, important for the expression of Crawford's ideas on literature and life. His ghost stories were collected in *Wandering Ghosts* (1911); the most famous is "The Upper Berth."

his writing in, and rejoiced to sail his own yacht in the teeth of a dangerous gale.

But though Crawford was a romantic figure, he always possessed what many romantics lack—moral sanity and a keen sense of responsibility. He never entertained a moment's doubt concerning the novelist's obligation to uphold the moral and spiritual ideals of the civilization to which he adheres, but the idea of teaching by means of the horrible example did not appeal to him. "For my part, I believe, that more good can be done by showing men what they may be, ought to be, or can be, than by describing their greatest weaknesses with the highest art."[5]

He had an astonishing capacity for assimilating experience, and though he wrote his novels at the rate of 6,000 words a day, he never cut corners. Before he wrote *Marietta* he studied glass blowing; for *Marzio's Crucifix* he made himself a silversmith; *The White Sister* shows an intimate knowledge not only of the life of a religious but also of the minute technicalities of Italian marriage and inheritance laws.

Yet Crawford never overloaded his novels with his own knowledge or permitted the reader's attention to be drawn away from the story itself.[6] Clinical analysis made no appeal to him. His theory of fiction was very simple. For him the novel was "a pocket-stage";

[5] It must not be supposed that Crawford was a prig. He was much criticized for *To Leeward* (1884), which involves the subject-matter of what is sometimes called "the French novel." In *Casa Braccio* a nun flees from her convent with a lover. Crawford was himself a faithful Catholic; for fiction he demanded a religion "of such grand and universal span as to hold all worthy religions in itself." Though he scorned Madame Blavatsky, he was attracted by Buddhism and various forms of occultism; there is a peculiar reference in *Mr. Isaacs* to "the Nirvana we all hope for in our inmost hearts, whatever our confession of faith." Those who know *The White Sister* only by the famous Lillian Gish film (1923) will find that the ending of Crawford's novel is considerably less uncompromising.

[6] This is not always a virtue. *Fair Margaret* (1905) contains a good characterization of the heroine herself and more particularly of Madame Bonani, the older prima donna who befriends her, but the author quite fails to achieve any such study of the life of an artist as Willa Cather was to turn out ten years later in *The Song of the Lark*. Instead he concerns himself with the adventures encountered outside the opera house. And the sequels—*The Prima Donna* and *The Diva's Ruby* (both 1908)—quite frankly go over into sensationalism.

if it failed to "amuse and interest," to fascinate and enthrall the reader, then it did not succeed in some other aspect; it was simply, aesthetically speaking, dead. And he knew, too, that aesthetic effect must always depend upon artifice, illusion. "The most dramatic scene of real life, if it actually took place on the stage of a theatre, would seem a very dull and tame affair to any one who chanced to find himself in the body of the house."[7]

Crawford's limitations as a novelist are simply that he was more broad than deep and that he lacked passion. "I am, I think," he said in 1881, "perfectly incapable of anything like enthusiasm, and I have not the slightest imagination." This harsh self-judgment was, of course, an overstatement, but the seasoned reader of Crawford knows what he meant. Crawford was more the "born story-teller" than any other writer of his time, yet he became a novelist more or less accidentally. With all his gifts—or perhaps because of them—he floundered long in his choice of career. The stuff of his first novel came to him by chance, and the idea of writing it down originated with his uncle, Samuel Howe, to whom he related it orally. *Mr. Isaacs* combined occultism and worldly splendor with a touch of facile idealism; in those days, when India was a new country in fiction, it could hardly have failed of success. Crawford had found his place in the world, and he devoted himself to his task with a faithful zeal which does all honor to him as a man, even driving himself, in his later years, into illness and melancholy, that he might continue to support his family upon the lavish scale to which his success had caused them to become accustomed. It would not be fair to say that he became cynical about it all, but he certainly did come to take up a professional attitude, and one can hardly believe that there were very many among his multitudinous books that he really felt impelled to write.

Crawford never wrote a book that was not worth reading or one

[7] In matters of technique, Crawford was capable of astonishing naïveté to the end, as may be seen from *The White Sister,* where readers are exhorted not to forget seemingly irrelevant incidents because their connection with "a singularly unexpected and dramatic conclusion" will presently appear, and told that they must take the author's word for that which lies outside their own experience "or else throw my book aside for a dull novel not worth reading."

which any slave of a good story could find it easy to put down. In general, he was at his best when he was most deeply in earnest, as in his Saracinesca stories—(experts have testified that he knew Italian character like an Italian)—and least effective in his melodrama. But this statement is less an indictment of melodrama as such than it is, as Ouida perceived, a recognition of the fact that melodrama was not really compatible with Crawford's gift. Essentially, his was a rather sober, and not at all a fanciful, way of looking at life. He was not, like Wilkie Collins or Joseph Shearing, a master of "atmosphere." Yet, for some reason, he could rarely keep melodrama from breaking in. *A Tale of a Lonely Parish* starts charmingly, quite in the Trollope manner. But for his climax Crawford seems to feel that he must bring Mary Goddard's worthless husband back from prison, involve him—and her—in perilous intrigue, and finally dispose of him. Even in *The White Sister,* where Angela Chiaramonte is conceived as a very large and strong character—even though she is not always a convincing or consistent one—the wicked Marchesa is cheap sensation fiction, and Angela's own discovery of a long-lost parent in her mother superior is cut from the same bolt.

The historical novels are likely to be stilted and artificial, striking no strong note of human reality, though *Via Crucis* has a nobility of tone which befits its subject. *In the Palace of the King* is theater—it furnished a very successful starring vehicle for Viola Allen—and it gains power through its observance of the unities. Philip II is a more conventional Spider of the Escurial than one might expect from a Catholic writer, but he is shaded with sufficient care to hold the interest. In books set in remoter epochs, Crawford's own idealism sometimes strikes a false note. The humility of Darius before his beloved is not credible in an ancient Oriental, nor is Khaled's refusal to take a second wife even though Zehowah herself has suggested it.

A Cigarette-Maker's Romance, which has been much praised, has a very sympathetic heroine in Vjera. Another short novel, *Marzio's Crucifix* (1887), is even better: indeed, Crawford never did a finer piece of work. Marzio is anticlerical. "You begin by knocking down, boy, if you want to build up." But he is a silversmith, and in his milieu the silversmith finds his reason for being in the making of chalices and crucifixes. This is the conflict upon which the tale turns.

It involves so serious a matter as a temptation to commit murder, and Marzio's salvation is achieved subtly and not conventionally. "If Christ had not died, I should not have made this crucifix. If I had not made it, it would not have frightened me. I should have killed my brother. It has saved me."

2. *Two Individualists: Miss Jewett and Miss Woolson*

In general, this book cannot concern itself with those writers, mainly "local colorists," who, though they may have written one or more novels, built their reputations in the field of the short story. Thus there is no specific consideration of Bret Harte (1836-1902), whose one novel, *Gabriel Conroy* (1875-1876), has never been considered important, nor yet of Mary E. Wilkins Freeman (1852-1930), who, though she published several novels, is known primarily for her brief pictures of New England village life and her top-flight ghost stories.

Sarah Orne Jewett (1849-1909), too, is generally thought of as a writer of short stories. But her case is somewhat different. So fastidious a judge of writing as Willa Cather placed *The Country of the Pointed Firs* (1896) with *Huckleberry Finn* and *The Scarlet Letter* as the three American books which "confront time and change" most "serenely." Few wise readers doubt that in her limited sphere she is one of the best of American writers. So far as New England at least is concerned, the local-color movement which began with *The Pearl of Orr's Island* came in her work to its finest flowering.

Miss Jewett's gift was not for the conventional kind of novel. She herself once humorously observed that while she had no difficulty with actors, scenery, or audience, there was never any play. She has the "play" also in her late, uncharacteristic Revolutionary War novel, *The Tory Lover* (1901), which, taking its point of departure from persons well known in the history of the author's own town, South Berwick, Maine, dramatizes the tragic division of loyalties which brought such misery to so many families as the break with the mother country drew near. It includes historical characters (John Paul Jones and Benjamin Franklin), and it has a wide-ranging plot, involving mystery and adventure, heroism and deadly peril, in America and on the high seas. But while it unquestionably proves that Miss Jewett knew all she needed to know about the novelist's craft, it remains, when all is said and done, but one historical romance among many others of its time.

The other two long continued stories—*A Country Doctor* (1884) and *A Marsh Island* (1885)—are slighter narratives. Of the two, *A Marsh Island* is the more successful. *A Country Doctor* was important to Miss Jewett for its portrait of her own father, who was at once a beloved practitioner, an accomplished man of science, and a gentleman of sound literary judgment who importantly influenced his daughter's literary career. As a child, she drove about the countryside with him. unconsciously absorbing the materials of her art, precisely as George Eliot did when she accompanied her father, the land agent. But Miss Jewett was too honest with herself to believe that *A Country Doctor* was much of a novel. It is a "modern" book, for all its love of the old ways, and it strikes the "feminist" note in its heroine's determination, shocking in her milieu, to become not a wife but a physician. But it lacks development, and this is not only because it makes no attempt to trace its heroine's intellectual or pre-professional growth. "Development" might also be said to be lacking in *A Marsh Island,* but there was less need for it here; for *A Marsh Island* merely probes the emotional uncertainties and adjustments of three engaging young people who, one summer, did not quite know their own hearts.

The real Sarah Orne Jewett, even as a novelist, is in the two books that are not "regular" novels at all: *Deephaven* (1877) and *The Country of the Pointed Firs.* Though these books include more varied material than they are sometimes given credit for having embraced, neither has a plot, and each comprises a series of sketches of Maine life.[8] Yet each makes a unified impression upon the mind.

And both, unfortunately, are indescribable, just as the *Cranford* of which the narrator of *Deephaven* is "often reminded" is indescribable. In their unspectacular and perfect symmetry, they simply refuse to stick out any handles for the historian to grab hold of. Yet their value for the historian is nearly as great as for the littérateur.

[8] There is an interesting study of the relationship of Deephaven to York, Maine, and to Miss Jewett's own South Berwick, in Babette Ann Boleman, "Deephaven and the Woodburys," *Col,* New Graphic Series, III (1939).

Here—in *The Country of the Pointed Firs* especially—are Miss Jewett's "actors" at their very best: Almira Todd, her mother, William, and the rest. For Miss Jewett knew the men and women—especially the women—of old Maine as no other writer of comparable talent has ever known them or ever can know them again.

She did not need to "work them up" for her stories, for she had them in her blood. Yet she knew that immersion alone was not enough; did she not warn Willa Cather of the necessity of achieving detachment from the people of whom she wrote, of learning how to take them "in their relations to letters, to the world"?

Her own world may seem, at first blush, a small one, her people simple and often eccentric. Unsympathetically viewed, Miss Joanna, who believes herself to have committed the sin against the Holy Ghost, is as monstrous an egoist as Cowper was himself under the same delusion. Miss Jewett might well have denied this, for she was one of those rare writers who have achieved tenderness without sentimentality. Didacticism and a febrile aestheticism were equally impossible for her: she was a great lady, but she was not a prude. And that small world of hers was capable of producing a great lady because it had inherited a great tradition. Miss Jewett herself witnessed the decline of her country as a center of world trade; she saw the coming of the mills and of the Irish immigrants. "I remember so many of our pleasures of which I have hardly said a word," says the narrator of *Deephaven*, artfully. The material, one gathers, is inexhaustible; is it not human nature? Miss Jewett's own reading ranged from the classics to the modern French and Russian novelists. She relished every quaint provincialism of her people, but what she wanted most was for the world to know "their grand simple lives." And there is such simple dignity about them that the reader feels no straining for effect when William's anointing with pennyroyal reminds the narrator of "A Dunnet Shepherdess" of "Medea's anointing Jason before the great episode of the iron bulls," or when Mrs. Hight's features are compared to those of "a warlike Roman emperor." Lowell compared Miss Jewett herself to Theocritus, and that was appropriate also. Kipling praised her for her grasp and vigor, and she was greatly admired by Henry James.

James also admired another woman writer in whom posterity does not share his interest: Cooper's grand-niece, Constance Fenimore Woolson (1840-1894). "A born New Englander, reared in Ohio, she has never been surpassed in her interpretation of the wild French *coureur de bois* surviving along the Canadian border; a Northerner, she was the first adequately to interpret the after-the-war South; and, though an American, she has been unsurpassed in her picturings of actual life in the Italy of her day."[9] She had a cosmopolitan mind: she was at home in Mackinac and the Great Lakes country; she wrote of the Great Smokies and the Blue Ridge before Charles Egbert Craddock; and her enchanting pictures of the Florida terrain (then a virgin land in fiction), especially in her finest and most ambitious novel, *East Angels* (1886), can bear comparison with the work of Marjorie Kinnan Rawlings today.

The full force of Professor Pattee's tribute to Miss Woolson cannot be gauged from reading her five novels alone, for much of her best work went into her short stories.[10] She was an artist of absolute integrity and a woman of true nobility of spirit. But she wrote slowly and painfully; she suffered many sorrows during her life; and she died prematurely, apparently under tragic circumstances. High as she stood with her contemporaries, one may still wonder whether she ever quite realized her full potentialities.

As a novelist, she began in 1882 with *Anne. Anne* is more "popular" than her other books—*The Wide, Wide World* (one might say) reworked upon a higher intellectual plane. It begins with the heroine's girlhood on Mackinac Island, moves on to her "finishing school" and her rich, eccentric relatives in New York, and ends with a murder mystery and a rather unsatisfying love affair, with the Civil War somewhat incidentally "thrown in." Compared to her other books, it seems naïve, yet not many of them have matched its charm. It was followed by a North Carolina novelette, *For the Major* (1883), which has been much admired by some good judges. But the heroine is a somewhat theatrical figure in girls' dresses and long blonde curls whose cross in life is the necessity of preserving

[9] F. W. Pattee, "CFW and the South," *SAQ*, XXXVIII (1939), 130-141.

[10] Some of these have been collected in *Castle Nowhere* (1875), *Rodman the Keeper* (1880), *The Front Yard* (1895), and other volumes; some are still buried in the files of *Harper's*, the *Atlantic*, etc.

her youth for the delectation of the aged and failing husband who believes her still to be a girl and rejoices to think of her in this aspect. Less unusual themes are employed in *East Angels* and in *Jupiter Lights* (1889), both of which contrast the self-sacrificing with the emotionally self-indulgent woman. Constance Woolson carried the devotion of her noble heroines to heights of quixotism where few readers of the present day are able to follow her; among the less admirable women, Garda Thorne, of *East Angels,* is a brilliant study of temperament, a woman so little amenable to ordinary standards that it seems almost beside the mark to call her "selfish." Take, for example, her great grief after the death of Lucian, which is altogether sorrow for her own loneliness: "I had to kill it, you know, or else kill myself. I came very near killing myself." Her last novel, *Horace Chase* (1894), is interesting for her attempt to portray an American businessman, whom she presents as not incapable of ruthlessness, yet able to rise to even greater magnanimity than James's "American."

Constance Woolson's pages are studded with observations which show her wise understanding of human nature. As early as *Anne,* she knows that "It is only in 'books for the young' that poorly clad girls are found leading whole schools by the mere power of intellectual or moral supremacy"; that "whim can be thoroughly developed only in feminine households"; and that the talk of women "over the dressing-room fire at night" is a "delightful mixture of confidence and sudden little bits of hypocrisy." The selfishness of Mrs. Rutherford, the professional invalid who victimizes Margaret Herold, in *East Angels,* is "summed up roughly in the statement that her views upon every subject were purely personal ones." In *Jupiter Lights* we are told that "women have miraculous power of really believing only what they wish to believe; for many women, facts, taken alone, do not exist." For all her seriousness, comedy lay well within Miss Woolson's range, as may be seen by the culture-specialists of *For the Major:*

Mrs. Rendlesham, who was historical, had made quite a study of the characteristics of Archbishop Laud, and the Misses Farren were greatly interested in Egyptian ceramics. Senator Ashley, among many subjects, had also his favorite; he not infrequently turned his talent for talking loose upon the Crimean War. This was felt to be rather a modern topic.

Such a passage may serve to indicate that Miss Woolson could, when she chose, "do" the eccentrics with whom so much of the pleasure of novel-reading has always been bound up. Mrs. Carew's rambling and senselessly allusive talk, in *East Angels,* is really wonderful, and no reader of *Anne* ever forgets the reticule in which Miss Vanhorn endlessly pursues her ever-elusive search for sugar-coated seeds, a clever use of a theatrical "property," carried far beyond the point at which the stage would be obliged to relinquish it.

It was natural that James should admire Miss Woolson. Both were devoted to Turgenev; both favored impressionism and the dramatic method; both cultivated the virtues of detachment. Her notebooks are not altogether unlike his. They were alike too in their preoccupation with the nuances of human character and with nice problems of conscience. James would readily have understood the spiritual torture of Eve Bruce, of *Jupiter Lights,* when she falls in love with the brother of the dipsomaniac whom she shot to save his wife and child when they were escaping from him in the South. Here is the "Should she tell him?" problem of shopgirl fiction on a new level. The situation between Owen and Sara, at the close of *For the Major,* is more subtly Jamesian in the girl's implied demand that her lover should preserve his faith in her in spite of the fact that all appearances are against her. "Men are dull," says Madam Carroll. "They have to have everything explained to them."

Miss Woolson's development of the situations in her novels does not, however, equal what James achieved. Her changes of mood are too frequent and not adequately prepared for; her emotional effects are too much "on again, off again." She was too fond of using demented women—and, in one instance at least, a demented man. Perhaps it was because she was essentially a short-story writer that she inclined toward the episodic type of development. I know that the contrast between Margaret and Garda is the very point of *East Angels,* but this fact alone does not seem to me to justify Miss Woolson in shifting the book's center of interest from one woman to the other as she does in the course of her narrative. And this kind of thing is even more troublesome when we come to Eve and Cicely in *Jupiter Lights*.

3. *S. Weir Mitchell: Medicine and Romance*

That distinguished Philadelphian, Dr. S. Weir Mitchell (1829-1914), neurologist and toxicologist of international reputation, was the author of some fifteen novels. Naturally the physician's interests and point of view are reflected in them. Even passing over such early tales as "The Case of George Dedlow" and "The Autobiography of a Quack" (later, 1900, expanded into a short novel), we still have, for example, the studies of insanity in *Thee and You* (1880)—where the fear of hereditary taint appears as a barrier in the way of marriage—in *John Sherwood, Ironmaster* (1911), and in *Westways* (1913); of dual personality in *Dr. North and His Friends* (1900); of alcoholism in *Circumstance* (1901); and of female neuroticism in *Roland Blake* (1886). But though Dr. Mitchell was a specialist among specialists, he never forgot that medicine is a part of life; as a man, as a citizen, he functioned, consequently in many aspects, and as a writer he handled many themes. Cowardice is not essentially a medical concern; neither is revenge and its effect upon the human being who wreaks it. But Mitchell treated both the first (*In War Time*, 1885) and the second (*Constance Trescot*, 1905), and he handled them wisely and compassionately.

It was another sign of the breadth of interest without which, in his crowded life, Mitchell could never have written fiction at all, that so few of his books should have confined themselves to the contemporary scene. It seems queer to speak of the novels whose action takes place during, before, or after the Civil War[11] as historical novels, for Mitchell himself served as a physician in that conflict; but the earliest of these did not appear until the war was twenty years behind him and the last not until 1913, when he was eighty-four. On the other hand, the two Quaker novelettes—*Thee*

[11] These books are *In War Time; Roland Blake; Far in the Forest* (1889), which takes place before the war on the northern Pennsylvania frontier; *Circumstance*, which is Philadelphia soon after the war; *Constance Trescot*, which is Boston and St. Ann, Missouri, soon after the war; and *Westways*, which begins before the war, in western Pennsylvania, and goes on into the conflict itself.

and You and *Hephzibah Guinness* (1880)—go back to the first dec-
ade of the century in Philadelphia, and all the world knows that
Hugh Wynne, Free Quaker (1897) has been the most successful
American novel about the Revolutionary War. Mitchell used Wash-
ington again, this time not as general but as president, in *The Red
City* (1907), which employed materials derived from the journal of
Elizabeth Drinker. But the only book in which he goes all out for
romance is *The Adventures of François* (1899).

Physicians have been called materialists, in literature and in life,
as far back as Chaucer. On that score, Dr. Mitchell's withers are
unwrung. "One gets, John," says Dr. Heath, of *John Sherwood,
Ironmaster,* "a great respect in my profession for the complexities of
this machine, a man." But Dr. Heath is not speaking by the book,
or for Dr. Mitchell. To him, man was never a machine. Meredith
admired *Roland Blake* for its "nobility," and the word applies to all
Mitchell's work. Like Roland, "he had that fine honor which is to
mere honor as is the flower to the leaf."[12] Toward women he is
always reverential. His treatment of such scoundrels as Darnell, in
Roland Blake, and Greyhurst, of *Constance Trescot,* testifies notably
to his compassion, for these are just the kind of human being that a
man like Mitchell must have found it difficult not to abhor. And
trying as the neurotic Octopia can be, she is presented as a human
being, not a pasteboard villainess: though she has contemplated
using blackmail in her brother's defense, when he himself turns to
it, she is genuinely shocked. Personally Mitchell was a devout man:
in *Constance Trescot,* he uses the heroine's unbelief, skillfully, as an

---

[12] Dr. Mitchell did avail himself, however, of the great man's time-hallowed
privilege of indulging his crotchets. Perhaps it is not fair to speak of his
dislike of Quakerism and spiritualism as prejudices. It is clear that as a
Philadelphian he had lived sufficiently in the presence of the Quaker refusal
to bear arms to be forced to think the problem through and reach a decision;
doubtless his considerable preoccupation with the theme shows that the
Quaker position had challenged him more deeply than he perhaps realized. The
special theme of *Hugh Wynne* is the rebellion of a Quaker boy to a position
in support of the Revolution and a place on Washington's staff. But his definition of mysticism (in *Dr. North and His Friends*) as a love of the mysterious
is merely childish, and he could be very trying too on the subject of the "new
woman."

element in her deterioration, and quite without indulging in propaganda.

Technically, Mitchell contributed little or nothing to the development of the novel. Though his methods of documentation in *Hugh Wynne* and in *François* are admired by some critics, they are in fact a little clumsy. I admit that *Characteristics* (1892) and its sequel, *Dr. North and His Friends,* are special cases, for these are essentially conversation-pieces, but it does not seem to me that even *Constance Trescot,* which Mitchell himself greatly admired, and which Professor Earnest considers his finest novel, has a very high degree of technical perfection.

With Mitchell, as with most novelists who have done pretty consistently good work without producing any universally accepted, indisputable masterpieces, the reader's choice among the materials available becomes largely a matter of personal taste. It would now be generally admitted that those critics of the 1890's who set *Hugh Wynne* above *Henry Esmond*—or even on a level with it—were not very discriminating readers. Yet the book does have an *Esmond*-like quality, and its suggestion of the pathos of distance does not lessen with time.[13] The closing reference to the *Morte d'Arthur* seems quite in harmony with the spirit of the book. *Thee and You* has a pretty, nostalgic atmosphere, but *Hephzibah Guinness* is a contrived thing, disfigured by Mitchell's dislike of Quakerism. *The Adventures of François* is very charming, and Mitchell has well integrated the French Revolutionary background with his gay but honest story of a *picaro's* life; *François* is equal to the best of Maurice Hewlett in kind. Of the more "psychological" books, like *In War Time, Roland Blake, Constance Trescot,* and *Circumstance,* perhaps it is enough to say that they are still very interesting stories, though probably not quite so powerful as they seemed to Mitchell's contemporaries. *Far in the Forest* and *When All the Woods Are Green* (1894) have quite naturally a special appeal to those who love the out-of-doors.

[13] Mitchell favored the Scott pattern in historical novels, with the historical personages themselves in the background. In preparing to write his own books, he steeped himself in knowledge of the period until he felt that if he had been set down in the city he was writing about, he "would know where the principal people lived, who were their children, what they ate and drank, what were their ways, their talk and their dress," etc.

4. *Some "Purpose-Novels" of the 1880's*

The 1880's also produced many *Tendenz-romane,* several of which it seems well to consider here. I begin with the never-acknowledged novels of John Hay (1838-1906), who was President Lincoln's secretary and biographer, and later distinguished as ambassador and Secretary of State and as champion of the "Open Door" policy in China, and with those of his close friend, Henry Adams.

Adams, neglected in his own time, has now become one of the glories of American literature; but his fame does not rest upon his novels nor even upon his political history, but rather on his great autobiography, *The Education of Henry Adams* (1918), "a study of Twentieth-Century Multiplicity," and the contrasting "study of Thirteenth-Century Unity," *Mont-Saint Michel and Chartres* (1904), to which the somewhat unexpected success of the *Education* so fortunately redirected attention.

The novels are *Democracy* (1880) and *Esther* (1884). In his introduction to the 1938 reprint of the latter, Robert Spiller has carefully pointed out the relevance of both fictions to Adams's thinking. They deal, he declares

with two of the most vital problems in human experience, the one with political, the other with religious faith. In each case the seeker for truth is a woman and the self-assumed embodiment of the idea is a man. . . . Both American diplomacy and traditional Christianity are cast aside; the intuitive wisdom of woman triumphs.

Democracy enjoyed a considerable vogue, both here and abroad. It is a study of corruption. Government officials are either venal or stupid: "I declare to you," says the veteran diplomat, Baron Jacobi, "that in all my experience I have found no society which has had elements of corruption like the United States." At their reception, the President and his wife, a "somewhat stout and coarse-featured" person, whom Mrs. Lee would not engage as a cook, stand "stiff and awkward by the door, both their faces stripped of every sign of intelligence," their hands stretched out to their visitors "with the mechanical action of toy dolls."

Esther deals with more attractive materials. Though Adams declared that he cared more for any dozen pages of this book than for the whole of his *History,* he nearly suppressed the novel, for the heroine is a portrait of his unfortunate wife, whose suicide seems to have been motivated by the same inability to believe that oppresses Esther Dudley.[14] In Marian Adams' case at least, the "intuitive wisdom of woman" accomplished little. Her husband never recovered from his grief, and after her death it came to seem to him that any unsympathetic reader of her story could only profane it. Nothing that Henry Adams ever did was untouched by the distinction of his mind, but his novels make their appeal to students of his thinking rather than to devotees of the art of fiction.

Distinction is hardly the hallmark of John Hay's novel, *The Bread-Winners* (1894), a bitter attack upon organized labor, and a sensation in its time. The scene is Cleveland at the time of the strikes and rioting of 1877, and the best one can say for Hay's hoodlums and scoundrels is that the "workers" have often enough been sentimentalized in American fiction so that we may, perhaps, be able to put up with a book like this to help restore the balance. In *The Bread-Winners* those active in the labor movement are "the laziest and most incapable workmen in town—men whose weekly wages were habitually docked for drunkenness, late hours, and botchy work." Since the cowardly mayor of "Buffland" will do nothing until he himself has been attacked, the first line of defense is formed by a company of Civil War veterans whom the wealthy, noble young hero organizes into a kind of vigilance committee. Hay exploits all his prejudices freely, not only on capital and labor but on subjects so far removed from it as spiritualism and Andrew Jackson. One need not doubt that he could have cited chapter and verse, in contemporary Cleveland and elsewhere, for all the horrors he portrays. But one may still feel that his understanding of the labor movement was not profound. *The Bread-Winners* is full of love and adventure; as fiction it is much livelier and more entertaining than Adams's novels; it is also better organized. But its tone seems vulgar in comparison.

The novels of Adams and of Hay are, if not quite curiosities, at

[14] See Katherine Simonds, "The Tragedy of Mrs. Henry Adams," *NEQ,* IX (1936), 564-582; cf. Harold D. Cater's introduction to *HA and His Friends* (HM, 1947).

best novels which make only a special appeal. The *Ramona* (1884) of Helen Hunt Jackson (1830-1885), on the other hand, is still a famous and favorite book all over America, and in southern California, where visitors to San Diego are still taken to the mission where two imagined characters were married, it has become something of a cult. *Ramona* has been thrice filmed, first as early as 1909, when D. W. Griffith made it into a one-reel Biograph, with Mary Pickford and Henry B. Walthall in the leading roles. As late as 1939 it came out in a fine new edition, illustrated from paintings by N. C. Wyeth.

Mrs. Jackson ("H.H.") was a poet, a journalist, and a crusader. In the 1870's she had written the "Saxe Holm" stories, which she never acknowledged, for *Scribner's Monthly;* and two more extended fictions—*Mercy Philbrick's Choice* (1876) and *Hetty's Strange History* (1877)—had been issued in the "No Name" series. But *Ramona* was her first (and last) long novel. (*Zeph,* 1885, was left unfinished at her death.) It was the richest fruit of her dedication of herself in her mature years to the cause of justice to the Indians. She herself was of the opinion that she had found in that dedication the purpose of her life, lamenting, as she faced death,

> That I have wasted half my day
> And left my work but just begun.

She had already made a frontal attack upon the problem in *A Century of Dishonor* (1881), and she wrote her novel because she felt the need of possessing herself—and her cause—of the emotional appeal which fiction can make. It is all the more remarkable, therefore, that her story should have been so little distorted by propaganda. To be sure, *Ramona* is not a great novel, but this is not because the author was committed to a cause; it is simply because she was not capable of creating great characters. The motivating force of her story was the hardships suffered by the Mission Indians when the establishment of American law in California led to the readjustment of ancient land claims. But the rich romantic feeling of the novel, the charm of the Franciscan fathers and the feudal life on the great Spanish *haciendas*—these things are quite as important by way of explaining its vogue as the propaganda element involved.

It is a little difficult to see why Mrs. Jackson should be reproached for her "sentimentalism," on the one hand, and, at the same time, criticized for having weakened her "case" by permitting Ramona herself, unlike Alessandro, to steer her ship into a safe harbor at last. Felipe's action as her rescuer has been very carefully prepared for, and Ramona's own ability to make terms with life is quite in harmony with her character, as conceived from the beginning of the book.

But the year 1888 brought a novel whose *réclame* was even greater than *Ramona's,* and whose influence, one hopes or fears, has not even yet spent itself. This was the *Looking Backward* of Edward Bellamy (1850-1898), the most widely-read of all American utopias.[15]

Looking Backward probably owed its special vogue to the fact that it set the realization of its hopes in no distant period or hard-to-visualize clime but in twentieth-century America—(its scene is Boston)—and promised their realization by deceptively simple means. Except for such things as the startling prophecy of the radio, the book makes no considerable demands upon the imagination. Moral shock, too, was carefully avoided: the change is made peacefully; religion remains a diluted form of Christianity; and sex never rears its ugly head. (Even the hideous clothes of the nineteenth century survive without great change.) It is true that modern readers, having experienced the blessings of conscription through two world wars and after, may shy at the element of gentle, resistless regimentation involved, but the men of the 'nineties lacked experience on that point.

Bellamy, who was the son of a Baptist clergyman in Chicopee Falls, Massachusetts, began his career not as a reformer but as a

[15] Bellamy impressed, among others, Mark Twain, Howells, Edward Everett Hale, T. W. Higginson, Frances E. Willard, and, more recently, Ida M. Tarbell, John Dewey, Upton Sinclair, Norman Thomas, and Heywood Broun. Among American novels, only *Uncle Tom's Cabin* can be said to have exercised a larger influence upon the American mind. In England, William Morris, horrified by Bellamy's reliance upon machinery, was inspired to write *News from Nowhere.* Elizabeth Sadler, "One Book's Influence," *NEQ,* XVII (1944), 530-555, discusses these matters in many aspects, commenting also upon the large amount of American fiction inspired by *Looking Backward:* there were sixty utopias between 1888 and 1900!

writer of romances.[16] He may, indeed, have overstated the social indifference of his early years: the influence upon *Looking Backward* of the American Marxian, Laurence Gronlund, seems clear.[17] Certainly the picture of Shays's Rebellion in Bellamy's historical novel, *The Duke of Stockbridge,*[18] shows sympathy for the underprivileged. Bellamy had a natural gift for fantasy, and he used this to build up a bit of machinery in *Looking Backward:* Julian West sinks into a mesmeric sleep in 1887 and is not roused until the year 2000. But despite the presence in the book of a conventionalized, yet rather charming, love-affair, the fictional content is thin: the "story" comprises mainly an exposition of the workings of utopia, set between inverted commas as having been spoken by Dr. Leete for West's enlightenment. The success of *Looking Backward* put an end to Bellamy's first career; he turned his back upon literature to devote himself (until tuberculosis killed him in his forties) to propaganda work; and though the later *Equality* (1897), which he wrote to meet the objections leveled against *Looking Backward* still pretends to be a novel, the pretense is not seriously maintained.

Absolute equality of income (or, rather, of goods and credit, since money has been entirely done away with), compulsory national service, and a complete state monopoly of all industry and production are the cornerstones of Bellamy's Brave New World. *Looking Backward* inspired a whole "Nationalist" movement, with "Bellamy Clubs" throughout the United States, and was importantly tied up with the temporary success of the Populist Party. Through translation into many languages, it extended its vogue abroad. As the twentieth century approached, interest flagged (as most reform-movements did under the baleful shadow of our nascent imperialism), but flared anew when the Great Depression of the 1930's inspired

[16] Howells thought these sufficiently accomplished to justify him in crowning Bellamy king of all early American romancers except Hawthorne. Cf. *Dr. Heidenhoff's Process* (1880) and *Miss Ludington's Sister* (1884). The best of his brief fantasies were collected posthumously in *The Blindman's Country* (1898).

[17] See W. F. Taylor's discussion in the enthusiastic chapter on Bellamy in *The Economic Novel in America.* Taylor also argues the influence upon *Looking Backward* of John Macnie's novel, *The Diothas* (1880).

[18] Serially, 1879; in book form, not until 1900.

the New Deal, Technocracy, the Townsend Plan, and other movements. Despite William Morris's criticism, it is not fair to call
Bellamy materially-minded—he was, indeed, an unselfish man of
unimpeachable idealism—but one may perhaps still venture to believe that he was comfortably Rousseauistic in his understanding of
human nature. For good or for ill, his program was much less
"impracticable" than his critics believed; during recent decades the
world has seemed to be moving clearly in his direction. So far there
are few signs that heaven on earth will be the result.

CHAPTER X

SOME SOUTHERN NOVELISTS OF THE 'NINETIES AND AFTER

The symmetry of form attainable in pure fiction cannot so readily be achieved in a narration essentially having less to do with fable than with fact. Truth uncompromisingly told will always have its ragged edges.

Billy Budd

1. The Finely-Wrought Art of James Lane Allen

Grant Knight's definitive study of the Kentucky novelist, James Lane Allen (1849-1925), is called *James Lane Allen and the Genteel Tradition.* Allen was, indeed, sometimes so genteel as to provoke a smile from a tougher-minded generation. Did he not refuse to read *Tom Jones?* But this is not the whole story about him.

Allen's literary manners were generally those of the Augustans, but his favorite novelist was Balzac. With *The Reign of Law* (1900) he brought the wrath of all American fundamentalism down upon his head; *The Bride of the Mistletoe* (1909) and *The Doctor's Christmas Eve* (1910) alienated perhaps the major portion of his remaining public. Before the end of the 'nineties, indeed, he had turned away from what he then thought of as the "feminine principle" which had inspired his earlier work to a larger "masculine principle," and he was well aware that this involved a shift "away from the summits of life toward the bases of life." In *Summer in Arcady* (1896), whose "full-breasted" young heroine uses a fine-tooth comb to remove the dandruff from her father's head, flings dumpling and gravy into her lover's face, and lifts "her rustling, snow-white petticoats high over the sheep and cattle traces in her path," he studied sex against a rural background as frankly, though not so tragically, as Hardy had studied it in the *Tess of the D'Urbervilles* by which Allen may have been influenced. For that matter, even *A Kentucky Cardinal* (1894) had revealed its author's awareness that love is not wholly a matter of making sonnets by moonlight under my lady's window. When Georgiana finds her betrothed kissing her young sister in the arbor, she silently forgives him: "Had she the penetration to discover that when a woman is engaged to a man she cannot deny him all things except at her own peril?" And in *The Choir Invisible* (1897), men are fervently exhorted not to wrong the women they love by putting them upon a pedestal.

Yet in a sense all these facts are misleading. The fundamental bent of Allen's mind *was* romantic and idealistic: he lived in the mood of the *Morte d'Arthur* to which he paid such impassioned tribute in *The Choir Invisible*. He may even have made a great mistake in ever trying to break away from the spirit of *The Choir Invisible*. Allen's was a very strange literary career, perhaps the most sadly aborted since Melville's. To us this comparison may well seem absurd, for Allen had not Melville's genius, but neither he nor his contemporaries knew that. He was one of the "great" writers of the 'nineties, a "best-seller" whom the critics ranked with Hawthorne. His first great change in type and method was in the direction of realism; this came when he wrote *The Reign of Law* and *The Mettle of the Pasture* (1903). From here he turned to Maeterlinckian symbolism and impressionism in the disastrous Christmas books which were so badly received that the last member of the proposed trilogy was never written, and with this failure he broke the back of his career. This is not to say that the books which followed—*A Cathedral Singer* (1916) and the rest—were poor books; Allen was never commonplace. The short pieces written at the very end of his life—*The Alabaster Box* (1923) and the tales collected in *The Landmark* (1925)—have some extraordinary things in them.[1] But none of the ambitious works planned during the last fifteen years ever got themselves written.

A Kentucky Cardinal combines a self-conscious, Barrie-like fantasy with a reverence for nature which suggests Thoreau; at the outset it seems hardly a more serious love story than Aldrich's

[1] Many critics esteem Allen more highly as a writer of short stories than as a novelist. The best of the early stories were collected in *Flute and Violin* (1891)

"Marjorie Daw." But before finishing its course, it has risen to something more vital than that, and though it has a happy ending, it haunts the memory with its poignant picture of willfullness and misunderstanding in love. But the masterpiece of the first period and perhaps of all Allen's work is *The Choir Invisible*,[2] a study of influence which takes both its title and its high-minded tone, though not its atmosphere, from George Eliot.

The theme of renunciation in love because of moral scruples has grown thin in fiction since Allen's time, but his treatment of it is quite justified by the results achieved. The book opens in 1795, and though it is, in no sense, a conventional historical novel, it does give, in its own highly spiritualized and indirect way, what must be a nearly complete picture of the Kentucky frontier: its imported gentilities and its native ruggedness; its religion and its rationalism; the reading of Tom Paine's *Age of Reason* at the crossroads and the classical curriculum at William and Mary. And the Kentucky Jacobins are already thinking of disunion in their anger against President Washington for his refusal to fling the nation into the European cockpit on the side of France.[3] "From every direction the forest appeared to be rushing in upon that perilous little reef of a clearing—that unsheltered island of human life, newly displaying itself amid the ancient, blood-flecked, horror-haunted sea of woods."

The realistic novels are less of a piece. *The Reign of Law* is one of the first American examples of the novel of religious doubt. "For in the light of the great central idea of Evolution, all departments of human knowledge had to be reviewed, reconsidered, reconceived, rearranged, rewritten." Allen's protagonist is much less sophisticated than the typical English hero of the Darwinian novel, for he is a product of the Kentucky hempfields as clearly as ever Clym Yeobright was the product of Egdon Heath; he is therefore all the more pathetically unqualified to cope with either his own doubts or the academic and ecclesiastical intolerance which they inspire. But his

[2] Though *The Choir Invisible* postdates *Summer in Arcady,* which is later in spirit, it was based upon the earlier *John Gray* (1893).

[3] For that matter, the shadow of the Civil War had been seen lowering over Henry Clay's world in *A Kentucky Cardinal.* Allen was to handle the Civil War more conventionally in *Sword of Youth* (1915), which includes an attractively sentimental picture of Lee at the close of the conflict.

return to the farm after having been expelled from college and the final love affair with the disagreeing but sympathetic Gabriella do not aid the unity of the book; neither does the somewhat exclamatory style in which Allen here chose to write contribute to its sense of reality.

Elements of uncertainty intrude too into *The Mettle of the Pasture*. Because he cannot bear not to be completely honest with her, Rowan Meredith tells his betrothed that he is the father of an illegitimate child. Her reaction is more intense than Hilda's at the sight of murder in *The Marble Faun*. How shocking is the scene in which the girl slips out of church because she cannot bear to confess that she is a miserable sinner while Rowan is making the same confession a few pews away! Ultimately, it is true, Isabel forgives her lover, and even marries him and bears him a child of her own; but the strain of what has gone before is so great that it costs him his life. Allen is not wholly on Isabel's side, and the story as he tells it is more convincing than this summary makes it sound. But he does not see—or at least state—the monstrous inhumanity of the proceedings quite definitely enough to make the ethical standing-ground of the novel entirely clear. "I am tired of it all," cries the dying Meredith. "I want to rest. Love has been more cruel to me than death."

The two Christmas books deal with painful themes: with "one of the persistent dreams of mankind—the dream of ideal love and ideal marriage with one who is unattainable," and with the hunger for youth which sometimes attacks hitherto happily married men at what it is now fashionable to call the male menopause. But nobody who had ever read any other novel in which these themes were treated would get any idea of the character of Allen's work from my description. Mrs. Ousley, for example, has no rival in her husband's affections. The drama works itself out upon what might almost be called a plane of abstraction, and the hideous cruelty of the position in which the two wives find themselves seems all the more chilling upon those frozen heights. There are children, not always convincingly handled, through whom, it seems, the final "solution," in the unwritten part of the work, was to have come. There is much Christmas lore; and *The Bride of the Mistletoe* is as much essay as fiction; for it is after her husband has read her a long,

Fraser-like account of Christmas customs and symbolism that Mrs. Ousley learns where she stands. There are power and beauty in these books, but there are suggestions, too, of the grandiose and the in-human, and it cannot be claimed that Allen has been entirely suc-cessful in communicating his ideas. Very few readers, surely, have ever grasped the real significance of Herbert's death in *The Doctor's Christmas Eve*.[4]

As a novelist[5] Allen is weakest in structure. His Preface to *The Bride of the Mistletoe* insists that the book "is not a novel; it has neither the structure nor the purpose of The Novel." He might per-haps have said the same of other books. He could rarely resist a digression; the panther-episode in *The Choir Invisible* (a display piece to match Simms's rattlesnake in *The Yemassee*), does not ad-vance the action in any way. In *The Mettle of the Pasture* unity is imperiled by the continual introduction of new characters, each of whom becomes in his turn the focus of interest. In short, Allen had very little of that steady, forward narrative movement which is always the mark of the born storyteller.

The world of Allen's novels is at once a thin world and a rich one. As novelists go, he had not many themes or interests. But if we compare him with the naturalists, the impingements upon his world seem overwhelming. To begin with, there was nature, nature "with the full metaphysical light upon it," as Pattee says, yet nature studied, at the same time, in the full light of modern scientific knowledge. And the human background is hardly less "thick": "The retreating wave of Indian life, the thin restless wave of frontier life, the on-coming, all-burying wave of civilized life—he seemed to feel close to him the mighty movement of the three."

His style, like Cabell's, is too mannered for the mood of the moment; with the mood of the moment, criticism, fortunately, has little to do. Unlike Cabell, he could be saccharine; but he could also create effects which were beautiful of their kind. The description of

[4] Grant C. Knight, *JLA and the Genteel Tradition*, p. 172.

[5] Allen's novels after the Christmas books, in addition to *Sword of Youth*, were *The Heroine in Bronze* (1912), a love story of New York; *The Emblems of Fidelity* (1919), an epistolary novel constituting a social comedy; and *The Kentucky Warbler* (1919), the story of a boy's growing into life, based on the experience of the ornithologist Alexander Wilson.

the great shield which is Kentucky at the beginning of *The Bride of the Mistletoe,* the comparison between books and trees in *The Mettle of the Pasture,* the discussion, in *The Choir Invisible,* of the difference between "light-houses" and "candles in our hands"—this last a passage as suggestive as the lucubrations of Plotinus Plinlimmon in Melville's *Pierre*—these are at least impressive rhetoric. He was capable of humor too, as in the social comedy of Pansy's visit to Mrs. Meredith in *The Mettle of the Pasture,* or, more briefly, in *The Reign of Law,* in the relieved determination of David's pious parents to tolerate his long-recognized peculiarities now that they know he is to study for the ministry. "And who had a right to understand a minister? He was entitled to be peculiar." But Allen's subtlety is more characteristic than his humor. It may be seen clearly in his analysis of Dr. Birney's selfish little daughter in *The Doctor's Christmas Eve.* Voltaire, we are told, might have had a voice like hers "if he had been a little girl." And Allen goes on to distinguish masterfully between Elsie and her brother Herbert by describing the elements in their father's life by which each was impressed. The girl responds to "what looked to her like his self-love; his care about what he ate and drank; his changing his clothes whenever he came home," to whatever made him the center of his little world. The boy is altogether different. "The earliest notion of his father the boy had grasped was that of always travelling toward the sick—to a world that needed him." "Actually his father had no business of his own: he merely drove about and enabled other people to attend to their business."

2. *"Epitaph of a Civilization"*

A reverential spirit toward the old South was shared by Thomas Nelson Page (1853-1922), F[rancis] Hopkinson Smith (1838-1915), and John Fox, Jr. (1863-1919). And though it was Page of whom it was said that he had written the epitaph of a civilization, the other two had a share in the writing.

All three men were romancers, and all three led very active lives. None, to be sure, saw service in the Civil War. Page and Fox were too young, and Smith (born in Baltimore), spent the war years earning a living in New York. But both Page's father and his uncle

were officers in the Confederate army, and his own first-hand knowledge of a Union raid was preserved in *Two Little Confederates*
(1888). Fox (many years later), organized a militant police force
which brought peace to the Cumberland mountains.

Page was the complete Southern gentleman—chivalrous, high-
minded, and devout (a biographer of Lee); steeped in classical literature from his youth (one of his last books was a study of Dante).
During World War I he was American ambassador to Italy. The
amazingly versatile Smith was more "modern." Where the other
two men were lawyers, he was an engineer; he built Race Rock
lighthouse and the foundation of the Statue of Liberty. Long before
he ever thought of literature, he had turned to painting as a hobby;
a friend of Abbey, Vedder, and Chase, he became an illustrator of
books; he once painted a picture a day for fifty-three successive days.
Indeed, Smith was over fifty when he began to write, but once he got
under way, he was far more prolific and wide-ranging than either of
his friends.

Page himself credited George W. Bagby (1828-1883) with having
broken away from the formal, artificial, idealistic tradition of the
earlier Southern literature; in Bagby himself he found a true picture
of what he called the "sweetness and simplicity and charm" of old
plantation life, and from him he derived his inspiration. He began,
naturally enough, with the short story (*In Ole Virginia,* 1887),
which, for that matter, he never relinquished; his novels are few.
The novelists he loved best were Fielding, Thackeray, Dickens, and
Hawthorne; he considered *Esmond* the finest of all novels, with
Bleak House a close second.

His own first novel was *On Newfound River* (1891); his most important was *Red Rock* (1898), which has long been regarded as a
kind of standard description of Reconstruction from the Southern
point of view. The Preface defends the old South against its enemies
—"Every ass that passes by kicks at the dead lion"—and in the
prewar portion of his novel Page is careful to permit the Southern
moderates to play the most conspicuous roles. It is interesting to
compare *Red Rock* with the coarser and more sensational picture of
Reconstruction painted by Thomas Dixon in *The Clansman* (1905),
which inspired *The Birth of a Nation.* Page does not omit the Klan

—he makes, too, a moderate use of standard Gothic properties, among them the inevitable mysterious ancestral portrait—but he centers attention upon the legal chicanery by means of which Southerners were defrauded by Northern shysters and scalawags. The book is very long and somewhat overloaded with detail; there is so much of it that sometimes one is not sure where the emphasis is supposed to fall.

Page covered the Reconstruction years again, much more lightly and picturesquely, in his last novel, *The Red Riders* (1924), which he never quite finished. The young hero of this book accidentally encounters Booth and his fellow-conspirators just before Lincoln's assassination; he also has a rather sentimental interview with the President himself. Thaddeus Stevens appears as "Senator Estovan," with his housekeeper and reputed mulatto mistress, Lydia Smith, under her own name. Again we have a picturesque account of the raiding of a plantation, but with gallant Northern officers rebuking and restraining the looters.

After *Red Rock,* Page's most important novel was *John Marvel, Assistant* (1909), which took him out of his beloved South altogether. Most of the action occurs in an unnamed large "Western" city, which is probably Chicago. Page preaches more in *John Marvel* than he did in his Civil War books, not only about the sins of the city but even about "the reeking putrescence of the so-called problem novel." But *John Marvel* itself is a "problem novel," involving trades-unionism (toward which the author is unfriendly), Socialism (which he views with surprising sympathy), anti-Semitism, municipal corruption, dishonest financial manipulation, white slavery, yellow journalism, courage and cowardice in the pulpit, and the exploitation of the poor. The book is well-informed, high-minded, surprisingly forward-looking, and generally sensible and right. But though the story is competently-handled, the characters are, for the most part, machine-made.[6]

Smith used his engineering experiences in *Tom Grogan* (1896)

[6] Page also published *Gordon Keith* (1903), in which Northerner and Southerner are contrasted, not quite fairly, in a New York setting, and a number of novelettes, some of them for children, of which the best is a charming idyll, *The Old Gentleman of the Black Stock* (1897).

and in *Caleb West: Master Diver* (1898). His knowledge of art and of artists becomes important in *The Fortunes of Oliver Horn* (1902) and in such stories as *The Romance of an Old-Fashioned Gentleman* (1907). Tom Grogan is a woman, carrying on her husband's stevedore business after his death, caring for her family, and fighting single-handed a union all of whose members are dirty spalpeens. In *Caleb West* the action revolves around the waywardness of the diver's child-wife, who is forgiven at last, somewhat in the manner of Little Em'ly in *David Copperfield*. Smith once told Professor Quinn that Bret Harte and Daudet (*Sapho*) had been important influences upon his work; but Harte's master, Dickens, must have been at least as important as either. Mr. Stidger, of *Oliver Horn,* and Gadgem, of *Kennedy Square* (1911), are obviously Dickensian characters; St. George, on the other hand, would have felt more at home in Thackeray. Richard Horn's reading from *The Cricket on the Hearth,* in *Kennedy Square,* is skillfully managed, to show its effect upon the mind of the heroine and, through her, at last, upon the unraveling of the plot.

The work upon which Smith's reputation as a writer was originally based, however, had nothing to do with either of his preliterary vocations but came exclusively out of his Southern inheritance. *Colonel Carter of Cartersville* (1891) exploits, with loving humor and delighted relish of eccentricity, the ruined gentleman of the old South. When he is informed that the grocer has called twice during a single evening, the Colonel is mortified to have missed him:

"The fact is I have not treated him with proper respect. He has shown me every courtesy since I have been here, and I am ashamed to say that I have not once entered his doors. His calling twice in one evening touches me deeply. I did not expect to find yo' tradespeople so polite."

Yet the Colonel has his fire-eating side. He challenges Klutchem to a duel because he believes that he has been insulted by him, and a hardhearted post-office department returns the letter for postage. By this time the Colonel is convinced that so far from Klutchem having wronged him, he has wronged Klutchem, and though the latter knows nothing of the intended challenge, he insists on waiting upon him to apologize. But when Klutchem, who is laid up with a nasty gout, will not go down to Wall Street to receive the apology properly in the presence of the Colonel's friends, the irascible old man grows indignant again and threatens him with a horsewhipping.

Smith was essentially a picturesque and "charming" writer, with a fondness for dramatic (sometimes melodramatic) scene, and a strong pictorial sense. He believed "in the ultimate triumph of good over evil, in the fundamental kindness of human nature." Except for *The Tides of Barnegat* (1906), which is mildly symbolical, he rarely achieved a tight structure. His most effective setting is the genteel Kennedy Square of old Baltimore, which he used both in *Oliver Horn* and in the novel which bears its name.

The central situation in *Kennedy Square* (1911)—the father's turning against his son because, under great provocation, he has violated the code of hospitality by fighting a duel with a guest—is not very believable, and the old man's generosity at the end (out of consideration for a happy ending), is as incredible as his cruelty at the beginning. If we can get over this hurdle, we shall find little more to criticize: Harry's own fortunes make for an interesting story, and so do the loyalty and devotion under adversity of his stalwart uncle St. George. The faithful Negroes are very appealing also, and Poe and John P. Kennedy add glamour to the book through their brief apearances.

Oliver Horn is a strange, impossible, yet very attractive mixture. Even the art schools of New York grow prudish when Oliver invades them: there are no naked models in the life classes. Neither is there any grossness in the bohemian artist-life into which the boy is plunged; a good deal of liquor is consumed, but it never seems to have any effect on anybody. Oliver's struggles to keep alive during the war, though autobiographical, are only indicated, not described. Yet for all this, *Oliver Horn* is a forward-looking, not a backward-looking, book.

Smith loved the charm of old Kennedy Square, but he was quite aware of the snobbery and provincialism upon which it rested, and the sheltered Sue Clayton, the girl of the old South, cannot hold a candle to the new woman, the artist Margaret Grant, whom Oliver meets in New York. Both Margaret and Oliver fight "the good fight of science and art against tradition and provincialism—part of that great army of progress which was steadily conquering the world!"

On the whole, one may well doubt that Smith's gentility was a more distorting medium than a number of very different prepossessions in contemporary fiction.[7]

Of John Fox's novels, the best, by common consent, are *The Little Shepherd of Kingdom Come* (1903) and *The Trail of the Lonesome Pine* (1908). Fox is differentiated from Page and Smith by the fact that his special field lay among the primitive people of the Cumberland whom he called "our contemporary ancestors." Often he brings them into contact with the aristocrats of the Bluegrass, thus creating a contrast which, as he presents it, strongly favors the mountaineers. The Civil War part of *The Little Shepherd* is conventional—Chad disappoints his friends by feeling impelled to fight for the North— but the opening section, which portrays the primitive life of the hills, Chad's association with Melissa and her family, and his determination to make something of himself under Major Buford's patronage, has a lovely radiance.

The Trail of the Lonesome Pine, despite its haunting title, makes less than might have been expected of its wonderful materials. There are actually three sources of interest in this book: the life of the mountaineers themselves, the love story between the mountain girl and the engineer,[8] and the study of the coming of industrialism to a primitive community. But even under adversity, the engineer is almost the stalwart "strong man" of the movies and red-blooded fiction, while the development of the girl, once she has been given "advantages," becomes ludicrous. It is true that she does not become a great singer, but Fox tells us clearly that she might easily have

[7] See also, among Smith's fictions, *Peter* (1908), a loosely woven narrative of considerable charm, whose elderly name-character serves as mentor and guide to a young Southerner, employed as clerk to a contracting engineer in New York; *Felix O'Day* (1915), which gives us an Irish baronet searching for his wife in the metropolis, and the posthumous *Enoch Crane* (1916), planned by Smith but written largely by his son.

[8] Fox discovered his central themes early: the mountain girl in *A Mountain Europa* (1894), the feud in *A Cumberland Vendetta* (1895). *Crittenden* (1900) concerns the Spanish-American War. Feuds and the coming industrialism are important again in *The Heart o' the Hills* (1913), which also has a tobacco-grower's war. *Erskine Dale, Pioneer* (1920) is an historical novel of Revolutionary times, whose hero, heir to a great Virginia estate, is brought up among Indians.

done so! These are the marks of a "popular" novel, and they explain why *The Trail of the Lonesome Pine* has been even more successful in the theater than between covers. (It also inspired a popular song.) On the stage, it furnished Charlotte Walker with one of her most successful roles; the silent film, in 1922, marked the screen farewell of the lovely Mary Miles Minter.

3. *Allotropes and Mary Johnston*[9]

The end of the 1890's and the opening years of the twentieth century witnessed a decided revival of interest in the historical novel. Among the most successful of these works (some of which are discussed elsewhere in this volume) were S. Weir Mitchell's *Hugh Wynne, Free Quaker* (1897), Charles Major's *When Knighthood Was in Flower* and Mary Johnston's *Prisoners of Hope* (both 1898), Paul Leicester Ford's *Janice Meredith* and Winston Churchill's *Richard Carvel* (both 1899), Maurice Thompson's *Alice of Old Vincennes* and Booth Tarkington's *Monsieur Beaucaire* (both 1900), and Robert W. Chambers's *Cardigan* (1901).

Of the writers here named, Mary Johnston was the one who enjoyed the most important career as an historical novelist and showed the greatest capacity for growth. Her early work, sometimes florid, is often conventional in its development; her last, most deeply creative, novels ventured into a realm where, in the present stage of human development and of the development of fiction, a complete realization of one's aim is very nearly impossible. But if she fell short of being a great novelist, she was unmistakably a great woman, and her books are full of nourishing food for the human spirit.

Mary Johnston was born, at Buchanan, Virginia, on November 21, 1870, the daughter of Major John W. Johnston, of the Confederate Army. She died, at Warm Springs, Virginia—a Socialist, a pacifist, and a mystic—on May 9, 1936.

She produced, in all, twenty-three novels. Fifteen are concerned, wholly or in part, with Virginia. Seven of these deal with colonial Virginia: *Prisoners of Hope, To Have and To Hold* (1900), *Audrey*

[9] This account of Mary Johnston's work is based upon the writer's article, "The World and Mary Johnston," *SR*, XLIV (1936), 188-206, which see for a fuller consideration of many of the points raised here.

(1902), *Croatan* (1923), *The Slave Ship* (1924), *The Great Valley* (1926), and *Hunting Shirt* (1931). The hero of *Lewis Rand* (1908) lives near Jefferson's Monticello. *The Long Roll* (1911) and *Cease Firing* (1912) are played against the epic background of the Civil War. *Miss Delicia Allen* (1933) opens in the 1840's and ends during the war; *Drury Randall* (1934) is built around the fortunes of a conscientious objector to the conflict. *Michael Forth* (1919) begins not long after the war and runs well into the twentieth century. *Hagar* (1913) does not open until well on toward 1900. *Sweet Rocket* (1920) has a contemporary setting altogether.

Of the non-Virginian novels, *Sir Mortimer* (1904) deals with the Elizabethan sea-rovers in the Old World and the New. England proper furnishes the setting for two books: Henry VII's England in *Silver Cross* (1922) and the seventeenth century in *The Witch* (1914). (Delicia Allen pays a visit to Victorian England.) *Foes* (1918) and the non-Virginian portion of *The Slave Ship* are set in eighteenth-century Scotland. The scene of *1492* (1922) is sufficiently indicated by its title. *The Fortunes of Garin* (1915) takes place in twelfth-century France. The series of stories presented in *The Wanderers* (1917) opens in prehistoric times and does not end before the French Revolution. *The Exile* (1927) takes place on an imaginary island in the not-so-distant future.

It is often assumed that Mary Johnston's work breaks sharply around the year 1918. Up to that time she had been writing historical romances of adventure. Thereafter she concerned herself with "mystical writing." But the facts do not support this convenient simplification.

Only the first five novels—*Prisoners of Hope, To Have and To Hold, Audrey, Sir Mortimer,* and *Lewis Rand*—are "straight" historical romances. These books are concerned mainly with personal problems; they owed their success to their exciting narrative and their rich backgrounds.

The two Civil War books mark the beginning of the sociological period. Here the drama of the individual is subordinated to the drama of a people. This aspect of Mary Johnston's work finds its fullest expression in *Hagar,* the suffrage novel. and it culminates in

The Wanderers, a series of studies in the changing relations between men and women.

The other books of the middle period are difficult to classify, looking backward as they do to the older romances, and at the same time foreshadowing the mystical tendencies of much later books. Essentially, however, I think they belong to the sociological group. In *The Fortunes of Garin,* we have, in addition to the love story, and closely involved in it, a picture of the collapse of the feudal system, and the theme of *The Witch* is the struggle for religious freedom.

Following *The Wanderers* came the three books in which the accumulating "inwardness" of Mary Johnston's previous writing reached its climax—*Foes, Michael Forth,* and *Sweet Rocket.* In the first two, the method is still that of the historical novel. In *Sweet Rocket* the story and the backgrounds are less important and the ideas more.

It should be clear that Mary Johnston never turned to the past to escape the problems of the present. In her thinking, the past controls the future, and the future remolds the past. The present is only a link between the two. Every man carries the past within himself, as the Blue and the Grey in *Cease Firing* feel endless vistas opening out behind them. But a man does not live in the past. Ian and Glenfernie, mortal foes, "had felled many forests" since the day when, coming suddenly upon each other, they might have flown at each other's throats.

This idea of growth as summing up the significance of all life lies at the root of Mary Johnston's interest in the pioneer. There is hardly a book in which the pioneer does not play an important role. In *The Witch* Joan and Aderhold choose to give up their lives rather than inhibit their development by conforming to obsolete creeds and practices. Hagar, like Miriam in *Michael Forth,* fights for the emancipation of women. Even in *Prisoners of Hope* the note of advance is sounded. Here, Betty Carrington, the little Puritan, is ridiculed by her friends because she doubts the righteousness of the slave system. Here, too, Landless gains the undying loyalty of the Indian, Monakatocka, when he disregards the color line and sucks the poison from the red man's snake bite. Finally, the love between Patricia Verney and an indentured servant outrages all the traditions of class.

Even pioneers see truth only in flashes, however, and they are not able to live steadily in the light which they perceive. There is Edward Cary, of *Cease Firing,* who hates war, yet consents to have a share in it. Sometimes bitterness, pain, and travail fall to the lot of the pioneer. Michael Forth grows almost without a sense of strain. But quite a different experience is that of David Scott in *The Slave Ship,* for David, with all his tremendous capacity, has a bad heritage, and he fights a bitter fight against cruelty and greed before, finally, he wins the victory.

Most of the characters in Mary Johnston's later novels are pioneers in the field of an expanding human consciousness. They believe that "There existed a consciousness surpassing old levels that we had known." They are inspired by the thought that "A part of the world is passing beyond old powers into new." They regard themselves as experiencing now what will someday come to be the common possession of the race. "Here and there, throughout the past, and often now I think in our own day, a man or woman lays hold upon faculties that someday all will lay hold upon."

The new development involves among other things a breaking down of the old barriers of space and time. When the Selkirks emigrate to America, they are conscious of the veritable presence of the daughter they have left behind them in Scotland. There is even communion between the living and the dead. Kirstie Mackay, of *The Great Valley,* had been kept away from the man she loved by religious prejudices in their respective families. And then he had died. Yet the victory was still with love. "Those silly giants had not kept them apart, nor had silly death!" And now "Kirstie Mackay moved with a dead lover in a land above a land."

"The holder-back is the sense of disunity." This is the great barrier that must be crossed before a human being can possess the Sense of the Whole. Some persons, some places diffuse an atmosphere which radiates harmony. Such persons are Mrs. Allison in *Foes,* Aunt Sarah in *Michael Forth.* Such a place is Sweet Rocket.

Different natures approach unity in different ways. Hagar's is the artist's power of merging with her materials. "She never lost the child's and the poet's power of coalescence." For Denny Gayde the mystic consciousness is all shot through with a sense of social obligation. "We've got to feel, 'if you are struck, I am struck. If you are wearing stripes, I am wearing stripes.' We've got to feel something more than brotherhood. We've got to feel identity." Paradoxically enough, they feel identity most keenly who are farthest along the road. Richard Kaye, of *The Exile,* does not feel superior to others who cannot share his views. "What is true of me is true of all others. One is at the dawn, one is in the hour before it, one is at midnight —that is all. Ahead of us are those in full day."

But a man has foes. When Glenfernie stands beside the Kelpie's Pool, and realizes that the man he had called friend has cruelly betrayed him, unity breaks for him into little pieces. And it must not be supposed that because Glenfernie finally forgives Ian, there is any Pollyanna optimism or any juggling of right and wrong. Hate possesses Glenfernie as completely as it has ever possessed a man. Had the author been content to treat her characters on the surface of life—to handle them as the ordinary novelist would have done it— the story must have ended with the death of Ian or of Glenfernie or of both. But she sees more of them than that, sees them, one might say, on several planes at once, the long inheritance of the past blending into the aspiration of the future. The book ends with reconciliation not because the author has a point to make or a theory to illustrate but because once all the elements of the situation have been taken into account, it can end in no other way. "My fellow man is myself," says Aderhold. And Michael Forth adds, "The very ones that a man calls foes—it is impossible not to love them."

This is, of course, essentially a religious problem, and it is not surprising that Aderhold should try to work out the idea of the relationship between God and man in the old philosophical terms of microcosm and macrocosm. The Kingdom of God is still to come, yet the Kingdom of God is here. No matter what calamities afflict mankind, they cannot wholly crush those whose hope is fixed on eternity. Joan and Aderhold suffer nearly everything that human beings can suffer, yet in the end—and the end is death—"pain did not win." There is something in human life that is essentially undefeatable, something in man that guns cannot kill. Jayme de Marchena, the narrator of *1492,* perceives, as Socrates perceived so long ago, that no harm can come to the good man. "Surely they who serve large purposes are cared for! Though they should die in prison, yet are they cared for!" It is in this faith that David Scott, too, at last painfully possesses his soul. "A time would come—a time would come—when Earth should put on heaven. I thought, I felt, I lived. I knew my work. I was uplifted."

But if she was a religious novelist, Mary Johnston was not a propagandist. She did not, like Mary Austin, for example, proselytize in behalf of her ideas. She was simply, as an artist, engaged in the reassembling, the reinterpretation, of her own spiritual experience and that of her time.

Of Mary Johnston's special gifts as an historical novelist, and of her influence, I have little space to speak here. As an historian of the theater, Professor Quinn has testified to the skill and knowledge with which, in *Audrey,* she recreates the Williamsburg theater of the early eighteenth century. Her war novels anticipated later developments by nearly a generation. We know that she exercised an important influence on Rafael Sabatini. That she also influenced Elizabeth Madox Roberts I cannot prove, but *The Great Meadow* inevitably recalls *The Great Valley,* and Mary Johnston's style is strongly suggested in *He Sent Forth a Raven.*

Some of the spontaneity, the full-bodied richness of the earlier novels undoubtedly disappeared from the later, leaner, more implicational books. And nowhere in her final phase did Mary Johnston again create such a character as Lewis Rand. Yet the last books must still stand as her most original contributions to the American novel.

One night in the early 1920's, Zona Gale gave a lecture on "Allotropes" at the University of Chicago.[10] The diamond is the allotrope of coal, she told us; J. W. Thomson had recently announced the discovery of an allotrope of water. From here Miss Gale went on to a fascinating discussion of the possibility of developing more allotropes in literature and in life—"the allotrope of the novel," for example, and "the allotrope of ourselves."

If the allotrope of the novel exists at all in our later American literature, it must be among such books as those of Mary Johnston, Elizabeth Madox Roberts, and Zona Gale herself that we shall have

[10] As "Scholarship and the Spirit," this lecture may now be read in her *Portage, Wisconsin and Other Essays* (K, 1928).

to look for it. Whatever else may be said about Mary Johnston, the people who stopped reading her in later years because the sword-and-cloak romance was outmoded had got it wrong in several different ways. As a number of gifted writers have since shown us, the sword-and-cloak romance is not dead. And in the usual sense Mary Johnston never wrote a sword-and-cloak romance, or if she did, she had certainly given up all that kind of thing long before the 1920's. The readers she lost in later years fell away not because they had outgrown her but because they could no longer keep up her pace.

CHAPTER XI

TOWARDS NATURALISM

John Jay Chapman once summed up all the laws of dramatic composition under one law: Something must be going on on the stage which interests the audience. Otherwise they will go away. It is even easier to close a book than it is to walk out of a theater. The first task of novelist and dramatist alike is to establish the emotional importance of his characters. If you do not care whether the hero gets his heart's desire or whether he breaks his neck, nothing else makes any difference either.

JULIAN FORREST

1. Naturalism and the Naturalists

Naturalism in modern fiction springs from *Le Roman Expérimentale* (1880) of Émile Zola and the twenty novels of the Rougon-Macquart series which are the aesthetic exemplification of the creed that Zola proclaimed. The naturalists attempted to apply Claude Bernard's theories of experimental medicine to the writing of fiction. They built as the scientist builds, on a basis of observed fact, and their method was to document their observations by the use of multitudinous details. Enthralled by the scientific materialism of the age of Darwin, they saw man as at once the sport and the product of his heredity and his environment. The naturalist may be a reformer, as Zola himself was—change the environment and you change the man—but, freedom of the human will having disappeared, he can pass no moral judgments. In his view of man and nature, he blinks nothing, but he views "evil" with the eye of a physician, never with the eyes of a judge.

Obviously, there are few consistent naturalists, either in life or in art. The "romantic" elements in Zola's own novels have often been commented upon. A writer's own "beliefs" are often much less important for his art than his temperament, and the needs of the particular work under consideration may, on occasion, take precedence of both. An artist enthralled by his daemon who finds, as Shelley did in "Adonais," that his philosophy threatens to abort his creation must consciously or unconsciously choose between junking his philosophy and junking his work. Mary Garden tells us that when she was on the stage she expressed and communicated emotions she had never felt as a woman. It is not surprising that the naturalistic "creed," which seriously lowers human dignity and places limitations upon the significance of human experience, should more often be found inadequate as an aesthetic frame of reference than, say, the affirmations of the Christian faith. Charles Child Walcutt goes so far as to say: "No perfectly naturalistic novels—i.e., no perfect embodiments of naturalistic theory in the structure of a novel—have been written, for if they were perfectly naturalistic they would not be novels but reports. . . ."[1]

Where did naturalism enter the American novel? In view of the considerations just adduced, this is not an easy question to answer. But at least we may, with some hope of profit, examine the works of a number of writers in whose work various naturalistic elements appear.

2. Hamlin Garland: "Veritism" and After

It would not be easy to justify the importance which, by common consent, attaches to the figure of Hamlin Garland by reference to his novels alone. It may be that Garland was more important as a man than he was as a writer. Certainly no man of letters ever had a wider acquaintance among his writing contemporaries or developed and recorded his friendships with greater diligence.[2] But except for *Rose of Dutcher's Coolly* (1895), the aesthetically mature Garland hardly touched, as novelist, that life of the Middle Border which he knew best of all, and of which alone, had he remained permanently faithful to his early, brave, brash pronunciamento in *Crumbling Idols* (1894), he ought to have written. It is true that if *Boy Life on the Prairie*

[1] See Charles C. Walcutt, "From Scientific Theory to Aesthetic Fact: The 'Naturalistic' Novel," *Quarterly Review of Literature*, III (1946), 167-179, and the references therein cited; also, Herbert Edwards, "Zola and American Critics," *AL*, IV (1932), 114-129.

[2] In *Roadside Meetings* (1930); *Companions on the Trail* (1931); *My Friendly Contemporaries* (1932); *Afternoon Neighbors* (1934).

(1899) and *Trail-Makers of the Middle Border* (1926) are to be classified as novels, this statement must be modified somewhat.[3] But it will remain anomalous that this author should have given the only perfect illustrations of the credo upon which he had defiantly staked his career in his short stories,[4] and left us the clearest impression of the influences upon his formative years in his autobiographical narratives, while using most of his full-length novels for the more romantic materials of a superficially observed Far West.

There are, to be sure, the four early novels which both Garland and most of his critics have been inclined to dismiss with a wave of the hand. All were published in 1892, and all save *A Spoil of Office* are brief. Both *A Spoil of Office* and *A Member of the Third House* add propaganda and crusading zeal to the more objective "veritism" of the *Main-Travelled Roads* whose author had been more concerned to portray the unhappy conditions of farm life than to find out a remedy. Both deal with political problems and corruption, and both are forward-looking sociologically but undistinguished as fiction. *Jason Edwards, An Average Man* is more like the *Main-Travelled Roads*. Frozen out of Boston by high rents and low wages, Jason and his family take the trail of promise to the Northwest, here to be squeezed by ruthless landlords and mortgage-holders and finally finished off by a cyclone. Walter Reeves, the self-made Boston newspaper man, who loves the musical daughter of the family, alone saves the book from an utterly hopeless ending by casting himself at last as a kind of unwillingly-accepted god from the machine; but in so brief a narrative, the love story makes for a degree of divided

---

[3] Both books are much less in the vein of literal recording than the rest of Garland's family chronicles. The *Trail-Makers* is one of a tetralogy embracing also *A Son of the Middle Border* (1917), *A Daughter of the Middle Border* (1921), and *Back-Trailers from the Middle Border* (1928). The three last named deal with the writer's own life and that of his family. *Trail-Makers* is a different matter; here we read how the father of Hamlin Garland came from New England to Wisconsin, how he won his bride, and how he fought in the Civil War. And this time, as if to indicate that he has mingled imagination with the facts that came to him through oral tradition, Garland, though still retaining a factual manner of narration, has employed fictitious names.

[4] *Main-Travelled Roads* (1891) and its successors. All that Garland wished to preserve is now contained in the later, enlarged editions of *Main-Travelled Roads* and in *Other Main-Travelled Roads* (1910).

unity. Much the best of these early books is *A Little Norsk,* which concerns two Dakota farmers who adopt a baby after her mother has frozen to death in a blizzard. Though suggesting in some aspects countless sentimental stories about men who have brought up girl children, *A Little Norsk* is differentiated from them by Garland's willingness to admit the complicating factor of sexual attraction as the girl grows up and again by the unromantic business of her marriage to a worthless young man who walks out on her when her baby is about to be born.

Garland himself had known farm life in Wisconsin, where he was born in 1860, in Dakota, but especially in Iowa, where, though a boy, he did a man's work and learned the meaning of toil. Except for the Bible and a few Sunday School books, he first savored "literature" in "Aladdin" and "Beauty and the Beast." From McGuffey's *Readers* he got his introduction to many English classics; at the same time he was bolting dime novels and the *New York Saturday Night.* In Boston, where he arrived in 1894, passionately in search of culture, he lived on next to nothing, like a monk in a cell, and put himself through an heroic course of reading in the Public Library. He accepted Darwin, Spencer, and the evolutionists; he discovered Whitman; new worlds opened out before him in Ibsen, Björnson, and other advanced European writers. He met Henry George and became a champion of the Single Tax; later, he enthusiastically accepted the Farmer's Alliance and the Populist Party.

The Western farm boy made influential friends at the Hub and registered surprising progress; he became a "professor" at the Boston School of Oratory, and, in his ill-fitting clothes, delivered lectures to Back Bay Brahmins on such aesthetic themes as the acting of Edwin Booth.

Yet his first piece of writing of any importance was a description of corn-husking in Iowa. Passionately as he loved Eastern culture, he knew that it was no source of material for him. "It was rather . . . a story already told, a song already sung." He was importantly influenced by *The Hoosier Schoolmaster,* which he encountered while it was running its serial course in a farm paper. In Boston he reviewed Joseph Kirkland's *Zury* for the *Evening Transcript,* and Kirkland's encouragement, when he stopped off to see him in

Chicago, furnished the immediate impulse which led to his own first fictions.

Garland left Boston and committed himself to Chicago in the great days when the city basked in the glow of the World's Columbian Exposition, when Stone and Kimball were establishing their remarkable publishing house and the midwestern metropolis was all set to become not merely "hog-butcher to the world" but the literary capital of America. Here he founded the Cliff Dwellers Club and married the sister of the great Chicago sculptor, Lorado Taft. About the time of World War I he moved to New York, where he felt, rightly as the event proved, that wider literary recognition awaited him. Still later he went to Hollywood, where, in 1940, he died.

As has already been indicated, Garland's first comprehensive statement of his literary ideals as a "Veritist" was made in *Crumbling Idols*. The fundamental demand of these pages is the demand that writers find inspiration in their own country, throwing off the dominion of the past, and making the common man the fundamental subject of esthetic concern. Garland's antiromanticism shows in his quotation from Eugène Véron: "We care no longer for gods or heroes; we care for men."

Garland was at this time so fanatical in his adherence to these principles that he saw even Shakespeare fading away into a "name," and so committed to the thesis that local color was "demonstrably the life of fiction" that if he had to choose between expressing fundamentals and expressing the "minute and characteristic aspects of the passing hour," he thought he would be content to let the fundamentals go. Scrapping the great writers of the past, he was ready to scrap their methods also, for he had embraced the impressionist cause in painting and it seemed to him that literature too had to go out for something like that. "Veritism discredits plots and formal complications. It deals with life face to face, and swiftly and surely from the individual artist's standpoint. Characters and the relation of groups of characters are coming to have more value than plot."

The novel which best exemplifies Garland's early ideals is, as has already been indicated, *Rose of Dutcher's Coolly*. Here he achieved what for a male writer must surely be pronounced an unusual feat: he reflected his own early ambitions and experiences in the story of a farm girl who gets an education for herself at the University of Wisconsin and then comes on to Chicago to become a writer. There is much in the book that is naïve, and it is too bad that the most interesting part—the girl's growing up—should have been so summarily treated. But the story has life in it, even today.

Especially interesting, in view of Garland's later intense dislike of the libertarian tendencies of current American fiction, is his treatment of sex in this book. He paints an idealized portrait of a very passionate woman, and the existence of passionate women who were also virtuous was hardly admitted by the average novel-reader of the time. On the farm, "the apparently shameful fact of sex faced . . . [Rose] everywhere." She runs naked through the corn and admires her beautiful body in the mirror; once she confesses to her father having shared in some childish sexuality. Later, Dr. Thatcher feels her attraction so strongly that he frankly tells his wife he thinks it wiser not to permit Rose to continue to live in their home. When the girl reads *The Scarlet Letter,* she ponders all its implications, and after seeing a play which is committed to the thesis of the double standard, she concludes that "A woman can set her foot above her dead self as well as a man."

In this connection, there is an impressive account of the appeal which the "naked majesty" of the circus riders makes to the girl's "pure wholesome awakening womanhood, with the power of beauty and strength and sex combined." Their leader, tawdry as he is in himself, becomes a shining ideal of grace, to be cherished in memory; as such, he has an important influence upon Rose's life. This is precisely the kind of experience which counts in the life of a sensitive youngster, yet how few writers have had the courage to use it without degrading it to buffoonery or obscenity!

No writer ever respected women more than Hamlin Garland, and sometimes he is frankly romantic in his treatment of them. Yet his honest handling of Rose is not uncharacteristic. Lee Virginia, of *Cavanagh* (1910), is pure and refined to all outward seeming, but when the hero thinks of her bad inheritance, she "stirs" his blood "to the danger-point." The uncultivated speech and manners of the heroine of *Money Magic* (1907) set our teeth on edge, yet we are intended to respect her and to sympathize with her, even when she is tempted to infidelity. Elsie Brisbane, of *The Captain of the Grey-Horse Troop* (1902), has all the advantages which these girls lack, but the reader is expected to be as patient as the hero in nursing her mind until she outgrows the prejudices of her early training and achieves her full womanly development.

After *Rose of Dutcher's Coolly,* Garland wrote over a dozen more novels, most of which were concerned with the West. Sometimes, as in *Money Magic,* he begins in the West and moves on, in this case to Chicago and New York. *Her Mountain Lover* (1901) gives us a Western hero in London. One of the least believable of his books, *The Light of the Star* (1904), concerns the New York stage, in which he had become interested both through his brother's career as an actor and his own friendship with James A. Herne, who was trying to bring realism into the theater. And two—*The Tyranny of the Dark* (1905) and *Victor Ollnee's Discipline* (1911)—reflect their author's lifelong interest in spiritistic phenomena.[5] More typical, however, are such stirring tales of Western adventure, organized around a Western, or national, problem as *The Captain of the Grey-Horse Troop* (justice for the Indians); *Hesper* (1903)—(the Cripple Creek mine "war" and the infringement of the rights of the individual by combinations of both labor and capital); and *Cavanagh, Forest Ranger* (conservation, in which Garland had come to be enlisted through his friendship with Theodore Roosevelt).

Howells thought *Money Magic* the best of Garland's later novels, and this is a reasonable view. The theme would have suited Howells himself, and Garland's execution is admirable in many ways. Whether Bertha Gilman, of Sibley Junction, Colorado, would ever have married Mart Haney if he had not been shot by a gunman and summoned her to what he believed his deathbed, so that he might make her his wife and leave his wealth to her, nobody will ever know. (He had already sold out his saloon and gambling interests in order to try to make himself worthy.) Unfortunately, however, he did not die, but survived as a wreck of his former self, and the young wife who had expected that what he had to give would satisfy all

[5] For the factual record of Garland's life in this aspect, see *The Shadow World* (1908); *Forty Years of Psychic Research* (1936); *The Mystery of the Buried Crosses* (1939).

her needs soon discovered that she was asking too much of herself. She hews to the line as long as the book lasts, though not without much misery both to her husband and to herself, but it is Mart who at last solves the problem by deliberately taking himself into an altitude where he knows his weakened heart can no longer function.

Garland is generally scolded for the change of temper which came over his fiction with his Western novels, and the more emotional brethren even accused him of having "betrayed" the sacred "cause" and "sold himself" for financial security and membership in the Academy. A conspicuous dissenter from this view was Howells, himself a realist and a Socialist, who had felt from the beginning that Garland was "unconsciously romantic at heart" and devoted to reality only because he "did not know unreality." There was never any fundamental change in Garland, Howells insisted; "he is always what he was: mindful of his own past, and tenderly loyal to the simplest life, as embracing not only the potentialities but the actualities of beauty, of sublimity." Garland himself may seem to agree with his critics when he speaks of the pleasantness of his later themes and the larger acceptability of his mellower books to editors and readers. That there was an element of worldly wisdom in the change he made is no doubt true, but it is not necessary to become hysterical about it. Writers do not usually turn away from their native material until they have exhausted the use they can make of it, and the truth of the matter is that, outside of *Main-Travelled Roads,* Garland's strongest social and economic convictions had never directly inspired his best work. Moreover, his radicalism was an agrarian radicalism; he belonged to the old Jeffersonian school. It was never possible for him to follow the labor movement along any of its later lines of development; both his temperament and his convictions forbade this.

His richest and most characteristic mood was achieved late, in *A Son of the Middle Border* and its successors. Here, if anywhere, he turned his America into literature:

It all lies in the unchanging realm of the past—this land of my childhood. Its charm, its strange dominion cannot return save in the poet's reminiscent dream. No money, no railway train can take us back to it. It did not in truth exist—it was a magical world, born of the vibrant

union of youth and firelight, of music and the voice of moaning winds—
a union which can never come again to you or me, father, uncle, brother,
till the coulee meadows bloom again unscarred of spade or plow.

3. *Stephen Crane, Harbinger*

It would be difficult to prove that Crane was influenced by Zola.
He was in no sense a bookish person, and in his short life there
was little time for reading. Most of the writers whom it was proper
to admire in his time he cordially detested; for good measure, he
also detested Oscar Wilde, whom it was most improper to admire.
He even confined his admiration of Mark Twain largely to *Life on
the Mississippi.* He had some admiration for Flaubert and later for
James, and he once declared, inaccurately, that his "creed" was
identical with that of Howells and Garland. Tolstoy he called "the
writer I admire most of all," yet he found grave faults even in *War
and Peace* and humorously declared that he would like to rewrite it
and show how it ought to have been done.

Crane was not a great writer—he died too young for that—but he
was a writer of amazing, almost miraculous, prescience. He points
the way for the naturalists in *Maggie, A Girl of the Streets;* he
anticipates the "stream-of-consciousness" writers in *The Red Badge
of Courage;* his poems were years ahead of the Imagists. *Maggie*
suggests such Englishmen as Arthur Morrison, William Pett Ridge,
and Edwin Pugh, but Crane got it straight from the Bowery. The
poems may have been influenced by Emily Dickinson or Olive
Schreiner, but to Amy Lowell they seemed more suggestive of the
French symbolists and of certain Chinese and Japanese poets whom
Crane certainly did not know. One cannot read the *Badge* without
thinking of Conrad's *Nigger of the Narcissus,* which came out three
years later. *The Monster* reminded Carl Van Doren of Sinclair
Lewis, "The Bride Comes to Yellow Sky" of Willa Cather, the
stories of fighting and rough adventure of Ernest Hemingway. In
these cases there was obviously no influence—upon Crane at any rate
—and I doubt that Zola exercised much more. In short, Stephen
Crane was that despair of the academic critic, a highly "original"
writer.

He was born, on November 1, 1871, in Newark, New Jersey, the

fourteenth and youngest child of a Methodist minister, and named
after the ancestor who was believed to have signed the Declaration
of Independence. Both his father and his mother were remarkable
persons. He studied briefly—or perhaps one should say he participated in sports—at Lafayette and at Syracuse; in 1891 he went to
New York to become a newspaper reporter. Nobody would publish
Maggie in 1893, but when it was privately printed it won Crane the
friendship and encouragement of both Garland and Howells. In
1894 *The Red Badge of Courage* made his reputation. Having written imaginatively of war, he was chosen by the powers-that-be to
see the monster at first hand, as war correspondent both in Greece
and in Cuba. Toward the close of his life he lived in England, where
Conrad, Wells, and others became his friends. He died of tuberculosis in the Black Forest, on June 5, 1900.[6]

When Crane was rediscovered in the 1920's, it became the fashion
to belabor the editors and critics of the 'nineties for the disgusting
Puritanism they showed when they failed to appreciate *Maggie*. The
truth is that the book is far from being a masterpiece; rereading it
today, one finds little justification for Howells's discovery of a
cleansing pity and terror in it. It is a remarkable book for its break
with current fashions in writing and in thinking, for Crane refused
either to sentimentalize his material or to moralize over it—("I had
no other purpose in writing 'Maggie' than to show people to people
as they seem to me")[7]—but the immaturity of the artist is seen
clearly in his evident determination to be as "dreadful" as possible,
and the drunken mother is broad enough to have stepped out of the

[6] No writer was ever favored with a more fantastic legend than Crane;
see Thomas Beer's Appendix. It is true that he led an almost insanely bohemian life; he married a Jacksonville "madam," who, incidentally, made him
a very faithful and devoted wife. (See H. R. Crane, "My Uncle SC," *Am
Merc*, XXXI, 1934, 24-29, and Thomas Beer, "Mrs. SC," *ibid.*, pp. 289-295.)
Berryman declares that he drank little and burned up cigarettes without smoking them, and that there is no evidence whatever for the legend that he used
opium. The testimony to his honor by those who knew him best is unassailable; Conrad declared that "there was in Crane a strain of chivalry which
made him safe to trust with one's life."

[7] He does not altogether avoid commentary; see the end of Section XVI.
Perhaps the most didactic passage in Crane is at the close of "The Blue Hotel"
—"Every sin is the result of a collaboration. . . ."

comic strip. It was surely a technical fault, also, to center the reader's attention at the outset not upon the girl who gives the story its name but upon her brother.

Sexually the book is timid. Maggie's seduction is passed over, quite in the Victorian manner; despite its title, the narrative is in no sense the history of a prostitute. Maggie turns to prostitution only for a moment at the end of the story, after both her lover and her family have deserted her, and rather than continue along that road, she kills herself.[8]

But between *Maggie* and *The Red Badge of Courage* an astonishing development has occurred. The story of the (unnamed) Battle of Chancellorsville from the point of view of a raw recruit who sees nothing of its general design, the book was indebted importantly to none of the older and more orthodox literary sources that have been claimed for it with the exception of the *Century's* historical series, "Battles and Leaders of the Civil War."[9] The rest came from oral tradition transformed by imagination, from the recollections of those who, like Crane's Henry Fleming, saw the war only as the Red Monster impinged malevolently or capriciously upon them.

It was no wonder that Conrad loved the *Badge;* Henry is a true Conrad hero. "He must accumulate information of himself. . . ." "He was about to be measured." "Without salve, he could not, he thought [after his initial flight in battle], wear the sore badge of his dishonor through life." Crane's psychological way with an adventure story is Conrad's also, and his impressionistic method of presentation; like *Lord Jim,* the *Badge* is something much more subtle than the conventional story of the man who first disgraces himself, then atones by his resolute handling of the second chance. And while it is not much of a novel, if by a novel you mean a complicated and

---

[8] *George's Mother* (1896), Crane's other novelette of the slums, attempts less than *Maggie,* but, within its limits, it is more completely realized. We understand both the nagging, pious woman and the young workingman who finds no escape from her loving tyranny except with his fair weather friends at the saloon.

[9] See, however, Thomas Beer's discussion (*SC,* p. 47) of Harry Castleman's "Frank" stories, which Crane read in his boyhood; L. U. Pratt, "A Possible Source for 'The Red Badge of Courage,'" *AL,* XI (1939), 1-10; H. T. Webster, "Wilbur F. Hinman's 'Corporal Si Klegg' and SC's 'The Red Badge of Courage,'" *AL,* XI (1939), 285-293.

highly organized narrative, no book was ever more successful in fusing the inner and the outer action to achieve an impression absolutely unified.

It was no accident but a point which must be grasped by anyone who would understand Crane that he should have written the *Badge* before ever he smelled powder. He told Garland that his knowledge of war had been gained at football. Later his experiences and observations in Greece brought him the happy conviction that the book was "all right," but in themselves they produced no better novel than the inconsequential *Active Service* (1899).[10] Richard Harding Davis, the most "successful" of the group of journalist-fictionists to which Crane in a sense belonged, once wrote:

A reporter can describe a thing he has seen in such a way that he can make the reader see it, too. A man of genius can describe something he has *never* seen, or any one else for that matter, in such a way that the reader will exclaim: "I have never committed a murder; but if I had that's just the way I'd feel about it."

That is why Crane failed as a reporter—in journalism and in fiction. He had to realize his material imaginatively. He could catch a whole aspect of the American scene in a paragraph: the melodrama theater in *Maggie;* evening in a small town in *The Monster.* But he could not transcribe.[11]

H. L. Mencken has acutely observed that "He had . . . no literary small talk; he could not manage what the musicians call passage-work." His characters tend to be figures of allegory, as in an early D. W. Griffith film. It is not surprising, therefore, that with the *Badge* his service as novelist should have been nearly completed. The love story of *The Third Violet* (1897) is of no more consequence than *Active Service;* and he left *The O'Ruddy* (1903), an old-fashioned Irish romance, to be written three-quarters by Robert

[10] He wrote more effectively of war in the short pieces in *The Little Regiment* (1896) and *Wounds in the Rain* (1900). *Whilomville Stories* (1900) are interesting for their unsentimental treatment of children. Berryman doubts his failure as a war correspondent. See Ames W. Williams, "SC, War Correspondent," *New Col,* I (1948), 113-123.

[11] The great story called "The Open Boat" is the most important exception to this statement. See Victor A. Elconin, "SC at Asbury Park," *AL,* XX (1948), 275-289.

Barr. Except for the novelette *The Monster* (1898), all his most significant later work was in the short story.

The Monster need not be discussed in extenso here, but one point should be made: it is no more essentially a horror story than *Maggie* is a study of sex. Four words give us all we know of Henry Johnson after he had been burned by the acid in rescuing the doctor's child: "He had no face." The doctor's unwise gratitude keeps him alive, and Crane uses his presence in the little town to test the decency and humanity of its inhabitants.

Vernon Loggins speaks suggestively of Crane's style as "a meaningful mingling of unexpected and curious words." The famous last sentence of Chapter IX in the *Badge*—"The red sun was pasted in the sky like a wafer"—has been lauded for its brilliance and excoriated for its artificiality. It is, of course, both brilliant and artificial; Crane was a great phrasemaker, but it would be too much to say that he never forced the note. Joseph Hergesheimer has rightly praised the dialect of the *Badge*—not "so much a dialect as it is the flexible and successful record of what promised to be the new language of a new land." Crane was far more of a "marvelous boy" than Chatterton ever was, for his talent was far more genuine. How much he would have developed if he had lived, it is difficult to say; his last work is not, in all its aspects, completely reassuring. In a sense he was one of those persons who do not need to live because they know all the answers beforehand. He pointed the way. He pointed many ways. And it is no disrespect to him to say that he did not in himself take the naturalistic novel very far.

4. *The Achievement of Frank Norris*

Frank Norris had only three more years of life than Crane. In some ways he was considerably less grown up at the time of his death. But unlike Crane he was most emphatically a novelist. And though his large conceptions still had something boyishly grandiose about them, he put an achievement behind him which still seems a large one.

Norris was born in Chicago, on March 5, 1870. His father had come from Michigan to earn a million dollars in the wholesale jewelry business; his mother had had theatrical experience. When the family moved to San Francisco in 1885, Chinatown, the Barbary Coast, and the Presidio each contributed its share toward quickening the son's imagination.

He knew already that business was not for him, but he had not yet discovered his destiny in literature. Instead, he studied art, first in San Francisco, then under Bouguereau, at the Atelier Julien in Paris. In 1890 he began four years as a college playboy at the University of California. He was much more serious at Harvard, where he studied under Professor Lewis E. Gates; here he wrote much of *McTeague* (1899) and all of *Vandover and the Brute* (published posthumously, 1914). He was in South Africa at the time of the Jameson raid, and served unimportantly as war correspondent in Cuba during the Spanish-American War. In 1896 he joined the staff of *The Wave* in San Francisco. S. S. McClure brought him to New York; he left McClure to join the new firm of Doubleday, Page and Company for whom he "discovered" both *Lord Jim* and *Sister Carrie*.

Besides *McTeague*, Norris had published, by the end of the century, three comparatively unimportant novels: *Moran of the Lady Letty* (1898), *Blix* (1899), and *A Man's Woman* (1900). He was now engaged heart and soul in realizing his great Epic of the Wheat, "an idea as big as all outdoors," from which he planned to go on to a trilogy about the Battle of Gettysburg.

The Octopus, which concerns the growing of the wheat in California, appeared in 1901, to open even the eyes that had been blind to the merits of *McTeague*. But *The Pit*, which deals with the selling of the wheat in Chicago, was left to appear posthumously in 1903; and *The Wolf*, which was to have pictured the consumption of the wheat in Europe, was never written, for Frank Norris died, on October 25, 1902, following an operation for appendicitis.[12]

Norris completely missed Zola—and apparently all modern French literature—during his years in Paris; here all his enthusiasm was for Froissart, the opera, fencing, and medieval armor and tapestry. He tried to paint an immense picture of the Battle of Crécy; and his first book, published at his mother's expense, was *Yvernelle* (1891), a romantic, chivalric poem in three cantos. There can be no question

---

[12] See the story, "A Deal in Wheat," in the collection of the same title (1903). D. W. Griffith made this into a one-reel Biograph film.

as to his enthusiasm for Zola during his college days and after-wards,[13] but it must not be forgotten that he interpreted Zola as a romanticist. Materialistic determinism was foreign both to Norris's buoyant nature and to his moral idealism, and even when he thought he was accepting it, he seems not fully to have grasped its implica-tions. "Norris accepted determinism only in so far as it appealed to his dramatic sense. . . . He followed Zola because the latter, in pre-senting man as the victim of external laws, allowed for big forces and hence big conflicts. . . ."[14]

The simple note of conflict is most clearly sounded in *A Man's Woman*—Norris's only really bad book[15]—and in *Moran of the Lady Letty*. Here Norris appears as one of the founders of the "red-blooded" school of Jack London. *Moran* was a deliberate attempt to write a short novel of adventure in the Stevenson tradition, but back of Stevenson lay its author's affection for the Scandinavian saga ma-terials he had first savored at Berkeley.[16] Norris had a weakness for "strong" women. The young Viking Moran fights, eats, swears, and drinks like a ruffian, and it is not until after Wilbur has slugged her in fair fight that she can bring herself to love him. As a love story, the book is bad; but it is good in so far as it savors of the sea, of the sagas, and of *Treasure Island*. Norris had sense enough not to permit

---

[13] See W. E. Martin, Jr., "FN's Reading at Harvard College," *AL*, VII (1935), 203-204. Lars Åhnebrink's *The Influence of Émile Zola on Frank Norris* (HUP, 1947) is a painstaking comparison between Norris's work and that of his supposed master.

[14] Franklin Walker, *Frank Norris*, p. 85. Zola was not, of course, the only literary influence upon Frank Norris. His mother read Scott and Dickens aloud to him during his formative years; the Dickens influence appears notably in many grotesques and type-sketches. Condy Rivers, of *Blix*, who is a self-portrait, has a tremendous admiration for Kipling and had "suffered an almost fatal attack of Harding Davis." Walker credits Davis's Van Bibber stories with some influence upon *Vandover;* Oscar Cargill thinks that Kipling's "The Mark of the Beast" was important here. A certain affinity with the spirit of Victor Hugo is evident, and there has recently been considerable tendency among students of Norris to credit Tolstoy with a strong influence upon him.

[15] This tale of Arctic exploration has some good qualities: it presents, for example, a good picture of life under extreme cold. But the action is hardly more than a series of grossly artificial settings for moral conflicts every bit as unconvincing as were ever the great "situations" in the old melodramas.

[16] For a more direct use of saga materials, see the story "Grettir at Dragney," in the short story collection called *The Third Circle* (1909).

Wilbur and Moran to marry. Instead, a vengeful Chinaman sticks a knife into the girl, and she and her ship float out to sea together.

Blix, a fictionized treatment of Norris's courtship of Jeannette Black, whom he married in 1900, and of his own beginnings as a writer, is much better. The simplest of all Norris's books, it catches the spirit of a sweet, absurd youth, and even when it seems ridiculous, it is endearing.

Norris seems more naturalistic in *McTeague* than he does in *The Octopus,* but this impression may be due merely to the more sordid character of his materials. Many critics have found the charming little romance of Miss Baker and Old Grannis, which furnishes one of the subplots, too *Cranford*-like for *McTeague.* I do not see why. Shall we object to McTeague's taking Trina and her mother to the Orpheum vaudeville? would a performance of Charles Reade's dramatic version of Zola's *L'Assommoir* have preserved the tone of the book better? The grotesquerie of Maria Macapa's tragedy is, perhaps, more questionable because less realistic; and the difficulty with McTeague's symbolic canary—surely the hardiest bird in all literature!—is simply that one cannot believe in him. McTeague's "sixth sense," which warns him of approaching danger, also creates some difficulty. As for *Vandover and the Brute,* its theme—the degeneration of a well-meaning young man through dissipation—is very naturalistic, very French; but Norris handles it in the spirit of an Anglo-Saxon moralist; this almost frightening book is surely one of the most powerful sermons ever preached. But the very title shows Norris's bias; the division of man's nature between body and soul is foreign to the whole spirit of naturalism.[17]

It would be unreasonable to go to Frank Norris for an elaborate theory of fiction, but this is not to say that there are no penetrating

[17] After the girl he has seduced commits suicide, Vandover sees himself responsible not only for the destruction of her life but "for the ruin of that something in her which was more than life." The sentence is characteristic of Norris. In *The Octopus* he plays about a bit with the old fertility cults, but in general he tends to shy at the very thought of sex, and one cannot help wondering whether some youthful disillusionment in the world of the Imperial Hotel which Vandover inhabits may have warped his outlook at this point. The beast symbol is very effective in *Vandover,* but why should poor McTeague be called a beast when he has done nothing else than feel honest passion for Trina?

observations in *The Responsibilities of the Novelist* (1903). There are as many definitions of romance as there are definers; Norris's definition is that romance is "the kind of fiction that takes cognizance of variations from the type of normal life." He knows that neither realism nor romance is an accident of geography, that there is "as much romance on Michigan Avenue as there is realism in King Arthur's Court." And he is as sure as Stevenson ever was that no novelist can represent life as it is.

But it is the word "responsibilities" that strikes the keynote. For Frank Norris public talent, no less than public office, was a public trust. The author of *McTeague* was in a strong position to plead without weakness for constructive reading matter for the "Very Young Girl." He sweeps away the cant that the novelist's personal morality does not affect his work and urges young writers that if they would succeed they must be good men as well as good novelists.

The book is not all as good as that. The discussion of education and educational problems[18] is that of a barbarian, and Norris's consideration of style is not much better. It would be absurd to say that Frank Norris was not an artist. His effects are coherent and carefully planned, and he knew how to build effectively toward an end. Yet he was capable, too, of very bad art. His references to Moran's "biceps and deltoids" must cause even his best friends to wince, and so does his rant about "the symphony of energy, coeval with the centuries, renascent, ordained, eternal." In one passage he praises Blix and Condy because "their brains were almost as empty of thought or of reflection as those of two fine, clean animals." There were times when he could be like them.

Yet it is precisely this kind of thing which makes Frank Norris such an interesting writer. It is very hard to say what he would have done with the years he never had. There was one whole side of him that was not artist at all but journalist, sociologist, reformer. His social consciousness was deepening toward the end of his life. Would the sociologist have killed the artist in him at last? Or would he have brought his varied rich endowments into harmony?

When the collected edition of Frank Norris's works was published, the publishers stamped the spine of the books with a sheaf of golden

[18] See "Salt and Sincerity," in *The Responsibilities of the Novelist.*

wheat. What this amounts to practically is a declaration that *The Octopus* is his greatest book. And so it is, though *McTeague,* the story of the unlicensed dentist whose fiber collapses under adversity, while his pretty little wife is increasingly possessed by the lust of gold until we find her at last wallowing naked in a bed full of gold pieces while her estranged husband starves outside her window, is the prime manifestation of its particular kind of power in American literature before Dreiser. But Norris himself told Howells that he did not get the whole truth into *McTeague,* and he was right.[19]

He did not get it all in *The Octopus* either, but he did get a good deal of it. There has been considerable discussion during recent years as to whether *The Octopus* is philosophically consistent.[20] Whether it is artistically unified would seem to be a more important consideration. The story, with its numerous subplots and its vast social and economic implications, is built around the struggle for land between the ranchers and the Southern Pacific Railroad; the locale is the San Joaquin Valley in California; the climax is furnished by the Mussel Slough tragedy of 1880. The tale of Annixter and Hilma Tree, of the man's redemption through his love for her, is well integrated with the main plot, but the story of Vanamee and Angèle Varian—"pure romance," Norris called it—"oh, even mysticism, if you like, a sort of allegory"—does not seem quite at home in the book. On the other hand, the fact that the ranchers who fight the railroad—and are destroyed by it—are not proletarians but agrarian capitalists does not seem very important. *The Octopus* is not a perfectly integrated novel, but it is full of life and of warm, generous feeling. After all, "a man's reach should exceed his grasp. . . ."

The Pit, which was by far Norris's best-selling novel, falls far below *The Octopus,* partly because grain-speculating in Chicago was a less rewarding subject than the one he had found in the earlier

[19] In 1923 Erich von Stroheim made *McTeague* into one of the best of American films, *Greed;* and again, as in 1899, cries of distress were heard from the tender-minded. See Louis Jacobs, *The Rise of the American Film* (HB, 1930), p. 346 ff.

[20] See H. W. Reninger, "Norris Explains 'The Octopus': A Correlation of His Theory and Practice," *AL,* XII (1940), 218-227; C. C. Walcutt, "FN on Realism and Naturalism," *AL,* XIII (1941), 61-63; George W. Meyer, "A New Interpretation of 'The Octopus,'" *CE,* IV (1943), 351-359.

book, and one less well suited to his own particular gifts and interests, and partly because there is a tendency to lose the main theme in the personal history of Curtis Jadwin and his wife. Suggested by Joseph Leiter's historic "corner" of 1897, the book ends with Norris's reaffirmation of his faith in this earth that we inhabit and in the wheat itself as triumphant over the men who had tried to control it for their paltry and selfish ends. Whether it was naturalism or not, it was an exhilarating expression of Frank Norris's idealism.

5. *Jack London and the Cult of Primitive Sensation*

The cult of raw meat and red blood to which Norris had occasionally lent himself was destined for the most extreme expression it was ever to find this side of pulp stories in the work of Jack London, one of the few American writers who have addressed a world audience. When he died at the same time as the Emperor Franz Joseph, the European press gave him the lion's share of its space.

London was born in San Francisco, on January 12, 1876, the unacknowledged, illegitimate son of "Professor" W. H. Chaney by Flora Wellman. Chaney, who was of Maine origin, was half scholar and thinker (with perhaps even a touch of genius in his make-up) and half charlatan, specializing in astrology. Flora was the erratic daughter of a good Ohio family of Welsh extraction.

A nervous, highly sensitive boy, Jack London spent an impecunious, unsettled childhood, selling newspapers to help support the family, assisting in the spiritualistic séances conducted by his mother, and hanging about the water-front saloons in Oakland and San Francisco. At fifteen, he became an "oyster pirate" in San Francisco Bay. He worked in a laundry; he shipped on a sealing voyage to Japan; he took to the road as a hobo and was clapped into jail. In 1897 he joined the gold rush to the Klondike.

But all the while he was living in another world with equal intensity. Irving's *Tales of the Alhambra* and Ouida's *Signa* had awakened his passion for literature, which was wisely guided by Ina Coolbrith, when she was librarian at Oakland. His formal schooling, at Oakland High School and the University of California, was brief, but he read and studied voraciously, sometimes as much as nineteen hours a day. He read Kipling, Stevenson, Melville, Shaw, Zola, Tolstoy, Flaubert, Hardy, and Conrad; Spencer, Darwin, Nietzsche, and Karl Marx; the standard philosophers and economists. When he began to write, he deluged the magazines with his manuscripts, as described in *Martin Eden.* The first story he sold went to *The Overland Monthly* for five dollars. He "arrived" in January, 1900, when "An Odyssey of the North" appeared in the *Atlantic,* and he was importantly sponsored, in the course of his ensuing career, first by S. S. McClure, and later by George Brett, of Macmillan.

He married Bess Maddern, a cousin of the actress Mrs. Fiske, then deserted her and their two daughters (though he continued to provide for them), for Charmian Kittredge. He went abroad to report the Russo-Japanese War. He sailed his own boat to the South Seas, where he picked up rare tropical diseases. He made incendiary speeches throughout the United States and twice ran for mayor of Oakland on the Socialist ticket. Though he earned a million with his pen, he was always in need of money, borrowing and demanding advances. He built up a vast patriarchal estate in California, pouring thousands upon thousands into his boat and into the mansion "Wolf House," which burned before he could move into it, and supporting hordes of workmen, dependents, and unfortunates. He died, probably by suicide, on November 22, 1916.

Jack London wrote fifty books in sixteen years. To the general public he is first of all the chronicler of the Klondike, of man and brute against the frozen north. Yet of the twenty books that can be called novels, only five are set, wholly or in part, in Alaska: *A Daughter of the Snows* (1902); *The Call of the Wild* (1903); *White Fang* (1906); *Burning Daylight* (1910); and *Smoke Bellew* (1912). The second of these, his first important achievement, is probably his most famous book; as all the world knows, it is the story of a dog who reverts to the ways of his savage ancestors. In *White Fang* London reversed the process; his other dog stories—*Jerry of the Islands* and *Michael, Brother of Jerry* (both 1917)—take place in the South Seas; so do *Adventure* (1911) and *Hearts of Three* (1920). *The Sea Wolf* (1904) and *The Mutiny of the Elsinore* (1914) are, of course, sea stories; *The Game* (1905) and *The Abysmal Brute* (1913) deal with prize-fighting. *Martin Eden* (1908) is a fictionized autobiography.[21] *The Valley of the Moon* (1913) and *The Little Lady of the Big House* (1916) have California settings; both are love stories, but *The Valley of the Moon* adds a far-ranging consideration of agricultural and industrial problems.

Five books on varied themes are bound together by a common element of fantasy or imagination. *Before Adam* (1906) describes the dream-life of a man whose racial memory is so freakishly powerful that he lives over in his sleep the experiences of a primitive ancestor. *The Iron Heel* (1907) tells of the fascist dictatorship (as we would now call it) which is imposed upon mankind by a dying capitalism and of the abortive First Revolt at Chicago in 1917. *The Scarlet Plague* (1915) pictures the return to barbarism which followed the destruction of all save a handful of human beings by a new and irresistible disease, early in the twenty-first century. In *The Star Rover* (1915), a California "lifer" learns how to escape the torture of the strait jacket by "the little death," which means that he discovers how to free his spirit from his body and to roam through his past lives.

Jack London always insisted that his books were not mere adventure stories; they had a meaning. Theoretically, he was materialist, Socialist, Darwinian, Nietzschean—all in one; and many of his admirers have trustingly envisioned him as perched upon the backs of all these horses, even when they were galloping furiously in different directions. Temperamentally he was closest to Nietzsche, as his supermen and superdogs attest, though his daughter declares roundly that "he was so enchanted by the philosopher's vocabulary and slogans that he noted little else." With Marxism he had much

---

[21] *John Barleycorn* (1913), though often spoken of as a novel, is a factual record, with some manipulation for literary effectiveness, of London's experiences with alcohol and a passionate plea for prohibition. "The pseudo-civilization into which I was born permitted everywhere licensed shops for the sale of soul-poison. The system of life was so organized that I (and millions like me) was lured and drawn and driven to the poison shops." It took him many years to learn to like alcohol. He drank first because in his milieu light, warmth, and camaraderie were to be found only in the saloons, and because he had to prove that he was a man among drinking men. What he really craved was candy! Given London's temperament, his argument is unanswerable. He was wrong only in his idealistic belief that once women were given the vote, they would put John Barleycorn out of business.

less in common, and it became progressively less important in his work as time passed. He believed in "leaders," and he rejected the ideal of universal brotherhood in favor of a passionately-held Anglo-Saxon racism. It is true that he claimed to have written *Martin Eden* to show that life is not worth living without Socialist sanctions, but he himself admitted that nobody had ever got this idea from the book itself. Socialism plays no part whatever in *The Valley of the Moon,* whose hero and heroine extricate themselves from the economic morass by calling up the pioneering spirit of their covered wagon ancestors. The truth of the matter seems to be that Marxism held Jack London, in so far as it appealed to him at all, in two contradictory ways: through his humanitarianism and love for the underdog and through his passion for sensation. Fabian methods he always scorned: the old order must go down in blood. Many Socialists complained, consequently, that *The Iron Heel* had set the cause back in the United States for many years. And when, at the end of his life, he had to choose between following the party line and supporting World War I, the party went down and out, though he asseverated loudly, of course, that it was not he by whom the cause had been betrayed.

How far his materialism was due to an uncritical reading of writers like Haeckel and how far to a natural reaction against what one supposes must have been the pretty rackety spiritualism of his mother, it would be difficult to say. But it is clear that it did not meet his own emotional needs, and when he is most creative, he is inclined to go beyond it. London's natural tone was wholesome and manly. He was kind, generous, patient, and forbearing; he fought aboveboard and he was incapable of holding a grudge. At the beginning, he was inclined to respond eagerly to life and to believe in its goodness; his thinking caused him to regard such reactions as dynamic illusions and vital lies; later still, John Barleycorn's "White Logic" destroyed these illusions and the taste of life turned bitter in his mouth. When Martin Eden falls in love, he finds his materialistic creed quite incapable of explaining his experience. In *The Sea Wolf,* London is obviously thrilled by the superman aspects of the brutal Wolf Larsen, but he chooses to tell the story from the point of view of the aesthetically sensitive Van Weyden, a believer in spiritual values. In *Before Adam,* the first example of cooperation among the brute-men calls up visions "of Damon and Pythias, of life-saving crews and Red Cross nurses, of martyrs and leaders of forlorn hopes, of Father Damien, and of the Christ himself. . . ." London was capable of finding the great fact of Anglo-Saxon history in its acceptance of the religion of Jesus; capable, too, of talking about "the divine possibilities" ahead of man. As he grew older, this note was more frequently sounded. The heroine of *The Valley of the Moon,* though free of "conventional religion," yet has a "deeply religious" nature, and the book leaves the impression that the universe itself is friendly to man and that human maladjustments are man-made. Finally, *The Star Rover* not only invokes the reincarnation hypothesis which had been specifically denied in *Before Adam* but throws over materialism in all its phases. Comte and Bergson are quoted to teach that "Matter is the only illusion" and that "There is no death. Life is spirit, and spirit cannot die."[22]

Writing to Jack London was never more than a means to an end, and the end was material advancement. "In a certain sense," Joan London observes shrewdly, "this attitude was typically working class. . . ." He wrote his thousand words a day, and when they were done he was finished. He never skipped a day because the spirit failed him, and apparently he was never caught up by his daemon and carried beyond the daily stint. He professed, indeed, to hate writing, and in his last years he was frankly cynical and un-painstaking about it; it was because he had betrayed his art that his art, at last, failed to save him from the forces that were destroying him.

The most important single literary influence upon him was probably that of Kipling. He valued "strength of utterance" above "precision of utterance," and in so far as he had a literary creed it was to have his characters tell the story by deeds and utterance, eliminating the author as much as possible. His style, characteristically

[22] I am not forgetting that these are dramatic utterances, nor do I argue that London underwent any kind of religious or philosophical conversion. There is no evidence to indicate that he believed in reincarnation; he used it as a literary device. The inadequacy of the materialistic frame of reference for his art is nevertheless clear.

simple and free-flowing, can be eloquent; sometimes it is repetitive and clumsy; it is hardly ever carefully wrought.

He was more storyteller than novelist, and he is rarely satisfying in his structure. In *Martin Eden* the hero's struggle for education and self-expression is quite convincing, but his success-story turns to caricature. London nearly always fails in *developing* his characters. Burning Daylight is comparatively believable in the Klondike, but he is merely ludicrous when he gets his money back from the Wall Street swindlers by merely drawing a bead on them; neither do we believe in his final abdication as a tycoon. *The Valley of the Moon* is a little of everything: an idealistic love story, an economic novel, a Pacific Coast travelogue, and a treatise on agriculture. Even *The Sea Wolf,* surely the best of the more ambitious novels by ordinary critical standards, is not all off the same bolt.

Perhaps London came closest to complete success in *White Fang* and *The Call of the Wild.* Theodore Roosevelt's accusation of nature-faking must be at least partially sustained, and if nature-faking is a greater fault here than in "Krazy Kat" or "The Nun's Priest's Tale," the reason is simply that London's books set up certain claims in the way of scientific accuracy that the other works never made. These two stories are, nevertheless, eloquent, impassioned, and spontaneous; they represent a daring and successful use of the imagination. And though the "red in tooth and claw" aspect is somewhat overplayed, it must be admitted that this is nicely overbalanced by the account of Scott's conquest of White Fang through love.

What place in American literature will finally be assigned to Jack London, it is still, more than a generation after his death, somewhat difficult to say. His daughter calls him "last of the writers to celebrate the American frontier, first to trumpet the battles on the frontier of social justice." Though neither her "first" nor her "last" is accurate, the statement is still very suggestive. His materials and his beliefs were more naturalistic than his art. As Professor Pattee has observed, he seems realistic when he is writing about a life that we do not know, but he is much less convincing when he gets upon our own ground. He wrote of "the stress and strain of life, its fevers and sweats and wild indulgences" as a lovesick boy writes about his sweetheart; he made a romance of savagery, the "survival of the

fittest," "the Law of Club and Fang," and "the Dominant Pri-
mordial Beast."

Some of this was adolescent daydreams. Some of it was wholesome, bracing tonic. Some of it was legitimate revolt against the
menace of "civilized" life in his time. To most of his readers he
meant courage and adventure, the vicarious fulfillment of their
action-desires in a world which seemed to be placing less and less
premium upon self-realization through physical activities. In America, at least, most of them were comparatively indifferent to his
radicalism, and probably his "primitivism" and "brutality" did them
little harm. In sexual matters he honored all the magazine-taboos.[23]

His challenge is, in the last analysis, the challenge of his own
personality. He was a hack writer of genius, and, as has been said
of Byron, the faults of his work were the faults of his life. In his
essay on Jack London,[24] Van Wyck Brooks quotes Lowes Dickinson's saying that "The Red-blood is happiest if he dies in the prime
of life; otherwise he may easily end with suicide." For civilized
men there is nothing else quite so artificial as primitivism, and the
vitality cult may well be a sign of deficient vitality. "He hated the
oblivion of sleep," so Jack London expressed it of his other self,
Martin Eden. "There was too much to do, too much life to live.
He grudged every moment of life sleep robbed him of, and before
the clock had ceased its clattering he was head and ears in the
washbasin and thrilling to the cold bite of the water." Such eager
appetence has its charm, but it may easily overreach itself in other
things besides alcohol. The strange thing about Jack London is his
clear-headed knowledge of himself. Both *Martin Eden* and *John
Barleycorn* attest that there were no limits to his courage and his
sincerity in facing the truth. But the knowledge that was given him

[23] He probably felt little sense of repression in doing this. Though he had
lived with coarse women, he never lost the typical American reverence for
good ones. As a student at Oakland High School, he was as shy with girls
as any of his immature classmates. Not until he sees the cherry-stains on Ruth's
lips can Martin Eden make himself believe that she is a woman of flesh and
blood and not a goddess. Hobart Bosworth, "My Jack London," *Mark Twain
Quarterly,* V, Fall-Winter, 1942-1943, pp. 2+, testifies to JL's "purity of mind
and cleanliness of thought," his dislike of filthy talk even among men.

[24] In *Sketches in Criticism* (Du, 1932).

was not a saving knowledge. Any time during his earlier life, he might, it would seem, have turned back upon the way he was traveling. He might even have stopped drinking. He chose not to do so, and he made his choice in the clear knowledge of what it entailed. Like Isadora Duncan, like Oscar Wilde, he threw away his extraordinary charm and squandered much of his genius. It does not matter very much whether his death was suicidal or not. His life was. If morphine had not killed him, uremic poisoning would soon have done the job. The night of November 21-22, 1916 simply set the seal upon decisions he had made long ago.

CHAPTER XII

VOICES OF THE NEW CENTURY

1901: Jan. 1: The new century came in with God knows what in its shut
hands and was welcomed. We may entertain devil or angel unawares.

S. Weir Mitchell

1. Mary Austin, Sybil

Carl Van Doren said of Mary Austin that her books "were wells
driven into America to bring up water for her countrymen, though
they may not have recognized their thirst." She was the foremost
sybil of our time. "What other woman," asked H. G. Wells, "could
touch her?" Yet her place in the history of the novel is a comparatively small one. In her own words, her work belonged "to the
quality of experience called Folk, and to the frame of behavior
known as Mystical." Disdaining "the male ritual of rationalization"
in favor of more direct, intuitional methods, she experimented with
"the utterly familiar and still mysterious and exciting stuff of ourselves." Her best work lies in that shadowy No Man's Land which
overlaps the boundaries of science, art, and scholarship.

As a small child, under a walnut tree in Illinois, Mary Austin one
day achieved a direct apprehension of God—"the experienceable quality in the universe." Later she learned about prayer—in California
from the Paiute Indians, and in Italy from Cardinal Merry del Val
and Mother Veronica of the Blue Nuns. She had gone to Italy in
what she supposed to be the last months of her life, after her physician had sentenced her to die of cancer of the breast, but she became
so much interested in what she found there that she forgot about her
tumor, and when she had time to think of it again it was gone.
Prayer, as she conceived it, was a curiously unemotional thing, less
a matter of asking God for favors than of placing yourself, through

carefully studied and practiced technique, where the healing, unifying power of the universe can get at you.

The Indians helped because they had known how to adjust themselves to the land they lived in; their morality, their religion, their economics were all a part of the pattern of their physical environment. Long before the days of the Imagists, Mary Austin found in the rhythm of Indian chants the basis of all authentic American poetry. And when Owens Valley was drained of its water to supply Los Angeles, she was crushed by what she regarded as an outrage against nature; to the day of her death she expected the parched land to revenge itself fearfully upon the city. Viewed from her background in middle America and the West, New York and the industrial East held a disproportionate place in surveys of the United States. She criticized Eastern seaboard culture for facing Europe instead of America and found fault with an interpretation of American life which "centered in New York, with a small New England ell in the rear, and a rustic gazebo in Chicago. . . ."

Such a writer must violate many orthodoxies and outrage many prejudices, and when the eccentricities of Mary Austin's personality are taken into account, nobody should be surprised to learn that she was as bitterly hated as she was passionately loved. She was a curious combination of arrogance and selfless humility: she gave herself up to be "used" by impersonal forces, but those upon whose toes she trampled called her "God's mother-in-law." Worse still, her admirers did not often understand her much better than her detractors. Indeed, she did not always understand herself, and even when she did, she was not always able to explain herself to others. Mary Austin conducted her explorations upon the frontiers of consciousness, and we have as yet no vocabulary which is adequate to describe the experiences of such persons. The next stage in the development of human personality was perhaps embodied as clearly in her as in any human being of our time. But it may be generations before we shall surely know.

Mary Austin never wrote a bad novel, yet it is hardly an exaggeration to say that she never produced a novel that was entirely successful. What the land meant to her was best expressed in such sketches and stories as those contained in *The Land of Little Rain*

(1903), *The Flock* (1906), *The American Rhythm* (1923), and *The Land of Journey's Ending* (1924). For her mystical experiences and what she came to believe about them, we must go to such books as *Christ in Italy* (1912); *The Man Jesus* (1915), later *A Small Town Man* (1925); *Everyman's Genius* (1925); *Experiences Facing Death* (1931); and *Can Prayer Be Answered?* (1934).

Mary Hunter was born in Carlinville, Illinois, on September 9, 1868, but after her graduation from Blackburn College, she moved with her family to a homestead near Bakersfield, California. In California she became a teacher, and in 1891 she married Stafford Wallace Austin, vineyardist, later school superintendent and manager of an irrigation project, but their only child was mentally defective, and the marriage ended in divorce. Mrs. Austin suffered great physical and mental agony; she taught in various localities; and she lived in close contact with Indians and came to understand their ways. Her first story was sold to the *Overland Monthly* in 1892, but she did not "make" the *Atlantic* until about the turn of the century, and her first book was not published until 1903. She was the friend of many distinguished writers both here and in England and of two presidents of the United States—Theodore Roosevelt and Herbert Hoover. With George Sterling and Jack London, she helped found the artist colony at Carmel. She tried living in New York but found herself unable to feel at home there. In 1925 she settled at Santa Fe and became tremendously interested in reviving Spanish-Indian folk culture. She died on August 13, 1934.

Mary Austin's first novel, *Isidro* (1905), was an historical romance of Spanish California in the days preceding the secularizing of the missions. It has a young hero designed for the priesthood, who falls in love with a girl disguised as a boy; it has murder, journeying friars and Indians, and a lost child restored to her father. The story, in other words, is conventional; it is the land that comes alive.

Mrs. Austin could probably have turned out any number of tales of this character, but 1905 was late to begin a course as historical romancer and she had no desire to sink into a groove. In 1908, with *Santa Lucia,* she turned to modern life and the problem of adjustment in marriage. She gets the feeling of the small Western college community exceedingly well, but her story has a continually shifting center of interest.

There is a deeper probing of the wrongs of women in a much better novel, *A Woman of Genius* (1912), which takes the form of the autobiography of a great actress, Olivia Lattimore. Olivia comes out of the same Middle Western world of whatnots and sexual repressions that Mary Hunter knew, and she makes her entry into the theater through amateur productions, community theatricals, and small barnstorming troupes playing the Middle West in the days when Chicago was still a producing center. She is even given a touch of the author's own mysticism: the Pan-like "Snockerty" is closer to the children of Taylorville than the God of the Sunday School can ever be, and in her darkest hour Olivia learns an experimental kind of prayer. Though Mrs. Austin was always ready to defend the small town against the rootless sophistication of the cities,[1] all that was valid in the "revolt" from the village that was to come upon us with Sinclair Lewis and *Main Street* is already implied in *A Woman of Genius*. So is everything that is important in woman's rebellion against man, for on its deepest level the book is a study of creative power, of its connection with sexual power, of how it is differentiated from sexual power, and of the conflict between art and love.

Mary Austin was less successful with the two other novels involving social considerations: *The Ford* (1917) and *No. 26 Jayne Street* (1920). The former gives an elaborate picture of the struggle between capitalist and farmer for water rights in California. Both here and in *No. 26 Jayne Street,* it is clear that Mrs. Austin, though herself often a rebel, is unfavorably impressed by the "sleazy" quality in American radicalism, primarily, it seems, because the radical, in his preoccupation with "causes" and other abstractions generally shows a tendency to forget human realities. In *The Ford,* however, the situation never seems quite clear cut, nor is there a satisfying climax. *No. 26 Jayne Street* is actually two books: the first part is merely a picture of American radicalism at the time of America's ill-starred entry into World War I; the rest, which is very Jamesian and very

---

[1] See, for example, in *Earth Horizon,* pp. 99-103, the stimulating discussion of Longfellow's importance for Midwestern culture, and on pp. 139-148, her brilliant desentimentalizing of the saloon.

well done, shows up the shallowness of one radical, Adam Frear, who is all for the new ways in political affairs while he continues to act the autocrat in his personal relationships. The predatory lover of the Dreiser school is precisely what will not go down with Neith Schuyler; she tells Adam to his face that what she objects to in him is his feeling that the "things we do ourselves can't be helped." The point of the book, of course, is that "we can't hope to have pure Democracy in politics until we get it in our fundamental relations."

I have disturbed chronology in order that I might consider Mary Austin's three "mystical" novels together. *The Lovely Lady* (1913) is an idyll, the story of a poor boy who became a rich man, dreamed of the Lovely Lady, was betrayed by her at last when he thought that she had appeared, and then found her in the very woman to whom he imagined he had condescended. *Outland* was written in collaboration with George Sterling and first published in London as "By Gordon Stairs." The American edition of 1919 carries upon its title page only the name of Mary Austin. This romance deals with the adventures of two Californians who make contact with a half-primitive, half-fairy race, living, quite unknown to Americans, in the Western forest. It is the kind of book which must succeed gloriously or utterly fail. For me, *Outland* does not succeed.

Mary Austin's last novel, *Starry Adventure* (1931)—she was at work upon a sequel when she died—is at once the most rewarding and the most disappointing of her fictions. The realization of New Mexico in the first half, of Gard's growing into life in full awareness of his country, and of his mystical sensitiveness—which is Mary Austin's adventure under the walnut tree transplanted to a new land —all this is first-rate, full-bodied, many-dimensioned fiction. Unhappily the second half, which is the study of Gard's relations with two women, is merely a bore. Though it seems cruel to say it, there are times when his sense of impending "starry adventure" suggests nothing better than the futile awareness of the feckless hero of "The Beast in the Jungle."

Mary Austin had no elaborate theory of fiction; when, as a young girl, she announced her determination to become a writer, and was asked by her unsympathetic family what kind of books she wanted to write, she replied, "All kinds." She very nearly did, but the experience hardly made her a novelist. In her article on the technique of the novel,[2] the principal point she makes is that "The democratic novelist must be inside his novel, rather than outside in the Victorian fashion of Thackeray or the reforming fashion of Mr. Wells." She also declares that "Characteristic art form is seldom perfected until the culture of which it is an expression comes to rest," but this may be merely a justification of her own limitations. When she began, her technique was rather advanced for its time. She has little formal exposition: she flings her reader into the situation to find his bearings as best he can. Sometimes her method makes for unnecessary obscurity. In later years, she was somewhat given to complaints that her readers did not get the point of her novels. If this be so, the fault was not altogether theirs.

2. *Robert Herrick, Idealist*

Robert Herrick was born in Cambridge, Massachusetts, on April 26, 1868. His oldest American ancestor, a nephew of the author of *Hesperides,* had settled at Salem in 1638; he was related to the Hales, the Mannings, the Hawthornes, and the Peabodys; his immediate forebears were lawyers, teachers, and clergymen. At Harvard, he was a contemporary of Santayana, William Vaughn Moody, Norman Hapgood, and Robert Morss Lovett; he nearly wrecked the *Harvard Monthly* when he sullied its chaste pages with the first English translation of Ibsen's *Lady from the Sea.* His teaching began at the Massachusetts Institute of Technology, but in 1893 William Rainey Harper lured him to the new University of Chicago, where he remained officially for exactly a generation, and where his students in "Advanced Composition" found him terrifyingly frigid in the classroom but sympathy and understanding itself in their personal conferences. During his later years the spot of earth dearest to his heart was York Village, Maine, but after his retirement from teaching, he brought his career to a rather amazing close as Government Secretary of the Virgin Islands. He died, at St. Thomas, on December 23, 1938.

"I think the one subject, consciously or unconsciously, always to be

[2] "The American Form of the Novel," *NR,* XXX, Apr. 12, 1922, Suppl., pp. 3-4.

found in my books [such is Herrick's own finding] is the competi-
tive system—its influences upon men and women." It is generally
viewed as an influence which makes for corruption. It corrupts not
only meat packers[3] and financiers;[4] neither does it stop with archi-
tects, builders, and engineers.[5] The painter goes down in the
struggle;[6] the scholar feels its corroding force in his traditional
"ivory tower";[7] the medical profession seems to be particularly susceptible.[8] But none of the men involved are melodramatic scoundrels,
for the disease in question is nothing more sinister than that "civilized self-interest" which Western men have been taught to praise.
Husbands go along with the current, and wives are incited by the
desire for a fine home, opportunities for their children, and other
goals not base in themselves. In his later years, Herrick was to criticize the proletarian novelists for their failure to perceive that the top
dogs, too, were "conditioned." "Bitter mockery, contempt are not
enough."

The involvement of women is somewhat less direct than that of
men. But because sex is the only other force in life that can compare
in power with "the spirit of possession," the woman herself may
easily become a source of corruption in her husband's world. Herrick
had no desire to return to "the squaw era," to rob the "bearers of the
sacred seed" of the privileges they have won. Neither did he believe
that in the present stage of their development women showed a
tendency to use their privileges wisely. "Tradition has taught them
for generations to work by fraud and wile, and their instinct warns
them against the ideal." In *Together,* Dr. Renault draws up a bitter
indictment of sterile, spendthrift, lazy, selfish women, and, as if that
were not enough, Herrick himself adds a highly rhetorical essay-
chapter in which he addresses his reader *in propria persona.*

Yet the proportion of unworthy, or even of worldly, women in
Herrick's novels is not higher than one would expect in an honest
picture of modern life. His worst woman is the scientist Serena

[3] *The Memoirs of an American Citizen.*
[4] *A Life for a Life.*
[5] *The Common Lot; Waste*
[6] *One Woman's Life.*
[7] *Chimes.*
[8] *The Man Who Wins; The Web of Life; The Healer.*

Massey, of *The End of Desire,* who is such a monster that the ideal-istic hero's passion for her grows incredible in the course of the narrative.[9] But over against her one may well place an idealized woman of another late novel, Dean Edith Crandall, of *Chimes.* In *The Common Lot* it is the husband who is dragged down by greed of gold; the wife is incorruptible. In *The Memoirs of an American Citizen,* the packer's noble sister is made the mouthpiece of the author's most passionate ideals.

More ordinary women are cherished also when their hearts are sound. Ernestine Geyer, the grotesque and ignorant "Laundryman" who befriends the selfish heroine of *One Woman's Life*—and suffers for it—is a thoroughly admirable woman. In Jinny, the common-place, estranged wife of Dr. Redfield's silly son in *The End of Desire,* we are made to admire a quite ungifted girl who is honestly trying to do her duty, and Serena's daughter May (like Venetia Phillips, of *The Common Lot,* before her), is sound also, beneath all her superficial modernity and libertarianism. In *The Real World,* Jack Pemberton's appreciation of the "simple humanity" of his worthless brother's vulgar mistress is about as far away from both snobbery and prudery as it is possible to go.

Adelle Clark, of *Clark's Field,* is a more important matter. Though she is introduced as a waif, Herrick deliberately deroman-ticizes, desentimentalizes her. In childhood she is dull and awkward. When, through the appreciation of real estate values in Clark's Field, she comes unexpectedly into great wealth, she cuts a wide swath— "almost aimless and lazy enough to be described as vicious." But her growth through folly, "through crude desire, through passion and pain and sorrow," to wisdom and magnanimity, even toward the worthless young husband who has been debauched by her wealth, and the assumption, at last, of her obligation toward society—all this is finely and compassionately described. "She, too, was a child of God! albeit she had lived many years and done folly and suffered sorrow before she could recognize it."

Another test case comes with that strangely unappreciated novel,

---

[9] Serena is a reworking, in darker colors, of Jessica Mallory, of *Chimes.* But Herrick gives Jessica at least one moment of wisdom and courage when she publicly opposes America's entrance into World War I.

Homely Lilla. This book is, in the best sense, a feminist document, and its heroine is as heroic a figure as Willa Cather's Ántonia—a vital, vibrant, unselfish woman, married to a prim, mean, cowardly, treacherous man. Lilla learns compassion through her wrongs, grows greater and kinder, not meaner and smaller. How admirable is her kindness to Valerie, whom she saves from going to pieces altogether at her husband's hands!

A dim sense of the necessity for forgiveness, for toleration, for pity as the ultimate reaction to life carried her up beyond her own irritation. It was the same about the war; men murdering each other like blind beasts, killing and maiming and torturing each other by the millions, without the power to stop; exciting each other to renewed excesses of killing and hate. "Men, men," she murmured, "and women too!" Will David have to be like that?[10]

It is dangerous to be dogmatic about literary influences in discussing a writer so widely read as Robert Herrick. In an interview he once described himself as having been brought up on the great Russian realists and the great English realists from George Eliot to Hardy. He praised Dostoevsky and accused Zola of having overplayed the sexual note for commercial reasons. In 1914 he berated the contemporary American novel for its sentimentality, prudery, and lack of real democratic and religious feeling. Few American writers after Howells seem to have been important to him. His early interest in Ibsen has tempted some writers to find not only Ibsen but Tolstoy and Strindberg in his women; this, however, is highly speculative. In his later years, he was somewhat inclined to welcome Albert Halper and other proletarian writers, but this was principally because he thought they had learned "that the function of the novel is to portray, not to argue," and because he saw in them a reaction against postwar decadence. Freudianism he always tends to classify

[10] Quoted from *Homely Lilla* (copyright, 1923, by Harcourt, Brace and Company). I admit that I am puzzled by one of Herrick's heroines, Cynthia Lane, of *Waste.* Though he was apparently aware of her shortcomings, he goes unaccountably "soft" on her; I would guess that she had a real life original who possessed some glamour for him that he did not succeed in communicating to the reader. In the novel she is captivating only in her girlhood appearance at the World's Columbian Exposition, and I have no faith in the forced happy ending of her love story.

with Christian Science, and he thought its influence upon fiction "disastrous both verbally and mentally."[11]

Four of the twelve novels Herrick published before World War I were described by the author himself as "idealistic." One other—*His Great Adventure* (1913)—is a story of incident, unparalleled in Herrick's career. The remaining seven are in the predominant realistic, socially-minded mode of the day. Taken together, they represent as comprehensive a picture and as serious a criticism of American society as the fiction of the time could offer. These novels are *The Man Who Wins* (1897), *The Gospel of Freedom* (1898), *The Web of Life* (1900), *The Common Lot* (1904), *The Memoirs of an American Citizen* (1905), *Together* (1908), and *One Woman's Life* (1913).

Among these books, *The Common Lot* is generally regarded as the work which established Herrick's reputation. *Together*—a long, and, to me, rather tiresome study of a number of marriages, all but one of which are unhappy—was by far his best seller. Perhaps *The Memoirs of an American Citizen* is most frequently spoken of as the best. It is, in a sense, the most dramatic of Herrick's books; here alone has he written in the first person. Like Thackeray's Barry Lyndon, the unscrupulous packer tells his own story in the full conviction that it justifies his conduct, but though he lands at last in the United States Senate, the reader is not deceived.

Such choices, however, are largely matters of taste. One could make a very good case for *The Web of Life,* a story of Chicago in the days of the Pullman strike, which, like the World's Columbian Exposition, the Panic of 1893, and the Haymarket Riot, is frequently to be encountered in Herrick's stories. *The Web of Life* involves suicide and the suspicion of murder, economic want, and marital

[11] In his autobiography, *All Our Years* (VP, 1948), Herrick's lifelong friend and colleague, R. M. Lovett, shocked by the novelist's acerbic picture of the University of Chicago, in *Chimes,* and his cruel caricatures of many campus personalities, including the first two presidents of the university, accuses him of dependence upon living models and of a willingness to sacrifice the amenities of private life to the convenience of his art. The University of Chicago was not the only quarter in which such offense was taken in the course of Herrick's career. He himself never publicly admitted such charges: see his article, "An Author's 'Models,'" *Literary Review*, III (1923), 905-906, and his letter, "The Necessity of Anonymity," *SRL,* VII (1931), 886.

irregularity; it commands more passion than Herrick usually achieves and justifies Howells's comment that it has "a poetic sense of Fate in it . . . and a pathos which the austere Nemesis of *The Common Lot,* for instance, does not indulge." Well worthy of attention, also, is *The Gospel of Freedom,* an international novel, whose heroine is a restless and wealthy American woman who must go abroad and play with fire before she learns that "There is no freedom and everyone is free," that freedom "is a state of feeling, of the spirit, not a condition of person," and that it is no more easily attainable in Paris than it was in Chicago.

The "idealistic" novels which Herrick himself said lay closest to his heart are *The Real World* (1901), *A Life for a Life* (1910), *The Healer* (1911), *Clark's Field* (1914), and the short story, *The Master of the Inn* (1908).[12] Herrick believed that all great art is necessarily idealistic and that the writer who confines himself altogether to the realistic method must perforce satisfy himself with surfaces alone. These "idealistic" books of his own he described as concerned "with large spiritual themes and the characters . . . types, the action almost always symbolic." *The Real World* carries an epigraph from Sir Thomas Browne, affirming that writer's faith "that this visible world is but a Picture [and an "equivocal" one] of the Invisible."

One may, however, accept Herrick's critical principles without necessarily regarding these books as his greatest achievements. The merits of *Clark's Field* have already been indicated. *The Master of the Inn,* though not perfectly proportioned, is a charming idyll. But both *The Real World* and *The Healer* fall between two stools: allegory and symbolism go just far enough to leave the reader with the uncomfortable feeling that the author is attempting a picture of the life we know and not quite succeeding. This is not true of *A Life for a Life,* a vision which turns apocalyptic in the end, with a picture of what is presumably the San Francisco Earthquake and Fire (though no city is ever named), but *A Life for a Life* can hardly be

[12] Blake Nevius, who has studied these books in the light of Herrick's fragmentary, unpublished autobiography, "Myself," and other MS material in the University of Chicago Library, presents an important study of them in "The Idealistic Novels of RH," *AL,* XXI (1949), 56-70. Cf. also H. Lüdeke, "RH, Novelist of American Democracy," *English Studies,* XVIII (1936), 49-57.

regarded as establishing Herrick's mastery of the allegorical method. He had not the imagination which is required to make such literature impressive. His symbolism is painfully obvious, and his eloquence turns readily to bathos.

Between 1914 and 1923 Herrick published no novel; then, with *Homely Lilla,* he emerged once more, the unsparing critic of a world profoundly modified by a war which he had first supported as a holy crusade, then completely rejected.[13] In his final phase he wrote five novels: *Homely Lilla* (1923), *Waste* (1924), *Chimes* (1926), *The End of Desire* (1932), and his utopia, *Sometime* (1933). Except for the last, which was surely as melancholy a curtain as a distinguished writer ever pulled down upon his career, he gained in power to the end.

To be sure, he was an even lonelier figure now than he had been in his prime. There was considerable justification for the attacks which University of Chicago men made upon *Chimes* on the score of unfairness and bad taste. But there was never any excuse for the view that, in *The End of Desire,* Herrick shared the sexual looseness which he professed to deplore. The novel is an extremely unpleasant picture of a profligate age, but the mood throughout is a mood of excoriation. The really important book of the last years is *Waste,* a review of the American adventure from before the Chicago World's Fair well into the postwar period. This novel is the work of a great American patriot who died just in time to escape having it borne in upon him that his countrymen are incapable of learning by experience.

Many faults have been found in Herrick's novels. He was a very prolific writer for one so lacking in invention; consequently, he is often repetitive. He had little humor, and both his dialogue and his situations frequently give the impression of having been contrived to make a point. He often used melodrama and coincidence. His method, too, is anything but austere for a younger contemporary of Henry James: "If Edward S. had left his post-office address, there

---

[13] In his article, "The War and Ourselves," *Survey,* LII (1924), 493-495, Herrick traces his change of attitude "from that of the fervid partisan of the Allies and their cause" (1914-1917) "to that of hesitation and doubt" (1917-1918) "to that of pacifist, flat and plain, as at present." It is traced, much more fascinatingly, as fiction, in both *Waste* and *Chimes.*

was no doubt that long before this Clark's Field would have been eaten up; there would have been no Adelle Clark—and no book about her and Clark's Field!"

It has been objected, too, that Herrick never "solves" the problems he poses. Even in his realistic novels, he is always on the side of the idealists, yet his idealists show deplorable judgment. Vickers, of *Together,* runs off with a worthless woman to save her from a brutal husband; when she leaves him, he gives her half his fortune and agrees to be saddled with the care of her daughter by another man; later, when his sister is in danger of trusting her life to an undesirable lover, he taunts the scoundrel into shooting him in the hope that his death may open her eyes! Herrick knows that Vickers is a fool. "Nevertheless," he says, "the heart of a Fool may be pure." So it may, but that even pure fools can solve such problems is worse than doubtful. There are elements of the fool, too, about Dr. Sommers, of *The Web of Life,* and Dr. Holden, of *The Healer,* who is also a boor. And this time, Herrick seems not to know it.

His "solutions," indeed, are likely to take one of two forms: either to become one of the "little people" or to withdraw from society altogether. Jackson Hart, architect of *The Common Lot,* does not regain his prostituted power until he goes back to work for his first, incorruptible employer at $200 per month; Hugh Grant, of *A Life for a Life,* still more strangely, returns to the ranks in the very bank he had regarded as corrupt. Dr. Sommers commits himself upon principle to a kind of monastic ideal: professional men, he thinks, have no right to ask anything beyond bare subsistence. And Holden, Renault, and the Master of the Inn all take refuge in the wilderness.

But a novelist's reading of life is not primarily a matter of devising panaceas, and Herrick's over-all view is both more adequate and more optimistic than many of his readers have discovered. Against this ideational background, even the suggested "solutions" themselves seem less evasive or sentimental than they might otherwise appear.

From his Puritan ancestors Herrick inherited the conviction that this world is a desperately wicked place, and the conduct of men, as he observed it in Chicago during one of the great periods of industrial development in the western world, did not cause him to change his mind. Yet life was beautiful as well as terrible, and it was because he believed in it so profoundly that war and greed and economic exploitation seemed to him so overwhelmingly evil. He knew that even through fellowship, even through love, man's passion for union, for completeness, can be achieved only for moments, and that it is nearly impossible for the very best of us to treat another human being with consistent justice and tenderness. Yet the meaning of life lies in the effort to do just these things.

Most of the comparisons that have been made between Herrick and James are meaningless, but he *was* like James in the sense that, for all his fastidious intellectuality, the thing he admired most was simple, unadulterated human goodness. In his novels, the impulse toward evil takes the form of social pressure to a larger extent than it did with the author of *The Scarlet Letter,* but he never forgets that social pressure itself is created by the lusts and the greeds of men. He had little faith either in science or in technology, and he trusted the new psychological pseudosciences least of all. All his hope was in the humanities, with their direct appeal to the heart and the will, their sympathy, imagination, and faith. He once objected to Zola, Hardy, and Norris that they tended to make man too much the product of the mere material forces brought to play upon him. It was his emphasis upon the will and upon the importance of the individual that saved Herrick from the Communist heresy, socialistic as some of his specific suggestions seem.

To save himself or to save society, in Herrick's novels, a man must first of all turn away resolutely from his sin. Jackson Hart, of *The Common Lot,* does not even understand his wife's objection to the morass of corruption into which he is sinking until he himself has suffered a change of heart and rejected evil because he loathes it. For the Will itself is creative; it "shapes and makes"; it draws the real out of the unreal; through suffering it brings peace. It is "singly, individually" that the vicious circle must be broken, not through politics, not through programs and panaceas, "but only by Will— the individual good will to renounce, working against the evil will to possess. . . ." Thus Herrick's outlook upon evil, both social and personal (and the two are one) is just as uncompromising—and just as encouraging—as that of the New Testament, and the most encouraging thing about it is that, accepting his philosophy, no man need wait for either God or the government to bring in the millennium; he can immediately begin to work upon it in the stuff of himself.

3. *Booth Tarkington, Success*

Beyond any other writer of his time, Booth Tarkington gave the "advanced" critics an opportunity for head-shaking and hand-wringing. He posed an entirely different problem from that suggested by, say, Myrtle Reed or Harold Bell Wright. Despite the enormous popularity of such writers, nobody ever attributed literary significance to their work. In Tarkington's case it was always recognized frankly that he had five or six times as much talent as any novelist really needs. He had great skill in structure; he created characters which became household words; his style combined ease, charm, and distinction. Yet he shied from tragedy (most of his characters find, with Virgil Adams, that just when you think you're "right spang against the wall," "something you never counted on turns up," and "somehow you kind of squirm out"); he had no truck with the fashionable indecency of his time; and, except for his interest in spiritualism, he persisted to the end of his days in being curiously "right-thinking." All in all, he seemed to have achieved just that romantic treatment of realistic materials which was Robert Herrick's definition of what the public wants.

The attack on Tarkington was based upon a number of assumptions, all completely unverified: (1) that the truth is always to be found with the extremists and never in the middle of the road; (2) that "new" ideas are necessarily better than old ones; (3) that if he had remained the Socialist he thought he was in his college days, he must have written better fiction; (4) that those who have no stake in the established order necessarily see its problems more clearly than those who have.

To say that these propositions are not necessarily valid is not, of course, to affirm that their opposites would own any superior validity. Of course the richly rewarded writer has his temptations. Yet there are writers who are quite sincere in holding conservative views; for them the real "betrayal" would lie in the direction of making terms with the economic radicalism and sexual libertarianism whose absence in their work the critics so pathetically lament.

There is every reason to suppose that Tarkington was such a writer. The limitations of his work were simply those imposed by his talent and his temperament. Unlike Joseph Conrad, whom he so much admired, he did not take up a "great" attitude toward human experience. Instead, he took up a sensible attitude, a clean, kindly, somewhat humorous attitude, just the kind of attitude one might expect of a man who came out of the world of James Whitcomb Riley, George Ade, Meredith Nicholson, and John T. McCutcheon. It was his conviction that writers do what they must, that there are no "good" conditions and no "bad" conditions for the *production* of a work of art, and that "prices" have nothing to do with the quality of the work turned out. "I have written things only as I thought they ought to be written." And as for having employed special devices to woo either editors or readers: "Really, I'd as soon have forged a check."

(Newton) Booth Tarkington was born in Indianapolis on July 29, 1869 and died there on May 19, 1946. The Reverend Thomas Hooker and Mary Newton, the Salem beauty, were among his New England ancestors; his grandfather was one of the "fathers of Indiana Methodism," his father, a legislator and lawyer. He was educated at Phillips Exeter, Purdue, and Princeton; like the hero of *The Gentleman from Indiana,* he impressed his college classmates with the conviction of his coming greatness. Yet he left college with his interests divided between literature and art, and his first five years of effort netted him a total of $22.50. Except for one term in the state legislature, his life was devoted altogether to writing. In addition to his novels, he wrote many plays in which such stars as Richard Mansfield, Otis Skinner, and George Arliss appeared, as well as film plays for his friend, Thomas Meighan. He was a notable collector of paintings and other *objets d'art*. In later years he divided his time between Indianapolis and "Seawood," his summer home, "The House That Penrod Built," at Kennebunkport, Maine. Twice married, he died childless.

Among American novelists, Tarkington was most influenced by Howells and Mark Twain. He admired such English realists as

Hardy and Bennett; in French literature, his taste embraced both realists and romancers—Balzac, Daudet, Dumas, and the autobiographers. His own inclination to both realism and romance was seen at the very beginning of his career when he published *The Gentleman from Indiana* (1899) and *Monsieur Beaucaire* (1900).[14] *Beaucaire*, the tale of a French prince masquerading as a lackey in Restoration Bath (and testing the cold heart of an English beauty), has been one of the longest-lived of the turn-of-the-century romances. *The Gentleman from Indiana* is a work of richer promise but lesser achievement. Here we have realism in the picture of the town, social consciousness in the young editor John Harkless's crusade against both political corruption and rowdyism, sentimentality in the love story, melodrama in the episode in which Harkless is supposed to have been murdered by the "White Caps," and comic opera unreality in Helen Fisbee's being able not only to run John's paper for him during his illness but actually to enlarge it, and finally to get him nominated to Congress! The other most ambitious book of the first period, *The Conquest of Canaan* (1905), which is the story of the outcast boy and girl of the town who come back and force their fellow-townsmen to accept them upon their own terms, has romantic elements also, yet it makes a more unified impression. Tarkington was to use the theme of vindication again in better books, as in *The Turmoil, The Midlander,* and *Mirthful Haven,* and Ariel Tabor's loneliness at the dance was to be reworked elaborately in *Alice Adams.*

[14] *Beaucaire* was written before *The Gentleman from Indiana,* and *Cherry,* which was not published until 1903, had preceded both. *Cherry* is generally regarded as more precious than *Beaucaire;* this impression is due to the style, for the story is told from the point of view of an elegant young prig. In *Beauty and the Jacobin* (1912), which, according to Tarkington, represented his first attempt to write from the inside of his characters out, he concerned himself with the French Revolution; in the late *Wanton Mally* (1932), he gave us French gallants and Restoration bucks again—this time with the significant addition of English Quakers—in a world of ruder adventures than those encountered in *Beaucaire. The Two Vanrevels* (1902), which goes back to the days of the Mexican War, is Tarkington's only "historical novel" of Indiana. Contemporary Europe furnished the setting for four novels: *The Beautiful Lady* (1905), *His Own People* (1907), *The Guest of Quesnay* (1908), and—much later—*The Plutocrat* (1927), in which a "self-made" American moves across the European scene.

The Penrod books[15] and *Seventeen* (1916) are something else again;[16] if William ("Silly Bill") Baxter has become the very type-figure of puppy love, Penrod himself comes close to folklore. Yet there has always been a serious division of opinion between those who praise these amusing books as a surpassingly truthful revelation of the youthful mind and those who profess to see the youngsters as knowingly, and sometimes even heartlessly, exploited for their enter-tainment value to older readers. There is some evidence, I think, to support both views, but there is no justification for seating Penrod beside Tom Sawyer; he lacks the poetry of Mark Twain's creation.

Tarkington's best period as a creator of character and portrayer of midwestern life may be said to begin with *The Flirt* (1913). But fine as the worthless heroine is, the book itself tends toward the same scattered impression as *The Gentleman from Indiana:* the setting and the small town characters are very convincing, but the whole story of Val Corliss's shady financial manipulations is melodrama. *Alice Adams* (1921) was much better, and so were the three novels afterwards (1927) bound together as *Growth: The Turmoil* (1915), *The Magnificent Ambersons* (1918), and *The Midlander* (1923).

The girl Alice Adams is both silly and lovable, and Tarkington's story about her is probably his most successful book. It achieves, for one thing, a simplicity and concentration which is rare in his work, and, though I confess I am somewhat surprised, so far as I know nobody has yet been ridiculous enough to suggest that it would have been a finer work of art if the heroine had turned on the gas in the last chapter instead of climbing the dismal stairs which lead to the business college. The hot, uncomfortable dinner party at which Alice's matrimonial hopes crash has been justly celebrated; here and elsewhere, it is Tarkington's special merit that he never permits us to forget that, though the stakes for which his people play seem

---

[15] *Penrod* (1914); *Penrod and Sam* (1916); *Penrod Jashber* (1929). In 1931 the three books were reissued in one volume as *Penrod: His Complete Story.*

[16] *Little Orvie* (1934) employs Penrod-like material built around a younger and less attractive boy. In *The Flirt*, Cora Madison's precocious young brother Hedrick ("He kissed an idiot") threatens at times to usurp the main interest. Florence, of *Gentle Julia* (1922), has been described as "a fourteen-year-old feminine Penrod."

small ones, basic life forces are involved in the struggle and human hearts are being broken.

Growth is not as fine as *Alice Adams* all the way through. Bibbs Sheridan, the third son of the fairy tale, develops into a business genius much too quickly, and Mary Vertrees's conduct at the dinner where she is playing for Sheridan is much too obvious to take anybody in. It is laying it on with a trowel, too, to have old Sheridan tell Bibbs that he would have more sympathy with his literary aspirations if he wanted to write advertising copy.

On the other hand, many of the criticisms that have been directed against this trilogy cannot be sustained. Difficult as it may be for the "intelligentsia" to believe it, many important businessmen do still consult spiritualistic mediums, precisely as Eugene Morgan, the pioneer builder of "horseless carriages," does at the end of *The Magnificent Ambersons.*[17] Given Eugene's temperament, moreover, his resultant forgiveness of the now smashed George Minafer is not out of character.

Neither is it true that George himself turns out too well in this book; for while the boy had been an insufferable snob, Tarkington had carefully prepared for the outcome by showing the existence of his fine qualities, alongside the bad ones, almost from the very beginning of the story. And if the novel contains no "scene" so elaborately developed as the dinner party in *Alice Adams,* it is still full of vividly glimpsed moments which refuse to die out of the memory: George murmuring echoes of Hamlet's melancholy at himself in the looking glass; George baiting Mrs. Johnson, who has circulated scandal about his mother; George forbidding Morgan the house because the boy thinks it disgraceful that his mother should marry again, and gazing at the photograph of his dead father (whom he did not love), for which he has now, belatedly, purchased a sixty-dollar silver frame; Lucy and George parting nonchalantly at the drugstore, where Lucy nearly faints the moment he has left her; the scene with Aunt Fanny upon the floor, where the boy first learns that she is penniless; the disappearance of the Amberson name from

---

[17] Professor Quinn (*American Fiction,* p. 601) to the contrary notwithstanding, Tarkington does not commit himself to the thesis that Eugene has talked to Isabel's spirit.

the list of "Most Prominent Citizens and Families," and the substitution of "Tenth Street" for "Amberson Boulevard"; George's frantic plea for reassurance after his mother's death, that he has done right in keeping her away from Morgan, and the pathetic cries from his bedside—"Mother, forgive me! *God,* forgive me!"

In *Growth,* moreover, Tarkington showed that he knew what is wrong with American cities as well as any muck-raking novelist of them all.[18] As an apostle of "progress," Dan Oliphant, of *The Midlander,* comes into his own at last, but he dies at the height of his achievement, miserably unhappy over the failure of his marriage with a worthless woman who has given him a worthless son, and his brother's valedictory sums up the author's conception of the significance of his life:

"Here's my brother spent all his days and nights—all his strength and health—just blindly building up a bigger confusion and uproar that smashes him; and then when he *is* smashed, it keeps on bothering and disturbing him—yes, and choking him!—on his very deathbed!"

Bibbs Sheridan, on the other hand, finds his love, yet the ending of *The Turmoil* is not conventionally "happy," for the man is left stranded in a work he never wanted to do.

The reality of Tarkington's bitch-women—Cora Madison, of *The Flirt;* Lena McMillan, a piece of soiled goods from the New York marriage counter, who marries Don Oliphant and destroys him; Laila Capper, the beast in the jungle of *Kate Fennigate* (1943); and the unpleasant heroine of *Image of Josephine* (1945)—the reality of these women has never been denied. Robert Cortes Holliday called Mariana, of *The Guest of Quesnay,* "a bit of cynical drawing almost Degasesque." But it is sometimes complained that when his women are not bitches, they are angels. It must be confessed that Tarkington has women, like Martha Shelby, of *The Turmoil,* whose charity seems as inexhaustible as the charity of God; Kate Fennigate, too, is less touching than, say, Alice Adams because she has no need to learn anything; she knows it all already. There are other girls, how-

---

[18] The short stories collected in *In the Arena* (1905) reflect Tarkington's interest in practical politics. *Ramsey Milholland* (1919), his closest approach to a war novel, is not important, for war was not among the subjects into which Tarkington possessed much insight.

ever, like the heroines of *Claire Ambler* (1928), *Mirthful Haven* (1930), and *Presenting Lily Mars* (1933), in whom both strength and weakness are carefully shaded.

No very striking new developments appeared in Tarkington's later novels; on the other hand, there was no serious falling-off of power. The knowledge of New England derived from his summers in Maine yielded *Mirthful Haven,* a picture of social conflict in a summer resort and fishing community, and the less serious *Mary's Neck* (1932). His life as a collector produced *Rumbin Galleries* (1937), which is developed episodically, in terms of comedy. His experience with the stage appeared in the brief *Harlequin and Columbine* (1918) and, more importantly, in *Presenting Lily Mars,* which, facile though it is in its plot development, is very knowing in its comprehension of the actor's temperament. The burdens imposed upon business and family life by the Depression and the New Deal are reflected in *The Fighting Littles* and *The Heritage of Hatcher Ide* (both 1941). *Women* (1925), *Young Mrs. Greeley* (1929), and *The Lorenzo Bunch* (1936) are other domestic novels of the later years. The last, unfinished novel, *The Show Piece* (1947), was a study of a self-centered young man.

Tarkington did not believe that either art or human nature had been importantly altered by any of the bewildering changes which have taken place in twentieth-century life; if one finds unaccustomed notes sounded in his later books, this is due merely to the increasing thoughtfulness of a mature man. In *The Conquest of Canaan* he had quite gratuitously developed a threat to Joe's final happiness in the suggestion, at the end, of the heroine's interest in the new minister, only that he might have the pleasure of dissolving it away. But in *Kate Fennigate,* the evil Laila achieves a "happy ending" of a very different character. Laila, who might very easily have been ruined, is left wallowing in prosperity and apparently quite victorious. Actually, she has been defeated, for she is caught in her own "encasement." She has been defeated not so much by Kate as by those qualities of character, embodied in Kate, which lie so far above her plane of being that she does not even know that they exist. Above all, she has been defeated by the decency of a man who could not sink to her level even when he was foolish enough to be fasci-

nated by her. The Indiana folk-artist is satirist as well as sentimentalist, and the satirical note did not decline in Tarkington's later books:
the "dear, good, beautiful people" of *The Gentleman from Indiana*
are, often enough, mostly fools. Tarkington did not believe that
critical judgment had much to do, one way or the other, with a
reader's response to an author; one liked or one disliked, rather,
according as "one vibrated, or did not vibrate, in sympathy with the
rhythm of the author's writing." He himself caught the American
rhythm with notable success, and many agreed with him that even
fools can be loved.

CHAPTER XIII

EDITH WHARTON: SOCIAL BACKGROUND AND ETHICAL DILEMMA

Order the beauty even of Beauty is.
THOMAS TRAHERNE (quoted by E. W. on the title-page
of *The Writing of Fiction*)

1. *The Making of a Novelist*

Because Edith Wharton is the acknowledged *grande dame* of American letters, she is sometimes dismissed as a "society novelist." This is nonsense. "Society women" do not write novels—novels of Mrs. Wharton's caliber at any rate; such fiction can only be written by artists. If the artist also happens to be a "society woman," that is, no doubt, an interesting, perhaps even an important, fact, but it does not become the whole truth about her. Like other writers, Mrs. Wharton was importantly conditioned, in some respects unfortunately, by the circumstances in which she was born and bred. Up to the time her husband's health broke down, she lived a "fashionable" life; she had both wealth and culture, and she never ceased to move at will in the most exclusive circles. But she "saw through" society early, and it was never its more superficial aspects by which she was enthralled. Her own social success was, as she saw it, distinctly qualified. After her marriage, she was a failure in Boston "because they thought I was too fashionable to be intelligent, and a failure in New York because they were afraid I was too intelligent to be fashionable." The members of her family never indicated any awareness of her artistic life: her novels were treated as a family disgrace, never to be spoken of under any circumstances.

Edith Newbold Jones was born in New York City on January 24,

1862, into a wealthy, middle-class family of merchants, bankers, and lawyers. The Revolutionary War hero, Major-General Ebeneezer Stevens, was an ancestor; a Huguenot great-grandfather participated in the founding of New Rochelle. She was privately educated, largely in the modern languages, and she knew Europe, from her earliest years, almost as well as Newport and New York. Not being allowed to read children's books or popular fiction, she was thrown back upon her father's small but carefully-selected library of French and English classics.

In 1885 she was married to Edward Wharton, of Boston; they lived in New York, at Newport, in Lenox, Massachusetts, and in Paris, and always traveled extensively. Though Mr. Wharton never shared his wife's intellectual interests, the marriage seems to have been successful until his mental breakdown. They were divorced in 1913, and Mrs. Wharton spent her later years in Europe. When the war came in 1914, she threw herself devotedly into relief work; by the time it ended, she and her colleagues had 5,000 refugees under their care and had established four colonies for displaced children and old people and four tuberculosis sanatoria.

She was decorated by both the French and the Belgian governments, and the last years of her life were crowded with honors, including an honorary doctorate from Yale and a Gold Medal from the National Institute of Arts and Letters. She died in France on August 11, 1937.

Edith Wharton began to "make up" stories before she had learned to read. At eleven she began her first novel with the words: " 'Oh, how do you do, Mrs. Brown?' said Mrs. Tompkins. 'If only I had known you were going to call I should have tidied up the drawing-room.' " Some of her youthful poetry was printed in the *New York World* and (through Longfellow's intercession), in the *Atlantic.*

Yet she did not begin her adult writing in earnest—poems first, then short stories—until about 1889. Her first book, an influential pioneering work on *The Decoration of Houses,* written in collaboration with the architect, Ogden Codman, Jr., appeared in 1897, but her first collection of short stories did not come until 1899, her first novelette until 1900, nor her first novel till 1902. *The House of Mirth,* the novel which established her reputation, was published in 1905, when she was forty-three years old.

Mr. Edmund Wilson, laboring a connection between genius and disease, explains all this by reference to Edward Wharton's illness.[1] It was out of her husband's neurasthenia that Mrs. Wharton became "a passionate social prophet"; she relieved her own emotional strain by denouncing her generation. After her divorce, she had nothing more to worry about; her later books, therefore, are not worth much, though, to be sure, Mr. Wilson does remark casually that he has not read many of them.

This kind of theorizing about literature is rarely much concerned with the facts of the case, yet the fascination it exerts for a certain type of mind appears to be irresistible. If Mr. Wilson had taken the trouble to read Robert Sencourt's *Cornhill* article about Mrs. Wharton,[2] he might have learned, to treat the subject here in only one aspect, that the tension in her emotional life did *not* come to an end with her separation from her husband.

The truth of the matter seems rather to have been that though the storytelling impulse was always there, the writer's *talent* developed slowly. Her kind of fiction depended upon maturity of outlook and considerable experience of the world. It may indeed be that during the early years of her marriage Mrs. Wharton was, in a measure, following false images of good. She herself speaks of her "discovery of that soul of mine which the publication of my first volume called to life." She was also a hesitant creature; there was more real humility about her than her sometimes formidable aspect indicated. It was the very best thing that could possibly have happened to her that, thanks to the failure of another novelist to deliver his work on time, *Scribner's Magazine* should have begun serializing *The House of Mirth* when only 50,000 words had been written, for the circumstance compelled Mrs. Wharton to do in six months what she had vaguely supposed would take eighteen; her doubts and hesitations perforce came to an end, and her self-confidence as a novelist was established for good and all.

[1] "Justice to Edith Wharton," in *The Wound and the Bow* (HM, 1941).
[2] *Cornhill Magazine,* CLVII (1938), 721-736.

2. *General Survey I:* Ethan Frome *and Others*

Edith Wharton published fourteen novels,[3] eleven novelettes,[4] eleven volumes of short stories,[5] two volumes of verses,[6] and twelve other books. Our concern here is with all the fiction except the short stories.

One novel—*The Valley of Decision*—is an elaborate historical novel which has often been compared to George Eliot's *Romola.* Three—*Ethan Frome, Summer,* and *"Bunner Sisters"*—deal with humble people in rural New England and in New York. Two—*A Son at the Front* and *The Marne*—are concerned with World War I. All the others represent the norm of Mrs. Wharton's fiction; they concern social and ethical problems among cultivated people, mostly Americans, at home and abroad.[7]

The Valley of Decision (1902) is the most spaciously varied of Mrs. Wharton's fictions, the richest in background and in "color." It testified to a culture which had obviously been absorbed *con amore* and not "worked up" for the occasion. Charles Eliot Norton, who admired it greatly, thought it less a novel than "a study of Italian thought and life during the latter part of the eighteenth century. . . . The material and spiritual scene and its significance are more interesting than the individual characters of the personages who are the actors in the drama." But though Mrs. Wharton herself

[3] She left a fifteenth, *The Buccaneers* (1938), partially completed; it was published by her literary executor.

[4] I have counted the contents of *Old New York* as four novelettes, rather than one long novel, and have included in my reckoning two pieces which Mrs. Wharton did not bring out between independent covers but included in collections of short stories: "Bunner Sisters" (in *Xingu*) and "Her Son" (in *Human Nature*). In my survey of Mrs. Wharton's work in this section and the next, I have marked the novelettes with asterisks.

[5] *The Greater Inclination* (1899); *Crucial Instances* (1901); *The Descent of Man and Other Stories* (1904); *The Hermit and the Wild Woman and Other Stories* (1908); *Tales of Men and Ghosts* (1910); *Xingu and Other Stories* (1916); *Here and Beyond* (1926); *Certain People* (1930); *Human Nature* (1933); *The World Over* (1936); *Ghosts* (1937).

[6] *Artemis to Actaeon* (1909); *Twelve Poems* (1926). Cf. Robert Sencourt, "The Poetry of EW," *Bkm*(NY), CXXIII (1931), 478-486.

[7] *The Age of Innocence* and *Old New York* have, of course, historical settings, but this does not affect their fundamental character.

felt that the book was not sufficiently "compact" or "centripetal" to be more than a "romantic chronicle," the struggle for liberalism described in it is not remote from the vital concerns of modern life, and one critic goes so far as to call it Mrs. Wharton's most American novel.

The war books need not detain us. They are not unskillfully done. There is a vivid picture of the terror and of some of the gallant, pitiful, or contemptible types it revealed. But in spite of the magnificence of Mrs. Wharton's own war work, everything she wrote about the conflict was vitiated by the superficiality of her own thinking. For her the war was a German assault upon "civilization," and in her mind "civilization" and "France" were synonymous terms. England merely hovered somewhere on the periphery, and her native land was presumably created only that it might, after disgraceful hesitation, finally rush to the aid of *la belle France*.

The other three pieces mentioned—or at least one of them, *Ethan Frome* (1911)—are very different. To its author's own intense annoyance,[8] *Ethan Frome* was often called her masterpiece. It is a cool, spare tragedy of a sensitive farmer in the back hills of New England, who is married to a mean, hypochondriac woman. Life renews itself for Ethan when Zeena's cousin Mattie comes to the house as a "hired girl." Confronting separation, the lovers choose death instead, by way of a sled steered down a steep hill, straight against a tree. But by the irony of fate, they achieve only mutilation, and all three persons live out their long lives in the frustration-filled farmhouse, where the wife is forced to undertake the lifelong care of the now helpless and querulous Mattie. Says Walter Fuller Taylor:

The tragic qualities of this story are enhanced by Mrs. Wharton's careful workmanship. Having to deal with the events of a whole generation, yet seeing that her theme would not bear the slow, expansive method of the

---

[8] See Edith Wharton, "The Writing of 'Ethan Frome,'" *Col*, Part XI (1932), and her Introduction to the "Modern Student's Library" edition (S, 1922). For the views of those who do not appreciate Ethan Frome, see Elizabeth S. Sergeant, "Idealized New England," *NR*, III (1915), 271-275, and John Crowe Ransom, "Mrs. W's Difficulty," *AR*, VI (1936), 271-275. Blake Nevius has recently argued—*NEQ*, XXIV (1951), 197-207—that *Ethan Frome* is not remote from the main themes of Mrs. Wharton's fiction. See, also, his "EW Today," *Pacific Spectator*, V (1951), 233-241.

full-length novel, she adopted the device of having the story built up, retrospectively, in the mind of an observer who is intelligent enough to comprehend the motives of all the actors. Not until after the apparent climax has been passed does she bring the reader himself face to face with the two women and thereby reveal, suddenly, the full extent of their calamity.[9]

The other New England novel, *Summer* (1917), is a seduction tale, generally considered much inferior to **Ethan Frome,* though there are dissenting voices. The worthless suitor of **"Bunner Sisters"* is unfortunately permitted to "take in" the reader, along with the poor women whom he captivates, but it is difficult to see how solidity of specification could go much farther than it does in this story or how any situation could be much more pitiful than the one described.

3. *General Survey II: The Body of Mrs. Wharton's Fiction*

From these books I pass to a discussion of the full-length, typical Wharton novels. *The House of Mirth* (1905) was its author's first extended picture—and indictment—of New York society. She had already learned "that a frivolous society can acquire dramatic significance only through what its frivolity destroys." What it destroys in this instance is Lily Bart.

When *The House of Mirth* appeared, a contemporary reviewer declared that

The young woman, whatever her training and standing, who drinks cocktails, smokes, plays cards for money, and indulges in an occasional oath, may not go to the bad, but she cannot escape becoming coarse and vulgar.

This is quite true, but what did the reviewer desire for Lily Bart? What she gets is death. This seems enough from the point of view of the mid-century, but perhaps 1905 was made of sterner stuff.

Moreover, Lily is not punished for her sins but for her virtues. Mrs. Wharton understood that society, which is profoundly corrupt, never objects to evil but only to indiscretion. You may be as wicked as you like, but you must play the game according to the rules. This Lily cannot do because she is above it. In the scandal which wrecks her she is wholly innocent, the victim of an unscrupulous woman

[9] *A History of American Letters.* Copyright, 1936, American Book Company.

who was not worthy to undo the latchets of her shoes. If she had been able to stoop to use the vulgar weapon of blackmail which chance had put into her hands, she could have crushed her adversary, or, failing that, have made herself impregnable. And the man she loved could not save her, for he was a poor creature who, as Constance Woolson would say, had to have everything explained to him. She remains a fragile bit of slightly corrupted beauty, the Portrait of a Lady with a difference.

The next novel, *The Fruit of the Tree* (1907), was much inferior, partly because the industrial problems upon which it opens were not Mrs. Wharton's material and partly because it lacks a center of interest. The sympathetic study of euthanasia must have seemed very daring in 1907, and one can still respond to Mrs. Wharton's scorn for physicians who regard their patients as "cases" rather than human beings.[10]

It was followed by *The Reef* (1912), which to Henry James seemed "a Drama . . . almost of the psychologic Racinian unity, intensity, and gracility." It is, indeed, Mrs. Wharton's most Jamesian long novel. Delayed by circumstances upon his journey into France to join the woman he expects to marry, George Darrow, in Paris, allows himself to drift into a careless liaison with a young girl. Some months later, having joined Mrs. Leath, he finds Sophy Viner installed in her family, as a governess and the fiancée of Mrs. Leath's stepson. The book is the probing of the situation in which all four persons thereupon find themselves. As Miss N. Elizabeth Monroe has said,

It resembles a musical composition in the way the theme is sounded in the first scene, then developed through the Paris incidents, falling into muted loveliness in the descriptive scenes at Givré, gaining in intensity as the complication grows, until it falls off in a kind of despair at the end. Every scene is fully developed yet never detaches itself from the course of the story.[11]

[10] Homer E. Woodbridge, *Nation*, LXXXV (1907), 514, describes resemblances between *The Fruit of the Tree* and Ibsen's *Rosmersholm*, though without asserting indebtedness.

[11] *The Novel and Society*, pp. 122-123. Copyright, 1941, by The University of North Carolina Press. Quoted by permission.

Neither marriage ever takes place, but the palm for courage and generosity goes at last to the girl.

The Custom of the Country (1913) again represents a falling off, though it is a more successful book than *The Fruit of the Tree.* It is not that the reader questions the reality of the much-married social climber, Undine Spragg. Undine succeeds where Lily Bart failed precisely because she knows not honor. But the perfect comment, again, was made by James: *The Custom of the Country* is "consistently, almost scientifically satiric." It reveals Mrs. Wharton in her least endearing aspect, as the superior observer of contemptible people.

In 1920 came one of Mrs. Wharton's fine achievements, *The Age of Innocence,* in which she managed to give a nostalgic picture of fashionable New York in the 1870's and at the same time to satirize it. The stability of society, which is more important than the happiness of any individual, is successfully upheld by May Archer, who does not even scruple to save her husband from running off with Ellen Olenska by whispering that she is about to bear his child. But the emancipated Countess, whom an unhappy European marriage had made an off-color member of the Newland clan (at the same time freeing her from most of the prejudices of the time) would have taken care of the matter, if necessary, quite without May's help, for she knows that honor is much more important than love, and that a human being cannot build on the pain of others and survive herself. Newland asks her:

"Then what, exactly, is your plan for us?" . . .

"For *us?* But there's no *us* in that sense! We're near each other only if we stay far from each other. Then we can be ourselves. Otherwise we're only Newland Archer, the husband of Ellen Olenska's cousin, and Ellen Olenska, the cousin of Newland Archer's wife, trying to be happy behind the backs of the people who trust them."

"Ah, I'm beyond that," he groaned.

"No, you're not! You've never been beyond. And *I* have," she said, in a strange voice, "and I know what it looks like there."

A pendant to *The Age of Innocence* was made up of the four novelettes published in 1924 under the title of *Old New York.* The most significant of these is **The Old Maid* (The 'Fifties), in which love is sacrificed again to social *mores.* When Charlotte Lovell gave her illegitimate child to be brought up by her sister, she did not know how she was delivering herself into another's power, nor what fierce hunger and jealousy would consume her own heart in years to come. *False Dawn* (The 'Forties) concerns the Italian primitives which Lewis Raycie outraged his father by purchasing for $5,000 upon the advice of such nobodies as Ruskin and Rossetti, and which, fifty years later, were worth millions. *The Spark* (The 'Sixties) is an incredibly rambling narrative for Mrs. Wharton yet one incredibly full of character. Hayley Delane's whole life has been illuminated by a chance hospital contact with a male nurse during the Civil War. "I don't think he believed in our Lord. Yet he taught me Christian charity." Of course the nurse was Walt Whitman. But years later, when the identification is made, and a friend reads to Hayley from *Leaves of Grass,* the conventionally-minded man can only regret that the great inspiration of his life was responsible for "all that rubbish." *New Year's Day* (The 'Seventies) is Mrs. Wharton's *Lost Lady.* Mrs. Hazeldean gets money to keep her dying husband in comfort in the only way a woman can and her reputation is ruined in consequence. But having no spiritual resources beyond her love, she lives a commonplace life thereafter. "She had done one great—or abominable—thing; rank it as you please, it had been done heroically. But there was nothing to keep her at that height."

Before *Old New York,* however, Mrs. Wharton had written *The Glimpses of the Moon* (1922), in whose Susy Branch she gave us, against a glittering European background, a social parasite with the stamina and executive efficiency which Lily Bart lacked. Susy's husband, Nick Lansing, shares her "sponging" with her, but is estranged when he learns that, to preserve their luxury, she has aided her hostess in a dishonorable intrigue. Both try mating with others but it doesn't work:

"Married. . . . Doesn't it mean something to you, something inexorable? It does to me. I didn't dream it would, in just that way. But all I can say is that I suppose the people who don't feel it aren't really married—and they'd better separate; much better."

This brings us to the final phase of Mrs. Wharton's work. In *The Reef* George Darrow's casual mistress had turned up as his prospective stepson's fiancée; in *The Mother's Recompense* (1925),

Kate Clephane's European lover reappears, in New York, to woo her daughter. The relationship between mother and daughter is many faceted, and the situation is thoroughly explored. But much of the novel is in Mrs. Wharton's "superior" vein—a consciously satirical picture of corrupt people. She fails to establish the importance of her central character; the reader oscillates between sympathy and contempt and never settles down comfortably with either.

In both *Twilight Sleep* (1927) and *The Children* (1928) we have moved into a world in which all standards have gone to pieces. Mrs. Manford, the rich woman of *Twilight Sleep* who drugs herself with her activities in behalf of often contradictory causes, is indeed an entirely decent woman, but she is a complete fool, the born prey of every unscrupulous charlatan who sets his fees high enough. (The Mahatma's "Holy Ecstasy" had reduced her hips after all else had failed.) This is all cleverly done, but it lives on a plane of caricature even broader than *The Custom of the Country*. In *The Children,* which, as Agnes Repplier remarked, "has all the force of satire and all the tenderness of compassion," the tangled milieu which has been created by successive divorces and remarriages is even more appalling, but the book is saved by Judith Wheater, "the disenchanted maiden for whom life seemed to have no surprises," and the most charming girl Mrs. Wharton ever created. She has been soiled, in a way, by the appalling society in which she has lived, yet she touches the imagination with the thought of something exquisite, utterly loyal and indomitable, capable of bearing anything. In comparison, Rose Sellers—a type that Mrs. Wharton had already used as Anna Leath in *The Reef* was to use again as Halo Tarrant in *Hudson River Bracketed* (1929) and its sequel, *The Gods Arrive* (1932)—seems an ideal rather than a human being, a modern sophisticated equivalent of Patient Griselda. Martin Boyne, who is temporarily in charge of Judy and all the little Wheaters of whom she is in charge finds considerable difficulty in deciding whether what he feels for her is amorous or paternal, but though the ambiguity wrecks his proposed marriage with Mrs. Sellers, the girl herself never suspects.

The two books I have already mentioned in connection with Halo Tarrant are not built around her but around her lover, Vance

Weston, who comes out of the Middle West, ranges through adventures amatory and otherwise, in New York and in Europe, and is presumably intended to develop into a great novelist. Though there is no falling-off in Mrs. Wharton's style nor yet in her sense of values, few readers have found Weston worth 1,000 pages. The novelist died over *The Buccaneers* (1938), which records the adventures of three American girls in London society of the 1870's, guided by a governess, Laura Testvalley, who had long teased her creator's imagination.

I have left myself little space for the four novelettes of which I have not yet spoken: *The Touchstone* (1900), *Sanctuary* (1903), *Madame de Treymes* (1907), and *"Her Son"* (1933). Over the last we need not linger. The other three are excellent examples of the author's skill in handling the ethical dilemma. Glennard, of *The Touchstone,* sells for publication, after her death, the love letters that had been written to him by a great woman. In *Sanctuary,* Kate Peyton, who had failed, in a crisis, to nerve her lover to act up to her ideal for him, finds the reward of all her striving when, years afterward, their son faces his own ordeal unflinchingly. *Madame de Treymes,* which echoes both "Madame de Mauves" and *The American,* contrasts French and American ideals of honor in a situation too complicated to admit of brief summary. These works are not, at every point, unassailable—the plot of *Sanctuary* is filled with improbabilities—but they all strike the note of nobility.

4. *Affirmation: Of Art and of Life*

Edith Wharton's primary interest was in the kind of fiction we call psychological: "real drama is soul drama." She is, therefore, inevitably indebted to the French masters who stressed this aspect and to her friends Paul Bourget and Henry James. But her people live not in a vacuum but in society, and she praises Balzac and Stendhal for their ability to see characters as the products of social forces.[12]

[12] To a certain extent, she seems to have realized that Fielding and Scott had also done something of this; she found another suggestion of it in *Moll Flanders.* She is not particularly strong in her appreciation of nineteenth-century British fiction, though she praises Thackeray, Trollope, and Jane Austen as creators of character. She also enjoyed Stevenson. She admits the

Art, for her, was primarily a matter of selection; the novelist's task is that of disengaging "crucial moments from the welter of existence" and making them vivid and meaningful. James said of her that she gave us her saturation "not in the crude state but in the extract." She rejected both the "slice of life" theory and the "stream-of-consciousness" technique, which, in her eyes, was merely a new-fangled form of it with Freudian trimmings.

Like James, she found the "differences and *nuances*," the "intensities and reticences," the "passions and privacies" that fiction needs in the "dense old European order" rather than in America. She knew that there are no trivial subjects *per se,* and she believed that it was precisely when dealing with apparent trivialities that the writer had need of the great attitude. She accepted the Jamesian ideal, but with a woman's passion for the concrete and consequent comparative indifference to ideational structures, she refused to develop Jamesian symmetry to anything like the lengths that the Master had carried it. She echoes James in her themes, her method, and sometimes even in names and specific situations, but her structure is much freer than his; and though she may have pondered her "angles of vision" as carefully as either he or Conrad, except in *Ethan Frome,* she generally makes the reader much less conscious of them.[13]

A story might begin for Edith Wharton with either the characters or the situation. If the situation came first, she was always very careful to let it lie in her mind until it had brought forth of itself the people it needed. It was an idiosyncrasy of her creative mind that her characters always came to her *with their names,* which she could

vividness of Dickens's characters but contends that they have life only in the world which he created for them. She seems to have regarded herself as the pioneer among truthful literary historians of New England, and she is very superficial when she accuses Sarah Orne Jewett and Mrs. Wilkins Freeman of having viewed their country through "rose-colored spectacles." Her most amazing blind spot, however, seems to have been Melville: she lumps *Moby-Dick, Lord Jim,* and *Rob Roy* together as "just 'good yarns,' in the old simple sense of the tale of adventure"! Elsewhere she sneers at Melville as having seen life "in terms of South Sea cannibals."

[13] There is an excellent comparison of Mrs. Wharton's technique and that of James in Joseph Warren Beach, *The Twentieth Century Novel.*

not change except at the cost of losing her hold upon them. She always knew the destiny of her people from the beginning, but she did not know how it would come.

For the substance of her story she relied upon narrative, in her view a suppler and more varied form than dialogue, which she reserved for culminating moments. Dialogue was wasteful and roundabout, imposing the limitations of the drama (for which she never greatly cared) upon the more "orchestral" novel. Setting never existed for her unless it could be made part of the action. Yet she was always conscious of "conducting" her narrative, and when she wrote dialogue she was only a recording instrument.

She used coincidence freely to bring about her situations, and it cannot be claimed that her motivation is always quite convincing. One is not sure, for example, that Ethan and Mattie would have attempted suicide, that Ralph Marvell and Count Raymond de Chelles would really have been taken in by Undine Spragg, that Nick Lansing would have left Susy when he did. Often Mrs. Wharton's workmanship is fine enough to cause us to overlook such things. But this is artifice rather than art.

In the early days Edith Wharton was often reproached for her lack of "categorical" morality. Perhaps it is because Charity Royall shows no sense of having done wrong that Régis Michaud calls *Summer* a "pagan" novel. Sophy Viner is similarly unrepentant, and Mrs. Wharton does not say whether she agrees with her or not. But she leaves no doubt of Darrow's guilt, for Darrow used the girl as a thing, without loving her, to bridge over a difficult time in his own life, and without ever considering the effect upon her.

Edith Wharton's successive novels survey a world growing progressively more promiscuous. She does not display the deepening bitterness and disgust of Robert Herrick over the spectacle, but nobody who reads her books with any intelligence can possibly believe that she thinks promiscuity "works." As Nona Manford realizes while she ponders the plight of her brother and his worthless wife, "Human nature had not changed as fast as social usage. . . ." Happiness is not possible for human beings until passion has been taught to obey the commands of reason. Like Martin Boyne, Edith Wharton lived to learn to marvel "at the incurable simplicity of the corrupt. 'Blessed are the pure in heart,' he thought, 'for they have so many more things to talk about. . . .' "

Most of what has been written about Mrs. Wharton's "coldness" is nonsense. She was trained in an austere aesthetic method, and her conception of the novel required that the artist should stand aloof from his material, always in supreme command of the effects which he creates. But though she is not sentimental, she can be called inhuman only by persons not capable of reading fiction which has been conceived upon a level of intellectual distinction, and we have unmistakable evidence of her compassion in private life.

She is, indeed, kind to many characters whom the charity of most of her readers has not been able to embrace. Her men in general are poor creatures; some woman must always make their decisions for them; about the only decision any one ever makes for himself is Ralph Marvell's when he takes his own life. Nor do they define their relationship to society much more successfully than their relationship to love. One critic attributes their weakness to Mrs. Wharton's "feminism," but this is quite beside the mark: Mrs. Wharton seems to like them. A more reasonable explanation is that unless a sensitive man happened to be an artist, there was really not very much for him to do in the world she knew best. Very likely, too, the influence of Walter Berry upon her was not a happy one at this point.

Henry James once told Edith Wharton that her only serious drawback as an artist was "not having the homeliness and the inevitability and the happy limitation and the affluent poverty, of a Country of your Own. . . ." The shortcomings of her world imposed serious limitations upon her art. Part of the fault was, I think, in her. Though she was enthralled by great poetry, and, like James, testified to her sense of the galling limitations of this world by writing excellent ghost stories, it is painful to learn that even as a child she never cared for fairy tales but was greatly taken by "the gods and goddesses of Olympus, who behaved so much like the ladies and gentlemen who came to dine." All aristocracies are, in a sense, artificial, but the American aristocracy, which is based on money, lacks culture, and is often hostile to fine art, must be, for an artist, the thinnest and most unrewarding of all. If Mrs. Wharton was not herself corrupted by it, her preoccupation, as an artist, with its concerns still made it necessary for her to take her reader into much unpleasant company and waste his time upon many trifling matters. She saw all this clearly, but since she was a realist, she could hardly be expected to read into her world qualities which it had never possessed. James, to be sure, in a sense, did just that; but James was less of a realist than Edith Wharton and more of a poet. She was, too, closer to determinism than he, and the fate of her people was more largely controlled by their environment. In so far as she and James shared common limitations in the way of material, the consequences were, therefore, more serious for her than for him.

In one of her short stories Edith Wharton presents "one of the women who make refinement vulgar." It would be grossly unjust to turn such a phrase against her; in one sense, no writer's taste was ever more impeccable. But there is a certain vulgarity in all satire and in every thought of superiority to another human being; in the vulgarity which inheres in an elegant malice such a novel as *The Custom of the Country* is drenched. It is also true that Mrs. Wharton's superb competence sometimes creates an impression of "slickness" which is not fair to her; her brilliant epigrams crackle about our ears until the mind wearies; surely this *must* be superficial stuff, or nobody could bring it off with such ease!

Edith Wharton paid a price for her shortcomings, but we should always remember that it is not *The Custom of the Country* upon which she was called to stake her fame. The real Edith Wharton is in the compassion with which she created Lily Bart and Charity Royall; in the noble symmetry of *The Reef* (itself, like sound architecture, an affirmation of Order), and in the stern, wintry integrity of *Ethan Frome,* where misery itself is turned to beauty; in the lofty highmindedness of women like Kate Peyton and, in a more worldly way, the Countess Olenska, and in the wistful, poetic charm of such touching visions as Martin Boyne's last glimpse of Judith Wheater.

CHAPTER XIV

ELLEN GLASGOW: TRIUMPH AND DESPAIR

Whether I wrote history or fiction, I would write of the South not as a lost province but as a part of the larger world; I would touch the universal chords beneath the minor variations of character.

E. G.: Preface to *The Miller of Old Church*

1. *Tradition and the Novelist*

Like Edith Wharton, Ellen Glasgow was a great lady. But she was a great lady of Virginia, and that made a difference. I am not thinking here of the "color" of the Southland, for she rebelled against swords and roses from the very beginning; when, upon the appearance, in 1925, of *Barren Ground,* her publishers proclaimed that realism had at last crossed the Potomac, both Stuart Sherman and Archibald Henderson were able to reply that the crossing had taken place twenty-five years earlier with *The Voice of the People* and that realism was heading north! Ellen Glasgow herself always felt that the South offered the novelist richer themes than any other part of America—"depth and a tragic past, and a gay and gallant pessimism"—and though she was never a regionalist, she well knew the value of her vital contacts with "the oldest roots of our Republic," which were also "the oldest roots of democracy," and of her tie with the land itself. Her work was forward- not backward-looking, and her range was wide; taken together, her novels constitute a picture of Virginia from 1850 to our own time, but their emphasis is always upon the men and the forces that are building the Virginia of the future and not upon the chauvinists who still bemoan the losses of the past. Like all really creative writers, Ellen Glasgow led a lonely life, estranged as fundamentally in her age from what seemed to her the inverted sentimentalism of writers like Caldwell and Faulkner— "ambitious amateurs, who imagine that they are realists because they have tasted a stew of spoiled meat"—as she had been in her youth from their evasively genteel elders. All of which, of course, is only another way of saying that she was the kind of writer who deserves to inherit a tradition because she alone knows how to employ it, rejecting whatever has become sterile and making full use of that which is still valid in it.

Ellen Glasgow was born in Richmond, Virginia, on April 22, 1874, and died in the same city on November 21, 1945. Her mother belonged to the Tidewater aristocracy; her father's Scotch-Irish ancestors had settled in the wilderness between the Blue Ridge and the Alleghenies. There were lawyers and teachers in the family, with an ironworks in the background, supplying cannon for the Civil War. The delicate child, too frail to go to school, studied her letters from *Old Mortality,* which she had already learned to love, along with the English and Scottish popular ballads, from the oral rendition of her Aunt Rebecca. While she was still very young, she read all the standard English poets and novelists, and she encountered Balzac, Flaubert, and Maupassant before she had done any important work of her own. Later came the Russians, "the greatest of all novelists." She studied the classical English economists and philosophers also and went on to Huxley and to Darwin, whom she calls the most important single influence upon her thinking.

Creation came, in the beginning, spontaneously. When she was three years old, one Little Willie popped into her consciousness, and for years she pursued his adventures from the moment she was tucked into bed at night until she fell asleep. At seven she wrote a story which she called "A Lonely Daisy in a Field of Roses." When she came across the manuscript toward the close of her life, it seemed to her that in it she had already discovered her own important theme—the struggle of the outsider for recognition and establishment. Her first novel, afterwards destroyed, bore the characteristic title, *Sharp Realities.*

Fielding's *Tom Jones* was for her the greatest English novel and his Amelia one of the most living women in fiction. Other novels for which she was ready "to die upon the literary barricades" were *War and Peace, The Brothers Karamazov, Clarissa Harlowe, David Copperfield,* the Barsetshire novels, *Remembrance of Things Past,* and *Le Vicomte de Bragelonne*. Among American writers she called Howells our greatest realist, who "made us see the poetry of the life he knew best." She welcomed the later American historical novel as a wholesome reaction from the puerilities of the futilitarian era. Southern writers she liked best when, like the author of *Uncle Remus*, they forgot elegance and explored the psychology of humble people who could be presented without sentimentality or pretense. Among her contemporaries she was partial to the gallantry and the disenchantment and the aesthetic sensitiveness of James Branch Cabell.

The purpose of fiction, as she conceived it, was "to increase our understanding of life and heighten our consciousness." She did not want to be either "realist" or "romancer"; she simply wanted to express the truth about human life, embracing both the world within and the world of external appearances. By the same token, she rejected both sentimentalism and cruelty. "Blood and irony" was what she was after; for blood means passion, warmth, vitality, and irony is "the safest antidote to sentimental decay."

Though she recognized the importance of form from the beginning of her career, aestheticism for its own sake never tempted her. She spared no pains to become as thoroughly acclimated in the world of her fiction as in that which her body inhabited, spending months, if necessary, reading background material that would contribute only a page or two of tangible print. She was capable of searching for a word or a phrase for hours, and then of getting up from her bed to write it down when it came to her unexpectedly in her sleep. It took many weeks to write the chapters in the first part of *Vein of Iron* which give us the viewpoints of the various characters, each in his own rhythm.

Yet her technique, as distinguished from her vision and her convictions, developed slowly and with infinite pains; as she herself realized, she did not begin to do her best work until after 1922. This was partly because, having grown up in a society largely indifferent to fine art, she came to her first novels with very little in the way of aesthetic theory behind her, but it was more because she was so constituted that she could not imitate the method of another writer, no matter how much she admired him; she had to proceed experimentally until, with much stumbling, she had at last made a way of her own.

2. *A Social History of Virginia*

Ellen Glasgow wrote nineteen novels.[1] Twelve of these she included in 1938 in the definitive "Virginia Edition" of her works, for which she wrote a series of prefaces comprising a self-evaluation which has been equalled or surpassed by only two other American novelists, Cabell and Henry James. These Prefaces were reprinted, along with an essay on *In This Our Life* (1941), in the book called *A Certain Measure* (1943), wherein she arranged her preferred fictions to make up a social history of Virginia,[2] a complete picture of the South in defeat, avoiding sentimentality and local color, and concentrating "more upon universal impulses than upon provincial behavior."

The first group is as follows:

I. *The Battle-Ground* (1850-1865)	Published 1902
II. *The Deliverance* (1878-1890)	1904
III. *The Voice of the People* (1870-1898)	1900
IV. *The Romance of a Plain Man* (1875-1909)	1909
V. *Virginia* (1884-1912)	1913
VI. *Life and Gabriella* (1894-1912)	1916

To these were added three Novels of the Country:

I. *The Miller of Old Church* (1898-1902)	1911
II. *Barren Ground* (1894-1924)	1925
III. *Vein of Iron* (1901-1933)	1935

and four Novels of the City:

I. *The Sheltered Life* (1910-1927)	1932
II. *The Romantic Comedians* (1923)	1926
III. *They Stooped to Folly* (1924)	1929
IV. *In This Our Life* (1938-1939)	1941

[1] Plus one volume of short stories, mostly ghost stories, called *The Shadowy Third* (1923). She also left a novelette, *Beyond Defeat,* a sequel to *In This Our Life,* and an autobiography, which have not yet been published.

[2] The original plan was to use *The Shadowy Third* in place of *The Romance of a Plain Man.* When the publishers made it clear that they wanted a novel, Cabell's vote was for *The Builders,* his objection to *The Romance of a Plain Man* being that it was told from the man's point of view. But Ellen Glasgow felt it safe to rely upon her intuitions to tell her how a man would feel.

I shall comment upon these books in the order in which their author arranged them.

The Battle-Ground studies two neighboring Virginia families against the backdrop of the Civil War. Its Negro folklore and its picture of the hero and heroine in childhood are very winning; in its account of the conflict it differs from other Civil War novels of the time less in its materials than in its intelligence; the doctor's "God damn war!" was daring in 1902 and not only on account of its profanity.

The central figure of *The Deliverance,* Christopher Blake, represents the old South dispossessed by upstarts; the book tells of his terrible revenge and of his attempted atonement after a change of heart. The scene is the tobacco fields, of which Miss Glasgow made a careful study, for she wanted her characters "projections of the landscape." But the plot is developed obviously, and Christopher is not a strong enough character for the role he is called upon to play. Neither is the conquest of hate through love entirely convincing; had she written the book when she was older, Miss Glasgow later declared, she would have given it a tragic ending.

The Voice of the People and *The Romance of a Plain Man* are a pair. In the first, the poor white trash Nicholas Burr, rises to political power; in the other, a workingman of the city achieves financial mastery. Taken together, the two books chronicle "the stubborn retreat of an agrarian culture before the conquests of the Industrial Revolution, and the slow and steady rise of the lower middle class." Nick is handled objectively, but because Miss Glasgow wished to do Ben Starr from the inside, and also because she believed that the autobiographical method, which had been traditionally associated with heroic action, might add irony to her tale, she wrote *The Romance of a Plain Man* in the first person. Neither book is quite satisfactory. *The Voice of the People* contains a realistic picture of a political convention (which the young lady author was smuggled in behind the scenes to witness); there is a good deal of charm in its old Southern types, and the love story owns a fragile idyllism. But the development of the plot is weak, and Nick's death, at the hands of a mob, as he stands at the summit of his career, lacks both force and inevitability. The first part of *The Romance of a Plain Man,* which is a fairly close imitation of the opening chapters of *Great Expectations,* was the most charming thing Miss Glasgow had yet done. But after the children grow up, the novel suffers from shifting centers of interest and from summary developments, which are only stated and not shown. As a child, Sally resembles Dickens's Estella, but, unlike Estella's, her characterization is not sustained; as Ben's wife, she is a plaster saint until, quite inexplicably, we come to the scene where she behaves like a spoiled baby in her determination to risk her neck by riding a dangerous horse. Finally, her health breaks, and we steer straight for a sentimental and evasive ending, with Ben quite unconvincingly relinquishing the goal of all his striving to devote himself, at long last, exclusively to her.

The last two novels of the first group—*Virginia* and *Life and Gabriella*—are again complementary. Both heroines are unfortunate in marriage, but their reactions are very different. Virginia is the old-fashioned masculine ideal—so comfortable for men!—which the General of the *Plain Man* had in mind when he declared that there was no more edifying sight under heaven than a woman bearing her wrongs beautifully. For Gabriella, on the other hand, love dies with respect, and she invests her energies in a business career in New York. Modern readers are much more likely to sympathize with Gabriella than with Virginia, but Virginia is not, therefore, necessarily a less successful characterization. Ellen Glasgow began painting her portrait in a mood of irony, but found herself yielding increasingly to a "sympathetic compassion." Both books are among the best of Ellen Glasgow's early novels, but both, I think, appeal mainly to women. *Barren Ground* is as much preoccupied with a woman, but this time the situation is viewed with a human, and not merely a feminine, eye.

The very best book before *Barren Ground* is *The Miller of Old Church.* Ellen Glasgow herself parallels it to *The Deliverance,* as another story of the plain countryman forging ahead in a later period and a different province. But none of her novels are as sociological as some of her descriptions of them, and the "feel" of *The Miller* is not at all like that of the earlier book. This time the rustics are as good as Hardy's, including Solomon Hatch, who feared that "a man that's gone wrong on immersion can't be trusted to keep his hands off the women," and Sarah Revercomb, who puts down the rector by being able to say the first chapter of Chronicles backwards, and who wears a crape veil to her son's wedding in the twentieth year of her widowhood because it was too costly to lay aside. The situation described at the beginning, with its overtones of mystery and its suggestions of ancient wrong, is fascinating; it is the only important weakness of the book that these mysteries are cleared up too early.

Then, in 1925, with *Barren Ground,* came a new "intuitive visitation" of power. This story of the betrayed girl who became at last the victor and not the victim is generally considered Miss Glasgow's masterpiece. Certainly it is her most spacious canvas; neither is any other of her novels quite so "strong." But it is a remarkable fact that never again after *Barren Ground* did Ellen Glasgow turn out a book which was not excellent. *The Romantic Comedians* is unquestionably her most brilliant and highly-unified novel, a scintillating combination of irony and compassion, the product of a single inspiration, poured out *mit einem Gusse.* And the wistful poignant beauty of *The Sheltered Life* will always make it, for some of Ellen Glasgow's readers, incomparably her most precious book.

In *Barren Ground* Ellen Glasgow first importantly celebrated that "vein of iron" without which the problem of human life seemed to her to admit of no solution. The phrase fascinates her; she uses it again and again, finally employing it as the title of a novel. What it means is that character is fate, that "imagination is a creative principle and depends little upon the raw material of life," that life itself is a struggle with barren ground and that one may "learn to live gallantly without delight," that it is impossible to defeat a human being who will not acknowledge defeat. After her betrayal Dorinda gives herself over to the destructive power of hate, and though in the end hate does not win, she always carries her scars. When one sums up the wrong things she does, they make a formidable list; even "reclaiming the abandoned fields" becomes at one time "less a reasonable purpose than a devouring passion." Yet she never forfeits the reader's sympathy. It is much the same with the life she leads and the imagined world in which she leads it. It is a hard world, a world cruelly stunted of its full development. But because human values have survived in it, it is shot through and through with magnificence. That survival and that consequence mark the difference between Ellen Glasgow and those of her contemporaries who did not have the stamina required to face life without an inner collapse.[3]

The last novel of the country, *Vein of Iron* itself, is the book in which Ellen Glasgow comes closest to the power of *Barren Ground*. *Vein of Iron* is the only story she ever wrote about the inland wilderness settled by her father's people. Ada Fincastle's struggle for adjustment in a marriage which soon loses its initial rapture, through years of war and depression, is less picturesque than Dorinda's battle in *Barren Ground,* but it is not essentially less heroic, and the girl herself has more charm. Her father, a philosopher whose books are prized by European savants but ignored in his own country, and her Calvinistic grandmother who refuses to speak to her when she learns that she is to bear a child out of wedlock, but comes to her instantly when labor begins: "Hold tight to me, Ada. Hold tight as you can. I won't let you go"—these are memorable figures. Both *Barren Ground* and *Vein of Iron* reflect the larger freedom which public opinion was beginning to permit novelists after World War I, but here again Ellen Glasgow differed from many of her contemporaries. If ever a woman had a "right" to love out of wedlock, it was Ada Fincastle. And if ever a woman courageously accepted the consequences of her deed, it was she. But "That is the greatest injustice in life—we cannot suffer anything alone, not even disgrace"—and Ada goes through the rest of her life feeling that she has been responsible for her grandmother's death.

The slight plot of *The Sheltered Life* culminates in a Southern lady's murder of a husband who sincerely loves her but finds it impossible to remain faithful to her. It is typical Glasgow irony that the lady should have been able to commit the crime only because she was not in complete possession of her faculties following an operation and that the husband should have been probably less guilty in his feeling for Jenny Blair than he had been in any of his

---

[3] *Barren Ground* goes soft only in the story of Dorinda's flight to New York, which is quite facile, with character largely at the mercy of circumstance, and the kind doctor playing a very convenient *deus ex machina* when Dorinda is hurt.

previous affairs. Miss Glasgow realized that George being what he is, his unfaithfulness to Eva really had very little to do with his affection for her. But the plot of *The Sheltered Life* does not matter very much, for it is a philosophical novel, an inquiry concerning what it is that endures in the flux of life. The action is viewed from two different points of view which might be described as those of youth and age, of thought and emotion—the viewpoint of Jenny Blair, the little girl who throws herself at George's head and becomes the almost innocent cause of his death, and that of her grandfather, General Archbald, "the civilized man in a world that is not civilized." As a boy he was a freak in his family because he hated sports; before the war sucked him up without making him believe in it, he had used to help runaway slaves to get away. He missed the woman he loved and was a faithful husband to another whom he did not love; after her death, when he wished to marry again, he gave up the plan out of consideration for other members of his family. This touching figure is most fully presented in Part II—"The Deep Past"—which is comparable to "Time Passes" in Virginia Woolf's *To the Lighthouse,* which was published five years earlier, and by which it was almost certainly influenced.[4]

The full effects of the postwar liberation in Miss Glasgow's novels were best shown in *The Romantic Comedians* and *They Stooped to Folly,* which give every sign of having been influenced by the author's friendship with Cabell—both view sex, in the Cabell manner, as furnishing the stuff of high comedy, a rare achievement in women's work—and which we know to have furnished her with relief after the solemnities of *Barren Ground* and the horrors of World War I. After Mrs. Honeywell died, everyone in Queenborough expected the Judge to marry the love of his youth, Amanda Lightfoot—"fifty-eight if a day, but marvelously preserved"; instead he chose Annabel Upchurch, aet. eighteen. What follows might have been a cheap tale indeed in the hands of a less fastidious writer: Ellen Glasgow made it a distinguished vessel to hold her most perfect blend of civilized wit and genuine compassion. At every

---

[4] In a review of Virginia Woolf's *Flush* (*New York Herald-Tribune Books,* Oct. 8, 1933), Ellen Glasgow called *To the Lighthouse* "the most beautiful and satisfying novel written in our time."

point, she resolutely avoids the easiest way. Annabel is not a "bad" girl, though she is certainly a fool; and though her husband has obviously been a much greater one, his creator is not afraid to permit him to behave like a Southern gentleman when his hour is upon him. Scott, Cervantes, and a few others—you can count the writers capable of such a mixture of the sublime and the ridiculous upon the fingers of one hand.

They Stooped to Folly, which of course takes its title from Goldsmith's famous quatrain, studies "the almost forgotten myth of the 'ruined' woman" in three embodiments, each representative of her age: "poor Aunt Agatha," who was crushed into retirement (until, in her old age, she emerged to discover the delights of the "movies" and the "banana split"); Mrs. Dalrymple, who was only tarnished—it was hard to believe that any woman "so well dressed and so skillfully repaired" could really have suffered in "the withering fires of remorse"; and Mr. Littlepage's secretary, the shameless Milly Burden, child of an age of "forsaken standards and distorted values," who insists that "being ruined is a state of mind" and perceives no reason why she should not speak of her experience quite freely.

Since all "woman myths" have been invented by men, it is suitable that *They Stooped to Folly* should make use of a man's reflecting consciousness. Though Mr. Littlepage's own marriage has been happy, he has always had "a secret leaning toward faithless husbands and other undesirable acquaintances." He finds it a pity that charm "is so often divorced from the cardinal virtues," and since he thinks of the modern revolt as "less immoral than experimental," it is natural that he should constitute himself Milly's protector. When his formidable daughter, Mary Victoria, who has been doing relief work in Europe, looks up the poor creature that had fathered Milly's child, and, out of sheer benevolence, marries him and brings him home with her, it seems to show her father "that intemperate virtue is almost as disastrous . . . as temperate vice." The entire action of *They Stooped to Folly* is confined to a six months span—even Milly's seduction, if it can be called that, is over before the book opens—but reflective interludes and soliloquies take us back into the past whenever we have need of such excursions.

The study of crumbling standards—and of the consequent need

for an anchor—is continued in Miss Glasgow's last novel, *In This Our Life*. Indeed, Roy, the "good" heroine of the book, first came into her creator's consciousness crying, "I want something to hold by. I want something good." Both Craig and Peter are contemptible weaklings, and both desert Roy for her younger sister, Stanley, the most worthless heroine Miss Glasgow ever created. Stanley and her invalid mother are the tyrants of the family. Asa Timberlake, the father, is the humane man, the brooding consciousness that we have already met in a considerably more heroic incarnation in the person of General Archbald. Asa speaks for the author in his judgment that the young people of the book—and of the age—"had never really broken through the tight shell of their egotism" and have no real design for living. They externalize their own inner disorder. Even when their instincts remain sound, "a decent world cannot be based on instinct alone."

In This Our Life is not Miss Glasgow's most attractive book, but when one remembers the condition of health—or, rather, of mortal illness—in which it was created, it becomes a miraculous achievement. For it Miss Glasgow received, at last, a long-overdue Pulitzer Prize.[5] Probably most readers remember longest such moments in it as that in which Asa is "suffocated by the longing to shield, by the savage and irrational instinct of parenthood" as he looks down upon the daughter from whom he had believed himself hopelessly estranged, lying "defenseless in sleep," or that in which Roy's control suddenly snaps when she sees her long-suffering father sitting down quietly in the night to try to sew a button on his clothes.[6]

[5] After having ignored her for many years, the prize-givers discovered Ellen Glasgow with a vengeance during her last years. In 1938 she was elected to the American Academy of Arts and Letters. In 1940 she received both the Howells Medal and the *SRL* Award for Outstanding Service to American Letters. In 1941 she was awarded the Southern Authors' Prize.

[6] Six of Ellen Glasgow's novels were excluded from the Virginia Edition. The first three of these were laid in New York: *The Descendant* (1897); *Phases of an Inferior Planet* (1898); and *The Wheel of Life* (1906). No one of these is very good, but the first is significant as marking her point of departure. It is a plea for the disinherited whose hero is an illegitimate poor white; the title-page flaunts an epigraph from the materialistic German philosopher Haeckel: "Man is not above Nature, but in Nature." Ellen Glasgow placed the scene of this novel outside Virginia because at this time the pull of inheritance and tradition was so strong that she felt she could not write

3. *The Last Citadel*

The values of Ellen Glasgow's fiction are those of a skeptical, urbane, tolerant, and highly civilized mind. Temperamentally she was always inclined toward the skeptical attitude as "the safety-valve of civilization"; having revolted against the genteel hypocrisies of the world of her youth, she clung gratefully to her hard-won "liberty not to believe" and "not to be glad." Alfred Kazin once spoke of her as combining the manners of a dowager with the mind of a nihilist, and it is difficult today to realize how shocking her extremely well-bred description of Cyrus Treadwell's brief, cruel encounter with his Negro mistress must have seemed in 1913. She was no more inclined to sentimentalize Negroes than white folks, but she handled the South's "peculiar institution" with no holds barred, and no abolitionist can have shocked one type of mind more than her quiet statement that she first heard the word "well-bred" when her mother applied it to an old Negro who used to work about the Glasgow house. That rough saint, Ben O'Hara, who has all the virtues and none of the graces, and whom Gabriella finally marries after she has shed her sentimental affection for Arthur Peyton, has no particular reality as a character, but his presence in her novel certainly testifies to the breadth of Ellen Glasgow's sympathies.

About the emotional life of mankind she is so level-headed as to be chilling. Again and again she expresses the idea that love is not very important except to those who have never had it. *In This Our Life* is a long keening over the tyrannies inseparable from family

unsentimentally of her native heath. *The Descendant* (like *Phases*) was published anonymously, and accepted, or so its author believed, because the publisher's reader mistook it for an unsigned work of Harold Frederic. Sara Haardt remarks wittily that Miss Glasgow "wrote a Bohemian novel of New York without ever going out unchaperoned." *The Ancient Law* (1908) records a man's struggle to rehabilitate himself after imprisonment. The other two books—*The Builders* (1919) and *One Man in His Time* (1922)—are more mature. *The Builders* concerns a bitch-woman who victimizes her husband and at the same time manages to put him thoroughly in the wrong. This novel serves as a vehicle for some of Ellen Glasgow's hopes for the new South. *One Man in His Time* goes back to an earlier period and involves the political struggle once more: its hero, Gideon Vetch, born in a circus tent, becomes governor of Virginia. Gideon's daughter, Patty, weds an aristocrat, thanks largely to the wisdom and tolerance of his cousin, Corinna Culpepper.

life. Yet even when her men are weakest, she is not bitter about them; neither does she idealize her women. Though she has been called a feminist, this is true only in a very qualified sense. It was no idolater of her own sex who permitted Ralph McBride to write home from the war that he was sick of women. "There's been no lack of women in this war. They've rushed for every horror as straight as ducks for a puddle."

Something of Ellen Glasgow's rebellion was, to be sure, outgrown with her youth. At eighteen she called herself the only Socialist in Richmond; in her maturity she knew that no social order that men can establish will function justly and humanely until men are themselves just and humane in their inner abiding place. And though none of the horrors of her time caused her to take her place with the "tired liberals," she did admit, in her later years, a feeling of sadness that "That liberal hope of which we dreamed in my youth appeared to have won no finer freedom than an age of little fads and the right to cry ugly words in the street."

The Roman Catholic critic, Elizabeth Monroe, not unnaturally finds that Ellen Glasgow's art only "appears to be objective" while actually being "oriented in her own skeptical and relativistic view of life." But even Miss Monroe admits that she tempers her "searing vision of disintegration with a vision of beauty blossoming in its midst, and with an ironic tolerance of good and evil as parts of a universal pattern."[7] Ellen Glasgow never pretended to be a happy woman; indeed she once spoke of herself as having achieved "the freedom of despair." She could not conceive how any person of imagination could enjoy—or, hardly, even desire—happiness in a world full of unimaginable suffering for man and beast. For her the great sin—the only real sin—was cruelty; like Arnold Bennett, she was oppressed by the pity of decay, the invulnerable, all-engulfing triumph of time. But if happiness perished, honor remained, and the power to endure, and the intelligence to adjust oneself to live an undefeated life even under the most unfavorable conditions. Her characters are, perhaps better Stoics than Christians. "He's found something," Ralph would muse aloud to Ada. "I don't know what to

[7] N. Elizabeth Monroe, *The Novel and Society*. Copyright, 1941, by The University of North Carolina Press. Quoted by permission.

call it. Invulnerability is as good a name, I suppose, as any other."

For all that, Ellen Glasgow was not a materialist, for she knew that the deeper truths call for intuition, and she claimed for herself "moments of mystic vision." Like Dorinda, she "never entirely abandoned her futile effort to find a meaning in life," and in her later years she suspected the *Shorter Catechism* and the Westminster Confession of having contributed more to her life than she had realized. Even in the black years during which her life ended, she refused to believe that civilization had at last taken the trail of the Gadarene swine to the abyss. She denied the term realist to writers without humor and defined true realism as "optimistic without being sentimental." There can be little doubt that Ada Fincastle's final summary of her faith is Ellen Glasgow's own, and it is as robust as that of Frank Norris at the end of *The Octopus:*

Shelters and systems and civilizations were all overwhelmed in time . . . by the backward forces of ignorance, of barbarism, of ferocity. Yet the level would steadily rise, little by little; in the end other unities would emerge from the ruins; and the indestructible will of the world was toward life.[8]

[8] *Vein of Iron,* copyright, 1935, by Ellen Glasgow.

CHAPTER XV

THEODORE DREISER,
THE MYSTIC NATURALIST*

I once believed that nature was a blind, stumbling force or combination of forces which knew not what or whither. . . . Of later years I have inclined to think just the reverse, i.e. that nature is merely dark to us because of her tremendous subtlety and our own very limited powers of comprehension.

T. D.: A Hoosier Holiday (1916)

1. *The Matrix*

Dreiser is generally regarded as the novelist above all others who fought the battle for naturalism in American fiction, and his monolithic novels are set up as its outstanding monuments. This view is not so much incorrect as it is one-sided, an oversimplification of the Dreiser problem; as we proceed, we shall see that it calls for modification in many ways.

Balzac was a far more important influence upon Dreiser's work than Zola—Dreiser himself went so far as to tell Mencken that he had "never read a line of Zola"—but an unpublished novel by a newspaper friend, "distinctively imitative of Balzac and Zola," was possibly more important than either of the French writers directly. Dreiser read the standard British nineteenth-century novelists; he read Hawthorne, Irving, and the New England poets; he admired the Tolstoy of *Ivan Ilyitch* and *The Kreutzer Sonata;* he read Hardy, Henry B. Fuller, and Hamlin Garland. He also read Ouida, Laura Jean Libbey, and Horatio Alger, Jr., and he was exposed vastly to a whole world of sentimental song and story that one would expect the brother of the composer of "On the Banks of the Wabash" to

---

* A small portion of this chapter appeared as a Dreiser memorial article in the *Chicago Sunday Tribune Magazine of Books,* on February 3, 1946. Copyright, 1946, by the Tribune Company.

have savored.[1] Even the unlikeliest of these writers left their marks upon him; to his own "self-analyzing eyes" he always seemed "somewhat more of a romanticist than a realist." "I revere James Whitcomb [Riley] with a whole heart," he writes. "There is something so tender, so innocent not only about his work but about him." And Dreiser himself would "hate to think it was all over with America and its lovely morning dreams."

Dreiser read in other fields also. It would be difficult to exaggerate the influence upon his thinking of Spencer, Tyndall, and Huxley, and later of Jacques Loeb's *The Mechanistic Conception of Life.* Yet one cannot but feel that environment must have counted more than any reading; like all of us, but more than most of us, Dreiser interpreted his reading in terms of his environment. His poverty-stricken background was culturally barren; he was flung, or he flung himself, into the world of the robber barons in the last golden age of ruthless individualism, which lives in his novels as nowhere else in our literature. Did not his superiors inform him at the outset that "life was a God-damned, stinking, treacherous game, that nine hundred and ninety-nine men out of every thousand were bastards"? Clumsy, ignorant, brooding, greedy, sensitive, passionate, pitiful, rebellious, and loving-hearted, Dreiser was himself an American tragedy; or, if he was not, then, precisely to the extent that he rose above his conditioning, did his life indicate the inadequacy of the "views" that he held.[2]

Theodore Dreiser was born at Terre Haute, Indiana, on August 27, 1871, the twelfth of thirteen children. His pious German Catholic father had once been prosperous, but a series of misfortunes had changed that, and the Dreiser children, like Jennie Gerhardt's family, picked up coal along the railroad tracks. The mother, who was of Mennonite background, and had a simple, loving, earthy temperament, had "psychic" sensitiveness; at one time, she saw the Blessed

---

[1] See H. L. Mencken, *A Book of Prefaces,* pp. 73-74. The lyric for "On the Banks of the Wabash" was written largely by Theodore Dreiser.

[2] According to George Jean Nathan (*The Intimate Notebooks of George Jean Nathan,* Knopf, 1932), Dreiser "discovered" the Russian ballet on his trip to Russia and came back urging that it be brought to America. After he "discovered" the Grand Canyon, he wondered why Americans were not made aware of it!

Virgin standing in the garden. The family moved to Evansville, Sullivan, and Warsaw; Theodore obtained menial jobs in Chicago; there was even a year at Indiana University, but this does not seem to have meant very much. Newspaper work began in 1892 on the Chicago *Globe* and continued in St. Louis, Toledo, Pittsburgh, and New York. Dreiser wrote hack fiction for Street and Smith and edited various magazines; from 1907 to 1910 he was editor-in-chief of the Butterick Publications, where he proved himself a mighty circulation builder and seems not to have disbelieved in the work he had to do. He also organized the National Child Welfare League. He had been married in 1898 under circumstances similar to those which obtained at Eugene Witla's mating in *The "Genius,"* and his "chemism" being similar to Witla's also, he later sought his freedom. Afterwards he formed a much more enduring relationship with a young cousin named Helen Richardson, but the refusal of the first Mrs. Dreiser to agree to a divorce prevented his marrying Helen until 1942. Though he had published his first novel as early as 1900, he did not come to be widely known among readers of fiction until he was "boomed" by H. L. Mencken and others in the early 1920's, and he did not find a really wide public or a generous critical acclaim until *An American Tragedy* came out in 1925. His later years were spent in Hollywood, where he died on December 28, 1945.

Consideration of Dreiser's philosophy of life is complicated at the outset by his own insistence that he didn't have any. As late as 1928 he declared that he was unable to make up his mind about anything or to catch any meaning from all that he had seen, and that he felt himself destined to pass on, quite as he came, confused and dismayed.[3] This statement, obviously, junks Spencer along with Aquinas; if you cannot make up your mind about anything, then you are no more materialist than Catholic; if you are not sure that anything is true, then everything may be false. But since a man who had nothing to say could hardly have felt impelled to write a whole shelf of books to say it, this is obviously not the whole story. Nor, indeed, did Dreiser quite claim that it was.

It was, clearly enough, the reading of Spencer's *First Principles* and kindred books—Huxley, Haeckel, Carl Snyder's *The World*

---

[3] See his statement in *The Bookman* (New York), LXVIII (1928), 25.

Machine, and others—during his newspaper days that stripped Dreiser of the few remaining rags and tags of his already abandoned Catholicism and convinced him that man was a mechanism and a poor one at that, with all his ideals, joys, and sorrows mere "chemic compulsions." This notion seemed to harmonize with the way life was lived in the newspaper world of a hard-boiled Chicago, and Dreiser tried to think by it and create by it. He speaks of his brother, Paul Dresser, as "one of those great Falstaffian souls who, for lack of a little iron or sodium or carbon dioxide in his chemical compost, was not able to bestride the world like a Colossus." And when it comes to people like Frank Cowperwood in his novels, the point seems to be not so much that ruthlessness in love and business is right as that the whole question of rightness or wrongness is beside the mark. "Nothing is proved; all is permitted." That is the way people are made, and there is nothing you can do about it. Given a Clyde Griffiths, a Roberta Alden, and a Sondra Finchley in the circumstances indicated, the only way out is through the electric chair.

It is easy to see how such a working hypothesis may, in the beginning, have helped Dreiser: it set him free as a man to follow his imperious passions, and it created a frame of reference for him as an artist. Only, it solved his problems by ignoring the most significant half of all of them, and of this, as he grew older, he seems to have become increasingly aware.

Temperamentally, Dreiser was more mystic than materialist. As a boy, he loved *The Water Babies,* by Charles Kingsley; "the metaphysical and mystic impulses which project life and which were suggested therein appealed to me strongly." The mother who saw the Virgin in the garden lived on in him; "signs" followed him all his life. He loved goodness, despite all his immoralism: in his mother; in Jennie Gerhardt; in Saint Francis of Assisi, whose paean in praise of poverty made his hair tingle to the roots; in the Christ-like "Doer of the Word" of whom he wrote in *Twelve Men.* Once, quite in the manner of Saint Francis, he himself tried to reason with a puff-adder, assuring the frightened and angry creature of his good-will, and he believed that he succeeded. And though in life he rebelled against his pious father, the old man's portrait as old Gerhardt (his Catholicism transformed into Lutheranism), is one of the most sympathetic in Dreiser's whole gallery. In *An American Tragedy,* Clyde Griffiths's evangelist-mother and the clergyman McMillan are as moving in their simple goodness as they could be in any novel written by a devout believer, and the same may be said of the Christian Science practitioner in *The "Genius."*

The materials of Dreiser's novels do not seem too exhilarating to most of his readers, but Dreiser himself loved life. "All life is good, all life, to the individual who is enjoying himself and to the Creator of all things." In spite of all dullness, suffering, and shame, he would gladly have lived his own life over again. Neither did he wish to deny that "everywhere I find boundless evidence of an intelligence or intelligences far superior to my own." He did not believe that nature was "a blind, stumbling force"; she only seemed so to us because of our limited knowledge. It is true that the creator of this world is not necessarily "the ultimate power or guiding force" of the universe. But the physical structure of life itself is "shot through with some vast subtlety that loves order. . . ." And he could not believe that the atoms were "toiling for exactly nothing"; who can be sure that the race itself is not "an embryo in the womb of something which we cannot see"? Evolution is still going on, and it is not necessary to believe that the present unsatisfactory position of man in the universe will be his permanent position. Meanwhile, men must "act in the name of tendencies," assume that their ideals are in some sense real; if they do not, "by so much is the realization of human ideals, the possibility of living this life at all decently, by any, made less."

2. Sister Carrie *and After*

It was Frank Norris who, in a sense, sponsored Dreiser's literary career when, as a "reader" for Doubleday, Page and Company, he became responsible for the ill-starred publication of *Sister Carrie* (1900) by that house.[4] The book was based upon the experiences of Dreiser's own sister, with some literary influence from George Ade's

[4] See Theodore Dreiser, "The Early Adventures of 'Sister Carrie,'" *Colophon,* Part V (1931); also, Dorothy Dudley's more elaborate account in *Forgotten Frontiers,* Chs. XXXI-XXXVI.

"Fable of the Two Mandolin Players and the Willing Performer." From the point of view of right-thinking people in the last year of the nineteenth century, the difficulty with the book was not merely that it told the story of a "kept" woman and her lovers but, even more seriously, the inevitable suggestion contained in it that rewards and punishments in this world have very little to do with either sins or virtues. Hurstwood, to be sure, suffers terribly, and the slow, horribly depressing decline of the once popular manager to destitution and suicide is by far the finest thing in the novel; certainly it is far more moving and interesting than anything that happens to the pussy-cat kind of girl who gives the book its name. But Drouet, the jaunty "drummer" who was Carrie's first protector, never fails to land on his feet—one feels at last not only that his future is safe but that he has immensely enjoyed his life—and Carrie herself achieves great success, as success for an attractive woman goes in our America.

Dreiser sentimentalizes Carrie—in his tender title, which "came" to him out of that mysterious region of "otherwhereness" before he had even chosen the theme of his book, and in the famous last paragraph, where he presents her as a seeker after beauty forever doomed to disappointment. But his characterization of the woman belies him. There is nothing of the pilgrim about Carrie; all she ever asked of life was a fair degree of creature comfort and a place of modest security in a world which seemed to have nothing for her so long as she remained a decent girl. But by the same token, if she is no pilgrim, she is utterly free of the guile and rapacity that "kept" women were supposed to display in novels when they were admitted there at all. Neither is Drouet, her seducer, the conventional wolf in sheep's clothing whom everybody had hissed in the old melodramas. "He loved to make advances to women, to make them succumb to his charms, not because he was a cold-blooded, dark, scheming villain, but because his inborn desire urged him to that as a chief delight."

There are faults in *Sister Carrie:* the heroine's rise to theatrical eminence is romantic in the bad sense; one is never quite convinced that Hurstwood would have taken the money; and if Carrie believed herself married to him, when in the world did she think he had been divorced? But the author's love for his essentially commonplace sinners still powerfully communicates itself to his readers, and for many the old Union Park district in Chicago speaks more eloquently of them than of any of the real persons who have lived there.

The heroine of *Jennie Gerhardt* (1911)—whose original was another sister of Dreiser's—is again a "kept" woman, but this time of a different sort. For Jennie, despite the irregularities of her life, *is* virtuous—at least if we accept Dreiser's definition of virtue: "Virtue is that quality of generosity which offers itself willingly for another's service. . . ."—and Lester is attracted to her because "Something about her—a warm womanhood, a guileless expression of countenance—intimated a sympathy toward sex relationship which had nothing to do with hard, brutal immorality." Once more it is economic considerations that lead to irregularity, but Jennie is Lester's wife in everything except the name; there is no unfaithfulness in her. In one aspect, Dreiser is like life itself: we can find in his novels the morals we bring to him. The orthodox reader may find in *Jennie Gerhardt* an impressive picture of the miseries incident to irregular unions, a powerful denunciation of the wrongs which women must suffer under such arrangements. Another type of reader will discover the moral issue in the question of love versus property; according to this view, Lester's sin would not be his union with Jennie[5] but his later sacrifice of her to position and wealth. That Jennie herself was vastly worth loving, and worth marrying, I think no reader has ever been able to doubt.

The next two novels—*The Financier* (1912, revised 1927) and *The Titan* (1914)—have a very different kind of theme; here is the Philadelphia and Chicago career of one of the most picturesque robber barons of American industry, Charles T. Yerkes. Dreiser

---

[5] Stuart Sherman ("The Barbaric Naturalism of Mr. TD," in *On Contemporary Literature*) was unconvinced alike by Jennie's yielding to Senator Brander and, later, by her going to live with Lester Kane, practically with her mother's sanction. Burton Rascoe (*Prometheans,* p. 247) was also skeptical on the second point but changed his mind when he learned of the real life basis of the story. This does not seem to me at all conclusive; that which is transcribed from life, and upon which, for that reason, the creative imagination has not had a chance to operate, is very often flat and unconvincing upon the printed page. I may add that I think the introduction of Lester Kane in *Jennie Gerhardt* infelicitous; he turns out a far more sensitive person than the casual young bounder who first cavalierly accosts Jennie seems to be.

presents him as Frank Cowperwood, a boy born without a conscience, who early in life made up his mind he was going to be a
lobster and not a squid.[6] Both here and in *An American Tragedy,*
which was based on the record of an actual murder case, Dreiser
keeps as close to the facts as Shakespeare sometimes did in his historical plays, but even when he follows his sources step by step, his
signature is unmistakable. The background of the Cowperwood
books is as elaborate as anything in fiction: high finance, ward politics, the traction business, even (when, at the close of the Philadelphia
chapter, Cowperwood is sent briefly to prison), legal machinery and
incarceration—all are here. New aspects of the hero's character
emerge as the story needs them; sometimes they are set forth in
terms of direct comment by the author himself instead of seeming
to emerge dramatically in the course of the action; yet it is only here
and there that the tycoon gets out of hand. Dreiser may tell us that
Cowperwood collected paintings, but he never makes those paintings real to us—or to him—nor yet a genuine factor in his development; and Dorothy Dudley is surely right when she declares that the
financier himself would never have said, "All of us are in the grip
of a great creative impulse," or that he would have understood such
a remark. I have my doubts, too, about his admiration for Lincoln.

Yet the character is fascinating, beyond all question, as Yerkes
must have been in life, and the contrast between the great generosity
of the man and his complete ruthlessness is part of the fascination.
To be sure, not all the tycoons were rapacious toward women, but
in this case one must grant, I think, that the man's business enterprises and his multitudinous amours are unmistakably the expres-
sions of a single personality.

In *The "Genius"* the background involves painting, journalism,
magazine publishing and editing, and finally medicine. To the
portrait of Eugene Witla aspects of both Dreiser and Everett Shinn
are said to have contributed. There is clearly much autobiography:

[6] See the early chapters of *The Financier,* as fine an example of the use of
Darwinian conceptions in fiction as can be found anywhere. Robert Elias
(*TD, Apostle of Nature,* p. 135) has called attention to Dreiser's "A Lesson
from the Aquarium," *Tom Watson's Magazine,* III (1906), 306-308, "wherein
he likened the behavior of human beings to the behavior of stort minnows,
hermit crabs, shark-suckers, and sharks. . . ."

Eugene turns agnostic, for example, after a course of reading in the British rationalists that must have been much like Dreiser's own. The book progresses through Eugene's rise as an artist—there is something of the same kind of romanticism here as in the account of Sister Carrie's success upon the stage—his marriage, his physical breakdown, his rehabilitation through hard labor, his rise to power and prosperity as editor and publisher, the loss of his position through his affair with Suzanne Dale, and his incomplete redemption through the shock of his wife's death in childbirth and his love for his baby daughter. It would be difficult to say whether the long succession of Eugene's amours or the gruelling obstetrical passage at the end was primarily responsible for the temporary suppression of the book; but tiresome as the "affairs" are, it should be said that *The "Genius"* is not pornographic; there is no lingering over the sexual act itself; for that matter, there are no such passages anywhere in Dreiser. Eugene never has physical relations with Suzanne; neither is her appeal for him mainly sensual. Of his connection with Frieda, Dreiser says: "Eugene was not one who . . . would persuade a girl to immorality for the mere sake of indulgence." Neither is he a dissipated man. His undoing is his sensitiveness to youth and beauty, especially the beauty of girls, which seems to him incomparably the most desirable thing in the world.

So it seems also to the hapless Clyde Griffiths, of *An American Tragedy* (1925), that plethoric book with which Dreiser came at last to his kingdom. The underprivileged boy, son of narrow and igno-rant evangelists, is supposed to be a victim of American class dis-crimination and economic inequality: as the "poor relation" of the owner of a collar factory, he has a foot in each of two worlds and feels at home in neither. "Getting ahead" is the only religion he knows, "parties" the only satisfying activity; for him the light of the ideal is refracted only through a woman's eyes. How, then, can he be expected to tie himself to a pregnant shopgirl who has now lost all the charm she ever had for him, at the very moment when his affair with the beautiful, wealthy, and socially prominent Sondra Finchley is making such unexpected progress.

Clyde did not drown Roberta at Big Bittern, but whether it was conscience or lack of nerve that blocked him, who shall say? Technically, the girl died in an accident, an accident from which the lover who wished her dead made no attempt to save her. But no strong defense could be built upon such a foundation, especially when the prosecution was being conducted by a politically ambitious (though not really dishonorable) man.

In *An American Tragedy* Dreiser attempted a complete picture of a trial—what happens in the courtroom and what happens behind the scenes. He was never greater than when probing the degree of guilt in Clyde's own mind. The boy who was a murderer and yet no murderer can find no certitude at any point: he is unsure of himself and he is unsure of God. Even when he has given the Reverend Mr. McMillan his "testimony," he is still tormented by doubt.[7]

The connection between *An American Tragedy* and Dreiser's "philosophy" has perhaps been sufficiently referred to elsewhere in this discussion. It must be clear, also, that if the word "tragedy" is to be applied to such characters and to such a story, it cannot be used in the classical sense. That young men can grow up in America with no higher ideals than those of a Clyde Griffiths is a national disgrace if not a national tragedy; and surely there can be no question that the book is deeply moving. A mechanist who fathers characters whose lives are without meaning and who are pushed about by forces completely outside their control has no right to move us so much! But Dreiser, as Eliseo Vivas has said, is a very inconsistent mechanist, and "in spite of his mechanism, few novelists respond to human beings as sensitively as he does."

Dreiser lived twenty years after the publication of his most successful book; in all this time, he published no novel. After his death we were given two more long fictions. One was *The Stoic* (1947), the concluding third, after we had long ceased to expect it, of the "Trilogy of Desire" which had been begun so long ago with *The*

[7] There are some incidental matters in *An American Tragedy* that should be glanced at in passing. Matthiessen called attention to the element of foreshadowing involved when, upon Clyde's first meeting Roberta, he invites her to enter a boat at the amusement park, and she asks, "Will it be perfectly safe?" Note, also, Dreiser's use of a sympathetic nature background at Roberta's death, somewhat in the manner of Elizabethan and older literature. Clyde's temptation is presented parabolically, in terms of conventional diabolism, like the temptation of Jesus in the New Testament. In Book II, ch. XLVI, italics are employed to indicate the workings of the subconscious mind.

Financier. The other was *The Bulwark* (1946). In both books, the main interest is religion.

The Stoic describes the last part of Frank Cowperwood's life in London traction enterprises—London was also Yerkes's final arena—his lonely death in New York, and the spiritual adventures of his last mistress, Berenice Fleming, after his passing. It is a somewhat tired book, in which events and personages are viewed largely from the outside; as a matter of fact, Dreiser did not quite finish it. Yet though he knew his English backgrounds much less intimately than he had known the materials employed in the first two thirds of his trilogy, the novel is still, in its first half at least, absorbing, and Cowperwood is still Cowperwood, even if he is endowed at times with a kind of psychic sensitiveness which causes him to take to "feeling" things "in the region of his solar plexus." But the part of the novel that everybody remembers longest is structurally only an epilogue; this is the account of Berenice's flirtation with Yoga, her finding of a spiritual way of life and her self-dedication to the service of humanity as a kind of memorial to her dead lover. As she sees it, Cowperwood's "constant search for beauty in every form, and especially in the form of a woman, was nothing more than a search for the Divine design behind all forms. . . ."

The idea behind all this is impressive enough, but its effective presentation hardly lay within Dreiser's range. Most readers, consequently, found themselves less interested in Miss Fleming's spiritual pilgrimage as the climax of an absorbing series of novels than for its autobiographical interest. As they read it they asked themselves an aesthetically quite irrelevant question: What has happened to Theodore Dreiser?

The Stoic might, in this aspect, have created a greater sensation than it did had it not been preceded into print by Dreiser's "Quaker novel," *The Bulwark.*[8] This is the story of Solon Barnes, who tries to be a faithful member of the Society of Friends, despite his growing wealth and the changing standards of the business world. It develops itself largely in terms of his struggle with his children; Etta goes to live with an artist in New York, and Stewart, half

[8] For a Quaker judgment of *The Bulwark,* see Carroll T. Brown, "D's 'Bulwark' and Philadelphia Quakerism," *Bulletin Friends Hist. Assn.,* XXXV (1946), 52-61. A letter of Dreiser's to Rufus Jones appears on p. 62.

innocently involved in a scandal, kills himself. Solon's wife dies and he himself is stricken with cancer, but his faith is triumphant over all, and he detaches himself from acquisitiveness. In the end, Etta comes back to him, and with Isobel, his unattractive oldest daughter, is his stay and comfort until he dies.

3. The End of the Road

The Bulwark was not altogether the product of Dreiser's old age. He began working on it while still collecting material for *The Titan,* and there are four or five early versions of it. Once it was actually announced for publication in 1916. But the book Dreiser was planning at that time was not the book that finally appeared. The original plan of having Solon die disillusioned was abandoned in response to the change in the writer's own ideology in later years.[9]

Persons who know only that Dreiser joined the Communist Party not long before his death may wonder at this simultaneous development in the direction of a religious attitude toward life and may ask themselves how the two affirmations can be reconciled. The answer is, of course, that they cannot, and that Dreiser's communism was a home-grown variety. He had always been a "sucker" for causes; in the course of his life, he had signed almost everything. One feels that he might quite as easily have joined the Society of Friends had a very persuasive advocate reached him at the psychological moment, or even the Congregational church of which Allen Hunter, who conducted his funeral services, was pastor. There he had taken communion the last Good Friday of his life and had been deeply moved. It was Thoreau and John Woolman that he was reading during his later years, not Karl Marx, and he expressed great admiration for the Quaker philosopher, Rufus M. Jones. He joined the Communists with much hesitation and many reservations, insisting that he had in no sense abridged his complete freedom of thought and action. He did not live long enough afterward to be disillusioned.

Enough has been said in these pages concerning Dreiser's approach to life to make it clear that his final attitude, though by no means consistent with all the views he had expressed in the past, represented no clear break with that past either. I have already

[9] See Granville Hicks, *Am Merc,* LXII (1946), 751-756.

quoted Eliseo Vivas' judgment that "few novelists respond to human beings as sensitively as he does." This statement does not apply merely to *An American Tragedy:* it applies to most of Dreiser's fiction.[10] One may sneer at his philosophy but not at the groping honesty with which it has been developed. One may deplore, also, his lack of selectivity, his failure to conceive a novel as a work of art. When Carrie approaches a department store, we must pause for a dissertation upon the nature of the department store and the role it plays in American life, and Cowperwood cannot even give the Yerkes Observatory to the University of Chicago without our being treated to a careful description of the grinding of the great lens! But even while one condemns these things, one realizes that a sense of life has been communicated. Every critic for a generation has had harsh things to say about Dreiser's style—the fruit of "a miscegenation of the gutter and the psychological laboratory"[11]—and every charge that has been made can be sustained. Yet, in essential matters, like all writers of genius, Dreiser has found his way home, and nobody really believes that *The Titan* would be a better book if it were rewritten in the manner of Meredith or Henry James.

Above everything else, one can never forget for long, while reading Dreiser, that one is concerned with a writer who actually abandoned *Sister Carrie* temporarily when he came to the story of Hurstwood's decline because somehow he "felt unworthy to write all that." Dreiser the creator broods over his world with a vast cosmic pity; one feels of him (different as he is), as John Buchan said of Scott, that he "loves mankind without reservation, is incapable of hate, and finds nothing created altogether common or unclean," that he "gathers all things, however lowly and crooked and broken, within the love of God." If the Creator of the universe is, in this aspect, anything like him, few souls will perish. And he who has refused to judge must surely be justified at the Judgment.

[10] Besides the novels, there are two volumes of short stories—*Free* (1918) and *Chains* (1927)—and two volumes of plays—*Plays of the Natural and Supernatural* (1916) and *The Hand of the Potter* (1918). There is probably considerable fiction in *A Gallery of Women* (1929), but *Twelve Men* (1919) must be factual in the main. See *The Best Short Stories of TD,* ed. Howard Fast (World, 1947).

[11] Paul Elmer More, "Modern Currents in American Literature," in *The Demon of the Absolute* (PUP, 1928).

CHAPTER XVI

IN THE SECOND DECADE

Art is a new world we . . . make out of ourselves to show the old world what itself is made of.

BOOTH TARKINGTON: *Presenting Lily Mars*

1. *Dorothy Canfield: "The Rhythm of the Permanent"*

Among the novelists of our time who have found their special theme in domestic life, none is better than Dorothy Canfield. She is often regarded as a merely "popular" writer, and criticism has done little with her work. Yet few novelists have had a richer intellectual background or enjoyed wider or more fructifying contacts with life. It is her great virtue that she has refused to shut her eyes to the horror and terror of human experience, at the same time declining to close her mind against the conviction that life itself is shot through with spiritual significance. Her principal limitations are a style which, though always competent, is never really characteristic or distinguished, and the fact that (in spite of her specialist's knowledge of French literature), she has never learned selectivity. Nearly all her novels are much too long. Characteristically, she wins the reader's absorbed attention in the first third of her narrative and then proceeds to bury him under masses of detail.

The daughter of an old Vermont family, Dorothy Canfield was born in Lawrence, Kansas, on February 17, 1879, while her father was a professor in the university there. James Hulme Canfield moved on to the chancellorship of the University of Nebraska, and the presidency of Ohio State, where, in 1899, his daughter took her bachelor's degree; her Ph.D. she acquired at Columbia after he had become librarian there. Her mother was a painter with a studio in Paris, and part of the girl's childhood was spent in France. She returned to that country, with her husband, John Redwood Fisher, to engage in relief activities during World War I; she has also spent some time in Norway, in Switzerland, and in Italy. But her official home, ever since her marriage in 1907, has been an old farmhouse near Arlington, Vermont. She is an authoritative writer on education and educational problems: as a young woman, she was secretary of the Horace Mann School; she served as the official interpreter of Madame Montessori and the Montessori method in the United States; she was the first woman member of the Vermont State Board of Education. She is also a musician and an accomplished linguist.[1]

Dorothy Canfield's first novel, *Gunhild,* the fruit of a trip to Norway, appeared in 1907, but attracted little attention. Her second, a study of the havoc which greed and snobbery can produce in marriage, which she caustically entitled *The Squirrel-Cage* (1912), was much more successful. Three years later, *The Bent Twig* established her reputation. Her position was strengthened by *The Brimming Cup* (1921), *Rough-Hewn* (1922), and *The Deepening Stream* (1930). Meanwhile she had also published two less significant novels: *The Homemaker* (1924) and *Her Son's Wife* (1926). She notably widened her range in *Bonfire* (1933) and *Seasoned Timber* (1939), widely varying pictures of Vermont town life.

In this commentator's judgment, Dorothy Canfield's best fiction is to be found in the first part of *The Bent Twig*—which tells of the childhood of the Marshall girls, in their intellectual, music-loving, and deliberately unfashionable state university environment, and of their first encounter with the glory and squalor of Chicago—and the first two-thirds of *The Deepening Stream,* up to the beginning of World War I.

The two chapters in *The Bent Twig* which describe the heroic battle of Judith and Sylvia Marshall against race prejudice, after it has been discovered that two of their school friends are part Negro, is really stirring, and, unlike much of Mrs. Fisher's work, it does not seem to have been arranged for the purpose of illustrating the author's values; instead, the values emerge spontaneously from the

[1] In addition to her novels, Dorothy Canfield has published a number of collections of short stories, among them *Hillsboro People* (1915); *Home Fires in France* (1918); *Raw Material* (1923); *Basque People* (1931); *Fables for Parents* (1937). *Understood Betsy* (1917) is already something of a "classic" among juveniles.

characters and the situation. I am less interested in Sylvia's progress through the university and in her mating, but toward the end of the novel, Austin's socialism, the tragic alcoholism of Arnold, and the death of Mrs. Marshall and her husband's consequent mental anguish introduce new elements of interest, as life opens out for Sylvia in terms of "an adventure perilous and awful beyond imagination."

The academic background again enriches *The Deepening Stream,* in which we are also invited to study the effect upon a growing mind of residence abroad and of living oneself into another culture and a different way of life (in this case, the French), and then later, in mature life, of a knowledge of, and growing into, the ways of Friends. "How he takes the dramatic quality out of things!" So Matey muses upon her Quaker father-in-law. "Later she perceived that his dry coolness was enemy only to melodrama, and that deflating its falsity, he allowed the real drama to emerge." There is no idealizing of family life in these pages. Professor Gilbert and his wife contend bitterly for domination in the family, and the fight exercises a warping effect upon the lives of their children, but the author knows too the strength of the bond between them. If I do not include among the best elements in this book its account of Adrian and Matey's war work in France, this is not because these chapters are not well done or written in an enlightened spirit, nor even because the war had become a somewhat hackneyed subject in fiction by 1930, but rather because the introduction of this element seems to me a somewhat intrusive theme, as if the author felt that she could not keep up our interest through a long book in her study of a happy marriage, without introducing some such extraneous interest.

Happy marriage is studied again in *The Brimming Cup,* with the cultured Vincent Marsh playing the serpent in a Vermont Eden. Only, since Vincent never comes to life, the wife's temptation remains perforce unreal and unmoving, and the chapter in which she finally reaches her decision has too much essay, argument, or preachment about it. The story of Gene and Nellie Powers and Frank Warner serves effectively to underline the main theme by presenting a parallel situation among less cultivated people who resolve it through violence. More successful is the contrast provided by what a Quaker would call Mr. Welles's "concern" for Southern Negroes. Because he is not seeking personal gratification or evading his responsibilities, Welles rightly moves out of security into a larger life. But Marise perceives clearly that for her to leave her husband and family in search of the "self-development" through passion which Vincent offers would be like going back to play with her dolls.

Rough-Hewn is an experimental novel, which describes the completely separate lives of the hero and heroine of *The Brimming Cup* up to the time of their mating. The structural problems are solved successfully, but Marise, who, unlike her husband, is the child of an unhappy marriage, seems less marked by her experiences than one might have expected. The contrast between the two is, therefore, less effective than it might have been; neither does the girl's early life become an important factor in her marital problems. I do not believe that Dorothy Canfield has been very successful in her attempt to write the chapters which deal with Neale from the boy's own point of view. She seems to feel that the way to make the boy real is to cram these chapters with football lingo, a mistake less commonly made by male writers, who know that many boys hate athletics.

At the beginning of *Her Son's Wife,* Mrs. Bascomb is presented as a figure of comedy, and the reader may have some difficulty in making his adjustment to the first pathetic and then heroic figure that she becomes after her foolish and hitherto comfortably dominated son brings an impossibly vulgar daughter-in-law into her home and life. Lottie first wrecks Mrs. Bascomb's happiness by the simple expedient of being herself; then she proceeds to offer her the means of building it up again by giving her a grandchild whom Mrs. Bascomb learns to adore. The conflict in the book is the grandmother's battle to save the little girl from what her mother would make of her, which she wins at the monstrous cost of working upon Lottie's weak mind to convince her that she is an invalid until at last the silly woman has actually become one. Irony and sentimentality are mingled at the close when, after the girl's departure for college, poor Lottie clings in trust and affectionate dependence upon the "Momma" who has at once destroyed her and taken upon herself the burden of her worthless life. But it is difficult to believe that the task could have been accomplished with so little in the way of tragic conflict as Mrs. Bascomb shows.

Another worthless heroine—of quite a different stamp—appears in *Bonfire*. This is Lixlee, child of "The Shelf," one of those backward, mountainous New England regions which had already appeared in American fiction in Edith Wharton's *Summer*. There is some room for difference of opinion concerning the complete reality of this woman, but Mrs. Fisher's account of her effect upon the community, through her marriage with Dr. Craft and the subsequent scandals in which she becomes involved, provides an interesting study. In their concern with communal affairs, both *Bonfire* and *Seasoned Timber* reflect growth in Dorothy Canfield's powers as a novelist.[2]

The educational background is used again in *Seasoned Timber*, whose central character is the head of an impoverished "academy" in a Vermont town. Here, too, the author has drawn upon her knowledge of Vermont folkways and has created many delightful local types. As usual, there is too much of the book, and the structure would have been better if the struggle recorded in the second half had been joined, in some vital fashion, with the first part, which concerns instead Timothy Hulme's love for the young teacher to whom he never declares himself and who weds instead his nephew Canby (who, incidentally, turns out rather too good to be true). As has already been indicated, Dorothy Canfield has always been an outspoken liberal, but never before had she spoken to such effect as here. *Seasoned Timber* appeared just as Americans were beginning to be most concerned about fascism, but Mrs. Fisher differed from many of her compatriots in hating fascism here as well as in Europe, and in education as well as in government. In *Seasoned Timber* the Day of Judgment arrives when a rich trustee leaves the academy a million dollars on condition that it transform itself into a fashionable school for boys and exclude Jewish students. In an out-of-the-way corner of America, an heroic fight is won and waged by men

[2] The passages in *Bonfire* which are written from the point of view of Henrietta the cat have been denounced as nature-faking! This surely is to display a painfully defective sense of humor. The passages in question are consciously whimsical; they are done with great skill; and they form a playful and effective contrast to the realistic body of the book.

and women who fully realize the price that they are going to have
to pay to retain their spiritual decency. It is greatly to Dorothy Canfield's credit as a realistic novelist that she should have dared to
make Timothy Hulme as amusing—and, at times, even as petty—
as he is heroic. If the fight for democracy is ever to be won in
America, she seems to be saying, it is petty, amusing, heroic people
like ourselves who must win it.

2. *The Sympathetic Realism of Elsie Singmaster*

Elsie Singmaster is our leading historian in fiction of the ways of
the Pennsylvania Germans. She was born, on August 29, 1879, at
Schuylkill Haven, Pennsylvania. Her father, John Alden Singmaster,
was a distinguished clergyman; her mother came of English Quaker
stock. As a child she lived in Allentown and other Pennsylvania
towns, and summered at Macungie, the village which, in her fiction,
she calls Millerstown. She was educated at Cornell and at Radcliffe
(from which she was graduated in 1907); two years before, she had
sold her first story. In 1912 she married the musician Harold Lewars
and went to live at Harrisburg; when he died, three years later, she
returned to her father's house, now established at Seminary Ridge,
on the battlefield of Gettysburg, where he had become president of
the Lutheran theological seminary. Here Elsie Singmaster has lived
ever since. She is an authority on Gettysburg, past and present; out
of the oral traditions of the great battle she has fashioned some of her
most characteristic work.

Her spiritual allegiance seems always to have been to her father's
side of the family:

I am fortunate [she writes] in having a mixed ancestry of English, German, and Dutch. I know of no pioneer ancestor who was not in America
by 1750, and of none who was not an American in spirit; but the per-
sistence of German in the section in which I lived gave me two tongues,
two literatures, and in a sense two civilizations. Later I perceived that
in their religious life, in their church music, in their love of the soil, . . .
[the Germans] presented a background of unmatched richness.

The anomaly in Miss Singmaster's career is that she is much better
known for her juveniles and the very large number of short stories

that she has published serially[3] than she is for her full-dress novels. Because she has never "written down" to her juvenile audience, it is sometimes difficult to differentiate between her stories for young people and her adult fiction. But it is probably safe to call *Katy Gaumer* (1915) her first real novel.

Compared to her later work, this book is episodic and loosely-knit. Yet it has much charm. The mystery of the lost communion set—its complications and its consequences in the life of John Hartman, who was responsible for getting it walled up in the church, and of William Koehler, who was accused of stealing it—is strongly suggestive of Hardy. In Katy herself Miss Singmaster had already discovered her characteristic heroine, the girl in love with life and hungry for learning who stumbles through her lack of practical selfishness. She was learning, too, how to enrich her foreground-drama by sketching in an elaborate background of the life of a whole community, an art which she brought to its highest point of development nearly twenty years later in her finest novel, *The Magic Mirror*.

In *Basil Everman* (1920), which is set in a little college town just north of the Mason-Dixon line, where the Civil War is still a live subject for controversy, Miss Singmaster found her most unusual subject, for the book is dominated by the personality of a young writer of genius who died unknown before the story began. Basil's posthumous discovery by a fatuous and amoral young editor, in whom Miss Singmaster rather cruelly caricatures the dilettante who is knowing in strictly literary matters and quite ignorant of life, brings considerable heart-searching to the people of Waltonville, and especially to his sister, wife of the president of the college, who, despite her passionate love for her brother, had always thought him "queer." Miss Singmaster manipulates her materials carefully: Basil lived, it turned out, quite irreproachably, and Eleanor Bent is not his bastard, as Mrs. Lister had feared, but the daughter of the village doctor and legitimately born besides. But to find this a flaw in the

[3] There are three volumes of collected short stories: *Gettysburg* (1913, enlarged 1930); *Bred in the Bone* (1925); and *Stories to Read at Christmas* (1940). Elsie Singmaster has also written about Gettysburg in *Emmeline* (1916); *John Baring's House* (1920); *A Boy at Gettysburg* (1924); and *"Sewing Susie"* (1927). These are all intended primarily for young readers.

book would be to become guilty of the same confusion between genius and irregularity which both Mrs. Lister and the editor made. On the very threshold of the 'twenties, *Basil Everman* set up a standard for all who believe in freedom and spontaneity for the artist, and at the same time flung down the gauntlet to the narrow, greasy-minded people who insist that a writer's imagination must work just like their own. One of the most stirring passages occurs at the point where the tyrannical Mrs. Scott is trying to discover where Eleanor "got the idea" for her "little story," and Dr. Green interposes:

"Out of her head, Mrs. Scott, where all authors that are worth while get theirs. That's where Shakespeare got his and where Basil Everman got his. Their heads are differently stocked from ours. You don't suppose they have to see everything they write about, do you? . . ."

Miss Singmaster was now fully launched into her most productive period. The next year, with *Ellen Levis* (1921), she returned to Pennsylvania and produced one of her two finest novels. And here, again, she is in the mood of the 'twenties, for Ellen is a girl who rebels against the narrow standards of her fanatical Grandfather Milhausen and the dying Seventh Day Baptist community over which he presides and forces her way out into a larger human world. Much of the action of *The Hidden Road* (1923) takes place in New York, but its heroine, Phebe Stannard, is another Pennsylvania girl (half English, like her creator), with a talent for music and a genuine capacity for scholarship, but with a special problem—the exaggerated importance she attaches to romantic love. More naïve than either of these girls, though equally hungry for self-improvement, is the heroine of a somewhat slighter book, *Keller's Anna Ruth* (1926). Anna Ruth's special handicap is poverty—or, rather, her father's miserliness; her own temporary collapse into ancestral ways when she comes into unexpected wealth after Keller's death seems inadequately prepared for.

Between *Ellen Levis* and *The Hidden Road,* Elsie Singmaster had produced a rather different sort of novel in *Bennett Malin* (1922), whose action begins in her own country but soon shifts to Cambridge, Massachusetts. The hero is a literary descendant of Sir Willoughby Patterne, a hopeless prig, utterly destitute of talent, who stakes everything upon his passionate desire to become a novelist who shall correct the faults of Dickens and Scott. Perhaps Miss Singmaster's quiet realism is better adapted to more sympathetic persons. Her Bennett is not a tragic hero, nor is he handled without compassion, but he might have interested the reader more if he had been treated with the elegant malice of an Edith Wharton or an Ellen Glasgow.

What Everybody Wanted (1928) is considerably less characteristic. The scene is laid in southern Pennsylvania and in Baltimore, and the people belong to a higher social stratum than the one the author knows best and sympathizes with most deeply. Miss Singmaster is rich in humor of the *gemütlich* variety, but a brittle Oscar Wilde kind of farce is not quite her dish. "Everybody" in this case are Mamma, still beautiful at forty-five, and her daughters, Marian and Arietta Lee. What they all wanted was Lucien Clement. It is the silly Arietta Lee who gets him, but both the others are thoughtfully provided for, Mamma through Mr. Obenchain, a wealthy Jew who is something of a "sport" in Miss Singmaster's fiction-world. This book contains six sections, each named for the character who tends to dominate it. But the author has not been rigid about point of view, and she will never be accused of imitating *The Awkward Age.*

In 1934, however, she returned triumphantly to her own material in *The Magic Mirror,* which is set at Allentown at the turn of the century. This book not only makes the people of a humble German household profoundly interesting, but it achieves as complete a vision of the life of a whole community and its surrounding countryside as I know in American fiction. It is full of Pennsylvania German dialect, folklore, and religious belief; it is, indeed, the richest of all Miss Singmaster's books. And this time the aspiring youth is not a girl but a boy, Jesse Hummer, who becomes a writer. Miss Singmaster was well advised to take her characters, in the course of the narrative, to the Bach Festival at Bethlehem, for she is always at her best in writing of sacred music.

Of late years Miss Singmaster has been increasingly concerned with historical fiction. As far back as 1917 she had produced a brief narrative called *The Long Journey,* in which she worked up from the Pennsylvania archives and other sources the story of the coming of Conrad Weiser to Pennsylvania, from a war-ravaged Palatinate, under the patronage of Queen Anne of England. Now, with *A High Wind Rising* (1942), she returned to Weiser, though the real hero of the book is his protegé, Bastian Schantz. *A High Wind Rising* covers the Pennsylvania frontier from 1728 to the French and Indian War. It is full of negotiations with the Indians, whisperings of approaching conflict between France and England, and finally the horrors of frontier warfare itself. The method is somewhat less direct than the author usually employs—perhaps she was influenced by her admiration for the work of Conrad Richter—and though the scene may not always be completely realized, there are vivid moments, many of them in connection with the love story, which involves Bastian's long quest for the briefly-glimpsed Ottilia; this is certainly the most romantic thing Elsie Singmaster has done. *Rifles for Washington* (1938) is a vivid story of a boy in the Revolution which would probably be better known than it is if it were not often regarded as a juvenile, and the same might well be said of *Swords of Steel* (1933) and of *I Heard of a River* (1948), which describes the German-Swiss settlement of Lancaster County. *I Speak for Thaddeus Stevens* (1947), on the other hand, is a biographical novel, based on original material, and attempting a rehabilitation of the Reconstruction statesman.

In *The Magic Mirror* an established writer sends Jesse Hummer a box of books which includes *César Birotteau, Eugènie Grandet, Cousin Pons, Far from the Madding Crowd, Fathers and Sons, The Mill on the Floss, Vanity Fair,* and *Madame Bovary*. She urges him to "write about persons and scenes with which he was familiar":

He must observe how the authors found material not only in adventure and in love between the sexes, which were the almost inevitable choice of the young writer, but in the love of friend for friend, in the devotion to honor of a ruined man, in the tenderness of a broken-hearted man for the poor, in the passion of the miser, in the selfish ambition of a conscienceless woman. He must note how a character was developed— a look, a phrase, a physical trait, and there stood the whole man. . . . She sent him one book with hesitation—of such materials also was great literature made. . . .

It is clear that E. M. Lawson's advice to the young writer is Elsie Singmaster's advice also. We have her own testimony for it that she does not always follow the Turgenev-James advice to begin with the characters:

> In the beginning my characters have a somewhat shadowy personality, suggested by an acquaintance or some of the traits of an acquaintance, or perhaps by someone seen only for a few moments. They may have their origin in the exigencies of the plot in which they are to figure. As the story develops they develop with it, until they become rounded beings. If they are suggested by a living person, they are very apt to cease to resemble him or her and become entirely different.[4]

Elsie Singmaster is a writer of idealistic temper and strict moral and religious principles who almost consistently employs the realistic method. Her books are likely to center about eager, ardent, aspiring, sensitive young people who draw themselves out of depressing surroundings and away from narrow, selfish associates to make something of themselves in the world of art, scholarship, and fruitful human relations. When they are lucky, they find one or two older persons about who are wise enough to understand what they are doing and kind enough to reach out a helping hand.

But there is never any evasiveness in their creator's presentation of them. She never idealizes them. However pious their surroundings, they have all the faults and weaknesses to be found in the characters of more sophisticated writers. Or perhaps Miss Singmaster is really the sophisticated writer, since she seems so much less surprised by what she finds than many of her contemporaries and also much less fascinated.

Keller's Anne Ruth is crowded with degraded small-town types. The heroine's brother becomes a bootlegger and is shot. The odor of decaying vegetables and of coal gas (by which both the elder Kellers are asphyxiated) clings round the book. Yet it is not degrading, for the author never forgets the humanity of her characters, of her readers, nor of herself.

Elsie Singmaster is sensitive enough to understand Miss Grammer's advice to Ellen Levis that it is unwise to be dependent upon other human beings for one's happiness, but she has much less sympathy with Cassie Hartman, who, having been hurt in her love for her husband, silently withdrew into herself until she became some-

[4] Quoted by Dayton Kohler, *Bkm*(NY), LXXII (1931), 621-626.

thing beautiful and inhuman. One must not ask too much of human beings. There is Emmanuel Hummer, of *The Magic Mirror,* who drives a beer truck and spends his evenings at Wagner's. Though the reader is quite conscious of his limitations, Hummer is a good man and we are in no danger of not respecting him fundamentally. His wayward son Stanley finds a happy ending through his union with a girl who had herself borne a child out of wedlock. Roger Keller, on the other hand, is not redeemed, but neither is he depicted, in his waywardness, as completely lacking either conscience or humanity. Life is tolerable in the end even for such a selfish fool as Alvin Koehler, and Naomi forgives Bennett Malin's inhumanity and even generously shares the blame for it. "He was not an angel fallen from a great height; he was a mortal who had stepped aside from the right path."

Miss Singmaster's heroines are faithful and passionate; when sexual irregularity occurs, its consequences are faced courageously, even in good families. In *The Hidden Road* we have a study of the power of desire in a girl's life, and Phebe is unquestionably the Singmaster heroine who comes closest to being soiled. But she suffers a change of heart after her escape; *The Hidden Road* is clearly its author's answer to the libertarians. Katy Gaumer is horrified when she finds herself falling in love with David Hartman after her unhappy experience with Alvin Koehler, and Ellen Levis longs desperately "for childhood, for innocence, for ignorance, for freedom from this consuming passion."

Though religion plays a considerable role in Elsie Singmaster's novels, she gives more attention to the numerous marginal sects scattered through southern Pennsylvania than she does to her own Lutheranism. Millie's religion, in *Ellen Levis,* is described as "a possession for eternity, but of little practical use in this life." The picture of the evangelist in *Bennett Malin* is hostile; neither does one feel any respect for Wilhelmina, of *The Hidden Road,* who makes it a rule to speak to every girl in school about her soul. But the skeptic, Dr. Levis, is a sympathetic portrait, and although his pious son Matthew is out of sympathy with him during his lifetime, he longs passionately for his counsel after the doctor is dead. The Lutheran watch night services in *The Magic Mirror* make an attractive picture. Marion, of *What Everybody Wanted,* finds her religious inspiration not through preaching, nor even through the Bible, but in Bach. Stanley Hummer comes to himself through a Hungarian Catholic girl, and his marriage turns out to be the best thing that ever happened to him. On the other hand, neither Ellen Levis, Phebe Stannard, nor Anna Ruth Keller can be said to have much religion; and having pictured Ellen's revolt against her Seventh Day Baptist inheritance, Miss Singmaster does not go on, as might have been expected, to chronicle her achievement of a more rational faith but seems content to allow her to meet the problems of her life upon the humanistic level.

The virtues of flamboyancy are not to be found in Elsie Singmaster's novels; she is not, in the ordinary sense of the term, a "brilliant" writer. Dayton Kohler has called her method "austerely Lutheran"; less sympathetic readers sometimes called it stolid. The present writer never fails to find her, within her range, richly satisfying. She is not the greatest or subtlest of American novelists, but she gives her readers an abundant impression of wholeness.

3. *Joseph Hergesheimer: "Brocade and Dream"*[5]

Joseph Hergesheimer is a Pennsylvania novelist of a different order. He was born in Philadelphia, on February 15, 1880, of German and Scottish ancestry. His father, an officer in the United States Coast Survey, was generally absent from home; his mother was "away spiritually." The delicate, solitary boy grew up in the devout Presbyterian household of his grandfather, a self-made man who had come to America as a printer's devil. Joseph Hergesheimer attended a Quaker school, and later studied painting, first at the Pennsylvania Academy of Fine Arts, and then in Italy. He first conceived the idea of becoming a writer when he met, and corrected proofs for, the English woman novelist, Lucas Cleeve; he couldn't, he thought, write any worse than that!

For fourteen years he scribbled without encouragement. His first

[5] A small portion of this discussion of Joseph Hergesheimer was embodied in my article, "Our Changing Literary Temper," published in the May 1945 numbers of *College English* and *The English Journal.* Copyright, 1945, by the University of Chicago Press.

two novels—*The Lay Anthony* (1914) and *Mountain Blood* (1915) —made little stir. But with *The Three Black Pennys* (1917) his reputation was established.

This was the first of his novels of the past, and it is still, in some ways, the most successful of them. The story of 150 years in the life of a family, against the background of the iron industry in Pennsylvania,[6] *The Three Black Pennys* suggests Butler, Bennett, and Galsworthy. But since Hergesheimer's preoccupation was with emotional problems, he did not "get up" his backgrounds like Bennett, and the originality of his book is perhaps sufficiently attested in the fear of its English publisher, Heinemann, that the narrative might be too exclusively American to hold British readers. In a sense, *The Three Black Pennys* is an experimental novel; its author's imagination fused the three episodes of which it consists into an organic unity by establishing his center of interest not in any one of the individual protagonists but rather in the "black," wayward strain, the occasional outcrop in the Pennys of a remote Welsh ancestor, which appears in all three.

Hergesheimer returned to the method of *The Three Black Pennys* in *The Foolscap Rose* (1934), in which paper replaces iron and steel, and, with modifications, in *The Limestone Tree* (1931), which portrays Kentucky from colonial times to the 1890's in ten different episodes. The author's understanding of our American past is at its best here; the book reveals scholarship infused with imagination; it tells us not only what our ancestors wore and what kind of houses they inhabited but how they thought and felt.[7] The unity of *The Limestone Tree* is more mechanical, however, than that of the *Pennys;* there are scores of characters to keep straight; and the general recapitulation and parallelism in the last chapter seems somewhat forced.

Java Head (1919) presented an entirely different problem.[8] Here

---

[6] Iron is background again in "Tubal Cain," one of the three novelettes in *Gold and Iron* (1918). Another of these, "The Dark Fleece," is worth comparing with *Java Head*.

[7] This same gift appears at its best in *Quiet Cities* (1928), Hergesheimer's best collection of short stories and one of his finest books.

[8] See Joseph Hergesheimer, "Scholasticus in se Scholia Facit, or 'Java Head' Revisited," *Princeton University Library Chronicle*, III (1942), 52-55.

is the Port of Salem during President Polk's administration, when a soulless, conscienceless commercialism (the opium trade) was encroaching upon the romantic, the heroic, the lovely past. And here is Gerrit Ammidon, a rebel more uncompromising than the Black Pennys themselves who returns from China with a Manchu wife, and creates one of the strongest contrasts in American fiction when he takes her with him to the family pew in the North Church. The story is told from the point of view of the various participants, including, climactically, that of Taou Yuen herself, for Hergesheimer wanted to show his readers what tawdry commercial values look like when viewed through the eyes of the changeless East. But this was an attempt in which complete success could hardly have been hoped for. Hergesheimer ought either to have handled Taou Yuen as Galsworthy handled Irene or else *Java Head* ought to have been written in collaboration with a Manchu novelist of genius. As it stands, he made it inevitable that he should be obliged to turn to melodrama for his solution.

There are no baffling technical problems of any kind in *The Bright Shawl* (1922), a vivid picture of Cuba in her days of bondage and of the idealistic young American who tried to deliver her. In *The Lay Anthony* the naïveté of the hero had seemed at times the naïveté of the author; we are beyond all that kind of thing now. *The Bright Shawl* has the charm of a slight, perfect thing, tossed off by an accomplished writer at the height of his powers. *Balisand* (1924) is a much more ambitious but less entertaining book, the portrait of a Virginia Federalist of the post-Revolutionary War period—his hard drinking, his gambling, his stern sense of honor within the boundaries of an artificial code. Of Hergesheimer's understanding of the period there can be no question. But the theme is somewhat indirectly presented, and the book seems overweighted with not too significant detail.

The first important modern novel was the much praised *Linda Condon* (1919), a somewhat Freudian study of soulless beauty. Linda escapes the sordidness of her mother's world, but only at the cost of emotional frigidity. Though she never learns to give herself to love, she holds the devotion of her husband and the adoration of the great sculptor, Dodge Pleydon, who never models her beauty, yet makes her, through the inspiration she holds for him, an inescapable part of the great art of the world.

But this is not the distinctive note of Hergesheimer's modern novels. That note was sounded first in *Cytherea* (1922), a study of dissatisfaction in a middle-aged, married man, overcome by the desire to seize, before it shall be too late, the erotic experience he has somehow missed in life, to merge with the Cytherea who is at once a vampire-doll and the goddess of his dreams. He has the misfortune to find his fate in the neurotic Savina Grove, who dies (ironically enough), from the strain of the experience and leaves her lover a stranded derelict in Cuba.[9]

Hergesheimer returned to the theme of *Cytherea* in a far more unpleasant novel, *The Party Dress* (1930), in which the same problem is considered from the woman's point of view. Further studies of drunkenness and infidelity among wealthy Americans appear in the short stories called *Tropical Winter* (1933); the novel, *Tampico* (1926), which is a full-length portrait of an unscrupulous American financier in Mexico, is set in the same kind of atmosphere.

Hergesheimer is one of the most difficult of our novelists to evaluate fairly. It would be absurd to say that he cannot create character, yet there are scenes in even his best novels in which the people seem altogether unreal. Perhaps the fundamental difficulty is that individual character does not seem very important to him; he "didn't much believe in the triumph or importance of the individual"; even the Pennys were to him like the notes in a piece of music, and valued individually in quite that way. He even persuaded himself that not to be interested in the individual was somehow "classical." Hergesheimer admitted frankly that he made his characters up to embody the qualities he admired but failed to find in himself—calmness, fidelity, hardness of body, "a distinguished resolution in body and mind," and, in the case of women, "a warm rich vitality of being."

[9] Mina Raff, the film star of *Cytherea*, shows the influence of Hergesheimer's admiration for Lillian Gish—see his article about her in *Am Merc*, I (1924), 397-402—but is in no sense a portrait of her. The film in which Lee Randon sees Mina is D. W. Griffith's production of *Way Down East* (1920), in which Miss Gish gave one of her finest performances. Lillian Gish never appeared in a Hergesheimer film, but Dorothy Gish was a brilliant figure as La Clavel in the film version of *The Bright Shawl*.

The women especially were created for his "personal reassurance and pleasure." But "the business of being a woman is universal and not individual." Lee Randon does not even remember Savina as an individual, once she has served his need—and destroyed him.

Hergesheimer's admirers insist that he is, above all things, the novelist of spiritual integrity, and there are books, like *Java Head,* of which this is certainly true. The influence of Conrad seems to have been important at this point. Others find themselves so stifled and smothered in fabrics, so worn out with physical sensation that values disappear altogether. Many years ago, Fanny Butcher spoke of his "five-sensitive writing."

Some of this carries over from Hergesheimer's experience as a painter. He has "used words precisely in the way I had used colors, striving for the same effects." But this is not all. And the $500,000 that *The Saturday Evening Post* paid him for his stories seems to have made it easier for him to become seduced by the luxury which intellectually he can only despise.

Hergesheimer does not like the age in which his lot has been cast; he may record its infidelities but he does not approve of them; he cannot rid himself of the notion that values were lost somehow with a simpler, less sophisticated America. Yet, in a sense, his love for this older America is a sentimental love, for he has no real anchors in the past. He clings tenaciously, as he himself has observed, only to its more superficial aspects: its faith is gone, but he remembers "the hour of its supper" and "its amazing breakfasts." Unfortunately a man cannot fend off a welter of materialism with even the finest and rarest antiques; neither is Duncan Phyfe one of the names given among men whereby we must be saved.[10]

There is a deep division here in Hergesheimer himself. He disliked the "literary pathology" and the "arrogant materialism" of his time, but he did not like the things the libertarians were attacking much better; his antipuritanism, his negative reaction to his narrow

[10] In the dedication of *Swords and Roses* (1929) to Mrs. Knopf, Hergesheimer laments the necessity of seeking in books the romance, "the simpler loveliness of the past," which the men of the period celebrated could know at first hand. But when he delved more deeply into the Civil War for his biography of *Sheridan* (HM, 1931), he was disabused of the notion that the period was romantic.

religious upbringing delivered him over to the very forces that were destroying the things he loved. As time went on, he felt himself out of harmony with his contemporaries; he was even shocked by them, despite his "not inconsiderable experience." He did not wish to reform them, but he accepted himself as having dated, and he wanted to rest.

Art itself began to retreat from him; indeed, he was getting "damned sick" of art. He had never been able to read many of the English novelists,[11] but in *The Lay Anthony* he had gone out of his way to call "Heart of Darkness" the most beautiful story of our time. In later years he lost the ability to read Conrad; he seems to have lost the ability to read all novelists except his friend and admirer Cabell. He had tried to cling to values in fiction even after they had grown dim in life. When he wrote *The Three Black Pennys,* he still saw that, in a satisfying work of art at least, consequences must follow Howat's adultery; he could not have been sure of that at a later date. *Linda Condon* seems to be a study in spiritual experience; actually it means only that, through Pleydon's adoration, Linda has somehow had her beauty perpetuated—surely not a very worthy goal to which to dedicate one's life! By 1931 Hergesheimer saw the novel itself as "dying." Three years later, at fifty-four, he published his last book.

4. *Sherwood Anderson: The* Cri de Coeur *as Novel*

Sherwood Anderson was the D. H. Lawrence of American literature. Like Lawrence, he attempted almost every literary genre; unlike him, he was entirely successful only with his sketches and short stories, which, unfortunately, lie outside my range in this book.[12] His novels are all unsatisfactory, and it is only because of

[11] In his youth Hergesheimer read Oliver Optic and Edward Ellis, later Ouida and The Duchess. Henry James, though he would seem to have a Iamesian problem in *Linda Condon,* he once denied ever having read. He did read the Lake Poets, Arnold, and Browning; also George Moore and Turgenev.

[12] Historically, *Winesburg, Ohio* (1919) ranks with Edgar Lee Masters's *Spoon River Anthology* (1916), Sinclair Lewis's *Main Street* (1920), and Zona Gale's *Miss Lulu Bett* (1920) as marking the "revolt from the village" which was such an important theme in the literature of the 1920's. But in Anderson the frustrated businessman is quite as important as the frustrated

the wide influence he acquired when in the 'twenties he was regarded as one of the liberators of American literature that he deserves extended consideration in this book.

What Anderson shared with Lawrence was his revolt against an industrialized civilization and his feeling that in order to recover mental and spiritual health men must learn to live more "natural" lives.[13] From this follows naturally the affection which both writers feel for animals, for Negroes of the primitive, African variety, for men who work with their hands, and for nonintellectual types in general. It is all, as Frederick J. Hoffman says, "a kind of Freudianized Rousseauism."[14] Craftsmanship is a way out from the blind alley into which we have wandered, but sex is a door more readily and universally accessible.

Sex plays a large part in Anderson's books, and he is much occupied with its more wayward manifestations. Many of his characters are perverts and other frustrated creatures. It is often complained that there is something morbid or unclean in the fascination which such persons have for Anderson. On the other hand, one must admit that there is something beautiful in the quite uncondescending compassion he feels for them, at least when it stops this side of mawkish sentimentality. Anderson praises Alfred Stieglitz for the something which happened to him that "sweetened the man's nature, made him a lover of life and a lover of men." The same thing obviously happened to Anderson. He hated and feared the "new suspicion of man by man . . . making more prevalent and more marked our human loneliness." And sex itself is less important in his books

villager. See William L. Phillips, "How SA Wrote 'Winesburg, Ohio,' " *AL*, XXIII (1951), 7-30. His later short stories were collected in *The Triumph of the Egg* (1921); *Horses and Men* (1923); and *Death in the Woods and Other Stories* (1933).

[13] For Lawrence's reaction to *Winesburg, Ohio*—"good, I think, but somehow hard to take in: like a nightmare one can hardly recall distinctly"— cf. B. W. Huebsch, "Footnotes to a Publisher's Life," *Col*, N. S. III (1937), 406-426.

[14] In *Dark Laughter*, Bruce likes "Sponge" and his "old woman" because they behave like "fox terriers, not quite human," especially when they are drunk. At the same time, he is haunted by "the deft quick hands of the old meat-cutter" and horrified when the government goes into " 'bunk-shooting' on the grand scale" in World War I.

for its own sake than as a possible point of assault against the lone-liness by which his people are always oppressed.[15]

Though Anderson is often called a naturalist, this is true only in a qualified sense. He shares the naturalistic faith in instinct, the naturalistic tendency to use aesthetically the stuff of common life, and the naturalistic determination not to permit his presentation to be warped by any conventional "moral" considerations. But he never approaches objectivity, and he is completely concerned with the life within. In his technique he is more expressionist than naturalist.

One hears much of the influence of the Russians upon him. Yet he never read many of the writers he was supposed to resemble until his attention had been called to them by his own reviewers. Hoffman has shown conclusively that there is very little evidence to show that he based his stories upon a careful study of Freud.[16] Anderson him-self has a good deal to say about his use of George Borrow and of the Bible, while Horace Gregory has argued the case for the influ-ence upon him of Melville and Mark Twain.[17]

He *was* influenced, unfortunately, by Gertrude Stein's experiments with words, and possibly also, as Paul Elmer More suggested, by her notions about the "continuous present." This might explain his curious mingling of past and present into "a kind of unprogressive circulation" and his trick of "beginning again and again and again." He gets drunk on words, and in his more apocalyptic moods he seems not to care whether he communicates an idea or not.

Sherwood Anderson was born at Camden, Ohio, on September 13, 1876. His father (one might say) was Windy McPherson—a wanderer, an odd-job man, an amiable incompetent, and a teller of tales. The mother may have been of German or Italian descent. Sherwood, who had little schooling, performed a variety of jobs, some of which familiarized him with saloons and racecourses at an

---

[15] The characteristic Anderson hero is not a libertine. Sometimes, as in that touching story, "I Want To Know Why" *(The Triumph of the Egg),* he is extremely fumbling and tentative in his approach to sex. Cf. also, in *Poor White,* Hugh's frustrated longing to go to the girl who is waiting for him in the next room: "Remember she's a good woman and you haven't the right."

[16] Frederick J. Hoffman, *Freudianism and the Literary Mind* (LSUP, 1945).

[17] In his Introduction to *The Portable SA.*

early age. In his teens he went to Chicago and got a job in a warehouse. After this, he served briefly in the Spanish-American War, and finally settled down, as a successful businessman, in a paint factory at Elyria, Ohio.

According to his own story, he awakened as suddenly to the aimlessness of a businessman's life as Saint Paul to his mistaken ways on the road to Damascus, walked out in the middle of a sentence he was dictating to his stenographer, leaving both business and family behind him. This is the central situation in Anderson's novels. He used it again and again. Actually it was much less dramatic than that. Even when he went to Chicago he did not at first devote himself exclusively to literature.[18]

In Chicago he was encouraged by Dreiser, Floyd Dell, Ben Hecht, Harry Hansen, Robert Morss Lovett, Llewellyn Jones, and others, and here he began contributing to *The Little Review*. His first book was *Windy McPherson's Son* (1916). In 1919 the short stories collected in *Winesburg, Ohio* established his reputation; in 1921 he received the Dial Award. *Dark Laughter,* his most successful novel, appeared in 1925. With the proceeds he bought a farm near Marion, Virginia, where he edited and published two small newspapers, one Republican and the other Democratic. His death, at Cristobal, in the Canal Zone, on March 8, 1941, was caused by his having swallowed a bit of toothpick in a tid-bit consumed at a farewell party in New York before he left for a South American tour.

Windy McPherson's Son opens upon a vivid picture of a boy suffering in revival meetings, yearning after beauty, and awakening to the sting of sex. From here we pass on to his business success, which is dull. The first part of the story of his marriage with Sue is straight out of the women's magazines. With the account of the couple's frustration in their desire for parenthood, the novel picks up again, only to become ridiculous in its record of Sam's wandering about America, savoring various experiences with common men, trying to aid strikers, searching for a philosophy of life, and getting drunk. There is little unity, and no pains are taken with transitions: Sam, for example, becomes a drunkard in one sentence. His relations with

---

[18] See Irving Howe, *Sherwood Anderson,* pp. 46-49, 51. Cf. Karl James Anderson, "My Brother SA." *SRL.* XXX, Sept. 4, 1948, pp. 6-7+.

Janet and Edith Eberly are not uninteresting in themselves, but Anderson merely "tells" us about them instead of portraying them, and he leaves the whole experience as a detached episode without building it into either the development of Sam's character or the development of the book. The ending, where Sam makes up with Sue by returning to her with a parcel of adopted children, is pure sentimentality.

In *Marching Men* (1917), the hero is still Sam McPherson, but this time he is called "Beaut" McGregor. He is the son of a coal miner who lost his life through heroic conduct in a mine accident. McGregor first attracts attention as a lawyer in Chicago, when he saves a petty criminal who had been "framed" to cover up tracks for the "big shots" in the First Ward. Though he loves the daughter of a capitalist, he gives her up because he cannot bear to break away from the milliner who has befriended him. Finally, he trains vast hordes of workmen to march ceaselessly through the streets of Chicago and scare the daylights out of everybody because nobody knows what they are marching for. They don't know. McGregor doesn't know. Anderson doesn't know. "The thing was hypnotic. It was big." But it fails to win credence, even upon a symbolical level.

Anderson addresses the reader directly whenever he takes the notion, and shows no scruples about letting any part of his story hang in the air at any time. Character is rarely portrayed in action. After McGregor decides to stay with Edith, we never hear of her again. The book is full of flashbacks which are never related in any vital way to the subject in hand.

The first part of *Poor White* (1920)—the story of Hugh McVey's shiftless youth in a small Missouri town, of the courage he imbibes from an energetic New England woman, and of his progress as an inventor—is much the best thing Anderson ever produced in a novel. His description of the change from an agricultural to an industrial community has been much praised. Indeed, all three of the novels so far considered are good so long as they keep to the village: it is odd that they should all go to pieces at about the same point. This one crashes with the introduction of the love story, partly because we are asked to establish a new center of interest in mid-narrative and partly because the tale itself becomes both dull and absurd.

There is more unity in Anderson's fourth and most scandalous novel, *Many Marriages* (1923), an expanded short story which is largely concerned with the events of a single night. Compared to what had gone before, *Many Marriages* is very objective. Anderson limits both time and space, begins at the end and looks back. Even here, however, the unity achieved is not perfect, for toward the end the point of view shifts from John Webster to his daughter.

The narrative starts simply, and rather winningly, as a kind of parable, probing the problem of a middle-aged man, a washing-machine manufacturer in Wisconsin, tied to a clod who does not want to live and would not know how to try. But the climactic scene, in which John Webster struts naked before an improvised altar and tries to justify himself to his daughter in an interminable monologue whose purpose is to awaken her awareness of life, with disturbing side glances at her sexuality, is too absurd even to be offensive, and his talk, whatever it may have done to the girl, only puts the reader to sleep. At the end, Webster runs off with his stenographer while his wife swallows poison.[19]

Dark Laughter (1925) returns to the aimless peripatetics of the first two novels—the pilgrimage without a goal. This time it is a newspaper man, Bruce Dudley, who walks out on his wife in Chicago, drifts down the Mississippi to New Orleans, and then back to Indiana, where he becomes involved in a particularly unmotivated love affair with his employer's wife. Régis Michaud speaks of *Dark Laughter* as "a sort of *sotto voce* monologue with musical interludes." The chorus is furnished by the deep sexual laughter of the spontaneous and uninhibited Negroes during the period when Bruce and Aline are coming together, a suggestive dramatic device which recalls O'Neill's chorus in *Lazarus Laughed*.

Anderson's last two novels were little regarded. By the time he

[19] In view of the sensation created by Dr. H. S. Canby, when, in his review of *Many Marriages,* now reprinted in his *Definitions,* Second Series (HB, 1924), he developed a parallel between Anderson's novel and *The Pilgrim's Progress,* it is interesting to note that Bunyan's masterpiece was one of the two titles Karl Anderson could remember as having been in the family home. Christopher Ward has a very amusing parody of *Many Marriages* in *The Triumph of the Nut* (Ht, 1923). Mark Van Doren's review of *Kit Brandon,* in *The Private Reader* (Ht, 1942) is also in parody style.

wrote *Beyond Desire* (1932) he had become very socially minded. The scene is a small Georgia mill town and the hero is Red Oliver, who comes home from college for the summer. Sex and the economic order combine to disturb him, and his unrest is reflected in that of the community, which is just undergoing industrialization. Red finally dies for the Communist cause in a strike, without ever quite making up his mind that he believes in it. Anderson's confused chronology is at its worst in this novel, and unity is menaced both by the long account of the "Mill Girls" in Book II and, more seriously, by the shift from Red and his problems to the frustrated Ethel in Book III. *Kit Brandon* (1936) is about a Southern mountain girl, daughter of a moonshiner, and her experiences as factory-hand, shop-girl, and bootlegger. The best part is the description of the mountain people; the end is mere adventure story.

It should be realized that Anderson's virtues as well as his faults made it difficult for him to write a successful novel. He was at his best in his burning, vivid realization of the moment; he believed, indeed, that "The true history of a life is but a history of moments," and, by his own admission, he had no hold on facts. He could not even write the story of his own childhood as a factual record: he had to turn it into fiction as *Tar* (1926). His virtues are those of the lyric poet, but unlike the best of such poets, he achieves no balance of the world without and the world within. His picture of the world without is shadowy; he fails to visualize either characters or background; everything else is sacrificed to a welter of moods.

This, of course, is limitation even in a short story. Robert Morss Lovett calls Anderson's stories centripetal, not centrifugal, and Virginia Woolf, who admired him, speaks of his tendency "to land . . . softly in a bog."[20] Nevertheless, both Chekov and Katherine Mansfield have taught us that a short story which is merely the expression of a mood can be very powerful, and when Anderson is at his best he is of their company. The novel calls for too much in the way of development and externalization to lie within the range of such a writer, especially when, as Lewisohn remarks of Anderson, he finds "continuity of utterance . . . almost insurmountably

---

[20] "American Fiction," in *The Moment and Other Essays* (HB, 1948).

difficult." All the memorable passages in Anderson's novels are vignettes.

It is one thing for a man honestly to admit that he is puzzled by life; it is quite another to make a cult of befuddlement and give the impression of playing the village idiot on purpose. Up until about 1923 Anderson was really groping; after that, he more or less went through the motions. His primitivism, too, suggests a literary attitude, and Rebecca West shows good sense when she remarks of the characters in *Many Marriages* that they "never seemed to attain the dignity of complete nudity; their complexes clung to them like dark woollen socks." Anderson has, to be sure, many "solutions." They range all the way from just walking out to joining the Communist Party. But one gathers that it was the walking out that he enjoyed most. He could not adjust himself to the ever-present condition of our life here: the compromise between the real and the ideal. As an artist, he was always limited to the particular effects he could secure within the range of an artfully simple, though, in its way, very accomplished, technique. When he got beyond that range, he could only cry, "I have a wonderful story to tell, but I know no way to tell it."

CHAPTER XVII

WILLA CATHER AND THE LOVELY PAST*

Long ago, sweetheart mine,
Roses bloomed as ne'er before.
EDWARD MACDOWELL

1. *Points of Departure*

Compared to Joyce or Faulkner or even Henry James, Willa Cather does not seem like a difficult writer. Yet there have been some extraordinary misconceptions concerning her.

She is, we are told, the historian of the Nebraska frontier. And though her workmanship is exquisite, her range is narrow.

Yet Elizabeth Monroe once remarked that Miss Cather embraces such themes as "a new settlement of the frontier by Swedes, Norwegians, Poles, Slavs, Bohemians, and the French, the contrast between the civilizations involved in this settlement, the sweep of American religious history, and the triumph of great personalities over the hardships of American life."[1]

This, surely, would not ordinarily be regarded as a narrow range.

Yet the matter cannot be disposed of so simply.

Far beyond that of most novelists, Willa Cather's was the artist's approach to life. The concrete held her, never the abstract; human beings, human consciousness. Like Niel Herbert, in *A Lost Lady*, she was concerned not with what men have thought but with what they have felt and lived; even her "anchors" were not ideas but "merely pictures, vivid memories."

Moreover, life flowered for her in a certain richness of personality

* There is some material in this chapter which, though much revised, appeared in my essay on Willa Cather in *The Sewanee Review*, XXXVII (1929), 221-239. Copyright, 1929, by the University of the South.

[1] *The Novel and Society*. Copyright, 1941, U of NC Press.

—"personal bravery, magnanimity, and a fine, generous way of doing things"—a creative attitude toward existence. This she found in pioneers of the flesh all the way from peasants to railroad builders —"A pioneer should have imagination, should be able to enjoy the idea of things more than the things themselves"—and in pioneers of the spirit: great artists, great scholars, and great saints.

Life is not yet so poor that the eager youth who looks for these things will not find them, wherever his lot may be cast. Willa Cather's formative years belonged to the Nebraska frontier; she found them there. That was an accident of geography.

She was later of the opinion that greatness had departed from American life, but that was when she was old and tired. In a way she always remained "faithful" to Nebraska, but this did not mean that she was a regionalist. It meant simply that she was the kind of writer who has his roots in the experiences of his formative years, who cannot write once he has been spiritually detached from his country. She herself was fond of saying that all the essential materials of her fiction were gathered before she was fifteen; after that she was only recollecting and reassembling.

There is, obviously, a limitation here. But it is a limitation of theme, interest, temperament, not a geographical limitation. It explains why Willa Cather was never a prolific writer. It explains, too, why, as she perceived in the kindred case of Katherine Mansfield, it took her a long time to find herself. "There had to be a long period of writing for writing's sake."

The range indicated is never shallow, and it is narrow only in the sense that a good many areas of human interest are rather deliberately ruled out. Crowding memories thronged the corridors of her brain: the episodic character of her fictions, which all commentators have noticed, was due quite as much to the richness and variety of the material besieging her and clamoring for admission as to any constitutional inability to master the problem of structure. She was past mistress of the vignette. Probably only those who have read all her books through in rapid succession can know how very many personages she has illuminated and vitalized for a moment—and then let go. It might also be justly urged that no two books could well be more different in tone and atmosphere than, say, *Death*

Comes for the Archbishop and *My Mortal Enemy,* or *My Ántonia* and *The Professor's House.*

To be sure, there are many excellent things that Miss Cather was never able to do. She knew the passion for the land, which grips men in lonely places; she knew the lust to create beauty. She knew, too, the meaning of noble, faithful friendship; but she was helpless when it came to sexual love. The singer's odyssey in *The Song of the Lark* is moving, but Fred Ottenburg is a ludicrously impossible character, and, to borrow an expression from Lord David Cecil, his mating with Thea is about as thrilling as the loves of the plants. Indeed, Willa Cather herself was not much interested in Thea's success as a singer; in later life, she wished she had ended the book at the point where the girl established herself. Success in general made no appeal to her imagination, nor does she seem to have got much satisfaction out of her own success. The kind of people she liked— "who had imagination and generous impulses"—could still exist in a moneyed society, but most of them were failures, "shut up in prison," while mean, narrow men like Bayliss Wheeler held the keys.

She herself became ever more conservative with advancing years. She scorned the crusade against the use of foreign languages during World War I—"Our lawmakers have a rooted conviction that a boy can be a better American if he speaks only one language than if he speaks two"—and she did not shrink from presenting Ántonia, in her final phase, as having almost forgotten her English through the exclusive use of Bohemian in her home. But by 1936 she was writing about the young man of German, Jewish, or Scandinavian extraction, whose English is "without emotional roots" and "merely a means of making himself understood," and who is, therefore, unable to relish *The Country of the Pointed Firs* properly. In her Prefatory Note to the collection of essays called *Not Under Forty* she throws down the gauntlet: "It is for the backward, and by one of their number, that these sketches were written."

Personally I can see no reason why a fine writer should be required to be in sympathy with the mood of her time. As Auclair tells Saint-Vallier, "Change is not always progress." It is much more important to be attuned to what Dorothy Canfield calls "the rhythm of the permanent," and sometimes this may even mean to be de-

liberately out of tune with the times.[2] Moreover, since Willa Cather
was, as we have seen, the kind of writer who can use only the themes
of her youth, any limitation that may be involved at this point would
be much less serious in her case than in a different kind of writer.
I agree that the late stories collected in *The Old Beauty* (published
posthumously in 1948), are, at times, almost a caricature of the best
of her earlier work. But how can we be sure that this is *because*
Miss Cather was fundamentally out of sympathy with her time?
May it not have been simply because she was old and sick? How do
we know that they would have been better stories if she had served
on as many committees as Theodore Dreiser? That she was, in her
later years, a difficult woman is, I think, undeniable; she had become
a world figure who could afford to indulge her crotchets, and the
range of her interests and sympathies was narrower than it had been
in her youth. But that is not quite the same thing.

2. Biographical

Willa Sibert Cather was born near Winchester, Virginia, of
English, Irish, and Alsatian forebears. The official date is December
7, 1876. The actual date was probably 1873 or 1874.[3] But her formative years were spent in Nebraska, on a ranch near Red Cloud, where
Bohemians and Scandinavians far outnumbered the native Americans. On her pony, the girl rode about the foreign settlements,
learning to see and to appreciate an alien point of view, grasping
eagerly, with the artist's unconscious zest, at the only life within
her reach.

I have never found any intellectual excitement more intense than I used
to feel when I spent a morning with one of these pioneer women at her
baking or butter-making. I used to ride home in the most unreasonable
state of excitement; I always felt as if they told me so much more than
they said—as if I had actually got inside another person's skin.

Willa Cather's early ambition was not to be a writer but a physician. A self-willed individualist even as a child, she had only two

---

[2] See Willa Cather's scornful discussion of "Escapism," in *Willa Cather on
Writing* (1949), pp. 18-29.
[3] See James R. Shively, *Willa Cather's Campus Years*, pp. 14, 115-119;
Mildred R. Bennett, *The World of Willa Cather*, p. 9.

years of formal schooling before she applied for admission to the University of Nebraska, but she had read the English classics with her two grandmothers and had studied Latin with an old British scholar. She was "literary" enough at the university, however, from which she was graduated in 1895; she was also considered very eccentric and unfeminine.[4]

Willa Cather did not publish her first book—the poems collected in *April Twilights*—until 1903. Meanwhile she was experiencing life, at home and abroad. "I couldn't have got as much out of those . . . years if I'd been writing."

Also, she wanted to acquire a competence, so that when she did begin to write she would not be at the mercy of commercialized magazines. She had newspaper experience on the Pittsburgh *Leader* and elsewhere;[5] she taught English in the high school at Allegheny, Pennsylvania. From 1906 to 1912 she was on the staff of *McClure's Magazine*, for four years as managing editor. She "ghosted" S. S. McClure's *Autobiography* and did editorial work on Georgine Milmine's *Life of Mary Baker G. Eddy*. Mildred Bennett believes that she also had a share in the writing of Ellen Terry's autobiography. When she felt that she had enough money, she gave up journalism, took a house at Cherry Valley, New York, and began work on *Alexander's Bridge*. In her later years she made her home in New York, with frequent trips to Europe, Canada, and the West. She died in New York on April 24, 1947.

3. *Studies in Fulfillment*

Alexander's Bridge (1912) was not in itself very important. It came out of "meeting some interesting people in London," plus a warm, youthful enthusiasm for Henry James. "Like most young writers I thought a book should be made out of 'interesting material,' and at that time I found the new more exciting than the familiar." *Alexander's Bridge* has an international setting—Boston,

---

[4] Shively, pp. 16 ff.; Bennett, p. 213.

[5] A good deal of Willa Cather's journalistic writing has been identified only recently. Besides Bennett and Shively, see Flora Bullock, "WC, Essayist and Dramatic Critic," *Prairie Schooner*, XXIII (1949), 393-401; George Seibel, "Miss WC from Nebraska," *New Col*, II (1949), 195-208; John P. Hinz, "WC in Pittsburgh," *New Col*, III (1950), 198-207.

Canada, London—and the central figure is an engineer. The weakness in the bridge is symbolically paralleled to the weakness in the man.[6]

Self-discovery came with *O Pioneers!* (1913). Actually, it was a rediscovery, since the early stories which James R. Shively has printed in *Willa Cather's Campus Years* now prove that she had already employed some of her basic themes while still an undergraduate. *O Pioneers!* and *My Ántonia* (1918) should be read together, though *My Ántonia* is the better book. Ántonia Shimerda, "a rich mine of life, like the founders of early races," is a greater creation than Alexandra Bergson. But both books have the same sense of reality, the same passionate honesty, the same somber, lonely beauty.

Alexandra is the kind of person Captain Forrester has in mind when he speaks of the West as having developed out of dreams— "the homesteader's and the prospector's and the contractor's. We dreamed the railroads across the mountains, just as I dreamed my place on the Sweet Water." She becomes the head of the family after her father's death, and it is her far-seeing vision, her faith in the land, which keeps her stolid and her vacillating brother tied each to his task in the "hard times" when they are asking only for release. Her self-denial is in marked contrast to their selfishness, and their greed for the land that she has won keeps happy marriage away from her for years.

Ántonia does not see the future of the land like Alexandra; she is a part of it. But her emotions run deeper, and she has none of the Swedish girl's stolidness. ("She was a Bohemian girl who was good to me when I was a child. I saw a great deal of her from the time I was eight until I was twelve. She was big-hearted and essentially romantic.")[7]

She comes out of an immigrant family which lacks the barest essentials of life. The father, a sensitive man of considerable cultiva-

[6] John P. Hinz, *AL,* XXI (1950), 473-476, points out the influence upon *Alexander's Bridge* of Ibsen's *Master Builder* and the Quebec Bridge disaster of Aug. 29, 1907. In a sense, the book foreshadows her later studies in frustration.

[7] For the real Ántonia, see Bennett, pp. 46-52. Her husband was "Neighbour Rosicky," of *Obscure Destinies.* When, in hospital, he was once required to identify himself, he declared proudly, "I am the husband of My Ántonia!"

tion, kills himself when he fails to make his adjustment to the New World wilderness. When, after her father's death, Ántonia goes to work in the fields like a man, she loses her "nice ways," as Jim's grandmother had said she would. Later, when the Italian Vannis come to Black Hawk, she develops the dance craze and all that goes with it. Nothing much happens to Ántonia except that she manages to get herself betrayed by a rascally railroad conductor and left with a baby to support. "She loved it from the first as dearly as if she'd had a ring on her finger, and was never ashamed of it." After this episode, Miss Cather leaves Ántonia for twenty years, then reintroduces her, the wife of a commonplace Bohemian and the mother of fourteen children, a battered woman who has lost her teeth but who still retains "the fire of life."

Between *O Pioneers!* and *My Ántonia,* Willa Cather wrote her longest novel, *The Song of the Lark* (1915). It begins about 1890 in the parsonage of a small town in Colorado, moves to Chicago and the life of a music student there in the early days of the Thomas orchestra, makes an excursion into the canyons of the Southwest (later to be so impressively presented in *The Professor's House*), and, passing over Thea's period of study abroad, ends in New York, where she is singing Wagnerian roles at the Metropolitan.

The Song of the Lark presents "Moonstone," Colorado, with extraordinary fidelity. The first section gives vivid pictures of various personages through whom the growing artist's sensibilities are awakened. There are Doctor Archie, whose skill and sympathy mean so much; the Kohlers, with their quaint German ways, forever planting trees to make shade; Professor Wunsch, the pitiful, derelict music-master; Ray Kennedy, the ill-starred young brakeman, who loves Thea, and whose life insurance is the means of launching her upon her career; and Spanish Johnny, with his sensitive spirit and his disreputable ways.

Miss Cather later virtually repudiated *The Song of the Lark*[8] on the ground that "the full-blooded method, which told everything about everybody" was not the right method for her. Moreover, "The book set out to tell of an artist's awakening and struggle. . . . It should have been content to do that." Yet the last part of the novel

[8] See "My First Novels (There Were Two)," in *Willa Cather on Writing.*

is by no means entirely unsuccessful; like George Moore's *Evelyn Innes,* it remains one of the best studies we have in fiction of the artistic life of a great stage artist.[9] Where it fails, as in Thea's affair with Fred Ottenburg, the trouble is not that Thea has "arrived" but that Willa Cather is writing outside her range.

4. Studies in Frustration

In *One of Ours* (1922) the frontier has become the Middle West. And now the protagonist is a man. This is the story of Claude Wheeler—simple, sensitive, unselfish—from his young manhood on a Nebraska farm, through the disastrous experiment of marriage with a cold, pious, shallow, and selfish woman, to his heroic death in World War I.

The old hardships of Ántonia's time are all forgotten now. But, alas! other things have been forgotten with them:

> The Old West had been settled by dreamers, great-hearted adventurers who were unpractical to the point of magnificence; a courteous brotherhood strong in attack but weak in defense, who could conquer but could not hold. Now all the vast territory they had won was to be at the mercy of men like Ivy Peters, who had never dared anything, never risked anything. They would drink up the mirage, dispel the morning freshness, root out the great brooding spirit of freedom, the generous, easy life of the great landholders. The space, the color, the princely carelessness of the pioneer they would destroy and cut up into profitable bits, as the match factory splinters the primeval forest.

Nobody has ever questioned that the picture of Nebraska in the first part of *One of Ours* is superbly done. Even Miss Cather's war is more exciting in Nebraska than it ever becomes in France. The frantic reading of newspapers, the hunting for old neglected maps, the strange, wild tugging at the heart, the wonder of a horizon really expanding at last to the breadth of the world—that all this is

---

[9] Miss Cather seems to have been less interested in music than in musical, especially operatic, personalities, and the opera is half drama. The portrait of Thea Kronborg was strongly influenced by Miss Cather's admiration for Olive Fremstad, who is said to have exclaimed, upon reading *The Song of the Lark,* "I can't tell where I end and you begin!" See WC, "Three American Singers" (Fremstad, Louise Homer, Geraldine Farrar), *McClure's Magazine,* XLII, Dec. 1913, pp. 33-48.

authentic must be recognized by everybody who lived through those terrible days.

Yet the charges that have been leveled against the book are many. It is charged that it breaks in the middle. It is charged that it poses a problem which is never solved. It is even charged that the author's own attitude toward the war is naïve.[10]

No doubt it would be possible to defend Miss Cather against these strictures. *One of Ours* is not primarily a study of marriage: Claude's marriage is over and done with before he leaves for France. And if his story is incomplete, so was the life of his generation. Claude himself knows before he dies that America will not achieve her war aims, yet he accepts the conflict as something that was put up to his generation. There is abundant evidence, in the letters of soldiers and elsewhere, that irrational as this attitude is, it did exist.[11]

It would be possible to do all this, but it would hardly be worth while. Subjected to the test of reading, the first part of Claude Wheeler's history is one book while the last part is another. And the last part is never more than a tour-de-force because it was not Willa Cather's material.

In the next book, the frustration involved is of a very different character. Marian Forrester, the heroine of *A Lost Lady* (1923),[12] is an artist who lived and wrought in terms of personal contacts. "Thirty or forty years ago, in one of those gray towns along the Burlington Railroad, which are so much grayer today than they were then," she was mistress of a house "well known from Omaha to Denver for its hospitality and a certain charm of atmosphere." But after the impoverishment, the illness, and at last the death of her husband—and after the nauseous Ivy Peters has replaced that generous man as the exemplar of "success" in his country—poor

[10] As by Heywood Broun: "It seems to Miss Cather that the war was not without purpose, since it gave a significance to the life of farm boys in Nebraska. The hero of the book loses his life and finds his soul. We happen to believe that there is such a thing as setting too high a price even upon souls, and war is too high a price."

[11] The book was, as a matter of fact, based on the letters of a relative who was killed in the war; see Bennett, pp. 14-15.

[12] Marian is Mrs. Silas Garber, wife of an ex-governor of Nebraska; see Bennett, pp. 69-76.

Marian is like a ship without a rudder. Unable either to "immolate herself . . . and die with the pioneer period to which she belonged," or to find a suitable object of devotion in the age of little things into which it has been her misfortune to survive, she descends to unworthiness. Willa Cather insisted that she did not try for a character study in Marian Forrester but only for an impression. But, as David Daiches has pointed out, the heroine's personal deterioration "is artfully linked to the background theme of the decline of the pioneering West." The subtlety with which the process is traced, and its influence indicated upon the boy, Niel Herbert, who has idealized Mrs. Forrester—

Lilies that fester smell far worse than weeds—

and the wonderful largeness and charity of his—and, by implication, the author's—attitude toward her make the brief novel a masterpiece of its kind.

The hero of *The Professor's House* (1925), Godfrey St. Peter, teaches history in a midwestern college within sight of Lake Michigan. His work on the Spanish explorers has brought him fame and the money to build a fine new house; only, unfortunately, he cannot tear himself away from his study in the old one. His elder daughter has grown wealthy and hard upon the proceeds of a patent left her by her fiancé, Tom Outland, the professor's most brilliant pupil, who was killed in the war. Her younger sister is embittered and estranged. Mrs. St. Peter is enjoying a second blooming, frankly basking in the flattery of her sons-in-law. To the professor himself all this means nothing—nothing except, increasingly as time goes on, anguish. He has fallen out of his place in the world, and looks back upon his career as that of another person. Nothing is real except what he began with in boyhood.

The Professor's House is Willa Cather's subtlest and richest—though not her greatest—book, a book full of nourishing food for the mind and spirit of a disillusioned, if not despairing, maturity. Its spirit is kept free of bitterness, for the professor drops his burden at last after he has been nearly asphyxiated in his old study; he knows now "that life is possible, may even be pleasant, without joy, without passionate griefs"; he faces the future with fortitude. But the failure of the life he lives—and of the age he lives in—to nourish his spirit is nearly complete.[13]

It must have been clear to Miss Cather that she could not go much farther along this particular road. Only one more way-station remained. It is the shortest and most cryptic novel she ever wrote—*My Mortal Enemy* (1926).

Myra Driscoll runs away from a rich, tyrannical, Irish uncle in Parthia, Illinois, to marry Oswald Henshawe. They live with actors, writers, and musicians in the Madison Square district in New York, and despite Myra's difficult temperament, they seem happy enough. But after Myra loses her health and Oswald his position, and they go to live in a miserable little jerry-built hotel on the Pacific Coast, their state is sad indeed.

Only two episodes in Myra's life are presented to the reader; the rest is told by implication. There are unforgettable moments, like the New Year's party in New York, where Madame Modjeska sits regal in the moonlight while her countrywoman sings the "Casta diva." Indeed the whole book has a profound and subtle suggestiveness which Miss Cather never surpassed. But important matters—like the question of Oswald's faithfulness—are left unpardonably obscure, and there are times when the story seems to have been written up to its tantalizing title.

5. *Retreat to the Past*

Where was Willa Cather to go from here? Not to "the banking system and the stock exchange"—that was as impossible for her as it had been for Henry James. But there was an unfailing haven of refuge. That was the past.[14]

Death Comes for the Archbishop (1927) is *My Ántonia's* only possible rival as Miss Cather's most important book. A fictionized account of the lives of Bishop Lamy and Father Macheboeuf, in New Mexico of the 1850's, *Death Comes for the Archbishop* is one

---

13 For Miss Cather's own views on *The Professor's House*, see *Willa Cather on Writing*, pp. 30-32.

14 Granville Hicks's attack on Willa Cather for her retreat to the past, *EJ*, XXII (1933), 703-710, now seems something of a curiosity of criticism. She was defended vigorously by Archer Winsten, *Bkm*(NY), LXXIV (1932), 634-640, and by J. Donald Adams, *The Shape of Books to Come*, pp. 120-125.

of the most lambent and luminous narratives in American literature.[15]

This work seems to have sprung from a literary and an artistic
inspiration:

Since I first saw the Puvis de Chavannes frescoes of the life of Sainte
Genevieve in my student days, I have wished that I could try something
a little like that in prose; something without accent, with none of the
artificial elements of composition. In the Golden Legend the martyrdoms
of the saints are no more dwelt upon than are the trivial incidents of
their lives: it is as though all human experience, measured against one
supreme spiritual experience, were of about the same importance. The
essence of such writing is not to hold the note, not to use an incident
for all there is in it—but to touch and pass on.

How could that be the right method for Willa Cather? Why was
she successful here, while in *One of Ours* she failed?

Because this time she was able to capture the remembrance of
things past which had always been necessary to awaken her creative
powers.

She had been interested in the Southwest, and in the Catholic
missionaries of the Southwest for fifteen years, long before she ever
thought of writing about them. Bishop Lamy himself had become
"a sort of invisible personal friend." Ten years before, she had considered the subject, but it refused to "come." Suddenly, it flowered,
and she canceled all other plans to devote herself to it.

I did not sit down to write the book until the feeling of it had so teased
me that I could not get on with other things. The writing of it took
only a few months, because the book had all been lived many times before
it was written and the happy mood in which I began it never paled.[16]

She adds that she used many of her own experiences, and some of
her father's experiences, in the book, and that writing it was like

[15] It is widely but erroneously believed that Willa Cather's French Catholic
books marked her own conversion to the Roman faith. "I'm an Episcopalian,
and a good one, I hope." But she did not join the church until 1922. "Miss
Cather found it difficult to believe. 'Faith is a gift,' she said; and she admitted
that even her Catholic books were written out of admiration for a faith she
could not quite accept." (Bennett, p. 137.)

[16] The quotations are from her letter to Michael Williams, *Willa Cather
on Writing*, pp. 3-13.

"a return to childhood, to early memories." In other words, *Death Comes for the Archbishop* was quite as "natural" a book for Miss Cather to write as *My Ántonia*.

Like *Death Comes for the Archbishop, Shadows on the Rock* (1931) deals with the past and has a Catholic background, but there the resemblances end. It began when Miss Cather found in the Louvre the diary of an apothecary who had served in Quebec under Frontenac. The book is simply a picture of life in that place toward the end of Frontenac's life, and the title gives a clue to its manner, method, and mood.[17] The loveliness of *Shadows on the Rock* is the loveliness of pale moonlight; its beauty is a beauty reflected and refracted through old chronicles and quaint legend of the past. Incident goes; color and movement go; the piece is played steadily, a bit monotonously, in a minor key. Here, and not in *Death Comes for the Archbishop,* is the real suggestion of Puvis de Chavannes.

6. *The Last Novels*

After *Shadows on the Rock,* Willa Cather published two more novels—*Lucy Gayheart* (1935) and *Sapphira and the Slave Girl* (1940).

Lucy goes to Chicago from Haverford on the Platte, falls romantically and adoringly in love with the great singer for whom she plays accompaniments, is crushed by his death, and has just begun her readjustment when she goes out skating on the Platte and breaks through the thin spring ice.

Lucy Gayheart was somewhat less warmly received than Miss Cather's earlier books. For this there were a number of reasons. It is a sweet, sad love story which had the misfortune to appear at a time when a number of writers had convinced a part of the public that, for some reason which was never made very clear, insensibility was somehow a virtue. None of its materials were new to Miss Cather, and because the heroine lacked the drive of some of her predecessors many readers found her less interesting. Finally, the

[17] This, I think, is not true of the much-discussed title of the preceding book, which was derived from Holbein's *Dance of Death* (see Footman, *AL,* X, 128). Much has been made of "comes *for*" rather than "comes *to*" as indicating the religious point of view. The title remains, nevertheless, macabre, and the book is anything but that.

book contains one unbelievable scene—that in which Lucy gets rid of Harry Gordon by lying to him about her relationship with Sebastian. Several explanations of this have been attempted, but the simplest and the soundest is that Miss Cather was plot-ridden, as Shakespeare often was before her.

Lucy Gayheart has a meaning. It even has, if you insist, a "moral." This is Lucy's discovery that "Life itself . . . [is] the sweetheart."

> She must go back into the world and get all she could of everything that had made him what he was. Those splendors were still on earth, to be sought after and fought for. In them she would find him. *If with all your heart you truly seek Him, you shall surely find Him.* He had sung that for her in the beginning, when she first went to him. Now she knew what it meant.

It is the bitterest kind of irony that chance—aided by a bit of temper—should have destroyed Lucy Gayheart just after she had learned the secret!

But the book does not really need this, significant as it is. Here is a moving bit of human life, presented (save in the one instance noted) with flawless art. That so many people should have had to ask what it "meant" (for unemployment, no doubt, the monetary system, and the Japanese adventure in Manchuria) was a lamentable commentary on how far our criticism had descended.

The other book, *Sapphira and the Slave-Girl,* represented for Miss Cather a deeper excursion into memory than any other that she essayed, for here alone has she written of Virginia. The story takes place before the Civil War; the Epilogue, composed in the first person, describes how the author was brought into contact with her materials. *Sapphira* enlarges Miss Cather's range also in that here, more extensively than in any other novel, she is concerned with the Negro race. The theme is a woman's base and groundless jealousy of a lovely slave girl. The book contains a number of echoes of earlier Cather novels; beautiful as it is, it seems a little pale and underdeveloped. Because the social history that she originally intended to include seemed to Willa Cather to obscure the theme of the book, she is said to have eliminated six pounds of manuscript.[18]

---

[18] I must add a word about Willa Cather's short stories. The first collection, *The Troll Garden* (1905) comprised (1) "Flavia and Her Artists," (2) "The

7. Literary Theory and Craftsmanship

Miss Cather's first great literary master was Henry James. Granville Hicks speaks of *Alexander's Bridge* as "her one book" which shows James's influence. The truth is that she shows James's influence in books of the most varied character—*My Ántonia, A Lost*

Sculptor's Funeral," (3) "The Garden Lodge," (4) " 'A Death in the Desert,' " (5) "The Marriage of Phaedra," (6) "A Wagner Matinee," (7) "Paul's Case." Of these (2), (4), (6), and (7) were reprinted in *Youth and the Bright Medusa* (1920), in which "Coming, Aphrodite!" "The Diamond Mine," "A Gold Slipper," and "Scandal" appeared for the first time. When the *Youth* collection was reprinted in the Autograph Edition, (4) was dropped. In 1932 came *Obscure Destinies,* comprising "Neighbour Rosicky," "Old Mrs. Harris," and "Two Friends." *The Old Beauty and Others* (1948) contained, besides the title-story, "The Best Years" and "Before Breakfast." Since Miss Cather's death, James R. Shively has also reprinted six stories she wrote in the 1890's in *Willa Cather's Campus Years.*

In addition to these, there are at least twenty-one stories by Willa Cather, in nationally-circulated magazines, twenty of which she never allowed to be reprinted. The exception is "Double Birthday," which she permitted Dale Warren to use in his *A Modern Galaxy* (HM, 1930).

The twenty-one stories are: (1) "On the Divide," *Overland Monthly,* XXVII (1896), 65-74; (2) "Eric Hermansson's Soul," *Cosmopolitan,* XXVIII (1900), 633-644; (3) "Jack-a-Boy," *Saturday Evening Post,* CLXXIII, Mar. 30, 1901, p. 4; (4) "El Dorado: A Kansas Recessional," *New England Magazine,* N.S. XXIV (1901), 357-369; (5) "The Professor's Commencement," *NEM,* N.S. XXVI (1902), 481-488; (6) "The Treasure of Far Island," *NEM,* N.S. XXVII (1902), 234-249; (7) "The Namesake," *McClure's Magazine,* XXVIII (1907), 492-497; (8) "The Profile," *McC M,* XXIX (1907), 135-140; (9) "The Willing Muse," *Century,* LXXIV (1907), 550-557; (10) "Eleanor's House," *McC M,* XXIX (1907), 623-630; (11) "On the Gull's Road," *McC M,* XXXII (1908), 145-152; (12) "The Enchanted Bluff," *Harper's Magazine,* CXVIII (1909), 774-781; (13) "The Joy of Nelly Deane," *Ce,* LXXXII (1911), 859-866; (14) "Behind the Singer Tower," *Collier's,* XLIX, May 18, 1912, p. 16+; (15) "The Bohemian Girl," *McC M,* XXXIX (1912), 421-443; (16) "Consequences," *McC M,* XLVI, Nov. 1915, pp. 30-32+; (17) "The Bookkeeper's Wife," *Ce,* XCII (1916), 51-59; (18) "Ardessa," *Ce,* XCVI (1918), 105-116; (19) "Her Boss," *Smart Set,* LX (1919), 95-108; (20) "Uncle Valentine," *Woman's Home Companion,* LII, February 1925, p. 7+, March 1925, p. 15+; (21) "Double Birthday," *Forum,* LXXXI (1929), 78-82.

Seven of these stories have their locale in the West, five wholly or largely in New York or some other large American city, two abroad, two in small American cities, one on the sea, and one in a small town in Pennsylvania. Scandinavians figure importantly in four, Bohemians in one, an Italian in one, Jews in two. Music is an important element in two, art in three, literature in one; the theater plays some part in three. One story has an educa-

Lady, My Mortal Enemy—wherever she chooses to present a story from the point of view of "some more or less detached, some not strictly involved . . . witness of reporter, some person who contributes to the case mainly a certain amount of criticism and interpretation of it."[19]

Flaubert and his contemporaries seem at one time to have meant much to her; Balzac she virtually repudiated when she repudiated the method of *The Song of the Lark*. She admired the simplification of economy of Turgenev and Prosper Mérimée. She admired Tolstoy and Hawthorne for their ability to assimilate setting, so that

tional background; two deal with the business world. Religion is important in one, and the church as an institution plays its part in two others. Four stories have a frame; three seem very Jamesian. Two are novelettes. Four seem to have no other purpose than to capture a mood or preserve the flavor of a personality. The great surprises are "Consequences," a psychic horror story, and "Behind the Singer Tower," which is drenched in the "social consciousness" for lack of which Willa Cather was reproached by Marxian critics. The most prescient tale is "The Enchanted Bluff," a kind of preliminary study for "Tom Outland's Story," in *The Professor's House*.

Mrs. Bennett mentions two more stories which I have not seen: "An Affair at Grover Station" and "The Conversion of Sum Loo," both published in *The Library* (Pittsburgh) in 1900. Neither have I seen "The Fear That Walked at Noonday," a combination ghost story and football story, written in collaboration with Dorothy Canfield, published first in a Junior Class yearbook of 1894, and reprinted in an edition of thirty copies by Ralph Allan in 1931. See articles by F. B. Adams, Jr., in my bibliography.

Students of these early stories should be warned that the first six among my twenty-one numbered items were written by Willa Cather only in part. The present writer was informed by her that the first two of these were college "themes" (though the second was actually produced after graduation), rewritten by her instructor and sent to market without her knowledge, and that the other four represent the collective efforts of a group of four young people, of whom she was one, working on Pittsburgh newspapers.

The four stories about artists and singers added to the Cather canon in *Youth and the Bright Medusa* all seem to me (for her) rather cheap, and "Paul's Case," that darling of anthologists, merely the case history of a particularly nasty brat. Of the stories in *Obscure Destinies*, "Neighbour Rosicky" is one of Miss Cather's most lovable Bohemians, and "Two Friends," though slight, is perfect of its kind, but "Old Mrs. Harris" fails to focus. There is nothing of importance in *The Old Beauty and Others*.

[19] David Daiches (*Willa Cather*, p. 19) is perhaps over-subtle when he sees in Willa Cather's studies of European emigrants in America "a transmutation of one of James's major themes" and an example of "James's legacy transplanted and put to new uses."

it seems to exist "not so much in the author's mind, as in the emotional penumbra of the characters themselves." She speaks admiringly of Conrad and of Stephen Crane.[20] According to Louise Bogan, she rejected Chekhov as despairing and bloodless.[21] The three American books which seemed to her to confront the future most serenely were *The Scarlet Letter, Huckleberry Finn,* and *The Country of the Pointed Firs.* To Sarah Orne Jewett she owed a special debt, for it was Miss Jewett who urged her to commit herself and her career to her own, at that time, unfashionable materials.

Once she had found her field, she gave herself to an unceasing search for simplification. She sloughed off sentimentality. She rose above her early awkwardness and prolixity. Rating power of observation and description as but a low part of the novelist's equipment, she soon came to believe that the novel was "overfurnished." And "a novel crowded with physical sensations is no less a catalogue than one crowded with furniture." She did not think of her writing as a means of exploiting her personality; instead, it was "a complete loss of self for three hours a day"; her ideal, therefore, was "to make things and people tell their story simply by juxtaposition," with as little comment as possible. She never hesitated to throw away a dozen fairly good stories in order to produce one that was really good. "Whatever is felt upon the page without being specifically named there—that, it seems to me, is created."

Technique for its own sake did not interest her, and she gives few signs of having lived through a period when the novel was becoming more and more experimental. As David Daiches has already pointed out, she actually begins *Death Comes for the Archbishop* with the "solitary horseman" of early nineteenth-century fiction. In the ordinary sense, she does not analyze her characters at all: she merely wishes to put her readers into a position where they can sense the essence of her people's individuality. Like Conrad, consequently, she has a sense of mystery hovering about many of them which does not at all make them seem less alive. Myra Henshawe and Sapphira Colbert are good examples of this.

[20] See, especially, her "When I Knew Stephen Crane," reprinted in *Prairie Schooner,* XXIII (1949), 231-236.
[21] *New Yorker,* VII, Aug. 8, 1931, pp. 19-22.

Above all else, Willa Cather is the novelist of memory. All her characters have a habit of recalling their past. Moreover, she characteristically throws the story itself into the past and looks back upon it, thus securing both detachment and what Nietzsche called "the pathos of distance." "In Haverford on the Platte the towns-people still talk of Lucy Gayheart." And even in mid-narrative we may encounter such passages as these: "Long, long afterward, when Niel did not know whether Mrs. Forrester were living or dead. . . ." and "In the old times, when Nancy and Mrs. Blake were alive, and for sixty years afterward. . . ." Closely connected with this is her fondness for epilogues. She does not like to end on a high note; she prefers to taper off slowly.

Her craftsmanship, consequently, is often pronounced defective in the matter of structure. The usual view is that only in *A Lost Lady* has she achieved a perfect narrative, and that the two French Catholic books solve the problem by evading it, through taking the form of a chronicle. As far as that goes, *A Lost Lady* itself is developed episodically. Yet except for *My Ántonia,* which suffers from a divided unity because the heroine disappears for a considerable time in mid-narrative, and *One of Ours,* whose failure I have already sufficiently adumbrated, none of Willa Cather's books, in the nature of their problem, require any higher degree of unity than she has seen fit to give them. It was, no doubt, immensely daring to interrupt St. Peter's story and inject an eighty-page account of Tom Outland's adventures in the Southwest, but to Miss Cather's way of thinking, the contrast thus achieved was very much the point of the book.

8. *"Life Hurrying Past . . ."*

When *O Pioneers!* was published, one reviewer declared that a scattered effect might have been expected in a novel "which takes its title from Whitman and which is dedicated to the memory of Sarah Orne Jewett, 'in whose beautiful and delicate work there is the perfection that endures.'" But it is precisely because Miss Cather was able to respond to both Whitman and Miss Jewett, because her soul was hungry for music and the arts, at the same time that her heart clung passionately to the land, that she became the fine novelist we knew. Her love of common things saved her from trifling, and her hunger for beauty preserved her from the provincialism that might otherwise have clouded her work. Jim Burden, of *My Ántonia,* studying Virgil and thinking of the "hired girls" on the farm, understands the connection: "It came over me, as it had never done before, the relations between girls like them and the poetry of Virgil. If there were no girls like them in the world, there would be no poetry."

As passionately as any of the moderns, Willa Cather believed in the fulfillment of the individual destiny. But her people have roots, and she does not present fulfillment in terms of a shrinking of responsibility. When it comes to a choice between the gaudy and the drab, between tinsel and substance, she is all for the substance, even if she must take the drab along with it.

She had an essentially French appreciation of civilization, of the amenities of life. There is actual passion in her relish of these things. When she first came into the Fields house at 148 Charles Street, Boston—"an American of the Apache period and territory"—she basked in "an atmosphere in which one seemed absolutely safe from everything ugly." At her best, she spiritualizes even material comforts. Bishop Latour's soup is "the result of a constantly refined tradition," with "a thousand years of history" in it; and the dying Madame Auclair is painfully conscious that she is leaving more than her "things" to her little daughter, "a feeling about life that had come down to her through so many centuries and that she had brought with her across the wastes of obliterating, brutal ocean." In short, Miss Cather is essentially a novelist for civilized people.

This point of view has its limitations. I do not know what Willa Cather would have said to Trollope's brash pronouncement:

All material progress has come from man's desire to do the best he can for himself and those about him, and civilization and Christianity itself have been made possible by such progress.

There are many passages in which she seems fundamentally in agreement with this. Doctor Archie tells Thea that all religions are good and all equally impossible to "live up to."

"I've thought about it a good deal, and I can't help feeling that while we are in the world, we have to live for the best things of this world, and those things are material and positive."

Even some things not among the "best" are admitted occasionally. Is Claude Wheeler right in his thought that "agreeable people" are made "by judicious indulgence in almost everything he had been taught to shun"? Is Lucy Gayheart more attractive for sharing the whisky in Harry Gordon's flask when she skates with him on the Platte?

Sanity, magnanimity, love of beauty, enthusiasm for living—these are the outstanding qualities of Willa Cather's work at its best. Magnanimity, especially, is a salient characteristic of her women. There is nothing in her books more touching than the picture of Alexandra at the close of *O Pioneers!* planning to get a pardon for the man who murdered her brother. Life escapes from us very quickly; it is not often that we save even so much of the past as the print of a girl's naked foot in a block of cement. Water is a better symbol, beautiful, but running away:

The stream and the broken pottery; what was any art but an effort to make a sheath, a mold in which to imprison for a moment the shining, elusive element which is life itself—life hurrying past us and running away, too strong to stop, too sweet to lose?

CHAPTER XVIII

JAMES BRANCH CABELL:
THE ANATOMY OF ROMANTICISM*

. . . it is only by preserving faith in human dreams that we may, after all, perhaps some day make them come true.

The Cream of the Jest

1. *Lichfield out of Poictesme*

James Branch Cabell has had the most curious career of any American writer. He began in the early 1900's "to write the very nicest kind of books—like Henry Harland's, and Justus Miles Forman's, and Anthony Hope's." The exuberant romanticism of some of these tales won their admirers, notably Mark Twain and Theodore Roosevelt; but most of the books speedily got down to nineteen cents in the department stores, while their critical reception may not unfairly be gauged by the "Tributes from the Press" which Mr. Cabell has impishly gathered together at the close of *Straws and Prayer-Books*. What it all seems to add up to is that, while the stories are worthless, the colored illustrations, which were by Howard Pyle, are superb. And that was the First Act.

Act Two began in 1919 with the suppression of *Jurgen*. At this point Mr. Cabell became a "protégé of the censor." The book itself went to forty dollars in the secondhand shops, and the Cabell Cause promptly became indistinguishable from the Right of the Artist To Express Himself Freely in Defiance of Puritan Inhibitions. Influential critics like Carl Van Doren, H. L. Mencken, Burton Rascoe, and Vernon Louis Parrington hailed Mr. Cabell as a great writer. The

---

* Under the title "Cabell: A Reconsideration," the larger part of this chapter appeared in *College English*, IX (1948), 239-246. Copyright, 1948, by the University of Chicago Press. Quotations from the writings of James Branch Cabell in this chapter are made by kind permission of the author.

old books were revised and brought back into print; the *Biography of the Life of Manuel*—"the most ambitiously planned literary work which has ever come out of America"—was completed; and the collected Storisende Edition came into being. That was the Second Act.

In the 'thirties the intellectual climate began to change, and Mr. Cabell found himself no more sympathetic toward the literary tastes of most of his contemporaries than he was in tune with their political convictions. Now a writer of established reputation, he was again as neglected as when he had been a tyro. And that was the Third Act.

The Fourth Act is now in progress. So far it has produced two novels and two nonfiction works—*Let Me Lie* (1947) and *Quiet, Please* (1952).

It is clear that Mr. Cabell refuses to stay dead even when we have got him comfortably buried. Is it too much to hope that a highly controversial figure may now be reasonably assessed and at least tentatively assigned to what one may hope will be his permanent place in our literature?

The biographical data may be briefly set forth.

James Branch Cabell was born of two distinguished Southern families, on April 14, 1879, in Richmond, Virginia. At seventeen, while yet in his junior year at William and Mary, he taught French and Greek in the college; he graduated, in 1898, with a high scholastic record. He has had some experience in newspaper work, both in Richmond and in New York; he has mined coal briefly in West Virginia; he has served several historical societies as genealogist and historian. He has been twice married and is the father of a son.

But it will take many more words to describe the ground plan of the *Biography*:

1. The Preface: *Beyond Life, Dizain des demiurges* (1919). The novelist John Charteris defines his and, by implication, Mr. Cabell's gospel of romanticism and outlines the three philosophies held and illustrated by the descendants of Manuel—the chivalrous, the gallant, the poetic, or (in other words) life viewed "as a testing; as a toy; and as raw material."

2. The Life and Legend of Manuel the Redeemer: *Figures of Earth: A Comedy of Appearances* (1921), deals with the earthly life of the Redeemer in Thirteenth-Century Poictesme; *The Silver Stallion: A*

Comedy of Redemption (1926), concerns the posthumous development of his legend.

3. The Three Themes of the Biography Illustrated: *The Silver Stallion* was to have been followed by *The Witch Woman,* which would have pictured the relations, through several centuries, between Ettarre, third daughter of Manuel and Niafer, and ten human lovers. But this project was wrecked by the time needed to prepare the Storisende Edition plus Mr. Cabell's rather strange determination to add nothing to the *Biography* after having passed his fifty-first birthday. What was to have been a *dizain* has dwindled, therefore, to a trilogy; fortunately, the trilogy illustrates the three main themes of the *Biography* and thus serves as an effective introduction to what follows. In *The Music from behind the Moon* (1926), Ettarre is loved by a poet; in *The White Robe* (1928), by a gallant bishop; in *The Way of Ecben* (1929), by a chivalrous king.[1]

4. The Chivalrous Attitude: *Domnei: A Comedy of Woman-Worship* (1920), which was originally published as *The Soul of Melicent* (1913), is the first novel to be devoted wholly to the chivalrous attitude. This theme is continued in the ten short pieces collected in *Chivalry: Dizain des reines* (1909), which concerns Henry III's queen, Alianora of Provence (who mated also with Manuel), and nine other women, wives of six English monarchs who, through her, inherited Manuel's life.

5. The Gallant Attitude: Gallantry is the exclusive theme of three books: *Jurgen: A Comedy of Justice* (1919); *The High Place: A Comedy of Disenchantment* (1923); and *Gallantry: Dizain des fêtes galantes* (1907). *Jurgen* is dominated by Manuel's second daughter, Dorothy la Désirée. The hero of *The High Place,* Florian de Puysange, French regency descendant of Manuel and of Jurgen, fails in his gallantry when he raises the coverlet which Jurgen wisely left unlifted; for beauty and holiness can blend only with the chivalrous and poetic attitudes but never with the gallant, which must perforce concern itself only with the surface of life. This the six heroes of *Gallantry* understand.

The continued exposition of the theme of gallantry in the *Biography* is partially interrupted by *The Line of Love: Dizain des mariages* (1905); chronicling the life of Manuel through ten generations, clear down to its introduction into the American Musgrave family,[2] *The Line of Love* presents all three attitudes.

---

[1] These three works have now been republished together, with a new introduction, as *The Witch-Woman: A Trilogy About Her* (FSY, 1948).

[2] In *The Lineage of Lichfield* (1922), Mr. Cabell has thoughtfully traced all these relationships for us in genealogical form.

6. The Poetic Attitude: *Something about Eve, A Comedy of Fig-Leaves* (1927); *The Certain Hour: Dizain des poètes* (1916). Gerald Musgrave, American hero of *Something about Eve,* is in the nineteenth generation from Manuel. Like Florian, Gerald fails; having resisted woman in many incarnations as siren, he succumbs to her in her deadliest aspect of domesticity and lives contentedly on Mispec Moor, while others, his own son finally among them, pass on to the marches of Antan. What *Gallantry* is to *The High Place, The Certain Hour* is to *Something about Eve.* Here are the earthly lives, as embodied in Shakespeare, Herrick, Pope, and others, of the ten images which Manuel shaped upon Upper Morven and to which Freydis gave life. Where Gerald Musgrave "failed, economically" with the poetic attitude, they succeeded. But they failed as human beings.

7. The Three Attitudes in Modern Virginia: In *The Cords of Vanity: A Comedy of Shirking* (1909), Robert Etheridge Townsend, Gerald's great-grandson, exemplifies gallantry. *(From the Hidden Way,* 1919, a collection of Townsend's verses, completes his portrait as a gallant; the play, *The Jewel Merchants,* 1921, dismisses the theme of gallantry from the *Biography.)* In *The Rivet in Grandfather's Neck: A Comedy of Limitations* (1915), Colonel Rudolph Musgrave, grandson of Gerald's brother, pursues chivalry under modern conditions. *The Eagle's Shadow: A Comedy of Purse-Strings* (1904), shows Felix Bulmer Kennaston, son of Townsend's mother's sister, attempting to maintain the poetic attitude.

But Felix gets another book, and a much better one, in *The Cream of the Jest: A Comedy of Evasions* (1917). Here, while the body of Felix inhabits Lichfield, his soul returns, through dreams induced by a sigil which turns out at last to be only half of a broken cold-cream jar, to the land of Poictesme, "so that, through this return, the perpetuated life of Manuel ends its seven hundred years of journeying at the exact point of its outset. The circle is thus made complete, as my last poet annihilates, through quite other means than were employed by my first poet, Madoc, the intervening twenty generations."

8. The Epilogue: *Straws and Prayer-Books: Dizain des diversions* (1924), a companion piece to *Beyond Life,* in which Mr. Cabell explains what prompted him to write the *Biography.*

9. Notes and Addenda: *Townsend of Lichfield: Dizain des adieux* (1930).

Poictesme, which so far as it is anything save a world of the imagination, is a medieval French province—Poitiers plus Angoulême— was born in 1905 of ignorance and annoyance. Making his characters perform in Tunbridge Wells—which he had never visited—the author of *Gallantry* found himself embarrassed by problems of local geography and determined that never again, when avoidable, would he lay his scene in an actual place. "I needed in my own little world to be omnipotent, and to move untrammeled by historic facts which any demiurge other than I had brought into being."[3]

The country grew through the years. John Bulmer discovered it in 1905.[4] Prince Edward Longshanks and Ellinor of Castile visited it in 1909, while traveling from northern France into Spain.[5] The story of *The Soul of Melicent* (1913), inhabited it wholly. New territories were staked out, new discoveries made in *The Cream of the Jest, Jurgen, Figures of Earth,* and *The High Place.* Its creator last visited the country in 1927 for *The White Robe.* By that time he had familiarized himself with its history from 1234 to 1750.

It now seems a real place to him. Maps have been drawn of it. Its bibliography "rivals in bulk that of any other French province."

Each of its leading personages has been commemorated in a biography; its laws and legends have been summarized; the development of its religion is known; a considerable section of its literature has been preserved; in at least one symphony[6] and a fair number of songs its music endures; and its relics in the way of drawings and paintings and mural decorations and sculpture are still tolerably numerous.[7]

But all this is superficial. Cabell's ignorance of the geography of Tunbridge Wells was a happy accident. Poictesme was destined for him. His kind of novel could have found its scene nowhere else, nor could he otherwise have satisfied his desire to write of life "not as it is but as it ought to be." Like Kennaston, he was foreordained to concern himself "with an epoch and a society, and even a geog-

---

[3] The wheel came full circle when, many years later, Frank C. Papé drew pictures of Poictesme for the illustrated editions of Cabell's books at his studio in Tunbridge Wells.

[4] See "In the Second April," in *Gallantry.*

[5] See "The Story of the Tenson," in *Chivalry.*

[6] *Jurgen,* a symphonic poem by Deems Taylor, written for the New York Philharmonic Orchestra, 1925.

[7] Cabell delights his admirers and annoys his detractors by inventing an elaborate bibliography from which he pretends to have derived his stories about Poictesme. Cf., for example, the elaborate list at the end of *Domnei* and Walter Klinefelter's charming *Books About Poictesme* (Chicago, The Black Cat Press, 1927).

raphy, whose comeliness had escaped the wear and tear of ever actually existing."

2. *"As It Ought To Be"*

Mr. Cabell's romanticism has been expounded in many places, notably through John Charteris in *Beyond Life* and Felix Kennaston in *The Cream of the Jest*. His views have an obvious kinship with Stevenson's: he knows, for example, that nothing could be more unreal, or even more unscientific, than the naturalistic approach to life, for the simple reason that living is essentially and inevitably a subjective process—"no man lives in the external truth, among salts and acids, but in the warm, phantasmagoric chamber of his brain, with the painted windows and the storied walls"—but his presentation is far more whimsical than Stevenson's and far less doctrinaire.

In his essay on Elinor Wylie, Cabell distinguishes between the golden, sunshiny, major romance of Scott and Dumas—the romance which proceeds from the writer's being in love with life—and the minor romance, illuminated by the moon, which "embellishes life because the writer has found life to be unendurably ugly." It is in making this latter approach that he has left himself open to the charge that he is merely an "escapist" who cannot "face life." The world of men does not "content nor even vitally concern" the artist; Kennaston cannot understand why anyone should wish to read books to be reminded of what life is like. Like Bernard Shaw, Mr. Cabell believes that "living is the only art in which mankind has never achieved distinction." No realist can ever be more than a copyist, and it is the untruth that makes men free. He even believes, or pretends to believe, that the artist does his best work in "that middle world" from which great conflicts, great causes, and great refusals are all barred out. And when he pitches his tent in Poictesme, he still prefers "to play with human passions, rather than . . . to consent to become their battered plaything."

But to stop here is to miss the figure in the carpet. Cabell says all these things, and in a way they are true; but they are not meant to be taken too literally. Cabell, like Madoc, is among those who forever hear "another music skirling," and it calls him, "remotely, toward his allotted doom." One cannot vilify that temperament without vili-

fying the creative imagination itself. The dreamer who believes—
and who may well be scientifically correct in believing—that "for
humankind the dream is the one true reality" can hardly be accused
of evasion when he writes of dreams; neither can an artist whose
dreams have been molded, through the ardent efforts of a lifetime
of creative activity, into one of the most unmistakable realms in
literature be safely dismissed as a mental masturbator.

But the case for Cabell is considerably stronger than that, for if
Poictesme is a "created" realm, it is not, for all its dreamlike beauty,
a realm from which either the problems or the pains of "real" life
have been excluded; as Mr. Mencken once remarked, Jurgen goes
about, among his monsters and demons, with all the solidity of a
Rotarian or a stockbroker. Indeed, Mr. Cabell's detractors attack him
on this ground also, for, in attacking Mr. Cabell, no holds are barred.
As he ruins the effect of his beautiful style by cocksureness and
vulgarity, so (we are told) does he destroy the romanticism of his
utopia by admitting humor, by altogether unsuitable references to
the needs of nature, by introducing an Eagle who is an obvious
caricature of Woodrow Wilson, and in a dozen other ways.

Basically, it is clear that Cabell shares the high regard of Ibsen
and of Conrad for dynamic illusions, vital lies.

To what does the whole business tend?—why, how in heaven's name
should I know. We can but be content that all goes forward, toward
something. . . . It may be that we are nocturnal creatures perturbed by
rumors of a dawn which comes inevitably, as prologue to a day wherein
we and our children have no part whatever. It may be that when our
arboreal propositus descended from his palm-tree and began to walk
upright about the earth, his progeny were forthwith committed to a
journey in which today is only a way station. Yet I prefer to take it
that we are components of an unfinished world, and that we are but
as seething atoms which ferment toward its making, if merely because
man as he now exists can hardly be the finished product of any Creator
whom one could very heartily revere. We are being made into something
quite unpredictable, I imagine; and through the purging and the smelt-
ing, we are sustained by an instinctive knowledge that we are being
made into something better. For this we know, quite incommunicably,
and yet as surely as we know that we will to have it thus.

And it is this will that stirs in us to have the creatures of earth and
the affairs of earth, not as they are, but "as they ought to be," which

we call romance. But when we note how visibly it sways all life, we perceive that we are talking about God.[8]

3. Of Phallic Comedy

None of this sounds very much like a writer whose most famous book was suppressed for a year and a half by the New York Society for the Suppression of Vice. Mr. Cabell's own opinion is that the theme of the *Biography* is the life of man, that Jurgen's principal interest was in exercising his brain rather than another organ, and that the proportion of sexual interest in his books is about the same as it is in life. Now it may be that Cabell's innuendo is only what he once called Gerald's sojourn with Maya of the Fair Breasts, that is, a parenthesis; but Gerald never reached Antan, and it must be admitted that Mr. Cabell's style is very parenthetical. To accuse John Sumner of having read an unintended sexual significance into the lance, the veil, and other "properties" in *Jurgen*[9] was clever dialectic; but it is difficult to believe that the misinterpretation took the author completely by surprise.

What attitude to take toward such things is another matter. One may, of course, decline to have anything to say to phallic comedy, on the ground that it is, as Gerald Musgrave would say, "un-American"—though I much fear that neither the native American tradition nor contemporary American life will sustain that view. One may accept it and still feel that there is too much of it in Cabell, as Jurgen was bored by the diversions of Anaïtis. Or one may frankly enjoy it and still balk at the numerous suggestions of perversity in *The High Place, The White Robe,* and elsewhere. Objections to many passages, it is true, disappear in the light of Cabell's mad logic: when Elissa, of *Smire,* announces her fixed rule never to disparage her late husband in his own bed, "no matter with whom I may happen to be sharing it," we have a keen commentary on human hypocrisy and inconsistency whose force in Cabell has not always been fairly recognized. And Gerald Musgrave, entangled in his unhappy liaison with Evelyn Townsend, who has given him "all,"

---

[8] From *Beyond Life.* Copyright 1919, 1927, by James Branch Cabell.
[9] See Guy Holt, *Jurgen and the Law* (McB, 1923).

and thrown herself upon his chivalry, is sure that there is no friendlier piece of counsel extant than the Seventh Commandment.

Cabell is well within his rights when he points out that his teachings on these matters have always been conservative, for Cabell is, above all else, the novelist of acquiescence. "To submit is the great lesson"; on that point he is as classical as Pope. "I have written sedately in praise of monogamy in *Jurgen,* and of keeping up appearances in *Figures of Earth,* and of chastity in *Something about Eve,* and of moderation in *The High Place,* and of womanhood in *Domnei,* and of religion in *The Silver Stallion.*" It is true that he adds slyly in another connection that "these volumes touch upon many other matters" and that their "spiritual message . . . is not wholly priggish." Jurgen himself declares in a passage which suggests a good deal concerning his creator that "it is eminently interesting to meditate upon strange pleasures, and to make verses about them is the most amiable of avocations; it is merely the pursuit of them that I would discourage, as disappointing and mussy."

4. *Nonbiographical*

Though I have taken some illustrations from other books, I have so far spoken specifically only of the *Biography of Manuel.* To distinguish the *Biography* from his other books, Mr. Cabell, upon its completion, lopped the "James" from his name and took to signing his books "Branch Cabell." Branch Cabell produced three volumes of belles-lettres known collectively as *Their Lives and Letters*[10] and two fictional trilogies: *The Nightmare Has Triplets,* comprising *Smirt* (1934), *Smith* (1935), and *Smire* (1937); and *Heirs and Assigns,* which embraces *The King Was In His Counting-House* (1938), *Hamlet Had an Uncle* (1940), and *The First Gentleman of America* (1942). With the publication of *There Were Two Pirates* in 1946, apparently convinced at last that the reading public was incapable of the discrimination that must be required in order to regard the use of "Branch Cabell" as anything more than an affectation, Mr. Cabell resumed his full name.

The King Was in His Counting-House "is based upon the notion

[10] *These Restless Heads* (1932); *Special Delivery* (1933); *Ladies and Gentlemen* (1934).

of writing about Cosimo de Medici, first Grand Duke of Tuscany, and the two sons who succeeded him, in somewhat the manner in which a Jacobean dramatist might have handled this theme." *Hamlet Had an Uncle* goes back of Shakespeare to the sagas. *The First Gentleman of America,* "a tale told in the Northern Neck of Virginia," when that country was known as Ajacan, is built around the struggle for America between Jean Ribaut and the founder of St. Augustine, Pedro Menéndez de Aviles; the book involves the Indian prince who was the first American to be subjected to the influences of European cosmopolitanism and manages to say a good word for the political policy which has since come to be known as isolationism.

The theme in all three novels is Cabell's favorite theme of compromise and adjustment. "The protagonist of each book, after his allotted jaunt, with youth to incite him, into outlandish regions, accepts more or less willingly his allotted place in the social organism of his own people and country." The "thrice used scenario" has, however, been "variously handled—as a saga, and as a melodrama, and as folklore."

The three parts of *The Nightmare Has Triplets,* on the other hand, comprise a single work. According to the author, this work "attempts to extend the naturalism of Lewis Carroll," to apply "an elaborate and unflinching naturalism" to the world of dreams. I do not think Cabell has really done that—as they tell me Joyce has in *Finnegans Wake*—nor can I believe that the attempt was very seriously made. Yet the Forest of Branlon is a less elaborate Poictesme, and the books Cabell has written about it are nearly as fine as the best of the *Biography*. Smirt, who is apparently an author's godlike conception of himself, is transformed to a shopkeeper through the will of a woman; in this aspect, as Smith, he is Lord of the Forest of Branlon. "Daily I created, in my own small kingdom, that beauty which derided time. For absurd loyalties my forest had made a haven; my forest fed magnanimity; my forest revived the hurt daydreams of youth." Smith fell asleep between the knees of Tana, and, when he woke up, he found a woman's skeleton perched behind him. "Among these depressing circumstances I had become Smire." But his visiting cards were still engraved *Poietes.*

Both *There Were Two Pirates* and *The Devil's Own Dear Son* (1949) have come out of Mr. Cabell's recent winters in Florida; indeed, he has ventured to group them with the book about *The St. Johns* (1943) which he wrote in collaboration with A. J. Hanna to make up a trilogy known as *It Happened in Florida. There Were Two Pirates* tells the story of the freebooter José Gasparilla and his other self. The picture of Gerald's affection for that "illusion," his little son, in *Something about Eve,* had already revealed Cabell's feeling for children, but the much more elaborate childhood episode in *There Were Two Pirates* is a much finer thing. It is true that, to give it the prominence it required, the story of the pirate's adventures had to be considerably curtailed, but it was worth the sacrifice.

The Devil's Own Dear Son lacks the wistful tenderness of *There Were Two Pirates* but it is far more hilariously entertaining. Its locale is neatly divided between St. Augustine, Florida, and Hell. There is a family connection between the hero, Diego de Arredondo Dodd, son of the proprietor of the Bide-a-While Tourist Home, and that José Gasparilla whom we already know; there are even sideglances toward the Forest of Branlon and toward Poictesme itself; Diego, at a crucial moment, mounts the Silver Stallion, despite the warning of his father, Red Samaël, the Seducer, that the creature "is nowadays an infirm and discredited animal." The book has a supernatural pattern, but its spirit is very worldly, and it is full of topical hits: lovingly satirical toward St. Augustine, bitterly critical of what Mr. Cabell considers the inanities of American foreign policy, and with side glances, in many moods, toward varied aspects of American life, including the novelists, the reviewers, and the book clubs.

5. *"To What Does the Whole Business Tend?"*

Nearly everything that can be said against Mr. Cabell's work has been said consummately—by Mr. Cabell. Madoc's songs are described by the best-thought-of connoisseurs as "essentially hollow and deficient in . . . red blood."[11] Miramon's personal taste in art is said to favor "the richly romantic sweetened with nonsense and

---

[11] *The Music From Behind the Moon.*

spiced with the tabooed."[12] Bulmer tells Townsend that he is sadly
passé: "That pose is of the Beardsley period and went out many
magazines ago."[13] Of Horvendile it is said that "he very irritatingly
poses as a superior person, that he is labored beyond endurance, that
he smells of the lamp, that his art is dull and tarnished and trivial
and intolerable."[14]

Moreover, Cabell is repetitive. Again and again, he gives us two
basic situations: "the encounter of two persons between whom love
has existed, and who speak together, as they believe, for the last
occasion in their lives," and the meeting with a former self. Jurgen's
standing "face to face with all that Jurgen had been and was not any
longer" was the one adventure which his biographer "lacked heart
to tell of."

That Mr. Cabell's virtues are those of a spontaneous, youthful
exuberance it would be foolish to claim. His is a matured, cerebrated
romanticism. He has combined all known mythologies and invented
his own; unless you have a specialist's knowledge of the field, you
will never know how much is scholarship and how much invention;[15] neither can you be sure whether a queer-looking name is an
anagram which you must solve to get the point of the episode in
which it figures—whether, indeed, the whole episode has a profound
inner meaning, or whether the surface beauty (or, as the case may
be, the surface hilarity) is supposed to be enough.[16] At its best,

[12] *The Silver Stallion.*

[13] *The Cords of Vanity.*

[14] *Something about Eve.*

[15] Cabell has read "some part" at least of all the important books available,
but he has not enjoyed all his reading. He praises Shakespeare (though he
likes both Marlowe and Congreve better), Dickens, Thackeray (he wishes
he had written *Henry Esmond*), Villon, Hans Christian Andersen, Machen,
De Coster's *Tyl Eulenspiegel,* and Gilbert and Sullivan. He does not care for
Rabelais, Boccaccio, Cervantes, Defoe, Fielding, Smollett, Jane Austen, Trollope, James, Meredith, and Hardy. Verse-making in general he regards as
belonging to the childhood of the race. He believes that the writings of Edgar
Allan Poe and "a tiny fraction of Mark Twain" enshrine all the literary
genius that has manifested itself in America. He enjoys the work of a number
of his contemporaries, but has no confidence in his judgment of it. He never
read Anatole France until after he himself had begun to be compared to
France.

[16] Some of Cabell's obscurity follows inevitably from the nature of his
work: he always describes the adventures of the heroes, for example, from
the point of view of the protagonist. But some of it is unnecessary and

Cabell's syncretism is capable of the superbly imaginative roll call of the poets in *Something about Eve* and of the later, more elaborate portrayal of Nero, Villon, Tannhäuser, and others, later in the same book. On the other hand, it may produce nothing better than the pseudo-bibliography at the end of *Domnei*.

A more serious criticism is suggested by Charteris when he declares that *Beyond Life* is "an apology for romance by a man who believes that romance is dead beyond resurrection." Of Alfgar in *The Way of Ecben* it is remarked that "This man attempts to preserve the sentiments of Ecben without any of the belief which begot them. This man yet kneels before an altar which his own folly has dishonored, and he yet clings to that god in whom he retains no faith."

Mr. Mencken catches a glimpse of the difficulty here when he remarks of *The High Place* that romance seems to have come to flower in a bloom that poisoned itself. And Howard Pyle, who was a great man in his way, saw the same thing much more clearly, from another angle, when, in 1907, he dealt young Cabell's career a body blow by refusing to illustrate any more of his stories for *Harper's Magazine* on the ground that they were "neither exactly true to history nor exactly fanciful."[17]

The connection between romanticism and religion is very close at this point. Mr. Cabell, one of the few churchmen among the literary leaders of the 'twenties, tells us that he has "some real faith and . . . a great many duplex envelopes." There can be no question as to his skepticism. *"Peut-être"* or *"Que-sais-je?"* is the motto of many of his characters; his is a world in which "who wins his love must lose her." Almost invariably the first act of his comedy sets up the goal, the second strives toward it, and the third falls short. But steeped in *Weltschmerz* though the whole Cabell cosmos is, hope yet refuses

unpardonable. Apparently nobody has ever understood the symbolism of the mirror and the pigeons. (McNeill, *Cabellian Harmonics,* Ch. X, attempts an unauthorized interpretation.) When Cabell himself speaks of the matter in *Special Delivery,* he declares only that this "is the secret which lay glowing at the inmost heart of my many books unseen by any beholder (I believe) save only me; the secret from which I drew a smug sense of superiority. . . ." This, I fear, *is* mental masturbation; there are no "secrets" in art, for art is communication. Cabell detests Joyce, but as he speaks these words we glimpse him on the road Joyce was traveling when he disappeared beyond the horizon.

[17] See Charles D. Abbott, *Howard Pyle, A Chronicle* (H, 1925), pp. 125-126.

to die. The Sphinx never gets beyond the extremely unsatisfactory opening paragraph which sums up the meaning of all life as we know it here; yet "one has but to turn over that page in order to begin upon the most splendid of romances."

Mr. Cabell has not been quite consistent in interpreting the religious implications of his romanticism. In *Straws and Prayer-Books* he sees the artist as inevitably a rebel, for the world that we inhabit does small credit to its Maker. The chivalrous Roland, of *Smith,* on the other hand, disclaims all desire to "dispraise our human life . . . [and] the brave earth which is its theater. I have found life very good. I praise life. It is only that a boy creates in his daydreams a life which is better." Much profounder than either of these utterances is Kennaston's conception of God himself as an Artist and of life as the romance that he is writing; from this Manuel's conception of the artist as sharing the creative activity of God follows inescapably. Kennaston, too, has at last an essentially sacramental conception of experience; after all his wanderings with Ettarre in the world of dreams, he perceives that "the ties of our ordinary life here in the flesh have their own mystic strength and sanctity. I comprehend why in our highest sacrament we prefigure with holy awe, not things of the mind and spirit, but flesh and blood."

Perhaps Mr. Cabell has never really made up his mind whether he accepts what Kennaston calls "the Christ-legend" as a good churchman should or only because of its "surpassing beauty." Paul Elmer More moved unerringly to the heart of the problem when he complained of Mr. Cabell's "failure to discriminate between ideas and ideals, that is between an intuition into the eternal truth of things behind the curtain of appearances and an attempt to wrap the hateful facts of reality in veils of deliberate illusion."[18] But is not this precisely the difficulty of the twentieth century, both for religion and for romance? And must not Mr. Cabell again stand clear of the insensitive charge that he is a trifler and a poseur?

[18] *The Demon of the Absolute* (PUP, 1928). In another essay in this volume, More credits Trollope with true religious feeling on the strength of a passage in *The Bertrams.* I believe that if he had read the letter called "Liturgy in Darkness" in Cabell's *Special Delivery,* he would have recognized the same thing here: "From the deep dark we cry out to a wisdom very far above our blunders, to a strength above our feebleness, and to a kindliness above our spites, our lewdness, and our busy hatreds."

"Why could You not let me believe, where so many believed?" cries Jurgen. "Or else, why could You not let me deride, as the remainder derided so noisily?"

Mr. Cabell's is a highly complex temperament, and his gallantry has often got in the way of his chivalry. But basically he accepts the universe (though with many grimaces), and there has never been any serious doubt where his heart lies. Like Jurgen, he lacks "the requisite credulity to become a free-thinking materialist." A child of the Golden Age might well feel that he is hostile to romance or even that he is irreligious. We, surely, ought to know better.[19] And the service he performed for imaginative literature, and for faith itself, when he carried their banners, at a slightly cocky angle, through the Dark Night of the materialistic, complacent, self-satisfied 'twenties, has never received anything like the recognition it deserves.

As for the ups and downs of Cabell's reputation, it is fortunate that literary questions are not settled by majorities. There are more good books dead than alive, and the only reason why we do not know what song the sirens sang is that nobody cared enough about it to write it down.

The sirens' songs are forgotten already, and Poictesme may in time join the lost Atlantis. But, for a little while yet, I think that it may provide a number of us with a welcome refuge from the Brave New World. Though there may be much, first and last, for which we have to forgive James Branch Cabell, he is still a unique and incomparable figure in American literature. As long as one copy of his books survives in the world, he will remind us that the wind bloweth where it listeth, that the artist is not subject to regimentation. He will never be the voice of a "party" or of a "movement"; he will never speak for anything smaller or more limited than the human spirit itself.

[19] I cannot honestly say that there are no passages in Cabell's work which seem blasphemous to me. But in the light of the author's vast knowledge of myth and comparative religion, it would be difficult to prove that the intention was blasphemous. It should be noted that in developing the legend of Manuel the Redeemer, Cabell was not thinking only of Christ. For parallels to Mithras, Huitzilopochtli, Tammouz, Heracles, Gautama, Dionysos, and Krishna, see Cover and Cranwell, *Notes on Figures of Earth,* Appendix A.

CHAPTER XIX

SINCLAIR LEWIS AND THE BABBITT WARREN

God help the country that has only commercial towns for its capitals.

JAMES FENIMORE COOPER

1. *The Road Ahead*

"The bad boy of American letters whose thoughts are on bent pins while the deacon is laboring in prayer"—so Parrington, twenty-five years ago, characterized Sinclair Lewis. But Lewis was never a revolutionary writer. Aesthetically and morally, he stayed close to the center of the stream; and he resembles both Tarkington and Mrs. Wharton (whom he greatly admired and to whom he dedicated *Babbitt*)[1] much more than, upon first consideration, he may appear to do so. Both Stuart Sherman and Régis Michaud compared *Main Street* to *Madame Bovary*, and Carl Van Doren described Babbitt's crisis as "a classic experience: a man in the midst of prosperity stopping to weigh and value his possessions."

Lewis was born, in Sauk Center, Minnesota, on February 7, 1885. Though his boyhood was literary and, in some aspects, rebellious, the future author of *Arrowsmith* greatly admired the medical tradition in his family. His father and three other relatives were, or had been, physicians, and the boy used sometimes to assist upon medical calls. At Yale he was a brilliant nonconformist, editor of a literary magazine, and author of "long mediaeval poems, with (O God!) ladys [*sic*] clad in white samite, mystic, won-der-ful." He also wrote about "the Little Ones and the gas-stove that was really a beastie,"

---

[1] In an article on "The Great American Novel," *YR*, XVI (1927), 646-656, Mrs. Wharton praised *Main Street* very warmly, naming, among its predecessors, *McTeague*, by Frank Norris; *Susan Lennox*, by David Graham Phillips; *Unleavened Bread*, by Robert Grant; and the work of George Ade.

and planned a great four-generation novel, *The Children's Children,* that, perhaps fortunately, never did get itself written.

He traveled to England on a cattle boat and in the steerage to Panama; he also roamed widely in the United States. Once he lived in a Socialistic community under Upton Sinclair (whom he paid off in *It Can't Happen Here*), and served as janitor of the group. He functioned as a newspaper reporter and held editorial positions on *Transatlantic Tales* and *Adventure.* He worked for Stokes and for George H. Doran. He made translations from French and German. For a long time he did not sell anything except jokes to *Life* and *Punch,* though Jack London, in his later years, bought "ideas" for stories from him and paid him ten dollars apiece for them. He was married first to Grace Livingston Hegger and then to Dorothy Thompson. Each woman gave him a son, and both marriages ended in divorce.

His first book was a juvenile, *Hike and the Aeroplane,* "by Tom Graham," published in 1912. The first novel was *Our Mr. Wrenn* (1914), which suggests the H. G. Wells of *Love and Mr. Lewisham* and *The History of Mr. Polly.* Four more novels followed with only moderate success; then, in 1920, *Main Street* made him the most famous novelist of his time. In 1926 he refused the Pulitzer Prize; four years later, he became the first American writer to be honored with the Nobel award. He died in Rome, on January 10, 1951.

Judged by his later achievement, all of Lewis's first five novels seem somewhat tentative. But they contain interesting examples both of his gift for turning a wary eye upon the Babbitt warren which produced him and also of his affection for its inhabitants. The romantic side of common things is stressed: a dreamy city clerk's life in *Our Mr. Wrenn,* the automobile and the airplane in *The Trail of the Hawk* (1915), the business woman's environment in *The Job* (1917). *The Innocents* (1917) is a Darby and Joan tale, in which the traditional, pre-*Main Street,* small-town literary values survive in a metropolitan environment, and *Free Air* (1919) is a love story of the West, the motor car, and the out-of-doors.

Some of these themes naturally gave Lewis a better opportunity than others. The Hawk, with his youthful, liberal rebellion, is obviously closer to his creator than is Mr. Wrenn; and it is (or was, in

1915) easier to get romantic about aviation than about stenography, though it should not be forgotten that the heroine of *The Job* moves on first to Babbitt's "profession" and then to hotel management, of which Lewis was to make so careful a study in *Work of Art*. The author himself once commented upon the interesting circumstance that when the real Hawk finally appeared in Lindbergh, he should have been, like Lewis's hero, of Scandinavian extraction, and should have hailed from the same part of the United States.[2]

2. Imp of Fame

Lewis planned *Main Street* as a noncommercial book; it might, he hoped, sell five or six thousand copies. The idea long antedated the war, but originally the central character was not Carol Kennicott, who marries the doctor of Gopher Prairie and becomes a frustrated apostle of sweetness and light to benighted Middle Westerners, but a small town lawyer. *Main Street* has been called the antithesis of Meredith Nicholson's conception of the Middle West as "the Valley of Democracy,"[3] but this is not entirely true. Carol is not always right nor her opponents always wrong. No young woman so unsure in her aims, so naïve and flighty in temperament, so ignorant concerning the nature of the forces opposed to her could have won the fight upon which this girl embarks. But in the main she holds her creator's sympathy and that of the reader also.

Gopher Prairie merchants oppose the co-ops because they know that a successful cooperative movement would seriously reduce their profits, and the Gopher Prairie librarian feels that her first duty is not to see that the books are used but carefully to preserve them. The woman's club covers all the English poets in one session and

[2] Cf. George L. White, Jr., *Scandinavian Themes in American Fiction* (U. of Penn., 1937), pp. 137-138. Much the fullest study of Lewis's early novels is John T. Flanagan, "A Long Way to Gopher Prairie," *Southwest Review*, XXXII (1947), 403-413.

[3] Nicholson's book of essays, *The Valley of Democracy*, was published by S in 1918. For his own, not wholly unfavorable, commentary on Lewis, see "Let Main Street Alone!" in *The Man in the Street* (S, 1921). Carolyn Wells burlesqued *Main Street* in her *Ptomaine Street, The Tale of Warble Petticoat* (L, 1921). On the other hand, Halford Luccock declares (*Contemporary American Literature and Religion*) that the Lynds documented its findings in *Middletown*.

goes on to "English Fiction and Essays" next week, and when the local pastor preaches on "America, Face Your Problems," he considers only Mormonism and Prohibition. Church members themselves have no real faith in Christian doctrine, and the village aesthete prefers the movies to standard literature because their purity is more carefully guarded through censorship. It all adds up to

an unimaginably standardized background, a sluggishness of speech and manners, a rigid ruling of the spirit by the desire to appear respectable. It is contentment . . . the contentment of the quiet dead, who are scornful of the living for their restless walking. It is negation canonized as the one positive virtue. It is the prohibition of happiness. It is slavery self-fought and self-defended. It is dullness made God.

Lewis was not the first writer to say all this, but no one else had ever dramatized it so effectively in the national mind. For *Main Street* had the good fortune to appear at the very moment when the American people were beginning to believe that they had been bulldozed into fighting a quite needless and useless war; having found out one sacred cow that gave Paris green instead of milk, they were not disinclined to turn a wary eye on other frauds elsewhere. In the era of "debunking" which ensued, there was inevitably a deplorable tendency, in which Lewis sometimes shared, to pour out the baby with the bath; nevertheless, a number of important truths were hammered home. From *Main Street* the novelist was to go on to the businessman, the scientist, and the clergyman; when, in the 1930's, Americans turned "earnest" again, his most important period had come to an end.

Lewis waited two years to bring out a successor to *Main Street*, and the result, *Babbitt* (1922), is called his masterpiece by most of the critics who do not, instead, choose its immediate successor, *Arrowsmith* (1925). Originally the action was planned to take place during twenty-four hours, and many have the impression that *Babbitt* is superior to *Main Street* in its structure. But the change of plan did not help, and severity in the matter of structure was never to fall within Lewis's range.[4] Where *Babbitt* is superior is in char-

[4] Howard Mumford Jones complains that Lewis's central situations are those of short stories, admitting little development, and that we know his characters almost as well at the beginning as we do at the end. In *Ann Vickers,*

acterization. The Zenith "realtor," superb in what has been called his "smoking room ignorance," has the kind of vitality associated with Dickens, Hogarth, and Daumier, and his name has already become a part of the language.[5] The basic trouble with Babbitt was that "he made nothing in particular, neither butter nor shoes nor poetry, but he was nimble in the calling of selling houses for more than people could afford to pay." His story, as Lewis tells it, is a merciless attack upon the cultural imbecility, the childishness, the coarseness, and the cowardice of too many solid American citizens; to read it now is to be taken back to the days following World War I, when decent men, shocked by Attorney-General Palmer's "raids," and sickened by the horrors of the Ku Klux Klan, began to fear that the mob spirit might really be going to rule America. Yet with great skill, Lewis never allows his hero to decline to a mere stalking horse. We know that in college he was "an unusually liberal, sensitive chap" who wanted to be a lawyer and take the cases of the poor for nothing; as a boy, we may suspect, he was not too distantly related to Penrod. Even while we know him, he dreams of "the fairy child" (who is no distant relative of Mark Twain's "My Platonic Sweetheart"), befriends the tragically sensitive Paul Riesling, rebels abortively against the repressions of the Good Citizens' League, and at last hopes wistfully that his foolish son may find the way he has somehow missed. Unhappily, the reader finds no reasonable ground to share this hope. As Maxwell Geismar says, *Babbitt* is a study in frustration, and the tone is muted throughout.

Arrowsmith, written after arduous specialized study and travel, with Paul de Kruif as technical adviser, has less wistfulness and more affirmation, for Lewis sincerely believed in the "values" of science,

---

an "aside" reveals, as early as p. 35, one aspect of the outcome of the story; on p. 347 Lewis intrudes to tell the reader about the new prison that has been built at Cumberland Gap since Ann worked there. One of the crucial elements in *Arrowsmith*—Leora's picking up the plague germ from a half-smoked cigarette—is casually reported, not presented as either "picture" or "scene," and not viewed from either Leora's point of view or that of any other character. As a technician, Lewis is experimental only in *Cass Timberlane,* where the main story is broken into by a series of vignettes describing the experiences of various husbands and wives.

    [5] *The Man Who Knew Coolidge* (1928), which is not a novel but a collection of monologues by the "booster" Lowell Schmaltz, is a pendant to *Babbitt.*

that is to say in "truth" established by an experimental process which can be checked by other investigators. So Arrowsmith prays:

"God give me unclouded eyes and freedom from haste. God give me a quiet and relentless anger against all pretense and all pretentious work and all work left slack and unfinished. God give me a restlessness whereby I may neither sleep nor accept praise till my observed results equal my calculated results or in pious glee I discover and assault my error! God give me strength not to trust in God!"

Arrowsmith stands with *Dodsworth* and *Cass Timberlane* as marking Lewis's closest approach to the realistic method, but every type of medical chicanery is pilloried somewhere in its pages, and one need only recall the "poetic" health officer, Dr. Almus Picker-baugh, the Kipling and Billy Sunday of health—with his addresses on such subjects as "The Pep of St. Paul, The First Booster" and his care never to disturb really dangerous forces—to be sure that Lewis had not chosen a subject which would allow him to make no use of his broader strokes.

The brushwork is much coarser, however, in the portrait of the Fundamentalist scoundrel, *Elmer Gantry* (1927).[6] One of the most vivid and amusing of Lewis's books, *Gantry* is also the most con-troversial, and not all the attacks upon it have been made by church-men. Walter Lippmann denounced it as "witch-burning to make an atheist's holiday" and an appalling illustration of "the bigotry of the antireligious." "A novelist who pretends to be writing in behalf of a civilized life," declared Mr. Lippmann, "ought not himself to behave like a barbarian."

That *Elmer Gantry* is caricature I do not see how anyone could deny, though I admit that no two informed readers would agree just where the exaggeration lies. The Village Atheist tradition has always been a minor but persistent note in the American symphony, and sometimes the unbeliever has exemplified the moral idealism of Christianity and its reverence for the individual better than those who have professed the Christian creed.

In any event, Mr. Lippmann's are not the fundamental objections that can be made to this book. Gantry is a swine, but it is not quite

---

[6] *Mantrap*, a story of the north woods, had intervened in 1926, but *Mantrap* represents a throwback to the pre-*Main Street* Lewis and has no significance beyond having furnished Miss Clara Bow with one of her best screen roles.

adequate to call him a hypocrite; in a way, he is perfectly sincere in his response if not to the religious, at least to the ecclesiastical, life. But he can neither control his passions nor keep his mind off the main chance, and the grossness of his nature obviates the possibility of the struggle and suffering which might make the study of such a temperament in a better or more sensitive man really moving. As he kneels in prayer, on the last page of the book, when he is welcomed back by his congregation, after having been "cleared" of the accusation brought against him by a woman, his heart fills with gratitude. In the same moment, he notices a new singer in the choir—"a girl with charming ankles and lively eyes, with whom he would certainly have to become acquainted."[7]

With *Dodsworth* (1929), the first and the most important period of Lewis's work ends. Dr. Canby has rightly remarked that this picture of the American businessman abroad is more like Howells than it is like Dickens. Dodsworth is specifically "not a Babbitt," and he thinks "rather well of Dreiser, Cabell, and so much of Proust as he had rather laboriously mastered. . . ." But he certainly does not behave or talk like an intellectual; Mr. DeVoto even doubts that he could have managed a corporation,[8] a doubt which may recall the questions many readers have asked of some of James's American businessmen abroad. Dodsworth is dragged about Europe by a worthless wife of whom his final repudiation probably gives the male reader the same sadistic pleasure which Margaret Mitchell was later to afford him at the end of *Gone With the Wind*. All in all, he is one of the most convincing Lewis characters, and he has his being in a book in which the Europe vs. America antithesis seems, for once, fairly stated.

[7] The book began, in Lewis's mind, with the vision of the egomaniac woman evangelist, Sharon Falconer, who hates the little vices and loves the big ones, and who dies heroically—and theatrically—in a tabernacle fire. Sharon is, nevertheless, a considerably less convincing figure than Elmer. For an account of some rather hysterical clerical reactions to *Elmer Gantry*, see A. B. Maurice, *Bkm*(NY), LXIX (1929), 52-53. A good antidote is Edward Shillito, " 'Elmer Gantry' and the Church in America," *XIX C*, CI (1927), 739-748. Lewis is somewhat more sympathetic toward religion in the later novels; his noblest cleric is the Negro preacher, Dr. Evan Brewster, of *Kingsblood Royal*.

[8] *The Literary Fallacy* (LB, 1944), p. 100.

3. *Wanderings and Divagations*

With *Ann Vickers* (1933), a book and a title both rather suggestive of Wells's *Ann Veronica,* Lewis entered upon a period of
experimentation. This is the story of a "career woman" who became
a social worker and a penologist, with (for the first time in Lewis),
rather disgusting erotic interludes. As a sociological report, *Ann
Vickers* is sometimes moving, but it is poor fiction from any point
of view. In its successor, *Work of Art* (1934), where he "got up"
the hotel business as thoroughly as Arnold Bennett did for *Imperial
Palace,* Lewis shocked all the paler critics by daring to suggest that
a good businessman was a more useful member of society than a
bad artist, but Isabel Paterson found the courage to hail the hero
as "the Forgotten Man who gets the necessary work of the world
done."[9]

There was a better reception in store for *It Can't Happen Here*
(1935)—"the hell it can't"—which dramatized the contemporary
fear of fascism by describing how a Huey Long-like dictator gained
control of the United States in the Election of 1936. In mood and
manner, the book is a kind of Wellsian fantastic romance—but with
sociology replacing science—and it should surprise nobody that it has
considerably more propaganda value than literary value. Nowhere
is the fable more incredible than in the role it assigns to Franklin D.
Roosevelt following his failure to win renomination at the end of
his first term.

In his next two books, Lewis seems to be drifting farther and
farther away from the fashionable "thinking" of the moment. In
The Prodigal Parents (1938), he uses Fred Cornplow, an automobile
salesman he would once have pilloried as another Babbitt, as a stick
to beat the young radicals with. *Bethel Merriday* (1940) came legitimately enough out of his own experiences with acting and playwriting. The story of a young actress was a good subject for him
at this time, for the people of the theater have always had the gift
of being able to withdraw at will from this unsatisfactory world

[9] Dr. Canby also defends the book in "SL's Art of Work," *SRL,* X (1934),
365, 373, where see, further, an excluded chapter.

which other people inhabit and enter a charmed circle of their own imagining.

In *Gideon Planish* (1943), on the other hand, he returned to the mood of his first successful novels—Elmer Gantry himself makes a brief reappearance—now directing his attack against the "philan-throbbers," with side-glances in the direction of the career woman. Prompted by his faithful and ambitious wife, the selfish, thirsty, and sexually-attractive Peony Jackson, Gideon is less of a scoundrel than Elmer but considerably more of a fool. Lewis is entirely serious about him; he has now reached the conclusion that the speaker's table has replaced Broadway as New York's Main Street; and even Gideon himself is sufficiently intelligent to be able to perceive at last that the real threat to American democracy comes from the pressure groups. The story, however, becomes less and less unified as it proceeds, and it produced no impact upon the public mind that was in any way comparable with that made by the novels of the 'twenties.

Revival of power came with *Cass Timberlane* (1945), a novel of considerable integrity and a patient study of marriage between an older man and a younger woman. This is the kindliest of all Lewis's mature books; the portrait of the wife might even be called sentimental. More dynamic was *Kingsblood Royal* (1947), which resembles most thesis-novels in that the thesis shows a tendency to swallow up the novel. It starts absorbingly with Neil Kingsblood's investigation of his ancestry because he has some reason to believe that he has royal blood in his veins; what he discovers is that he is 1/32 Negro, the descendant of an heroic pioneer. From here on the best of the book is talk—discussion of Neil's proper course and of the disabilities under which "his people" suffer. But the man himself behaves in an incredibly quixotic manner, which finally puts it quite out of his power to serve either the needs of his family or the interests of the Negro race. What it all adds up to, therefore, is not very believable.

Lewis's last two novels attached a melancholy kind of epilogue to his career. *The God-Seeker* (1949)—which, alone among his books, is set in the past—concerns vagaries of the missionary movement on the Minnesota frontier in the 1840's. Evangelism is pitted against humanism, and humanism wins. The author shows an understanding of the various forces involved and is not unfair in his treatment of them. In his account of race-relations he is on the side of the Indians but he does not sentimentalize them. A good deal of love and adventure is thrown in, and in the last part—which is very loosely connected—we see Aaron as a successful industrialist. There are many historical characters, and Major Brown's talk would be quite at home in *Babbitt*. But the book as a whole is a little pale. And Lewis's admirers in general seem to think it kinder to say as little as possible about the posthumous *World So Wide* (1951), which is the American businessman in Europe all over again. An elderly Dodsworth is briefly involved.

4. *Under Which King, Bezonian?*

Lewis was always more inclined to express his admiration for gifted contemporaries than to talk about the great writers of the past, but his affinities to Dickens[10] and to Mark Twain are readily apparent. As a boy he called Dickens his favorite novelist, and as late as 1939 he described himself as "a romantic mediaevalist of the most incurable sort." Coming from a writer of his complexion, this may have a touch of perversity in it, but it does point to a strain in Lewis that was often overlooked. He wanted "warmth and lucidity" in his novels; what he liked best in *Main Street* were the "purple passages" that nobody else had noticed. His special gift for mimicry —seen in its most undiluted form in *The Man Who Knew Coolidge* —was a tie with both the great writers I have mentioned, and he apparently went far beyond either of them in his habit of talking his novels out while he was writing them.[11]

But whatever Lewis wanted to be, what he was, first of all, was not a romanticist, and not even a realist, but a satirist. Confusion has been created at this point by his tremendous surface reality, his marvelous gift for describing gadgets, and his Hemingway-like capacity for setting down dialogue which seems accurate recording

[10] Dickens paid his own compliments to Main Street in *Martin Chuzzlewit* and *American Notes* and to the Gantry type of cleric in *The Pickwick Papers* and elsewhere.

[11] The best account of this is in *The Intimate Notebooks of George Jean Nathan* (K, 1932).

but which is really, of course, in both writers, very highly selective. His books are as rich in "properties" as a David Belasco stage production, and when he himself appeared on the stage he seems to have used properties quite in the Belasco manner.[12] He is intensely topical also: probably no other novelist ever referred in print to quite so many of his contemporaries.[13] So Dorothy Canfield exclaims in *Bonfire:* "Really Sinclair Lewis is a phonograph record!"

But none of this is realism: it is only verisimilitude. The clue to the Lewis method lies in his annoying and illusion-shattering use of obviously "phony" names, which he mixes up, quite arbitrarily with the real names he employs. He has, indeed, invented a State of Winnemac, which is bounded by Michigan, Ohio, Illinois, and Indiana![14] But there is more to it than that, more also than Lewis's obvious clowning when he gives us Sanderson Sanderson-Smith of *Gideon Planish* who is at once an advocate of nudism, Thomism, cricket, and the black mass, or Mr. Knife who has sparkling quotations from Dr. Frank Buchman painted on his cuspidors. What I am really talking about is the larger-than-life quality which seems less closely related to folklore in Lewis than it does in Dickens only because Lewis's trappings are more modern and his tone somewhat "hard-boiled." Babbitt is not merely a booster: he is a composite portrait of all the boosters who have ever lived. At his best, he is even the Quintessence of Boosterdom! In *Elmer Gantry* the villain hero is made to cover as much territory as possible by being first a Baptist and then a Methodist! I am not forgetting that Lewis documented with great care, but documentation never yet produced true realism. When Mrs. Stowe and Charles Reade used it, it produced

[12] See Robert van Gelder, *Writers and Writing,* p. 78.

[13] I have noticed only one error: the reference, in *Arrowsmith,* to the first cowboy hero of the screen, Broncho Billy (G. M. Anderson), as "Cowboy Billy Anderson."

[14] In *It Can't Happen Here,* Franklin Roosevelt runs for president against "Buzz" Windrip, who is compared to Huey Long, Father Coughlin, and an imaginary radio priest, Bishop Prang. "Billy" Sunday, the evangelist, appears, with characteristic lingo, in *Babbitt,* as Mike Monday; in *Ann Vickers,* his contemporary, "Gypsy" Smith, has evidently suggested a name for Gypsy Jones. The Smith Brothers' Catsup Factory is mentioned in *Elmer Gantry.*

magnificent melodrama. Strangely enough, nothing can produce realism except imagination.

This aspect of Lewis's work was noticed by all his most careful readers, but, as might have been expected, it was reserved for James Branch Cabell to write the most impressive description of it. Cabell finds Lewis's characters "superb monsters, now and then a bit suggestive of human beings," portrayed "with loving abhorrence." The pleasure of reading about them he compares, on the one hand, to that derivable from the comic strip "Mr. and Mrs." and the radio program "Amos and Andy," and, on the other, to that which emanates from the great classical satirists. It is, in a word, "the pleasure . . . of seeing a minimum of reality exaggerated into Brobding-nagian incredulity."[15]

Another widespread error about Lewis is the idea that he regarded Babbitt as the typical American and that he hated him. On the contrary, Lewis always insisted both that the Zenith booster merely represented "one type of American" and that "Actually, I like the Babbitts." No doubt the satirist in general loves the things he hates (as the lyric poet cherishes his grief), for the worse he finds them, the better they serve his creative purposes. H. L. Mencken, to whom Lewis dedicated *Elmer Gantry* must have come to enjoy the utterances of the "booboisie," as he collected them in the old *American Mercury,* quite as much as he relished Brahms. But these considerations do not quite cover the Lewis case. The conflict between satire and sympathy runs all through his work: Carol's last view of Main Street is both mystic and loving, and it was as early as 1928 that Lewis declared that his own utopia would not differ notably from that of the editor of *The Saturday Evening Post,* and that he did not wish to do away with the Babbitts but only wished that they might learn "to talk of the quest for God oftener than of the quest for the best carburetor." As time goes on, sympathy deepens and satire declines. In *It Can't Happen Here* Lewis mistrusts all panaceas and

[15] James Branch Cabell, "Goblins in Winnemac," in *Some of Us* (McB, 1930). Constance Rourke, *American Humor* (HB, 1931), goes at the matter from a somewhat different angle when she calls Lewis a fabulist and writes some fascinating notes on those aspects of the American folk tradition which lie behind this phase of his work.

rejects all revolutions, and by the time he reached *The Prodigal Parents* he was ready to plump for the Babbitts as themselves responsible for all the achievements of civilization. Coming from him, this rhapsody has its comic side, but the attentive reader finds it less a repudiation of his earlier work than a development of it.

But what, finally, did Lewis believe in? who were his gods? and to what did he adhere? His most specific commitment is, as we have seen, to the scientific method: he once stated that he had enjoyed writing more than he could have enjoyed any other career except working in a research laboratory. It may seem odd that, like H. G. Wells, though himself an artist, he should have been more inclined to believe in science than in art. Yet when, early in life, he considered a scholastic career, it was not science but a professorship of English literature that seemed to beckon him. Lewis mistrusted "intellectuals" and was uneasy in their society; perhaps he was repelled by the flummery and affectation often associated with artists; perhaps, too, he had heeded Bernard Shaw's advice to beware of all artists except very great artists.

In itself, this is clearly an inadequate gospel. Not many men can solve the human problem for themselves in the laboratory—or, for that matter in the studio; if everything in the marketplace is futility, then the outlook is dark indeed. Arrowsmith's withdrawal to the wilderness at the end of the novel which bears his name recalls the "solution" offered some time ago in a number of novels by Robert Herrick.

Actually, as a matter of fact, Lewis believed in more than science. It is true, however, that his characters are more successful in rebellion than in affirmation. One can defend Lewis at this point by urging that there is no point in asking a man whose gift is essentially that of a critic, a satirist, for a "programme." Lewis's general failure to create spiritually adult human beings seems to have been rooted in something deeper than choice of method, however; Arrowsmith himself, though he rarely forfeits the reader's sympathy, "stumbled and slid back all his life and bogged himself in every obvious morass."

Religiously, Lewis probably considered himself an atheist, but it is easy to agree with Dorothy Thompson that God was never taken in by that. In the last analysis, Lewis was an American liberal who believed in the free life. He denied ever having done propaganda for anything, or "against anything save dullness." In a sense, this is true; in another sense, it is misleading. Even before *Main Street,* the heroine of *The Job* begins to suspect "that life is too sacred to be taken in war and filthy industries and dull education; and that most forms and organizations and inherited castes are not sacred at all." Many years later, Ann Vickers is shocked at the idea of Russell wanting to go into business; a professional man, she thinks, has almost "mystical" loyalties to his calling, "and if he has to give it up, it's tragic to him." Perhaps Lewis himself, like many other Americans, did not really understand how much the American tradition meant to him until it was threatened, from without and, far more seriously, from within. From where Doremus Jessup stands, the differences between Babbitts and Arrowsmiths do not seem fundamental. "No American whose fathers have lived in this country for over two generations is so utterly different from any other American." So Doremus rejects murder as a method of government, which is the totalitarian state—"men's souls and blood are not eggshells for tyrants to break"—and so he rejects also, the more dangerous tyrannies that grow up in our own hearts: "Blessed be they who are not Patriots and Idealists, and who do not feel that they must dash right in and Do Something About It, something so immediately important that all doubters must be liquidated—tortured—slaughtered!"[16] Sinclair Lewis pricked the bubble of American complacency when we most needed a gadfly to sting us, and he called us back to the tradition of American independence at a time when many of his countrymen were ready to go whoring after strange gods. In these capacities—in spite of all limitations of art and of insight, and in spite of the tragic errors of his life—he served his country well, and he deserves to be held in grateful remembrance.

---

[16] As for moral questions in the narrower sense of the term, debauchery is generally treated rather severely in Lewis's pages—though drinking is omnipresent—but in the later novels even such noble characters as Neil Kingsblood and Doremus Jessup go in for extra-marital love-making. There are compassionate accounts of Lewis's own last, broken days in Perry Miller, "The Incorruptible SL," *AM,* CLXXXVII, Apr. 1951, pp. 30-34, and in Alexander Manson and Helen Camp, "The Last Days of SL," *Saturday Evening Post,* CCXXIII, Mar. 31, 1951, p. 27+. See also Dorothy Thompson in her column for the Bell Syndicate following Lewis's death, which was reprinted in *Book-of-the-Month Club News,* April 1951, and in her other article, "SL: A Postscript," *AM,* CLXXXVII, June 1951, pp. 73-74.

CHAPTER XX

ERNEST HEMINGWAY: LEGEND AND REALITY

"You are all a lost generation."—Gertrude Stein to E. H.

"A rose is a rose is an onion."—*For Whom the Bell Tolls*

1. *In his Time*

The widespread breakdown of traditional standards of conduct which took place during and after World War I, and by which we are still afflicted, has notably affected American fiction. It appeared in the work of many trashy novelists of no lasting significance whose attitude is accurately reflected in Warner Fabian's title, *Flaming Youth* (1923). It gave a new freedom, especially in the consideration of sexual matters, to established writers, and it brought a special, temporary vogue, generally for the wrong reasons, to James Branch Cabell, most of whose admirers never did understand what he was driving at. But there were other, younger men who must be regarded as special products of the age of "freedom." Among these were F. Scott Fitzgerald, the foremost historian of the jazz babies, in whom their tragedy was incarnate, and the erudite music critic, Carl Van Vechten, who spoke for the ultra-sophisticated, sometimes with a deliberately cultivated perversity.[1] And then, besides all these, there was Ernest Hemingway.

In the realm of the arts, Hemingway is one of the most famous of modern men. Like Byron a hundred years ago, like Mark Twain, like Jack London, like Stephen Crane, in more recent times, he is a living legend. It is interesting to note that only Mark Twain, among the men here named, lacked what it is simplest to call "Byronic" elements in his character or career. Hemingway's critical fortunes have ebbed and flowed but his public has known no wavering.

---

[1] Both Fitzgerald and Van Vechten are considered briefly in the Appendix.

Despite his long silences, every book is awaited as an event, and his failures seem to awaken almost as keen an interest as his successes.

The reasons for this extraordinary vogue are somewhat difficult to define. I do not mean that Hemingway is not a good writer. Within his limitations he is even a superb writer. But those limitations *are* sharply defined, and it is no special observation of mine that the reading public has never in general shown any tendency to agree with Croce that "Technique either does not exist or it coincides with art itself"; they do not, in other words, often "go for" a writer because of his technical skill. Doubtless it is true that many persons whose outward lives do not in the least resemble that of a typical "Hemingway character" are still conscious of the spiritual dislocation of which he has made himself the outstanding fictional spokesman in our time. Yet none of these explanations seem completely to cover the case.

Like Sherwood Anderson, Hemingway is, for many reasons, not essentially a novelist; he himself told Lillian Ross that all his novels had begun as short stories.[2] There are six long fictions, but as novels only two of them count: *A Farewell to Arms* (1929) and *For Whom the Bell Tolls* (1940). *The Torrents of Spring* (1926), the brief burlesque with which he signalized his emancipation from Anderson's influence, is merely an amusing bit of clowning, and both *To Have and Have Not* (1937) and *Across the River and into the Trees* (1950) are poor novels, though the latter has some interest as a portent. And though I know Hemingway's special admirers will consider the statement outrageous, I must still record my judgment that, considered as a novel, *The Sun Also Rises* (1926) seems to me a slight thing, successful as it has been in teaching young people how to waste their lives.

Ernest Hemingway was born, on July 21, 1898, into a prominent family in the wealthy, conservative suburb of Chicago known as Oak Park. His father was a well-known physician and passionate amateur sportsman. His mother had talent both in music and in

---

[2] Her "Profile" of Hemingway, *New Yorker,* XXVI, May 13, 1950, pp. 36+, gives us the most intimate view of him that has yet appeared. The short stories originally published in *In Our Time* (1925), *Men without Women* (1927), and *Winner Take Nothing* (1933) have now been collected, with a few new ones, in *The Fifth Column and the First Forty-Nine Stories* (1938).

painting. In 1917 he was graduated from Oak Park High School in the same class with the writer of these lines. During his senior year he had played on the football team, conducted a weekly "column" in the school paper, *The Trapeze,* and taken part in a number of other activities. His obiter dicta in his "column," which was, I think, influenced by B.L.T.'s celebrated "Line o' Type," in the *Chicago Tribune,* were often very amusing, though there was no indication that he was destined to become a famous writer. In his capacity as class prophet, I recall that he saw a brilliant future for me as a baseball player, no doubt on the ground of my notorious indifference to all kinds of athletic sports.[3] At this time, Hemingway was a handsome, friendly, and courteous boy who seemed equally enthusiastic about the sermons of the famous Dr. William E. Barton at the First Congregational Church (which was the family temple), and the performances of the Chester Wallace Players at the Warrington Theater. I have since read that he was lonely in high school, that he had once run away from home, and that he was sometimes regarded as a "tough guy." These things may or may not have been true; all I can say is that there was nothing in my contacts with Hemingway to cause me to suspect them. I had no classmate whom I recall with greater pleasure.

In our class yearbook, Ernest announced that he intended to go to the University of Illinois; instead, he got himself a job on the *Kansas City Star,* from which he passed on to war service in Italy. In the summer of 1918 he acquired a phenomenal number of wounds by the explosion of a trench mortar bomb. I believe he was the first American casualty in Italy; at any rate, he received high honors and was feted by the Italian people. After the war he returned to Chicago and married; then he joined the staff of the *Toronto Star,* in whose behalf he again went abroad. In Paris, he associated with Ford Madox Ford, Ezra Pound, and Gertrude Stein, and became famous while still in his twenties. Except for *The Little Review* (which had no money), no major American magazine printed one of his stories until the *Atlantic* and *Scribner's* did so in 1927. *Poetry* had used

[3] *The Tabula* (the Oak Park High School yearbook) for 1917 and the file of the weekly *Trapeze* (1916–1917) must be the earliest and rarest of all Hemingway "items."

some of his verses four years earlier, and he had appeared in "little" magazines in Europe. His first publication between covers was the slim *Three Stories and Ten Poems* which came out in Paris in 1923. From 1928 to 1938 he lived at Key West, Florida, where he earned a great reputation as a sportsman. He was variously involved in both the Spanish civil war and in World War II. With his fourth wife, Mary Welsh—(his third was the novelist Martha Gellhorn)—he now lives a semipatriarchal life in Cuba. I do not envy him his fame but I do envy him his cats. At the last count I have seen, the number was fifty-two, but it will be larger by the time these words are printed.

2. *Some Considerations of Method*

Hemingway's characters are soldiers, sportsmen, prizefighters, and matadors; his world of fiction swarms with perverts, drunkards, and prostitutes. He is greatly preoccupied with death and violence; more alcohol is consumed in his stories than in any other writer since Rabelais; and the conventional sexual ethic is often absent altogether. Because of the "unpleasant" character of his subject-matter, he has often been carelessly classified with the naturalists, but Malcolm Cowley was surely right when he pointed out that his true place was with such "haunted and nocturnal writers" as Hawthorne, Poe, and Melville, all of whom "dealt in images that were symbols of an inner world."[4] Obviously he creates by dramatizing his own experiences, but he is much better when he makes fiction of them than he is when he tries to present them in autobiographical or semi-autobiographical works, like the somewhat tortuous *Death in the Afternoon* (1932) and *The Green Hills of Africa* (1935), or the notorious *Esquire* articles of the same period.

His first, most precious, and most obviously apparent, gift for writing is his marvelous capacity for sensitiveness to impressions. This has sometimes been compared to Thoreau's; it also suggests that of Gerard Manley Hopkins (in such poems as "God's Grandeur"), and of Katherine Mansfield, to whom Mr. Burgum has compared Hemingway also in his narrative technique.[5] For Hemingway, it would seem, the world is created anew every morning, and

---

[4] See Cowley's introduction to *The Portable Hemingway* (VP, 1944).
[5] See J. K. M. McCaffrey, *EH, The Man and His Work*, pp. 316-317.

so vivid and refreshing is his rendering of it that material nature itself often seems in his pages to take on a moral significance. It is interesting for more than one reason to note in this connection that Hemingway does not smoke because the use of tobacco would interfere with his sense of smell.

Perhaps the prime example of Hemingway's ability to render sense-impressions vividly is the description of the washing and preparing of the trout in *The Sun Also Rises,* but others can be found in almost every book. Take, for instance, the "feel" of Maria's poor cropped head in *For Whom the Bell Tolls,* like the fur on a marten.[6] Nor has this capacity deserted Hemingway with growing maturity, as witness the picture of the breaking of the ice on the lagoon of *Across the River,* when the Colonel goes duck-shooting.

All this—and everything else—is described in the sparest and most athletic style conceivable. Hemingway's ideal is a prose "without tricks and without cheating," and Joseph Warren Beach speaks suggestively of the "self-denying ordinance" he has passed upon himself in his attempt to see how far he can go with "a mere notation of objective facts." The influence of Gertrude Stein and of Sherwood Anderson was important in helping him to find himself as a stylist, but he never followed Miss Stein into unintelligibility. His writing is (characteristically) simple to the point of brutality, concrete, emphatic as the rain of bullets, largely monosyllabic and innocent of subordination, as rich in "and's" as the English Bible.

This does not mean that Hemingway is easy reading, for he is intensely implicational, and in his pages juxtaposition is very important. He rarely interprets his juxtapositions for us: he will tell us what his characters said or did, but he leaves us to our own resources in the matter of interpretation. George Snell has spoken suggestively of his "submerged" meanings. He uses key phrases as a composer uses them, and Beach compares him, in this aspect, to James, though Hemingway employs the device more for emotional effect than, as James does, for clarification of meaning.[7]

---

[6] The discussion of odor in *For Whom the Bell Tolls,* Ch. XIX, involves the same sensitiveness but its method is synthetic; it builds up into a tour-de-force comparable to such literary spoofing as Sterne's disquisition on noses.

[7] See George Hemphill, "Hemingway and James," *KR,* XI (1949), 50-60.

Hemingway has the same kind of stylistic distinction in writing that a man needs in other aspects to be successful in a fight or a game. There are many effects which such a style cannot achieve. When it is not successful, it may easily give the painful effect of having burlesqued itself. But it can be very effective upon its own ground.[8]

3. *Significances*

The brutality of the Hemingway fiction world has led many readers to think of the author as a kind of caveman of literature. Nothing could be farther from the truth. Hemingway has the sensitive modern's interest not only in literature, painting, and music, but in the problem of the meaning and values of human life. Cowley has spoken of his heroes as "brutal and reckless by day but wistful as little boys when alone at night with the women they love." There are curious spots of sensitiveness in even his worst characters, and his own attitude toward them sometimes exemplifies what Principal Adeney of Manchester once described as "the most touching form of grace . . . which is known as mercy, kindness to the helpless, and especially the undeserving." Hemingway gives the impression of being a phenomenally sensitive man who has been terribly hurt by life, and who dwells upon horrible things partly to convince himself that he can "take it," and partly because he does not dare ever to let life catch him "off guard" again. It is the fashion to ascribe all this to his experiences in World War I and to make him the very type and symbol of the generation whose illusions were destroyed by that war. I do not deny the general soundness of this opinion, but neither do I believe that Hemingway would have been capable of taking precisely a sunny view of human existence even if there had been no war. *In Our Time* presents evidence that he encountered horror and terror even in his boyhood, at least on the hunting and fishing trips he made with his father in Michigan, and that he never

---

[8] There has been surprisingly little information made available concerning specific literary influences upon Hemingway. In the milieu in which he first began seriously to write, Flaubert would seem to have been inescapable. The writer to whom Hemingway himself has paid the warmest tribute is Mark Twain. Edmund Wilson has an interesting passage on Hemingway's possible relationship to Kipling. See McCaffrey, p. 354 ftn.

thereafter quite got them off his mind. I believe also that he was deeply moved by his father's suicide.[9] He was determined to blink nothing, to leave no aspect of the dark side of human experience unexamined. If he were to survive, he would survive on no basis of evasion, and if he were to cling fast to any values, it must be because experience itself had demonstrated that nothing could destroy them. Hemingway never wanted to write about everyday life—the poor, dear, foolish life that Howells loved so much. Instead, he wanted to concern himself with the ultimate crises of human experience, to surprise the human soul (if there was a soul) naked as it faced up to an ultimate challenge. In this sense—in his unceasing preoccupation with the problems of conduct—it must be admitted that those admirers are right who discern in him a profoundly "moral" writer. But what values does he affirm?

He formulates little. About as close as he has come to a categorical statement is the notorious pronouncement that that is moral which makes you "feel good afterward." And this does not get us very far.

When you ask about Hemingway's values, it is necessary, first, to make it clear whether you are talking about the Hemingway of *For Whom the Bell Tolls* or the Hemingway of *The Sun Also Rises*. For they are not quite the same Hemingway.

Yet they have some things in common. Both respect courage (and refuse ever to admit defeat). Both achieve integrity as craftsmen. Hemingway has his share of bluster and swagger, but in his inner abiding place he has been generally incorruptible in his attitude toward his art.

This may be enough to secure salvation, for unselfish devotion to art is the service of order, and the father of order is God. But drop the matter there, and we may still have to leave Hemingway with the brilliant technicians who have little or nothing to say about life.

The world of *The Sun Also Rises* is a world of drunken promiscuity, shot through with streaks of pity. Whatever Hemingway's "views" might have been, his objective method of presentation could

[9] This probably suggested the suicide of Robert Jordan's father in *For Whom the Bell Tolls*. I greatly admired Dr. C. E. Hemingway and would not speak of so painful a matter if it had not already been referred to in print, and inaccurately. It occurred in 1928, not "when Ernest was a boy."

have allowed him no chance to moralize over his sinners, and it does not necessarily follow that *The Sun Also Rises* is an immoral book. In its portrayal of the moral disorder inseparable from war, it may, indeed, be more wholesome and salutary than *For Whom the Bell Tolls*. I am, I must confess, less inclined than many critics to prostrate myself in admiration before the nymphomaniac Lady Brett Ashley, when she decides to give up the bullfighter lest she should poison his youth with her corruptions. The act itself was unquestionably right, but with that kind of woman one can never be too sure about motives. Further, I share Jake's own skepticism of the view that he and she would have been each other's salvation if circumstances had made it possible for them to love each other. Nowhere in literature have I found a group of people to have sold themselves to the devil so cheaply and got so little satisfaction out of it.

War is horror again in *A Farewell to Arms,* whose hero musters himself out, makes "a separate peace," when his interests and those of Catherine Barkley demand it. (As Shaw once pointed out, any war in history could have ended at any moment that the soldiers engaged in it should have developed sense enough to shoot their leaders and go home.) Hemingway had often used sex, as he used drink, to blot out painful thought, but when passion turns to love in his world, it is at once taken up into the quest for meaning. The affair between Catherine Barkley and her patient, Lieutenant Frederic Henry, begins casually and sensually enough, but it develops into an overwhelming romantic ardor of the classical variety, which thinks in terms of "forever"—and the world well lost—which is unblessed by conventional social sanctions only because of the disturbed conditions under which it flowers, and which culminates in an effect of overwhelming pathos when Catherine dies in childbirth. Both here and in *For Whom the Bell Tolls,* Hemingway ponders the special character of the relationship in anything but a libertarian spirit; old Pilar warns Robert Jordan not to think lightly of Maria because she has come to him, in the midst of revolution, without benefit of clergy, and the young man himself ponders the cruel destiny of lovers for whom a whole life must be telescoped within a few weeks of time. In Maria's case there is, moreover, one further complication. This is her imperious need, if she would survive as an emotional being, to be reconciled to life and the fundamental life-experiences after the outrages she has suffered at the hands of the fascists in the Spanish war.

Few male critics at any rate have been dishonest enough to declare that Catherine and Maria—or even Renata, in *Across the River*—do not appeal to them; but remembering the submissive character of these females, a good many have accused the author of infantilism in his treatment of love; his women, they allege, represent a boy's erotic fantasies, like the film stars that come to Robert Jordan in his dreams. Even Margaret Anderson subscribed to this view when she told an incredulous Hemingway that to be a great book *A Farewell to Arms* would have to deal "with something a little higher in the scale—say a love experience with some quality of awareness in it."

There is a point here but it would seem more or less irrelevant to Hemingway's aesthetic problem. He might well ask why the prerogatives which from time immemorial have been accorded writers of romance should be denied to him. If we are going to refuse to accept Jordan and Maria because they fall in love at first sight and give themselves to each other in haste, what becomes of Romeo and Juliet, Pelléas and Mélisande, and all the rest? We have no reason to suppose that Shakespeare ever asked himself whether the two of Verona were psychologically well qualified to build a life together and establish a good family, for he was writing neither a Kinsey report nor an Edith Wharton or Dorothy Canfield novel about family relationships. And neither was Hemingway.

Robert Penn Warren has shown how Frederic's encounters with the priest lend religious significance to *A Farewell to Arms* by pointing up the quest for meaning behind his careless life. "In the end, with the death of Catherine, Frederic discovers that the attempt to find a substitute for universal meaning in the limited meaning of the personal relationship is doomed to failure."[10] It may be that this consideration bulks larger in the critic's mind than it did in that of the author. The love experience in *For Whom the Bell Tolls* is not quite the same as in *A Farewell to Arms*. Frederic Henry could hardly have been capable of Robert Jordan's sense of mystical union

[10] *KR*, IX (1947), 1-28.

with Maria, even through separation and death. And for Jordan there is no conflict between love and duty, for both he and Maria are completely devoted to the Loyalist cause. This time the separate peace is "out."

Hemingway passed to *For Whom the Bell Tolls* through the ante-room of his worst novel, *To Have and Have Not,* whose central figure is Harry Morgan, Florida adventurer—"snotty and strong and quick, and like some kind of expensive animal." His history, which is a combination of three short stories, one of which has been inflated with largely irrelevant material, is as unsatisfactory aestheti-cally as morally. It would be too much to say that the reader is never made to feel sympathy for Morgan and his coarse wife, yet when all is said and done, the man *is* a criminal and a murderer, and Heming-way's attempts to glorify him into something more are simply a manifestation of the same kind of sentimentality that Thackeray flayed in the popular novels of more than a hundred years ago. As Harry lies dying of his wound, he mutters, "No matter how a man alone ain't got no bloody f——ing chance." Hemingway comments, "It had taken him a long time to get it out, and it had taken him all his life to learn it." If this be "social consciousness," it seems a curi-ously unsatisfying variety.

The Spanish play, *The Fifth Column,* which followed the year after, was not much more satisfying; it may best be regarded as a finger-exercise for the *Bell.* This, the most "successful" of Heming-way's novels, takes its title from Donne (the Random House edition of whose work is said to have been sold out after it appeared!) :

No man is an *Iland,* intire of it selfe; every man is a peece of the *Continent,* a part of the *maine;* if a *Clod* be washed away by the *Sea, Europe* is the lesse, as well as if a *Promontortie* were, as well as if a *Mannor* of thy *friends* or of *thine owene* were; any man's death dimin-ishes me, because I am involved in *Mankinde;* And therefore never send to know for whom the *bell* tolls; It tolls for *thee.*

Robert Jordan is no conscript; neither has he, like Hemingway's earlier heroes, stumbled into war or embraced it in the spirit of adventure. He is here in Spain because he believes that the battle for human freedom is going to be lost or won in this peninsula, and he wishes to be counted against the dragons and with the gods.

Whether he is right or wrong in his judgment, and whether one accepts or rejects the political implications which are currently being read into Donne's statement, the irresponsibility of *The Sun Also Rises* is clearly gone. And this time the spire of meaning does unmistakably raise itself out of the fable.[11]

4. *A Question of Adequacy*

Whether all this is adequate as a philosophy of life—or, what is more to the point here, adequate as a frame of reference for art as important as that which Hemingway, with his talents, ought to be producing—I am quite willing to allow each reader to decide for himself. But I should be untrue both to Hemingway and to my own standards of value if I were to evade stating frankly at this point that I myself do not believe it to be anything of the kind.

I am troubled at the outset by what seems to me the adolescent overemphasis which Hemingway places upon action. Herbert Muller calls *Green Hills* "The Rover Boy in the Congo." In the brief but illuminating sketch which he wrote for Georges Schreiber's *Portraits of Self-Portraits*,[12] Hemingway made two contradictory statements about himself: "He would rather read than do anything except write, and nothing can make him so happy as having written well." And: "If he had not spent so much time at . . . [fishing and shooting], at ski-ing, at the bull ring, and in a boat, he might have written much more. On the other hand, he might have shot himself." Here Hemingway seems to confirm those who have accused him of using action as an opiate. There is no suggestion here of the healthy praise of the joy of living which glorifies the ninth section of Browning's "Saul." Instead, one thinks of Gamaliel Bradford's suggestive remark about the hunting-passion of Theodore Roosevelt:

[11] No doubt one reason why *Across the River and into the Trees* disappointed so many critics is that it contained no suggestion that *For Whom the Bell Tolls* was ever written. Describing the last days in love and sport of an American colonel in Italy, it is more like *The Sun Also Rises* than it is like anything that Hemingway has written since, but it is a wistful, gentle *Sun Also Rises,* definitely autumnal in its spirit. If it has any spiritual significance, it perhaps indicates that a spirit long defiant of death has begun to make terms with him.

[12] Houghton Mifflin Company, 1936.

"He did not stop to think what a cruel reflection upon life it is that the best thing in it is the passion that makes us forget it."

I feel all this the more keenly about Hemingway because I believe that in spite of all his scrupulous honesty and fundamental kindliness of spirit, he has fallen victim to the fate he most wished to avoid: he has suffered himself to be "taken in." He went to extravagant lengths to avoid just that. He stripped his art of fine qualities it might otherwise have possessed; as a man, he set his feet upon some of the most dangerous roads that a man can travel. Yet he has been "taken in." He has been "taken in" by bullfighting; he has been "taken in" by hunting; he has been "taken in" by war.

Hemingway has never killed like an animal or a savage. That kind of killing is comparatively harmless. He has killed like a highly sensitive, pitiful, civilized man who feels himself under a terrible compulsion to kill because something has gone terribly wrong in his thinking. Even in *For Whom the Bell Tolls* the morality of killing is debated, pro and con, at wearisome length. And in *The Green Hills of Africa* and *Death in the Afternoon* Hemingway has written upon this subject some of the unhealthiest pages in our literature. He has romanticized killing; he has obliged himself to find a moral meaning in it; he has prated horribly about killing as an art. He has been "taken in" by these things far more completely than any sentimental old maid of the Friendship Village school was ever "taken in" by moonlight and roses. Surely if one cannot live without illusion, if one must romanticize something, it is better to romanticize beauty than ugliness, healthier to romanticize life than death and the things that make for death.

With war the situation is more complicated than it possibly can be with reference to either bullfighting or killing for sport. For all his experience of war, Hemingway is not, in the usual sense, a militarist; indeed his early books probably contributed to strengthen the pacifist feeling of their time. But by the time he edited his anthology, *Men at War,* in 1942, he was writing, like all the brass hats and professional patrioteers, "I hate war, BUT—" And it cannot, surely, be quite without significance that the hero and heroine of the book which is rightly considered the most meaningful he has written should be committed up to the hilt to a thesis whose vanity has been demonstrated by two world wars and untold millions of heartbreaks: War is the sum of all evil, but this war is different! If we only destroy these scoundrels now, then we shall have peace upon earth forevermore!

Justice Oliver Wendell Holmes is quoted by Max Lerner in his essay on Hemingway as having spoken of those who "must share the passion and action of . . . [their] time at peril of being judged not to have lived." There are such men, and it may be that Hemingway is one of them. One and all, they run grave moral peril; neither do they ever lead independent lives. Such men are more at the mercy of circumstances than others. They have their lives chosen for them by the accidents of their time. And the same thing happens to their thinking also. They catch their philosophy like a disease from their surroundings; they do not make themselves, in a different sense from that in which Donne used the word, islands in the sea of corruption which is the mundus about them. And that is what a man must do not only if he would save his soul but if he would establish in himself one of those centers of healing which in time are to save the world.

It is interesting to compare Hemingway at this point with the writer he seems most to admire—I mean Mark Twain. The resemblances go deeper than technical considerations. To Mark Twain also, life showed her horrors at an early age, and they ate into his soul as deeply as they have eaten into Hemingway's. It cannot be claimed that the effect upon his spiritual development was altogether happy; reinforced by the personal sorrows of his later years, the resultant disillusionment led him as far along the road to spiritual nihilism and despair as a man can go if he intends to come back. But though I believe him to have made serious errors in the interpretation of his experience, the one thing Mark Twain never, never did was to consider the possibility of reconciling himself with life by accepting life's evil or by making himself a part of the suffering and sorrow by which he had been oppressed. To the last breath he drew on earth, he knew that the unpardonable sin is putting pain into the world.

Lady Brett Ashley is a true Hemingway character when she finds herself falling in love with Romero. She can't help it. She has never in her life, she declares, been able to help anything. Later, to be sure, she has her moment of revulsion, but moments of revulsion are not enough. So far as this world at least is concerned, she goes to hell. Obviously, if you lose the freedom of the will, there can be no morality, and without morality, the novel, which, by its terms and conditions, is a study of human conduct, cannot possibly have any meaning either. Even in the hands of as great an artist as Ernest Hemingway, moral aimlessness has not proved a promising theme. That he has preserved in art the tragic disillusion of a certain class of people during one of the most trying hours in human history is undeniable, but one need not feel, therefore, that, for art, these people are very important. Faith in values did, after all, survive the war, terrible as it was, and they survived a second and still more terrible war, and they still survive today, in spite of unutterable menace and confusion. But you must know where to look for them. The principle was clearly enunciated six hundred years ago by a great and steady-eyed writer who perhaps understood the corruptions of mankind as well as Ernest Hemingway but whose spirit was never shaken:

> Men moste axe at seyntes if it is
> Aught fair in hevene; why? for they conne telle;
> And axen fendes, is it foule in helle.

CHAPTER XXI

NOVELISTS OF THE 'TWENTIES

The "great American novel," for which prophetic critics yearned so fondly twenty years ago, is appearing in sections.

EDWARD EGGLESTON, 1892

1. *John Dos Passos: The Collectivist Novel*

Temperamentally, John Dos Passos is an aesthete; in untroubled times, or without a driving conscience, he might well have given himself up to Amy Lowell imagism, or written a series of books like his early, nonfiction *Rosinante to the Road Again* (1922).

He was born in Chicago, on January 14, 1896. His father, the son of a Portuguese immigrant and a Quaker lady, became a corporation lawyer and a writer upon legal subjects; his mother was of Maryland extraction. Both sides of his family had been involved in the Civil War. "The Mason Dixon line," says Mr. Dos Passos, "was the first fence I ever sat on."[1]

As a child, he knew Mexico, England, and the Continent, as well as varied localities in his own country; from his graduation, *cum laude,* at Harvard in 1916, he proceeded to medical service in World War I.

The war was the first great influence upon his work, and it yielded his first important novel, *Three Soldiers* (1921).[2] There were two other influences later on: his awakening to the injustices in American life through his labors for the Harlan County, Kentucky, miners and for Sacco and Vanzetti,[3] and his subsequent disillusionment

---

[1] Quoted from the thirty-six-page untitled brochure which Houghton Mifflin Company issued in 1946 to signalize the publication of their special three-volume edition of *U.S.A.,* illustrated by Reginald Marsh.

[2] As well as its predecessor, *One Man's Initiation—1917* (1920), which was a kind of dress rehearsal for *Three Soldiers.*

[3] Dos Passos was jailed in Boston for demonstrating before the State House. See his tribute to Sacco and Vanzetti in *In All Countries* (1934).

with the radical movement, which has now turned him not only against the Communist Party but also against the New Deal and its inheritance, so that he jibes, "Writers of the world, unite. You have nothing to lose but your brains." In the Preface to the 1945 reprint of *One Man's Initiation,* which was entitled *First Encounter,* Mr. Dos Passos rejected all "short cuts to a decent ordering of human affairs" and declared that "The quality of the means we use will always determine the ends we reach."[4]

Literary influences upon his work are another matter. The resemblances between his prose and that of the Imagists and stream-of-consciousness writers are obvious. Like his friend Ernest Hemingway, he was acquainted with Gertrude Stein. The influence of Jules Romains has been urged; he himself influenced Sartre, who once called him "the best novelist of our time." His thinking probably did not escape the influence of Marx, but Gibbon and Thorstein Veblen, of whom he did a "Biography" in *U.S.A.* may well have cut deeper.

By a "collectivist" novel is here indicated a type of fiction in which the emphasis is not upon the life story of a single individual but rather upon the life of a social group, the individuals involved being significant merely as they illustrate the operations of "forces." Even the early "art-novel," *Streets of Night* (1923), which Dos Passos criticism in general has either condemned or ignored, divides itself between three hardly proper young Bostonians. There is a somewhat similar division in *Three Soldiers,* though here the most highly developed of the young men, John Andrews, the frustrated musician, certainly interests both the author and his readers more than either of the others.

Andrews is, indeed, a typical Dos Passos hero, the aesthetic revolutionary, a beauty-devoted young man with an intense social consciousness in whom a good deal of the author's temperament has clearly been expressed. This was the first important American fiction in which World War I was "debunked"—as Dos Passos saw it, American doughboys died to protect the Morgan investments—and the first to emphasize the dehumanizing horror and obscenity of

---

[4] His mature views on political and economic questions have been set forth in *The Ground We Stand On* (1941) and *The Prospect Before Us* (1950).

war. (In Europe, it had been preceded by the work of Latzko and Henri Barbusse.) When it was published it shocked many readers by its frankness, and it is still fair to call it one-sided in the sense that unfortunately most Americans did not react to military regimentation quite like the Dos Passos protagonists. It remains true, however, that, here and elsewhere, Dos Passos said something that badly needed saying and called attention to glossed-over and neglected unpleasant truth.

Three Soldiers was his only important novel before *Manhattan Transfer* (1925), the first full-fledged collectivist book. This time the protagonist is the city itself, which is portrayed from the 1890's up to the time the book appeared. Of the multitudinous characters, many appear but once, some several times, a few repeatedly. The "leading" characters, if there are such, are Jimmy Herf, a newspaper man, and the actress Ellen Thatcher, whom he loves and loses. Even when a "story" is suggested, it is told in terms of climacteric scenes, the development that lies between them being inferred. The principle of organization suggests the cinema's montage: separate "shots" combine into an over-all impression of the metropolis but not into a plot. There are lyrical epigraphs and something of what in *U.S.A.* was to be called "Newsreel" material. Commercialism is already a force for evil, but the revolutionary feeling of *U.S.A.* has not yet been developed. Basically, *Manhattan Transfer* seems aesthetic, rather than social, in its inspiration.

The three parts of *U.S.A.* (1937) were published separately as *The 42nd Parallel* (1930), *Nineteen-Nineteen* (1932), and *The Big Money* (1936). Actually, *U.S.A.* is one novel in three parts, or—since there was no more reason why it should stop after nearly 1,500 pages than at 500 or 2,500—perhaps one should call it rather a gigantic fragment. Its technique seems well adapted to describe the aimless lives of its characters. Dos Passos could not very well have had them *all* kill themselves, but it is difficult to think of any other decisive action of which most of them could have been capable.

In *U.S.A.* Dos Passos tries to do for the nation what *Manhattan Transfer* had done for the metropolis, but this time he goes in for a lesser degree of disconnectedness by limiting himself to the life-stories of twelve main characters—six men and six women—whose histories are narrated in installments which sometimes overlap, so that one reads about many of them under both their own and others' headings; the public relations man, J. Ward Moorehouse, for example, draws a number of them into his orbit.

Their histories are interrupted by (1) "Biographies"; (2) "Newsreels"; and (3) "The Camera Eye." These terms indicate: (1) twenty-five sketches of persons prominent in the American life of the time, ranging all the way from Woodrow Wilson to Rudolph Valentino; (2) jumbles of newspaper items and headlines, quotations from popular songs, and other ephemerae of the period, all set down upon the page in the same kind of confusion in which they existed in contemporary minds;[5] and (3) stream-of-consciousness musings, "acting as the small self-portrait in a painting," a device through which the author was enabled to comment upon his material.[6]

"Device" is the right word for these features, yet each does make its contribution. The "Camera Eye" sections, needlessly obscure, are written in that annoying kind of loose rhythmic prose that reads as if it had been turned out by a machine. Some of this "artiness" carries over into the "Biographies," which seem to me to have been somewhat overpraised. It has been suggested that the Biographies try to create a modern mythology; it has also been said that this material is needed to counterbalance the aimlessness of the fictional characters. Yet many of the biographees, famous though they were, were spiritual failures, and Dos Passos is quite as likely to do his best work with those whom he despises as with those, like Debs and Randolph Bourne, whom he admires. Personally I have found great pleasure in the "Newsreels," though, strictly speaking, they are neither fiction nor any other kind of original writing, and I cannot be sure that they would be extraordinarily effective with readers unable to recall many of the events alluded to. The juxtapositions, at any rate, are often extremely clever. In "Newsreel XIX," for example, we have scare headlines proclaiming "BILLIONS FOR ALLIES" and "UPHOLD NATION CITY'S CRY," snatches from the song *Over There,* the information that the Colt Patent Firearms

---

[5] In the Houghton Mifflin brochure we are told that the Newsreels "were incorporated into the technical plan after the novels had been started" (p. 10).

[6] *Loc. cit.*

Manufacturing Company has just announced an annual profit of 259 per cent and cut "a $2,500,000 melon," and the proclamation of a plan "TO KEEP COLORED PEOPLE FROM WHITE AREAS." Thus was the world made safe for democracy.

The later trilogy, *District of Columbia* (1952), does not tell a connected story. The first of the series, *The Adventures of a Young Man* (1939), describes Glen Spotswood's disillusionment with Communism, his falling out of favor with the Loyalists in Spain, and his contrived killing by Franco's men. In *Number One* (1943), which was obviously inspired by the career of Huey Long,[7] the story is told by Glen's older brother, Tyler, the aspiring dictator's secretary. The third and most important novel is *The Grand Design* (1949), an uncomplimentary picture of New Deal Washington, where crackpots and sinister interests juggle with the planet's destiny and with human lives. To such minor New Dealers as his foreground characters, Paul Graves and Millard Carroll, Dos Passos grants a naïve sincerity, but there is little to be said for Judge Oppenheim (in whom the reviewers found suggestions of Felix Frankfurter), for Walker Watson (who combines the least attractive traits of Henry Wallace and Harry Hopkins), or for the hovering, sinister background-figure of the President (symbolized by an overlong, up-tilted cigarette-holder), who is as savagely and powerfully sketched as any of the biographees in *U.S.A.* Glen Spotswood's father is a devastating portrait of a pro-war, interventionist radio commentator. As reading-matter, *The Grand Design* is absorbing; as a work of art, it suffers from the inevitable division of interest inherent in the very idea of the *roman à clef*.

In 1951, Dos Passos published *Chosen Country,* which looks like the beginning of a third trilogy. The love story in this book is certainly the best thing of its kind that he has written; in other aspects, *Chosen Country* illustrates its author's familiar faults and virtues. There are the usual topical materials. The disconnected chapters which break in upon the story from time to time were probably intended to enrich the book by helping the reader to understand the

[7] This theme has also been used by Adria Locke Langley, *A Lion Is in the Streets* (Whittlesey House, 1945) and by Robert Penn Warren, *All the King's Men* (1946). See, also, *It Can't Happen Here,* by Sinclair Lewis.

men and forces that created the world in which the hero and heroine have to live. But it would be hard to maintain that no irrelevancies have been included.

It has, perhaps, already been made clear that no other American novelist has ever dared to deal with American life on quite the scale of John Dos Passos. I can think of no other book in which the "feel" and color of so many varied phases of American experience, in so many different walks of life and so many different parts of the country, has been caught so effectively as in *U.S.A.;* no matter where you grew up, you can hardly avoid saying to yourself from time to time: "Yes, it really *was* like that!" From this point of view, Dos Passos is abundantly entitled to his audacious title,[8] and it is very remarkable that he should have been able to achieve such vividness while using so deliberately flat a style and limiting his characterization so strictly to behavioristic notation.

From another point of view, the appropriateness of the title might well be challenged. Nearly everything which makes the U.S.A. a tolerable place to live in is left out of the Dos Passos chronicle; his characters are endurable only while they are children. Characteristically they seek only their own ends and stop swilling liquor only while they copulate. Their brutality matches their sensualism: they can neither control their appetites nor honestly face up to the consequences of indulging them. In such a world, for example, children become not something to be borne and cherished but something to be murdered before they are born. Even the consecrated social worker, Mary French, smokes cigarettes until her mouth is parched and drinks until she staggers in the streets. Though there are episodes, like "Daughter's" tragedy, which are moving, one can well understand why Dick Savage, for example, should be ashamed to belong to the human race. The only trouble is that he never seems to make much effort to prevent the race being ashamed of him.

To be sure, it is part of Mr. Dos Passos' thesis that the conditions which exist in the United States produce the kind of people that he

[8] There are, of course, some errors: Chicago has a Coliseum but not a "Colosseum." Theodore Roosevelt was shot, during the 1912 campaign, not in Duluth but in Milwaukee. It is oculists, not opticians, who put drops in people's eyes.

describes. So they do, but to pretend that they produce nothing else is vicious nonsense. If this were true, the United States could never have produced Mr. Dos Passos. And neither the art of fiction nor any "cause" that a novelist may hold dear is to be served by blowing out the gas to see how dark it is.

It is not only conservative critics who have entered complaints along this line. Radicals have pointed out that the revolution itself could be of no use to such people as Dos Passos has described. But Mr. J. Donald Adams's objection is particularly interesting:

The opportunities for the individual have never "dried up" in the United States [declares Mr. Adams], except in the degree to which they have been curbed by governmental restriction, and that is a circumstance over which the "little man" can, if he will, exercise a measure of control.[9]

As far as it goes, this is quite true and badly needs saying. But it is not the whole truth. It is not *only* "governmental restriction" that can curb freedom in the United States; capitalistic exploitation can achieve the same end, and has often done so. From his own point of view, Dos Passos has always been a defender of the American Republic. Not he has changed but the times. Once the Republic was menaced by "extended Capitalism." Now the danger emanates from "extended Communism."[10] He has fought both.

Nevertheless, the limitations suggested here present aesthetic, even more than moral, problems. Again and again Mr. Dos Passos' readers have complained of his failure to create memorable characters. We do not care for his personages deeply enough to remember them; even in *U.S.A.* one runs into another and we retain a clear recollection of only isolated scenes. To James T. Farrell all the Dos Passos people seem to have "the same eyes and the same nose." It is true that part of this is Mr. Dos Passos' intention and that another part results inevitably from his methods of discontinuity and behavioristic notation. Along this line, Mr. DeVoto speaks of Dos Passos' intention "to reduce personality to a mere pulsation of behavior under the impersonal and implacable drive of circumstance." But the defense cannot proceed very far along this line, for, as we

---

[9] *The Shape of Books To Come* (VP, 1944), p. 76.
[10] From the brochure, p. 9.

all know, novelists tend to choose methods as well as themes—or to have them chosen for them—with their own limitations in mind. It is not reassuring to hear Mr. Dos Passos declare that "It seems to me that history is always more alive and interesting than fiction." This belief would not a priori be likely to conduce to the production of fiction more interesting than history. It would not be well for Mr. Dos Passos' reputation as a novelist if the "Newsreels" should survive longest of his work.

2. *The Inner Vision: Elizabeth Madox Roberts*[11]

Elizabeth Madox Roberts (born in 1886) was the opposite kind of novelist to John Dos Passos; his characters have no inner lives and hers have nothing else. Her people are the rural folk of the Bluegrass region, and she herself came of a family that had been identified with Kentucky since the days of Daniel Boone. But she lived also in Colorado and in California, and she was educated at the University of Chicago, where, like so many in her time, she was encouraged in her writing by the great mediaeval scholar, Edith Rickert, who had herself published novels.[12] Greatly handicapped by ill-health during her early life, Miss Roberts did not reach Chicago until 1917. She published verses in 1915 and 1922 but she did not get round to her first novel, *The Time of Man,* until 1926, when she was forty years old, after which she very shortly found herself enjoying an international celebrity. She produced six more novels, two collections of short stories,[13] and one more book of verse[14] before death took her, on March 13, 1941, at the age of fifty-five.

The Time of Man, My Heart and My Flesh (1927), *The Great Meadow* (1930), and *He Sent Forth a Raven* (1935) are Miss Roberts's important novels. *The Great Meadow,* which concerns

[11] Quotations from the writings of Elizabeth Madox Roberts in this section are copyright by The Viking Press, Inc., or by the author.

[12] Edith Rickert (1871-1938): *Out of the Cypress Swamp* (Methuen, 1902); *The Reaper* (HM, 1904); *Folly* (Baker & Taylor, 1906); *The Golden Hawk* (B. & T., 1907); *Severn Woods* (HB, 1930).

[13] *The Haunted Mirror* (1932); *Not by Strange Gods* (1941).

[14] Her three collections of verse are *In the Great Steep's Garden* (Colorado Springs, The Gowdy-Simmons Printing Co., 1915); *Under the Tree* (1922); *Song in the Meadow* (1940).

Boone's country before the Revolution, was the fourth novel to be published, but it had been conceived before any of the others and was held in mind for fifteen years before it got itself down on paper. Meanwhile, that *jeu d'esprit, Jingling in the Wind* (1928), which was third in order of publication, had been written concurrently with *The Time of Man* and *My Heart and My Flesh,* to give the author relief from their more somber preoccupations.

Jingling in the Wind is one of Elizabeth Roberts's three minor novels. This gay tale of a rainmakers' convention is a blend of Robert Nathan fantasy (there are conversations with a snake and a spider) and a satirical observation worthy of Sinclair Lewis; not the least interesting pages are those in which, with one eye upon Chaucer, the characters pause beneath the liquidambar tree to tell each other stories. Yet it does not seem to make a wholly unified impression. *A Buried Treasure* (1931) may best be described in musical terms[15] as a fantasia or as variations upon the theme of the discovery by an old couple of a pot of gold—its effect upon them and upon the community in which they live. Though it can hardly be claimed that everything in this novel is organically related, the performance is still a brilliant one, and a higher degree of intensity, or quality of excitement, is achieved than is often the case in Miss Roberts's books. In her last novel, *Black Is My Truelove's Hair* (1938), on the other hand, the loss of Fronia's thimble not only seems too trifling to serve as an effective center of interest; it breaks in upon the study of Dena's love-experience (which itself achieves a somewhat fizzling conclusion); and it is much too wasteful and long-drawn out a means of bringing the girl to her second, and presumably true, love to be justified upon that score.

The most obviously interesting thing about *The Time of Man,*

[15] Musical analogies often occur to the readers of Elizabeth Roberts's fiction, and she herself often created under musical inspiration. She told Grant Knight that she had played Victrola records of Beethoven's Ninth Symphony while writing *My Heart and My Flesh* and the same composer's Sixth while at work upon *A Buried Treasure.* This novel was based upon a neighboring farmer's story that he had found a pot of Spanish coins, dating from before 1803. Miss Roberts added that she thought of the book as a comedy in five acts and that she meant it to be an experiment in the presentation of shifting points of view: compare Philly's attitude toward the treasure with Ben's.

technically considered, and the one by which contemporary reviewers were most impressed, was its treatment of the kind of characters that were generally encountered in writers like Sherwood Anderson with a degree of subjectivity more often associated with Virginia Woolf or Dorothy Richardson. There is no "plot" in this book. We meet Ellen Chesser in adolescence, go through marriage and child-bearing with her, watch the crisis precipitated by her husband's cruelty and unfaithfulness, and, at the end of the book, after Jasper has been driven away from home, falsely accused of barn-burning, we are with her and her children again upon the road, where we found her with her parents at the beginning. The book has poetic sensitiveness and keen humanity. It is true to primitive humanity and to humanity at large. Certainly such episodes as Jonas Prather's confession of sin—his horror over the hideous resemblance between his own mother and the prostitute's child—are done with great power. And if Ellen Chesser was not so sharply defined a character as Willa Cather's Ántonia or the heroine of Ellen Glasgow's *Barren Ground,* she still caused a good many readers to think of these personages. For that matter, she was the most vivid character that Elizabeth Roberts was ever to create.

In *My Heart and My Flesh* Miss Roberts invaded Faulkner's world of miscegenatory degradation (before he had created it), but she handles her subject-matter so obliquely that the impression of horror is softened and dulled. This novel anticipated the interest in abnormal mental states that was to mark the fiction of the 1940's; its experimentation in matters of form—with dialogue printed sometimes like the speeches in a play—recalled Melville. It was much too "unpleasant" a book to achieve the popularity in store for *The Great Meadow,* which is generally regarded as one of the finest historical novels of our time.

In *The Great Meadow* Miss Roberts did not shy at traditional themes: there is an Indian raid; Daniel Boone is a character; there is even an Enoch Arden situation. But she never concerned herself with the accumulation of historical detail, for she wrote the historical novel as if it were poetry, with Berkeleian idealism and the pioneering spirit so curiously blended that it was difficult to tell where one ended and the other began. To Diony there is no being for the world without a mind to know it:

> Her whole body swayed toward the wilderness, toward some further part of the world which was not yet known or sensed in any human mind, swayed outward toward whatever was kept apart in some eternal repository, so that she leaped within to meet this force halfway and share with it entirely.

At the end of the book, Miss Roberts relates her tale to its historical background by ending the war and resolving the domestic situation at the same moment:

> For a little while, . . . [Diony] felt that the end of an age had come to the world, a new order dawning out of the chaos that had beat through the house during the early part of the night.

But if *The Great Meadow* is Elizabeth Madox Roberts's most completely wrought and thoroughly satisfying novel, the much more difficult *He Sent Forth a Raven* (which, as Grant Knight has pointed out, was influenced by her admiration for *Wuthering Heights*), is larger in conception and reveals more of her spirit. The characters, too, have a larger purchase upon the imagination.

When Stoner Drake's second wife dies, he vows never to set his foot upon God's earth again. This vow is kept. He runs his large farm from the chimney corner, from his bedroom, and from a bridge connecting the house with the other farm buildings. Here he blows upon his great horn, summoning his family and the farm workers to obey his will.

His daughter Martha he breaks and destroys by a cruel and unjustified accusation of harlotry flung in her face and in that of the lover who comes to woo her. But his granddaughter Jocelle is not so easily broken. For her, when she is outraged, Stoner Drake renews his vows, but neither outrage nor tyranny can crush her spirit. When the curtain falls at last, "She had drawn life out of Wolflick where a lonely tomb closed over, had closed over Drake years ago."

About these three the minor figures are grouped: Johnny Briggs, an eccentric itinerant preacher, mumbling eternal blessings he only half understands; the half-mad Dickon, author of a jumbled *Cosmography* in which the whole mystery of creation is explained;

Walter, who is consumed with rage when World War I breaks into his life, who violates Jocelle in his agony, then rushes off to die in battle; and, finally, the conscientious objector, Jocelle's lover, Logan Treer, the man of the future. "I was at the very heart of the age, at the beginning of what's to come after."

The theme of this puzzling book is clearly the agony of our time. "We are still waiting for the waters to dry and the dove to find a foothold, a resten place for the sole of her foot." Jocelle is the raven whom Stoner Drake, unknowing, sends forth into the flood of war, and it is Jocelle, aided by Logan, who finds dry land at last. Walter's rape of Jocelle is, of course, the violence done by war to life itself— "Wiped his dirty filth on my body"—and Miss Roberts does not gloss over its horror. To Dickon mankind is "an atomic stench," and Jocelle herself, at the height of her agony, hears the cackling hen "screaming over the monstrous awfulness of the thing she had done; she had continued life." But in the greatness of her spirit the girl refuses to accept this point of view, refuses even to turn in disgust from sex itself: "she would not see Walter again until she had known her own lover; she would have her own; she would be vindicated." Neither does she, like Martha, hate her violator. Along with the rest, he was, as Logan finally helps her to see, "the *unknowing* soldier . . . out to kill and get killed to make fifty rich men richer." The book closes with the old promise of new life: "Seedtime and harvest, and cold and heat, and summer and winter, and day and night shall not cease."[16]

Elizabeth Madox Roberts's "poetic" insight and method[17] were at

[16] Hardly any of the reviewers even pretended to understand *He Sent Forth a Raven*, but Miss Roberts approved of a review by Grant Knight in a Lexington paper. What he wrote there he repeated substantially in his article, "Bluegrass and Laurel, The Varieties of Kentucky Fiction," *SRL*, XXVIII, Jan. 6, 1945, pp. 12-13, to which my own account is indebted.

[17] The folk ballads of the Southern mountains echo all through Elizabeth Madox Roberts's novels, from *The Time of Man* to the last novel, *Black Is My Truelove's Hair*, which takes its title from a ballad. There are many passages in her work which have a greater affinity with modern poetry than with modern fiction. As examples cited almost at random, note the powerful symbolism of the evil pullet who sucks her own eggs in *A Buried Treasure*, the prisms in the window-box and the terrifying image of blackness and emptiness which Dena achieves while sitting beside Lantry on the bed and

once her greatest gift as a novelist and her sharpest limitation. She wrote about what interested her: even *The Great Meadow* is less concerned with the Dark and Bloody Ground than with its reflection in Diony's mind. For this reason she is quite capable of passing over a crucial event in half an easily-overlooked sentence, embedded in the middle of a long paragraph—Martha's whole life is wrecked in a brief passage at the end of Chapter III in *He Sent Forth a Raven*—and then of lingering for many pages over the elucidation of a mental state.

Miss Roberts could do vivid descriptive passages as well as any writer when it suited her purpose, but even here her emphasis is likely to be mental. Take, in *Black Is My Truelove's Hair,* the sounds of the night as Dena hears them during her flight from Langtry; take her body as she lies naked in the sun, or her legs as, beside the road, she draws on the long silk stockings which reach almost to the top of her thighs (and especially her complicated, minutely-rendered state of mind as she does so). Take, as best of all, the description of the carnival, so living, yet so marvelously uncluttered with detail, and with most of the action taking place inside Dena's mind.

It is inside the mind that Miss Roberts's world—and that of her characters—lies, and once they have laid hold upon it they cannot be dispossessed. After Conway has been burned to death, the heroine of *My Heart and My Flesh* finds herself not deprived but possessed of him thrice over: "the Conway of the first fact," whom she had known in life; the "charred, shrunken ember," lying in his coffin, half a mile up the street; and the "third fact," which "had already begun to supplant the first," and which is "the fact of him as a memory, as finished, as perpetual now and unchanged." To Jocelle the presence of one man makes another seem more real. "She looked at the face suddenly and saw the hidden and absent one." Looking

gazing into the blackness of his mind, in *Black Is My Truelove's Hair*. The same thing is illustrated, along with Miss Roberts's tendency to shift from outer to inner action in the same novel, where Dena lets ner mind get fastened upon the lost thimble until it grows as big as a mountain: "Dena climbed to the top of the thimble and looked down into it. Or, reversed, the thimble stood as a round mountain peak with a tall thicket around the bottom in which were giant owls looking out."

back into the life of her forebears, Diony sees herself "as the daughter of many, going back through Polly Brook through the Shenandoah Valley and the Pennsylvania clearings and roadways to England, Methodists and Quakers, small farmers and weavers, going back through Thomas Hall to tidewater farmers and owners of land." She even sees her own life *as it might have been* if the Indians had succeeded in taking her. "She saw herself from the distance, a long dim vista reaching down from Ohio." Andy Blair, of *A Buried Treasure,* speaks of himself as lucky, and immediately, in his wife's eyes, "A tall, slow-moving man, who might at any instant become elegant, stood as a fog around Andy and then went out quickly." This same wife, Philly, has the gift of entering imaginatively into others' lives, going with Imogene Cundy "into her marriage morning" and seeing her, the first day of her married life, in Giles Wilson's house. Dena Jones has this same capacity, enjoying the carnival, before she has any idea that she may be able to attend, through savoring the pleasure of her friends who will be there. And to Ellen Chesser, in the presence of Sallie Lou, whom she suspects of having supplanted her with Jonas, the gift becomes torture:

She felt Sallie Lou winding through her body and calling to her. In another moment she knew what it would be to kiss Sallie Lou's mouth and what it would be to want to kiss there. She felt near to Jonas on the instant, nearer than she had been for many months. She felt herself merge with Jonas.

This last example admirably exemplifies what Mark Van Doren called Miss Roberts's "fluidity."

Naturally both Miss Roberts's fluidity and her overwhelming inwardness had an important influence upon her style. Jeremy, of *Jingling in the Wind,* certainly speaks for his creator in his disquisition upon the limitations of words as a means of conveying the quality of experience, their recalcitrance, their lewdness and waywardness. Miss Roberts adds, characteristically, "He was by reason of his tastes inclined toward the practices and pleasures of poetry, and was thus the most practical of men. . . ."[18] As to the practical

[18] Alexander M. Buchan, *Southwest Review,* XXV (1940), 463-481, sums up the effects produced by Miss Roberts's style "in her own phrases": "1) an agreeable 'monotony'; 2) a 'fluid speech,' which, as she terms it elsewhere, is

side of it, opinions may differ, and even the pleasure depends upon the reader's own cast of mind. There is a quality of monotony that is undeniable, for while Elizabeth Roberts's style was as unmistakable as that of Henry James, it was far less varied and vital, and one can well understand the objections of those who feel that her narratives are less clothed in her individual manner than embalmed in it. It is true, as her special admirers have always insisted, that her kind of poetic insight is the very thing that is needed to save the novel from its exhausted naturalism and sentimentalism, but in her case (as, long ago, in Meredith's) one may still be permitted to doubt whether further development will be assured until this insight has been wedded to a somewhat sounder narrative method than either writer was quite able to achieve. Apart from all such considerations, the books remain, capable of meaning everything to those to whom they mean anything at all.

3. *Romance and Fantasy: Elinor Wylie, Robert Nathan, and Thornton Wilder*[19]

For all their materialism, the 1920's still witnessed a revival of interest in romance and fantasy. Cabell was the star example, but being often given to hidden meanings that could be terribly "real," and having at the same time a reputation for the kind of naughtiness that the age valued, Cabell represented something less of a break with the time-spirit, in this aspect, and required less reorientation of his readers, than certain other writers who made even less of an effort to meet them upon their own ground.

Of these the most brilliant was the exquisite and neurotic Elinor

'half-rhymed experience'; 3) a break in this fluid speech, brought about by a 'few, hard, tender sayings'; 4) the use of words to 'heighten reality,' and to dig down to the 'roots of human life.'" Ernest E. Leisy (*The American Historical Novel*, p. 118) pays this tribute to the style of *The Great Meadow:* "By taking the living speech of the Kentucky hills and laying strong emphasis on its archaisms and racy figurativeness, she solved the problem of reproducing authentic pioneer dialogue. She transcended the effect of literal realism with an infusion of folk poetry that is essentially a reverie illuminating the universal values of human nature."

[19] Quotations from the novels of Elinor Wylie and Robert Nathan in this section are copyright by Alfred A. Knopf, Inc.

Wylie[20] (1885-1928), who loved silver, clear crystal, and the austere New England landscape, and whose filigreed style, whether in prose or in verse, never even remotely suggests the cruel turbulence of her own emotional being. "The facts of her life as they have been related to me," writes Carl Van Vechten, "were completely at variance with her character as I was acquainted with it." It is difficult to avoid the lyrical note in speaking of Elinor Wylie: thus Joseph Auslander describes her as "glittering ambiguously still, revealed in defiant flashes, riding the fox and hunting the unicorn and wearing always on her spacious forehead the sardonic and lovely stigmata," and even the Quaker Dr. Canby works out a detailed comparison between her and the bird of paradise. All four of her novels and nearly all her important poems[21] were published during the last seven years of her life. Like Shelley's, her career was cruelly aborted: both spirits had the courage to confront agony, but neither knew how to endure the gritty mediocrity and infuriating meanness of this life.

It is difficult to summarize Elinor Wylie's novels. Except for the exquisiteness and the erudition which characterize all four of them, they are not in the least alike; even the style transforms itself to the likeness of the theme while ever remaining just miraculously hers. It is remarkable, too, that such gossamer should be able to support so much learning; she would not even introduce a frontier bluestocking into *The Orphan Angel* until Carl Van Doren had attested her possibility by reference to a forgotten novel by Caroline M. Kirkland.

The first of the quartette—*Jennifer Lorn* (1923)—is a sustained satirical comedy of the days of Warren Hastings, which somehow blends humor, complete disillusioned worldliness, and extreme exoticism, though perhaps without achieving a completely unified emotional effect. It had never occurred to Elinor Wylie that a novel ought not to be "artificial," for she knew that the only kind of art that is not "artificial" is bad art. "At that very moment, by one of those pleasing coincidences more common in romantic fiction than

[20] So called from the name of her second husband. She was born Elinor Hoyt into a distinguished and fashionable Pennsylvania family; she died Mrs. William Rose Benét.

[21] See *Collected Poems of Elinor Wylie* (K, 1932).

among the ineptitudes of mortal life . . ."—thus, boldly, she links two episodes in *The Venetian Glass Nephew. Jennifer Lorn* brings us the fabrics and *objets d'art* of the eighteenth century, its culture, its vaulting ambition, its heartlessness, and even its orientalism. It has, too, the least idealized of all lovely heroines. Elinor Wylie's mind assimilated the most diverse literary materials and made all that she seized her own. We have Van Doren's word for it that Gerald is partly Darcy of *Pride and Prejudice,* whom Elinor admired in her youth, but who ever guessed it from the text?

In *The Venetian Glass Nephew* (1925), she moved more daringly —though playfully—into the supernatural. Here is a brief tale which, for the convenience of those to whom beauty is not enough, has been interpreted as a study of the conflict between art and nature, and in which, as might have been expected from Elinor Wylie, art wins, hands down. Virginio is literally a man of glass, created by a wonder-worker for a Venetian cardinal of the eighteenth century who has no nephew of his own. But the lovely Rosalba, whom he weds, is flesh and blood. There is no trouble about the most important thing of all: that has been thoughtfully provided for. But "the lighter contingencies of courtship" are another matter, for Virginio "cannot support the rigors of hide-and-seek or the excitement of a bout of blindman's-buff." Fortunately, Rosalba's love is of the heroic variety. She gives her body to be burned, submits to the embrace of Brother Fire, and becomes consequently the Glass Nephew's porcelain bride. "In a porcelain vessel filled with clear water a rose may live for a little while, but out of clay a rose may rise alive and blooming, set on the roots of elder roses. There is a difference, but it does not matter."

Much the longest and most popular of Elinor Wylie's novels, *The Orphan Angel* (1926), an enchanting picaresque narrative, lighted by a radiant moon, is based upon a "just suppose" speculation. Suppose Shelley not to have been drowned off Via Reggio but rescued by a passing ship and carried to America. Shelley's passion for republican principles being what it was, and America being in 1822 the land of untouched freedom, the idea becomes a fascinating one. Emily Clark speaks of the combination in Elinor Wylie of a fastidious love of elegance with what she herself called her "johnny-cake side." Both aspects find expression in this book as in nothing else she ever did; as Stephen Vincent Benét remarked, the tramp across the virgin land, from Boston to San Diego, on a romantic quest for Silver Cross (Sylvie La Croix), may seem like a fairy tale, yet every stage of it could be traced upon a map. Elinor Wylie's long-distance love affair with Shelley was as passionate as Amy Lowell's with Keats;[22] there were times when she was more Shelley than Shelley was himself; her dream image of him, consequently, was truer than that which many biographers have achieved. The end of the novel finds him still unmated; perhaps it would have been too much to ask of Elinor Wylie that she should give him to another woman, even of her own creating.

The last novel, *Mr. Hodge and Mr. Hazard* (1928), though slightly linked with *Jennifer Lorn,* is the hardest of all to describe. Perhaps it is the least definite and significant of the four as to theme, but it is the most successful in creating the atmosphere of a period, and it certainly contains the best novelist's prose. Mr. Hazard, returning to England from the East in 1823, is Shelley in a way, but then he is also Elinor Wylie. He is the Ghost of the Romantic Period; perhaps he is even literally a ghost. Numerous passages suggest the personages of the passing Romanticism and the coming Victorianism; the latter appears notably in Mr. Hodge. "The period-perfume has been pushed to the background," says Henry Lüdeke, "and the psychological study of complex human relations is beginning to take its place. . . . On the whole the book seems to suggest that, had she lived, Elinor Wylie would have developed a light and realistic social comedy."[23]

The work of Robert Nathan (born, New York City, 1894) is more extensive and bears a more single imprint. Up to *One More Spring* (1933)—that enchanting story of a group of derelicts (a ruined antique-dealer, a violinist, a banker, and a prostitute), living in a tool-shed in Central Park—he addressed a small though devoted audience; it seems odd that it needed the Depression to make this

[22] See Julia Cluck, "EW's Shelley Obsession," *PMLA*, LVI (1941), 841-860, and, in the "Fugitive Prose" section of *Collected Prose,* " 'Excess of Charity,' " and "Mr. Shelley Speaking."

[23] "Venetian Glass: The Poetry and Prose of EW," *English Studies,* XX (1938), 241-250.

fine artist a "success"! It is hard to realize, too, that Mr. Nathan has
now published nearly twenty-five works of fiction. His publisher
compared *Journey of Tapiola* (1938) to *Candide*. Surely no writer
has ever cultivated a small and modest garden more intensively.

Like Tapiola's friend, the canary Richard, who aspires to be a
baritone, Mr. Nathan sees little to admire in musicians who cannot
speak to the ear, poets who cannot address the mind, and painters
who do not know how to draw; like the scholar Henry Pennifer, of
Winter in April (1938), he objects to novelists who "begin at the
bottom, and then . . . go still further down." If you think that books
must smell bad because life itself smells, he is likely to reply that the
real trouble is with your nose. Nathan has complained of Thomas
Wolfe that he "puts all his life into his books as into a garbage pail";
he cannot understand why a writer should be expected to "throw
himself around," or why it should be more necessary to "air personal
antagonisms and irritations" in a book than it is in a friendship.[24]
Both in prose and in verse,[25] he dislikes the willfully complicated and
the obscure. He loves gentle people, even when they are "failures";
neither can he believe that there is anything "more real than the
hopes and griefs of children" or that a labor union is "more actual
than a doll."

Yet he is not out of touch with his times. Even fairy stories like
The Woodcutter's House (1927) reflect the vulturism of earth, and
his children, like Walter de la Mare's, can be surprisingly callous. In
his pages, the Jews do not cease to be difficult even when they trek
toward the Gobi Desert after their expulsion from Europe in *Road
of Ages* (1925). *They Went On Together* (1941) gives us war
refugees in Europe, and *The Sea-Gull Cry* (1942) brings two of them
to Cape Cod. The Nathan method is not limited to themes of gentle
fantasy. It has by this time encompassed various aspects of terror
and disaster—did not Hollywood get one of its greatest "storm
scenes" from *Portrait of Jennie* (1939)?—and in *Road of Ages* it
embraced a theme of epic proportions.

[24] See Robert van Gelder's interview with Nathan in *Writers and Writing*.
[25] The fullest collection of Nathan's poems is now in *The Green Leaf* (K,
1950). His only volume of nonfiction prose is *Journal for Josephine* (K, 1943).

Mr. Nathan's first novel, *Peter Kindred* (1919), which was obviously based upon his own experiences at Phillips Exeter, at Harvard, and in a New York advertising agency, is generally called a false start. But though the names of its hero and heroine were taken from *Joan and Peter,* the book is far from being a mere tribute to H. G. Wells. It is three times as long as anything Nathan has written since: he had not yet learned how to choose the significant detail. But though his style has not yet been developed, there are signs that it is on the way, and a number of the Nathan attitudes—sensitiveness to youth and grief for youth's peculiar vulnerableness, love of music,[26] religious awareness commingled with skepticism, even the painful sense of the Jew's maladjustment in a Gentile world—all are already here.

The style arrived two years later with *Autumn,* a tale of rural New England, still a bit uncertain in its fable, in which the reader's attention is divided between young lovers and an older man who sympathizes with them and tries to guard them. *Autumn* was followed by two finer books—*The Fiddler in Barly* (1926) and *The Woodcutter's House;* both use talking birds, insects, and animals for satirical commentary upon human behavior, and *The Woodcutter's House* even adds the Little Green Man, a minor god who represents a unique employment on Nathan's part of conventional fairy lore.

These three books and the much later *But Gently Day* (1943) employ a rural setting. *The Sea-Gull Cry* and *Long After Summer* (1942)—like part of *Portrait of Jennie*—are staged at Cape Cod. The people of *The River Journey* (1949) float down the Mississippi from a small town in Iowa, while *Mr. Whittle and the Morning Star* (1947) takes place in a college town. *The Married Look* (1950) reflects its author's residence in California. *Road of Ages* and *They Went on Together* are, of course, European, and *Jonah* (1925) goes back into the old Bible world, while *There Is Another Heaven* (1929) makes the jump into Eternity. All the rest are New York City

[26] Nathan is an accomplished musician, both as composer and as executant, and his love of music is reflected in several novels, perhaps most strikingly in the notable description of one of Lotte Lehmann's song recitals in *Winter in April.*

novels.[27] What other novelist has so often described Central Park so delightfully or in so many seasons or moods?

Immediately after *Autumn,* Nathan wrote a much more fantastic book in *The Puppet Master* (1923). The dolls talk, marry, and quarrel, and at its best this book is very good indeed, though the episode in which the puppet Mr. Aristotle mutilates his wife and then commits suicide strikes some readers as both mawkish and sadistic; it sounds an unhealthy note of which I am never conscious again in Nathan, except, perhaps, for a moment, at the death of the young rat Micah in *Tapiola's Brave Regiment.*

Jonah, a retelling of the most fairy-tale-like narrative in the Old Testament, with a somewhat detailed account of the prophet's earlier life, including his disillusioning love affair with Prince Ahab's daughter Judith, who loved him but turned him down upon being convinced that he would ruin her socially, is still one of the most daring and far-reaching of Nathan's books. Outside of a few brilliant passages in Roark Bradford, there is nothing in contemporary American literature to match God's conferences with Jonah, with Moses and Noah in heaven, and with the Whale, who, being an ignorant creature, unaware of future exegesis, expects the swallowing of Jonah to be "horrid," but who agrees to perform Jehovah's bidding when assured that it will earn him a place in history.

Jonah is not, of course, Nathan's only supernatural story. The heroine of *The Bishop's Wife* (1928) is nearly seduced by the angel who comes to help her husband build the cathedral; Death joins the human characters on *The River Journey;* and in *Mr. Whittle and the Morning Star,* God argues with the man who feared that the world was going to be destroyed by the atom bomb quite as in the old days he argued with Jonah. The bomb figures again, importantly, in *The Innocent Eve* (1951), in which a terrifying, yet strangely idealistic, Lucifer comes to New York, looking very much like a delegate to the United Nations, for the purpose of getting possession of it. (One is not quite sure at the end of the book whether it would have been better or worse for humanity if he had succeeded.) *There Is Another Heaven* touchingly explores the sad plight of the converted

[27] *The Enchanted Voyage* (as I show elsewhere), only in part.

Jew who cannot feel at home in a fundamentalist heaven.[28] And if fourth-dimensional novels, or novels based on J. W. Dunne's theory of Serial Time,[29] are to be called novels of the supernatural, then *Portrait of Jennie, But Gently Day,* and *The Married Look* would all need to be added to the list.

All these books date from the early years of Mr. Nathan's career or else they are very recent. In his middle period, his norm was set rather by such works as *The Enchanted Voyage* and *Winter in April.* In their tone and development, both these works represent Nathan's art at its best, but some readers find it easier to achieve Coleridge's "willing suspension of disbelief" when they leave the plane of the actual altogether than when they are asked to contemplate Hector Pecket's unseaworthy sailboat traveling down the highways from the Bronx to Virginia. For similar reasons, it is hard to accept the assembling of all the characters of *The Orchid* (1931) at the carousel; and both the raiding of the dress shop in *Winter in April* and the benevolent kidnaping of the heroine in *Long After Summer* smack a bit too much of Hollywood farce.

"Development" may seem an odd word to apply to Mr. Nathan's very brief fictions; in a sense, they are not developed at all. *The Orchid* and *Mr. Whittle* are the two which come closest to boasting a "plot." The personages are introduced; they are involved in a situation; then the situation is resolved through some single, often accidental, sometimes sensational, event. Such are the Easter Sunday accident in *One More Spring,* the jailing of Mr. Pecket in *The Enchanted Voyage,* the children's floating out to sea in *The Sea-Gull Cry,* the circus fire in *The River Journey,* and the rattlesnake bite in *The Married Look.*

[28] In *The Bishop's Wife* Mr. Cohen explains why he has not submitted to conversion: "No, my friend; if I do not turn Christian like so many others, it is not because of the religious practices. It is because I do not want my grandchildren to hate the Jews. . . . I do not buy my way up, so that I too, can spit down on my people. Do you think I love the Jews so much? How can I tell, when I am one? But I am sick of those who hate them, because I am sick of hate." Cf. Nathan's own statement, "On Being a Jew," *Scribner's Magazine,* XCIII (1933), 372-373.

[29] See Wagenknecht, *Cavalcade of the English Novel,* pp. 464-465, and the Introduction to the reprint of *Portrait of Jennie* in *Six Novels of the Supernatural* (VP, 1944).

One of the prime elements in Nathan's charm is, of course, his style. He has used it often for impressionistic pictures of the city:

Here in the city the mild October day is drawing to its close. Already a star shines in the cool sky which is a little green, like the inside of a melon. In the south and the west there is a rose in the air above the blue shadowy buildings, but in the east it is almost dark.[30]

But he can do the country also:

The evening deepened around them, the green sky faded and darkened, the stars appeared one by one. A fox barked far off on the mountain, and a dog answered from across the valley. The hush of the night, the fading sky and the bright, sinking moon, the cold air with its faint smell of earth, of wood-smoke and dung, made a mystery and a silence around him, and his heart filled with longing for the world's beauty, for the immemorial hush of evening, for young girls singing in the dark, and the cold, sweet air of nightfall in other lands, in other years, far off and forgotten . . . over the same brown earth, under the same white moon.[31]

The same style works quite as well in describing Eternity:

The Styx lay silent. No oar disturbed the serenity of those bitter waters, on whose dark bosom lilies and weeds floated without movement. Charon's skiff, half drawn up on land, waited in vain; and slowly rotted. Its master slept; and dreams of past glories caused him to smile.[32]

And when Nathan desires grandeur, he can achieve even that:

So saying, the Lord blessed Leviathan, who sank sadly back to the depths of the sea; and, turning from the shore, the Light of Israel rolled like thunder across the valleys toward Golan.[33]

Though Mr. Nathan seems a strange combination of Christian, Jew, and skeptic, his hunger for God runs necessarily through all his work. Perhaps He abides at last, as Henry Pettifer conjectures, "somewhere in the spirit of man, far off from prayers and passions, . . . [in] a place as cool and still as air." But on other occasions He is something warmer and closer than that:

[30] *Winter in April.*
[31] *But Gently Day.*
[32] *There Is Another Heaven.*
[33] *Jonah.*

. . . Because God is at the end of everything. He has to be; there's nothing beyond Him. If you were to go right out of the world, He's all you'd find. And if you went down deep into your heart, that's where He'd be. . . .[34]

Thornton Wilder has attracted more critical attention and inspired more passionate partisanship than either Nathan or Elinor Wylie. His has been a very curious career. He began with *The Cabala* (1926), achieved sensational success with *The Bridge of San Luis Rey* (1927), went on to *The Woman of Andros* (1930) and *Heaven's My Destination* (1934), and then failed to bring out another novel for fourteen years. Then, in 1948, he published *The Ides of March*. Meanwhile he had won success as playwright (*Our Town,* 1938, etc.), and for some reason best known to himself had served as a kind of barker for Gertrude Stein upon her American tour.

Mr. Wilder was born in Madison, Wisconsin, on April 17, 1897, but his parents hailed from New England and his background was clerical, literary, and scholastic. He spent part of his childhood in China, while his father was consul-general at Hong Kong. He studied at Oberlin, Yale, and Princeton, and he has taught at both Harvard and the University of Chicago. He served in both world wars. Critics have found Proust, Gide, Joyce, and Anatole France important influences upon him. He admits that he has found difficulty in writing about the world he lives in, and though he respects the literary pamphleteers, he sees no reason why all writers should follow their lead.

The Bridge of San Luis Rey was not published in the expectation of any particular sales. How could a slim, exquisitely-wrought, intensely "literary" work, which did not even tell a connected story, and which, besides all its other shortcomings, had the misfortune to have been conceived as a philosophical novel set in eighteenth-century Peru—how could such a book possibly have been expected to whip up its own steam to become a runaway best seller, pick up the Pulitzer Prize, get itself filmed twice, and even achieve the crowning distinction of being serialized in the Hearst newspapers? Yet all these things happened.

Even *The Cabala* might have been expected to do better, for

[34] *But Gently Day.*

learned as it is, and remote as it must seem from the issues of modern life—("Here's a group of people losing sleep over a host of notions that the rest of the world has outgrown several centuries ago: one duchess's right to enter a door before another; the word order in a dogma of the Church; the divine right of kings, especially of Bourbons")—it is surely sophisticated enough, and decadent enough, so that it might have reasonably made an appeal to those who were then reading *South Wind* with rapture and were soon to take up with *Point Counterpoint*. It is true that it is suggested at the end that the Cabalists themselves are the ancient Roman gods grown weak and old, but that curious notion is not insisted upon with sufficient force to make it anything more than a pleasant fancy.

Unlike *The Bridge of San Luis Rey*, however, *The Cabala* did not have the advantage of dealing—and in terms congenial to the temper of the age—with a subject which interests the men of the twentieth century quite as much as it held Job's contemporaries—the mystery of evil. When the Bridge falls, on July 20, 1714, Brother Juniper cannot avoid asking himself, "Why did this happen to *those* five?" He devotes himself, accordingly, to the study of their lives, and what he learns makes up (though not as he formulated it), the series of narratives which constitute the body of the book. Though Wilder "spares" the reader Brother Juniper's generalizations, we are told that "He thought he saw in the same accident, the wicked visited by destruction and the good called early to Heaven." But the Church finds the book in which his conclusions are set forth heretical, and both he and it are burned in the marketplace.

This is one of the most unusual ideas around which any modern novel has been built, and in the cool, distant manner in which Wilder has chosen to treat it, it is a minor masterpiece. It is not a "novel" really; we are not asked, nor given the time, to live our way into these people's lives; for the most part, we are merely told what happened to them, not shown. Yet they are as vividly presented as characters in a *conte* can be: the Marquesa de Montemayor (who has been suggested by Madame de Sévigné); the Perichole, who brings all the glamour of the theater into the book with her; and Esteban, for whose grief, after his brother's death, we are even made to feel a little pity.

The Woman of Andros, which is based in part upon the *Andria* of Terence, goes even farther afield. Though it has two climaxes— for it is the story of the learned *hetaera* Chrysis and also of her hapless young sister Glycerium (both in their relations with the sensitive young Greek Pamphilus)—the book is more concentrated, in everything except fundamental idea, than is *The Bridge.* It is the idea that has puzzled some readers of *The Woman of Andros,* though actually it is clear enough. Wilder is pointing up the hopelessness of the pre-Christian world. Both at the beginning of the story and again at the end, our imagination is directed to "the land that was soon to be called Holy and that even then was preparing its precious burden."[35] Yet the Greek spirit is not maligned. For though Chrysis sees human beings in general as merely enduring "the slow misery of existence," her courage is superb: "I want to say to someone . . . that I have known the worst that the world can do to me, and that nevertheless I praise the world and all living. All that is, is well."

In *Heaven's My Destination* Wilder evidently attempted to answer those critics who had been berating him for his refusal to write about contemporary life. The author has admitted Gertrude Stein's influence upon this work. It was not a happy influence, for it led him studiously to avoid taking up an attitude toward his hero, who is a noble idealist one moment and an unconscionable prig the next. Sinclair Lewis, whose field Wilder here invaded, would have made himself clearer. Yet the dominant tone is satirical, and a picaresque novel whose hero is forever getting himself into trouble for his innocence and idealism, his militant evangelicalism, his opposition to tobacco and alcohol, his pacifism, and his incorrigible proselytizing is perhaps sufficiently unusual so that his history ought to be forgiven a certain failure to achieve complete singleness of effect.

Whether Mr. Wilder has resumed the novelist's career with *The Ides of March,* or whether that historical "fantasia" is to remain *sui generis* among his later works, it is as yet too early to say. *Sui generis*

---

[35] It is interesting to compare this with Robert Nathan's contrast of Hebraism and Hellenism in *Jonah.* "You Jews," so God declares to Moses, "you do not understand beauty. With you it is either glory or despair." And the last words of the book are: "And with a sigh He looked westward to the blue Aegean. Warm and gold the sunlight lay over Greece."

from one point of view it is bound to be, for it is an elaborate account of the events leading up to Caesar's assassination, told in terms of a series of documents, presented with a great show of pseudo-critical and scholarly apparatus.[36] Though *The Ides of March* smells of the lamp beyond any of Wilder's other novels, it has many brilliant things in it. But because of its specialized character, it does little to strengthen the hope of his admirers that he may yet become, in the usual sense of the term, an important American novelist.

Wilder is generally classified as definitely a Christian writer. He once told a German interviewer that he was trying to describe "this magic unity of purpose and chance, of destiny and accident," and in the Preface to his collection of plays, *The Angel That Troubled the Waters* (1928), he declared his hope "to discover the spirit that is not unequal to the great religious themes, yet which does not fall into a repellent didacticism." Perhaps it is an exaggerated fear of didacticism that has so far kept him from a direct attack upon any of the great distinctively Christian themes: "the most exhausting of all our adventures is that journey down the long corridors of the mind to the last halls where belief is enthroned." *The Woman of Andros* suggests the Christian view only by contrast; in *Heaven's My Destination* the author's attitude is at best ambivalent. Even *The Bridge of San Luis Rey* seems thoroughly agnostic in its relationship to the special problem it poses. "There is a land of the living and a land of the dead and the bridge is love, the only survival, the only meaning.' Whatever answer this may be to the problem of suffering, and whatever comfort may be derived from it, it is hard to perceive that it is distinctively Christian.

[36] Oddly enough, a similar method has been used in a recent British novel about Caesar, this time primarily in his relations with Cleopatra: *A Goddess to a God* (M, 1948), by John L. Balderston and Sybil Bolitho. Though published after *The Ides of March,* it was not influenced by it. From the book itself I can perceive no particular reason why *A Goddess to a God* should have reached a narrower public than the Wilder work. But the finest Roman novel of recent years is *The Fates Are Laughing,* by W. P. Crozier (HB, 1945).

CHAPTER XXII

NOVELISTS OF THE 'THIRTIES

> . . . History tells lies about real persons and fiction tells truth through the mouths of unreal ones. OLIVER WENDELL HOLMES

1. Gargantua as Novelist: Thomas Wolfe

One of the prime literary sensations of the 1930's, Thomas Wolfe was far from being a typical figure of his time. If he was marvelously free from the characteristic faults of twentieth-century aesthetes, he was also apparently unable to learn anything from their technical achievement. His imitations of Joyce have somewhat obscured this fact, but his imitation of Joyce is all on the surface; even his so-called basic theme of the Search for the Father was more or less superimposed; so far from being the inspiring force behind his work, it was first suggested to him, as an unifying device, by his editor, Maxwell Perkins. In the same way, his chants and soliloquies and prose poems were less an attempt to go along with contemporary experiments in the novel-form than the fruit of a romantic, sentimental exuberance, pouring itself out through the means most immediately available. Wolfe loathed the glib, decadent, eclectic, rootless intellectualism of the metropolitan sophisticates whose slimy trail sprawls across so much contemporary art. The Cambridge variety he castigated in his picture of Professor Hatcher's playwriting circle in *Of Time and the River,* and the more corrupt New York growth was finally rejected in George Webber's break with Mrs. Jack and her world in *You Can't Go Home Again.* Neither did pink attract him in either its aesthetic or its political sense. His roots were in Longfellow's America, in the world of Ridpath's history and John L. Stoddard's lectures, and his rhetorical eloquence stemmed directly from his father's "spouting" of the poetry that men loved in the nineteenth century. Even Shaw was not sufficiently concerned with the whole of society to satisfy him; in O'Neill he deplored a "backward tendency" toward the primitive. He made as spectacular a pageant of his bleeding heart as any early romantic. If his vogue proved nothing else, it at least proved that a novel innocent of "form," a welter of details and images far beyond anything the early Victorians produced, could still enthrall the modern reader—at least if it had some four-letter words in it, a reasonable amount of profanity and physical horror, and a frank, even brutal, treatment of certain aspects of experience that the Victorians had ignored. The enthusiasm of his admirers did not always do much credit to the penetrating intelligence upon which they prided themselves, but it did show, reassuringly, that they still had more heart in them than one might have supposed, and that a primitive sexuality was not the only genuine emotion to which they were capable of responding.

Thomas Wolfe was born at Asheville, North Carolina, on October 3, 1900. Pennsylvania and North Carolina joined in his background. He studied at the state university, then at Harvard, where he tried playwriting under George Pierce Baker and nearly got a play produced by the Theater Guild. For six years he taught English at Washington Square College. His first novel, *Look Homeward, Angel,* was published in 1929, its successor, *Of Time and the River,* in 1935. His death, which was caused by heart and kidney ailments following an attack of pneumonia, occurred at Baltimore on September 15, 1938.

Wolfe's four monolithic novels are really one novel—or the gigantic prelude to a novel. The plan, as set forth in the "Publisher's Note" preceding *Of Time and the River,* comprised these "six books, in the order of their appearance, together with the time plan which each follows":

> *Look Homeward, Angel* (1884-1920)
> *Of Time and the River* (1920-1925)
> *The October Fair* (1925-1928)
> *The Hills Beyond Pentland* (1838-1926)
> *The Death of the Enemy* (1928-1933)
> *Pacific End* (1791-1884)

What was published was quite different. After Maxwell Perkins had persuaded Wolfe to omit the introductory account of his ancestors, originally intended for inclusion in it, *Look Homeward, Angel* appeared as a fairly coherent account of Eugene Gant's (Wolfe's) childhood and youth in Catawba (North Carolina) and his college years at Pulpit Hill (Chapel Hill). But when *The October Fair* came to Perkins's desk in 1933, it was twelve times the length of the ordinary novel and included much more than we now know as *Of Time and the River*. Wolfe had the worst case of *cacoëthes scribendi* in literary history: when he corrected themes for his freshmen in New York his comments were sometimes longer than what they had written. In writing his novel, he had apparently been piling up material helter-skelter and quite without regard for sequence. The train-ride which makes up the first section in *Of Time and the River* originally ran 100,000 words. Indeed it was not Wolfe who decided that the time had come to stop writing in 1933; it was Perkins. Thereupon author and editor set to work with equal passion and agony to carve a novel out of two feet of manuscript, discarding the irrelevant and the intractable and supplying fresh links where they were needed. Sometimes Wolfe's additions would take up more space than the material discarded; once, indeed, the new stuff was so good that, though he doubted its relevance, Perkins had not the heart to throw it out. As published, *Of Time and the River* confined itself entirely to the first part of the *October Fair* manuscript—Eugene's experiences at Harvard and his European tour—leaving for later publication the account of the 1925-1928 years, "a period of greater certitude ... dominated by the unity of a single passion." This, the long affair with Mrs. Jack, became the second half of *The Web and the Rock,* posthumously published in 1939. In an essentially futile attempt to secure some measure of objectivity,[1] Wolfe had changed his hero from Eugene Gant to George Webber, and had been obliged to use the first half of *The Web and the Rock,* consequently, to build up a fresh background for his new *alter ego* and to tell the story of his early life. *You Can't Go Home Again,* published in 1940, continues Webber's history through his developing literary career, his retreat to the little people in the slums of Brooklyn,

---

[1] After *Of Time and the River* had appeared, Wolfe left Scribners for Harpers; consequently it fell to Edward Aswell instead of Maxwell Perkins to prepare *The Web* and its successors for publication.

his final break with Esther Jack and her corrupt theater world, and his visit to Germany. The most significant development is the growth of the hero's social consciousness, away from his earlier extreme individualism, through his contacts with the terrors of the Great Depression in America and with emergent fascism abroad.[2]

Wolfe was the most autobiographical of all American novelists. In some cases he apparently could not substantially alter even the names of the persons who had inspired his characters; in writing of Eugene Gant he sometimes calls him "he" and sometimes "I." He defends himself on this point by urging that all fiction is autobiography; so, in a sense, it is; but the very terms of the defense employed show that he never understood the difference between playing variations upon your own experiences and using the creative imagination to project yourself into other lives. He cites Lowes' interpretation of the use Coleridge made of his reading, but he fails to mention the fact that when Coleridge wrote "The Rime of the Ancient Mariner" he had never sailed on the sea.

Indeed, Wolfe lacked selective power almost altogether. "I do too much of everything. . . ." His hunger for life went almost to the length of madness. He was a glutton for experience. He wanted to read all the books, eat all the food, drink all the liquor, know all the people, and love all the women in the world. It is said that he once talked to a friend in a restaurant for sixteen hours. And the past was, for him, as clamorous as the present: there were "a thousand buried, nameless, and forgotten lives, ten thousand strange and secret tongues alive now, urgent, swarming in his blood, and thronging at the gateways of his memory." He uses all the words in the dictionary, but the one word he really needs often gets lost in the shuffle. His books almost *happened*. He created in a demonic frenzy, brought forth in travail, and sometimes failed to recognize the child. Talk rambles on in bald obviousness, as if writer and characters alike were not only saying and writing, quite without reflection, the first thoughts that occurred to them but all the others as well. Wolfe once

[2] The fragment *The Hills Beyond* (H, 1941) gets the history of George Webber's maternal ancestors as far as 1880. "The Web of Earth," a monologue of Eugene's mother, Eliza Gant, is included in the volume of short fiction called *From Death to Morning* (S, 1935).

wrote 80,000 words to record a conversation that was supposed to fill five minutes of dramatic time.

Consequently, his books are full of irrelevant material. Bascom Pentland's story, to take but one example, has no real connection with the theme of *Of Time and the River*, yet it is narrated at length. Even the people in Pentland's office must be described minutely, though we are never to see them again. What Eugene observes from the window of a train passing through small towns is developed as elaborately as if Engene himself were involved in it—to say nothing of the fact that much of it he would not have been able to see at all.

Coupled with Wolfe's intensity, this abundance makes for a tension or violence so extreme that it destroys the meaning of all experience, for when eating one's breakfast is as intense a business as watching one's father die, one soon finds it impossible to be moved by either event. The critic who remarks that Wolfe alone has preserved in fiction the normal American family life of his time sets one wondering uncomfortably where he may have grown up. The truth is that the jungle is a peaceful place compared to Wolfe's domestic interiors. Even when Ben gives his brother a watch, he must do it violently, and there is so much power in old Gant's dying that it seems more vigorous than anybody else's life.[3]

Of course this intensity was Wolfe's great gift, or would have been if he had ever learned to control it, as Dickens did, instead of being carried away by it. Again and again he was betrayed into the kind of rant that always lies treacherously in wait for eloquent writers. Of the glories and terrors of being young he babbled as naïvely as any young nineteenth-century romantic of *Licht, Liebe, Leben*. At his worst, he makes Ella Wheeler Wilcox sound like a very restrained and sophisticated writer. Women nearly always bring out the pulp-writer in him: "The girl's beauty that night was almost unbelievable." But how many pulp-writers have ever been guilty of

---

[3] Some of Wolfe's exaggerated passages were, of course, intended humorously. But such burlesque titles for modern paintings and plays as "Portrait of a Nude Falling Upon Her Neck in a Wet Bathroom" and "You Shall Be Free When You Have Cut Your Father's Throat" are too broad to be very amusing. Moreover, Wolfe can be quite as extreme when burlesque is farthest from his mind, as when George Webber presents himself to Esther Jack as utterly desolate because he has lost his "squeal."

writing "She was a virgin, crisp like celery"? Eugene's early affair with Laura is Tarkington material, quite shorn of Tarkington's irony. In general, I think it fair to say, Wolfe observed women less than he smelled them. George Webber approaches Esther like a cannibal, and his apostrophes to the "Boston bitch" Ann reveal a poverty of language and imagination that would shame a stevedore. Esther begins her nerve-wracking scenes with him on a level of dignity but soon descends to billingsgate and at last finds a rant to match his own.

Much of this Wolfe himself would have agreed with, for as time went on he tried increasingly to be more objective as well as more representative and less inclusive. His own modest, yet dignified, statement of his aims and evaluation of his progress in *The Story of a Novel* (Scribners, 1926), is very winning, even though not particularly reassuring. His determination to drop Eugene Gant for George Webber was as arbitrary as Trollope's sudden decision to slaughter Mrs. Proudie after he had heard her severely criticized, but it was considerably less decisive. For while Wolfe now began calling Eugene George, he was still thinking about himself, and as soon as he reached the love-affair, he began to use Wolfe's own experiences, first written up as Gant's, without even troubling to change the name he had given the woman in the moment of Gant's meeting with her. There is no question that the awakening of Wolfe's social consciousness, especially as it is reflected in *You Can't Go Home Again,* is all to his honor as a man, and it is generally agreed that he did achieve a measure of objectivity both here and in *The Hills Beyond,* though some believe that he achieved it at the cost of considerable sacrifice of vitality.[4] His hope for society was a noble hope, but he found no real way to implement it, and we shall never know whether, if he had lived, he would have found means to remedy the perceived shortcomings of his art. As it is, he was an undoubtedly fascinating writer whose aspiration far exceeded his achievement.

---

[4] It is interesting that at least one critic, Pamela Johnson, should find the Gant books more objective than the Webber books. In the former, she argues, we see other people vividly through Eugene's eyes; in the latter, the mere fact that he was, in a measure, detaching himself from the central character set him free to concentrate exclusively upon him, and Webber, consequently, fills the world.

"Excuse the length of my letter," wrote Pascal; "I had no time to write a short one."

2. Chamber of Horrors—Southern Exposure

Because both use freely materials involving Southern decadence and degeneration, William Faulkner and Erskine Caldwell have often been mentioned together. As the less significant of the two writers, Caldwell (though he began a little later), may well be considered first.

Erskine Caldwell was born in rural Georgia, on December 17, 1903, the son of a Presbyterian clergyman. He attended, among other schools, the University of Virginia and the University of Pennsylvania, and he has held a wide variety of jobs, ranging all the way from war correspondence to physical labor. He lived for a number of years in Maine but now makes his home in the Southwest.

He has been most admired for his short stories.[5] The novels which have attracted attention are, first of all, *Tobacco Road* (1932), which Jack Kirkland made into a play that ran seven and a half years on Broadway, and *God's Little Acre* (1933). Except for *Georgia Boy* (1943)—a comparatively mellow work for Caldwell, and one which raised vain hopes in some quarters that he might be turning to a more "normal" kind of character—the only novel of recent years that has been taken seriously is *Tragic Ground* (1944). At the moment, indeed, Caldwell seems destined for survival only in the mansions of subliterature. His sales continue enormous—largely in twenty-five-cent, paper-covered editions, decorated with crude pictures of half-naked women—but his critical stock is now so low that it is difficult to believe he ever enjoyed the acclaim which was given to him only a few years ago.

Caldwell's typical characters are sharecroppers and degenerate poor whites of the Deep South,[6] and except for the Faulkner of *Sanctuary,* perhaps no writer not avowedly pornographic has ever so consistently devoted himself to a record of sexual degradation. I am

[5] Collected in *Jackpot* (1940) and in *Stories* (1944), with an introduction by H. S. Canby.
[6] The hero of *A House in the Uplands* (1946) is a plantation owner, but he behaves as badly as Jeeter Lester himself.

not for a moment questioning Mr. Caldwell's claim that his purpose in writing of such horrors is to awaken the conscience of the nation to the iniquity of the social and economic conditions which, in his view, have produced them. His own nonfiction sociological writing[7] creates a strong presumption of sincerity, and the indictment of lynching in *Trouble in July* (1940), of the wartime iniquity of luring country people to the towns for emergency jobs and then abandoning them to want in *Tragic Ground,* and of other crimes against the helpless elsewhere[8]—all this is perfectly valid as far as it goes. My concern is entirely with Mr. Caldwell's success as a writer. I do not believe that, in general, he makes out an effective case or that his fictions serve the cause he professes to hold dear. His characteristic personages are the weirdest of grotesques—Miss Saunders, the social worker of *Tragic Ground,* is as incredible as the people she tries to help—by which I do not at all mean that I doubt the existence of equally degraded or foolish people: I simply doubt that the comic strip attitudes in which Mr. Caldwell presents them have any correspondence with either reality or fine art.

Caldwell's method is to describe the most hideous behavior conceivable with an air of innocent insouciance. This is presumably what one of his admirers has spoken of as "the essential naïveté, pureness of heart, and social consciousness" of his work! ("When I use a word," said Humpty Dumpty, "it means just what I choose it to mean—neither more nor less.") If you are going to rely upon mere outrageousness for your effects, you cannot of necessity achieve anything better than shock value. Caldwell's people are quite as callous in other things as they are in sex, as when Jeeter and his wife leave the grandmother's body lying in the road where she has been run down by an automobile without even trying to find out whether she is dead. Such people do not awaken sympathy nor even pity; even considered strictly as grotesques, they are not interesting. If

[7] See *Some American People* (1935), *Tenant Farmer* (1935), *You Have Seen Their Faces,* with Margaret Bourke-White (1937), *Say! Is This the U.S.A.?* (1941). Mr. Caldwell is also the editor of the "American Folkways" series (1940+).

[8] *This Very Earth* (1948) relates the calamities which overtake a farmer-family after they are forced into town; *A Place Called Estherville* (1949) concerns a mulatto brother and sister in the same predicament.

they awaken anything besides disgust, it is a kind of Rabelaisian mirth, and there are times, as in the account, in *Tobacco Road,* of the degraded woman preacher, Sister Bessie, and the sixteen-year-old boy whom she has persuaded to marry her (on the Lord's instigation), by buying him an automobile, when they can be as funny as they are outrageous.[9] Yet Caldwell insists that he did not intend them to be laughed at; if this is true then he has surely failed in communication.[10] Nor is the situation improved when callow philosophizing is piled on top of wallowing. I grant that it may sound impressively D. H. Lawrence to declare that "There was a mean trick played on us somewhere. God put us in the bodies of animals and tried to make us act like people." Yet I am not much impressed by the remedy for such complexes which seems to be suggested in *God's Little Acre* in the scene in which Will Thompson, who has already copulated with one sister-in-law, strips another naked, in his own wife's presence, tearing her clothing to shreds, and gains such power from his use of her that he heroically rushes back to the idle mill and turns the power on! All three of the women involved and Will's father-in-law to boot are overwhelmed with admiration for his heroic conduct; for once they have encountered a man who lives as God intended him to live.[11]

William Faulkner is, of course, a very different story, and Faulkner's reputation has never been so high as it is today. Whatever may legitimately be urged against him, few competent critics can doubt

[9] *Journeyman* (1935) studies the career of a rascally male preacher, a primitive Elmer Gantry.

[10] There are exceptions to this statement. One feels that under other conditions Floyd, of *Tragic Ground,* might have made something of his life, for he is still man enough to kill the scoundrel who seduces his young daughter. But what shall be said of Spence Douthit and his wife, who manifest no indignation or distress when Mavis becomes a prostitute at thirteen?

[11] Mr. Caldwell's first two novels, bravely entitled *The Bastard* and *Poor Fool* (both 1930), are described even by his admirers as a conglomeration of almost unreadable horrors. Later titles not hitherto mentioned are *The Sure Hand of God* (1935), which concerns a woman of easy virtue looking for a husband for her daughter and a man to pay her own bills, and *Episode in Palmetto* (1950), which describes the amorous exploits of a young schoolteacher. *All Night Long* (1942) came out of Mr. Caldwell's experiences reporting the German-Russian war. *The Courting of Susie Brown* and *Lamp for Nightfall* have been announced by DSP-LB for 1952.

that his is the most powerful imagination among contemporary American novelists.

He was born, in New Albany, Mississippi, on September 25, 1897, of a family long prominent in public affairs. His great-grandfather, Colonel William Falkner,[12] railroad builder and Civil War hero, was the author, among other books, of a popular novel called *The White Rose of Memphis* (1881). The Colonel might have made a very good hero for one of his grandson's novels (which are, indeed, said to contain much family history). When he arrived in Ripley, Mississippi, at the age of ten, having walked all the way from Middleton, Tennessee, to make his home with an uncle, he found that relative in jail, under accusation of murder. He himself became a mighty duelist, but he was slain in cold blood in 1899 by an old friend and railroad associate whom he had just defeated for the legislature.

These facts may give something of the flavor of the "Deep South" which has produced William Faulkner and of which he is a part. His home is in Oxford, Mississippi (the "Jefferson" of his fiction). He served with the Royal Air Force in the First World War. He has supported himself by doing physical labor of various kinds and by holding sundry odd jobs. Once he roomed in New Orleans with Sherwood Anderson. More recently he has done his stint in Hollywood, and one of the best of the many stories told about him is that when he got there and received his assignment, he asked and obtained permission to do his writing "at home," but that when the studio officials sought him, he was not, as they had expected him to be, at Santa Monica but in Oxford. Spiritually, at any rate, he has never been away.

Yet Faulkner's report upon the land of his heart is not that of a realist. In his most characteristic work, he has chosen instead to function upon the level of legend and myth. He has created an imaginary Yoknapatawpha County in northern Mississippi. Here are the Compsons and the Sartorises, the McCaslins and the degenerate Snopses; the aristocrats, the poor whites, and the postwar commercial exploiters of the South; Negroes, Indians, poor farmers,

---

[12] Though the present-day novelist is called "Faulkner" on all his title-pages, *Who's Who in America* still gives "Falkner," pronounced fawk'-nẽr.

and once-wealthy plantation owners. Faulkner has not got all of his work into the Yoknapatawpha saga, as Cabell got all of his up to 1930 into the *Biography of Manuel*. The first two novels, for example, are out. *Soldier's Pay* (1926) is one of our bitterest fictions about the wrecked soldier's return after World War I; *Mosquitoes* (1927) is a sophisticated conversation piece in the manner of the early Aldous Huxley. *Pylon* (1935) is built around a flying meet in New Orleans. *Sartoris* (1929) was the first of the Yoknapatawpha series, and *The Sound and the Fury* (1929), *As I Lay Dying* (1930), *Sanctuary* (1931), *Light in August* (1932), *Absalom, Absalom!* (1936), *The Wild Palms* (1939), *The Hamlet* (1940), and *Intruder in the Dust* (1948) all belong to it.

The novels and the short stories[13] are elaborately interrelated. Both persons and events may be treated supplementarily or sequentially in works written years apart. There are inconsistencies and contradictions also, for no writer was ever less interested than Faulkner in a mere mechanical or schematic unity. Apparently the pattern of family and social relationships described in a novel goes on developing in his mind long after the book has been published, and his knowledge of his people and their relations with each other is continually being enlarged.

The complications of the Yoknapatawpha saga can only be suggested here. The deepest roots go back to *Absalom, Absalom!*, which begins with the building of Sutpen's Hundred by naked slaves back in the 1830's. Thomas Sutpen establishes himself in the community by marrying into the respectable Coldfield family, and his story is viewed in retrospect, as his sister-in-law, old Miss Rosa, tells it to Quentin Compson, upon the eve of his departure for Harvard in 1909. To proceed very summarily, Sutpen has been married before, and has had a son known as Charles Bon, by a West Indian woman whom he discarded when he learned that she had Negro blood. Charles later falls in love with his half-sister, Judith Sutpen, and is murdered by her brother Henry. (At the end of the book, Henry burns to death in the conflagration which consumes Sutpen's Hundred in the best Gothic tradition.) Sutpen too is murdered, by a

[13] Now available in part in *The Collected Stories of William Faulkner* (RH, 1950).

poor white whose daughter he had taken unto himself in a vain attempt to beget a son.

Not all the story is told by Miss Rosa; some of it Quentin pieces out from other sources. Much of it he tells to his Canadian roommate at Harvard in a vain attempt to help him to understand the South. But Quentin himself is involved in a family tragedy as harrowing as that of the Sutpens—and this is the theme of *The Sound and the Fury*. His father is a drunkard, his mother a selfish, neurotic fool; his brother Benjy an idiot; his sister Candace a nymphomaniac; and the only really responsible member of the family, his brother Jason, such a monster of cruelty that the others seem amiable beside him. Quentin loves Candace so much that to save her from a forced marriage, he pretends to have had incestuous relations with her, but the expedient fails to work, and he drowns himself in the Charles River. There is another Quentin in the book, Candace's daughter (not by her husband), who is named after her uncle and inherits the sensual proclivities of her mother; any chance she might have had of escaping the general doom is effectually frustrated by the cruelty with which Jason drives her into fierce rebellion.

In one of Faulkner's novels, a chorus-character admits that the persons whose actions constitute the story "ain't human." Every kind of offense, legal and moral, that can be committed appears somewhere in Faulkner's pages, every variety of physical horror, every type of degeneracy, every phase of abnormal behavior. I once amused myself by making a list of these things, but I shall not print it, for I am convinced that, except perhaps in *Sanctuary,* which was avowedly written as a "shocker" and to make money, then rewritten lest it should shame his more serious works, such a summary would be as unfair to Faulkner as it would wrong the Elizabethan dramatists to list all the sensational aspects of the plots of plays like *Hamlet* and *The White Devil.* Encountered as Faulkner presents them, the horrors are in general less nauseating than the summary would be, partly because of his indirect and involuted methods of presentation, partly because classical literature has trained us to accept as myth many horrors over which we would gag in the newspapers, and partly because the discerning reader generally feels that he can be sure of the author's own scale of values. In 1931 Faulkner declared that he still felt too young and inexperienced to have produced a "real novel," but that he hoped, say in five years, to turn out a *Clarissa* or a *Tom Jones,* a book resting upon "one of the few fundamental truths which mankind has learned." In 1950, upon being awarded the Nobel Prize for Literature, he attempted to define these truths: "love and honor and pity and pride and compassion and sacrifice":

I decline to accept the end of man. . . . I believe that man will not merely endure; he will prevail . . . because he alone among creatures has a soul, a spirit capable of compassion and sacrifice and endurance. The poet's, the writer's duty is to write about these things. It is his privilege to help man endure by lifting his heart, by reminding him of the courage and honor and hope and pride and compassion and pity and sacrifice which have been the glory of his past. The poet's voice need not merely be the record of man, it can be one of the props, the pillars, to help him endure and prevail.[14]

The usual reaction to this statement, among readers who were not Faulkner specialists, was "How can a man who writes like Faulkner believe such things?" I do not think it completely covers the case to say that it is *because* he believes such things that Faulkner can write as he does—and retain his sanity; yet the retort has point. Malcolm Cowley has compared Faulkner with Hawthorne. He is nowhere more like him than in what Hawthorne's daughter once described as her father's "religious . . . Christlike choice of mental companionship (pity) with the greatest of all mourners, those who have sinned. . . ." I have spoken of Candace Compson, for example, as a nymphomaniac. So she is, but she is also a human being, and as we follow her story, we understand the love which Quentin feels for her. Nor is Candace an isolated instance. To say that *As I Lay Dying* is the story of how the Bundrens cart the putrefying corpse of their mother across the country in the heart of summer, to bury it, in accordance with her last wish, in her old home, sounds merely disgusting, yet the book is full of beauty, wisdom, and even, on occasion, charm; and the Bundrens themselves, simple as they are, emerge in almost an heroic aspect, carrying out, under overwhelm-

---

[14] For the complete text of Faulkner's address, see *New York Herald-Tribune Book Review,* Jan. 14, 1951, p. 5.

ing difficulties, what they themselves regard as a sacred duty to their dead. There is much that may be questioned in Evelyn Scott's tribute to Faulkner,[15] but she is right when she finds in *The Sound and the Fury* a "reassertion of humanity in defeat that is, in the subjective sense, a triumph." Nor is this merely because Faulkner has, as she asserts, achieved "the conquest of nature by art." Humanity is not utterly contemptible, even in its most degraded aspects: it still wears what in *Huckleberry Finn* is called "the Lord's mark." "The result . . . is an exaltation of faith in mankind."

Moreover, Faulkner has his decent characters: Lena Grove and Byron Bunch of *Light in August,* the sewing machine man of *The Hamlet,* Dilsey of *The Sound and the Fury,* the convict who aids the pregnant woman during the Mississippi flood in *The Wild Palms,* Gavin Stevens and his nephew and their friend, old Miss Habersham, of *Intruder in the Dust,* who do not stop even at exhuming dead bodies to save the Negro Lucas Beauchamp from the lynchers.

Like all myths, Faulkner's fables are concerned with larger matters than the fate of their individual characters. But it is not necessary to accept, say, the detailed allegorical interpretation which George O'Donnell works out for *Sanctuary* to perceive that Faulkner's ethic has social, as well as personal, implications. The tragedy of a South brooded over by the ghosts of the past is never off his mind— "Yesterday won't be over until tomorrow, and tomorrow began ten thousand years ago"—but because the problem of the South is a human problem, the implications of the struggle cut through all sectional boundaries.

In the South itself it is clear that Faulkner's heart is with the old ways: otherwise he could not be so bitter against those who are destroying them. Mr. Cowley has noted that Popeye, the impotent villain of *Sanctuary,* is always described in mechanical terms, which suggests that he is a "compendium of all the hateful qualities of finance capitalism." But there is no chauvinism in Faulkner's attitude toward his country. He has sometimes been called a Negro-hater. On the contrary, some of his most attractive characters are Negroes. About the "peculiar institution" he is as bitter as Harriet

[15] *On WF's "The Sound and the Fury"* (Cape & Smith, 1929).

Beecher Stowe. Slavery and miscegenation—here is the cancer in Southern society, and it sent its corruptions pulsing through the blood stream of the whole body politic until it produced such horrors that the worst symbols he can devise no doubt seem pale to Faulkner for the purpose of portraying them. The war, the evil of the carpetbagger regime, the degenerate Scopses overrunning the country as they overrun the hamlet of Frenchman's Bend—all have followed from this basic wrong. In *Intruder in the Dust* we get Faulkner's maturest statement of what the South must do to be saved and of what the rest of America can do to help her. It is an indictment of the shame of a nation and a picture of human beings facing up to their responsibilities toward inherited evil. There is no facility about it, and it will bring no comfort to anybody who believes that passing laws in Washington is going to help very much. But at no point is the Negro slandered or his rights denied.

Slavery and miscegenation are both wrong for the same reason— that they involve treating human beings as if they were things. And it is at this point that Faulkner's reading of history and his interpretation of the significance of the human drama as a whole coalesce. As Warren Beck has said, his theme is "that man, when passion-ridden and irrationally seeking privilege or sensation or escape, plunges on toward stultification and tragedy." What the exploiters have come to possess they can only destroy; it becomes a curse to them; for nature cannot be owned. "The right attitude toward nature is . . . associated with the right attitude toward man, and the mere lust for power over nature is associated with the lust for power over other men. . . ." To live successfully, you must give yourself up to life.

It is very unfortunate that a writer who thus reads the human drama should have been so often misunderstood in an age which has such desperate need of just such a reading. But it is largely Faulkner's own fault, for he has been extremely eccentric in method and style—and often, too, in his choice of materials.

A writer's procedure in these matters is governed by two things: his theme and purpose; his temperament and experience of life. No intelligent reader is, at this date, disposed to deny Faulkner the privilege of using whatever materials he needs to convey his vision.

The point is that when it comes to human degradation, he often uses more than he needs, thus betraying a morbid imagination or an overbearing tendency toward sensationalism or both, and thus inevitably alienating many readers who ought to be on his side.[16] Even the admiring George O'Donnell calls *Light in August* a failure because the degenerate Joe Christmas, who ought to have been the antagonist, runs away with the story and usurps the place of the protagonist instead.

With style and method the situation is the same. Faulkner once told a class at Chapel Hill that he had never given form in fiction a moment's thought. This was obviously not a serious statement; nobody can read through the recent "Critical Appraisal" by Campbell and Foster without perceiving that Faulkner has given form in fiction as serious consideration as Joyce himself. At the same time, it would be difficult to deny that he has often indulged in such willful caprice as to make his books virtually unreadable except by those who, as Joyce once expressed it with reference to himself, are prepared to devote their whole lives to the task. Here, again, one does not deny the author's "right" to use any method he needs to get his story told in the most effective possible way. The trouble is that many of Faulkner's devices seem only to prevent the story from getting itself told. I know it is the thesis of some of his more fanatical admirers that a bad sentence is not a bad sentence when he writes it, but I cannot believe that such indulgence will really serve Faulkner's needs in the long run or that he himself could be content to survive as the darling of a coterie. The truth is that when he is at his worst Faulkner's style is barbarous—barbarous in its abundant sclecisms, barbarous in its intolerable purple passages, and barbarous, most of all, in its unending, anaconda-like involutions.[17] That it is

[16] Vincent F. Hopper, "F's Paradise Lost," *VQR,* XXIII (1937), 405-420, seeks to explain Faulkner's preoccupation with evil on the ground of his "Swiftian abhorrence of the animal propensities of man and a Miltonic dissent from the evils of the world."

[17] The most careful discussions of Faulkner's style (in addition to that in Campbell and Foster) are in Joseph Warren Beach, *American Fiction, 1920-1940,* p. 152 ff.; Conrad Aiken, "WF: The Novel as Form," *AM,* CLXIV (1939), 649-654; Warren Beck, "A Note on F's Style," *Rocky Mt. R.,* VI, Spring-Summer, 1942, p. 5+.

at the same time the style of a man of genius I freely grant, but this does not cancel out the barbarisms. Faulkner once declared that he writes out of an inner compulsion and that it is a mistake for the reader to try too hard to understand him. This is as charming in its way as Sir Walter Scott's cavalier attitude toward the "problems" of fiction, but posterity has made Sir Walter pay a heavy price for his derelictions. It is impossible not to regret that Mr. Faulkner seems disposed to surrender the problem of communication quite so easily. One can only hope that, under the stimulus and encouragement of the Nobel Prize, his best work lies yet before him.[18]

3. *Return to History*

With some important exceptions, already noted, the 1920's were in general a here-and-now-minded period. The 'thirties witnessed the first great revival of historical fiction since the turn of the century.

Among those who built a sustained and sustaining career upon the historical novel, the largest reputation, probably, was won by the Maine novelist Kenneth Roberts (b. 1885). But the greatest single successes were the *Anthony Adverse* (1933) of Hervey Allen (1889-1949) and the *Gone With the Wind* (1936) of Margaret Mitchell (1900-1949).

For a full account of the return to history (which is still one of our dominating literary interests), the reader must turn to Ernest E. Leisy's *The American Historical Novel*.[19] The need to escape from an America which seemed, during the years of the Great Depression, inexplicably to have failed to fulfill all its golden promises must, in the nature of the case, have encouraged many readers to retreat to the past. Many persons found themselves fighting as bitter a battle for survival as Scarlett O'Hara herself after the Civil War. It was exhilarating to watch Scarlett fight and win; even if she did not always employ the most genteel means, at least she did not lie down and die. Futilitarianism and deflation of values had been very smart during the 'twenties, when our economic future seemed secure, but

---

[18] Though *Requiem for a Nun* (1951) was not generally hailed by its reviewers as a satisfactory work of art, it is, in some aspects, a hopeful book in its reference to Faulkner's future.

[19] University of Oklahoma Press, 1950.

they would not do now. And as the depression years passed on into the war years, with their bitter policy debates and their conflicts of fundamental principles, Americans more and more felt the need of returning to the Rock Whence We Were Hewn and of re-examining the basic postulates upon which American thinking and living had been based since the birth of the nation. There were even times when the historical novel almost seemed to supply a "retreat" in the religious sense of the term, and when enlightenment, not swashbuckling, became the object of the quest.

Both Allen's novel and Margaret Mitchell's occasioned a good deal of sniping. Much of this was thoroughly picayunish, the inevitable result, in an envious world, of overwhelming success. *Gone With the Wind* was the fastest-selling novel in literary history; by the summer of 1949, when a drunken driver killed its author in the streets of Atlanta, it had sold 6,000,000 copies in thirty languages, not including pirated editions. During the war the Nazis banned it as far as their influence extended, yet it is said that Hitler insisted upon viewing the film when a print turned up in occupied Paris. People who have no standards of their own are always obliged to apply curiously irrelevant criteria to the assessment of literature. To the man in the street "success" is the somewhat vulgar guarantee of excellence, but the super-aesthete is no more intelligent when he assumes that any work which exerts a very wide appeal must necessarily be second-rate. It is worth remembering that Margaret Mitchell enjoyed the warm encomia of many established novelists. Early in 1937 Kenneth Roberts was complaining bitterly to himself about the sales of *Gone With the Wind* in comparison to the reception being accorded his own work. But when he finally read the novel it seemed to him "a bully book" that "well deserved" its success. And Harrison Smith's obituary notice for Miss Mitchell in *The Saturday Review of Literature* virtually cried "peccavi" for the strictures of an earlier editor.[20]

Before he published *Anthony Adverse,* Hervey Allen, who had been a soldier and a teacher, was best known as a poet and a biog-

[20] See Bernard DeVoto, "Fiction Fights the Civil War," *SRL,* XVII, Dec. 18, 1937, p. 3+, and supplementary discussion, XVII, Jan. 8, 1938, pp. 8-9; Harrison Smith, *SRL,* XXXII, Sept. 3, 1949, p. 23.

rapher of Poe. He is said to have spent five years on his novel and to have had thirty dollars left in his purse when he sent it to his publisher. *Anthony Adverse* is not, of course, essentially an American book; it opens in Italy, and it ranges, before it has finished, through three continents; it has, as the saying is, everything in it except the kitchen stove. If there is anything to be said against it, it is just this: the author seems to have set out deliberately to produce a romantic novel in which one man should encounter every aspect of experience, yield to every temptation, and scale every aspiring height which the world over which Napoleon's shadow fell could afford.

Allen himself used to declare that his book was "modern" because far-reaching travel is characteristic of our time; he also pointed out that he had been influenced by Joyce, and that his work was more classical than romantic, both because of its almost mathematically exact structure and because it subordinated the individual to the whole. As he conceived it, the problem of the historical novelist was "to shape his story out of meaningless data with a form and pattern which have human meaning, rich, if possible, in emotional and philosophical values." Into this design the source material must be fitted, but the atmosphere and tone of the finished work are never "of the actual world"; neither are they to be obtained "by gluing facts together into a kind of composite photograph in the album of the past."[21]

Allen was right to object[22] to the loose popular description of his work as a "picaresque" novel, for Anthony is no rogue but a pilgrim whose life-story is intended to shadow forth the life of man; but if the book is "modern" it is so only in the sense that the temporal provides a frame for the eternal. It has been called a fleshly book, but

[21] Hervey Allen, "History and the Novel," *AM*, CLXXXIII, Feb. 1944, pp. 119-120. *Anthony's* literary sources are multitudinous; when the silly cry of plagiarism was raised, Allen struck savagely at his critics in a long article, "The Sources of 'Anthony Adverse,' " *SRL*, X (1934), 401+, which vies with similar revelations by Kenneth Roberts as the most enlightening account we have of how historical novels are made. This article quite obviated the necessity of John A. Kinneman's "Anthony Adverse or Theodore Canot," *Journal of Negro History*, XXX (1945), 304-310.

[22] In his Introduction to the three-volume edition of *Anthony Adverse*, illustrated by Edward A. Wilson, and published by the Limited Editions Club in 1937.

its sexual passages are no more superbly realized than many other adventures—what the child Anthony saw from the great tree in the Convent of Jesus the Child, for example. The contrast between flesh and spirit lies, indeed, close to the heart of the author's meaning, and few books have done fuller justice to the dual aspect of our lives. Moreover, the novel's vivid realization of sensuous impression is matched by the suggestiveness of its symbolism, which, though sometimes mechanically developed, is rarely inappropriate. Of a later work Allen once stated that he tried to achieve consistency in characterization by working out a complete biography for every character, though only a small portion of it could actually be used in the novel. And one of the best things about *Anthony Adverse* is its vivid realization of even minor characters and the way in which even minor episodes possess their own background and atmosphere.[23]

Though *Gone With the Wind* lacks the metaphysical overtones of *Anthony Adverse,* it gains force through its closer and more obvious unity. Margaret Mitchell's father was president of the Atlanta Historical Society; his daughter had been steeped in the materials of her novel all her life. She worked on it for years, for her own entertainment, writing the last chapter first, as she had always used to do her newspaper work. She did not write consecutively; neither did she verify her references. That drudgery she left until the book had been accepted, and it took her eight months.[24]

[23] Unlike Margaret Mitchell, Allen continued to write fiction after his great success but never again really struck fire. The Civil War novel, *Action at Aquila* (1938), though admirably vivid, was obviously not designed as a major work. *The Disinherited* was planned as a series of six novels which should record American development from the wilderness to the Civil War. Allen lived to write three of these novels: *The Forest and the Fort* (1943), *Bedford Village* (1944), and *Toward the Morning* (1948). They are by turns impressive and exasperating, and their theme seems a long time emerging. All three were republished in 1950, in a somewhat cut version, together with the fragment of a fourth, as *The City and the Dawn.*

[24] The story of how Macmillan's Harold Latham discovered the manuscript of *Gone With the Wind* on a scouting trip in Atlanta is one of the most diverting true fairy tales of the modern book trade; it sent half the publishers in America out on the road in search of similar bonanzas! See the news item in *Publishers' Weekly,* CXXIX (1936), 2513. Mr. Latham himself told the story more elaborately in *Book-of-the-Month Club News,* June 1936; his article was reprinted, with other interesting items, in a pamphlet, *Margaret Mitchell and Her Novel "Gone With the Wind"* (M, 1936).

Gone With the Wind abounds in action and is filled with the nostalgic atmosphere suggested by its superb title, yet the principal interest lies in character—in the character, first of all, of its selfish heroine, Scarlett O'Hara, and the man, Rhett Butler, in whom at last she meets her match, and upon her misapprehension of whom she misses her best chance of happiness. Margaret Mitchell refused either to sentimentalize her characters or to slander them; at the close of the penultimate chapter she shows us very clearly just what a sentimental ending for her book would have involved—and then shies away from it. For a Southern Civil War novel, *Gone With the Wind* is rather remarkably on the realistic side, and it is far more antiwar than prowar.

The Southern belle as an opportunistic adventuress was a rather astonishing theme to begin with (though Scarlett does not belong to the old aristocracy), but the author knew her people. The young woman's determination to stop at nothing to win economic security may have cost her her soul, but it was her Southern sentimentalism that destroyed her chances for happiness in this world. Superbly executive as she was in all practical affairs, she mooned her life away over a schoolgirl fixation upon Ashley Wilkes, that honorable, gentlemanly fool, who had to wait until his wife was dead before he found out that she, not Scarlett, was the woman he really loved! The destruction is all the more devastating because Margaret Mitchell never took the easiest way—for all her marrying, Scarlett is really a cold woman sexually—and because the ending is not, in the classical sense, "tragic." Character is fate. The action is viewed consistently from the woman's point of view, and Rhett Butler might easily have been a Rochester-St. Elmo kind of hero, yet somehow he is not. Miss Mitchell kept the mold—and filled it with life. Her psychology may not cut very deep but it is sound, and her sense of values is sound also. There is never a moment when we do not see around her principals, yet neither ever forfeits our psychological sympathy. As for the "good" heroine, Melanie Hamilton Wilkes, she is saved from priggishness (though sometimes only by a hair), not only by the stubborn determination with which she defends her friends and her principles but also by her narrowmindedness in all that touches the simply sacred "cause." To realize how well Margaret Mitchell did by her, one need only recall Amelia Sedley.

Kenneth Roberts's distinguishing mark as a novelist in his capacity to combine really breathless action with a solidity of specification which creates a strong air of reality. This effect is not achieved by chance. In common with other successful writers of his kind, Mr. Roberts knows that the novelist has to plug up a great many holes that the historian can afford to leave open. Historians of Benedict Arnold's Quebec expedition, for example, may content themselves by recording the bare fact that at one point a whole company suddenly ran out of provisions. But a novelist "who is trying to make that expedition come to life" must explain exactly how this circumstance came about.

Most novelists supply such explanations from their "imagination." This Roberts is not willing to do. He must find out what really happened if the facts are in any way discoverable. Perhaps this procedure may involve some reflections upon the character and power of his imagination. But limitation or not, his method helps to account for the characteristic quality of his fiction. He admits that the experiences of the men who marched against Ticonderoga did not come to seem real to him until he had read the diary of Henry Sewall in the unique existent copy of the *Maine Farmer* for June 29, 1872, the copy that the printer took home with him the night his print shop at Augusta burned, destroying all the rest of the edition. Nor did the statement of Major Robert Rogers' biographer that no copy of the court-martial proceedings against Rogers had survived deter Kenneth Roberts from undertaking a search. They turned up at last, in England, at the Colonial Office repository in Canterbury. For *Arundel* he "rounded up," among other things, "all available references to Abenaki Indians, histories of most towns in southern Maine, and all known diaries, documents, letters, and biographies" dealing with the expedition against Quebec. There were "not quite enough" of these to fill a freight car. He also traveled carefully over the route followed by Arnold and his army and made sure "of the exact location of barricades, defending forces, and houses in old Quebec at the time of Arnold's attack."[25]

[25] The source material for *Northwest Passage* was reprinted in part in the

Roberts is never deterred by the difficulties involved in a theme nor yet by the fact that his presentation of it may run counter to current convictions and prejudices. Benedict Arnold is the hero of both *Arundel* (1930) and *Rabble in Arms* (1933), while the immense *Oliver Wiswell* (1940) gives us the American Revolution from the Loyalist point of view. But *Oliver Wiswell* is less pro-British than it is antiwar and pro-common sense; it is neither "Hurray for Sam Adams and to hell with King George" nor vice versa, but rather "To hell with both of 'em." General Howe is as great an ass as in any pro-Revolutionary book, and it would be impossible to excoriate the arrogance and stupidity of British policy more furiously. Roberts believes—or, at least, Wiswell believes—that almost all persons thrust into authority in time of war go mad. Politicians start wars for honest men to fight, then refuse to prosecute them with any vigor or intelligence, and never have sense enough to know when and where to stop:

I thought of all the wars of which I'd read, and clearly saw at last that not one of them—not one—had brought one solitary benefit that couldn't have been attained by peaceful means if only those who fought them had been content to wait—had been wise enough to make the concessions that all human beings must make if they're to live in amity.[26]

Oliver Wiswell and *Northwest Passage* (1937) are Roberts's most ambitious books. The latter falls into three divisions: The 1759 expedition against the Indian town of St. Francis is followed by an interlude in London, in which Rogers is attempting to gain influential friends and money and to consolidate his plans for the expedition in search of the Northwest Passage (while the narrator, Langdon Towne, serves an apprenticeship to painting), and this, in turn, by an account of Rogers' career as governor of Michilimackinac. Roberts has been severely criticized, here and elsewhere, for sprawling structure, yet there is no agreement as to which part of the book is best! Bernard DeVoto, who compares the London interlude favorably to Thackeray's novel, *The Virginians,* finds in Part Three the

second volume of the limited edition. *March to Quebec* (1938) reprints *Arundel* source material.

[26] Copyright 1941 by Doubleday & Company, publishers.

"hunger and desire of the nation just about to break westward into the untrodden lands" as nowhere else in our fiction.

Roberts has also produced two stirring sea stories of the War of 1812 period: *The Lively Lady* (1931) and *Captain Caution* (1934). *Lydia Bailey* (1947), which takes in Toussaint L'Ouverture's uprising in Haiti, thrilling adventures among the Barbary pirates, and other things, is perhaps the most "romantic" of his works thus far, but it is no less firmly grounded than its predecessors upon solid historical knowledge.

Among contemporary women writers of historical novels, probably the foremost reputation belongs to the Worcester, Massachusetts writer, Esther Forbes, whose roots carry back to the beginnings of New England and one of whose ancestors perished in a Cambridge jail while under accusation of witchcraft. Miss Forbes' friends have playfully pointed out that she has found the perfect way to write historical novels: she takes copious notes in a handwriting so illegible that she is never able to decipher them; then when she comes to write, she is thrown back, as a creative writer should be, upon the knowledge she has been able to assimilate!

Her first novel, *O, Genteel Lady* (1926)—which was one of the very first Book-of-the-Month Club selections—was a period piece which probably owed its success to its picturesque introduction of famous nineteenth-century men of letters on both sides of the Atlantic. But her second, *A Mirror for Witches* (1928), was a brilliant and terrifying tour-de-force, a combination of twentieth-century psychology and seventeenth-century superstition which, in less skillful hands, would surely have come a terrible cropper. The quagmires of psychology—and physiology—did engulf Miss Forbes in *Miss Marvel* (1935), of which Dr. Canby remarked wittily that she made the mistake of dressing her chicken in the parlor. With a full-bodied novel about a New England community of 1639, *Paradise* (1937), she found her way again,[27] and she has never since lost it. *The General's Lady* (1938) is a Revolutionary War tragedy, which might easily have become either a conventional adventure story or a con-

[27] Since Miss Forbes took time out from *Paradise* to write *Miss Marvel*, this is not quite an accurate statement.

ventional murder tale but stubbornly refused to do either.[28] Her longest, and in some ways her most impressive, novel to date is *The Running of the Tide* (1948), which brings us to Salem in the days of her glory and of her decline, presenting a moral problem in the great tradition of New England fiction and telling the moving story of an increasingly abortive love affair against the suitable background of the port's failing trade.[29]

Unlike Miss Forbes and Mr. Roberts, Howard Fast (b. 1914) has not given quite all his attention to the historical novel.[30] Neither has he devoted all of his historical fiction to the same period. *The Last Frontier* (1941) concerns a disgraceful Indian war of 1878, while *Freedom Road* (1944) provides a counter-irritant to such works as *Gone With the Wind* and *The Birth of a Nation* by glorifying the Negro "statesmen" of the Reconstruction period, and *The American* (1946) praises Vachel Lindsay's "Eagle That Is Forgotten," Governor Altgeld of Illinois, who committed political suicide because it seemed to him his duty to release the Chicago anarchists who had been imprisoned after the Haymarket riot. Fast went farthest afield in *My Glorious Brothers* (1948), which tells the heroic story of the Maccabees, between the Old Testament and the New, and in *Spartacus* (1952), which deals with the slave revolt against the Roman Republic.

His special field, however, is the American Revolution, to whose varied aspects he has now devoted no fewer than five novels: *Two Valleys* (1933), *Conceived in Liberty* (1939), *The Unvanquished* (1942), *Citizen Tom Paine* (1943), and *The Proud and the Free*

[28] Among Miss Forbes's discarded manuscripts is another Revolutionary War novel, a plea for tolerance toward dissenting minorities. According to Dale Warren, she dropped this when, like so many other interventionists, she jettisoned tolerance during the early years of World War II. By this time one might reasonably expect her to have regained her equilibrium; unless she thinks Kenneth Roberts stole her thunder with *Oliver Wiswell*, perhaps we may still see this novel.

[29] She is an authority on Paul Revere; see her *Paul Revere and the World He Lived In* (1942). A fictional offshoot of this book was *Johnny Tremaine* (1943), a really admirable story of a boy in Revolutionary Boston, designed for young readers.

[30] *Place in the City* (1937) and *The Children* (1947, serially 1937) deal with life in New York City tenement and slum districts, while *Clarkton* (1947) concerns s⸀rikes and strike-breaking in a Massachusetts milltown.

(1950). *The Unvanquished,* in which he pictured Washington's development from a fox-hunting Virginia gentleman to a leader of men, was a considerable success, and W. E. Woodward published a new biography of Paine to answer his novel.

Fast represents the propagandist as historical novelist. No matter where he goes in search of a subject, he never fails to see any historical crisis as a struggle between entrenched privilege and the proletariat. And for all his talents, his heart is never in the story he has to tell but always in the sermon he has come to preach. His historical background and coloring are likely, therefore, to seem somewhat thin and facile; the reader has some difficulty in getting out of our own time because he knows that the author himself is firmly entrenched there.

Even less than Howard Fast has August Derleth devoted himself exclusively to the historical novel. Mr. Derleth was born in 1909 in the heart of the Black Hawk country, at Sauk City, Wisconsin (the Sac Prairie of his books). Here he has lived all his life, and here is now an institution and a leading citizen.

Many of the settlers in this part of Wisconsin were German Catholics, but others were "Freethinkers," adherents of the historic, nineteenth-century humanist "movement" which stemmed from the University of Prague. Liberty and piety have both been cherished in this region—the Sauk City cemetery is still divided into three sections, with Catholics on one side, Protestants on the other, and the Freethinkers lying between them!—and both liberty and piety live in Mr. Derleth's pages. One of the most versatile and prolific of modern American writers, he is poet, essayist, anthologist, and writer of "general" books, as well as novelist, who has published a considerably larger number of titles than the years of his life. His own publishing company, Arkham House, which he established in 1939 to preserve between covers the work of his friend H. P. Lovecraft, has gone on to bring out many other volumes of literature of the supernatural.[31]

[31] Howard Phillips Lovecraft (1890-1937), of Providence, Rhode Island, wrote under the inspiration of Edgar Allan Poe and Arthur Machen, and was published during his lifetime mainly in the pulp magazines. He is excluded from this chronicle by the fact that all his significant works are short stories.

Derleth's "Sac Prairie Saga" is not all fiction.[32] The historical novels are *Still Is the Summer Night* (1937),[33] *Wind Over Wisconsin* (1938),[34] *Restless Is the River* (1939),[35] and *Shadow of Night* (1943).[36] Characteristically, these are loosely woven chronicles whose people, often of European origin and sometimes of noble blood, have a way of carrying over from one book to another. Wisconsin grows from wilderness to settled community before our eyes, with all American history behind it as a frame of reference.

What Mr. Derleth has that is lacking in a writer like Howard Fast—or that is lacking, for that matter, in modern novelists generally—is a country. He belongs. He writes of a land and a people that are bone of his bone and flesh of his flesh. In his fictional world, there is a unity much deeper and more fundamental than anything that can be conferred by an ideology. It is clear, too, that he did not get the best, and most fictionally useful, part of his background material from research in the library; like Scott, in his Border novels, he gives rather the impression of having drunk it in with his mother's

Arkham House has published these Lovecraft books, the first two of which are already valuable and scarce: *The Outsider and Others* (1939); *Beyond the Walls of Sleep* (1944); *Marginalia* (1944); and *Something About Cats and Other Pieces* (1949). A popular edition of *Best Supernatural Stories of HPL*, edited by Derleth, has been issued by World (1945). HPL's own *Supernatural Horror in Literature* and Derleth's *HPL: A Memoir* were both published by Ben Abramson in 1945. Offshoots of Derleth's Arkham House are Mycroft and Moran (publishing detective stories) and Stanton and Lee (general publishers).

[32] An excellent introduction to Derleth's work is *Wisconsin Earth, A Sac Prairie Sampler* (Stanton and Lee, 1948), which comprises the novel *Shadow of Night*, the short stories *Place of Hawks* (1935), and *Village Year: A Sac Prairie Journal* (1941). Of his novels of contemporary life the most important is probably *The Shield of the Valiant* (1945), whose central figure is a young novelist, Steve Grendon, obviously the author's *alter ego*. The principal plot element is provided by the love of a banker's son for a girl from the wrong side of the tracks, but the value of the book lies primarily in its attack upon witch-hunting and bigotry. See also *Evening in Spring* (1941) and *Sweet Genevieve* (1942). *Country Growth* (1940) and *Sac Prairie People* (1948) are short stories.

[33] Sac Prairie in the 1880's.

[34] The 1830's, including the Black Hawk War.

[35] 1839-1850: the coming of "civilization."

[36] 1852-1857. *Bright Journey* (1940), which concerns the northwest fur trade from 1812 to 1843, is not strictly a part of the Sac Prairie series.

milk. The many descriptions of the land itself, which show that the author is fundamentally a poet, may annoy readers who are in a hurry to get on with the story; it may also be objected that some historical characters and events are too obviously introduced or referred to. Yet the Sac Prairie novels touch the authenticity and integrity of the best kind of historical fiction at many points. In *Wind Over Wisconsin* Mr. Derleth does not really need Black Hawk to hold the reader's interest, for Chalfonte's domestic life seems quite as important as anything that happens to a man out of history. A more highly unified book is *Shadow of Night,* the story of one who comes to Sac Prairie to kill the man who had slain his brother in a revolutionary uprising in Europe and who was unable to carry out his plan, partly because the human being he found in Wisconsin simply would not coalesce with the hated image he carried in his mind, partly because he fell in love with his enemy, and perhaps most of all because he found that he was simply not a killer. *Shadow of Night* is essentially a psychological novel. Its problem recalls Mary Johnston's in *Foes;* its tense atmosphere is somewhat suggestive of the work of Joseph Shearing.

Another pronounced individualist among writers of historical novels is Conrad Richter, who was born in 1890 in Pine Grove, Pennsylvania. Mr. Richter has had a much more varied and down-to-earth career than is at all common among novelists,[37] and he now belongs as much to the Southwest as he does to Pennsylvania. If he resembles any other modern American writer, it is not one of the historical novelists but Willa Cather.

This resemblance appeared strongly in his first novel, *The Sea of Grass* (1937), the story of a cattle baron of the old Southwest—Mr. Richter had already studied the type and sympathetically recorded his hopeless fight against "progress" in the story "Smoke on the Prairie" in *Early Americana* (1936)—and his wayward but exquisite wife, who was well portrayed by Katharine Hepburn in the film version. The book's warm, romantic feeling for the land suggests Willa Cather; so does its nostalgic wistfulness and the

---

[37] The amazing—and surely, unique—development of Mr. Richter's career upon its literary side is traced by Bruce Sutherland, "CR's Americana," *NMQR,* XV (1945), 413-422.

way in which Mr. Richter holds his subject away from him. The events recorded in *The Sea of Grass* do not happen while we read about them: they happened long ago. And, as in *My Ántonia* or *A Lost Lady,* the narrator is more observer than participant.

A Lost Lady, however, is more strongly suggested by one of Mr. Richter's minor works, *Always Young and Fair* (1947), which has a Pennsylvania small-town setting after the Spanish-American War. It is the story of a woman who, like one of Meredith's sentimental idiots, withdraws from the world after losing her lover in the war (though she herself never really loved him), and who continued her perverse way of life until the romantic image she had created of herself was suddenly shattered, after which she promptly proceeded to lose all sense of values. In any other writer's hands, this would have been morbid or distasteful or both. Mr. Richter actually succeeded in making it charming.

But there is no suggestion of Willa Cather or of any other writer except Conrad Richter in the author's masterpiece—the trilogy, written in the backwoods vernacular, which comprises *The Trees* (1940), *The Fields* (1946), and *The Town* (1950). This work describes the life of Ohio pioneers from the eighteenth-century days of forest wilderness to the 1860's. The matriarch, Sayward Luckett, and her agnostic New England husband, Portius Wheeler, lawyer and judge, are the dominating characters, though Guerdon's short-lived and occultly-gifted child might well be expected to touch modern readers as deeply as Little Eva and Paul Dombey moved their grandparents. Yet individual characterization is not the prime virtue of these rich and satisfyingly earthy books. They pulse from beginning to end with the passion of the land, the flesh, and the spirit. They have American blood and the American heartbeat in them. Here, if anywhere in fiction, modern readers can learn what it meant for a people to pit themselves against a wilderness.[38]

My choice of historical novelists for discussion in this section can no doubt be attacked as arbitrary. I wish there were space to speak of

---

[38] The Richter canon thus far is completed by *Tacey Cromwell* (1942), a Western story about a "bad" woman with a heart of gold, and *The Free Man* (1943), a brief and legendlike story, possibly underdeveloped though based on thorough historical knowledge, about a Palatinate German who moves from indentured servant to freeman at the time of the Revolution.

Herbert Quick (*Vandemark's Folly,* 1922), of James Boyd (*Drums,* 1925, and other books), of Bess Streeter Aldrich (*A Lantern in Her Hand,* 1928), of Evelyn Scott's experimental Civil War novel, *The Wave* (1929), of T. S. Stribling, especially in *The Forge* (1931), of Stark Young (*So Red the Rose,* 1934), of Rose Wilder Lane (*Free Land,* 1938), and of the Catholic novels of Helen C. White and her sister, Olive B. White. (Of these only Helen's *Dust on the King's Highway,* 1947, concerns an American theme, though Olive's powerful study of religious persecution under Elizabeth I, *Late Harvest,* 1940, is certainly not without application to modern problems.) Some critics prefer the work of Walter D. Edmonds (*Drums Along the Mohawk,* 1936, and other novels) to that of Kenneth Roberts. With *The First Rebel* (1937), Neil Swanson set out on an immense series of novels which should describe the advance of the American frontier as far as the Mississippi. Archie Binns has been praised for his novels of the far Northwest (*The Land Is Bright,* 1939), as has Le Grand Cannon for *Look to the Mountain* (1942) and its successors. At fifty-five Thomas B. Costain began what looks like a long series of spectacularly successful romantic novels with *For My Great Folly* (1942), and Samuel Shellabarger was even a little older when he wrote *Captain from Castille* (1945). In 1946, the eighteenth-century scholar, Odell Shepard, scored a success with *Holdfast Gaines,* written in collaboration with his son, Willard Shepard. This was followed in 1951 by *Jenkins' Ear,* "A Narrative Attributed to Horace Walpole, Esq."

4. *Two Kinds of Novelist: Steinbeck and Marquand*

Diverging tendencies in contemporary fiction could hardly be better illustrated than in the work of John Steinbeck and John P. Marquand. Both "arrived" in a big way near the end of the 'thirties, Marquand in 1937 with *The Late George Apley,* Steinbeck two years later with *The Grapes of Wrath,* the story of the Dust Bowl migrants, their trek to California and their disillusionment there, which became the most controversial American novel about a social problem since *Uncle Tom's Cabin.* But neither novelist was a beginner. Marquand had years of success in the "slicks" behind him,[39]

---

[39] The early Marquand had written historical romances (*The Unspeakable Gentleman,* 1922, and *The Black Cargo,* 1925) and stories of the present day

and Steinbeck had already scored one considerable "success," both between covers and in the theater, with *Of Mice and Men* (1937).

The great change in Mr. Marquand's career reminds one of his own Jim Calder in *Wickford Point* (1939). Jim had done magazine stuff so long that nobody believed him capable of "serious" work. The critics have had—and are still having—the same trouble with Mr. Marquand. People ought to stay classified! You have to go on reading them when they don't. And it's even worse when a "popular" writer not only turns "serious" on you but insists upon having his cake and eating it too. Mr. Marquand serialized part of *Point of No Return* (1949) in *The Ladies' Home Journal* while another part appeared in *The Atlantic Monthly!* He is also guilty of having "made" the covers of *Time* and *Newsweek* on the same date.

If we can forgive this one irregularity, however, we shall find Mr. Marquand's decorum irreproachable in every other respect. He is today our foremost practitioner of the social novel as Edith Wharton, F. Scott Fitzgerald, and Sinclair Lewis all understood that term. The hero of *H. M. Pulham, Esquire* (1941) admits frankly that he does not like the new novels:

The characters in them, ever since the twenties, were always struggling with internal emotional conflicts that revealed themselves in sexual irregularities, and they were never like anyone I knew. They were farmers in the Dust Bowl or traveling salesmen or people who lived at Palm Beach or on the Riviera, never decent, honest-to-goodness men or women.[40]

Mr. Marquand's own characters are often very unlovely persons indeed—certainly they are no "better" than many of Mr. Steinbeck's people—and they frequently say and do things by which Mrs. Wharton, in her earlier phase, at least, might have been shocked. But the change is in our deteriorating *mores,* not in Mr. Marquand. To the end of the chapter, he believes in good manners and he believes in God.

(*Warning Hill,* 1930). *Ming Yellow* (1935) is a "thriller" of modern China, and there is a whole series of books (*Thank You, Mr. Moto,* 1936, etc.) about a fascinatingly suave Japanese secret agent. In his excellent study of Marquand in Gardiner's *Fifty Years of the American Novel,* pp. 125-126, Charles A. Brady shows that the novelist's later themes have already emerged in the early work.

[40] Copyright 1940, 1941, by John P. Marquand and Adelaide H. Marquand

It is true that his faith is sometimes obscured by his method, which is consistently that of the satirist. Perhaps, indeed, his tone is determined less by faith than by pragmatic habit. He was born in Wilmington, Delaware, on November 10, 1893. He has seen considerable, wide-ranging military service; he has done newspaper reporting and advertising in New York; yet he is as New England as the Amy Lowell of "Lilacs"; was not his grandfather a brother of Margaret Fuller? His virtues as a novelist are those which come from thorough immersion in the life described; he himself judged *B. F.'s Daughter* (1946) inferior to his best work because of his comparative unfamiliarity with the locale involved. He has "debunked" Beacon Hill "aristocracy" and Harvard snobbery (he worked his own way through that institution), the New England literary tradition (there is a fourth-rate poet in the *Wickford Point* background), patriotism, the advertising game, banking, and publishing. He has also "debunked" the Freudians, the "sociological survey" and the "foundations" boys, and other rebels against established ways, in much the manner in which old Samuel Butler used to turn suddenly and rend the emancipated, who had supposed, all along, that he was on their side. But Marquand differs from Butler, and from all savage satirists, not only in his gentility but in his refusal to take up a superior attitude toward those who are, when all is said and done, his own kind. Whether writers—as in *Wickford Point* and *So Little Time* (1943)—or businessmen—as in *The Late George Apley* and *H. M. Pulham, Esquire*—his heroes have an unhappy (though not unvarying), way of marrying the wrong woman and of being dominated by her, and then finding themselves, in middle life, oppressed by the uneasy feeling that their whole lives have been a futility, yet of going on in the old groove, if for no other reason because they believe themselves to have passed the point of no return. For all their weakness, they have a wistful charm that is very appealing, and Marquand is very good at throwing the pathos of distance over a vanishing way of life. When he finished with George Apley he was a little surprised to find that he "amounted to more than I had intended." This affectionate attitude would lead to falsification with many writers but not with Mr. Marquand, who evidently sees no less clearly because he loves. The picture of Aunt Sarah's way of life in *Wickford Point* shows how close he could come to the *Cranford*-mood if he chose. Being a satirist, he generally does not choose. Indeed, he is more likely to shatter the spell even after he has created it, as when Grandfather blames his indigestion on "that God-damned water from the red pump."

Essentially Marquand has only one central character—the middle-aged New England gentleman (sometimes living in New York), who is under tremendous pressure to conform, from his inheritance, from his family, from the society in which he lives. In some books— in *So Little Time,* which is a study of America being sucked into Europe's wars for the second time within a generation, and in the novelette, *Repent in Haste* (1945), which deals with an unsuccessful "war marriage"—he is more topical than usual,[41] but this considera-tion involves no change of method. In *Wickford Point,* Jim Calder, who has no wife, finally breaks away from the victimizing relatives whose moral deterioration even surpasses their financial decline; this, however, is not typical. The usual fate of the Marquand hero is acquiescence. In *H. M. Pulham, Esquire,* the "suitable" wife not only fails to bring her husband happiness but comes very close to betraying him. Yet when he meets the New York girl, Marvin Myles, again, he realizes that he would have been no better off with

[41] War in general is not treated too respectfully by Mr. Marquand. The Civil War Apley hired a substitute, "much to his own regret," as he could not be spared from his nationally important (and personally profitable) work. (Incidentally the shadow of savage labor policies hovers in the background of the Apley story.) When George's son, John, goes to the Mexican border in 1916, at President Wilson's behest, his father gives him his blessing, the more readily since all his friends are going and he will be traveling "with a distinctly Boston battery." After 1914 George himself becomes a violent fire-eater, about as intelligent in his patriotism as he is later in another aspect when he conscientiously patronizes a bootlegger to show his contempt for a law which infringes his personal liberty. As a patriotic gesture, he plows up a magnificent lawn to plant vegetables, allowing a number of fields which might have been used for the same purpose to lie fallow. Neither H. M. Pulham nor Charley Gray, of *Point of No Return,* is able to get much satis-faction out of his war record, though Pulham has been decorated for valor. He knows that at least fifty lives would have been saved if he had had sense enough to surrender. In *Melville Goodwin, U.S.A.* (1951), which appeared after this chapter had been written, Mr. Marquand achieves what seems, for a satirist, a rather surprisingly sympathetic portrait of a general.

her, for Marquand is as clear as Wolfe or Cabell that "We can't go back."

This is perhaps not quite true in *The Late George Apley,* which is by all means the most experimental in form among Mr. Marquand's books and technically quite the most brilliant. *Apley* takes the shape of a discreet "Life and Letters" of a solid Boston and Milton citizen, prepared by a typical Beacon Street memoirist for private circulation in an edition of fifteen copies. It is not news at this date that the novel sold considerably more than that: it must be, far and away, the most "successful" of all "literary" novels. George Gissing's *The Private Papers of Henry Ryecroft* is no doubt as famous a work but it certainly has not achieved anything like a comparable circulation. The satire is directed quite as much against Mr. Willing, the memoirist, as it is against George Apley himself, and Mr. Willing, unlike his subject, is set forth completely upon his own terms and left to condemn himself through the superficiality of his thinking and the limitations of his style. Marquand was never to trust the intelligence of his readers to quite the same extent again, and his later books are more conventional in form. Technically their outstanding quality is their use of the "flash back," which Marquand employs perhaps more extensively than any other novelist has ever ventured, though I think there is an element of artificiality about the structure in *Point of No Return.* He has an engaging way, too, of adding depth to his novels by offering a wholly inferential treatment of the more important themes while the foreground is occupied with trivialities, such as, for example, the very unpromising business of the class reunion upon which *H. M. Pulham, Esquire* opens. When Thomas Apley is in decline he suddenly remarks one day to his wife that he wonders whether it might not have been better after all "if George had married that little Irish girl." Mary Monahan was a Catholic, and she lived in South Boston; obviously it wouldn't have "done." Only, unfortunately, there was nothing else in life that George ever really wanted.[42] When Thomas dies he leaves a million to Harvard to be used for the benefit of "deserving Protestant

---

[42] It is too bad that the Mary Monahan episode should have been spoiled by bringing her back into the book at a later stage to extricate George Apley from a somewhat melodramatic difficulty.

students" from the Milton area, and his son is compelled, upon the advice of his lawyers, to pay a considerable sum to a New York hussy who claims old Thomas as the father of her child, not, of course, because George believes the story but simply to protect his father's name from scandal. But in spite of all variations from book to book, the reader always knows where to "have" Mr. Marquand.

With Mr. Steinbeck, on the other hand, it is the very cream of the jest that nobody ever has any idea where to have him. This makes his books a very exciting reading adventure, but it also means that, though (if you count *The Pearl,* 1948), he has now published a round dozen of novels, his position in our fiction, and even his future, remain, a dozen years after *The Grapes of Wrath,* quite undefined and hypothetical.

John Steinbeck was born in Salinas, California, on February 27, 1902. His father was treasurer of Monterey County; his mother had been a schoolteacher. The elder Steinbeck was of Prussian extraction, via New England; the mother's forebears hailed from northern Ireland. The son attended Stanford University, where he interested himself in marine biology but did not take a degree. He has been a ranch-hand and a chemist in a sugar-beet factory; he has worked in a fish-hatchery and as caretaker of an estate on Lake Tahoe. When Madison Square Garden was rebuilt he was one of the hod-carriers. He once lost a newspaper job in New York because he would not confine himself to factual reporting.

He has known want; at one time he and his wife lived on twenty-five dollars a month, subsisting largely on the fish they caught in Monterey Bay. All his early books sold very badly. The turn in his fortunes came when Ben Abramson, the Chicago bookseller, interested Pascal Covici in his work. Covici brought out *Tortilla Flat* (1935) after nine publishers had turned it down.

According to Steinbeck's pioneer biographer, Harry T. Moore, the writers Steinbeck most admires are Dostoevsky, Tolstoy, Hardy, Milton, George Eliot, and Willa Cather. There are others whom he once admired but has since repudiated, among them Cabell, whose influence can be seen in his first novel, *Cup of Gold* (1929). "The bulk of Steinbeck's reading among current books," says Mr. Moore, "is scientific, economic and sociological."

Of the novels Mr. Steinbeck has published since *The Grapes of Wrath* suddenly catapulted him toward the leadership of American fiction, only *Cannery Row* (1945) seems to have pleased many readers, and *Cannery Row* is merely a reworking of the kind of material he had used earlier in his career in *The Pastures of Heaven* (1932) and *Tortilla Flat. The Moon Is Down* (1942), which is based upon the Nazi invasion of Norway but does not actually portray it, was widely condemned, though often for the wrong reasons, and when *The Wayward Bus* came along in 1947 the reviewers were unable to make up their minds about whether it was to be taken literally or allegorically, or about anything else, for that matter, except that it was a *Grand Hotel* kind of hotel, definitely oversexed. *Burning Bright* (1950), which, like *Of Mice and Men* and *The Moon Is Down,* was conceived as a play, but which, unlike them, failed on Broadway, scrapped all codes, accepting murder as standing on the same innocent plane as adultery.

This is a somewhat dismaying circumstance, especially when one recalls Steinbeck's expressed hope, in his early days, for a steadily expectant audience of about 20,000 readers, with never a best-seller. "A single best-seller can ruin a writer forever." But it is less ominous than it might be when we remember that Steinbeck has never been a predictable or classifiable writer.

His relation to naturalism, for example, is difficult to define. *The Grapes of Wrath* has been widely considered a naturalistic novel, yet the last scene, where Rose of Sharon gives her breast to a starving man (though indebted to Maupassant), is sheer symbolism, and Barker Fairley is quite right in calling attention to the "rhythmical" and "repetitive" elements in the novel as a whole, its affinities "with poetry and folk-lore and the oral literature of the Continent, with popular tales, workers' songs, and even the spirituals." Symbolism was nothing new to Steinbeck's novels. The moon and the valley, both often with a sexual signification, appear in his books again and again, and special symbols enter with special themes. When Tom Joad's captured tortoise is set free, it starts off toward the Southwest again because that is the way life is moving. Steinbeck uses color symbolism also, and he is evidently as sensitive to music as was Elizabeth Madox Roberts, for Moore cites Steinbeck's own authority for his statement that *Cup of Gold* was worked out after the pattern of Dvořák's *Symphony from the New World*. Moore credits Steinbeck, too, with the capacity for a kind of Blakian—or Celtic—"sensitiveness," and we are not surprised when the dogs of *Tortilla Flat* are vouchsafed a manifestation of Saint Francis of Assisi. *In Dubious Battle* (1936) is a novel about a Communist-led strike, but it greatly disappointed Communists by its failure to hew to the party-line. "You can only build a violent thing with violence." In *The Grapes of Wrath* the hope of amelioration is centered in governmental paternalism of the New Deal variety. Frederic I. Carpenter has shown that the preacher Casy, in this novel, combines Emersonian transcendentalism with Whitman's "earthy democracy" and the "pragmatic instrumentalism" of William James and John Dewey. "Jim Casy translates American philosophy into words of one syllable, and the Joads translate it into action."[43]

These things sometimes go unrecognized because they are combined with other elements which readers are not accustomed to encounter in this connection. There has, for example, been much head-shaking over the fact that the author of *The Grapes of Wrath* should have begun his career, in *Cup of Gold,* by glorifying the ruthless individualism of the pirate Henry Morgan. Now there are many differences between *Cup of Gold* and Steinbeck's later work. But *Cup of Gold* does not glorify the ruthless individualism of Henry Morgan. On the contrary, it shows very clearly that that kind of ruthless individualism does not work.[44]

Strange combinations—and contradictions—nevertheless remain, and the four-letter words which shocked so many readers of *The Grapes of Wrath,* suggest only the least important of them. Casy says

[43] "The Philosophical Joads," *CE,* II (1941), 315-325. Woodburn Ross grapples with some of the problems involved in Steinbeck's thinking and feeling in "JS: Earth and Stars," *U. of Missouri Studies,* XXI (1946), 177-191—which treats Steinbeck's basic ideas and mental processes—and in "JS: Naturalism's Priest," *CE,* X (1949), 432-438—which is concerned with his religious feeling. Burton Rascoe comments on Steinbeck's belief in psychic forces, his conviction of the importance of "humility, benevolence and friendliness," etc. in *EJ,* Coll. ed., XXVII (1938), 205-216.

[44] See Percy H. Boynton, *America in Contemporary Fiction,* pp. 242-243, 257; F. I. Carpenter, "JS, American Dreamer," *Southwest Review,* XXVI (1941), 454-467.

that these words "ain't bad" to him any more. They are simply words that people use, without meaning any harm by them. So far as Casy's milieu and Steinbeck's novel are concerned, this is quite correct, though for many of the readers of 1939 the shock was still so great as in many cases to short-circuit communication. But there are other, more serious problems.

There is the obvious D. H. Lawrence-ism of *To a God Unknown* (1933), for example, whose hero kills himself as a living sacrifice to bring rain, and there is the glorification of immorality and irresponsibility (so long as they are coupled with kindliness of spirit), in *The Pastures of Heaven, Tortilla Flat,* and *Cannery Row*.[45] *Of Mice and Men* is unsatisfactory because it tries to squeeze tragedy out of characters who lack tragic stature and in Lennie's case even human significance. The dream of the little piece of land is as sentimental as anything on a colored calendar; even George admits that, if once he were delivered from the burden one cannot believe he would ever have assumed, he would only take his fifty "bucks" to the "cat house." Here the sweet simplicities of the Friendship Village school turn to a glorification of idiocy, and James T. Farrell is quite just when he declares that *Of Mice and Men* has "all the mannerism and none of the substance of genuine realistic writing."

Mr. Steinbeck's feeling that in this world "success" is generally associated with hardness and cruelty is not hard to understand nor difficult to accept, and it is very easy to pass on from that perception to a glorification of the vices of the unsuccessful along with their gentleness. There is more than this to say, however. If Steinbeck is anything, he is kind, yet there is an element of sadism in his work, and violence and degradation often seem to fascinate him for their own sake. Edmund Wilson has observed that he does not humanize his animals in the manner of Kipling and other writers; rather he shows a tendency to drop human beings to the animal level. Some writers attribute his preoccupation with such things to his training in biology. He seems to try to apply an optimistic theory of naturalistic determinism to all human affairs—a sort of notion that every-

---

[45] In *Tortilla Flat* this is modified to a certain extent by the "literary" element in the book, which has obviously been designed as a humorous variation on the theme of the *Morte d'Arthur*.

thing works for the best, however wasteful the process may seem. Along this general line, Woodburn Ross, who stresses Steinbeck's affinities with Hume, Rousseau, and especially Comte, writes:

. . . he is a man of two worlds. As a believer in the inductive, scientific method he must record what he sees, he must write realistically. But as a man of powerful affections and intuitions he must reflect irrational attitudes which are justifiable only in terms of the desires of the human spirit. He is therefore at the same time brutal and tender, rational and irrational, concrete and abstract.

The nonfiction *Sea of Cortez* (1941) poses a special problem here, for it was written in collaboration with the scientist Edward F. Ricketts, and it is difficult to tell to what extent the ideas expressed in it should be attributed to Steinbeck himself, or whether, if it is Steinbeck's own philosophy that is here set forth, we are to take the book as indicating a permanent shift or attitude or merely as the expression of a mood.[46] *Sea of Cortez,* at any rate, represents a turning-away from all social problems—it was written just before America's entry into World War II—to seek absorption in a piece of scientific research which is pursued for its own interest and without raising any questions about the commonweal. Indeed, the idea that scientific research involves any social obligations seems to be categorically denied. At the same time the validity of "teleological thinking" is denied also, but upon the not precisely amoral ground that it tends to make "great tenderness" and "all-embracingness" more difficult to achieve. The thing to do is to understand the situation. Once that has been accomplished, apologies are unnecessary. The "why" of the matter is no longer important. It just "is."

Upon this basis one critic has suggested that the war may have destroyed the faith expressed in *The Grapes of Wrath* and left Steinbeck where Hemingway was grounded after World War I. If this is true, the resultant disillusionment is probably not unconnected with the author's disappointing record during the postwar years. But the evidence is not all in, and it would be unwise to

[46] It may be that Steinbeck's own *The Log from the Sea of Cortez,* announced for 1952 publication, but not yet available as this chapter is written, may answer this question.

dogmatize. There are passages in *The Grapes of Wrath* itself that are not far from *Sea of Cortez.* That there are some elements which make for confusion in Steinbeck's thinking seems to be clear enough, and it is not unreasonable to suggest that his art might benefit if he should ever succeed in getting them straightened out. Personally I gravely doubt that if he were to slough off his mysticism, as some of his critics advise him, it would help him to solve his problems, but he may very well need to be rescued from certain confusing elements of primitivism and irrationality. Today he stands in the position of many men who, unable to accept inherited authority or to rest content amid the aridities of futilitarianism, give the impression of perpetually starting to build upon fresh foundations.

As of today, again, *The Grapes of Wrath* remains his most important novel, a book which none of its readers will ever forget. It has many faults: its characters, sometimes described formally, like studies in still life, range all the way from blanks, through symbols and grotesques, to solid reality; it has only a loose sort of unity, with no real climax or termination. Sometimes, too, Steinbeck analyzes where he ought to portray. The intercalary chapters, directly influenced by Pare Lorentz's documentary films, *The River* and *The Plow That Broke the Plains,* and of his radio drama, *Ecce Homo,* enlarge the dispossession of the Joads by relating it to the experiences of thousands of their compatriots. The very violence of the reactions awakened by the book shows that, with all its faults, it had life in it. At the very lowest reckoning, it will be a permanent part of this generation's remembrance of a dark hour in American history, an hour whose bitterness is still an important part of our inheritance.

CHAPTER XXIII

A NOTE ON THE FICTION OF THE 'FORTIES AND AFTER

We have relished our lostness with peculiar vanity, as though no young folk before had ever been so magnificently abandoned; we have pitied ourselves for being simply men on earth. Cause or no cause, we have made more fuss about living than any folk ever known.

The Garretson Chronicle

No detailed account of the novels of the 1940's can be given here. A good many of the books published during this decade by writers previously established have already been considered, and few of the new writers have yet got far enough in their careers to make anything like a considered approach to the evaluation of their product possible. We have become accustomed to living through three or four crises per annum—most of which manage to arrive just before an election—and we are all painfully familiar with numerous persons who are fully persuaded that the world was not created, either for good or for evil, until they were ready to come into it. Yet in spite of these persuasions—and the circumstances which have occasioned them—the past still refuses to die and men continue to enjoy many of the books which their fathers enjoyed and to try to produce others like them. To cite here but one example, one may note that the vogue of the monolithic historical novel, established by the success of *Gone With the Wind* and *Anthony Adverse,* continued throughout the decade and still continues. I will mention here but three examples: *House Divided* (Houghton Mifflin, 1947), by Ben Ames Williams (b. 1889); *Remembrance Rock* (Harcourt, Brace, 1948), by Carl Sandburg (b. 1878); and the *Raintree County* (Houghton Mifflin, 1947), of the ill-starred Ross Lockridge, Jr. (1914-1948).

Of these the last is by far the most important. Ben Ames Williams has, of course, long since established himself as a novelist, both in the historical and the contemporary field, and it is no disrespect to him to say that his *House Divided* differentiates itself from other good Civil War novels primarily by the fact that it runs to more than 1,500 pages. A picture of a Southern family which discovered in the course of the conflict its kinship to Lincoln, and a study of the influence of that discovery upon the lives of its members, the book is absorbing in its narrative, competent in its characterizations, and sound in its sense of values. *Remembrance Rock*, the first and presumably the only novel of a distinguished poet and historian, has more literary quality, but though it contains much absorbing fiction, its preeminent virtues are those of poetic insight and interpretation. To read a thousand pages of fiction is a wearing task, even when a continuous story is told which surges to a dramatic climax, but the task becomes much greater when one is asked to follow four un- connected stories—a Puritan story, a Revolutionary story, a Civil War story, and a World War II story—each with its scores of char- acters to be kept in mind. The pattern of the book is the pattern of the American dream, and its theme seems to be the necessity of preserving a sense of continuity and of holding firmly to a great past if we would solve the problems which now confront us. What attitude he wished us to take up toward them Sandburg did not say. In *Raintree County*, on the other hand, poetic insight was married to all the gifts of the born novelist. Professor Tindall has hailed this book as having given us the subtleties that we have hitherto been obliged to seek in marginal novelists like Joyce and Virginia Woolf in a full-bodied, absorbing narrative in the great tradition.[1] It does that but it does more than that; it comes as close as any novel has ever come to getting the essential American experience within the covers of a book, and it achieves this feat by transcending the his- torical level and interpreting that experience also upon the level of myth. Even so confirmed an Easterner as Henry Seidel Canby felt, upon completing it, that he understood, at last, what was meant by the saying that the Middle West is the heart of America. It is true

---

[1] W. Y. Tindall, "Many-Leveled Fiction: Virginia Woolf to Ross Lockridge," *CE*, X (1948), 65-71.

that *Raintree County* has its crudenesses, but these are a part of its endearing youth, and if they were lacking it would be farther away in spirit from the life which it interprets. The action takes place in rural Indiana between 6 A.M. and midnight on July 4, 1892, but it is broken into by numerous flash backs which cover the years from 1844 on down. The teeming sense of life which *Raintree County* communicates caused its author to be compared to Thomas Wolfe, but Lockridge attained a control over his materials which Wolfe never knew. Touch this book, as the old saying goes, and you touch a man, for the life of a man informs it, and it may well have been the strain of tearing it out of himself, under peculiarly difficult conditions, that cost Ross Lockridge his life. We shall never know what American fiction lost by his tragic death.

I remarked a moment ago that few of the new writers of the 1940's were yet ripe for evaluation. The most serious considered critical attempt that has been made along this line is John W. Aldridge's *After the Lost Generation* (McGraw-Hill, 1951), a book which, despite all its high and mighty flourishes and almost offensive surety, reveals both critical acumen and a sound sense of values. Yet it is hardly an exaggeration to say that *After the Lost Generation* is almost as much a study in psychiatry as a study in literature. For some strange reason, Mr. Aldridge seems to be primarily interested in the writers who embody and express the moral bankruptcy which is our heritage from two world wars and the surpassing folly that has succeeded. He has excluded, he tells us, Robert Penn Warren, James Gould Cozzens, Tom Lea, Nelson Algren, Walter Van Tilburg Clark, and Lionel Trilling because they were too old to have been crucially affected by the ordeal of his own generation, and he has excluded Jean Stafford, Mary McCarthy, Shirley Jackson, Howard Nemerov, Eudora Welty, Carson McCullers, and a dozen others because he did not find their work particularly relevant to his theme. The writers to whom he has devoted himself (following his preliminary consideration of Hemingway, Fitzgerald, and Dos Passos, whom he regards as the lost generation writers most influential in the 1940's) are Alfred Hayes, b. 1911,[2] Vance Bourjaily

---

[2] Alfred Hayes (Howell, Soskin): *All Thy Conquests* (1946); *Shadow of Heaven* (1947); *The Girl on the Via Flaminia* (1949).

(b. 1922),[3] Norman Mailer (b. 1923),[4] John Horne Burns (b. 1916),[5] Irwin Shaw (b. 1913),[6] Merle Miller (b. 1919),[7] Gore Vidal (b. 1925),[8] Paul Bowles (b. 1911),[9] Truman Capote (b. 1925),[10] and Frederick Buechner (b. 1926).[11] These persons have not been selected primarily as "war writers," in the sense that they have written about the war, though many of them have done that, but rather as manifestations of the contemporary collapse of values. "If . . . [the writer] remains true to his insight, he cannot avoid describing the situations of his time as they predominantly are, that is, as meaningless, valueless, and futile." Bourjaily, for example, does not deal with battle; instead, he brings us a fuller and blacker picture of the degradation of youth which war brings about than any book that came out of World War I. Oddly enough, it does not seem to have occurred to Mr. Aldridge that if values were really gone, it would not be possible for him to find all these writers, despite their outstanding talents, essentially failures.

As for the "war novels," in the narrower sense of the term, their characteristic note, as Mr. Aldridge sees it, is "an elaborate documentation of wartime misery, ranging from the suffering of the common soldier under the fascist hierarchy of the American Army to the suffering of civilians in countries dominated by a corrupt American occupation force." They "stress the cruel disparity between our ideals and our practice, the ideals which won us the war and the practices which lost us the peace." Norman Mailer's *The Naked and the Dead,* which is generally regarded in the trade as the book

[3] Vance Bourjaily: *The End of My Life* (S, 1947).

[4] Norman Mailer (R): *The Naked and the Dead* (1948); *Barbary Shore* (1951).

[5] John Horne Burns (H): *The Gallery* (1947); *Lucifer with a Book* (1949).

[6] Irwin Shaw: *The Young Lions* (RH, 1948). Cf. Bergen Evans, *CE,* XIII (1951), 71-77.

[7] Merle Miller: *Island 49* (Crowell, 1945); *That Winter* (Sloane, 1948); *The Sure Thing* (Sloane, 1949).

[8] Gore Vidal (Du): *Williwaw* (1946); *In a Yellow Wood* (1947); *The City and the Pillar* (1948); *The Season of Comfort* (1949); *A Search for the King* (1950); *Dark Green, Bright Red* (1950).

[9] Paul Bowles: *The Sheltering Sky* (ND, 1949); a new novel, *Let It Come Down,* is announced by RH for publication early in 1952.

[10] Truman Capote: *Other Voices, Other Rooms* (RH, 1948).

[11] Frederick Buechner: *A Long Day's Dying* (K, 1950).

which broke down the postwar buying public's resistance to war novels, was the first fiction to attempt a comprehensive picture of the evil of war "within a philosophical framework." As a picture it succeeded, but Mailer was unable to make his protest against war dramatically effective because it was clear that the lives of his characters had already been devoid of values even in peacetime. In *The Gallery,* John Horne Burns got values into his essay-sections ("Promenades") while his fiction ("Portraits") remained futilitarian. But *The Young Lions,* by Irwin Shaw, and *This Winter,* by Merle Miller, are even worse because here a deliberate warping of material has taken place. Shaw distorts in obedience to a "polemical purpose," and Miller merely disregards logic. Aldridge, indeed, regards *This Winter* as a foolish book about slick and hollow people and Miller himself as a master journalist without convictions who gives "a touch of phoniness" to everything he writes. He is almost equally severe on *The Young Lions* which he finds filled with "pointless embroidery" and unified in structure but not in meaning. Only its negative, evil character, Diestl, is entirely convincing.

Gore Vidal has written about the war and also about other themes, particularly homosexuality. Aldridge grants him sincerity and determination but finds his work vitiated by "spiritual nothingness" and "spreading aridity of soul." His "frantic productivity" itself testifies to the "urgency of his need in his search for values," and his books since *Williwaw* make up a record "of stylistic breakdown and spiritual exhaustion." Truman Capote's *Other Voices, Other Rooms* was essentially a homosexual fantasy, signalizing a retreat to a private world. It is implicational, filled with symbolism (or, as Mr. Aldridge puts it, metaphors), and elaborate juxtapositions and interrelationships. Capote has "technical skill largely divorced from insight." His work is "a concoction and not a synthesis." Paul Bowles takes his people to Africa in search of sensation and spiritual emptiness and finally sacrifices his theme to melodrama and violence. Frederick Buechner writes a novel "in strict observance of all the rules but in which the game for which the rules were devised never gets round to being played."

Now there is nothing sacrosanct about Mr. Aldridge's judgments. Even those who are prepared to grant that he is entirely right in his evaluation of the work which his young novelists have thus far produced may wish to argue, in some cases, that the talent which has appeared is sufficiently remarkable to deserve more encouragement than he appears inclined to offer. *A Long Day's Dying,* for example, is, in its way, an amazing book. At the very beginning of his career, Frederick Buechner actually knows a good many of the technical secrets that it took Henry James his lifetime to search out. It is quite true that he has so far manifested none of the spiritual insight which James needed his technical skill to express, and this is the circumstance which attaches to his achievement itself a touch of the monstrous. But it is certainly much too early in the game to rule out the possibility that he may still prove capable of growth. Capote's, on the other hand, is a dazzling, unhealthy talent, perhaps the most startling American fiction has known since the debut of Faulkner. Perhaps Capote has been influenced by Faulkner; perhaps he traces back to that side of the Gothic tradition that began with M. G. Lewis. Yet there is humanity in *Other Voices, Other Rooms,* alongside all the pyrotechnics, and an uncanny ability to create a weird world that comes alive.[12]

All this, of course, has an element of wishful thinking in it. And the mere fact that such judgments as Mr. Aldridge's can be entered by a conscientious and competent critic *who is himself a part of his time* is surely not without significance. At the very least, it testifies to a widespread sickness of soul among the youngest generation of the most talented American writers which is a frightening thing. For one cannot dismiss Aldridge's criticisms, as many persons rightly or wrongly dismissed Paul Elmer More's condemnation of *Manhattan Transfer* as "an explosion in a cesspool" on the ground that

---

[12] Second novels by Capote: *The Grass Harp* (RH, 1951) and by Buechner: *The Seasons' Difference* (K, 1952) were published while this book was going through the press. *The Seasons' Difference* seems to indicate increasing preoccupation with the religious theme on Mr. Buechner's part, but it leaves me still unwilling to prophesy concerning his future. His use of the children in this novel is one more indication of Jamesian influence. *The Grass Harp* is, from one point of view, more encouraging, for, though it is, in a sense, even more marginal than *Other Voices,* it does show Truman Capote, for all his strangeness, capable of producing minor art of great charm and even, at times, of a curiously radiant quality. Certainly this book will attract many whom *Other Voices* repelled.

it merely represented the pontifical condemnation of an older generation which either could not or would not understand.[13]

Mr. Aldridge's list of war novels is not, of course, complete.[14] He says nothing, for example, of the *Mr. Roberts* (Houghton Mifflin, 1946) of Thomas Heggen (1919-1949) or of James A. Michener's (b. 1907) *Tales of the South Pacific* (Macmillan, 1947), both of which met spectacular success on the stage, the latter as the phenomenal Rodgers and Hammerstein musical hit, *South Pacific*. He says nothing of John Hersey (b. 1914). Hersey's episodic and overrated *A Bell for Adano* (1944), a story of the American occupation of Italy, appeared when many persons still believed in the war, but Hersey did not junk his idealism even when he told one of the most hideous stories in human history, the tale of the extermination of Polish Jewry in *The Wall* (1950).[15] And, of course, Aldridge came too early to consider James Jones's (b. 1921) hard-boiled story of the peacetime army in Hawaii up to Pearl Harbor, *From Here to Eternity* (Scribners, 1951), whose language has made it one of the most eagerly fought-over pieces of contemporary fiction.

I do not propose to discuss these works here, nor have I space to consider many of the writers whom Mr. Aldridge merely mentions or passes over altogether. Carson McCullers (b. 1917)[16] has learned simplicity in Hemingway's school, and though she often gives the impression of having tried to mention as many unpleasant things as possible, she can hardly be denied a deep human feeling, especially for children. In her first and most ambitious novel, *Boston Adventure* (1944), Jean Stafford (b. 1915), was only partly successful. The summer resort portion of the book, when Sonie Marburg

[13] Mr. Aldridge's agreements and disagreements with the leading reviewers may be studied by looking up the various titles mentioned in *The Book Review Digest*.

[14] See "The Novels of the Second World War," *Publishers' Weekly*, CLIV (1948), 1802-1808.

[15] Technically *The Wall* is interesting for its presentation of a story in terms of an elaborate *dossier*. The attempt to achieve verisimilitude through mock-documentation has rarely been carried to such lengths in fiction.

[16] Carson McCullers (HM): *The Heart Is a Lonely Hunter* (1940); *Reflections in a Golden Eye* (1941); *The Member of the Wedding* (1946). In 1951 all three novels were reprinted in an omnibus: *The Ballad of the Sad Café*. See Dayton Kohler, *CE*, XIII (1951), 1-8.

was a child, has a fine authenticity, but Miss Stafford's account of life on Beacon Hill is as fantastic as it is dull. Her other two, briefer novels—*The Mountain Lion* (1947) and *The Catherine Wheel* (1952)—show an uncanny understanding of the terrors of childhood and an insight into the tortured ways of the human heart unsurpassed since Katherine Mansfield. But Miss Stafford, too, seems tightly bound to the Catherine wheel of frustration.[17] Eudora Welty (b. 1909) and Shirley Jackson (b. 1919) are so far primarily short story writers; of their work as novelists there may be time to speak hereafter.

Robert Penn Warren, who was born in Kentucky in 1905, and who has had a long career as college professor and critic—he is also a poet and a writer of short stories—can hardly be called a young writer, but he did not publish his first novel, *Night Rider,* until 1939, and it was not until the smashing success of his third, *All the King's Men,* in 1946—the second was *At Heaven's Gate* (1943)—that he became widely known to the general public. As I have already remarked elsewhere, *All the King's Men* was obviously suggested by the career of Huey Long. It was followed, four years later, by *World Enough and Time,* Mr. Warren's reworking of the Kentucky Tragedy.

Mr. Warren is considered by some critics the most gifted American novelist of recent emergence. At his best he is capable of powerful conceptions and a genuine splendor of utterance. And though he is often quite unnecessarily coarse, he is no futilitarian. It is unfortunate that his spectacular virtues should be balanced by equally spectacular defects.

He might, indeed, be a better novelist if he were less of a poet and less of a thinker. He has a passion for superimposing philosophical significance upon sociological themes in such a fashion that the sociology comes to seem distorted and the philosophizing forced. In itself, his ambition to make his novels a significant interpretation of life whose meanings shall involve far more than the lives of the people he describes in them is perfectly legitimate. But it does not always lead him in the direction of a sound narrative technique.

World Enough and Time, which is the most elaborately wrought

[17] Jean Stafford's books are published by HB.

of Mr. Warren's novels, is probably the most thoughtful and the most intellectual among the many studies of the Kentucky Tragedy that have been made. It is, too, a solid, convincing picture of old Kentucky life. More than one critic has been reminded by it of Melville's *Pierre*. But this is something of a left-handed compliment, for while *Pierre* is unmistakably a work of genius, nobody would call it a completely successful novel.

Warren psychologizes the old tale of passion and revenge and oversubtilizes the motives of the actors to such an extent that the fable itself loses the power to move us as it does in the less ambitious versions by Simms and Joseph Shearing. The villain seems frankly incredible through most of the narrative; only toward the end do we learn that he did not do the unbelievable thing which we have until now been asked to credit provisionally. Neither does the hero become more attractive because he does not act to avenge his wife until after he has been tricked into action by the unbelievable Wilkie.

Warren shows his tendency toward anticlimax when he fails to end the Kentucky Tragedy at the gallows but instead carries the principals off for a series of wild adventures among the Indians. To a lesser extent, this same failure, or unwillingness, to limit his canvas, appears also in *All the King's Men*. It is significant that Jack Burden should admit to himself that "I had forgotten that the story of Judge Irwin, which seemed so complete in itself, was only a chapter in the longer story of the Boss. . . ." The story of Cass Mastern is not even that, yet in some ways it is the most compelling thing in the book. "For Judge Irwin and Cass Mastern do not resemble each other very closely." Perhaps all the material included has a philosophical unity, but it can hardly be said to be unified in terms of fiction. "This has been the story of Willie Stark, but it is my story too." So it is, but there are times when it seems neither.

Another writer with an academic background is Gerald Warner Brace (b. 1901), a professor in Boston University.[18] The completely

---

[18] Brace's great-grandfather, John Pierce Brace (1795-1872), editor of the *Hartford Courant,* and a teacher, at Litchfield, Connecticut, of Harriet Beecher Stowe, who always remembered him affectionately, wrote, among other things, *Tales of the Devils* (1847), an attack upon Bulwer-Lytton in the form of a "sequel" to *Ernest Maltravers,* and *The Fawn of the Pale Faces* (Appleton, 1853), a Cooper-like romance of Indian times, round about Hartford. For

unforced and unexpected success of *The Garretson Chronicle* (1947), which became a best-seller without anybody having expected it or planned for it, proved that it is possible for a fine book of highly individual quality to make its own way even in hectic days. Mr. Brace had begun in 1936 with *The Islands; The Garretson Chronicle* was Opus #4. All his books had been well reviewed, but the box office returns on the first three had not been sensational.

Bernard DeVoto has said that every novelist has but one novel to write and that he writes it over and over. This is not quite true in Brace's case, for he has given himself a holiday from his novel in two out of his five books thus far—*The Wayward Pilgrims* (1938) and *A Summer's Tale* (1949)—both of which partake in a measure, the second more than the first,[19] of the fantasia. Brace's essential story is one which he shares with Elsie Singmaster and many other novelists—the tale of the sensitive youngster who is making his terms with life. From another point of view one might say that the story itself does not matter very much: it is merely a vehicle for conveying the meaning of his New England inheritance. *The Garretson Chronicle,* for example, which, despite the author's own tendency to prefer *Light on a Mountain* (1941),[20] seems to me incomparably Brace's richest book and the one in which his essential meaning is most clearly expressed, has not been idly named. Its structure is very loose and rambling—for a time we even lose the boy who is supposed to be telling the story—and its theme is

memorabilia of his career, see Emily N. Vanderpoel, *More Chronicles of a Pioneer School,* etc. (N. Y., Cadmus Book Shop, 1927). His son, Charles Loring Brace, founded and directed the New York Children's Aid Society, where Horatio Alger lived for a time and whence he derived much of his material.

[19] In *A Summer's Tale,* which takes place on an imaginary island off the coast of Maine, we have the ultimate expression of Brace's worship of islands and also the best extant example of what a "summer novel" has come to be like in a thoughtful and troubled age. *A Summer's Tale* is utopia, comic opera, a tale of deering-do, and a local color piece. It embraces a burlesque on fifth columnists, journalists, and the American navy, and it is a highly romantic love story with echoes of the great verses of Spenser and Sir Thomas Wyatt sounding through its cadenced prose.

[20] Brace's (at this writing, 1952) next novel, *The Spire,* will be, in a sense, a sequel to *Light on a Mountain,* recording further adventures of Henry Gaunt and his sister Sylvia.

nothing more than a feeling about life and a way of life. In so far as the great tradition of New England culture has been able to survive in our world, you will find it in these books, which are the work of a man who has no being apart from it but who is too honest to blink any of the difficulties involved in the business of utilizing his inheritance.

For Brace, the New England tradition is not Beacon Street and the Harvard Yard primarily (though it embraces both) but the back country in Vermont and New Hampshire and the islands off the coast of Maine. He is like Willa Cather and like Edith Wharton (who is rarely given credit for so much homeliness), in his feeling that craftsmanship is quite as important as books and the work of the hands as distinguished a product of civilization as the product of the brain. Brace himself might well have written more novels if he had not built so many boats. The ideal is harmony between hand and brain, but in practice conflict is often involved, a conflict frequently connected, in Brace's pages, with the welling up of some primitive darkness within the personality itself. Of adolescence the Garretson chronicler writes: "For some, it may pass easily; it may even be a straight, clear passage like any other time of life; but for me it turned into a long confusion, partly happy enough, and partly dark and shameful." In Morton Gaunt, of *Light on a Mountain,* the darkness long survives adolescence, and wins at last, though the author has fortunately not followed the story through to its black denouement. Edgar Thurlow's fight, in *The Islands,* is waged mainly upon the vocational level. He "learned to read and write, though he grudged it; but the rest of his learning came from pipewrenches and ax handles, from watching his father measure honestly to the sixteenth inch." In the end he turns his back upon Beacon Street and the wholly understanding spinster who has offered him the opportunity to become a Harvard-trained engineer and goes back to Maine.[21] Farthest from him spiritually is Henry Gaunt, the "good" hero of *Light on a Mountain,* for in Henry the intellectual interest is so overwhelming that the conflict between the two sides of life

[21] It is interesting to compare Brace's account of this matter with Jean Stafford's queer impression of a somewhat similar circumstance in *Boston Adventure.*

can hardly be said to exist; Ralph Garretson achieves a balance which is probably closer to Brace's ideal.

In the last analysis, however, the Brace world is neither a region nor a craftsman's paradise; it is a world of human relationships. Henry Gaunt is a part of his country; he knows "that his trip to the peak and down by the Sargent place was actually a search for some sort of truth to base a life on." But that living truth is no mere emanation of the landscape. "My boy," cries Henry's favorite teacher, Professor McCann, "if you don't like people you're doomed. That's straight from the oracle—if you don't like people you might as well give up right now; sure as fate you'll end in despair and madness." It is the lack of this quality in him that defeats Randall Garretson, despite many excellent gifts: "His intention was forever kindly, rational, peaceable, but only somewhere touched with inhumanity."

Benedict Thielen, a Princeton man, born in New Jersey in 1902, who divides his time between Key West and Martha's Vineyard, has yet to write his *Garretson Chronicle,* which, being interpreted, means that the reading public has not yet, in any effective way, discovered him. There is no excuse for the neglect which Thielen has met with from public and critics alike; it is not a happy augury for American fiction that so fine and individual a writer can reach the half-century mark still virtually unrecognized. Thielen's short stories (necessarily excluded from consideration here), have been welcomed by periodicals as unlike each other as *The Yale Review* and *The New Yorker* but even they remain largely uncollected.[22] And his four novels (issued through three different publishers), have been almost completely disregarded; in the Boston area, where this chronicle was completed, there is no work of his authorship listed in the card catalogue at the Public Library, the Athenaeum, nor even the Harvard Library!

If Thielen were a difficult writer or one whose work involved an unusual assault upon the moral prejudices or sensibilities of his

---

[22] Some of Thielen's short stories have been printed in *Dinosaur Tracks and Other Stories,* published in London by Secker and Warburg in 1937. *Stevie* (Dial Press, 1941) is something of a cross between the short story and the novel.

readers, this situation might be more easily explicable. He is mildly experimental, mildly realistic, and apparently somewhat skeptical and relativistic. But these tendencies, in far more extreme forms, have not prevented widespread recognition for other writers.

His characteristic method as a novelist is to study the events of a single happening or event upon various lives or to explore the experience of various individuals involved in a particular situation. In his first novel, *Deep Streets* (Bobbs-Merrill, 1932), almost all the characters have their fate determined by the gift of a five-dollar bill, made unpremeditatedly by Dr. Bodley, a somewhat fatuous retired professor of literature, to his servant-girl, Katy Schultz, on the morning of her nineteenth birthday. Crime, death, disfigurement, economic ruin, and moral corruption are all brought to people most of whom never heard of Dr. Bodley, and all without greatly straining the probabilities; the novel is a rather impressive dramatizing of Mark Twain's thesis in *What Is Man?*, though it must be admitted that Thielen has loaded the dice pretty heavily in presenting accident consistently as a force for evil, never for good.

There followed a simple, straightforward narrative called *Women in the Sun* (1933). This story is told from the point of view of a lawyer who tries to escape temporarily from the shoddy complexities of modern life by hiring himself out for the season to an Italian vineyardist, and who ironically finds himself promptly involved in an emotional imbroglio involving the two daughters of the family and the worthless young loafer whom the younger girl has married. The religiosity of the older daughter unfortunately turns out to have been merely a surrogate for unavailable love, and the results of her exposure to the lawyer's skepticism and the husband's lust are not happy. The wife's pregnancy and the teeming life of the vineyard contribute notably to the atmosphere in which this tale of civilized doubt and natural passion unfolds itself.

Both Thielen's best novels were published in the 1940's. In *The Lost Men* (Appleton-Century-Crofts, 1946), members of the bonus army that was driven out of Washington in 1932, are caught in the Florida hurricane on Labor Day, 1935. In *Friday at Noon* (Holt, 1947), the household goods of a family of five are auctioned off after the mother's death. As each article goes under the hammer, we get flash backs into the experience of the various members of the family and explore their several memories as these cluster about the articles in question.

In its most characteristic aspects, Thielen's work bears its obvious resemblances to that of Henry James and Virginia Woolf, by both of whom he has certainly been directly or indirectly influenced. But if he shows influence, he is not an imitator. Mrs. Woolf might indeed have found herself at home with the materials of *Friday at Noon,* but neither she nor James could possibly have attempted *The Lost Men,* nor would either have thought of writing a psychological novel which culminated in a catastrophe of nature that reminded reviewers of Conrad and George Stewart. It is true that neither of these novels is a full-blooded cumulative narrative; neither "arrives" at a great climax in the conventional dramatic sense of the term climax; it is true also that the plan of *Friday at Noon* has required the materials of the novel to submit to a certain measure of "arrangement." Nor does *Women in the Sun* itself move on to the violent ending which memories of *Cavalleria Rusticana* and other peasant tragedies might have led the reader to expect. The pattern of human experience has been altered; human beings have learned something new about themselves; and life moves on. And in the process they, and the reader himself, have explored the situation in a way that deserves to be called illuminating:

> He felt the moment. He saw himself again deep sunk in it. The fullness of this rich and throbbing moment lapped him round. Life closed over him and he was deep again in the center of its warm sweet core. He saw the moment still, but now it was cold. Now it was over. It was another man who had known it, not he.[23]

Forrest Rosaire (b. 1902), who studied under Robert Herrick at the University of Chicago, and who now lives in California, is less given to experimentation. Mr. Rosaire has so far brought out but two novels, both published by Knopf. *East of Midnight* (1945), whose exquisite title comes from an old fairy tale, is somewhat heavily psychiatric, though it contains (on pp. 357-359) a paean in praise of love which it is simple justice to call a modern scripture

---

[23] From: *The Lost Men,* copyright, 1946, by Benedict Thielen. Reprinted by permission of the publishers, Appleton-Century-Crofts, Inc

worthy of comparison with Saint Paul's. *The Uneasy Years* (1950) is a far more interesting story of family life on Chicago's Northwest side, and it is informed by the same touching compassion as the earlier book. This compassion is directed, first, toward the father, who is one of those unfortunate people who fail to provide decently for their families not through any lack of good-will but simply because they are possessed by an unquenchable thirst for creation (in this case, painting) without a shred of artistic ability. But in the family crisis brought to a head by Mrs. Conmee's inheritance it is that woman of bronze who is really tested and who comes closest to moral failure, and it is the husband whose love for his family is at last shown in the most self-forgetful way. Only the unconquerable devotion of their daughter Jean to both her parents prevents a catastrophe. Welcome relief in a very serious novel is supplied by the younger brother's love affair, a delightful business reminiscent of Tarkington, and all the more welcome because it becomes an integral part of a highly developed but always convincing plot.

Such writers as these and others (some of whom are considered in the Appendix) may perhaps help to remind us that the apostles of degradation and moral nihilism do not yet have things quite their own way in the American novel. A knowledge of history is always a good antidote to despair, and unwholesome tendencies in American fiction are nothing new. In the first chapter of this volume it was pointed out that the most frequently recurring themes in the books produced by the first generation of American novelists were incest, seduction, and suicide. Yet the novel—and the nation— were then at the beginning, not the end, of their development. After *Charlotte Temple* and *The Power of Sympathy* came Cooper and Hawthorne and Melville and Mark Twain and Howells and Henry James and many another writer whose works have added glory to American life.

Critics of the novel do not always show good judgment in deciding whom to discuss and whom to pass over in silence. Critics and reviewers are busy people, and there are many more books being published than anybody has time to read. The very outrageousness of the writers who devote themselves to shameless things often attracts to them a larger amount of attention than they would otherwise have commanded, a fact of which they themselves may well be presumed to be cannily aware. But the critic can hardly avoid his share of responsibility for the misplacement of emphasis which results.

The plain truth of the matter is that many reviewers and many reviewing media are nowadays quite indifferent to literature as an art. The novels to which they devote their attention are generally those who reflect "tendencies" in American life. And since they have a nose for news, the more extreme the "tendency," the better the chance that the novel in which it is expressed may be widely noticed.

In the long run, however, the public chooses its own books, and they are not always the books that are most chattered over at cocktail parties and literary teas. I do not imagine that *The Yearling* (1938), by Marjorie Kinnan Rawlings (b. 1896),[24] ever cut much of a figure at the cocktail parties, but no novel of our time has been more deeply loved.

"When the literary class betray a destitution of faith," wrote Emerson, in "New England Reformers," "it is not strange that society should be disheartened and sensualized by unbelief. What remedy? Life must be lived on a higher plane."

The American novelist has come into possession of a rich heritage, and he will not be content to play ducks and drakes with it forever. Even in this atomic age there are still Americans who believe with one of the best novelists of our recent past that "the indestructible will of the world . . . [is] toward life."

[24] Mrs. Rawlings is published by Scribners. All her books deal with the Florida backwoods. Among other works, she has written two novels besides *The Yearling: South Moon Under* (1933) and *Golden Apples* (1935).

NOTES ON NOVELISTS NOT CONSIDERED IN THE TEXT

> But say it is my humour. Is it answer'd?
> *The Merchant of Venice*

This Appendix supplements the foregoing chapters by attempting brief accounts (often more informational than critical), of the work of a number of writers whom space considerations obviated the possibility of including in the text. I am well aware that some of these deserve far more extended consideration than I have been able to give them; some of the others are "popular" writers, often excluded from literary history altogether, whose activities must, it seems to me, be taken into consideration by anyone who would achieve an understanding of the American literary scene.

But what of the many writers who are not mentioned at all, either in the Appendix or in the text? About all I can say is that, among contemporaries especially, I have been able to do little more than choose representatives of various schools and tendencies. I do not flatter myself that anybody else would make just the selection that I have made. But I have not been guided merely by my own tastes and prejudices. It is true that some names are here primarily because I think they have been neglected elsewhere. But it is also true that I have omitted some writers whom I like very much and that I have included others whose work I do not enjoy at all.

This is my answer-in-advance to the queries I shall receive as to just why So-an-So was left out. But it is not an answer that can be expected to satisfy anybody. Many special cases have been carefully considered, and I cannot record the ensuing debates here. I finally decided not to include Katherine Anne Porter, for example, because she does not seem to me primarily a novelist, and I excluded Anne Douglas Sedgwick because, despite her American birth, her work belongs to English, rather than to American, literature.

The symbols following the names of many of the authors indicate the principal publishers of their works.

ALDRICH, Thomas Bailey (HM) (1836-1907), was a poet, editor of the *Atlantic,* etc., a "man of letters" who worked in varied fields. Though usually regarded as a Boston Brahmin, the last flower of the genteel tradition, he was born at Portsmouth, N. H., and always thought of himself not as "genuine Boston" but as "Boston-plated." Portsmouth is the scene of the episodic and semiautobiographical *The Story of a Bad Boy* (1869), which preceded Mark Twain's revolt against the Sunday School type of boys' book with *Tom Sawyer.* Other fictions are *Prudence Palfrey* (1874), *The Queen of Sheba* (1877), and *The Stillwater Tragedy* (1880). All are love stories with an element of mystery in them; the last-named also deals with the labor problem from an antiunion point of view. Structurally Aldrich's novels are ramshackle, but his characterizations are often as sound as his cool, polished, slightly wistful style. In beautiful prose he captured New England in that happy hour when the rigors of Puritanism were past and the horrors of the Brave New World not yet even approaching the corner. His *Life* was written by Ferris Greenslet (1908); see Alexander Cowie, "Indian Summer Novelist," *NEQ,* XV (1942), 608-621.

ASCH, Sholem. See DOUGLAS, Lloyd.

AUSTIN, Jane G. (HM) (1831-1894), published her first book as early as 1859, but her reputation rests on her four romances of the Plymouth colony. Those who wish to follow the chronological sequence of events recorded should read them in this order: *Standish of Standish* (1889), *Betty Alden* (1891), *A Nameless Nobleman* (1881), *Dr. LeBaron and His Daughters* (1890). Though Mrs. Austin was more concerned to create an admiring picture of her ancestors than to create enduring fiction, her stories are still useful to give young readers an entertaining introduction to New England history.

BARNES, Margaret Ayer. See FERBER, Edna.

BAUER, Florence Marvyne. See DOUGLAS, Lloyd.

BEACH, Rex. See RHODES, Eugene Manlove.

BIRD, Robert Montgomery (1806-1854), was a Philadelphia physician, a novelist, and a dramatist who furnished Edwin Forrest with some of his most successful plays. His two elaborate novels of the conquest of Mexico—*Calavar* (1834) and its sequel, *The Infidel* (1835)—preceded Prescott and established Bird's own authority in the field. *The Hawks of Hawk Hollow* (1835) takes place in the Delaware Water Gap at the close of the Revolution. *The Adventures of Robin Day* (1839) is a far-ranging picaresque tale of a derelict boy. *Sheppard Lee* (1836) is an entertaining story about a shiftless man who learns how to escape from his difficulties by causing his spirit to transfer itself to the vacated tenement of one newly dead. Though the supernatural part of the story is managed with skill, the real interest is in social criticism. But Bird's most important novel is *Nick of the Woods* (1837), which has become part of the American mythology. This is an excellent story of the Kentucky forest, simpler and probably more sensational than Cooper, whose charity toward the Indian Bird did not share. In his normal aspect, Nick, or the Jibbenainosay, is a peaceful Quaker, derisively named Bloody Nathan. But the slaughter of his family has released his other, fiendish self, and he gives himself secretly to dreadful vengeance upon his foes. There is a biography by Clement E. Foust, *The Life and Dramatic Works of RMB* (Knickerbocker Press, 1911); see C. B. Williams's introduction to his edition of *Nick* (ABC, 1939).

BOYLE, Kay (HB), b. 1903, is one of our leading experimental novelists. She has had wide experience in Europe and in America, in various walks of life, and has known both comfort and economic insecurity. A poet and short story writer who has been influenced by Gertrude Stein, she inspires enthusiasm in those who share her interest in language and her penchant for somewhat "advanced" themes, while more conservative readers often accuse her of waywardness and lack of discipline, of indulging in "orgies of sensibility," and of concentrating attention upon technique rather than theme. She has been much concerned with the theme of love facing disease and death: see *Plagued by the Nightingale* (1931) and *Year Before Last* (1932). *Gentlemen, I Address You Privately* (1934) involves Lesbianism; and a whole series of novels concerns the coming of the Nazi terror; these include *Primer for Combat* (1942), *Avalanche* (1944), and *1939* (1948). *Monday Night* (1938) is a horror story. See Robert van Gelder's interview with Kay Boyle, in *Writers and Writing* (S, 1946).

BROMFIELD, Louis (H), b. 1896, is one of the most prominent living American novelists. He began with the tetralogy called *Escape—The Green Bay Tree* (1924), *Possession* (1925), *Early Autumn* (1926), and *A Good Woman* (1927)—which is a social chronicle or family type of novel, involving American industrialism and its effects, particularly on the lives of the women of the family, and stressing the theme of personal freedom and the need to escape from a dominating tradition. Among his many other novels mention may be made of the following: *The Farm* (1933) is based on the records of the author's own Ohio family through a hundred years. In *The Rains Came* (1937) and *Night in Bombay* (1940) he pictures modern India. *Mrs. Parkington* (1943) contains a portrait of the energetic aged widow of a "robber baron." In *Wild Is the River* (1941) he allowed himself the luxury of writing a lush romantic novel of Civil War New Orleans; *Colorado* (1947) is a "Western." More experimental are *The Strange Case of Miss Anne Spragg* (1928), a study of influence, involving the supernormal, and *Twenty-Four Hours* (1930), which follows the guests at a dinner party through the ensuing crises in their lives. *The Wild Country* (1948) is the story of a sensitive boy's ordeal, told in retrospect. Though he has lived much in France, Mr. Bromfield's roots are in the Middle West; he has been deeply interested in political problems and in agriculture.

BROWN, Alice (HM, M) (1857-1948), was the last survivor among the women-writers who recorded the older New England. She was poet and playwright as well as novelist; like Sarah Orne Jewett and Mary E. Wilkins Freeman, with whom she is often compared, she is probably best known for her short stories: *Meadow-Grass* (1895), *Tiverton Tales* (1899), etc. But she was a much more varied and prolific novelist than either of the others. Among her many titles are *Fools of Nature* (1887), *Margaret Warrener* (1901), *The Mannerings* (1903), *Paradise* (1905), *Rose MacLeod* (1908), *The Story of Thyrza* (1909), *John Winterbourne's Family* (1910), *Robin Hood's Barn* (1913), *The Prisoner* (1916), *Bromley Neighborhood* (1917), *Old Crow* (1922), *Dear Old Templeton* (1927), *Jeremy Hamlyn* (1934), and *The Willoughbys* (1935). The first named deals with spiritualism, and the supernatural always remained a special field for Alice Brown; if such novels as *The Wind Between the Worlds* (1920) and *The Kingdom in the Sky* (1932) are not the best of their kind, they do serve as a reminder that her preoccupation with New England village life did not mean that she lacked poetry and imagination.

BUCK, Pearl S. (John Day), b. 1892, grew up in China, where her parents were missionaries. She herself became a missionary. Later she revolted against the orthodox missionary point of view. She is the foremost interpreter in fiction of Chinese life; she thinks her novels about China in Chinese, and what has been called their Biblical style is really a Chinese style. Sometimes she shocks Western readers by describing Chinese customs from the Chinese point of view, not feeling it necessary to violate the integrity of her work by breaking in upon it to announce that she personally does not approve of what is taking place. Yet she inclines to think that she was handicapped by not being allowed to grow up among her own people. She never wanted to write about the Chinese as such; she wanted to write about people; the people she knew best just happened to be Chinese. Her fame was established by the trilogy, *The House of Earth*, which comprises *The Good Earth* (1931), *Sons* (1932), and *A House Divided* (1935)—a work more epic than dramatic in its development. The unnamed heroine of *The Mother* (1934) embodies the human instinct for survival. In *The Patriot* (1939) and in *Dragon Seed* (1941) and its sequel, *The Promise* (1943), Mrs. Buck dramatized the tragic conflicts of contemporary Chinese history. Other novels involving Chinese themes and characters are *East Wind: West Wind* (1930); *Pavilion of Women* (1946); and *Kinfolk* (1949). Her only historical novel, *Peony* (1948), concerns the Jews in China a hundred years ago. *This Proud Heart* (1938), *Other Gods* (1940), and *Portrait of a Marriage* (1945) concern American themes. An outspoken advocate of racial equality, Pearl Buck has also written widely in the nonfiction field. See her "Advice to Unborn Novelists," *SRL*, XI (1935), 513+, and Phyllis Bentley's discussion of her work, *EJ*, XXIV (1935), 791-800.

BURNETT, Frances Hodgson (S and others) (1849-1924), was born in Manchester, but came to the United States with her financially-ruined family and settled in Tennessee at the close of the Civil War. She wrote stories from childhood; as a young girl she marketed them for bread. Primarily she has always been known as "the author of *Little Lord Fauntleroy*" (1896), one of the best modern romantic stories for young readers, which serenely holds its own in a "hard-boiled" age in spite of having been roundly condemned by all critics who are really serious about keeping in tune with the time-spirit. Mrs. Burnett used her early life in Tennessee as material for some of her fiction, but she was too cosmopolitan in her outlook to take her place with the "local color" writers. Her reputation was made with *That Lass o' Lowrie's* (1877); among the most substantial of her many novels are *Through One Administration* (1883), *A Lady of Quality* (1896), *In Connection with the DeWilloughby Claim* (1899), *The Shuttle* (1907), *T. Tembarom* (1913), and *The Head of the House of Coombe* (1913). Her interest in religion may be seen in *The Dawn of a Tomorrow* (1896) and *The Secret Garden* (1911), while her special skill with supernatural themes is shown in *In the Closed Room* (1904) and *The White People* (1917). A number of her works were successful on stage and screen. See Vivian Burnett's biography, *The Romantick Lady* (S, 1927).

CABLE, George W. (S) (1844-1925), was born of a New England mother, and himself lived in New England after 1885; here he not only continued his creative writing but wrote nonfictionally about many aspects of American life, made joint lecture tours with Mark Twain, and interested himself deeply in the Negro problem and other good "causes." But he was born in New Orleans, and his most significant work—the short stories collected in *Old Creole Days* (1879); the long novel, *The Grandissimes* (1880); and the novelette, *Madame Delphine* (1881)—

introduced American readers to the ancient civilization of that city, These books are as rich in atmosphere and as exotic in tone as any in our literature; in some aspects they seem less Anglo-Saxon than French. Men and women of many tongues and races appear in them, representatives of many human strata; fierce creatures of the swamps rub elbows with hypersensitive products of civilizations already decadent, and the demimonde clings to the fringes of respectable society. Cable wrote about the Civil War and Reconstruction in *Dr. Sevier* (1885); *John March, Southerner* (1894); *The Cavalier* (1901); and *Kincaid's Battery* (1908). *Gideon's Band* (1914) concerns old times on the Mississippi; *Bylow Hill* (1902) has a New England setting and involves mental illness. There is no doubt about Cable's delicate art in the minds of those who have the patience to read him, but both his structural deficiencies and his over-elaborate use of dialect have thinned out the ranks of the faithful during recent years. There is a biography by Lucy L. C. Bikle, *GWC: His Life and Letters* (S, 1928).

CALDWELL, Taylor. See FERBER, Edna.

CARROLL, Gladys Hasty. See CHASE, Mary Ellen.

CATHERWOOD, Mary Hartwell (HM, Ce, etc.) (1847-1902), was born in Ohio but spent most of her life in Indiana and Illinois and at Mackinac Island. She published her first novel in 1875, but her first real success was *The Romance of Dollard* (1889). Mrs. Catherwood is primarily the novelist of the French settlement of the New World. Among her best-known books are *The Story of Tonty* (1890); *The Lady of Fort St. John* (1891); *Old Kaskaskia* (1893); *The Spirit of an Illinois Town* (1897); *Spanish Peggy* (1899); and *Lazarre* (1901), which is one of many novels devoted to the lost Dauphin. She also produced *In the Days of Jeanne d'Arc* (1897). See M. L. Wilson, *Biography of MHC* (Newark, Ohio: American Tribune Printery, 1904).

CHASE, Mary Ellen (M), b. 1887, distinguished scholar and teacher, preserves in her fiction the ways and ideals of the Maine ancestors of whom she wrote nonfictionally in *A Goodly Heritage* (Ht, 1932). Her principal novels are *Mary Peters* (1934), and *Silas Crockett* (1935), both of which concern seagoing families, and *Windswept* (1941). Somewhat similar in spirit are the Maine novels of Robert P. Tristram COFFIN (M), b. 1892, another writer of academic background, better known as a poet—*Red Sky in the Morning* (1935) and *John Dawn* (1936)—of Gladys Hasty CARROLL (M), b. 1904—*As the Earth Turns* (1933), *A Few Foolish Ones* (1935), etc.—and Rachel FIELD's (M) (1894-1942) mellow and perhaps more romantic novel, *Time Out of Mind* (1935).

CHILD, Lydia Maria Francis (1802-1880), was a reformer primarily interested in slavery and poverty. But she wrote four novels. *Hobomok* (1924), which goes back to Plymouth and Salem, has an English girl wedded to a noble savage who gives her up when her former lover returns—"Enoch Arden" with the other solution. Longfellow used it as a source for "The Theologian's Tale." It also has a secondary character who bids her lover speak for himself. *The Rebels* (1825) deals with Boston before the Revolution. *Philothea* (1836), which Poe admired, is probably the earliest American novel about classical Greece. Her last novel, *A Romance of the Republic* (1867), reflects her abolitionism. Whittier edited her *Letters* (HM, 1883), with a biographical introduction. See Margaret F. Thorp in her *Female Persuasion* (YUP, 1949).

CHURCHILL, Winston (M) (1871-1947), was born in St. Louis but later made his home in New Hampshire, where he performed valiant service as a political reformer and very nearly became governor. Most of his novels are either historical romances, involving crises in American history, or *Tendenzromane*. In the first group are *Richard Carvel* (1899), which concerns the Whig-Tory impasse of Revolutionary days; the Civil War novel, *The Crisis* (1901), most famous of all Churchill's books, set in St. Louis because the influence of both North and South was strong in that city; and *The Crossing* (1904), in which the George Rogers Clark expedition figures. *Coniston* (1906) deals with the political boss and *Mr. Crewe's Career* (1908) with big business in politics; in *A Far Country* (1915) the central character is a corporation lawyer. Women are the foreground-characters in *A Modern Chronicle* (1910) and in Churchill's last novel, *The Dwelling-Place of Light* (1917). But the most sensational of the problem-novels was *The Inside of the Cup* (1913), presenting the problem of the modern church as it confronts the challenge of modern thought and of modern social and economic conditions. Churchill's method is the same in both types of fiction: he builds up an elaborate background and allows divergent views to be expressed. He lacked spontaneity and he created no important characters, but he was a good craftsman who brought important themes before the consciousness of a vast public. See Richard and Beatrice Hofstadter, "WC: A Study in the Popular Novel," *American Q.*, II (1950), 12-28.

CLARK, Walter Van Tilburg. See RHODES, Eugene Manlove.

COFFIN, Robert P. Tristram. See CHASE, Mary Ellen.

COOKE, John Esten (1830-1886), was a prolific Virginia romancer, best known for *The Virginia Comedians* (1854). The strength of this book lies in its pictures of the theater at Williamsburg, the Governor's ball, the races at Jamestown, and, at the end, the opposition to the Stamp Act. But the characterization is elementary, and the story is virtually over at the end of the first volume, when the actress Beatrice Hallam (inspired by the Author's admiration for Kate Bateman), has finally evaded the brutal young aristocrat Effingham and wedded Charles Waters, whose radicalism is clearly the author's own. The comparatively ununified second volume was later published separately as *Captain Ralph;* if this arrangement be followed, then *Henry St. John, Gentleman* (1859) becomes the last novel of a trilogy. *Fairfax* (1868) presents the young George Washington; the careers of Stonewall Jackson and of Lee contributed to *Surry of Eagles'-Nest* (1866) and *Mohun* (1869), in which Cooke sought to use his Confederate war experiences; *The Heir of Greymount* (1870) was a Reconstruction novel. In his later years, Cooke clung to what he himself now considered an outmoded romanticism, believing himself too old to learn new ways. He enjoyed conjuring up a bookish atmosphere by pretending that he was editing an old manuscript, in the manner of Thackeray's *Henry Esmond.* This trick, already employed in *The Virginia Comedians,* saw service again in his story of King Charles I, *Her Majesty the Queen* (1873), and in the brief and charmingly, though artificially, archaic *My Lady Pokahontas* (1885). See John O. Beaty, *JEC, Virginian* (ColUP, 1922).

COZZENS, James Gould (HB), b. 1903, one of the most capable of contemporary American novelists, has probably attracted less critical attention than he deserves because of his pronounced individualism and his refusal to illustrate any "trend." His first important novel was the brief *S. S. San Pedro* (1931), which was based on the *Vestris* disaster. Among its successors have been *The Last Adam* (1933), *Men and Brethren* (1936), *The Just and the Unjust* (1942), and *Guard of Honor* (1948). These concern, respectively, a country doctor in Connecticut, an Episcopal clergyman in New York, the lawyers involved in a New England murder trial, and life at an army air base. In each instance Mr. Cozzens gets up his background with fine authenticity without committing himself as to his personal "views." See Granville Hicks, "The Reputation of JGC," *EJ,* XXXIX (1950), 1-7.

CRADDOCK, Charles Egbert, pseud. Mary Noailles Murfree (HM) (1850-1922), staked out the Cumberland Mountains claim in the "local color" movement. Though she made her reputation with a volume of short stories—*In the Tennessee Mountains* (1884)—she wrote many novels, among them *The Prophet of the Great Smoky Mountains* (1885); *In the Clouds* (1887); *The Despot of Broomsedge Cove* (1888); *In the "Stranger People's" Country* (1891); *The Juggler* (1897); *The Ordeal* (1912). In her later years she wrote historical novels and studies of the contemporary American scene. Miss Murfree was a scholarly woman; she had poetic feeling, a famous gift for description, and a highly individual style. Her mountaineers are vividly presented, and their expurgated speech is presented with sufficient care to erect a barrier between the author and an age impatient of dialect. Consult Edd W. Parks, *CEC* (UNCP, 1941).

CURWOOD, James Oliver. See RHODES, Eugene Manlove.

DAVENPORT, Marcia. See FERBER, Edna.

DAVIS, Rebecca Harding (HM, H, S) (1831-1910), was the wife of the Philadelphia editor, L. Clarke Davis, and the mother of Richard Harding DAVIS (S) (1864-1916). Though modern critics sometimes call her melodramatic and didactic, she took "this commonplace, this vulgar life" as her field, and, in her early work at least, she deserves to be remembered as a pioneer realist in American fiction. Though born in Pennsylvania, Mrs. Davis lived also in other sections of our country; her fiction is varied in theme and setting, mature in outlook, and sophisticated in its technique. She first showed her mettle in a short piece, "Life in the Iron Mills," published in the *Atlantic* in 1861; she wrote realistic, unsympathetic stories of the Civil War before De Forest. *Margret Howth* (1862) deals with poverty and industrialism in an Indiana milltown; *Waiting for the Verdict* (1868) concerns the Negro problem; *John Andros* (1874) attacks political chicanery and the whisky lobby. Other novels are *Dallas Galbraith* (1868); *A Law Unto Herself* (1878); *Dr. Warrick's Daughters* (1896); and *Frances Waldeaux* (1897). She produced an autobiography, *Bits of Gossip* (HM, 1904). Compared to his mother, Richard Harding DAVIS seems, despite his manliness and charm, a comparatively facile writer, more likely to be remembered for his short stories—*Gallegher* (1891); *Van Bibber* (1892)—than for such romantic and adventurous novels as *The Princess Aline* (1895), *Soldiers of Fortune* (1897), *The Bar Sinister* (1903), and *Vera the Medium* (1908). There are biographical introductions in the collected "Crossroads Edition" of his *Novels and Stories,* 12 vv. (1916); see, also, Fairfax Downey, *RHD: His Day* (S, 1933).

DELAND, MARGARET (HM, H) (1857-1945), laid the scene of many of her stories in "Old Chester," which may have been suggested by her birthplace, Manchester, Pennsylvania. See *Old Chester Tales* (1898); *Dr. Lavendar's People* (1903); *Around Old Chester* (1915); *An Old Chester Secret* (1920); *New Friends in Old Chester* (1924). As the titles show, most of the Old Chester chronicles are short stories, and Dr. Lavendar (a clergyman, not a physician), is very important in them. But Dr.

Lavendar is also important in *The Awakening of Helena Ritchie* (1906), which, with its sequel, *The Iron Woman* (1911), is generally regarded as Mrs. Deland's best achievement. Her first novel was *John Ward, Preacher* (1888), an American *Robert Elsmere*. Primarily, Mrs. Deland was not a local color writer but a disciple of George Eliot, concerned first of all with ethical problems. She was less pontifical in her presentation of them than Mrs. Humphry Ward, and though she sometimes gives the impression of having manipulated her situation in the interest of her ethical teaching, she was never really the dogmatist. Other novels by Mrs. Deland include *Sidney* (1890); *Philip and His Wife* (1894); *The Rising Tide* (1916); *The Vehement Flame* (1922); and *The Kays* (1926). *Golden Yesterdays* (1941) is an autobiography.

Douglas, Lloyd C. (HM) (1877-1951), exemplifies the popular religious novel of our time. A well-known clergyman, he began his career as novelist when the stuff of *Magnificent Obsession* (1929) forced its way in upon him while he was trying to write a nonfiction book. Bunyan had exactly the same experience with *The Pilgrim's Progress*. Among the phenomenally successful novels which followed were *Forgive Us Our Trespasses* (1932), *Green Light* (1935), *White Banners* (1936), and *Invitation to Live* (1940). All concern various aspects of the problem of living a Christian life in the complicated modern world. Probably Douglas's best narratives are his last two novels, which use New Testament characters—*The Robe* (1942) and *The Big Fisherman* (1948). *The Robe* played havoc with its publishers' paper supply during the war; in Chicago they advertised it with posters on the platforms of the Elevated stations. In his uncompleted autobiography, *Time Remembered* (1951), Douglas says that *The Robe* had its source in his preacher-father's reading aloud of *Ben-Hur* and a childhood visit to Barnum and Bailey's Circus! *The Big Fisherman* is credited with the largest advance sale of any novel ever published. By the time this book appeared, the Biblical novel was enjoying a widespread vogue in America and enlisting the talents of more accomplished novelists than Lloyd Douglas. Among these were Gladys Schmitt, b. 1909, with her heavily-sexed *David the King* (Dial, 1946); Florence Marvyne Bauer (BM), with two Biblically- and archaeologically-learned novels, *Behold Your King* (1945) and *Abram, Son of Terah* (1948); and Sholem Asch (P), b. 1880, who has tried to build a bridge between Jewish and Christian minds with his New Testament trilogy: *The Nazarene* (1939), *The Apostle* (1943), and *Mary* (1949). Since Mr. Asch still writes in Yiddish, though he has lived many years in the United States, his books belong to the American novel only by a certain extension of the term. A distinctively Christian novelist of more recent emergence than Lloyd Douglas is Elizabeth Yates (CM), b. 1905. She is distinctly feminine in her approach, and her work is comparable in some aspects with that of Elizabeth Goudge in England. Miss Yates has published *Wind of Spring* (1945), *Nearby* (1947), *Beloved Bondage* (1948), and *Guardian Heart* (1950).

EGGLESTON, Edward (S, Ce, etc.) (1837-1902), was born in Indiana but had a cultivated Virginia background. He began life as a Methodist circuit rider and ended it as an historian. The book which established his fame, *The Hoosier Schoolmaster* (1871), was rightly described by him as "the file-leader in the procession of American dialect novels." Eggleston, who had been influenced by Taine, resented the unending exploitation of New England regionalism in fiction while the rest of the country was neglected. He added many scholarly notes, as well as a valuable Preface, to the 1892 "Library Edition" of the book. Eggleston stayed in Indiana for *The End of the World* (1872), built around the Millerite notion that the end of all things would occur on August 11, 1843, and *Roxy* (1878), but he went to Minnesota for *The Mystery of Metropolisville* (1873), to Ohio for *The Circuit Rider* (1874), and to Illinois for *The Graysons* (1887), in which the young Abraham Lincoln, as counsel for the defense, saves the hero from a trumped-up accusation of murder. Eggleston's realism was as advanced as the main body of his reading public would accept, but it did not preclude considerable use of stock situations from old-fashioned, conventional, romantic fiction. With his last, and one of his best novels, *The Faith Doctor* (1891), he boldly invaded New York City. See William Peirce Randel, *EE* (King's Crown Press, 1946), with elaborate bibliography.

ERSKINE, John (BM) (1879-1951), led three lives: he was a scholar and professor of English, a gifted musician, and a novelist. As novelist he began in 1925 with *The Private Life of Helen of Troy,* a witty and mildly cynical examination of some of the problems involved in Helen's readjustment to her old life in Sparta after the Trojan War. Though it shocked both classicists and moralists, the story appealed to bookish tastes and, at the same time, to the smart, sophisticated, "debunking" tendencies that were so popular at the time. Erskine went on to treat other famous personages in *Galahad* (1926), *Adam and Eve* (1927), *Penelope's Man* (1928), *Tristan and Isolde* (1932), *Solomon, My Son* (1935), *The Brief Hour of François Villon* (1937), *Casanova's Women* (1941), and *Venus, The Lonely Goddess* (1949). *The Start of the Road* (1938), describing a hypothetical episode in Whitman's early life, and *Give Me Liberty* (1940), in which Patrick Henry appears, come closer to the historical novel. *Uncle Sam in the Eyes of His Family* (1930) is a kind of allegory, and *Mrs. Doratt* (1941) is an experimental novel in which the author himself appears. *Unfinished Business* (1931) sends a dead man back from the other world. *The Voyage of Captain Bart*

(1943) is an adventure story. *Sincerity* (1929), *Bachelor of Arts* (1934), and *Forget If You Can* (1935) concern modern American Life. See W. S. Knickerbocker, *SR*, XXXV (1927), 154-174.

FAIRBANK, Janet Ayer. See FERBER, Edna.

FARRELL, James T. (Vanguard), b. 1904, admires Dreiser, Proust, and Joyce, and holds "a functional concept of character, viewing it as a social product embodying the reciprocal play of local influences. . . ." Sometimes regarded as Dreiser's successor, he goes far beyond Dreiser in his brutal realism, and he possesses a far more doctrinaire mind. A somewhat unorthodox Marxian, Farrell has set forth his theories about literature in *The League of Frightened Philistines* (1945), *Literature and Morality* (1947), etc. His special field is the life of poverty-stricken Irish Catholics, damned by their milieu, in revolt against inherited ideals, in the slums of South Side Chicago. The Studs Lonigan trilogy—*Young Lonigan* (1932), *The Young Manhood of Studs Lonigan* (1934), and *Judgment Day* (1935)—records the progressive damnation and self-destruction of a young "slob." The promiscuous heroine of *Ellen Rogers* (1941) drowns herself in Lake Michigan. But Danny O'Neill, to whom Mr. Farrell has apparently given a good deal of his own character, lifts himself above his milieu and becomes a writer. Danny is the hero of *A World I Never Made* (1936), *No Star Is Lost* (1938), *Father and Son* (1940), and *My Days of Anger* (1943). There are other novels also and many short stories, for Mr. Farrell is very prolific. He sometimes uses stream-of-consciousness technique and various devices similar to those employed in John Dos Passos' documentary novels. His books have long been a battleground between the advocates of restraint in fiction and devotees of the new frankness. See the discussions of his work in Oscar Cargill's *Intellectual America,* in Joseph Warren Beach's *American Fiction, 1920-1940,* and W. M. Frohonk's *The Novel of Violence in America;* also, R. M. Lovett, *EJ,* XXVI (1937), 347-354.

FERBER, Edna (D), b. 1887, exemplifies the popular woman novelist of twentieth-century America whose books are usually best-sellers. Among others in this class are Kathleen NORRIS (D), b. 1880; Mary Roberts RINEHART, b. 1876; Janet Ayer FAIRBANK (HM) (1878-1951), and her sister, Margaret Ayer BARNES (HM), b. 1886; Fannie HURST (H), b. 1889; Frances Parkinson KEYES (Messner), b. 1885; Taylor CALDWELL (S), b. 1900; and Marcia DAVENPORT (S), b. 1903. All these women have aimed at mass circulation and have consequently concerned themselves with themes which interest the average reader and handled them in a manner which the average reader can comprehend. They attempt little or no technical experimentation, and their principal appeal is to readers of their own sex. But they all know how to tell a story, and some of them sometimes produce a book which interests even readers of quality fiction. Perhaps Kathleen NORRIS—*Mother* (1911); *Certain People of Importance* (1922), etc.— is the most domestic of the group. She is essentially a California writer, as Janet Ayer FAIRBANK—*The Smiths* (1925); *The Bright Land* (1932)—and Margaret Ayer BARNES— *Years of Grace* (1930); *Within This Present* (1933); *Edna His Wife* (1938), etc.—have their roots in Chicago and the Middle West. Mary Roberts RINEHART is best known for her mystery stories—cf. *The Circular Staircase* (1908)—but she has also tried her hand at many other types of fiction; in *K* (1915) she utilized the medical knowledge acquired as the wife of a physician. Frances Parkinson KEYES used her European residence and the familiarity with political life which she developed as the wife of a United States Senator who had been governor of New Hampshire in *Senator Marlowe's Daughter* (1933) and her Boston girlhood in *Joy Street* (1950); *Crescent Carnival* (1942) and *Dinner at Antoine's* (1948) deal with Louisiana. In her first novel, *Of Lena Geyer* (1936), Marcia DAVENPORT described a singer's life with the competence one might have expected from the daughter of Alma Gluck; *The Valley of Decision* (1942) has an industrial background; the title of *East Side, West Side* (1947) defines its theme. Taylor CALDWELL began with a bitter attack on the munitions-makers in *Dynasty of Death* (1938), a theme continued in some of her later books, but she has ranged as far afield as Richelieu's France in *The Arm and the Darkness* (1943) and the days of Genghis Khan in *The Earth Is the Lord's* (1941). Fannie HURST has studied women in business and in various types of emotiona! relationships in *Lummox* (1923), *Appasionata* (1926), *Back Street* (1931), *Imitation of Life* (1933), etc. Edna FERBER herself began as a sympathetic student of women in business not only in the Emma McChesney stories but in such novels as *Dawn O'Hara* (1911), *Fanny Herself* (1917), and *So Big* (1924), in which a woman becomes a truckfarmer and brings up a disappointing son. But Miss Ferber's distinctive note is a warm, vigorous, sometimes romantic treatment of various aspects of the American past in different parts of our country. The most popular and the most picturesque of her novels is *Show Boat* (1926); from the Mississippi locale of this novel she passed on to Oklahoma during land rush days in *Cimarron* (1889), to the fortunes of a Connecticut family in *American Beauty* (1931), to lumbering in Wisconsin in *Come and Get It* (1935), to New Orleans and Saratoga in the 1880's in *Saratoga Trunk* (1941), and to the development of Seattle in *Great Son* (1945). Miss Ferber and Mrs. Rinehart have published autobiographies: *A Peculiar Treasure* (1933) and *My Story* (1931, 1948). There are interviews with a number of the women mentioned in this paragraph in Robert Van Gelder's *Writers and Writing*.

FIELD, Eugene (S) (1850-1895), was not a novelist but a poet and short-story writer. But two works, posthumously published, both in 1896, might be described, for want of a more exact term, as novels. *The House* deals humorously with the trials and tribulations of acquiring and equipping a dwelling-place. *The Love Affairs of a Bibliomaniac,* which has a thin thread of narrative, often snapped, is devoted to the author's great passion, book-collecting, and contains many charming comments on favorite books.

FIELD, Rachel. See CHASE, Mary Ellen.

FINNEY, Charles G., b. 1905, an Arizona newspaper man, born in Missouri, great grandson of the founder of Oberlin College, has written three very individual novels. *The Circus of Dr. Lao* (Ben Abramson, c. 1935), which had its origin in a dream and was influenced by the author's experiences in China, belongs to the school of fantastic romance of which Cabell is the most distinguished exemplar; it is a heady mixture—bawdy, hilarious, and sometimes terrifying. Allegorical tendencies appear again in *The Unholy City* (Vanguard, 1937), which nobody seems to have liked, but the neglected masterpiece is *Past the End of the Pavement* (Ht, 1939), a touching and hilarious account of the adventures of two boys in a small midwestern town, who, to the consternation of their neighbors, devote themselves to collecting specimens of some of the less popular among God's creatures. It is difficult to understand why this book has not taken its undisputed place among the few classics about boy-life that have been written in America.

FISHER, Vardis (Caxton Printers, D, H, Vanguard), b. 1895, the Idaho novelist, is a stalwart and highly individual figure. Fisher's work has been described as "philosophical naturalism"; unlike many naturalists, he is highly subjective, and he uses his novels to express a philosophy in which a Lawrencian demand for freedom from all misconceptions which prevent human beings from developing in their own orbits and according to the demands of their own nature is only one element. Those who dislike Fisher call him morbid and egocentric; there is no violence or horror from which he turns away, and the quivering sensibilities of his characters often seem ludicrous to more "normal" people. He made his reputation with a tetralogy all of whose titles were derived from Meredith's *Modern Love—In Tragic Life* (1932), *Passions Spin the Plot* (1934); *We Are Betrayed* (1935), and *No Villain Need Be* (1936). His most popular book was his comparatively objective historical novel about the Mormons, *Children of God* (1939); he has also written about the Comstock Lode in *City of Illusion* (1941) and about the Donner Party tragedy in *The Mothers* (1943). He is now engaged in the most ambitious task any American novelist ever set for himself: a series of novels known as *The Testament of Man,* tracing human development from the dawn of consciousness. By 1951 six of these had been published. *Darkness and the Deep* (1943) and *The Golden Rooms* (1944) concern primitive man. *Intimations of Eve* (1946) and *Adam and the Serpent* (1947) involve the establishment of basic relations between men and women. *The Divine Passion* (1948) is set in the days of the patriarchs, and *The Valley of Vision* concerns King Solomon. There is a sympathetic account of Fisher's work in George Snell's *The Shapers of American Fiction.*

FITZGERALD, F[rancis] Scott [Key] (S) (1896-1940), was dismissed by Parrington as "A bad boy who loves to smash things to show how naughty he is; a bright boy who loves to say smart things to show how clever he is." More recently, John O'Hara has informed us that "All Fitzgerald was was our best novelist." It is difficult to sympathize with either of these judgments, though the second is quite in tune with the current Fitzgerald revival. Fitzgerald never smashed anything—except himself, and many of the things he said are not "smart" but sound and true. He first attracted attention with *This Side of Paradise* (1920), which was less a book than a manifesto, the Number One expression of the spirit of postwar youth in its gaudier manifestations. Persons encountering this novel for the first time today, and reading it along with post-World War II fiction, can hardly fail to be impressed by its innocence, for Fitzgerald himself was a liberal, a man of good will, sexually decent, and as little able to throw off his Irish Catholic puritanism as his Celtic charm. He used similar materials in his second novel, *The Beautiful and Damned* (1922), but he is far more in earnest here, and he has also begun to learn how to build a novel. But he is still romantic and sentimental in the worshipful adoration he accords his young wastrels even while the realist in him is honestly reporting all their selfishness, ignorance, and folly. The hero of *The Great Gatsby* (1925) is a wealthy young bootlegger whose inability to free himself from the spell of the shallow girl who had captivated his youth leads to tragedy. Fitzgerald painted Gatsby's portrait with a more mature compassion than he had previously revealed, but the book is not without its undeveloped possibilities. It probably deserves, nevertheless, to be regarded as his masterpiece, though some of his admirers have reserved this title for the long and complicated *Tender Is the Night* (1934). Here the downfall of various Americans—and, by implication, of a society— is studied against a Riviera background. Whatever merits the novel may have, few deny that it is confusing and faulty in its development. The author died over *The Last Tycoon* (1941), a study of the motion picture industry with far-reaching sociological implications, but this work did not get far enough to make an authoritative judgment possible. Fitzgerald unquestionably had extraordinary gifts, but one cannot but feel that those who call him a great novelist are taking a good deal on faith, perhaps describing the writer he might have been rather than the writer he actually was. He might not have achieved his full potentialities even if he had learned to leave liquor alone, for there was a naïve immaturity about him to the end of the chapter. As long as he lived he bemoaned having been unable to play football when he was at Princeton and his failure to get overseas during the war, yet he himself saw through the war as clearly as any man of his generation. He had a way of being taken in by the things he could see through. Perhaps the revival of interest in Fitzgerald and his work is simply another testimony to the inability of human beings to resist the appeal of the lovely, erring mortal who has the stuff of a legend in him. If he had been capable of the kind of discipline that means well-ordered living and complete achievement as an artist, he might well have been less stimulating to the imagination. Fitzgerald's short stories were published in a number of collections: *Flappers and Philosophers* (1921), *Tales of the Jazz Age* (1922), etc.; see *The Stories of F. Scott Fitzgerald* (1951). Arthur Mizener wrote his biography, *The Far Side of Paradise* (HM, 1951), and Budd Schulberg's novel, *The Disenchanted* (RH, 1950) is said to have been suggested by Fitzgerald's career. There is an anthology of criticism, edited by Alfred Kazin, *FSF, The Man and His Work* (World, 1951).

FLINT, Timothy (1780-1840), was the pioneer novelist of the West. A New Englander by birth—clergyman, schoolmaster, editor—Flint traveled widely and helped make Cincinnati a literary center. The hero of *Francis Berrian* (1826) gets involved in the Mexican revolution of 1822. *The Life and Adventures of Arthur Clenning* (1828) is a *Robinson Crusoe* story, with an English heiress added (to whom Clenning marries himself by the Episcopal service), and a young female savage to take the place of Friday. *George Mason, The Young Backwoodsman; or, "Don't Give Up the Ship"* (1829) is set in the Mississippi Valley; *The Shoshonee Valley* (1830) deals with the Oregon territory. Flint's travel and historical books were highly regarded; his *Recollections of the Last Ten Years* was republished by Knopf in the "Americana Deserta" series (1932). There is a biography by J. E. Kirkpatrick, *TF, Pioneer, Missionary, Author, Editor* (Cleveland, Ohio, Arthur H. Clark Co., 1911). With Flint should be mentioned James HALL (1793-1868) and Caroline M. KIRKLAND (1801-1864). Hall was a native of Philadelphia who became a Cincinnati lawyer. One of his books, *Harpe's Head, A Legend of Kentucky* (1833), is sometimes called a novel, but he is essentially a short story writer. Mrs. Kirkland, the mother of Joseph KIRKLAND (1830-1894), who wrote *Zury: The Meanest Man in Spring County*

(1887) and its sequel, *The McVeys* (1888), and who influenced Hamlin Garland, treated the West more realistically than Hall in her dataistic *A New Home—Who'll Follow? or, Glimpses of Western Life* (1839), the account of a settlement in Michigan.

FORD, Paul Leicester (DM) (1865-1902), great grandson of Noah Webster, was a trained historian and bibliographer. His novel of the Revolution, *Janice Meredith* (1899), was one of the most popular romances of its time. *The Honorable Peter Stirling* (Ht, 1894), which tells the story of a "practical idealist" who became a political boss out of pure benevolence, was widely read because it was believed, on somewhat uncertain evidence, to be based on the early life of Grover Cleveland. Ford tried the "Western" in *The Great K. and A. Train Robbery* (1897). *The Story of an Untold Love* (1897), *Wanted: A Matchmaker* (1900), *Wanted: A Chaperon* (1902), etc., are slighter, lighter fictions.

FREDERIC, Harold (S, ACC, etc.) (1856-1898), survives today mainly as the author of *The Damnation of Theron Ware* (1896), a study in the defection of a young Methodist minister which is considerably less than the realistic masterpiece it is often considered to be. Frederic's other most serious novels are *Seth's Brother's Wife* (1887) and *The Lawton Girl* (1890), which involve industrialism and sexual irregularity; *In the Valley* (1890), which concerns the American Revolution; and *The Copperhead* (1893), which is remarkable for its sympathetic presentation of an unpopular point of view. Frederic's last novels— *March Hares* (1896); *Gloria Mundi* (1898); *The Market Place* (1899)— are in lighter vein; some have English settings. The 1924 A. & C. Boni edition of *The Damnation of Theron Ware* has an introduction by R. M. Lovett; see Charles F. Walcutt, "HF and American Naturalism," *AL,* XI (1939), 11-22.

FULLER, Henry B[lake] (1857-1929), wrote two kinds of novels. *The Chevalier of Pensieri-Vani* (Ce, 1890) and *The Chatelaine of La Trinité* (Ce, 1892), *The Last Refuge* (HM, 1900), and *Gardens of This World* (K, 1929) are exuberant, somewhat meandering, and mildly frivolous novels with glittering European backgrounds; *The Cliff-Dwellers* (H, 1893), *With the Procession* (H, 1895), *On the Stairs* (HM, 1918), and, less importantly, *Bertram Cope's Year* (Seymour, 1919) and *Not on the Screen* (K, 1930) are unflattering social studies of Fuller's native Chicago. Sterne, Thackeray, Cervantes, and Daudet have all been discerned in his romantic pieces—Lowell and Norton warmly admired the *Chevalier*—and the Chicago novels have been compared to the work of almost all the modern naturalistic and realistic writers. Dreiser owned having been influenced by *With the Procession,* and Howells once called

Fuller his successor. He also experimented with poetry and drama and wrote many book-reviews and editorials. He is an intensely civilized writer, extremely intelligent, sometimes brilliant, and often slightly mordant. He hated his environment and was fundamentally out of sympathy with his times. In so far as he has a special theme it is the predatory role played by spoiled and prosperous women in a commercialized civilization. He generally gives the impression of writing more for his own delectation than for that of the public and he never took the trouble to direct or to distort his considerable talents in such a way as to command a wide audience. See Constance M. Griffin's *HBF, A Critical Biography* (U. of Pa. Press, 1939), with full bibliography and some hitherto unpublished pieces.

GALE, Zona (M, ACC, etc.) (1874-1938), Wisconsin liberal and champion of many good causes, was perhaps more impressive for her personality, and for the interest of her thinking about the art of fiction, than she was in her narrower aspect as a novelist. Yet her achievement as a novelist was not negligible. She began with an out-and-out fantasy, *Romance Island* (1906); her Friendship Village stories and other early books gave her a place with the homely school of Midwestern folk sentiment generally associated with Indiana. But *Birth* (1918) was an achievement of a different order; the central figure is an insignificant failure in whom the reader is compelled to recognize heroic qualities. Her great success, both as a novel and as a play, was *Miss Lulu Bett* (1920), the tale of a domestic drudge who revolted, generally associated with the "revolt from the village" school. Other aspects of frustration and fulfilment were studied in later novels, which were marked by mystical sensitiveness and increasing interest in symbolism: *Faint Perfume* (1923); *Preface to a Life* (1926); *Borgia* (1929); *Papa La Fleur* (1933); *Light Woman* (1937); and *Magna* (1939). For her own statement of her views, see *Portage, Wisconsin, and Other Essays* (K, 1928). Her biography is by August Derleth, *Still Small Voice* (ACC, 1940).

GRANT, Robert (S) (1852-1940), distinguished Boston jurist, was essentially a social satirist in fiction. His attitude toward the novel was much like that of his friend, Edith Wharton. He began with such light fiction as *The Confessions of a Frivolous Girl* (1880), but passed on to substantial work in *The Chippendales* (1909) and its sequel, *The Dark Horse* (1931). His first important novel, *Unleavened Bread* (1900), has a Becky Sharp-like heroine, Selma White, whom he reintroduced in *The High Priestess* (1915). One of his special themes is divorce: see *The Undercurrent* (1904); *The Orchid* (1905); *The Bishop's Granddaughter* (1925). Grant tried to write of Boston society from within (feeling that even Howells' sympathies had been largely with the newcomers) and to distinguish between the things that had run to seed in the old Puritan morality and that which was still worth saving. His autobiography, *Fourscore* (HM, 1934) includes fairly detailed commentary upon his fiction.

GREY, Zane. See RHODES, Eugene Manlove.

GUTHRIE, A. B., Jr. See RHODES, Eugene Manlove.

HALL, James. See FLINT, Timothy.

HOLLAND, J[osiah] G[ilbert] (S) (1819-1881), was a self-made man, a native of Massachusetts. Physician, educator, and editor, first, of the Springfield *Republican,* which he developed into one of the leading American newspapers, then of *Scribner's Monthly* (later the *Century*), which he founded in 1870, he exercised a large influence upon American letters. Holland published poetry, essays, and lay sermons as well as novels. The ethical and religious note was always strong in his work, but he was never, as has so often been stated, a clergyman. In early days he used the pseudonym, Timothy Titcomb. His first novel, *The Bay-Path,* appeared in 1857; this was followed in 1860 by *Miss Gilbert's Career.* But all three of his important novels appeared in the 1870's: *Arthur Bonnicastle* (1873); *Sevenoaks* (1875); *Nicholas Minturn* (1876). Holland was a disciple of Dickens: the influence shows in his humor, his methods of characterization, and his themes, and most of all in his humanitarianism. *Arthur Bonnicastle,* though partly autobiographical, has very clearly been influenced by *Great Expectations.* It is interesting to compare the predatory financier of *Sevenoaks,* who is said to have been based on Jim Fisk, with later, more amoral considerations in fiction of similar characters. Though Dr. Holland eschewed subtlety and worked in the primary colors, his novels are still extremely readable. See Harry H. Peckham, *JGH in Relation to His Times* (U. of Pa. Press, 1940).

HOUGH, Emerson. See RHODES, Eugene Manlove.

HOWE, E[dgar] W. (1853-1937), was a Kansas journalist whose *The Story of a Country Town* (1883), which was praised by Howells and Mark Twain, is considered an important early naturalistic novel, sounding the note of revolt against an idealized picture of rural and small town life. Though Howe does not rule out sensational events, his style has a quiet, dignified integrity, and the impression he leaves on the reader's mind is drab and a little dull. Disillusioned as he is, he is no rebel; his detachment imposes the cool distance of art upon what might have been a harrowing and frenetic tale, and the final mood is that of a kind of hopeless reconciliation. See his own introduction to the DM 1927 edition of *The Story of a Country Town* and Carl Van Doren's "Prudence Militant," *Ce,* CVI (1923), 151-156.

HUGHES, Langston. See WRIGHT, Richard.

HURST, Fannie. See FERBER, Edna.

HURSTON, Zorah Neale. See WRIGHT, Richard.

JUDD, Sylvester (1813-1853), was a Unitarian clergyman, born in Massachusetts, pastor at Augusta, Maine. His *Margaret* (1845), which describes, in an eighteenth-century setting, the spiritual growth of its heroine and finally, the regeneration of a community, is the novel above all others which dramatizes the Transcendentalism of Emerson and Alcott. *Richard Edney* (1850) has a contemporary urban setting. Still Transcendental in its ideal, it is less exuberant than *Margaret* and more realistic, more socially- and less spiritually-minded. See Philip Judd Brockway, *SJ (1813-1853), Novelist of Transcendentalism, University of Maine Studies,* Second Series, No. 53, 1941.

KENNEDY, JOHN PENDLETON (1795-1870) was a Baltimore gentleman of Liberal views and scholarly tastes, member of Congress and Secretary of the Navy under Fillmore, who advocated gradual emancipation and supported the Union cause in the Civil War. Both before and after the conflict, he worked zealously for reconciliation. Each of his novels is an individual achievement. *Swallow Barn* (1832) is the kind of book Irving might have written if Irving had been a Southerner, a graceful picture of planation life in the Old Dominion, sympathetically recorded just before its decline. *Horseshoe Robinson* (1835), which concerns the Revolution in South Carolina, leading up to the Battle of King's Mountain, is a full-dress, Cooper kind of historical novel, one of the most famous in our literature and one of the most intelligent and restrained. Decidedly more atmospheric and romantic is *Rob of the Bowl* (1838), which involves the quarrel between Catholic and Protestant in sixteenth-century Maryland. Kennedy backed Peary's expedition to Japan and Kane's second Arctic voyage; he believed in Morse's telegraph long before public opinion was willing to entertain the thought of such possibilities. Provost of the University of Maryland, he was the virtual founder of the Peabody Library. After the war he became president of the board of directors of the Baltimore and Ohio Railroad. See the introductions to J. B. Hubbell's edition of *Swallow Barn* (HB, 1929) and to E. E. Leisy's edition of *Horseshoe Robinson* (ABC, 1937).

KEYES, Frances Parkinson. See FERBER, Edna.

KIRKLAND, Caroline M. and Joseph. See FLINT, Timothy.

McCUTCHEON, George Barr (DM) (1866-1928), was the author of *Graustark* (1901), the American equivalent of Anthony Hope's *The Prisoner of Zenda* (1894), i.e., a tale of derring-do involving a dashing American hero in a tiny imaginary kingdom in the Balkans, who runs through a series of obvious plot-devices and, at the end, wins the hand of the passionate, high-minded, and much-intrigued-against princess. *Graustark* had five sequels; the best-known is *Beverley of Graustark* (1904), which was responsible for the Christian name of countless American girls; the last appeared as late as 1927. In the only careful attempt that has been made to study these novels, Grant C. Knight ("The 'Pastry' Period in Literature," *SRL,* XXVII, Dec. 16, 1944, pp. 5 ff.) finds *The Princess Aline* (1895), by Richard Harding Davis, the earliest important American example of the *Graustark*-type of novel and gives George Ade's *The Slim Princess* (1907) some of the credit for ending the epidemic; he also tries to assess the sociological significance of the phenomenon. McCutcheon's *Brewster's Millions* (1903) was a farce almost as successful, on the stage as well as between covers, as *Graustark* itself; another great hit was *Castle Craneycrow* (1902). In *The Sherrods* (1903) he assayed a more realistic kind of novel, a tragic love story with a rural setting in his own Indiana. His brother, John T. McCutcheon, the great cartoonist of the *Chicago Tribune,* writes of him in *John McCutcheon's Book* (Caxton Club, 1948), pp. 278-280.

MORLEY, Christopher (D, Li), b. 1890, has written comparatively realistic novels in *Human Being* (1932) and especially in *Kitty Foyle* (1939), the story of a "white collar girl" recorded in the stream-of-consciousness manner. But essentially he is too much the man of letters really to settle down to the business of being a novelist; he inherits the bookish tradition of the English essayists, and he is most himself when he is sharing with his readers his own tremendous gusto about books and about life. His first fictions—*Parnassus on Wheels* (1917) and *The Haunted Bookshop* (1919)—are very bookish, and the most admired— *Where the Blue Begins* (1922), the story of a philosophical quest in which all the characters are dogs, and *Thunder on the Left* (1925)— involve the element of fantasy. *Pandora Lifts the Lid* (1924) is a take-off on pirate stories, and *The Trojan Horse* (1937) retells the story of Troilus and Cressida with entirely too much dependence on the idea that it is very funny to have telephones in Troy. *The Man Who Made Friends with Himself* (1949) includes almost everything. See Richard D. Altick, "Average Citizen in Grub Street," *SAQ,* XLI (1942), 18-31.

NEAL, John (1793-1875), was a Maine Yankee of Quaker background and of powerful but undisciplined imagination, nursed on Godwin, Byron, and Brown. *Logan* (1822), *Seventy-Six* (1823), *Randolph* (1823), *Brother Jonathan* (1824), etc. are both humanitarian and wildly sensational. *Rachel Dyer* (1828), on the other hand, is a very sober novel about the Salem witch-trials, which the author hoped might be received "as some sort of atonement for the folly and extravagance of my earlier writings." Yet in the 1860's he was scribbling dime novels for Beadle. Neal regarded "classical English" as the deadest of all dead languages and self-consciously set to work to develop an American literature. Yet he spent part of his life in England and became the first American to write for the great English reviews. Some of his books have incidental sources of interest: *Brother Jonathan* (the longest early American novel) is a New England legendry; *The Down-Easters* (1833) exploits provincial character-types; *True Womanhood* (1859) reflects the Evangelicalism of the 1850's. His *Wandering Recollections of a Somewhat Busy Life* (1869) is still the principal source of information about Neal.

NORRIS, Kathleen. See FERBER, Edna.

PAULDING, James Kirke (1778-1860) was, like Cooper, a New Yorker whose novels enjoyed an international vogue. He was also a man of affairs (Secretary of the Navy under Van Buren), a critic, an essayist, and the author of a play, *The Lion of the West,* in which James H. Hackett acted for many years. Paulding admired Maria Edgeworth but thought Scott far inferior to Fielding, who was, for him, the ideal novelist, with *Tom Jones* as the ideal novel. Paulding differed from Fielding in that he was no master of the architectonics of fiction, but he had an interesting mind and considerable charm. *Koningsmark* (1823) deals with the Swedes in Delaware in the middle of the seventeenth-century; the hero is a Finn, and William Penn is among the characters. It contains much criticism of current social and political tendencies and of current romantic fiction. *The Dutchman's Fireside* (1831) combines a comedy of wooing and Dutch manners with the not quite harmonious material furnished by war hazards on the frontier. Based, like Cooper's *Satanstoe,* on Mrs. Grant's *Memoirs of an American Lady,* it is often compared to the Cooper work, but there are few real resemblances between them. *Westward Ho!* (1832) concerns the movement from Virginia to Kentucky; *The Old Continental* (1846) has an affinity with Cooper's *The Spy; The Puritan and His Daughter* (1849) moves from the Old World to the New. Cf. Amos L. Herold, *JKP, Versatile American* (ColUP, 1926), and Parrington's feeling tribute, in *The Romantic Revolution in America,* pp. 212-221.

PHELPS, Elizabeth Stuart (HM) (1844-1911) won fame in her 'twenties as the author of *The Gates Ajar* (1868), which is less a novel than a conversation-piece concerning the future life; designed to bring comfort to women who had suffered losses during the Civil War, it was even more popular in England than at home. There were two sequels: *Beyond the Gates* (1883) and *The Gates Between* (1887). *Within the Gates* (1901) is a dramatized version of *The Gates Between*. Elizabeth Stuart Phelps was the daughter of Austin Phelps, a distinguished theologian; her mother, also named Elizabeth Stuart Phelps, wrote fiction, and one of her stories, *The Sunny Side* (1851), sold more than 100,000 copies. Feminist, prohibitionist, antivivisectionist, and homeopathist, the younger woman was aware of the conflict in her veins between "the reformer's blood and the student's blood"; though she knew that it is the province of the artist to portray life as it is, she insisted that, above all else, "life *is* moral responsibility." Her mature religious fictions, of which the most noteworthy is *A Singular Life* (1894), whose hero lives out, to his martyrdom, a life of heroic service to the Gloucester fishermen (and which, incidentally, boasts one of the most delightful heroines in American literature), are neither pietistic nor lacking in humor. *Come Forth* (1890), a Biblical pastiche about Jesus and Lazarus which she wrote in collaboration with her husband, Herbert D. Ward, can easily hold its own beside the popular Biblical novels of the 1940's. Elizabeth Stuart Phelps never feared unpleasant themes. She deals with illegitimacy in *Hedged In* (1870) and with unhealthy conditions in factories and the struggle between capital and labor in *The Silent Partner* (1871). *Dr. Zay* (1882) concerns the new professional woman. *The Story of Avis* (1877), an ambitious novel probing the conflict between love and art in a woman's soul, was, despite its structural deficiencies, one of the most powerful fictions of its time. A very prolific writer, Elizabeth Stuart Phelps wrote a number of other novels and many short stories; among these are such fine pieces as "The Madonna of the Tubs" and "Jack the Fisherman," both based on her summers at Gloucester, and *The Supply at Saint Agatha's* (1896), in which her gift for the supernatural story is seen at its best. She also wrote an autobiography, *Chapters from a Life* (1896). See Mary Angela Bennett, *ESP* (Univ. of Pa. Press, 1939).

PHILLIPS, David Graham (ACC) (1867-1911), a native of Indiana and a newspaper man prominent in the "muck-raking" movement of the early 1900's, carried his journalistic and reforming instincts over into his twenty-three novels with sufficient force to mislead Frank Harris into calling him the greatest American novelist. His posthumous *Susan Lennox: Her Fall and Rise* (1917), which was at first suppressed, was praised by Edith Wharton. Among the best-known of his early novels, exposing evils in government and business are *The Great God Success*

(1901), *The Master Rogue* (1902), which attacked the Senate, and individual senators by name, *The Cost* (1904), *The Deluge* (1905), and *The Conflict* (1911). His later novels, which included *The Price She Paid* (1912) and *Old Wives for New* (1908), revealed more interest in sexual problems. Though far more of a reformer and idealist than Dreiser ever dreamed of being, Phillips sometimes offended the same sensibilities that found Dreiser's early novels intolerable. Phillips was murdered by a lunatic who imagined that he had depicted his family in one of his novels. There is a biography by Isaac F. Marcosson, *DGP and His Times* (DM, 1932); see Granville Hicks, *Bkm* (NY), LXXIII (1931), 257-266.

PORTER, Eleanor H. See WIGGIN, Kate Douglas.

PORTER, Gene Stratton. See WIGGIN, Kate Douglas.

PROKOSCH, Frederic (H), b. 1908, is one of the best philosophical novelists of recent emergence. His work bears some affinity to the old travel-narratives and to the country-house novels of such writers as Thomas Love Peacock. He uses symbolism freely, and his style is suggestive of modern poetry; indeed, he himself is a poet. Several of his volumes lie close to the political events of their time, and he may be said to possess what Henry James once described as "the imagination of disaster." *The Asiatics* (1935) and *The Seven Who Fled* (1937) have Asian settings, and *Storm and Echo* (1948) involves a trip into Africa. *The Skies of Europe* (1941), *The Conspirators* (1943), and *Age of Thunder* (1945) employ recent European history, while *Night of the Poor* (1939) and *The Idols of the Cave* (1946) have their setting in the United States.

REED, Myrtle (P) (1874-1911), was the most popular woman novelist of the first decade of the twentieth century. Typical titles are *Lavender and Old Lace* (1902), *The Master's Violin* (1904), *A Spinner in the Sun* (1906), and *A Weaver of Dreams* (1911). Her publishers printed them, in black and red, on excellent paper, with ruled borders, and bound them in decorated lavendar cloth. Myrtle Reed's books are pleasant, dreamy, little love stories; she wrote just well enough to persuade the uncultivated reader that she wrote beautifully; and her extreme sentimentality was counteracted by her genuine humor. Once, in *The Shadow of Victory: A Romance of Fort Dearborn* (1903), she attempted the historical novel. *The Book of Clever Beasts* (1904), a take-off on the nature-fakers, was praised by Theodore Roosevelt.

RHODES, Eugene Manlove (HM) (1869-1934), the cowpuncher novelist of New Mexico, has had more admirers among connoisseurs than any other writer of "Westerns." Rhodes was a writer of integrity and distinction, and his allusive style was merely one expression of a cultivated mind. Vigorous as he was, the lyrical note lay well within his range, and he was as capable of memorably thoughtful passages as any writer whose special field is a more sophisticated society. Among his novels are *Stepsons of Light* (1921), *Copper Streak Trail* (1922), *The Trusty Knaves* (1933), *Beyond the Desert* (1934), and *The Proud Sheriff* (1935); the best introduction to his work is now the omnibus edited by Frank V. Dearing, *The Best Novels and Stories of EMR* (1949). His wife, May D. Rhodes, wrote his biography, *The Hired Man on Horseback* (HM, 1938), which includes an essay by Bernard DeVoto and a bibliography by Vincent Starrett. The best-known and most successful of the more or less "standard" writers of "Westerns" were probably Rex BEACH (H) (1877-1949), whose special field was the Klondike gold rush—*The Spoilers* (1905), which made motion picture history, *The Barrier* (1908), *The Silver Horde* (1909), etc.—; Stewart Edward WHITE (D) (1873-1946), a naturalist and a man of sensitive spirit—*The Blazed Trail* (1902), *The Silent Places* (1904), etc.—; and James Oliver CURWOOD (BM, D) (1878-1927), who wrote about Canada and Hudson's Bay— *The Courage of Captain Plum* (1908), *River's End* (1919), *The Valley of Silent Men* (1920), etc. *The Virginian* (M, 1902), by Owen WISTER (1860-1938), was something of a special case; another, much later, was *The Covered Wagon* (ACC, 1922), by Emerson HOUGH (1857-1923), which aided notably by a great film, brought an almost forgotten primitive means of transportation back into the consciousness of the American people as a romantic symbol, typifying the courage and hardiness of their ancestors. More phenomenally "successful" than any of these, and pretending to much less literary quality, were the works of Zane GREY (H) (1875-1939): *Riders of the Purple Sage* (1912) and sixty-two others. They sold altogether 19,000,000 copies, and kept their author's name on the best-seller list continually from 1917 to 1925, a record no other writer has equalled. Of recent years a number of writers of individual talent have used Western materials but departed notably from the old formulas: see, for example, Walter Van Tilburg CLARK's (b. 1909) socially- and politically-conscious *The Ox-Bow Incident* (RH, 1940) and the books of A[rthur] B. GUTHRIE, Jr. (Sl), b. 1901: *The Big Sky* (1947) and *The Way West* (1950).

RICE, Alice Hegan. See WIGGIN, Kate Douglas.

RINEHART, Mary Roberts. See FERBER, Edna.

ROE, E[dward] P[ayson] (DM) (1838-1888), New York state Presbyterian clergyman, chaplain in the Civil War, discovered a huge, uncultivated audience for fiction with his novel of the Chicago Fire, *Barriers Burned Away* (1872). There followed *Opening of a Chestnut Burr* (1874), *His Sombre Rivals* (1883), *Driven back to Eden* (1885), *He Fell in Love with His Wife* (1886), *The Earth Trembled* (1887), and others. Roe was capable of astonishing crudeness and naïveté. But he had the courage to choose themes worthy of the largest talents, and his gift for breathless narrative and sensational incident never failed to please the "young" and the "common people" to whom he avowedly addressed himself. He has been given credit for helping to break down the prejudice against fiction in Evangelical circles. His sister, Mary A. Roe, wrote *EPR, Reminiscences of His Life* (DM, 1899).

RöLVAAG, Ole (H) (1876-1931) was born on the Island of Donna, on the edge of the Arctic Circle, came to the United States in 1896 to live with his uncle on a farm in South Dakota, and finally became a professor at St. Olaf College. His novels, written in Norwegian, deal with pioneer life in Dakota. They are realistic in spirit, blinking none of the cruel hardships of pioneer life but also expressing human aspiration and hope for the future. The most successful are *Giants in the Earth* (1927) with its sequels, *Peder Seier* (1928) and *Peder Victorious* (1929). See Parrington's discussion in *The Beginnings of Critical Realism in America* and Percy H. Boynton, *EJ*, XVIII (1929), 535-542.

SCHMITT, Gladys. See DOUGLAS, Lloyd.

SEDGWICK, Catharine Maria (1789-1867), "the Maria Edgeworth of New England," began with religious writings and finished with juveniles and tales making a moral or sociological "point." But she owes her fame to her historical novels and to the books which look forward to the New England novel of manners. *Hope Leslie* (1827) is a rich, rambling novel of seventeenth-century Massachusetts and of a girl who chooses to remain with the Indians who have abducted her rather than to return to her own people. *The Linwoods* (1835) deals with Revolutionary New York. *A New England Tale* (1822) is concerned with Friends, *Redwood* (1824) with Shakers. *Married or Single* (1857) reflects the contemporary interest in Spiritualism. See Mary E. Dewey, *Life and Letters of CMS* (H, 1872).

SHELDON, Charles M. (1857-1946), a Congregational clergyman of Topeka, and one-time editor of *The Christian Herald,* published much didactic fiction, including *In His Steps* (1896), which has been called the best-selling novel in American literary history. Defective copyright threw the book into the common domain, and so many editions have appeared that no accurate sales-figures are available. Frank L. Mott

(*Golden Multitudes,* Ch. XXVIII) rejects the widely-accepted estimate of 8,000,000 for the United States and 12,000,000 more abroad. He estimates 2,000,000 for the United States and 6,000,000 for world-wide sales. The book describes the revolution in the city of Raymond which follows the pledge made by a group of church members to their pastor that for one year they will take no action without first asking themselves, "What would Jesus do?" The movement spreads to nearby Chicago, where it ties in with settlement work, the war on the saloon, etc. Though *In His Steps* has no literary quality whatever, it still carries a challenge to the Christian conscience. It is the outstanding example among a vast number of American religious books, most of which never get into literary history. In 1921 Sheldon published a sequel, *In His Steps Today* (Revell, 1921). See his autobiography, *Charles M. Sheldon: His Life and Story* (Do, 1925), and his introduction to the 1949 Permabooks edition of *In His Steps.*

SINCLAIR, Upton (VP, etc.), b. 1878, the picturesque Socialist reformer who once nearly became governor of California, is the foremost modern American propaganda novelist. He is also one of the most prolific writers in American literary history and one of the most popular American writers abroad. His first successful novel was *The Jungle* (1906), based upon his investigations in the Chicago Stock Yards, which inspired a Federal investigation and led to passage of the Pure Food Act. *King Coal* (1917) was inspired by the Colorado coal strike of 1914-1915. *100%* (1920) is based on the Tom Mooney case. *Oil!* (1927) involves the Teapot Dome scandal, films, and popular evangelism in southern California. *Boston* (1928) concerns Sacco and Vanzetti. In 1940, just when it was beginning to appear that Sinclair might be played out as a novelist, he began publishing a series of novels which dramatized contemporary history up to the end of the Second World War: *World's End* (1940); *Between Two Worlds* (1941); *Dragon's Teeth* (1942); *Wide Is the Gate* (1943); *Presidential Agent* (1944); *Dragon Harvest* (1945); *A World To Win* (1946); *Presidential Mission* (1947); *One Clear Call* (1948); and *O, Shepherd, Speak!* (1949) The hero of this series is Lanny Budd, who witnesses the rise of the Nazi movement, with first-hand contacts with Hitler and Goering, and who acts as the personal representative of President Roosevelt abroad. These books became a staple article in the American book trade and were more respectfully reviewed than Sinclair's work in general had been. But this record does not, by any means, exhaust either the range or the extent of Sinclair's work. He began his career by scribbling West Point novels for Street and Smith! In 1903 he wrote a novel, *Prince Hagen,* in which he brought a Niblung to America; the same year he brought out the story of a modern Chatterton in *The Journal of Arthur Stirling. They*

Call Me Carpenter (1922) brings Christ out of the stained-glass window; *The Millennium* (1929) pictures the end of capitalism in the year 2000; *Roman Holiday* (1931) parallels contemporary and ancient Roman civilization. In *Another Pamela* (1950) Sinclair reworks the materials of Richardson's *Pamela* in the modern setting. Like Harold Bell Wright's, Sinclair's novels must be judged primarily as tracts. At his worst he has probably equaled the worst of Wright, but he has amazing range and vigor. See his autobiography, *American Outpost* (1932), and Floyd Dell's *US, A Study in Social Protest* (Do, 1927). There is a good general estimate by Robert Cantwell in Malcolm Cowley's *After the Genteel Tradition*.

STOCKTON, Frank R. (S) (1834-1902) is remembered, first of all, for the literary sensation of "The Lady or the Tiger?" (1882), the most famous trick story in American literature. But he also wrote a number of entertaining novels, of which the best known are *Rudder Grange* (1879), which was so popular that it inspired two sequels, *The Rudder Grangers Abroad* (1891) and *Pomona's Travels* (1894), and that charming burlesque of desert island romances, *The Casting Away of Mrs. Lecks and Mrs. Aleshine* (1886). (*The Dusantes,* originally published separately in 1888, is Part IV of later editions of the *Casting Away*.) Stockton's comedy is what is generally known as the "zany" variety, but it has none of the brittleness now commonly associated with that type. His imagination was gay, florid, impudently insouciant, and childlike— he wrote many fairy tales and supernatural stories, and was one of the star performers for *St. Nicholas* in its golden days—and his characteristic atmosphere is that of the extravaganza. Among his other novels are *The Late Mrs. Null* (1886); *The Great War Syndicate* (1889), which, with *The Great Stone of Sardis* (1897), anticipated modern destructive inventions; *Ardis Claverden* (1890); *Squirrel Inn* (1891); *The Adventures of Captain Horn* (1895); *The Associate Hermits* (1899); *A Bicycle of Cathay* (1900); and a gay pirate story, *Kate Bonnet* (1902). There is a collected "Shenendoah Edition" of his Works, 23 vv. (1899-1904); see Martin I. Griffin, Jr., *FRS, A Critical Biography* (U. of Pa. Press, 1939).

TAYLOR, Bayard (P) (1825-1878) was poet, essayist, world-traveler, lecturer, diplomat, journalist under Horace Greeley, and translator of Goethe's *Faust*. In the eyes of his contemporaries he was a far more distinguished writer than he has been considered by posterity. His literary ideals were those of the New England school but he worked with less sense of inner compulsion and a larger eye to the main chance. He wrote four novels. The first, *Hannah Thurston* (1863), which was strongly influenced by *Pride and Prejudice,* considers most of the reform movements of the nineteenth century, especially (from a conservative standpoint) "women's rights." In *John Godfrey's Fortunes* (1864), the important literary influence is that of *David Copperfield,* but the material is Taylor's own. This novel is a realistic tale with a romantic ending, detailing its hero's progress in New York journalism and giving a good satirical picture of the affectations of aesthetes and bohemians of various sorts. With *The Story of Kennet* (1866), a minor, or at least a regional, classic whose fame has endured to this day, Taylor found himself as a novelist. Here he gives a knowledgeable picture of the Pennsylvania farming country in which he himself had been born and bred, plus vivid characterizations of rural folk in whose culture Quakerism is the dominating element, though none of the leading characters of the novel are themselves Friends. There is considerably more sensationalism in his last novel, *Joseph and His Friend* (1870). See Richard Croom Beatty, *BT, Laureate of the Gilded Age* (UOP, 1936).

TOURGÉE, Albion W. (1838-1905) was born in Ohio, fought in the Civil War, and subsequently became a judge in North Carolina. McKinley made him consul at Bordeaux, where he died. His career as fictionist was dedicated to the novel of purpose, and his most important concern was with the Reconstruction problem. Seven books cover "the life of a generation from the rise of the Anti-Slavery sentiment, through the Rebellion to the end of the Reconstruction Era, and on into the days of the New South and its elements of hope." In the order in which the events recorded occurred, these are *Hot Plowshares* (1883); *Figs and Thistles* (1879); *A Royal Gentleman* (1881); *A Fool's Errand* (1879); *Bricks Without Straw* (1880); *John Eax, etc.* (1882); and *Black Ice* (1887). The most successful was *A Fool's Errand,* which was compared to *Uncle Tom's Cabin* and caused its author to be dubbed "the Victor Hugo of America." The central character is a Northerner who, like Tourgée, settled in the postwar South, defied public opinion and risked his life, but whose sweetness of spirit was recognized by his neighbors after his death. The best-known incident in this novel was very closely reproduced in Nancy Hale's novel, *The Sign of Jonah* (S, 1950). *With Gauge and Swallow, Attorneys* (1889), loosely connected short stories on legal themes, involves some "detective" interest; in *Out of the Sargasso Sea* (1893) Tourgée tried his hand at an historical novel about Columbus. But outside the Reconstruction series, his most important novel is *Murvale Eastman, Christian Socialist* (1889), which is a better book than Sheldon's *In His Steps* but not nearly so good as *A Singular Life,* by Elizabeth Stuart Phelps. Tourgée's contemporary vogue must have been due more to his compelling themes than to his art, for he never learned how to arrange the stuff of fiction so as to form what Galsworthy once called a "spire of meaning." His plots are melodrama, and his long expository passages often stop the story altogether. Yet he is never dull.

See Roy F. Dibble, *AWT* (Lemcke & Buechner, 1921), which is strangely unsympathetic in its critical judgments; compare George J. Becker, "AWT: Pioneer in Social Criticism," *AL,* XIX (1947), 59-72.

VAN VECHTEN, Carl (K), b. 1880, is a distinguished music critic and the author of the best of all books about cats, *The Tiger in the House* (1921), whose seven novels remain something of a monument to the cultured sophistication upon which the 1920's prided themselves. The first, *Peter Whiffle* (1922), was a fascinating trifle in the Beerbohm-Aldous Huxley manner, the imaginary biography of a cultivated dilettante, notable chiefly for its amazing allusiveness. It was followed by *The Blind Bow-Boy* (1923) in which intelligence, perversity, and vulgarity are curiously commingled. With *The Tattooed Countess* (1924) and *Nigger Heaven* (1926) Van Vechten showed an ambition to move on from the *hors d'oeuvres* to the *entrée* of the fictional feast. The *Countess,* probably his most satisfying story, is set in his native Iowa; *Nigger Heaven* marks the literary discovery of Harlem and is by no means exclusively concerned with night clubs. *Spider Boy* (1928) satirizes Hollywood; *Firecrackers* (1925) and *Parties* (1930) concern the more frivolous aspects of New York life. See Van Vechten's "Notes for an Autobiography," *Col,* Part III (1930).

WALLACE, Lew (1827-1905), Indiana lawyer with a distinguished record in the Mexican War and the Civil War, later Governor of New Mexico and Minister to Turkey, wrote three spectacular historical novels: *The Fair God* (HM, 1873); *Ben-Hur* (H, 1880); *The Prince of India* (H, 1893). The first concerns the conquest of Mexico; the last has the Wandering Jew as its central figure. But both were dwarfed by the success of *Ben-Hur,* which, as an institution among American novels, can only be compared with *Uncle Tom's Cabin, Looking Backward,* and *In His Steps.* The book was translated into many languages, and has even been issued, in a modified form, under the auspices of the Holy See. The Klaw and Erlanger stage production of 1899 ran until 1920, and the chariot race became part of Barnum and Bailey's Circus. In 1925 came the Metro-Goldwyn-Mayer cinema, the biggest film since Griffith's *Intolerance.* Wallace combined considerable learning—he read extensively for all his novels—with a gift for sensational incident and great dramatic "scenes," and he knew how to utilize his life experience even when he was writing of the far away and long ago: the military portions of *The Fair God* make use of his own Civil War campaigns. In the case of *Ben-Hur* he added the power of an evangel, for he claimed to have been converted by his reading for this novel into a believer in Christianity as a supernatural religion. See Irving McKee, *"Ben-Hur" Wallace* (U. of Cal. Press, 1947).

Wiggin, Kate Douglas (HM) (1859-1923) is, as a writer, so completely identified with rural New England that it is difficult to remember that she was born in Philadelphia and that she organized, in San Francisco, the first free kindergarten for poor children west of the Rockies. (Her writings on kindergarten work are authoritative.) As fictionist, Mrs. Wiggin established her reputation with a sentimental classic, *The Birds' Christmas Carol* (1887). But her natural bent was toward comedy, and her greatest triumph was *Rebecca of Sunnybrook Farm* (1903), whose adorable young heroine was reasonably described by Thomas Bailey Aldrich as "the nicest child in American literature." (Her further adventures were recorded in the episodic *New Chronicles of Rebecca,* 1907.) Probably Mrs. Wiggin's most considerable novel was *The Story of Waitstill Baxter* (1913), but *Rose o' the River* (1905), *The Old Peabody Pew* (1907), *Susanna and Sue* (1909), *Mother Carey's Chickens* (1911), etc. were all widely read and loved. Her work is somewhat more "popular" than that of Sarah Orne Jewett and Mrs. Wilkins Freeman; it partakes more of the character of the idyll and makes a somewhat freer use of sentiment. See, also, the work of the Kentucky writer, Alice Hegan Rice (ACC) (1870-1942), especially *Mrs. Wiggs of the Cabbage Patch* (1901) and *Lovey Mary* (1903). In its connection with the cult of the child, Mrs. Wiggin's work also suggests that of a number of other writers, among them Eleanor H. Porter (Page, HM) (1868-1920) and the Canadian writer, L. M. Montgomery (Page) (1874-1942), whose *Pollyanna* (1913) and *Anne of Green Gables* (1908) respectively, were widely read. Not even the author's death could stop the *Pollyanna* books, which were continued by other writers. Gene Stratton Porter (D) (1868-1924), who was a naturalist as well as a novelist, had a young hero, instead of a young heroine, in her most popular book, *Freckles* (1904). Eleanor H. Porter also tried the boy protagonist in the very successful *Just David* (1916). Consult Mrs. Wiggin's autobiography, *My Garden of Memory* (1923).

Wister, Owen. See Rhodes, Eugene Manlove.

Wright, Harold Bell (ACC, H) (1872-1944), an untrained preacher turned novelist, was scorned by the critics and regarded by his admirers as almost Shakespeare's equal. A Chicago publishing house devoted itself entirely to his work, pioneering in an intensive program of exploitation such as had never before been applied to the marketing of books. Wright tapped a hitherto largely untouched market; many of his "fans" bought virtually no other books. His most popular titles were *The Shepherd of the Hills* (1907), *The Calling of Dan Matthews* (1909), *The Winning of Barbara Worth* (1911), *The Eyes of the World* (1914), and *When a Man's a Man* (1916). He continued writing until 1942 but his vogue declined after World War I. Total sales ran over 10,000,000 copies. Wright took much material direct from life and checked his data carefully, but he always began with his "message"; according to his own statement, the characters of *The Eyes of the World* bore the names of abstract qualities until the final copy was made. His special vogue was due to his crude dramatizations of "standard," safe and sound American values; beyond any other writer of his time, he reveals the moral and emotional basis upon which the folk functioned. See F. L. Mott's chapter in *Golden Multitudes* and Hildegarde Hawthorne's "The Wright American," in *The Bookman Anthology of Essays,* ed. John Farrar (Do, 1923).

WRIGHT, Richard (H), b. 1908, wrote *Native Son* (1940), the story of a "bad nigger," based upon the actual career of a Chicago criminal. Though not free of sensational elements, it was intended as an indictment of society, and it caused Wright to be hailed as the "best Negro writer" and the author of "a Negro *American Tragedy.*" In England, Rosamond Lehmann found "grandeur" and "moral importance" in his work. In his autobiography, *Black Boy* (1945), Wright documented his novel by describing the horrible conditions under which he himself had been forced to grow up. His *Uncle Tom's Children* (1938) contains four stories describing various aspects of Negro life in the South. Langston HUGHES (K), b. 1902, gives a happier view of Negro life in *Not Without Laughter* (1930), whose setting is a small town in Kansas, but his short stories, in *The Ways of White Folks* (1934), are better known. Zorah Neale HURSTON (Li), b. 1903, refuses to admit any obligation to use her art to express her racial consciousness, but she is a specialist in the field of Negro folklore, which she has used with imaginative power in *Moses: Man of the Mountain* (1939). Her novels— *Jonah's Gourd Vine* (1934), *Their Eyes Were Watching God* (1937), and *Seraph on the Suwanee* (1948)—are all set in the South.

YATES, Elizabeth. See DOUGLAS, Lloyd.

SELECTED BIBLIOGRAPHY WITH ANNOTATIONS

The difference between a good student and a bad one may be instantly and unerringly gauged by their respective attitudes toward bibliography.

WELFORD DESTINN

This bibliography has been made with the same ends and aims as that in *Cavalcade of the English Novel*. It would obviously be absurd to lay any claims to completeness, but my ideal has been fairly comprehensive.

I have in general excluded book reviews and unpublished theses, and I have not attempted any extensive listing of works in foreign languages.

The exclusion of theses has not been due to any lack of appreciation on my part of the important materials therein contained. But most of the people who use this book will not have access to unpublished theses; moreover, in dealing with so vast and inexhaustible a subject as the one to which this book is devoted, some arbitrary limitations become inevitable. I have chosen to draw mine at the confines of print.

In general, I do not hold myself responsible in this bibliography for works which had not been published *and indexed* by June 1, 1951, at which time the task of putting my manuscript into final form began. I have, however, included a considerable number of items which did not become available until after this date; some titles have, in fact, been added as late as galley-proof. These works, it must be evident, I did not have an opportunity to read in time for my own pages to be influenced by them.

Readers should notice that general works, and works treating a considerable number of writers, are listed only at the beginning of the bibliography and not under the individual authors, and also that works which have been adequately described in footnotes are not listed again in this section. When the title of a book or an article is merely the name of the author with which it deals, or when it is not sufficiently descriptive to give the reader an adequate idea of the contents of the article, the title has generally been omitted in bibliographical references. In dealing with writers like Hawthorne and Melville, who have been very extensively written about, I have sometimes grouped under the names of the periodicals in which they appeared, articles of purely biographical, not critical, interest, without mentioning either their authors or their titles. I regret this summary method of dealing with them and adopted it only as a last resort when it became a choice between doing this and leaving such materials out altogether.

In addition to the usual sources of bibliographical information—such as the *Readers' Guide,* the *International Index,* the *Annual Bibliographies* of the Modern Humanities Research Association, and the annual bibliographies in *PMLA*—the bibliographies in the *Literary History of the United States* have been very useful, as has Lewis Leary's *Articles on American Literature Appearing in Current Periodicals, 1920-1945* (DUP, 1947), which is a cumulation of the quarterly bibliographies published in *American Literature;* see the "Addenda" in *AL,* XXII (1950), 61-74. For the later writers, the bibliographies in Fred B. Millett's *Contemporary American Authors* have also been useful.

The following abbreviations are employed not only in this section but also in the Appendix and in the footnote references throughout the book:

ABC	American Book Company	Du	E. P. Dutton & Co., Inc.
ACC	Appleton-Century-Crofts and their predecessors D. Appleton & Co. and D. Appleton-Century Co.	DUP	Duke University Press
		EJ	*English Journal*
		ELH	*Journal of English Literary History*
AL	*American Literature*	*ES*	*English Studies*
AM	*Atlantic Monthly*	*Fort*	*Fortnightly Review*
Am Merc	*American Mercury*	FSY	Farrar, Straus & Young and Farrar, Straus & Co.
Am Sp	*American Speech*		
Ant R	*Antioch Review*	FW	Funk & Wagnalls Co.
AR	*American Review*	H	Harper & Brothers
AWS	American Writers Series	*HaM*	*Harper's Magazine*
B&L	Boni and Liveright	HB	Harcourt, Brace & Co.
Bkm(L)	*Bookman* (London)	HM	Houghton Mifflin Co.
Bkm(NY)	*Bookman* (NY)	Ht	Henry Holt & Company
BM	The Bobbs-Merrill Company	HUP	Harvard University Press
BPLQ	*Boston Public Library Quarterly*	ISLL	*University of Illinois Studies in Language and Literature*
Ce	The Century Company	*JEGP*	*Journal of English and Germanic Philology*
Ce	*Century Magazine*		
CE	*College English*	K	Alfred A. Knopf, Inc.
CM	Coward-McCann, Inc.	*KR*	*Kenyon Review*
Col	*Colophon*	L	Longmans, Green & Co.
ColUP	Columbia University Press	Li	J. B. Lippincott Co.
CoM	*Cornhill Magazine*	*LA*	*Living Age*
CorUP	Cornell University Press	LB	Little, Brown & Co.
D	Doubleday & Company, Inc. and their predecessors, Doubleday, Page & Company and Doubleday, Doran & Company	*LM*	*London Mercury*
		LSUP	Louisiana State University Press
		LTLS	*London Times Literary Supplement*
Dal R	*Dalhousie R*	M	The Macmillan Company
DM	Dodd, Mead & Co.	McB	Robert M. McBride & Co.
Do	George H. Doran Company	ML	Modern Library
DSP	Duell, Sloan & Pearce, Inc.	*MLJ*	*Modern Language Journal*

MLN	Modern Language Notes	SEP	Saturday Evening Post
MLQ	Modern Language Quarterly	Sl	William Sloane Associates
MP	Modern Philology	SM	Scribner's Magazine
NAR	North American Review	SP	Studies in Philology
ND	New Directions	SR	Sewanee Review
NEQ	New England Quarterly	SRL	Saturday Review of Literature
NMQR	New Mexico Quarterly Review	S&S	Simon & Schuster
NQ	Notes and Queries	SoR	Southern Review
NYHTB	New York Herald-Tribune Books and New York Herald-Tribune Book Review	UCP	University of Chicago Press
		UKCR	University of Kansas City Review
NYTBR	New York Times Book Review	UNCP	University of North Carolina Press
OUP	Oxford University Press		
P	G. P. Putnam's Sons	UOP	University of Oklahoma Press
Pac Spect	Pacific Spectator	UPP	University of Pennsylvania Press
PMLA	Publications of the Modern Language Association of America	UTQ	University of Toronto Quarterly
PQ	Philological Quarterly	UTSE	University of Texas Studies in English
PR	Partisan Review		
PUP	Princeton University Press	VP	Viking Press
QQ	Queen's Quarterly	VQR	Virginia Quarterly Review
RH	Random House	XIX C	Nineteenth Century and After
RES	Review of English Studies	YR	Yale Review
S	Charles Scribner's Sons	YUP	Yale University Press
SAQ	South Atlantic Quarterly		

For bibliography of American fiction, see Lyle H. Wright, *American Fiction, 1774-1850, A Contribution Toward a Bibliography,* revised edition (Huntington Library, 1948). See also Oscar Wegelin, *Early American Fiction, 1774-1830: A Compilation of the Titles of Works of Fiction,* revised edition (Peter Smith, 1929); Otis W. Coan and Richard G. Lillard, *America in Fiction: An Annotated List of Novels That Interpret Aspects of Life in the United States,* revised edition (Stanford Univ. Pr., 1945). For Southern fiction, see also two bibliographies by Janet M. Agnew: *A Southern Bibliography: Fiction, 1929-1938* (LSUP, 1939) and *A Southern Bibliography: Historical Fiction, 1929-1938* (LSUP, 1940).

The three most important books devoted exclusively to the history of the American novel are Carl Van Doren, *The American Novel, 1789-1939,* revised edition (M, 1940); Arthur Hobson Quinn, *American Fiction, An Historical and Critical Survey* (ACC, 1936); and Alexander Cowie, *The Rise of the American Novel* (ABC, 1948). The Van Doren book, which supersedes the author's two earlier works—*The American Novel* (M, 1921) and *Contemporary American Novelists* (M, 1922)— is a comparatively brief but highly competent survey of the whole period indicated in its title. Quinn's is the most detailed study of American fiction in general—short story and novel together, and contains a great deal of information, particularly about the older novelists, which is not elsewhere available. It is not, in general, very sympathetic towards "modern" tendencies in the novel. Cowie's book, which virtually stops with Henry James, is the best book on the period covered.

See also the ff., not all of which are confined entirely to the American novel: Grant Overton, *An Hour of the American Novel* (Li, 1929); Pelham Edgar, *The Art of the Novel from 1700 to the Present Time* (M, 1933); Harry Hartwick, *The Foreground of American Fiction* (ABC, 1934); Herbert J. Muller, *Modern Fiction* (FW, 1937); Gordon H. Gerould, *The Patterns of English and American Fiction* (LB, 1942); George Snell, *The Shapers of American Fiction, 1798-1947* (Du, 1947).

Grant C. Knight covers the 1890's in *The Critical Period in American Literature* (UNCP, 1951). The twentieth century is considered by Frederick Hoffman in *The Modern Novel in America, 1900-1950* (Regnery, 1951). *Fifty Years of the American Novel, 1900-1950, A Christian Appraisal* (S, 1951), is an excellent symposium by Catholic critics, edited by Harold C. Gardiner, S. J. It is devoted mainly to Wharton, Dreiser, Glasgow, Cather, Lewis, Marquand, Fitzgerald, Dos Passos, Faulkner, Hemingway, Wolfe, Steinbeck, Farrell, and Warren. BM have announced Orville Prescott's *In My Opinion: An Inquiry into the Contemporary Novel* for spring 1952.

The American novel also comes in for extended treatment in many books devoted to American literature in general. Of these the most extensive was for many years *The Cambridge History of American Literature,* edited by W. P. Trent, John Erskine, Stuart P. Sherman, and Carl Van Doren, 4 vv. (M, 1917-1921, 1927). More recently we have acquired *Literary History of the United States,* edited by Robert E. Spiller, Willard Thorp, Thomas H. Johnson, Henry Seidel Canby, and others, 3 vv. (M, 1948) and *The Literature of the American People,* by Kenneth B. Murdock, A. H. Quinn, Clarence Gohdes, and George F. Whicher, edited by A. H. Quinn (ACC, 1951). All these works contain valuable bibliographies, and the third volume of *LHUS* is an unparalleled survey of American bibliographical resources, including a guide to manuscript materials. See, further: Vernon Louis Parrington, *Main Currents in American Thought,* 3 vv. (HB, 1927-1930); Grant C. Knight, *American Literature and Culture* (Long and Smith, 1932); Ludwig Lewisohn, *Expression in America* (H, 1932), later known as *The Story of American Literature* (RH, 1939); Walter Fuller Taylor, *A History of American Letters* (ABC, 1936), with valuable bibliographies by Harry Hartwick; Alfred Kazin, *On Native Grounds* (Reynal & Hitchcock, 1942); Russell Blankenship, *American Literature,* revised ed. (Ht, 1949). Many novelists are considered in Van Wyck Brooks, *The Flowering of New England* and its successors, *New England: Indian Summer, The World of Washington Irving, The Times of Melville and Whitman,* and *The Confident Years, 1885-1915* (Du, 1936,

1940, 1944, 1947, 1952). The *Dictionary of American Biography* (S, 1928-1936, 1944) is valuable for reference.

The ff. books contain material as indicated: Henry C. Vedder, *American Writers of Today* (Silver, Burdett, 1894) (Mark Twain, Howells, James, Aldrich, Crawford, etc.); John Erskine, *Leading American Novelists* (Ht, 1910) (C. B. Brown, Cooper, Simms, Hawthorne, Stowe, and Bret Harte); Frederic T. Cooper, *Some American Story Tellers* (Ht, 1911) (Wharton, Tarkington, Norris, Herrick, Crawford, Glasgow, etc.); Harry A. Toulmin, *Social Historians* (Badger, 1911) (Page, Cable, Craddock, J. L. Allen, J. C. Harris); John Macy, *The Spirit of American Literature* (D, 1913) (Cooper, Hawthorne, Mark Twain, Howells, James); John C. Underwood, *Literature and Insurgency* (Kennerley, 1914) (Mark Twain, Howells, James, Wharton, etc.); F. L. Pattee, *A History of American Literature Since 1870* (Ce, 1915); Joyce Kilmer, ed., *Literature in the Making* (H, 1917) (Howells, Tarkington, Herrick, J. L. Allen, Glasgow, etc.); Helen and Wilson Follett, *Some Modern Novelists* (Ht, 1918) (Howells, James, Wharton); C. Lewis Hind, *Authors and I* (John Lane, 1921) (Howells, James, Wharton, Crane, Anderson, R. H. Davis); D. H. Lawrence, *Studies in Classic American Literature* (A. & C. Boni, 1923) (Cooper, Hawthorne, Melville); John Macy, ed. *American Writers on American Literature* (Liveright, 1931) (a valuable survey, including many studies of distinguished writers by their successors); Yvor Winters, *In Defense of Reason* (Morrow, 1947) (Cooper, Hawthorne, Melville, James).

The most comprehensive listing of contemporary American novelists, with bibliographical and biographical (not critical) data is Harry R. Warfel, *American Novelists of Today* (ABB, 1951). See also Fred B. Millett, *Contemporary American Authors* (HB, 1940) and Annie R. Marble, *A Study of the Modern Novel, British and American, Since 1900* (ACC, 1928). There is a good deal of information about contemporary novels and novelists in Helen E. Haines, *What's in a Novel* (ColUP, 1942), and in Bernard DeVoto, *The World of Fiction* (HM, 1950). Valuable essays on authors published by Alfred A. Knopf will be found in *The Borzoi, 1920* and *The Borzoi, 1925*.

For other studies of contemporary American novelists see the works listed hereinafter, generally or as indicated: Régis Michaud, *Mystiques et Réalistes anglo-saxons d'Emerson à Bernard Shaw* (Paris, Colin, 1918) (James, Mark Twain, London, Sinclair, Wharton); Ernest Boyd: *Portraits: Real and Imaginary* (Do, 1924) (Dreiser, Cabell, Hergesheimer); Percy H. Boynton, *Some Contemporary Americans* (UCP, 1924) (Wharton, Tarkington, Dreiser, Cabell, Cather); John Farrar, ed., *The Literary Spotlight* (Do, 1924); Joseph Warren Beach, *The Outlook for American Prose* (UCP, 1926); Elizabeth Drew, *The Modern Novel* (HB, 1926); P. H. Boynton, *More Contemporary Americans* (UCP,

1927) (Melville, Hergesheimer, Anderson, Lewis); Régis Michaud, *The American Novel Today: A Social and Psychological Study* (LB, 1928); Grant Overton, *The Women Who Make Our Novels,* revised ed. (DM, 1928); J. C. Squire, ed., *Contemporary American Authors* (Ht, 1928) (Wharton, Dreiser, Lewis, Hergesheimer, Cather); T. K. Whipple, *Spokesmen* (ACC, 1928) (Dreiser, Anderson, Cather, Lewis); F. L. Pattee, *The New American Literature, 1890-1930* (ACC, 1930); Emily Clark, *Innocence Abroad* (K, 1931) (Cabell, Glasgow, Hergesheimer, Van Vechten, Wylie, etc.); J. W. Beach, *The Twentieth Century Novel* (ACC, 1932); Georges Schreiber, *Portraits and Self-Portraits* (HM, 1936) (Lewis, Hemingway, Dos Passos, Upton Sinclair, etc.); Malcolm Cowley, ed., *After the Genteel Tradition* (Norton, 1937) (Dreiser, Cather, Anderson, Lewis, Cabell, Dos Passos, Hemingway, Wolfe); Ford Madox Ford, *Portraits from Life* (HM, 1937) (James, Crane, Dreiser); Vernon Loggins, *I Hear America* (Crowell, 1937); C. John McCole, *Lucifer at Large* (L, 1937); P. H. Boynton, *America in Contemporary Fiction* (UCP, 1940) (Hergesheimer, Cabell, Anderson, Dreiser, Cather, Lewis, Dos Passos, Wolfe, Steinbeck, etc.); N. Elizabeth Monroe, *The Novel and Society* (UNCP, 1941) (Wharton, Glasgow, Cather); Maxwell Geismar, *Writers in Crisis* (HM, 1942) (Hemingway, Dos Passos, Faulkner, Wolfe, Steinbeck); J. Donald Adams, *The Shape of Books to Come* (VP, 1944); Pierre Brodin, *Les Écrivains Américains d l'entre-deux guerres* (Brentano's, 1945); James Gray, *On Second Thought* (U. of Minn. Pr., 1946) (reprints with later comments reviews of many novels); Robert van Gelder, *Writers and Writing* (S, 1946) (interviews with many novelists); Edwin B. Burgum, *The Novel and the World's Dilemma* (OUP, 1947) (Stein, Hemingway, Faulkner, Richard Wright, Saroyan, Steinbeck, Dreiser, Wolfe); M. Geismar, *The Last of the Provincials* (HM, 1947) (Lewis, Cather, Anderson, Fitzgerald); Lloyd Morris, *Postscript to Yesterday* (RH, 1947); John Peale Bishop, *Collected Essays* (S, 1948); Claude E. Magny, *L'Âge du Roman Américain* (Paris, Editions du Seuil, 1948) (Dos Passos, Hemingway, Faulkner, Steinbeck); William O'Connor, ed., *Forms of Modern Fiction* (U. of Minn. Pr., 1948); Guillermo de Torre, *Valoración Literaria del Existencialismo* (Buenos Aires, Ollentay, 1948) (Dos Passos, Hemingway, Faulkner, Steinbeck); W. M. Frohock, *The Novel of Violence in America* (Southern Methodist Univ., 1950) (Dos Passos, Wolfe, Farrell, Cain, Faulkner, Caldwell, Steinbeck, Hemingway); Josephine L. Jessup, *The Faith of Our Feminists* (Richard R. Smith, 1950) (Wharton, Glasgow, Cather); Edmund Wilson, *Classics and Commercials* (FSY, 1950); J. Donald Adams, *Literary Frontiers* (DSP, 1951). Many important critical essays on contemporary novelists are reprinted in Morton D. Zabel, *Literary Opinion in America,* revised ed. (H, 1951).

Among the works devoted to special types of novel, mention may be made of Morris E. Speare, *The Political Novel* (OUP, 1924); Lucy

Lockwood Hazard, *The Frontier in American Literature* (Crowell, 1927); George A. Dunlap, *The City in the American Novel, 1789-1900* (U. of Penn., 1934); Halford E. Luccock, *Contemporary American Literature and Religion* (Willett, Clark, 1934); Nick A. Ford, *The Contemporary Negro Novel* (Meador, 1936); James H. Barnett, *Divorce and the American Divorce Novel, 1858-1937* (U. of Penn., 1939); Joseph Mersand, *Traditions in American Literature: A Study of Jewish Character and Authors* (Modern Chapbooks, 1939); W. F. Taylor, *The Economic Novel in America* (UNCP, 1942); V. L. Parrington, Jr., *American Dreams: A Study of American Utopias* (Brown U. Pr., 1947). Best sellers have been studied by Frank L. Mott, *Golden Multitudes* (M, 1947) and James D. Hart, *The Popular Book* (OUP, 1950).

Chapter I: Brockden Brown and the Pioneers

GENERAL. The pioneering account of *The Early American Novel* is Lillie D. Loshe's (ColUP, 1907), but there is now a fuller and richer account in Chapters I-III of Cowie's *Rise of the American Novel*. For one type of early American fiction, see Herbert Ross Brown's richly entertaining *The Sentimental Novel in America, 1789-1860* (DUP, 1940).

THE POWER OF SYMPATHY has been edited by Milton Ellis, 2 vv., for the Facsimile Text Society (ColUP, 1937). See, further, Ellis, "The Author of the First American Novel," *AL*, IV (1932-1933), 365-368, and two articles by Tremaine McDowell, "The First American Novel," *AR*, II (1933), 73-81, and "Last Words of a Sentimental Heroine," *AL*, IV, 174-177.

MRS. ROWSON. The definitive edition of *Charlotte Temple* is that of Francis W. Halsey (FW, 1905). The fullest modern study is R. W. G. Vail, "SHR, The Author of 'Charlotte Temple,'" *Proceedings of the American Antiquarian Society*, XLII, Part I (1932), pp. 47-160. There is a fine essay by Constance Rourke in *The Roots of American Culture* (HB, 1942).

MRS. FOSTER. *The Coquette* has been edited by H. R. Brown for the Facsimile Text Society (ColUP, 1939). For historical backgrounds, cf. Caroline Dall, *The Romance of the Association; or, One Last Glimpse of Charlotte Temple and Eliza Wharton* (Cambridge, John Wilson, 1875) and Charles K. Bolton, *The Elizabeth Whitman Mystery* (Peabody Hist. Soc., 1912). Cf. also R. L. Shurter, "Mrs. HWF and the Early American Novel," *AL*, IV (1932-1933), 306-308.

ROYALL TYLER. See Frederick Tupper, "RT, Man of Law and Man of Letters," *Proc. Vt. Hist. Soc.*, 1928, pp. 65-101.

GILBERT IMLAY. See Ralph L. Rusk, "The Adventures of GI," *Ind. U.*

Studies, X, No. 57, 1923; O. F. Emerson, "Notes on GI," *PMLA*, XXXIX (1924), 406-439.

H. H. BRACKENRIDGE. The authority on B is Claude M. Newlin; see his *The Life and Writings of HHB* (PUP, 1932). For a briefer account, cf. int. to his edition of *Modern Chivalry* (ABC, 1937). See also John Dos Passos, *The Ground We Stand On* (HM, 1941).

BROCKDEN BROWN. The last collected edition was that of David McKay, 6 vv. (1887). *Wieland* has been edited by F. L. Pattee (HB, 1926), *Edgar Huntly* by David Lee Clark (M, 1928), and *Ormond*, by Ernest Marchand (ABC, 1937). William Dunlap wrote *The Life of CBB*, 2 vv. (Philadelphia, James P. Parke, 1815); the fullest modern study is Harry R. Warfel, *CBB, American Gothic Novelist* (U. of Florida Pr., 1949). See also Lulu R. Wiley, *The Sources and Influence of the Novels of CBB* (Vantage Press, 1951). The following older articles are still of interest: E. T. Channing, *NAR*, IX (1819), 58-77; John Neal, *Blackwood's*, XVI (1824), 415-428; W. H. Prescott, *Biog. and Critical Miscellanies* (Bentley, 1845); Margaret Fuller, *Papers on Literature and Art*, II (Wiley & Putnam, 1846); Anon., *American Review*, I (1848), 260-274; R. H. Dana, Sr., *Poems and Prose Writings*, II (Baker & Scribner, 1850); H. T. Tuckermann, *Mental Portraits* (Bentley, 1853); Richard Garnett, *Cornhill*, N.S. XIII (1902), 494-506. Martin S. Vilas may be said to have inaugurated the modern study of B with his badly-written *CBB, A Study in Early American Fiction* (Burlington, Vt., Free Press Assn., 1904). Cf. also Walter Just, *Die Romantische Bewegung in der Amerikanischer Literatur: Brown, Poe, Hawthorne* (Berlin, Mayer and Müller, 1910); Max Fricke, *CBBs Leben und Werke* (Hamburg, Otto Meissners Verlag, 1911). There are three important studies by D. L. Clark: "BB and the Rights of Women," *U. of Texas Bulletin*, No. 2212 (1922); "BB's First Attempt at Journalism," *UTSE*, VII (1927), 155-174; "Unpublished Letters of CBB and W. W. Wilkins," *ibid.*, XXVII (1948), 75-107. Other modern criticism includes: Annie R. Marble, *Heralds of American Literature* (UCP, 1907); Warren B. Blake, "BB and the Novel," *SR*, XVIII (1910), 431-443; Carl Van Doren, "Minor Tales of BB," *Nation*, C (1915), 46-47; Edith Birkhead, *The Tale of Terror* (Constable, 1921); G. E. Woodberry, *Lit. Memoirs of the Nineteenth Century* (HB, 1921); B. M. Stearns, "A Speculation Concerning CBB," *Penn. Mag. Hist. & Biog.*, LIX (1935), 99-105; Howard W. Hintz, *The Quaker Influence in American Literature* (Revell, 1940); William Peden, "Thomas Jefferson and CBB," *Maryland Q.*, No. 2 (1944), 65-68; C. C. Cole, Jr., "BB and the Jefferson Administration," *Penn. Mag. Hist. & Biog.*, LXXII (1948), 253-263; John G. Frank, "The Wieland Family . . . ," *Monatshefte*. XLII (1950), 347-353.

Chapter II. The Novel Established: The Age of Cooper and Simms

COOPER. The first definitive collection of C's novels (W. A. Townsend, 1859-1861) was notable for the illustrations of F. O. C. Darley. HM's "Household Edition" carried introductions by C's daughter, Susan Fenimore Cooper. P published the lavish "Leatherstocking Edition" (1895-1900), later reprinted in cheaper form as the "Mohawk Edition." Important modern edited texts included *The Deerslayer* by Gregory L. Paine (HB, 1927), *The Spy,* by Tremaine McDowell (S, 1931), and *Satanstoe,* by R. E. Spiller and J. D. Coppoch (ABC, 1937). The standard bibliography is Spiller and Philip C. Blackburn, *A Descriptive Bibliography of the Writings of JFC* (Bowker, 1934). Spiller's *JFC, Representative Selections,* "AWS" (ABC, 1936) lists writings about C.

There is no authorized biography. C's grandson, JFC, edited his *Correspondence,* 2 vv. (YUP, 1922). S. F. Cooper wrote of her father in *Pages and Pictures from the Writings of JFC* (Townsend, 1861); in "Small Family Memories," included in *Correspondence,* I; and in two *AM* articles: "A Glance Backward," LIX (1887), 199-206, and "A Second Glance Backward," LX (1887), 474-486.

The first general biographical and critical study was Thomas R. Lounsbury (HM, 1882). W. B. S. Clymer (Small, Maynard, 1900) is a brief biography, based on Lounsbury. Mary E. Phillips (John Lane, 1913) and Henry W. Boynton (Ce, 1931) are sympathetic studies of C's personal aspects. R. E. Spiller, *FC, Critic of His Times* (Minton, Balch, 1931) is a scholarly biography, set in the context of C's intellectual development. The most elaborate study for the period covered is Marcel Clavel, *FC, sa vie et son oeuvre: La jeunesse, 1789-1826,* and its complementary history of criticism, *FC and His Critics* (both, Aix-en-Provence, Imprimerie Universitaire de Provence, 1938). The latest general study is James Grossman (Sl, 1949).

The following books and articles are of varied interest: W. G. Simms, *Views and Reviews,* I (Wiley & Putnam, 1845); Francis Parkman, *NAR,* CLIV (1852), 147-161; *Memorial of JFC* (P, 1852); H. T. Tuckermann, *NAR,* CLXXXV (1859), 289-316; S. G. Hilliard, *AM,* IX (1862), 52-68; John Esten Cooke, "C's Indians," *Appleton's Journal,* XII (1874), 264-267; Brander Matthews, *Americanisms and Britticisms* (H, 1892); William Winter, *Old Shrines and Ivy* (Moffat Yard, 1892); Leon H. Vincent, *American Literary Masters* (HM, 1906); W. C. Brownell, *American Prose Masters* (S, 1909); T. W. Higginson, *Carlyle's Laugh* (HM, 1909); E. E. Hale, Jr., "American Scenery in C's Novels," *SR,* XVIII (1910), 317-332; James Routh, "The Model of the Leatherstocking Tales," *MLN,* XXVIII (1913), 77-79; Preston A. Barba, "C in Germany," *Ind. U. Studies,* No. 21 (1914); W. B. Cairns, "British

Criticisms of American Writings, 1815-1833," *U. of Wisc. Studies Lang. & Lit.,* No. 14 (1922); Eric Partridge, "FC's Influence on the French Romantics," *MLR,* XX (1925), 174-178; F. L. Pattee, *Am Merc,* IV (1925), 289-297; Margaret M. Gibb, *Le Roman de bas-de-cuir; étude sur FC et son influence en France* (Paris, Champion, 1927); Louise Pound, "The Dialect of C's Leatherstocking," *Am Sp,* II (1927), 479-488; G. C. Bosset, *FC et le roman d'aventure en France vers 1830* (Paris, Vrin, 1928); Régis Messac, "FC et son influence en France," *PMLA,* XLIII (1928), 1199-1201; R. E. Spiller, "C's Notes on Language," *Am Sp,* IV (1929), 294-300; J. A. Russell, "C, Interpreter of the Real and Historical Indian," *Jour. of Amer. Hist.,* XXIII (1930), 41-71; T. McDowell, "The Identity of Harvey Birch," *AL,* II (1930), 111-120, and "JFC as Self-Critic," *SP,* XXVI (1930), 508-516; Ernest A. Baker, *The History of the English Novel,* VII (Witherby, 1936); Yvor Winters, *Maule's Curse* (ND, 1938); Edward P. Vandiver, Jr., "JFC and Shakespeare," *Sh. Assn. Bull.,* XV (1940), 110-117; several articles in *New York History,* XXII (1941), 18-51, including a report of the sesquicentennial celebration; Phyllis Bentley, in *London Calling,* ed. Storm Jameson (H, 1942); Roy H. Pearce, "The Leatherstocking Tales Re-examined," *SAQ,* XLVI (1947), 524-536; H. H. Scudder, "C and the Barbary Coast," *PMLA,* LXII (1947), 784-792; Walter Sutton, "C as Found," *UKCR,* XVI (1949), 3-10; R. H. Pearce, "Civilization and Savagism: The World of the Leatherstocking Tales," *English Institute Essays, 1949* (ColUP, 1950); Charles Anderson, "C's Novels Spurned in the Maintop," *MLN,* LXVI (1951), 388-391; Max L. Griffin, "C's Attitude Toward the South," *SP,* XLVIII (1951), 67-76; James Grossman, "JFC: An Uneasy American," *YR,* XL (1951), 696-709.

Thackeray burlesqued C in *Novels by Eminent Hands* and Bret Harte in *Condensed Novels.* Cf. also John V. A. Weaver's burlesque review, "FC, Comic," *Bkm*(NY), LIX (1924), 13-15. Balzac's piece on "FC and Walter Scott" is reprinted in Katharine P. Wormeley's *The Personal Opinions of Honoré de Balzac* (LB, 1908).

SIMMS. There is no inclusive edition of S's novels. Alexander Cowie edited *The Yemassee* for ABC (1937). For bibliography, see Alexander Samuel Salley, *A Catalogue of the Salley Collection of the Works of WGS. . . .* (Columbia, S. C., printed for A. S. Salley by The State Co., 1943) and Oscar Wegelin, *A Bibliography of the Separate Writings of WGS. . . .* Third Edition, revised. (Hattiesburg, Miss., The Book Farm, 1941). Salley's edition of S's *Sack and Destruction of the City of Charleston, S. C.* (Atlanta, Oglethorpe U. Pr., 1937) contains important material. *The Letters of WGS,* edited Mary C. Simms Oliphant and Alfred Taylor Odell has been announced by U. of S. C. Press. The fullest general study is still W. P. Trent's inadequate *WGS* (HM, 1892). See, further: Edward F. Hayward, "Some Romances of the Revolution," *AM*, LXIV (1889), 627-636; Samuel A. Link, *WGS, the Novelist, the Poet* (Nashville, Tenn., Barbee & Smith, 1896); G. W. Whaley, "A Note on S's Novels," *AL*, II (1930), 173-174; Hampton M. Jarrell, "S's Visits to the Southwest," *AL*, V (1933), 29-35, with which cf. W. S. Hoole, "A Note on S's Visits to the Southwest," *AL*, VI (1934), 334-336; W. G. Hoole, "WGS's Career as Editor," *Georgia Hist. Q.*, XIX (1935), 47-54; R. I. McDavid, Jr., "'Ivanhoe' and S's 'Vasconselos,'" *MLN*, LVI (1941), 294-297; John W. Higham, "The Changing Loyalties of WGS," *J. Southern Hist.*, IX (1943), 210-223; F. H. Deen, "A Comparison of S's 'Richard Hurdis' with its Sources," *MLN*, LX (1945), 406-408; A. T. Odell, "WGS in the Post-War Years," *Bull. Furman U.*, XXIX, No. 3 (May 1946), pp. 5-20; J. Allan Morris, "Gullah in the Stories and Novels of WGS," *Am Sp*, XXII (1947), 46-53; C. H. Holman, "The Influence of Scott and Cooper on Simms," *AL*, XXIII (1951), 203-218. On the Indian specifically, see Jason A. Russell, "The Southwestern Border Indians in the Writings of WGS," *Education*, LI (1930), 144-157, and A. Keiser, *The Indian in American Literature*. J. A. Morris, "The Stories of WGS," *AL*, XIV (1942), 20-35, gives the best account of S's short fiction. S is a character in DuBose Heyward's novel, *Peter Ashley* (FR, 1932).

Chapter III. The Soul's Romance: Hawthorne

The best edition of H is the Old Manse Edition, 22 vv. (HM, 1900), who publish all books in this list not otherwise accredited.

There are bibliographies by Nica C. Browne (1905) and Wallace H. Cathcart (Cleveland, Rowfant Club, 1905). An elaborate listing of material about H: *NH, An Annotated Bibliography*, by Nouvart Tashjian and D. Eckerman (New York, William-Frederick Press) is in preparation; see, also, the bibliography in Austin Warren, *NH: Representative Selections* (ABC, 1934). Other recent collections of H material are in Malcolm Cowley, *The Portable H* (VP, 1948) and Mark Van Doren, *The Best of H* (Ronald Press, 1950). There is an *Analytical Index to the Works of NH* by E. M. O'Connor (1882).

NH and His Wife, 2 vv. (H, 1884), by Julian Hawthorne, is the basic biographical study. See also the same author's *H and His Circle* (H, 1903), *The Memoirs of JH* (M, 1938) and the ff. magazine articles: "The Salem of H," *Ce*, XXVIII (1884), 3-17; "Scenes of H's Romances," pp. 380-397; "H's Philosophy," XXXII (1886), 83-93; "Problems of 'The Scarlet Letter,'" *AM*, LVII (1886), 471-485; "H, Man of Action," *SRL*, III (1927), 727-728—cf. pp. 725, 866, 916; "The Making of 'The Scarlet Letter,'" *Bkm*(NY), LXXIV (1931), 401-411; "NH's Blue Cloak: A Son's Reminiscence," *ibid.*, LXXV (1932), 501-506.

H's younger daughter, Rose Hawthorne Lathrop wrote of him in *Memories of H* (1897); his son-in-law, George P. Lathrop, produced *A Study of H* (1876); his grand-daughter, Hildegarde Hawthorne, wrote *Romantic Rebel* (ACC, 1932) for young readers.

The following are early books about H not written by members of the family: H. A. Page, pseud. Alexander Japp, *Memoir of NH* (London, Henry S. King & Co., 1872); J. T. Fields (1876); Henry James (M, 1879); R. H. Stoddard (S, 1879); Moncure D. Conway (Walter Scott, 1890); Horatio Bridge, *Personal Recollections of NH* (H, 1893); Annie Fields (Small, Maynard, 1899); G. E. Woodberry (1902), L. Dhaleine, *H, sa vie et son oeuvre* (Paris, Hachette, 1905); F. P. Stearns, *The Life and Genius of NH* (Li, 1906); F. B. Sanborn, *H and His Friends* (Torch Press, 1908); Helen A. Clarke, *H's Country* (Baker & Taylor, 1910); M. Clare (D, 1912); Caroline Ticknor, *H and His Publisher* (1913); G. E. Woodberry, *H: How To Know Him* (BM, 1918).

With the 1920's, H biography became very psychological: Lloyd Morris, *The Rebellious Puritan* (HB, 1927); Herbert Gorman, *H, A Study in Solitude* (D, 1927); Julien Green, *Un puritan homme de lettres, NH* (Paris, Editions des Cahiers Libres, 1928); Newton Arvin (LB, 1929); Bliss Carman (Palo Alto, N. Van Patten, 1929); L.-E. Chrétien, *La Pensée morale de NH* (Paris, Didier, 1932); Elisabeth Reti, *H's Verhältnis zur New-England-Tradition* (Rüstringen, Wiechmann, 1935); Edward Mather, *NH, A Modest Man* (Crowell, 1940).

Few of these later books were entirely satisfactory. Until very recently the best modern comprehensive study of H in book-form was in F. O. Matthiessen, *American Renaissance* (OUP, 1941). During the 'thirties and 'forties very important work about H was being published serially by such scholars as Randall Stewart, Arlin Turner, Manning Hawthorne, and a few others.

The best biography of H is now Randall Stewart (YUP, 1948). The best general biographical-critical study is Mark Van Doren (Sl, 1949). Robert Cantwell, *NH, The American Years* (Rinehart, 1948) promises to be the most detailed biography of H but does not always reflect good judgment. Louise Hall Tharp, *The Peabody Sisters of Salem* (LB, 1950) is both sound and delightful. Jane Lundblad's *NH and European Literary Tradition* (HUP, 1947) concerns largely H's relationship to Balzac, the Gothic novels, and Madame de Staël. Cf. N. F. Doubleday, "H's Use of Three Gothic Patterns," *CE*, VII (1946), 250-262.

Vernon Loggues, *The Hawthornes* (ColUP, 1951) tells the story of the family in America from the early 1600's to 1934.

N. Arvin's *The Heart of H's Journals* (1929) is a useful abridgement, but all previous editions of H's Journals have now been superseded by Stewart's editions of *The American Notebooks* (YUP, 1932) and *The English Notebooks* (Modern Language Association, 1941), which have been newly edited from manuscript. A similarly definitive edition of the *French and Italian Notebooks* is being prepared by Norman H. Pearson. The authenticity of Samuel to Pickard's *H's First Diary* (1897) is still disputed; cf. *Dial*, XXXIII (1902), 155.

A complete collection of H's Letters is in preparation. The largest collections now available are in *Love-Letters of NH* . . . 2 vv. (Chicago, Society of the Dofobs, 1907); *Letters of H to William D. Ticknor, 1851-1864* (Newark, The Carteret Book Club, 1910); in *NH and His Wife* and some other biographical works. Scattered letters and other biographical data will be found in *NEQ*, V (1932), 237-263; VI (1933), 445-469; XI (1938), 66-88; XII (1939), 173-184, 235-241, 726-730; XIII (1940), 246-279; XVII (1944), 418-423; XX (1947), 209-231; in *AL*, XVI (1945), 316-331, XXIII (1951), 360-362; in *Col*, N.S. II (1937), 262-282; in *Huntington Lib. Q.*, VII (1944), 387-395; in *More Books*, XIX (1944), 263-279, 303-311; XX (1945), 299-315; XXI (1946), 43-53, 254-263. Granville Hicks, "A Conversation in Boston," *SR*, XXXIX (1931), 129-141, is a charming half-fictionized account of the Peabody milieu.

Hitherto unpublished material is made available in E. L. Chandler, "H's 'Spectator,' " *NEQ*, IV (1931), 289-297; N. H. Pearson, "A Sketch by H," *NEQ*, VI (1933), 136-144; three articles by R. Stewart, "H's Contributions to 'The Salem Advertiser,' " *AL*, V (1934), 327-341; "H's Speeches at Civic Banquets," *AL*, VII (1936), 415-423; "Two Uncollected Reviews by H," *NEQ*, IX (1936), 504-509; Arlin Turner, "H, at Martha's Vineyard," *NEQ*, XI (1938), 394-400.

See, also, these H symposia and special items: *The H Celebration at the Wayside, Concord, Mass., July 4-7, 1904* (1905); *The Proceedings in Commemoration of the One Hundredth Anniversary of the Birth of NH, Held at Salem, Mass., June 23, 1904* (Essex Institute, 1904) and *Dedication of the NH Memorial . . . at Salem, Mass., Dec. 23, 1925* (Salem, 1926). *The Critic* published a "Hawthorne Number" in July 1904.

Studies of H's sources up to 1936 are well summarized by A. Turner in "H's Literary Borrowings," *PMLA*, LI (1936), 543-562. See, further, *AL*, IX (1938), 403-410; X (1938), 311-318; XVI (1944), 26-28; *BPLQ*, III (1951), 244-246; *NEQ*, XIV (1941), 664-678; XVI (1943), 432-443; XVII (1944), 597-604; *MLN*, LXI (1946), 14-21; *UTSE*, XVIII (1938), 140-162; A. Turner, "H's Methods of Using His Source Materials," *Studies for William A. Read* (LSUP, 1940).

Various special topics are considered in: H. M. Belden, "Poe's Criticism of H," *Anglia*, XXIII (1901), 376-404; T. T. Munger, "Notes on 'The Scarlet Letter,' " in *Essays for the Day* (1904); B. M. Woodbridge, "The Supernatural in H and Poe," *Colo. College Publ.*, Lang. Series, II, Nos. 26-28, pp. 135-154 (1911); E. C. Ross, "A Note on 'The Scarlet Letter,' "

MLN, XXXVII (1922), 58-59; H. E. Thorner, "H, Poe, and a Literary Ghost," *NEQ*, VII (1934), 146-154; R. Stewart, "H in England: The Patriotic Motive in the Note Books," *NEQ*, VIII (1935), 3-13; C. A. Manning, "H and Dostoevsky," *Slavonic R.*, XIV (1936), 417-424; R. Stewart, "The Concord Group," *SR*, XLIV (1936), 434-446; A. Turner, "A Note on H's Revisions," *MLN*, LI (1936), 426-429, and "H as Self-Critic," *SAQ*, XXXVII (1938), 131-138; J. C. Matthews, "H's Knowledge of Dante," *UTSE* (1940), pp. 157-165; Harold P. Miller, "H Surveys His Contemporaries," *AL*, XII (1940), 228-235; N. F. Doubleday, "H's Criticism of New England Life," *CE*, II (1941), 639-653, and "H's Satirical Allegory," III (1941), 325-337; Valadimir Astrov, "H and Dostoevski as Explorers of the Human Conscience," *NEQ*, XV (1942), 296-319; Charles H. Foster, "H's Literary Theory," *PMLA*, LVII (1942), 241-254; A. Turner, "H and Reform," *NEQ*, XV (1942), 700-714; N. F. Adkins, "Early Projected Works of NH," *Bibl. Soc. of Am. Papers*, XXXIX, No. 2 (1945), pp. 119-145; Bertha Faust, *H's Contemporaneous Reputation* (U. of Penn., 1939); R. H. Fogle, "The Problem of Allegory in H's 'Ethan Brand,'" *UTQ*, XVII (1948), 190-203; R. B. Heilman, "H's 'The Birthmark': Science as Religion," *SAQ*, XLVIII (1949), 575-583; L. Daumer, "The Case of Tobias Pearson: H and the Ambiguities," *AL*, XXI (1950), 464-472; Mary E. Dichmann, "H's 'Prophetic Pictures,'" *AL*, XXIII (1951), 188-202; Q. D. Leavis, "H as Poet," *SR*, LIX (1951), 179-205, 426-458; Andrew Schiller, "The Moment and the Endless Voyage: A Study of H's 'Wakefield,'" *Diameter*, I (1951), 7-12.

The following books and articles are mainly of a more or less general critical character: Emile Montégut, "Un romancier pessimiste en Amérique," *Revue des deux Mondes*, XXVIII (1860), 668-703; E. P. Whipple, *Character and Characteristic Men* (1866); R. H. Hutton, *Essays in Literary Criticism* (J. H. Coates & Co., 1876); Anthony Trollope, *NAR*, CXXIX (1879), 203-222; H. W. Longfellow, *Prose Works*, I (1885); Charles C. Starbuck, *Andover R.*, VII (1887), 31-46; R. H. Hutton, *Literary Essays*, Revised edition (M, 1888); Leslie Stephen, *Hours in a Library*, I, Revised edition (P, 1894); G. W. Curtis, *Literary and Social Essays* (H, 1895); W. D. Howells, *My Literary Passions* (H, 1895); J. A. Noble, *Memories and Impressions* (Dent, 1895); F. P. Stearns, *Sketches from Concord and Appledore* (P, 1895); Lewis E. Gates, *Studies and Appreciations* (M, 1900); W. D. Howells, *Heroines of Fiction*, I (H, 1901), and "The Personality of H," *NAR*, CLXXXVII (1903), 872-882; Bliss Perry, *The Amateur Spirit* (1904); Paul Elmer More, *Shelburne Essays*, I and II (1904, 1905); P. H. Frye, *Literary Reviews and Criticisms* (P, 1908); B. Perry, *Park Street Papers* (1908); Henry A. Beers, *Four Americans* (YUP, 1919); Carl Van Doren, "The Flower of Puritanism," *Nation*, CXI (1920), 649-650; G. E. Woodberry,

Literary Memoirs (HB, 1921); Stuart P. Sherman, *Americans* (S, 1922); Robert Lynd, *Books and Authors* (P, 1923); Osbert Burdett, *Critical Essays* (FF, 1925); N. Arvin, "The Relevance of H," *New Student,* VII, No. 18 (1928), pp. 3-5; R. E. Spiller, "The Mind and Art of NH," *Outlook,* CXLIX (1928), 650-652+; A. Birrell, *Et Cetera* (Chatto, 1930); Herbert Read, *The Sense of Glory* (HB, 1930); H. W. Schneider, *The Puritan Mind* (Ht, 1930); H. S. Canby, *Classic Americans* (HB, 1931); Carlos Kling, "H's View of Sin," *Personalist,* XIII (1932), 119-130; Herbert Read, *The Sense of Glory* (HB, 1938); Walter Blair, "Color, Light, and Shadow in H's Fiction," *NEQ,* XV (1942), 74-94; O. L. Zangwill, "A Case of Paramnesia in H," *Character and Personality,* XIII (1945), 246-260; Van Wyck Brooks, *A Chilmark Miscellany* (D, 1948); Kathryn Carlisle, "Wit and Humor in NH," *Bard R.,* III (1949), 86-93; Irving Howe, "H on American Fiction," *Am. Merc.,* LXVIII (1949), 367-374; S. B. Liljegren, "Some Notes on H and H Research," *Studia Neophilologica,* XXI (1949), 1-12; H. B. Parkes, "Poe, H, and Melville: An Essay in Sociological Criticism," *PR,* XVI (1947), 157-165; R. E. Spiller, "The Closed Room and The Haunted Chamber," *SRL,* XXXI, Nov. 6, 1948, p. 14; John T. Flanagan, "The Durable H," *JEGP,* XLIX (1950), 88-96; Norman H. Pearson, *H's Usable Truth and Other Papers, Presented at the 50th Anniversary of N. Y. Lambda Chapter, Phi Beta Kappa* (Canton, N. Y., 1950); Donald A. Ringe, "H's Psychology of the Heart and Head," *PMLA,* LXV (1950), 120-132; John W. Shroeder, " 'That Inward Sphere': Notes on H's Heart Imagery and Symbolism," *PMLA,* LXV (1950), 106-119; Harrison Smith, "H: The Sombre Strain," *SRL,* XXXIII, Nov. 18, 1950, p. 18+; Q. D. Leavis, "H as Poet," *SR,* LIX (1951), 179-205, 426-458.

Chapter IV: The Ambiguities of Herman Melville

The Standard Edition of M's *Works* was published by Constable, 1922-1924. But this will surely be superseded by the edition now being published by Hendricks House, under the editorship of Howard P. Vincent.

A convenient introduction to the study of M is Williard Thorp's *HM, Representation Selections* (ABC, 1938), where see further bibliography. See, also, Raymond Weaver, *HM, Mariner and Mystic* (Do, 1921); John Freeman (M, 1926); Lewis Mumford (HB, 1929); Vega Curl, *Pasteboard Masks, Fact as Spiritual Symbol in the Novels of HM* (HUP, 1931); Charles R. Anderson, *M in the South Seas* (ColUP, 1939) —cf. the author's exciting account of his adventures while writing this book in "The Romance of Scholarship: Tracking M in the South Seas," *Col,* N.S. III (1938), 259-279; Stanley Geist, *HM, The Tragic Vision and the Heroic Ideal* (HUP, 1939); F. O. Matthiessen, in *American*

Renaissance (OUP, 1941); William Braswell, *M's Religious Thought* (DUP, 1943); William Ellery Sedgwick, *HM, The Tragedy of Mind* (HUP, 1944); Richard Chase (M, 1949); Geoffrey Stone (Sheed & Ward, 1949); Nathalia Wright, *M's Use of the Bible* (DUP, 1949); Newton Arvin (Sl, 1950). William H. Gilman's *M's Early Life and "Redburn"* (N. Y. U. Pr., 1951), Leon Howard's *HM, A Biography* (U. of Cal. Pr., 1951), Jay Leyda's immense accumulation of material in *The M Log,* 2 vv. (HB, 1951), and his volume of selections, *The Portable Melville* (VP, 1952) did not appear early enough to be used extensively in the writing of this book. *M's Quarrel with God,* by Lawrance Thompson, has been announced for 1952 by PUP. Works in foreign languages include Karl H. Sundermann, *HM's Gedankengut, eine kritische Untersuchung seiner weltanschaulichen Grundideen* (Berlin, A. Collignon, 1937); Walter Weber, *HM, eine stilistische Untersuchung* (Basel, Philographischer Verlag, 1937); Jean Simon, *HM, marin, métaphysicien, et poète* (Paris, Boivin, 1939); Jean Giono, *Pour saluer M* (Paris, Gallimard, 1941).

For letters and bibliographical material see Meade Minnigerode, *Some Personal Letters of HM and a Bibliography* (Brick Row Book Shop, 1922); Michael Sadleir, *Excursions in Victorian Bibliography* (Constable, 1922); V. H. Paltsits, *The Family Correspondence of HM, 1830-1904, in the Gansevoort-Lansing Collection* (N. Y. Pub. Libr., 1929). A more extensive bibliography and a more extensive collection of letters are in preparation. The following journals have appeared: "Journal of M's Voyage in a Clipper Ship," *NEQ,* II (1929), 120-125; *Journal Up the Straits, Oct. 11, 1856-May 5, 1857,* ed. R. Weaver (The Colophon, 1935); *Journal of a Cruise to the Pacific Ocean, 1842-1844, in the Frigate United States,* etc., ed. C. R. Anderson (DUP, 1937); *Journal of a Visit to London and the Continent, 1849-1850,* ed. Eleanor Melville Metcalf (HUP, 1948). For additional letters and biographical data, see also: *AL,* II (1930), 281-283; IX (1937), 26-48, 49-55; XI (1939), 23-38; XV (1943), 251-261; XIX (1947), 169; *BPLQ,* II (1950), 327-347; *ELH,* XI (1944), 76-83; *MLN,* LIX (1944), 52-55, 56-59; LXIV (1949), 241-245; *MLQ,* X (1949), 168-173, 377-388; *Month,* IV (1950), 180-186; *More Books,* XXII (1947), 203-208; *Nation & Athenaeum,* XXIX (1921), 712-713; *New Col.,* I (1948), 239-255; *NEQ,* VIII (1935), 99-105, 405-408; X (1937), 526-531; XXIII (1950), 97-99; *N. Y. History,* XV (1934), 144-159; *N. Y. Pub. Libr. Bull.,* LII (1948), 362-369; *NQ,* CLXXII (1937), 254-258, 272-276; *PMLA,* LXVI (1951), 613-625; *PQ,* XV (1936), 1-15; XVI (1937), 344-357; XVII (1938), 1-17; XIX (1940), 370-379; *UKCR,* III (1937), 254-262.

Various special topics are considered in the following: Leon Howard, "M and Spenser," *MLN,* XLVI (1931), 291-292; Russell Thomas,

"M's Use of Some Sources in 'The Encantadas,'" *AL*, III (1932), 432-456; Jean Simon, "Recherches Australiennes sur HM," *Revue Anglo-Amér.*, XIII (1935), 114-129; R. Thomas, "Yarn for M's 'Typee,'" *PQ*, XV (1936), 16-29; C. R. Anderson, "Contemporary American Opinions of 'Typee' and 'Omoo,'" *AL*, IX (1937), 1-25; L. S. Mansfield, "M's Comic Articles on Zachary Taylor," *AL*, IX (1938), 411-418; W. Thorp, "'Grace Greenwood' Parodies 'Typee,'" *AL*, IX (1938), 455-457; James M. Purcell, "M's Contributions to English," *PMLA*, LVI (1941), 797-808; W. Thorp, "Did M Review 'The Scarlet Letter'?" *AL*, XIV (1942), 302-305; Elizabeth S. Foster, "M and Geology," *AL*, XVII (1945), 50-65—cf. discussion by T. Hillway, *AL*, XXI (1949), 232-237, and E. Foster, XXII (1951), 479-487, and two articles by Hillway on related themes: "M's Use of Two Pseudo-Sciences," *MLN*, LXIV (1949), 145-150, and "M as Critic of Science," *MLN*, LXV (1950), 411-414; E. S. Oliver, "A Second Look at 'Bartleby,'" *CE*, VI (1946), 431-439; Herbert W. Schneider, *A History of American Philosophy* (ColUP, 1946), in which the author attempts to formulate M's philosophy; E. S. Oliver, "'Cock-a-Doodle-Doo!' and Transcendental Hocus-Pocus," *NEQ*, XXI (1948), 204-216; M. M. Sealts, Jr., "M's Reading. . . ," *Harvard Libr. Bull.*, II (1948), 141-163 and continuation; J. W. Nicol, "M's Soiled Fish of the Sea," *AL*, XXI (1949), 338-339; Harry R. Stevens, "M and Music," *Musicology*, II (1949), 405-421; R. W. B. Lewis, "M on Homer," *AL*, XXII (1950), 166-176; L. I. Lutwack, "HM and 'Atlantic Monthly' Critics," *Hunt. Libr. Q.*, XIII (1950), 414-416; M. M. Sealts, Jr., "Did M Write 'October Mountain'?" *AL*, XXII (1950), 178-182; M. L. Williams, "Some Notices and Reviews of M's Novels in American Religious Periodicals, 1846-1849," *AL*, XXII (1950), 119-127; Charles A. Fenton, "'The Bell-Tower': M and Technology," *AL*, XXIII (1951), 219-232; T. Hillway, "M as Amateur Zoologist," *MLQ*, XII (1951), 159-164.

The following deal with *Moby-Dick* alone: A. McK. MacMechan, *The Life of a Little College* . . . (HM, 1914); E. L. Grant Watson, *LM*, III (1920-1921), 180-186; A. Birrell, *LA*, CCCVIII (1921), 659-661; H. M. Tomlinson, *Lit. R.*, II (1921), 141-142; W. W. Wells, "'Moby-Dick' and Rabelais," *MLN*, XXXVIII (1923), 123; A. S. W. Rosenbach, *An Introduction to HM's "Moby-Dick"* (Kennerley, 1924); C. Van Doren, *Bkm*(NY), LIX (1924), 154-157, and *Ce*, CX (1925), 494-501; H. M. Tomlinson, *HaM*, CLII (1926), 618-621; W. S. Ament, *AL*, IV (1932), 39-47; Leon Howard, *MLN*, XLIX (1934), 310-311; R. S. Forsythe, *NQ*, CLXXII (1937), 296; R. G. Berkelman, *EJ*, Coll. ed., XXVII (1938), 742-755; A. W. Parks, *SR*, XLVII (1939), 130-132; R. P. Blackmur, *The Expense of Greatness* (Arrow Editions, 1940); David Potter, *Journal Rutgers U. Libr.*, III (1940), 62-65; S. W. D. Scott, *AL*, XI

(1940), 91-98; T. O. Mabbott, *NQ*, CLXXXI (1941), 47-48—cf. Charles Duffy, pp. 278-279; William White, *NQ*, CLXXXI (1941), 403; Henry A. Myers, *NEQ*, XV (1942), 15-34; F. Pirano, *Convivium*, XV (1943), 209-243; C. C. Walcutt, *MLN*, LIX (1944), 304-310; W. H. Auden, *NYTBR*, Dec. 16, 1945, p. 1+; Joseph Jones, *UTSE* (1945-1946), pp. 51-71, and *AL*, XVIII (1946), 35-37; John C. McCloskey, *PQ*, XXV (1946), 20-31; George Arms, *NQ*, CXCVI (1947), 187-188; M. Belgion, *SR*, LV (1947), 108-125; William Hull, *Etc.*, V (1947), 8-21; W. Thorp, Introduction to his edition of *Moby-Dick* (OUP, 1947); Rudolph von Abele, *Am Merc*, LXV (1947), 592-598; R. L. Cook, *Accent*, VII (1948), 102-109; W. L. Heflin, *AL*, XX (1948), 323-327; M. M. Sealts, Jr., *Papers Bibl. Soc. of Virginia*, II (1949), 104-114; G. H. Mills, *UTSE* (1950), pp. 231-248; Harry Slochower, *Am. Q.*, II (1950), 259-269; Donald Weeks, *Am. Q.*, II (1950), 165-176; Mellicent Bell, *PMLA*, LXVI (1951), 626-648; R. E. Watters, *UTQ*, XX (1951), 155-168. Gordon Roper's "M's 'Moby-Dick,' 1851-1951," *Dalhousie R.*, XXXI (1951), 167-179, is a useful survey of a century of criticism.

The rest is general criticism of M: FitzJames O'Brien, *Putnam's Mag.*, IX (1857), 384-393; H. S. Salt, *Scottish Art R.*, II (1889), 186-190; W. C. Russell, *NAR*, CLIV (1892), 138-149; F. J. Mather, Jr., *Review*, I (1919), 276-278; Viola Meynell, *LA*, CCCIV (1920), 715-720; H. H. Hudson, *Freeman*, III (1921), 156-157; Leonard Woolf, *Nation & Athenaeum*, XXXIII (1923), 688; C. Van Doren, *Ce*, LXXXVI (1924), 272-277; H. P. Marshall, *LM*, XI (1924-1925), 56-70; J. W. N. Sullivan, *Aspects of Science*, Second series (Collins, 1926); V. W. Brooks, *Emerson and Others* (D, 1927); H. S. Canby, *Classic Americans* (HB, 1931); Lloyd Morris, *Open Court*, XLV (1931), 513-526; Stephen A. Larrabee, *SAQ*, XXXIV (1935), 410-418; J. C. Powys, *Enjoyment of Literature* (S&S, 1938); Lorena M. Gary, *SAQ*, XXXVII (1938), 41-45; R. H. Gabriel, *The Course of American Democratic Thought* (Ronald, 1940); Leon Howard, *MLQ*, I (1940), 195-206; R. E. Watters, "M's Metaphysics of Evil," *UTQ*, IX (1940), 170-182; Ben D. Kimpel, *AL*, XVI (1944), 29-32; H. W. Wells, *SAQ*, XLIII (1944), 46-51; E. Opitz, *Contemporary R.*, CLXX (1946), 348-353; Carlos Baker, *NYTBR*, Aug. 10, 1947, p. 2; William S. Dix, "HM and the Problem of Evil," *Rice Inst. Pamphlet*, XXXV, July 1948, pp. 81-107; Jay Leyda, Introduction to *The Complete Stories of HM* (RH, 1949); R. W. Short, "M as Symbolist," *UKCR*, XV (1949), 38-49; R. E. Spiller, *SRL*, XXXII, May 14, 1949, p. 19; Walter Webber, "Some Characteristic Symbolism in HM's Works," *ES*, XXX (1949), 217-224; W. H. Auden, *The Enchafèd Flood* (RH, 1950); M. Cowley, *NR*, CXXIII, Oct. 30, 1950, pp. 24-26; A. Kazin, *PR*, XVII (1950), 67-75; R. E. Spiller, *SRL*, XXXIII, Nov. 25, 1950, pp. 24-25; C. Merton Babcock, "M's Backwoods Seamen," *Western Folklore*, X (1951), 126-133.

Chapter V: Mrs. Stowe and Some Contemporaries

GENERAL. Most of the writers considered in Part I have been inadequately studied. The best general references are Cowie's *Rise of the America Novel,* Brown's *The Sentimental Novel in America,* and Frank L. Mott's *Golden Multitudes: The Story of Best Sellers in the United States* (M, 1947). There are important background materials in E. Douglas Branch, *The Sentimental Years, 1836-1860* (ACC, 1934) and in F. L. Pattee, *The Feminine Fifties* (ACC, 1931). For individual writers, see *Bibliography of the Works of Susan Warner and Anna Bartlett Warner* (Highland Falls, N. Y., Book Hill Press, 1923); Regis L. Boyle, *Mrs. E. D. E. N. Southworth, Novelist* (Catholic U. of America Pr., 1939); Robert P. Eckert, Jr., "Friendly Fragrant Fanny Fern," *Col,* Pt. XVIII (1934). A biography of *Augusta Evans Wilson,* by William Perry Fidler, has been announced by the U. of Alabama Press.

ALCOTT. LMA is published by LB. The authorized biography is Ednah D. Cheney, *LMA: Her Life, Letters and Journals* (LB, 1889). Later biographies include Cornelia Meigs, *Invincible Louisa* (LB, 1933) and Katharine Anthony (K, 1938); but everything else on LMA has now been superseded by Madeleine B. Stern, *LMA* (UOP, 1950). Louise Gulliver has published *LMA: A Bibliography* (LB, 1932). Short studies include Gamaliel Bradford, *Portraits of American Women* (HM, 1919); Katharine Fullerton Gerould, *Modes and Morals* (S, 1920); Marion Talbot, "Glimpses of the Real LMA," *NEQ,* XI (1938), 731-738; E. L. Adams, "LMA's Doomed Manuscripts," *More Books,* XVII (1942), 221-222; Leona Rosenberg, "Some Anonymous and Pseudonymous Thrillers of LMA," *Papers Bibl. Soc. Am.,* XXXVII (1943), 131-140.

ALGER. See Herbert R. Mayes, *Alger, A Biography Without a Hero* (Macy-Masius, 1928). There are two articles: F. L. Allen, *SRL,* XVIII, Sept. 17, 1938, pp. 3-4+; Stewart Holbrook, "HA Was No Hero," *Am Merc,* LI (1940), 203-209. In 1945 Crown published an omnibus of four Alger novels, *Struggling Upward and Other Works,* with int. by Russel Crouse.

MRS. STOWE. Mrs. S's books are published by HM, who are responsible for everything in this note not otherwise accredited. Biographical studies have been published by Florence T. McCray, *The Life-Work of the Author of "UTC,"* (FW, 1889); *Charles E. Stowe, Life of HBS (1889); *Annie Fields, Life and Letters of HBS (1897); *C. E. Stowe and L. B. Stowe (1911); M. F. Crow (ACC, 1913); Constance Rourke, *Trumpets of Jubilee* (HB, 1927); *L. B. Stowe, Saints, Sinners, and Beechers (BM, 1934); Catherine Gilbertson (ACC, 1937). Works marked with a * are "authorized." But the fullest and finest biography of Mrs. Stowe is now Forrest Wilson, *Crusader in Crinoline* (L, 1941). Hazel Harrod has published "Correspondence of HBS and Elizabeth Barrett Browning," *UTSE*, XXVII (1948), 28-34. Special topics are treated in Grace E. MacLean, *"Uncle Tom's Cabin" in Germany* (ACC, 1910); E. Lucas, *La Littérature anti-esclavagiste au dix-neuvième siècle; étude sur Madame Beecher Stowe et son influence en France* (Paris, E. de Boccard, 1930); T. McDowell, "The Use of Negro Dialect by HBS," *Am Sp*, VI (1931), 322-326; Frank J. Klingberg, "HBS and Social Reform in England," *Am. Hist. R.*, XLIII (1938), 542-552; J. M. Purcell, "Mrs. S's Vocabulary," *Am Sp*, XIII (1938), 230-231. The fullest critical study is in an unpublished Ph.D. thesis by John R. Adams in the Library of the U. of S. Cal. See, further, Nassau W. Senior, *Essays on Fiction* (L, 1864); F. A. Shoup, " 'Uncle Tom's Cabin' Forty Years After," *SR*, II (1893), 88-104; A. Fields, *Authors and Friends* (1896); W. A. Guerry, *SR*, VI (1898), 335-344; G. Bradford, *Portraits of American Women* (1919); E. K. Maxfield, " 'Goody Goody' Literature and Mrs. S," *Am Sp*, IV (1929), 189-202; Grace Seiler, *CE*, XI (1949), 127-138.

HOLMES. Since Holmes is not essentially a novelist, no general bibliography is given here. His books are published by HM. See H. H. Clark, "Dr. H: A Reinterpretation," *NEQ*, XII (1939), 19-34; E. Roditi, "OWH as Novelist," *Accent*, I (1945), 23-33. Clarence P. Oberndorfer's *The Psychiatric Novels of OWH* (ColUP, 1943), which is based upon the assumption that H was "a precursor of Freud," consists of abridgments of the novels with introductions and "psychiatric annotations."

DEFOREST. For biographical information, see the introductions to H's 1939 reprint of *Miss Ravenel's Conversion* and the YUP editions of two non-fiction works: *A Volunteer's Adventures* (1946) and *A Union Officer in the Reconstruction* (1948). For criticism, see W. D. Howells, *My Literary Passions* and *Heroines of Fiction*, II; Clarence Gordon, "Mr. DeF's Novels," *AM*, XXXII (1873), 611-621; Clara F. McIntyre, "JWDeF, Pioneer Realist," *U. of Wyo. Publ.*, IX (1942), No. 1.

Chapter VI: "The Lincoln of Our Literature": Mark Twain

All books in this bibliography not otherwise accredited are published by H, who have published several sets of MT's books, including the Mississippi Edition and the Uniform Trade Edition. The standard bibliography is Merle Johnson, *Bibliography of MT, Samuel Langhorne Clemens* (revised edition, 1935). For a fuller listing of writings about MT, see books by Ferguson and Wagenknecht, noted below, and F. L. Pattee, *MT, Representative Selections* (ABC, 1935). A better volume of selections, with excellent introduction, is Bernard DeVoto, *The Portable MT* (VP, 1946).

The following MT items do not appear in collected editions (see also the list in Wagenknecht, pp. 281-282; Ferguson, pp. 336-337): *The Curious Republic of Gondour* (Boni & Liveright, 1919); *Sketches of the Sixties,* by Bret Harte and MT (San Francisco, John Howell, 1926); *Adventures of Thomas Jefferson Snodgrass,* ed. Charles Honce (Covici Friede, 1926); *The Washoe Giant in San Francisco,* ed. Franklin Walker (S.F., George Fields, 1938); *Letters from the Sandwich Islands,* ed. G. Ezra Dane (Stanford U. Pr., 1937, 1938; Chicago, Lakeside Pr., 1939)—cf. *AL,* XXI (1949), 252; *Letters from Honolulu,* ed. John W. Vandercook (Honolulu, Thomas Nickerson, 1939); *MT's Travels with Mr. Brown,* ed. F. Walker and G. E. Dane (K, 1940); *Republican Letters,* and *Washington in 1868,* ed. Cyril Clemens (International MT Soc., 1941, 1943)—cf. *AL,* XIII (1942), 439-440; XIV (1943), 430-431; XVI (1944), 32-34; *MT's Letters in the Muscatine Journal,* ed. E. M. Branch (MT Assn. of America, 1942); *The Letters of Quintus Curtius Snodgrass,* ed. E. E. Leisy (University Press in Dallas, 1946); Walter F. Frear, *MT and Hawaii* (Lakeside Pr., 1947), which reprints all MT material bearing on Hawaii, with an exhaustive discussion. The definitive edition of the often surreptitiously printed *1601: or, Conversation as It Was by the Social Fireside in the Time of the Tudors* . . . , with bibliography and collations, was edited by F. J. Meine (MT Soc. of Chicago, 1939). See, also, the only complete edition of *Life on the Mississippi,* with suppressed passages restored, and discussion by E. Wagenknecht and Willis Wager (Heritage Press, 1944).

Albert Bigelow Paine wrote the authorized *MT, A Biography,* 3 vv. (1912) and edited MT's *Letters,* 2 vv. (1917), *Speeches* (1910), *Autobiography,* 2 vv. (1924), and *Notebook* (1935). (See DeLancey Ferguson, "The Uncollected Portions of MT's Autobiography," *AL,* VIII, 1936, 37-46). A third volume of autobiography, *MT in Eruption,* was edited by Bernard DeVoto (1940). See also *MT's Letters to Will Bowen,* ed. Theodore Hornberger (U. of Texas Pr., 1941); *MT, Business Man,* ed. Samuel C. Webster (LB, 1946), which includes discussion as well as correspondence: *MT in Three Moods* (Friends Huntington Libr., 1948), *MT to Mrs. Fairbanks* (Hunt. Libr., 1949), and *The Love Letters of MT* (1949), all ed. Dixon Wecter. For uncollected letters and other fresh MT material, not elsewhere available, see Coley B. Taylor, *MT's Margins on Thackeray's "Swift"* (Gotham House, 1935) and the ff. serials: *AL,* II (1930), 25-53, VII (1936), 453-455, VIII (1936), 47-51, 304-305, X (1938-1939), 343-349, 468-488, XI (1939), 78-81, 247-259, XIII (1942), 405-410, XVII (1945), 348-352, XVIII (1946), 299-307, XIX (1947), 219-230, XX (1948), 111-128, 446-449, XXI (1950), 456-463, XXII (1950), 290-307; *HaM,* CXCII (1946), 106-109—cf. DeVoto's commentary, pp. 309-312; *Ind. Mag. Hist.*, XLVI (1950), 363-367; *Iowa Jour. Hist. & Pol.*, XXVIII (1930), 268-270; *Jour. Rutgers U. Libr.*, XXI (1947), 30; *MLN*, XLIV (1929), 256-259; *Pac. Hist. R.*, XVIII (1949), 110-111; *Pac Spect*, II (1948), 485-490; *SAQ*, XLII (1943), 262-269; *Slavonic & East European R.*, XXII (1944), 37-38.

The ff. books about MT have been published: Archibald Henderson (Stokes, 1911)—the pioneer critical study; W. D. Howells, *My MT* (1911); Mary Lawton, *A Lifetime with MT, The Memories of Katy Leary . . .* (HB, 1925); Friedrich Schönemann, *MT als literarische Persönlichkeit* (Jena, Walter Biedermann, 1925)—until Bellamy appeared, the most elaborate critical study, a book which considerably influenced Brashear; Clara Clemens, *My Father MT* (1931); Bernard DeVoto, *MT's America* (LB, 1932); Minnie M. Brashear, *MT, Son of Missouri* (UNCP, 1934)—the best study of MT's first environment; Edward Wagenknecht, *MT, The Man and His Work* (YUP, 1935)— the fullest study of MT's personality; DeVoto, "MT: The Ink of History" and "MT and the Limits of Criticism," in *Forays and Rebuttals* (LB, 1936); Ivan Benson, *MT's Western Years* (Stanford, 1938); George Ade, *One Afternoon with MT* (MT Society of Chicago, 1939); Edgar H. Hemminghaus, *MT in Germany* (ColUP, 1939)—which is really concerned with MT's books in Germany; Opie Read, *MT and I* (Reilly & Lee, 1940); DeVoto, *MT at Work* (HUP, 1942), which includes, among other things noted elsewhere, the "Boy's Manuscript," the original form of *Tom Sawyer;* C. Clemens, *Young Sam Clemens* (Portland, Me., Leon Tebbetts Editions, 1942); DeLancey Ferguson, *MT, Man and Legend* (BM, 1943), excellent critical biography; S. B. Liljegren, *The Revolt against Romanticism in American Literature as Evidenced in the Works of S. L. Clemens* (Upsala, A-B Lundequistska Bokhandeln, 1945); W. C. S. Pellowe, *MT, Pilgrim from Hannibal* (New York, Hobson Book Pr., 1946); Leon Lemonnier, *MT, l'homme et son oeuvre* (Paris, A. Fayard, 1947); E. M. Mack, *MT in Nevada* (S, 1947); Gladys C. Bellamy, *The Literary Apprenticeship of MT* (UOP, 1950); Edgar M. Branch, *The Literary Apprenticeship of MT* (U. of Ill. Pr., 1950); H. S. Canby, *Turn West, Turn East, MT and Henry James* (HM, 1951). A book on MT by the late Dixon Wecter, intended as a definitive study of the early years has been announced by HM. Caroline T. Harnsberger, *MT at Your Fingertips* (Beechhurst Press, 1948) is a kind of topical index.

Further biographical data about MT will be found in the ff. serials: *AL*, VIII (1936), 304-305; XI (1939), 247-259; XII (1940), 333-355; XIII (1942), 398-405; XVI (1944), 198-203; *Huntington Lib. Q.*, VIII (1945), 359-377; *Iowa Jour. Hist. & Pol.*, XXVII (1929), 409-456, 507-547; XLII (1944), 192-198; *Minn. History*, XVII (1936), 369-384; XVIII (1937), 28-35; *Mo. Hist. R.*, XXI (1926), 188-201; XXV (1930), 23-29;

XL (1945), 159-173; *Ohio State Arch. & Hist. Q.*, XLVIII (1938), 69-73; *Pacific Hist. R.*, XV (1946), 336-347; *William and Mary Coll. Q. Hist. Mag.*, XV (1935), 294-298.

The ff. deal with special topics, as indicated: LANGUAGE: Alma B. Martin, *A Vocabulary Study of "The Gilded Age"* (Inter. MT Soc., 1930); R. L. Ramsay & F. G. Emberson, *A MT Lexicon, U. of Mo. Studies*, XIII, Jan. 1938; also *Am Sp*, II (1927), 233-236; XVII (1942), 174-176; XXII (1947), 88-98; *U. of Mo. Studies*, X (1935), 1-53. MT AND GERMAN: *Am. Germ. R.*, VII (1940), 10-11; *Anglia*, LXV (1940), 206-213; *AL*, XIII (1941), 257-264; *MLQ*, VI (1945), 459-478. FOLKLORE: Victor R. West, "Folklore in the Works of MT," *U. of Neb. Studies in Lang. Lit. and Criticism*, No. 10 (1930). MISCELLANEOUS: *AL*, XIII (1941), 29-43; XIV (1942), 66-70; XIX (1947), 139-157; XXIII (1951), 355, 357, 357-359; *Col*, Part I (1930), N.S. II, No. 2 (1937), pp. 189-196; *Hunt. Lib. Q.*, VIII (1945), 359-377; *MLN*, LXIII (1948), 221-228; *PQ*, XXVII (1948), 276-279; *Scand. Studies*, XIV (1937), 159-167; *UTSE*, 1949, pp. 257-270.

The ff. are critical studies: H. D. Sedgwick, *The New American Type* (HM, 1908); W. L. Phelps, *Essays on Modern Novelists* (M, 1910); Stuart Sherman, *On Contemporary Literature* (Ht, 1917); B. Matthews, "MT and the Art of Writing," *HaM*, CXLI (1920), 635-643; H. H. Peckham, "The Literary Status of MT," *SAQ*, XIX (1920), 332-340; Gamaliel Bradford, *American Portraits, 1875-1900* (HM, 1922); Frank Harris, *Contemporary Portraits*, IV (Brentano's, 1923); F. L. Pattee, "On the Rating of MT," *Am Merc*, XIV (1928), 183-191; B. DeVoto, "MT and the Genteel Tradition," *Harv. Grad. Mag.*, XL (1931), 155-163; A. V. Goodpasture, "MT, Southerner," *Tenn. Hist. Mag.*, Ser. II, Vol. I (1931), 253-260; C. Hartley Grattan, in *American Writers on American Literature*, ed. John Macy (Liveright, 1931); Constance Rourke, *American Humor* (HB, 1931); Sir John Adams, "MT, Psychologist," *Dal R*, XIII (1934), 417-426; Richard D. Altick, "MT's Despair: An Explanation in Terms of his Humanity," *SAQ*, XXXIV (1935), 354-367; Newton Arvin, *NR*, LXXXIII (1935), 125-127; Anthony Deane, in Royal Society of Literature, *Essays by Divers Hands*, XIV (1935); Gabriel de Lautrec, *Mercure de France*, CCLXIV (1935), 69-82; T. Dreiser, "Mark the Double Twain," *EJ*, XXIV (1935), 615-627; Leon Lemmonier, *Grande Revue*, CXLIX (1935), 76-88; W. L. Phelps, *YR*, XXV (1935), 291-310; R. Ellis Roberts, *Fort*, No. 827 (1935), 583-592; Owen Wister, *HaM*, CLXXI (1935), 547-556; O. J. Campbell, "Twain versus Clemens," in *Essay Annual*, ed. E. A. Walter (Scott, Foresman, 1936); W. Fischer, *Die neueren Sprachen*, XLIII (1936), 471-480; H. H. Waggoner, "Science in the Thought of MT," *AL*, VIII (1937), 357-370; George Feinstein, "MT's Idea of Story Structure," *AL*, XVIII (1946), 160-163; John W. Hollenbach, "MT, Story-Teller, at Work," *CE*, VII (1946), 303-312; C. O. Parsons, "The Devil and Samuel Clemens," *VQR*, XXIII (1947), 582-600; Van Wyck Brooks, *A Chilmark Miscellany* (D, 1948); Rufus A. Coleman, "Trowbridge and Clemens," *MLQ*, IX (1948), 216-223; Ray B. West, Jr., *UKCR*, XV (1948), 92-104; E. Wagenknecht, *SRL*, XXXIV, Jan. 20, 1951, pp. 25-26.

There are two periodicals devoted to MT: *The MT Quarterly* (International MT Society, 1936 ff.) and *The Twainian* (MT Research Foundation, 1939 ff.). Articles published in these periodicals are generally not listed separately in this bibliography.

Chapter VII: The American Mirror: William Dean Howells

H's novels before *Annie Kilburn* (1888) were published by HM, thereafter by H, except for *The Leatherwood God* (Ce). A proposed collected edition achieved but six volumes (H, 1911). There is an extensive *Bibliography of WDH* (including criticism of H's work) by William M. Gibson and George Arms (N. Y. Pub. Library, 1948). See also the briefer bibliography by the same writers in *WDH, Representative Selections,* ed. Clara M. and Rudolf Kirk (ABC, 1950), whose long introduction is the best general account of H. Another recent collection is H. S. Commager, *Selected Writings of WDH* (RH, 1950).

There are two, important, book-length critical studies: Delmar Gross Cooke (D, 1922) and O. W. Firkins (HUP, 1924). An earlier study by Alexander Harvey (Huebsch, 1917) has little value. See, also, Susanne Königsberger, *Die Romantechnik von WDH* (Düsseldorf, G. H. Nolte, 1933).

Most of H's own books of autobiographical significance have been mentioned in my text and notes. The official biography is Mildred Howells, *Life in Letters of WDH*, 2 vv. (D, 1928). See also the *Letters* of Mark Twain and Henry James. Further letters and other biographical data will be found in *Americana*, XXXVII (1943), 257-295; *AL*, X (1938-1939), 78-80, 492-494, XVIII (1946), 165-168, XXI (1949), 49-55, XXIII (1951), 489-490; *Bibliophile Society of Boston, Twenty-Seventh Annual Report*, 1929, pp. 17-56; *Canadian Bookman*, II (1920), 9-12; *Journal Rutgers U. Library*, IV (1941), 33-44, VIII (1944), 9-13, X (1946), 1-19; *MLN*, LXVI (1951), 266-267; *NEQ*, XVII (1944), 580-591, XXIV (1951), 84-89; *Ohio Arch. & Hist. Q.*, LIII (1944), 39-51; *Studia Neophilologica*, XXII (1949), 48-61.

The following are critical studies: T. W. Higginson, *Short Studies of American Authors* (Lee & Shepard, 1880); W. C. Brownell, *Nation*, XXXI (1880), 49-51; T. S. Perry, *Ce*, XXIII (1882), 680-685; G. H. Badger, *International R.*, XIV (1883), 380-386; Henry James, *Harp. Weekly*, XXX (1886), 394-395; J. M. Robertson, *Essays Toward a Critical Method* (Unwin, 1889); H. T. Peck, *The Personal Equation*

(H, 1898); Cornelia A. P. Comer, *Critic*, XXXV (1889), 1021-1025;
A. Schade von Westrum, "Mr. H and American Aristocracies,"
Bkm(NY), XXV (1907), 67-73; H. Garland, "Sanity in Fiction,"
NAR, CLXXVI (1903), 336-348; W. L. Phelps, *Essays on Modern
Novelists* (M, 1910); H. James, "A Letter to Mr. H," *NAR*, CXCV
(1912), 558-562; W. B. Trites, *Forum*, XLIX (1913), 217-240; H. M.
Alden, *HaM*, CXXXIV (1917), 903-904; Edith Wyatt, *Great Com-
panions* (ACC, 1917); Francis Hackett, *Horizons* (Huebsch, 1918);
Henry B. Schwartz, "The Americanism of WDH," *Methodist R.*, CI
(1918), 226-232; D. G. Cooke, "The Humanity of WDH," *Texas R.*,
VII (1920), 6-25; John Erskine, *Bkm*(NY), LI (1920), 385-389; Henry
A. Lappin, *Catholic World*, CXI (1920), 445-453; Booth Tarkington,
HaM, CXLI (1920), 346-350; A. L. Bass, "The Social Consciousness
of WDH," *NR*, XXVI (1921), 192-194; James M. Dixon, "The Ideals
of WDH," *Personalist*, II (1921), 35-46; Rowland Grey, *Fort*, CXV
(1921), 154-163; James F. Muirhead, "H and Trollope," *LA*, CCCVIII
(1921), 304-309; May Tomlinson, *SAQ*, XX (1921), 360-367; H. M.
Jones, *Freeman*, VII (1923), 163; Carl Van Doren, *The Roving Critic*
(K, 1923); Albert Mordell, "WDH and the Classics," *Stratford Monthly*,
N.S. II (1924), 199-205; W. L. Phelps, *H, James, Bryant, and Other
Essays* (M, 1924); Edmund Gosse, *Silhouettes* (S, 1925); O. W. Firkins,
SRL, V (1949), 774-775; C. H. Grattan, *Am Merc*, XX (1930), 42-50;
George E. de Mille, *Literary Criticism in America* (Dial Pr., 1931);
A. H. Starke, "WDH and Sidney Lanier," *AL*, III (1931), 79-82;
Newton Arvin, *NR*, XCI (1937), 227-228; Owen Wister, *AM*, CLX
(1937), 704-713; Lucy L. Hazard, "H a Hundred Years Later," *Mills Q.*,
XX (1938), 167-172; W. F. Taylor, "WDH, Artist and American,"
SR, XLVI (1938), 288-303; Forrest Reid, *Retrospective Adventures*
(FF, 1941); George Arms, "The Literary Background of H's Social
Consciousness," *AL*, XIV (1942), 260-276; John P. Pritchard, *Return
to the Fountains* (DUP, 1942); Arms and Gibson, " 'Silas Lapham,'
'Daisy Miller,' and the Jews," *NEQ*, XVI (1943), 118-122; Robert B.
Sinclair, "H in the Ohio Valley," *SRL*, XXVIII, Jan. 6, 1945, pp. 22-23;
Edwin S. Morby, "WDH and Spain," *Hispanic R.*, XIV (1946), 187-
212; Gibson, "Materials and Form in H's First Novels," *AL*, XIX
(1947), 158-166; V. W. Brooks, *A Chilmark Miscellany* (Du, 1948);
E. H. Cady, "H in 1948," *UKCR*, XV (1948), 83-91, and *The Gentleman in America* (Syracuse U. Pr., 1949); H. S. Commager, *The American Mind* (YUP, 1950); Virginia Harlow, "WDH and Thomas Sergeant
Perry," *BPLQ*, I (1949), 135-150; Lloyd Morris, "Conscience in the
Parlor," *Am. Scholar*, XVIII (1949), 407-416; John K. Reeve, "The Way
of a Realist: A Study of H's Use of the Saratoga Scene," *PMLA*, LXV
(1950), 1035-1042; Herbert Edwards, "H and Herne," *AL*, XXII
(1951), 432-441; Lionel Trilling, "WDH and the Roots of Modern

Taste," *PR*, XVIII (1951), 516-536; J. L. Woodress, Jr., "H's Venetian Priest," *MLN*, LXVI (1951), 266-267.

Special Howells numbers and sections appeared as follows: *Book News Monthly*, XXVI, June 1908; *Boston Evening Transcript*, Feb. 24, 1912; *Harper's Weekly*, LVI, Mar. 9, 1912, pp. 27-34; *New York Sun*, Feb. 25, 1917; *NAR*, CCXII (1920), 1-20; *American Academy of Arts and Letters, Proceedings*, II, July 1, 1921, pp. 1-21.

Chapter VIII: The American as Artist: Henry James

There are two collected editions of HJ's fiction: The New York Edition, 26 vv. (S, 1907-1909, 1917), and the so-called New and Complete Edition, 35 vv. (London, M, 1921-1923). HJ's non-fiction has never been collected.

LeRoy Phillips has produced the standard *Bibliography of the Writings of HJ*, revised edition (CM, 1930). The best check-list of writings about HJ is in L. N. Richardson, *HJ, Representative Selections* (ABC, 1941). This is reprinted in part in F. W. Dupee's anthology of HJ criticism, *The Question of HJ* (Ht, 1945). It is supplemented by Eunice C. Hamilton, "Biographical and Critical Studies of Henry James, 1941-1948," *AL*, XX (1949), 424-435, and Viola Dunbar, "Addenda . . . ," *AL*, XXII (1950), 56-61.

There is at this writing no formal biography of HJ, though Leon Edel is said to have one in preparation. F. O. Matthiessen, *The James Family* (K, 1947) is an important collection of biographical materials, with selections from the writings of all the Jameses. Simon Nowell-Smith has made an anthology of biographical materials about HJ, *The Legend of the Master* (S, 1948), where further see bibliography.

The largest collection of letters is still Percy Lubbock, *The Letters of HJ*, 2 vv. (S, 1920). See also *Letters to an Editor* [Clement Shorter], privately printed (1916); *"A Most Unholy Trade," Letters on the Drama* (Cambridge, Mass., Dunster House, 1923); *Letters of HJ to Walter Berry* (Black Sun Press, 1928); *HJ: Letters to A. C. Benson and Auguste Monod* (S, 1930); *Theatre and Friendship*, ed. Elizabeth Robins (P, 1932); "Three Letters to Joseph Conrad," in *Twenty Letters to Joseph Conrad*, ed. G. Jean-Aubry (First Edition Club, 1936). Other letters will be found in *AL*, XXIII (1951), 131-133; *AM*, CLXXVIII, Aug. 1946, pp. 118-121; *BPLQ*, I (1949), 43-60; *Colby Lib. Q.*, I (1943), 34-44, Series III (1951), 23-26; *Harv. Grad. Mag.*, XLI (1933), 189-200; *LM*, VI (1922), 492-501; *NEQ*, XXII (1949), 173-192; *Jour. Rutgers U. Lib.*, XII (1949), 54-58; *PMLA*, LXVI (1951), 886-910; *YR*, XIV (1924), 205-208, XXXVIII (1949), 410-433. Other biographical data appears in *AL*, XXI (1949), 35-48, XXIII (1951), 302-314; *Commonweal*, LI (1950), 394-397; *Horizon*, XIV (1946), 52-60; *UTQ*, X (1940),

125-138. See, also, I. D. McFarlane, "A Literary Friendship—HJ and Paul Bourget," *Cambridge J*, IV (1950), 144-161. Books and articles about William James and other members of the James family will also be found useful.

The Notebooks of HJ, ed. Matthiessen and Kenneth B. Murdock (OUP, 1947) are of prime importance.

The following studies are published between covers: Elisabeth L. Cary, *The Novels of HJ, A Study* (P, 1905); Ford Madox Hueffer (Secker, 1916); Rebecca West (Ht, 1916); Joseph Warren Beach, *The Method of HJ* (YUP, 1918), the most elaborate study of technique— see also his *Twentieth Century Novel* (ACC, 1932); S. B. Liljegren, *American and European in the Works of HJ, Lunds Universitets Arskrift*, N.F. Avd. 1, Bd. 15, Nr. 6 (1920); Theodora Bosanquet, *HJ at Work* (Hogarth Press, 1924); Herbert L. Hughes, *Theory and Practice in HJ* (Ann Arbor, Edwards Brothers, 1926); Pelham Edgar, *HJ, Man and Author* (HM, 1927); M. R. Garnier, *HJ et la France* (Paris, Chamion, 1927); Lotte Borchers, *Frauengestalten und Frauenprobleme bei HJ* (Berlin, Greifswald, 1929); Cornelia P. Kelley, *The Early Development of HJ, ISLL*, XV, Nos. 1-2 (1930)—a model of scholarly investigation and the standard work in its field; Leon Edel, *The Prefaces of HJ* (Paris, Jouve, 1931); E. M. Snell, *The Modern Fables of HJ* (HUP, 1935); Stephen Spender, *The Destructive Element* (HM, 1935); Noël France, *HJ, peintre de la femme* (Alençon, Imprimerie Alençonnaise, 1942); Richard N. Foley, *Criticism in American Periodicals of the Works of HJ from 1886 to 1916* (Catholic U. of Am. Pr., 1944); F. O. Matthiessen, *HJ, The Major Phase* (OUP, 1944), an indispensable study of the last three great novels; Osborn Andreas, *HJ and the Expanding Horizon* (U. of Wash. Pr., 1948)—non-professional criticism; Elizabeth Stevenson, *The Crooked Corridor* (M, 1949)—excellent critical study; F. W. Dupee, *HJ* (Sl, 1951)—the latest, comprehensive general study, and a very good one; H. S. Canby, *Turn West, Turn East, Mark Twain and HJ* (HM, 1951).

The following list of briefer critical studies of HJ consists of the outstanding items included in Richardson's list, plus a fuller listing of material published since his book appeared: T. W. Higginson, *Short Studies of American Authors* (Lee & Shepard, 1880); Edgar Fawcett, *Princeton Review*, N.S. XIV (1884), 68-86; W. D. Howells, *HaM*, LXXVII (1888), 799-800; Norman Hapgood, *Literary Statesmen and Others* (Herbert S. Stone, 1897); Howells, *NAR*, CLXXVI (1903), 125-137; Joseph Conrad, *NAR*, CLXXX (1905), 102-108; Anna B. McGill, *Poet-Lore*, XVI (1905), 90-96; H. G. Dwight, *Putnam's Monthly*, II (1907), 164-170, 433-442; W. C. Brownell, *American Prose Masters* (S, 1909); Morton Fullerton, *LA*, CCLXV (1910), 643-652; E. Preston Dargan, *NR*, VII (1916), 171-174; Walter de la Mare, *LA*, CCLXXXIX

(1916), 122-125; Dixon Scott, *Men of Letters* (Hodder & Stoughton, 1916); John Freeman, *The Moderns* (Crowell, 1917); James Huneker, *Unicorns* (S, 1917); Edith Wyatt, *Great Companions* (ACC, 1917); W. B. Cairns, "Character-Portrayal in the Work of HJ," *Univ. of Wisc. Studies in Lang. & Lit.*, No. 2 (1918); Lawrence Gilman, *NAR,* CCVII (1918), 130-135; Arthur Waugh, *Tradition and Change* (Chapman & Hall, 1919); Anon., "The Novels of HJ," *LTLS*, May 12, 1921, pp. 297-298; W. L. Randell, *Fort,* CXVI (1921), 458-469; Gamaliel Bradford, *American Portraits, 1875-1900* (HM, 1922); Edmund Gosse, *Aspects and Impressions* (S, 1922); Dorothy Bethurum, "Morality and HJ," *SR,* XXXI (1923), 324-330; Robert Herrick, "A Visit to HJ," *YR,* XII (1923), 724-741; André Gide, *YR,* XIX (1930), 641-643; Matthew Josephson, *Portrait of the Artist as an American* (HB, 1930); V. J. McGill, "HJ, Master-Detective," *Bkm*(NY), LXXII (1930), 251-256; Herbert Read, *The Sense of Glory* (HB, 1930); Desmond McCarthy, *Portraits,* I (M, 1932); Pelham Edgar, "HJ, The Essential Novelist," *QQ,* XXXIX (1932), 181-192; Robert Cantwell, "No Landmarks," *Symposium,* IV (1933), 70-84, and "The Return of HJ," *NR,* LXXXI (1934), 119-121; Stephen Spender, "A Moral Writer in Search of a Moral Subject," *LM,* XXXI (1934), 128-133; Cantwell, "A Warning to Pre-War Novelists," *NR,* XCI (1937), 178-180; A. J. A. Waldock, *James, Joyce, and Others* (Williams & Norgate, 1937); Yvor Winters, "HJ and the Relation of Morals to Manners," *AR,* IX (1937), 482-503; Dorothy M. Hoare, *Some Studies in the Modern Novel* (Chatto, 1938); John C. Neff, "HJ the Reporter," *NMQR,* VIII (1938), 9-14; L. C. Knights, "HJ and the Trapped Spectator," *SoR,* IV (1939), 600-615; Forrest Reid, *Private Road* (FF, 1940); Ferner Nuhn, *The Wind Blew From the East* (H, 1942); Witter Bynner, *SRL,* XXVI, May 22, 1943, p. 23+; Leon Edel, "HJ and the Poets," *Poetry,* LXII (1943), 328-334; Spender, "A World Where the Victor Belonged to the Spoils," *NYTBR,* Mar. 12, 1944, p. 3; Isidor Schneider, "The Rediscovery of HJ," *New Masses,* LV (1945), 22-24; Quentin Anderson, "HJ and the New Jerusalem," *KR,* VIII (1946), 515-566; E. K. Brown, "Two Formulas for Fiction: HJ and H. G. Wells," *CE,* VIII (1946), 7-17, and "J and Conrad," *YR,* XXXV (1946), 265-285; Katherine Hoskins, "HJ and the Future of the Novel," *SR,* LIV (1946), 87-101; Paul Rosenfeld, "The HJ Revival," *Commonweal,* XLIII (1946), 329-332; Adeline R. Tintner, "The Spoils of HJ," *PMLA,* LXI (1946), 239-251; Edward Crankshaw, *Nat. R.,* CXXIX (1947), 73-77; L. C. Knights, *Explorations* (George W. Stewart, 1947); Sylva Norman, *Fort,* CLXVII (1947), 380-382; Clinton Oliver, "HJ as a Social Critic," *Ant R,* VII (1947), 243-258; Edward Sackville-West, *New Statesman & Nation,* n.s. XXXIV (1947), 273; Gertrude Stein, *Four in America* (YUP, 1947); W. H. Auden, "HJ and the Artist in America," *HaM,* CXCVII (1948), 36-40; J. W. Beach,

"The Sacred and Solitary Refuge," *Furioso*, III (1948), 23-27; F. R. Leavis, *The Great Tradition* (Stewart, 1948); Francis Thompson, *Literary Criticisms*, ed. T. L. Connolly (Du, 1948); L. Edel, "HJ and 'The Outcry,'" *UTQ*, XVIII (1949), 340-346; P. Rahv, *Image and Idea* (ND, 1949); Edouard Roditi, "Oscar Wilde & HJ," *UKCR*, XV (1949), 52-56; A. Berland, *UKCR*, XVIII (1950), 94-108; H. S. Canby, "HJ and the Observant Profession," *SRL*, XXXIII, Dec. 2, 1950, pp. 11-12+; G. K. Chesterton, *The Common Man* (Sheed & Ward, 1950); Robert P. Falk, "HJ's Romantic 'Vision of the Real,'" *Essays Critical and Historical Dedicated to Lily B. Campbell* (U. of Cal. Pr., 1950); Gorham B. Munson, "The Real Thing: A Parable for Writers of Fiction," *UKCR*, XVI (1950), 261-264; H. B. Rouse, "Charles Dickens and HJ: Two Approaches to the Art of Fiction," *XIX C Fiction*, V (1950), 151-158; R. W. Short, "Some Critical Terms of HJ," *PMLA*, LXV (1950), 667-680; Edward Stone, "HJ's First Novel," *BPLQ*, II (1950), 167-171, and "HJ's Last Novel," *ibid.*, 348-353; H. M. Walbrook, *Fort*, CXXXIII (1950), 680-691; R. P. Blackmur, "The Loose and Baggy Monsters of HJ: Notes on the Underlying Classic Form in the Novel," *Accent*, XI (1951), 129-146; B. Dort, "Un roman de la connaissance: 'Les Ambassadeurs' d' HJ," *Cahiers du Sud*, XXXIII (1951), 329-333; E. G. Fay, "Balzac and HJ," *French R*, XXIV (1951), 325-330; M. Nathan, "Les 'Ambassadeurs' et les Carnets de J," *Critique*, VII (1951), 492-498; A. Pierhal, "HJ, le Civilisé," *Hommes et Monde*, VI (1951), 413-420; John H. Raleigh, "HJ: The Problem of Empiricism," *PMLA*, LXVI (1951), 107-123; E. Sackville-West, *SRL*, XXXIV, Jan. 20, 1951, pp. 24-25; E. Stone, "HJ and Rome," *BPLQ*, III (1951), 143-145; Arthur L. Scott, "A Protest against the James Vogue," *CE*, XIII (1952), 194-201.

The following articles deal with more specialized or technical themes: *AL*, XVI (1945), 279-293; XVIII (1946), 71-88, XX (1949), 385-400, XXI (1949), 279-291—cf. XXIII (1951), 130-131, XXI (1949), 292-297, XXII (1950), 245-253—cf. XXIII (1951), 128-130, XXII (1951), 424-431, XXIII (1951), 315-322; *ES*, XXIX (1948), 33-47; MLN, LXIII (1948), 303-310; *NEQ*, XXIV (1951), 169-178; *Pac Spect*, IV (1950), 352-360; *PMLA*, XL (1925), 433-434; *Revue Anglo-Amér.*, IX (1932), 1-13, 112-122; *UKCR*, XVII (1950), 109-118.

The following periodicals have published special HJ numbers: *The Egoist*, Jan. 1918; *The Little Review*, Aug. 1918; *The Hound and Horn*, Apr.-May 1943; *The Mark Twain Quarterly*, Spring 1943; *The Kenyon Review*, Autumn 1943. *The New Republic* published a section "In Honor of William and Henry James," Feb. 15, 1943. These issues are not analyzed in the foregoing bibliography. There have also been many articles about HJ in recent volumes of *Scrutiny*. Some of these have been mentioned in my notes.

Chapter IX: Novelists of the 'Eighties

F. Marion Crawford. C's novels were published by M. He set forth his conception of fiction in *The Novel: What It Is* (M, 1893). Maud Howe Elliott, *My Cousin FMC* (M, 1934) is the closest approach to a life and letters. There are further biographical data in G. P. Brett, *Outlook,* XCI (1909), 915-917; Mary Crawford Fraser, *Collier's,* XLV, Apr. 23, 1910, pp. 22-24; L. Collison-Morley, *XIX C and After,* CXLII (1947), 302-308. For critical evaluation, see M. F. Egan, *Am. Cath. Q.,* XVII (1892), 621-633; Janetta N. Robinson, *Westminster R.,* CXXXVII (1892), 379-393; W. P. Trent, *SR,* II (1893), 239-256; Ouida, *Critical Studies* (Unwin, 1900); Anon., *Edinburgh R.,* CCIV (1906), 61-80; Elbridge Colby, *Am. Cath. Q.,* XLII (1917), 679-687; Hugh Walpole, *YR,* XII (1923), 673-691; Adolphe B. Benson, "MC's 'Dr. Claudius,'" *Scan. Studies and Notes,* XII (1933), 77-88; Grace Chapman, *LM,* XXX (1934), 244-253.

Sarah Orne Jewett. SOJ's books (and books about her, unless otherwise stated) are published by HM. Carl J. Weber has *A Bibliography of the Published Writings of SOJ* (Colby College Library, 1949). For letters, see Annie Fields, *Letters of SOJ* (1911); C. J. Weber, *Letters of SOJ Now in the Colby College Library* (Colby College Library, 1948), with supplements in *Colby Library Q.,* Series II (1949-1950), 201-206, 216-218; see also his "New England Through French Eyes Fifty Years Ago," *NEQ,* XX (1947), 385-396. There are book-length studies by F. O. Matthiessen (1929) and by Jean Sougnac (Paris, Jouve, 1937). Perhaps the best introduction to SOJ is the two-volume *The Best Stories of SOJ,* comprising *The Country of the Pointed Firs* and selected short stories, ed., with introduction, by Willa Cather; see also Cather, *Not Under Forty* (K, 1936). Critical studies include: C. M. Thompson, *AM,* XCIV (1904), 485-497; E. M. Chapman, *YR,* III (1913), 157-172; Edward Garnett, *Friday Nights* (K, 1922); Martha H. Shackford, *SR,* XXX (1922), 20-26; C. H. Grattan, *Bkm*(NY), LXIX (1929), 296-298; O. B. Floyd, "SOJ's Advice to a Young Writer," *YR,* XXVI (1937), 430-432; Anon., "The New England Spirit," *LTLS,* Nov. 22, 1947, p. 602.

Constance Fenimore Woolson. CFW's books were published by H. Clare Benedict's *CFW,* enlarged edition (London, Ellis, 1932), is a collection of biographical materials and literary remains, not a biography. There are additional Woolson materials in the same author's *Voices Out of the Past* (1929) and *The Benedicts Abroad* (1930), the trilogy constituting *Five Generations.* There is a modern biography by John D. Kern, *CFW: Literary Pioneer* (UPP, 1934). See also Jay B. Hubbell,

"Some New Letters of CFW," *NEQ,* XIV (1941), 715-735. Important critical essays are Henry James, in *Partial Portraits* (M, 1888); John Hervey, *SRL,* VI (1929), 268; L. N. Richardson, *SAQ,* XXXIX (1940), 18-36.

S. Weir Mitchell. SWM's books were published by Ce, including an "Author's Definitive Edition," 16 vv. (1913-1914). His biography was written by Anna Robeson Burr, *WM, His Life and Letters* (Duffield, 1929); B. R. Tucker, *SWM* (Badger, 1914); see also C. W. Burr, *SWM, Physician, Man of Science, Man of Affairs* (Philadelphia College of Physicians, 1920). The most authoritative study is now Ernest Earnest, *SWM, Novelist and Physician* (UPP, 1950); see also his "SWM as Novelist," *American Scholar,* XVII (1948), 314-322. David M. Rein's *SWM as a Psychiatric Novelist* is announced for spring 1952 by International Universities Press. See also Max Farrand, "Hugh Wynne, A Historical Novel," *Washington Hist. Q.,* I (1907), 101-108; A. H. Quinn, *Ce,* CXX (1930), 139-148; Charles R. Brown, *They Were Giants* (M, 1934); F. E. Schelling, "SWM, Poet and Novelist," in *Shakespeare Biography and Other Papers* (UPP, 1937); L. N. Richardson, "SWM at Work," *AL,* XI (1939), 58-65.

Henry Adams and John Hay. *The Bread-Winners* was published by H, Adams's novels by Ht. For Adams, see M. E. Speare, *The Political Novel* (OUP, 1924), Ch. XII; R. E. Spiller's introduction to the 1938 reprint of *Esther* (Scholars' Facsimiles & Reprints); and R. P. Blackmur, *SR,* LI (1943), 281-304. For Hay, see the introduction by his son, Clarence L. Hay, in the 1911 edition of *The Bread-Winners* and W. R. Thayer, *The Life of John Hay* (HM, 1915), Ch. XVII.

Helen Hunt Jackson. There is a biography by Ruth Odell (ACC, 1939), where see elaborate bibliography. Cf. also Allen Nevins, "HHJ, Sentimentalist vs. Realist," *American Scholar,* X (1941), 269-285. *Ramona* is published by LB.

Edward Bellamy. B's publisher was HM. There is an important biography by Arthur E. Morgan, *EB* (ColUP, 1944), where see bibliography. Morgan has also edited *The Philosophy of EB* (King's Crown Pr., 1945). See, further, W. D. Howells, *AM,* LXXXII (1898), 253-256; Caroline Ticknor, *Glimpses of Authors* (HM, 1922); Robert L. Shurter, "The Literary Work of EB," *AL,* V (1933), 229-234—cf. his "The Writing of 'Looking Backward,'" *SAQ,* XXXVIII (1939), 254-261; John H. Franklin, "EB and the Nationalist Movement," *NEQ,* XI (1938), 739-772; Alan Seager, *They Worked for a Better World* (M, 1939); Charles A. Madison, "EM, Social Dreamer," *NEQ,* XV (1942), 444-466; Mark

Van Doren, Jacques Barzun, and Max Eastman, in *The New Invitation to Learning,* ed. Van Doren (RH, 1942); Albert W. Leir, "EB: Utopian," *Ethics,* LV (1945), 131-144; Louis Filler, "EB and the Spiritual Unrest," *AM. Jour. Econ. & Soc.,* VIII (1949), 239-249; A. Mann, "Solomon Schindler: Boston Radical," *NEQ,* XXIII (1951), 453-476.

Chapter X: Some Southern Novelists of the 'Nineties and After

James Lane Allen. JLA's principal publisher was M. As stated elsewhere, the definitive study is Grant C. Knight, *JLA and the Genteel Tradition* (UNCP, 1935), where see further bibliography. See also John W. Townsend, *JLA, A Personal Note* (Louisville, Courier-Journal Printing Company, 1928), to which his *JLA, Still Kentucky's Greatest Writer* (Lexington, Bluegrass Bookshop, 1948) is a pendant. There is further critical comment in E. B. Brown, *AM,* LXXIX (1897), 104-110; L. W. Payne, *SR,* VIII (1900), 45-55; Anon., "JLA," *LA,* CCLXI (1909), 689-696; Harry A. Toulmin, Jr., *Social Historians* (Badger, 1911); John B. Henneman, *Shakespearean and Other Papers* (Sewanee, Tenn., University Press, 1911).

Page, Smith, Fox. All three writers were published by S, who brought out a collected Plantation Edition of Page, 18 vv. (1906 ff.), and a Beacon Edition of Smith, 23 vv. (1902 ff.). There is a brief biography of Page by his brother, Rosewell Page, *TNP, A Memoir of a Virginia Gentleman* (S, 1923), but there is no biography of Smith, and for Fox only an amateurish work by Harold E. Green, *Towering Pines* (Meador, 1943). Page himself wrote of Smith, *SM,* LVIII (1915), 305-313, and of Fox, *SM,* LXVI (1919), 674-683. For criticism of Page, see Charles W. Kent, *SAQ,* VI (1907), 263-271; George W. Cable, *Book News Monthly,* XXVIII (1909), 139-141; A. C. Gordon, *SM,* LXXIII (1923), 75-80; Edwin Mims, *AM,* C (1907), 109-115. Ronald Tree, *Forum,* LXIX (1923), 1137-1142, deals with Page as ambassador to Italy. The best account of Smith's aims and theory of fiction is A. S. van Westrum, *Lamp,* XXVIII (1904), 383-389. There are two articles by Theodore Hornberger which deal with the connection between Smith's painting and his writing: *UTSE,* XXIII (1943), 162-192, and *AL,* XVI (1944), 1-10.

Mary Johnston. Except for *Sir Mortimer,* all MJ's books through *The Wanderer* (1917) were published by HM. *Sir Mortimer, Foes, Michael Forth,* and *Sweet Rocket* were published by H, and all the others by LB, who also later took over *Michael Forth. Sweet Rocket* is included in E. Wagenknecht, ed., *Six Novels of the Supernatural* (VP, 1944). See John Farrar, *The Literary Spotlight* (Do, 1934); Grant Overton, *Cargoes for Crusoes* (Do, etc., 1924).

Chapter XI: Towards Naturalism

HAMLIN GARLAND. G's books were published mainly by H and M. The Sunset Edition and the Border Edition (both H) are partial collections. HG's own abundant autobiographical records (all M) have been indicated in the text. For students of his fiction the ff. articles by HG should prove interesting: *Arena*, VI (1892), 669-676, VII (1893), 513-524; *Forum*, XVII (1894), 690-698; *NAR*, CLXXVI (1903), 336-348; *World's Work*, XX (1910), 13569; *Bkm*(NY), LIX (1924), 257-262; *SRL*, VII (1930), 347; *EJ*, XX (1931), 355-364. The first edition of *Crumbling Idols* was reproduced in the Scholars' Reprints and Facsimiles series, 1951. The best general account of HG's work in print is in W. F. Taylor, *The Economic Novel in America*. See, further: Anon., *AM*, LXXVI (1895), 840-844; M. T. Blanc, *Revue des deux Mondes*, CLVII (1900), 139-180; W. D. Howells, *NAR*, CXCVI (1912), 523-528; Edwin W. Bowen, *SR*, XXVII (1919), 411-422; H. L. Mencken, *Prejudices*, I (K, 1919); Zona Gale, "National Epics of the Border," *YR*, XI (1922), 852-856; Allen Nevins, "G and the Prairies," *Lit. R.*, II (1922), 881-882; F. L. Pattee, *Tradition and Jazz* (Ce, 1925); Ruth M. Raw, "HG the Romanticist," *SR*, XXXVI (1928), 202-210; F. L. Mott, "Exponents of the Pioneers," *Palimpsest*, XI (1930), 61-66; Albert Keiser, *The Indian in American Literature* (OUP, 1933); Claude Simpson, "HG's Decline," *Southwest R.*, XXVI (1941), 223-234; John T. Flanagan, "HG, Occasional Minnesotan," *Minn. Hist.*, XXII (1941), 157-168; J. S. Goldstein, "Two Literary Radicals: G and Markham in Chicago," *AL*, XVII (1945), 152-160. The Summer, 1940 issue of the *Mark Twain Q.* was a Garland memorial number.

STEPHEN CRANE. *The Work of SC*, 12 vv., ed. Wilson Follett, was published by K (1925-1926). *The Red Badge of Courage* is available in ML and elsewhere. See, also, *Sullivan County Sketches*, ed. Melvin Schoberlin (Syracuse U. Pr., 1949); L. U. Pratt, "An Addition to the Canon of SC," *Research Studies, State Coll. of Wash.*, VII (1939), 55-58. There are two good collections of short stories: *Men, Women, and Boats*, ed. Vincent Starrett (ML, 1921), and *Twenty Stories*, ed. Carl Van Doren (K, 1940); *Twenty Stories* contains both *Maggie* and *The Monster*. There are four bibliographies: V. Starrett, *SC, A Bibliography* (Philadelphia, Centaur Book Shop, 1923); B. J. R. Stolper, *SC, A List of His Writings and Articles about Him* (Public Library of Newark, N. J., 1930); Ames W. Williams and V. Starrett, *SC, A Bibliography* (Glendale, Cal., John Valentine, 1948); Herbert F. West, *A SC Collection* (Dartmouth Coll. Lib., 1948). The pioneering biography was T. L. Raymond, *SC* (Carteret Book Club, 1923); this was more or less superseded by Thomas Beer, *SC, A Study in American Letters* (K, 1926), which is fascinating reading. More recent and more extensive is John Berryman, *SC* (Sl, 1950), which is excellent save for its wildly speculative final chapter. For evaluation, see Joseph Conrad's introduction to Beer's biography; Max J. Herzberg's to later edition of the ACC *Badge;* and the introductions by Joseph Hergesheimer, Robert H. Davis, Wilson Follett, Carl Van Doren, W. L. Phelps, Amy Lowell, Thomas Beer, Willa Cather, H. L. Mencken, Sherwood Anderson, and Charles Michelson to the several volumes of the *Work.* See, further: H. G. Wells, *NAR,* CLXXI (1900), 233-242; Edith Wyatt, *Great Companions* (ACC, 1917); J. Conrad, "SC: A Note Without Dates," *Bkm*(NY), L (1920), 529-531; Edward Garnett, *Friday Nights* (K, 1922); V. Starrett, *Buried Caesars* (Covici-McGee, 1923); Floyd Dell, "SC and the Genius Myth," *Nation,* CXIX (1924), 637-638; Carl Van Doren, *Am Merc,* I (1924), 11-14; W. Follett, *Bkm*(NY), LXVIII (1929), 532-537; H. Garland, *Roadside Meetings* (M, 1930); F. M. Ford, *Portraits from Life* (HM, 1937); Russell B. Nye, "SC as Social Critic," *Mod. Q.,* XI, Summer, 1940, pp. 48-54; Caroline Gordon, *Accent,* IX (1949), 153-159; Abraham Feldman, "Crane's Title from Shakespeare," *Am. Notes & Queries,* VIII (1950), 185-186; John W. Schroeder, "SC Embattled," *UKCR,* XVII (1950), 119-129; Anon., "Badge of Courage," *LTLS,* No. 2575 (June 8, 1951), p. 356; Scott C. Osborn, "SC's Imagery: 'Pasted Like a Wafer,'" *AL,* XXIII (1951), 362. Letters and biographical information will be found in *Academy,* LIX (1900), 116; *AL,* VII (1935), 82-84, X (1939), 460-71, XV (1943), 279-287; *Am Merc,* VII (1926), 291-297; *Bkm*(NY), LXIX (1929), 225-235, 367-374; *NQ,* CLXV (1933), 243, CLXVI (1934), 240-241; *Twenty Letters to Joseph Conrad* (see under James); Ralph D. Paine, *Roads of Adventure* (HM, 1922).

FRANK NORRIS. FN's writings were collected in the "Argonaut Manuscript Edition," 10 vv. (D, 1928), which was reprinted in an untitled trade edition the same year. For additional material, see *Two Poems and "Kim" Reviewed,* ed. Harvey Taylor (San Francisco, H. Taylor, 1930); *FN of "The Wave," Stories and Sketches from the San Francisco Weekly,* ed. Oscar Lewis (San Francisco, The Westgate Press, 1931); also, see W. E. Martin, Jr., "Two Uncollected Essays by FN," *AL,* VIII (1936), 190-198. The two most important studies are Franklin Walker, *FN, A Biography* (D, 1932) and Ernest Marchand, *FN, A Study* (Stanford U. Pr., 1942), which contains a bibliography. See also Marius Biencourt, *Une Influence du Naturalisme Français en Amérique: FN* (Paris, Marcel Giar, 1933). For further criticism, consult: W. D. Howells, *NAR,* CLXXV (1902), 769-778; H. Garland, *Critic,* XLII (1903), 216-218; D. H. Clift, *Pacific Monthly,* XVII (1907), 313-322; Edith Wyatt, *Great Companions* (ACC, 1917); C. C. Dobie, "FN, or, Up From

Culture," *Am Merc,* XIII (1928), 412-424; C. H. Grattan, *Bkm*(NY), LXIX (1929), 506-510; E. Wagenknecht, "FN in Retrospect," *VQR,* VI (1930), 313-320; E. Peixotto, *SRL,* IX (1933), 613-615; Paul H. Bixler, "FN's Literary Reputation," *AL,* VI (1934), 109-121; E. E. Cassady, *AL,* XIII (1941), 134-141; R. L. Duffus, *NYTBR,* June 8, 1947, p. 5; C. C. Walcutt, "FN and the Search for Form," *UKCR,* XIV (1947), 126-135, and "The Naturalism of 'Vandover and the Brute,' " in W. V. O'Connor, ed., *Forms of Modern Fiction* (U. of Minn. Pr., 1948); Irving McKee, "Notable Memorials to Mussel Slough," *Pac. Hist. R.,* XVII (1948), 19-27—cf. Gordon W. Clark, XVIII (1949), 501-504. See also the critical and biographical prefaces, of widely varying importance which various critics contributed to the collected edition.

JACK LONDON. Most of JL's books are published by M. The fullest and most intimate biography is Charmian London, *The Book of JL,* 2 vv. (Ce, 1921); the best is Joan London, *JL and his Times, An Unconventional Biography* (D, 1939), which is utterly honest, compassionate, based upon wide knowledge and excellent judgment, surely the best book any daughter ever wrote about her father. The only other attempt at a general biography based upon original sources is Irving Stone, *Sailor Horseback* (HM, 1938)—cf. T. K. Whipple, *Study Out the Land* (U. of Cal. Pr., 1943). Philip S. Foner has edited a selection from JL's writings with social implications, *JL, American Rebel* (Citadel Pr., 1947).

Charmian London has also published *The Log of the Snark* (M, 1915); *Our Hawaii* (M, 1917, 1922); *JL and Hawaii* (Mills & Boon, 1918); *The New Hawaii* (Mills & Boon, 1923).

Further biographical data will be found in: Martin Johnson, *Through the South Seas with JL* (DM, 1913); L. R. Livingston, *From Coast to Coast with JL* (Erie, Pa., A-No. 1 Pub. Co., 1917); Georgia L. Bamford, *The Mystery of JL,* etc. (Oakland, Cal., The Author, 1931); Joseph Noel, *Footloose in Arcadia* (Carrick & Evans, 1940); William McDevitt, *JL's First* (San Francisco, Recorder-Sunset Pr., 1946). Shannon Garst, *JL, Magnet for Adventure* (Messner, 1944) is a biography for young readers. Edward B. Payne, *The Soul of JL* (London, Rider, n.d.) is based upon alleged spirit communications; cf. Upton Sinclair, "Is This JL?" *Occult R.,* LII (1930), 394-400, LIII (1931), 10-14. To these the ff. material, published serially, may be added: *Bkm*(NY), XLIV (1916), 151-156; *Craftsman,* IX (1906), 607-619; *Ind. Mag. of History,* XXXVIII (1942), 407-410; *Masses,* X (1917), No. 9, Issue 73; *Palimpsest,* VII (1926), 129-158; *Seven Arts,* I (1917), 522-530. Rose Wilder Lane's "Life and JL" appeared serially in *Sunset* between Oct. 1917 and May 1918. The JL memorial numbers of *Overland Monthly* for May 1917 and May 1932 contain a variety of biographical as well as critical materials.

The following material is mainly of a critical character: Grace I. Colborn, *Bkm*(NY), XLIV (1917), 441-451; E. Preston Dargan, "JL in Chancery," *NR*, X, Apr. 21, 1917, Pt. 2, pp. 7-8; L. S. Friedland, "JL as Titan," *Dial*, LXII (1917), 49-50; Wilfrid Lay, "'John Barleycorn' under Psychoanalysis," *Bkm*(NY), XLV (1917), 47-54; H. L. Mencken, *Prejudices*, I (K, 1919); Grace U. Silver, "JL's Women," *Overland*, N.S. LXXIV, July 1919, pp. 24-28; E. W. Bowen, "JL's Place in American Literature," *Reformed Church R.*, 4th ser., XXIV (1920), 306-315; Lewis Mumford, *NR*, XXX (1922), 145-147; F. L. Pattee, *Sidelights on American Literature* (Ce, 1922); E. Sainte-Marie Perrin, "Un Romancier Californien, JL," *Revue des deux Mondes*, CLXXI (1922), 171-191; Franz Jung, *JL, Ein Dichter der Arbeiterklasse* (Vienna, Verlag für Literatur und Politik, 1924); Calvin B. Houck, "JL's Philosophy of Life," *Overland*, LXXXIV (1926), 103 ff.; C. H. Grattan, *Bkm*(NY), LXVIII (1929), 667-671; Stephen Graham, *The Death of Yesterday* (Benn, 1930); C. C. Walcutt, "Naturalism and the Superman in the Novels of JL," *Papers Mich. Acad. Science, Arts and Letters*, XXIV (1938), Part IV, pp. 89-107; Alison Bishop, "JL in a Confident Mood," *BPLQ*, III (1951), 312-314. Special subjects are treated in Ed Morrell, *The Twenty-Fifth Man, The Strange Story of EM, the Hero of JL's "Star Rover"* (Montclair, N. J., New Era Pub. Co., 1924); K. Groos, "Die Verwendung der Eidetik als Kunstmittel in JL's Roman, 'Martin Eden,'" *Zeitschrift für angewandte Psychologie*, XXXIII (1929), 417-438; Anders Kruskopf, "Martin Eden of Sonoma," *Am. Scan. R.*, XXXI (1943), 347-348.

Chapter XII: Voices of the New Century

MARY AUSTIN. Among MA's novels, *Santa Lucia* was published by H, *The Lovely Lady* by D, *Outland* by B & L, and the rest by HM. The principal source of information about her is her autobiography, *Earth Horizon* (HM, 1932). There are two important biographical studies: Helen M. Doyle, *MA, Woman of Genius* (Gotham House, 1939) and T. M. Pearce, *The Beloved House* (Caxton Printers, 1940). An abridgement of Dudley Wynn's New York University thesis, *A Critical Study of the Writings of MA* was published by the Graduate School of Arts and Science in 1941. For further critical and biographical comment, see: Lincoln Steffens, "MA and the Desert," *Am. Mag.*, LXXI, June, 1911, pp. 178-181; Carl Van Doren, *Many Minds* (K, 1924); Henry Smith, "The Feel of the Purposeful Earth," *NMQR*, I (1931), 17-33; Louise M. Field, *Bkm*(NY), LXXV (1932), 819-821; Mabel Major, "MA in Fort Worth," *NMQR*, IV (1934), 307-310; Elizabeth S. Sergeant, *SRL*, XI (1934), 96; Carl Van Doren, *NYHTB*, Aug. 26, 1934, p. 6; Arthur E. DuBois, *Southwest R.*, XXII (1937), 140-148; Dudley Winn,

"MA, Woman Alone," *VQR*, XIII (1937), 243-256; Louis Adamic, *My America* (H, 1938); Michael Williams, "Views and Reviews," *Commonweal*, XXXI (1939), 224-225; Vernon Young, "MA and the Earth Performance," *Southwest R.*, XXXV (1950), 153-163.

ROBERT HERRICK. Among H's novels, *The Man Who Wins* was published by S, *Clark's Field* by HM, *Homely Lilla* and *Waste* by HB, *The End of Desire* and *Sometime* by FR, and all the rest by M. The ff. are H's most important critical utterances concerning fiction: "The Background of the American Novel" and "The American Novel," *YR*, III (1914), 213-233, 419-437; "New England and the Novel," *Nation*, CXI (1920), 323-325; "The New Novel," *NR*, XXX (1922), 17-19; "What Is Happening to Our Fiction?" *Nation*, CXXIX (1929), 673-675; "What Is Dirt?" *Bkm*(NY), LXX (1929), 258-262; "Writers in the Jungle," *NR*, LXXX (1934), 259-261. For general critical comment, consult Harold Nielsen, *Poet-Lore*, XIX (1908), 337-363; W. D. Howells, *NAR*, CLXXXIX (1909), 812-820; Edwin Björkman, *Voices of Tomorrow* (Kennerley, 1913); Harry Hansen, *Midwest Portraits* (HB, 1923); Granville Hicks, "RH, Liberal," *NR*, LXVII (1931), 129-130; Newton Arvin, "Homage to RH," *NR*, LXXXII (1935), 93-95; R. M. Lovett, *NR*, XCVII (1939), 302.

BOOTH TARKINGTON. BT's "regular" publishers, D, brought out two collected editions—the Autograph (1918 ff.) and the Seawood (1922 ff.) —and trade editions of all books not otherwise here accredited. *Cherry, The Conquest of Canaan, The Turmoil,* and *Seventeen* were published by H. There are bibliographies by Barton W. Currie, *BT, A Bibliography* (1932)—cf. his "Hints to Tarkingtonians," *Col*, Pt. IX (1932)— and, more extensively, by Dorothy R. Russo and Thelma L. Sullivan, *A Bibliography of BT, 1869-1946* (Ind. Hist. Society, 1949), a delightful book, indispensable to serious study. *The World Does Move* (1928) contains reminiscences of BT but is not a formal autobiography. *Your Amiable Uncle* (BM, 1949) contains letters written from Europe to BT's nephews, 1903-1904. Some of BT's views on life and art are expressed in his essays, *Looking Forward and Others* (1926). Some installments of an unfinished autobiography, "As I Seem to Me," were published in *SEP* during July and August, 1941. The only book-length critical study is Robert Cortes Holliday, *BT* (1918); see Holliday's further comments on BT in *Broome Street Straws* (Do, 1919), *Men and Books and Cities* (Do, 1920), and *In the Neighborhood of Murray Hill* (Do, 1923). Asa D. Dickinson's pamphlet, *BT, A Sketch* (1926) contains a variety of useful material. Further critical comment will be found in C. H. Garrett, *Outlook*, LXXII (1902), 817-819; A. B. Maurice, *Bkm*(NY), XXIV (1907), 605-616; James Branch Cabell, *Beyond Life* (McBride, 1919); R. Ellis Roberts, "Mr. BT Through British Eyes,"

LA, CCC (1919), 541-545; Edith F. Wyatt, *NAR,* CCXVI (1922), 499-512; Marc Holys, "Un Romancier Régionaliste Américain, BT," *Le Correspondant,* CCXCII (1923), 644-662; Russell Doubleday, *Lit. Digest Int. Bk. R.,* II (1924), 224-225; Elizabeth F. Corbett, "T and the Veiled Lady," *AR,* II (1925), 601-605; Joseph Collins, *Bkm*(NY), LXV (1927), 12-21; A. B. Maurice, *Bkm*(NY), LXVIII (1928), 445-448; Alfred P. Dennis, "Getting BT Educated," *World's Work,* LIX (1930), 57-60; Kenneth Roberts, *I Wanted To Write* (D, 1949), pp. 361-374— also consult index.

Chapter XIII: Edith Wharton: Social Problem and Ethical Dilemma

Except for *The Reef* (ACC), EW's fiction before 1917 was published by S; except for *A Son at the Front* (S), thereafter by ACC. For bibliography, cf. L. McC. Melish, *A Bibliography of the Collected Writings of EW* (Brick Row Book Shop, 1927) and Lavinia R. Davis, *Bibliography of the Writings of EW* (Portland, Maine, Southworth Press, 1933).

EW published an autobiography, *A Backward Glance* (ACC, 1934). There is a biographical *Portrait of EW* by Percy Lubbock (ACC, 1947). Further biographical data appear in Hamlin Garland, *Afternoon Neighbors* (M, 1934); Mrs. Winthrop Chanler, *Autumn in the Valley* (LB, 1936); Logan P. Smith, *Unforgotten Years* (LB, 1939); Janet Flanner, *An American in Paris* (S&S, 1940).

EW set forth her literary principles in *The Writing of Fiction* (S, 1925). See also these articles by EW: "The Vice of Reading," *NAR,* CLXXVII (1903), 513-521; "The Criticism of Fiction," *LA,* CCXXXII (1914), 204-211; "Henry James in His Letters," *QR,* CCXXXIV (1920), 188-202; "Character and Situation in the Novel," *SM,* LXXVIII (1925), 394-399; "The Great American Novel," *YR,* XVI (1927), 646-656; "Visibility in Fiction," *YR,* XVIII (1928), 480-488; "Tendencies in Modern Fiction," *SRL,* X (1934), 433-434; "Permanent Values in Fiction," *SRL,* X (1934), 603-604.

The most elaborate critical study of EW is in French: E. K. Brown, *EW, Étude Critique* (Paris, Librarie E. Droz, 1935). The fullest study in English is unfortunately unavailable to most readers; this is Olga Avendaño de Valdivia's "EW," which was serialized in the *Andean Quarterly* during 1943-1944. Robert Morss Lovett's *EW* (McB, 1925), though highly competent, shows no great sympathy with its subject. Katharine Fullerton Gerould's *EW, A Critical Study* (ACC, 1922) is a pamphlet.

The ff. books and articles contain critical evaluations of EW's work: Anna McC. Sholl, *Gunton's Mag.,* XXV (1903), 426-432; Louise C. Willcox, *Outlook,* LXXXI (1905), 719-724; C. L. Franklin, *Bkm*(NY), XXIV (1906), 259-260; Charles Waldstein, "Social Ideals," *NAR,*

CLXXXII (1906), 840-852, CLXXXIII (1906), 125-136; H. G. Dwight, *Putnam's Monthly*, III (1908), 590-596; Hildegarde Hawthorne, *Women and Other Women* (Duffield, 1908); H. D. Sedgwick, *The New American Type* (HM, 1908); Calvin Winter, *Bkm*(NY), XXXIII (1911), 302-309; Edwin Björkman, *Voices of Tomorrow* (Kennerley, 1913); H. W. Boynton, "Mrs. W's Manner," *Nation*, XCVII (1913), 404-405; Henry James, *Notes on Novelists* (Dent, 1913); Robert Herrick, "Mrs. W's World," *NR*, II (1915), 40-42; James Huneker, *Ivory, Apes, and Peacocks* (S, 1915); Percy Lubbock, *Quarterly Review*, CCLXXXIV (1915), 604-616; Francis Hackett, *Horizons* (Huebsch, 1918); Régis Michaud, Mystiques et Réalistes . . . (Paris, Colin, 1918); Charles K. Trueblood, *Dial*, LXVIII (1920), 80-91; H. S. Canby, *Definitions* (HB, 1922); Grant Overton, *American Nights' Entertainments* (ACC, etc., 1923); Joseph Collins, *Taking the Literary Pulse* (Do, 1924); G. Overton, *Cargoes for Crusoes* (ACC, etc., 1924); W. L. Cross, *Bkm*(NY), LXIII (1926), 641-646; Stuart P. Sherman, *The Main Stream* (S, 1927); Catherine Gilbertson, *Ce*, CXIX (1929), 112-113; Katherine Mansfield, *Novels and Novelists* (K, 1930); Frances T. Russell, "EW's Use of Imagery," *EJ*, XXI (1932), 452-461, and "Melodramatic Mrs. W," *SR*, XL (1932), 425-437; H. S. Canby, *SRL*, XVI, Aug. 21, 1937, pp. 6-7; Wilson Follett, "What EW Did—and Might Have Done," *NYTBR*, Sept. 5, 1937, p. 2+; E. K. Brown, *Etudes Anglaises*, II (1938), 16-26; Q. D. Leavis, "HJ's Heiress," *Scrutiny*, VII (1938), 261-276; C. John McCole, "Some Notes on EW," *Cath. World*, CXLVI (1938), 425-431; Agnes Repplier, *Commonweal*, XXIX (1938), 125-126; Hester Chapman, *New Statesman & Nation*, XXIX (1945), 43; F. J. Hoffman, "Points of Moral Reference: A Comparative Study of EW and Scott Fitzgerald," *English Institute Essays*, 1949 (ColUP, 1950); Leo Lerman, "The Gilded Era of EW," *NYTBR*, Aug. 27, 1950, p. 1+; Louis Auchincloss, "EW and her New Yorks," *PR*, XVIII (1951), 411-419.

Chapter XIV: Ellen Glasgow: Triumph and Despair

Among EG's novels, the first two—*The Descendant* and *Phases of an Inferior Planet*—were published by H, and the last two—*Vein of Iron* and *In This Our Life*—by HB, who also published the critical prefaces collected in *A Certain Measure* (1934), where see also bibliography. All the others were published by D. The Old Dominion Edition (D, 1929-1933) contains *The Deliverance, The Battle-Ground, Virginia, The Voice of the People, The Miller of Old Church, Barren Ground, The Romantic Comedians,* and *They Stooped to Folly.* The contents of the limited, signed Virginia Edition (S, 1938) are described in the text. For bibliography of EG's own writings, see, further, W. H. Egly, *Bull. Bibl.,* XVII (1940), 47-50.

The following are critical articles by EG about her own work and that of others (some are reprinted in part in *A Certain Measure*): "The Dynamic Past," *Reviewer*, I (1921), 73-80; "The Novel in the South," *HaM*, CLVIII (1928), 93-100; "The Biography of Manuel," *SRL*, VI (1930), 1108-1109; "What I Believe," *Nation*, CXXXVI (1933), 404-406, reprinted in *I Believe*, ed. C. Fadiman (S&S, 1938); "A Memorable Novel of the Old Deep South," *NYHTB*, July 22, 1934, pp. 1-2; "One Way To Write Novels," *SRL*, XI (1934), 335+; reprinted in *What Is a Book?* ed. Dale Warren (HM, 1935); "Santayana Writes a Novel," *NYHTB*, Feb. 2, 1936, pp. 1-2; "Elder and Younger Brother," *SRL*, XV, Jan. 23, 1937, pp. 3-5. See, also, EG and Branch Cabell, *Of EG, An Inscribed Portrait* (Maverick Press, 1938); this is mostly by Cabell, whose portion of it was reprinted in his book, *Let Me Lie*.

The ff. comprise critical articles and reviews about EG by other writers: Isaac F. Marcosson, "The Personal EG," *Bkm*(NY), XXIX (1909), 619-621; A. M. Tyler, *Book News Monthly*, XXX (1912), 843-848; Louise M. Field, *EG, Novelist of the Old and the New South* (D, 1923)—pamphlet; Archibald Henderson, "Soil and Soul," *SRL*, I (1925), 907; G. Overton, "EG's Arrow," *Bkm*(NY), LXI (1925), 291-296; Dorothea L. Mann, *Bkm*(NY), LXIV (1926), 265-271; Edwin Mims, "The Social Philosophy of EG," *Jour. Social Forces*, IV (1926), 495-503; Stuart Sherman, *Critical Woodcuts* (S, 1926); Anice P. Cooper, *Authors and Others* (D, 1927); E. R. Richardson, "Richmond and Its Writers," *Bkm*(NY), LXVIII (1928), 449-453; Virginius Dabney, "A Prophet of the New South," *NYHT Mag.*, Aug. 25, 1929; Sara Haardt, "EG and the South," *Bkm*(NY), LXIX (1929), 133-139; D. L. Mann, *EG* (D, 1927), a pamphlet containing criticism by J. B. Cabell, Joseph Collins, and Carl Van Vechten; Kenneth B. Murdock, "Folly and the Ironist," *VQR*, V (1929), 596-600; Isabel Paterson, "Rue with a Difference," *NYHTB*, Aug. 4, 1929, p. 1+; Stuart Sherman, Sara Haardt, and Emily Clark, *EG: Critical Essays* (D, 1929), pamphlet; J. B. Cabell, *Some of Us* (McB, 1930); Julian R. Meade, *Writer*, XLII (1930), 239-241; Friedrich Brie, *EG* (Universität Freiburg, 1931); William R. Parker, *EJ*, XX (1931), 187-194; Stark Young, "At Sheltered Valley," *NR*, LXXII (1932), 100-101; Léonie Villard, "L'oeuvre d'EG, Romancière Américaine," *Revue Angl.-Amer.*, XI (1933), 97-111; J. S. Wilson, *VQR*, IX (1933), 595-600; S. Young, *NR*, LXXV (1933), 101-102; D. S. Freeman, *SRL*, XII, Aug. 31, 1935, pp. 11-12; J. S. Wilson, *VQR*, XI (1935), 620-626; J. Donald Adams, *NYTBR*, Dec. 18, 1938, p. 1+; H. S. Canby, *SRL*, XVIII, Sept. 10, 1938, pp. 3-4+; H. M. Jones, *NYHTB*, July 24, 1938, pp. 1-2; J. S. Wilson, *VQR*, XV (1929), 121-126; H. Brickell, *VQR*, XVII (1941), 121-126; H. M. Jones, *SRL*, XXIII, Mar. 29, 1941, pp. 5-6; J. S. Wilson, *VQR*, XVII (1941), 317-320; Paula Snelling, "EG and her South," *No. Ga. Review*, VI (1941), 26-27; Grace

Stone, *SR*, L (1942), 289-301; J. D. Adams, *NYTBR*, Dec. 2, 1945, p. 2; H. S. Canby, *SRL*, XXVIII, Dec. 22, 1945, p. 13; Malcolm Cowley, *NR*, CXIII (1945), 805; H. S. Commager, *The American Mind* (YUP, 1950); H. Blair Rouse, "EG in Retrospect," *Emory U. Quar.*, VI (1950), 30-40; Fredson Bowers (ed.), *English Studies in Honor of James Southall Wilson, University of Virginia Studies*, IV (1951); Frederick P. Mc-Dowell, "EG and the Art of the Novel," *PQ*, XXX (1951), 328-347.

Chapter XV: Theodore Dreiser: The Mystic Naturalist

Most of D's novels are now published by the World Publishing Company. For bibliography, see Edward D. MacDonald, *A Bibliography of the Writings of TD* (Philadelphia, Centaur Book Shop, 1928); Vrest Orton, *Dreiserieana* (New York, privately printed, 1929); Ralph N. Miller, *A Preliminary Checklist of Books and Articles on TD* (Western Michigan College Library, 1947).

TD's autobiographies—*Dawn* (1931) and *A Book About Myself* (1922), later renamed *Newspaper Days*—are important for the understanding of his milieu; only less important are *A Hoosier Holiday* (1916) and *A Traveler at Forty* (1913). For his philosophy, see *Hey-Rub-a-Dub-Dub* (1920); "If Man Is Free, So Is All Matter," *Forum*, XCVIII (1937), 301-304; "Good and Evil," *NAR*, CCXLVI (1938), 67-86. His views on political and social questions will be found in *Dreiser Looks at Russia* (1928); *Tragic America* (1931); and *America Is Worth Saving* (1941).

Dorothy Dudley's biography, *Forgotten Frontiers, Dreiser and the Land of the Free* (Smith and Haas, 1932), was reissued by Beechhurst Press, 1946, with some alterations as *D and the Land of the Free*. It contains much valuable information, not always happily presented. The pioneering critical study between covers was Burton Rascoe, *TD* (McB, 1925). More important than either of these are Robert H. Elias, *TD, Apostle of Nature* (K, 1948) and F. O. Matthiessen, *TD* (Sl, 1951). Biographical material of a more specialized character will be found in E. D. MacDonald, "D Before 'Sister Carrie,'" *Bkm*(NY), LXVII (1928), 369-374; in C. O'N. Haley, "The Dreisers," *Commonweal*, XVIII (1933), 265-267—cf. pp. 330, 389; in three articles by John F. Huth, Jr., "TD: 'The Prophet,'" *AL*, IX (1937), 208-217; "TD, Success Monger," *Col*, N.S. III (1938), 120-133; "D and Success: An Additional Note," *ibid.*, pp. 406-410; and in Myrta L. Avary, "Success and D," *ibid.*, 598-604. More extensive is Helen Dreiser's *My Life with Dreiser* (World, 1951). See also Frank Harris, *Contemporary Portraits*, II (The Author, 1919); Walter Tittle, "Glimpses of Interesting Americans," *Ce*, CX (1925), 441-447; Marguerite Tjader, *Twice a Year*, XIV-XV (1926-1947); Albert Mordell, "My Relations with TD," *Critic and Guide*, V (1951), 1-17.

For further critical commentary, see: Randolph Bourne, *The History of a Literary Radical* (Huebsch, 1920); H. L. Mencken, *A Book of Prefaces* (K, 1917); E. H. Smith, *Bkm*(NY), LIII (1921), 27-39; E. Garnett, *Friday Nights* (K, 1922); R. L. Duffus, *Am Merc,* VII (1926), 71-76; Search-Light, pseud. Waldo Frank, *Time Exposures* (B&L, 1926); R. Ellis Roberts, *Bkm*(L), LXXI (1926), 158-159; Milton Waldman, *LM,* XIV (1926), 283-291; C. R. Walker, "How Big Is D?" *Bkm*(NY), LXIII (1926), 146-149; John Freeman, "An American Tragedy," *LM,* XVI (1927), 607-614; Stuart Sherman, *The Main Stream* (S, 1927); Martin Gilkes, *New Adelphi,* II (1928-1929), 178-181; G. B. Munson, *Destinations* (J. H. Sears, 1928); Robert Shafer, "An American Tragedy," in Norman Foerster, ed., *Humanism and America* (FR, 1930); Clifton Fadiman, "D and the American Dream," *Nation,* CXXXV (1932), 364-365; F. R. Leavis, *For Continuity* (CUP, 1933); Charles Le Verrier, "Un grand romancier américain: TD," *Revue Hebdomadaire,* XLII (1933), 280-294; I. Schneider, *SRL,* X (1934), 533-535; Eliseo Vivas, "D, An Inconsistent Mechanist," *Ethics,* XLVIII (1938), 498-508; C. C. Walcutt, "The Three Stages of TD's Naturalism," *PMLA,* LV (1940), 266-289; C. Arnavon, "TD and Painting," *AL,* XVII (1945), 113-126; H. M. Jones, *NYTBR,* Jan. 13, 1946, p. 5; Francis Ludlow, "Plodding Crusader," *CE,* VIII (1946), 1-7; W. O. Ross, "Concerning D's Mind," *AL,* XVIII (1946), 233-243; C. C. Walcutt, "Naturalism in 1946: D and Farrell," *Accent,* VI (1946), 263-268; John T. Flanagan, *Southwest R.,* XXXI (1948), 408-410; H. L. Mencken, *New Yorker,* XXIV, Apr. 17, 1948, pp. 43-57; Max Lerner, *Actions and Reactions* (S&S, 1949); V. W. Brooks, *UKCR,* XVI (1950), 187-197; M. Jones, "Balzac aux Étars-Unis," *R. Litt. Comp.,* XXIV (1950), 230-232; Lionel Trilling, *The Liberal Imagination* (VP, 1950); Joseph J. Kwiat, "D and the Graphic Artist," *American Quarterly,* III (1951), 127-141; Florence Leaver, "TD, Beyond Naturalism," *Mark Twain Quarterly,* IX, Winter, 1951, pp. 5-9. There are several pieces about TD in James T. Farrell's *The League of Frightened Philistines* (Vanguard, 1945) and *Literature and Morality* (Vanguard, 1947). *The Book Find News* issued a Dreiser number in March 1946 (Vol. II).

Chapter XVI: In the Second Decade

DOROTHY CANFIELD. Through *The Bent Twig* (1915), DC's novels were published by Ht, thereafter by HB. Biographical material will be found in Sarah N. Cleghorn's autobiography, *Threescore* (Smith & Haas, 1936), and in W. L. Phelps, *Autobiography with Letters* (OUP, 1939). For criticism, see F. Schoenemann, "DC, eine neue Amerikanischer Roman-schriftstellerin," *Lit. Echo,* May 1922, pp. 973-978; Lynn Harold Hough, *The Lion in His Den* (Ass'n. Pr., 1925); Zephine Humphrey, *Woman*

Citizen, X (1926), 13-14; Dorothea L. Mann, *B*ⱪ*m*(NY), LXV (1927), 695-701; Elizabeth Wyckoff, *B*ⱪ*m*(NY), LXXIV (1931), 40-44; J. J. Firebaugh, "DC and the Moral Bent," *Ed. Forum*, XV (1951), 283-294—cf. "Mrs. Fisher Reads Professor Firebaugh," *ibid.*, pp. 294-298.

ELSIE SINGMASTER. Most of ES's fiction, including all the novels, are published by HM. Except for reviews of individual books, the only critical study of importance is Dayton Kohler's, which is listed in the text.

JOSEPH HERGESHEIMER. JH's books are published by K. JH has written of his life, his backgrounds, and himself in *The Presbyterian Child* (1923), *From an Old House* (1925), and "Some Veracious Paragraphs," *B*ⱪ*m*(NY), XLVIII (1919), 8-12. See also Burton Rascoe, "Contemporary Reminiscences," *Arts and Decoration*, XXI, August 1924, p. 36+; Jerome B. Gray, "An Author and His Town," *B*ⱪ*m*(NY), LXVII (1928), 159-164; Carl Van Vechten, "How I Remember JH," *Yale U. Library Gazette*, XXII (1948), 87-92. For JH's attitude toward art, fiction, and his own work, see his introduction to the 1930 edition of *The Three Black Pennys* and the following items by JH: *Hugh Walpole, An Appreciation* (Do, 1919); "The Feminine Nuisance in Literature," *YR*, X (1921), 716-725; "The Profession of Novelist," *NR*, XXX, Spring Lit. Suppl., Apr. 12, 1922, pp. 14, 16; "George Moore," *Lit. R.*, IV (1923), 361-362; "Art," *Am Merc*, IX (1926), 257-263; "James Branch Cabell," *Am Merc*, XIII (1928), 38-47; "Biography and Bibliographies," *Col*, Part VIII (1931); "The Lamentable Trade of Letters," *Am Merc*, XXV (1932), 262-268. The ff. are critical studies of JH: W. Follett, "Factualism versus Impressionism," *Dial*, LXVI (1919), 449-451, and "JH," in *The Borzoi* (K, 1920); H. S. Canby, *Definitions* (HB, 1921); James Branch Cabell, *JH, An Essay in Interpretation* (Chicago, The Bookfellows, 1921); *Straws and Prayer Books* (McB, 1924), and *Some of Us* (McB, 1930); E. Garnett, *Friday Nights* (K, 1923); Llewellyn Jones, *JH, The Man and His Books* (K, 1923); J. W. Beach, *The Outlook for American Prose* (UCP, 1926); H. L. Mencken, *Prejudices*, V (K, 1926); Berthe Gagnot, "Un Romancier Américain: JH," *Revue Anglo-Amér.*, III (1926), 505-510; Upton Sinclair, *Money Writes!* (A. & C. Boni, 1927); H. S. Canby, *American Estimates* (HB, 1929); Sara Haardt, "JH's Methods," *B*ⱪ*m*(NY), LXIX (1929), 398-403; Stephen Graham, *The Death of Yesterday* (Benn, 1930); Geoffrey West, *VQR*, VIII (1932), 95-108; Leon Kelley, *SR*, XL (1932), 171-193; C. Fadiman, "The Best People's Best Novelist," *Nation*, CXXXVI (1933), 175-177—cf. J. W. Krutch, p. 291.

SHERWOOD ANDERSON. SA's first four novels have most recently been published by VP. *Dark Laughter* was published by B&L, *Beyond Desire* by Liveright, and *Kit Brandon* by S. There are two good omnibus collections: *The SA Reader,* ed. Paul Rosenfeld (HM, 1947) and *The Portable SA,* ed. Horace Gregory (VP, 1949), which includes *Poor White.*

SA wrote of his own career in *A Story-Teller's Story* (VP, 1924), in *Tar, A Midwest Childhood* (B & L, 1926), and in *SA's Memoirs* (HB, 1942). See also *SA's Notebook* (B & L, 1926), *The Modern Writer* (Lantern Press, 1926), "On Being Published," *Col,* Part I (1930). Cleveland B. Chase, *SA* (McB, 1927) is a brief, mainly critical study; N. Bryllion Fagin, *The Phenomenon of SA* (Baltimore, The Rossi-Bryn Co., 1927) is able but extremely subjective. Irving Howe's *SA* (Sl, 1951) is an excellent critical and biographical study. James Schevill's *SA, His Life and Work* (U. of Denver Pr., 1951) is fuller on the biographical side. There is a series of biographical articles by W. A. Sutton in *Northwest Ohio Q.,* XIX (1947), 99-114; XX (1948), 20-36; XXII (1949-1950), 39-44, 120-157. See, further, *Berkeley,* No. 1 (1947), pp. 1-4, 30-38; *Newberry Library Bulletin,* Second series, No. 2 (1948), which contains a description of the SA Papers in the Library; and the Sept.-Oct. 1941 number of *Story* (Vol. XIX), a memorial number containing letters and many contributions of biographical and critical value.

For further consideration of SA, mainly critical in character, consult: F. Hackett, *Horizons* (Huebsch, 1918); Nelson A. Crawford, *Midland,* VIII (1922), 297-308; Paul Rosenfeld, *Dial,* LXXII (1922), 29-42; T. K. Whipple, *Lit. R.,* Mar. 11, 1922, pp. 481-482; Alyse Gregory, *Dial,* LXXV (1923), 243-245; Harry Hansen, *Midwest Portraits* (HB, 1923); S. P. B. Mais, *Some Modern Authors* (Grant Richards, 1923); J. Collins, *Taking the Literary Pulse* (Do, 1924); Floyd Dell, *Looking at Life* (K, 1924); Waldo Frank, *Salvos* (B&L, 1924); R. M. Lovett, *EJ,* XIII (1924), 531-539; P. Rosenfeld, *Port of New York* (HB, 1924); V. F. Calverton, *The Newer Spirit* (B&L, 1925); J. Collins, *The Doctor Looks at Biography* (Do, 1925); Carl Van Doren, "Sinclair Lewis and SA," *Ce,* CX (1925), 362-369; J. W. Beach, *The Outlook for American Prose* (UCP, 1926); Stuart Sherman, *Critical Woodcuts* (S, 1926); David C. Alexander, *Letters,* I, Feb. 1928, pp. 23-29; Paul Elmer More, *The Demon of the Absolute* (PUP, 1928); Rebecca West, *The Strange Necessity* (D, 1928); Wyndham Lewis, *Paleface* (Chatto, 1929); Rachel Smith, *SR,* XXXVII (1929), 159-163; Margaret Anderson, *My Thirty Years' War* (Covici-Friede, 1930); C. Fadiman, *Nation,* CXXXV (1932), 454-456; Bernard Faÿ, "Portrait de SA, Américain," *Revue de Paris,* Oct. 15, 1934, pp. 886-902; W. Frank, *In the American Jungle* (FR, 1937); Burton Rascoe, *Before I Forget* (D, 1937); R. M. Lovett, *VQR,* XVII (1941), 379-388; Lionel Trilling, *KR,* III (1941), 293-302; Russell H. Barker, *CE,* III (1941), 293-302; N. B. Fagin, *SAQ,* XLIII (1943),

256-262; L. Trilling, *NYTBR*, Nov. 9, 1947, p. 1+; John T. Flanagan, "The Permanence of SA," *Southwest R.*, XXXV (1950), 170-177.

Chapter XVII: Willa Cather and the Lovely Past

WC's first book, *April Twilights*, was published by Badger (later, 1923, enlarged, by K), her second, *The Troll Garden*, by McClure, Phillips & Co. Her first four novels were published by HM and everything since *My Ántonia* by K. HM published the collected Autograph and Library editions (1937 ff.).

For WC's views on fiction, see *Not Under Forty* (1936) and *Willa Cather on Writing* (1949). See, also, the Prefaces to the 1922 edition of *Alexander's Bridge* and the 1932 edition of *The Song of the Lark*, and "Portrait of the Publisher as a Young Man," in *Alfred A. Knopf: Quarter Century* (Privately printed, 1940), and, in a different vein, "Nebraska: The End of the First Cycle," *Nation*, CXVII (1923), 236-238.

The first book about Willa Cather, René Rapin, *WC* (McB, 1930), has little value. Mildred R. Bennett's *The World of Willa Cather* contains invaluable information about biography, backgrounds, and the sources of stories and characters. Elizabeth Shepley Sergeant's *WC: A Memoir* has been announced by Li for 1952 publication. David Daiches, *WC* (Cornell U. P., 1951) is at present the fullest critical study. See, also, Yvonne Hardy, *L'oeuvre de WC* (Rennes, Imprimeries Obertheir, 1947). James R. Shively's *Writings from WC's Campus Years* (UOP, 1950) sheds light on WC's early development. See, also, Frederick B. Adams, Jr., "WC. Early Years: Trial and Error," *Col*, New Graphic Series, Part III (1939), 89-100, and "WC. Middle Years: The Right Road Taken," *ibid.*, Part IV (1939), pp. 103-108. Other personal data are given in Grant Overton's *The Women Who Make Our Novels*; Burton Rascoe, "Contemporary Reminiscences," *Arts and Decoration*, XX, April 1924, p. 28; Walter F. Tittle, "Glimpses of Interesting Americans," *Ce*, CX (1925), 309-313; Elizabeth Moorhead, *These Too Were Here* (U. of Pittsburgh Pr., 1950).

For critical comment, consult: H. L. Mencken, in *The Borzoi, 1920;* Lloyd Morris, *NAR*, CCXIX (1924), 641-652; Thomas Beer, in *The Borzoi, 1925;* Stuart Sherman, *Critical Woodcuts* (S, 1926); E. S. Sergeant, *Fire Under the Andes* (K, 1927); Rebecca West, *The Strange Necessity* (D, 1928); Henry van Dyke, *The Man Behind the Book* (S, 1929); Pierre Chamaillard, "La Cas de Marian Forrester," *Revue Anglo-Américaine*, VIII (1931), 419-428; L. Kronenberger, *Bkm*(NY), LXXIV (1931), 134-140; C. Fadiman, *Nation*, CXXXV (1932), 563-565; Robert McNamara, "Phases of American Religion in Thornton Wilder and WC," *Cath. World*, CXXXV (1932), 641-649; E. K. Brown,

"WC and the West," *UTQ*, V (1936), 544-566; Margaret Lawrence, *The School of Femininity* (Stokes, 1936); Robert H. Footman, "The Genius of WC," *AL*, X (1938), 123-141; H. M. Jones, *SRL*, XVII, Aug. 6, 1938, pp. 3+; S. V. Benét and Rosemary Benét, *NYHTB*, Dec. 15, 1940, p. 6; Bernard G. Faÿ, "Borrowings from Anatole France by WC and Robert Nathan," *MLN*, LVI (1941), 377; George L. White, Jr., *SR*, L (1942), 18-25; E. K. Brown, "Homage to WC," *YR*, XXXVI (1946), 77-92; H. S. Canby, *SRL*, XXX, May 10, 1947, pp. 22-24; Dayton Kohler, *CE*, IX (1947), 8-18; M. D. Zabel, *Nation*, CLXIV (1947), 713-716; Bernard Baum, "WC's Waste Land," *SAQ*, XLVIII (1949), 589-601; Edward A. and Lillian D. Bloom, "WC's Novels of the Frontier: A Study in Thematic Symbolism," *AL*, XXI (1949), 71-93; H. S. Commager, "Traditionalism in American Literature," *XIX C*, CXLVI (1949), 311-326; J. P. Hinz, "WC: Prairie Spring," *Prairie Schooner*, XXIII (1949), 82-89; Bloom and Bloom, "WC's Novels of the Frontier: The Symbolic Function of 'Machine-Made Materialism,'" *VTQ*, XX (1950), 45-50; E. K. Brown, "WC: The Benjamin D. Hitz Collection," *Newberry Lib. Bull.*, Second series, No. 5 (1950), 158-160; Josephine Jessup, *The Faith of Our Feminists* (Smith, 1950); René Rapin, *Etude de Lettres*, XXIII (1950), 39-50; George Schloss, *Hudson R.*, III (1950), 151-156.

Chapter XVIII: James Branch Cabell: The Anatomy of Romanticism

The Storisende Edition of *The Works of JBC*, 18 vv. (1927-1930), comprising the *Biography of the Life of Manuel* was published by McB, who also published or republished trade editions of all JBC's books up to 1937, with the exception of *The Music From Behind the Moon* (John Day), as well as all books by other writers in this bibliography not otherwise accredited. *Smire* was published by D, books between *Smire* and *There Were Two Pirates* by FR, later books by FSY. The Storisende Prefaces were reprinted in *Preface to the Past* (McB, 1936).

The fullest bibliography is by I. R. Brussel (Philadelphia, Centaur Book Shop, 1932). There are a number of letters by JBC in *Frances Newman's Letters,* ed. Hansell Baugh (Liveright, 1929). John Macy edited a volume of selections, *Between Dawn and Sunrise,* with an introduction (1930).

Carl Van Doren, *JBC* (revised ed., 1932) is the best general study. Don M. Bregenzer and Samuel Loveman (eds.), *A Round Table in Poictesme* (Cleveland, Colophon Club, 1924) is a symposium to which a number of well-known writers contributed. Warren A. McNeill, *Cabellian Harmonics* (RH, 1928) studies C's style. See, also, H. L. Mencken's pamphlet, *JBC* (1927); James P. Cover, *Notes on "Jurgen"* (1928); John P. Cranwell and J. P. Cover, *Notes on "Figures of Earth"* (1929). Joseph Hergesheimer contributed a Preface to the 1920 edition of *Domnei*, Wilson Follett to the 1920 edition of *The Cords of Vanity*, Harold Ward to the 1922 edition of *The Cream of the Jest*, and Edwin Björkman to the 1923 edition of *The Eagle's Shadow*. The ML reprint of *Beyond Life* has an Introduction by Guy Holt.

See the ff. critical articles: W. Follett, *Dial*, LXIV (1918), 392-396; John Gunther, *Bkm*(NY), LII (1920), 200-206; Hugh Walpole, *YR*, IX (1920), 684-698; H. B. Fuller, "One on a Tower," *Freeman*, III (1921), 186-187; R. M. Lovett, *NR*, XXVI (1921), 187-189; E. Björkman, *Lit. Digest Int. Bk. R.*, I, Dec. 1922, pp. 40+; Vincent Starrett, *Buried Caesars* (Covici-McGee, 1923); Aleister Crowley, *Reviewer*, III (1923), 907-914; Percy H. Boynton, *Some Contemporary Americans* (UCP, 1924); Paul Jordan Smith, *On Strange Altars* (A. & C. Boni, 1924); J. W. Beach, *The Outlook for American Prose* (UCP, 1926); Stuart Sherman, *The Main Stream* (S, 1927); J. Hergesheimer, *Am Merc*, XIII (1928), 38-47; E. R. Richardson, "Richmond and Its Writers," *Bkm*(NY), LXVIII (1928), 449-453; Edward N. Hooker, *SR*, XXXVII (1929), 193-203; J. H. Palmer, "JBC, Dualist," *Letters*, II, Feb. 1929, pp. 6-14; Harvey Wickham, *The Impuritans* (Dial Pr., 1929); H. S. Canby, *American Estimates* (HB, 1930); Ellen Glasgow, "The Biography of Manuel," *SRL*, VI (1930), 1108-1109; Clara F. McIntyre, "Mr. C's Cosmos," *SR*, XXXVIII (1930), 278-285; Allan Tate, *NR*, XXXI (1930), 201-202; Gay W. Allen, "Jurgen and Faust," *SR*, XXXIX (1931), 485-492; Harlan Hatcher, "On Not Having Read JBC," *Bkm*(NY), LXXII (1931), 597-599; William R. Parker, "A Key to C," *EJ*, XXI (1932), 431-440; C. Fadiman, *Nation*, CXXXVI (1933), 409-410; N. Nabeshima, "On JBC," *Studies in Eng. Lit.* (Imperial U., Tokyo), XIII (1933), 365-379; V. Pollak, *Die Literatur*, XXXV (1933), 323-325; B. Rascoe, *Prometheans* (P, 1933); Maurice LeBreton, *Revue Anglo-Américaine*, XI (1933-1934), 112-128, 223-237; Leon Howard, "Figures of Allegory," *SR*, XLII (1934), 54-66; E. T. Sehrt, "Die Weltanschauung JBC's," *Englische Studien*, LXXII (1938), 355-399; Paul G. Brewster, "'Jurgen' and 'Figures of Earth' and the Russian Skazki," *AL*, XIII (1942), 305-319; Raymond B. Himelick, "C, Shelley, and the 'Incorrigible Flesh,'" *SAQ*, XLVII (1948), 88-95.

Chapter XIX: Sinclair Lewis and the Babbitt Warren

SL's novels before *Free Air* were published by H; thereafter through *Dodsworth* by HB; thereafter through *Bethel Merriday* by D; and from there on by RH. D also published his *Selected Short Stories* and the play *Jayhawker*, with Lloyd Lewis, both in 1935.

SL furnished a special introduction to the edition of *Main Street* published in 1937 by the Limited Editions Club, with pictures by Grant Wood; see also his "Main Street's Been Paved!" *Nation*, CXIX (1924),

255-260. Other articles by SL are "Self-Conscious America," *Am Merc,* VI (1925), 129-139; "Mr. Lormer and Me," *Nation,* CXXVII (1928), 81; "Breaking into Print," *Col,* N.S. I, No. 2, Winter 1937, pp. 217-221. His first wife, Grace H. Lewis, wrote of him in *Half a Loaf* (Liveright, 1931). *From Main Street to Stockholm: Letters of SL, 1919-1930,* ed. *Harrison Smith* (HB) and *The Man From Main Street: A SL Reader* (RH) have been announced for 1952 publication. There are some SL personalia in Edward F. Murphy, *Yankee Priest* (D, 1952).

For criticism and commentary, see: Archibald Marshall, "Gopher Prairie," *NAR,* CCXV (1922), 394-402; Stuart Sherman, *Points of View* (S, 1924); Oliver Harrison, pseud. Harrison Smith, *SL* (HB, 1925); Grant Overton, *Bkm*(NY), LXI (1925), 179-185; Carl Van Doren, "SL and Sherwood Anderson," *Ce,* CX (1925), 362-369; Louis Wann, "The 'Revolt from the Village' in American Fiction," *Overland,* LXXXIII (1925), 298-299, 324-325; Search-Light, pseud. Waldo Frank, *Time Exposures* (B & L, 1926); Walter Lippmann, *Men of Destiny* (M, 1927); W. J. McNally, "Mr. Babbitt, Meet SL," *Nation,* CXXV (1927), 278-281; Frances T. Russell, "The Young Mr. L," *U. Cal. Chron.,* XXX (1928), 417-428; Michael Williams, *Catholicism and the Modern Mind* (Dial Pr., 1928); F. T. Russell, "The Growing-Up of SL," *U. Cal. Chron.,* XXXII (1930), 319-324; H. L. Binsse and J. J. Trounstine, "Europe Looks at SL," *Bkm*(NY), LXXII (1931), 453-457; H. S. Canby, *Am-Scan. R.,* XIX (1931), 73-76; Christian Gauss, "SL vs. his Education," *SEP,* CCIV, Dec. 26, 1931, pp. 20-21+; Richard Hülsenbeck, *LA,* CCCXXXIX (1931), 479-482; H. M. Jones, *VQR,* VII (1931), 427-432; E. A. Karlfeldt, "SL and the Nobel Prize," *SRL,* VII (1931), 524-525; Lewis Mumford, *Current History,* XXIII (1931), 529-533; Annie R. Marble, *The Nobel Prize Winners in Literature* (ACC, 1932); C. Van Doren, *SL: A Biographical Sketch,* with Bibliography by Harvey Taylor (D, 1932); S. J. Woolf, *Drawn from Life* (Whittlesey House, 1932); F. Mowbray Velte, *Mod. Librarian,* III (1933), pp. 129-134 ff.; W. R. Benét, "The Earlier L," *SRL,* X (1934), 421-422; V. F. Calverton, "SL, The Last of the Literary Liberals," *Mod. Mo.,* VIII (1934), 77-86; C. Van Doren, "The Real SL," *NYHT Mag.,* Feb. 17, 1935, pp. 5+; H. S. Canby, *Seven Years' Harvest* (FR, 1936); E. M. Forster, *Abinger Harvest* (HB, 1936); G. Hicks, "SL and the Good Life," *EJ,* Coll. Ed., XXV (1936), 265-273; J. M. Murry, "The Hell It Can't," *Adelphi,* XI (1936), 321-327; V. F. Calverton, "The Prodigal SL," *Mod. Mo.,* X, Feb. 1938, pp. 11-13+; Lloyd Morris, "SL, His Critics and the Public," *NAR,* CCXLV (1938), 381-390; Joseph E. Baker, "SL, Plato, and the Regional Escape," *EJ,* College Ed., XXVIII (1939), 460-468; Thomas D. Horton, "SL: The Symbol of an Era," *NAR,* CCXLVIII (1940), 474-493; Benjamin Stolbert, *Am Merc,* LIII (1941). 450-460; Leo and Miriam Gurko, "The Two Main Streets of SL," *CE,*

IV (1943), 288-293; Warren Beck, "How Good Is SL?" *CE*, IX (1948), 173-180—cf. Russell Ames, "SL Again," *ibid.*, X (1948), 77-80; Jay Lewis, *Other Men's Minds* (P, 1948); Virginia Woolf, *The Moment and Other Essays* (HB, 1948), pp. 118 ff.; Lewis Gannett, "SL: 'Main Street,'" *SRL*, XXXII, Aug. 6, 1949, pp. 31-32; H. S. Commager, *The American Mind* (YUP, 1950); G. W. Johnson, "Romance and Mr. Babbitt," *NR*, CXXIV, Jan. 29, 1951, pp. 14-15; J. W. Krutch, *Nation*, CLXXII (1951), 179-180; Harrison Smith, "SL: Remembrance of the Past," *SRL*, XXXIV, Jan. 27, 1951, pp. 7-9+.

There has been considerable foreign comment on SL. The following are representative utterances: Fernand Baldesperger, *Correspondant*, CCCI (1925), 835-854; Luc Durtain, *Revue Hebdomadaire*, XXXVIII (1929), 554-564; André Bellessort, *Correspondant*, CCCXXIV (1931), 119-128; Arnold Zweig, *Die Literatur*, XXXIII (1931), 185-186; Bernard Faÿ, *Revue de Paris*, May 15, 1934, pp. 401-416; Leo von Hibler, *Anglia*, LIX (1925), 448-460; R. de Villeneuve, *Mercure de France*, CCLXXX (1937), 286-307; J. Loiseau, *Études Anglaises*, II (1938), 120-133; M. Brion, *Revue de deux Mondes*, Feb. 15, 1951, pp. 723-729; A. Siegfried, *Figaro*, No. 1980, Jan. 19, 1951, pp. 1, 7.

Chapter XX: Ernest Hemingway: Legend and Reality

Except for the anthology *Men at War* (Crown), EH's books are published by S. The ML editions of *The Sun Also Rises* and *A Farewell to Arms* have introductions by H. S. Canby and Ford Madox Ford respectively. The Limited Editions Club *For Whom the Bell Tolls* (1942) has an introduction by Sinclair Lewis and pictures by Lynd Ward.

For bibliography see Louis H. Cohn, *A Bibliography of the Works of EH* (RH, 1931); Lee Samuels, *A Hemingway Check-List* (S, 1951), which lists EH's contributions to periodicals as well as his books, including non-fiction. Cf. L. H. Cohn, "A Note on EH," *Col*, N.S. I (1935), 119-122.

EH's views on literature and many other subjects may be found in *The Green Hills of Africa*.

John K. M. McCaffrey's *EH: The Man and his Work* (World, 1950) is an anthology of critical studies on EH. Materials contained in this anthology are not listed separately hereinafter.

For further criticism, see: L. W. Dodd, "Simple Annals of the Callous," *SRL*, IV (1927), 322-323; Robert Littell, "Notes on H," *NR*, LI (1927), 303-306; E. Wilson, "The Sportsman's Tragedy," *NR*, LIII (1927), 102-103; P. Rosenfeld, *By Way of Art* (CM, 1928); Robert Herrick, "What Is Dirt?" *Bkm*(NY), LXX (1929), 258-262—cf. pp. 641-647; Dorothy Parker, "The Artist's Reward," *New Yorker*, V, Nov. 30, 1929, pp. 28-31; Margaret Anderson, *My Thirty Years' War* (K, 1930); Lewis Galantière, "The Brushwood Boy at the Front," *Hound and*

Horn, III (1930), 259-262; Arthur Dewing, *NAR*, CCXXXII (1931), 364-371; Laurence Leighton, *Hound and Horn*, V (1932), 519-539; R. M. Lovett, *EJ*, XXI (1932), 609-617; Clifton Fadiman, *Nation*, CXXXVI (1933), 63-64; Storm Jameson, "The Craft of the Novelist," *English R*, LVIII (1934), 28-43; Wyndham Lewis, *Men Without Art* (Cassell, 1934); Bernard DeVoto, *Forays and Rebuttals* (LB, 1936); V. F. Calverton, "EH: Primevalite," *Mod. Mo.*, X, Dec. 1937, pp. 6-7; Kenneth Campbell, *Am Merc*, XLIV (1938), 288-291; Hugh Allen, "The Dark Night of EH," *Cath. World*, CL (1940), 522-529; B. DeVoto, *Minority Report* (LB, 1940); David Daiches, *CE*, II (1941), 725-736; Eleanor M. Sickles, "Farewell to Cynicism," *CE*, III (1941), 31-38; M. Cowley, "H and the Hero," *NR*, CXI (1944), 755+; G. Hicks, "Twenty Years of H," *NR*, CXI (1944), 524+; R. B. West, Jr., "EH: Death in the Evening," *Ant R*, IV (1944), 569-580; Lloyd Frankenberg, "Themes and Characters in Hemingway's Latest Period," *SoR*, VII (1942), 776-788; Max Lerner, *Public Journal* (VP, 1946); R. B. West, Jr., "EH: The Failure of Sensibility," *SR*, LIII (1945), 120-135; Robert Daniel, "H and His Heroes," *QQ*, LIV (1948), 471-485; Mario Praz, "H in Italy," *PR*, XV (1948), 1086-1100; D. S. Savage, *Hudson R.*, I (1948), 380-401; Caroline Gordon, "Notes on H and Kafka," *SR*, LVII (1949), 215-226; Francis Hackett, "H: 'A Farewell to Arms,'" *SRL*, XXXII, Aug. 6, 1949, pp. 32-33; Norman Cousins, "H and Steinbeck," *SRL*, XXXIII, Oct. 25, 1950, pp. 26-27; B. R. Redman, "The Champ and the Referees," *ibid.*, pp. 15+; Evelyn Waugh, "The Case of Mr. H," *Commonweal*, LIII (1950), 97-98; Carlos Baker, "The Mountain and the Plain," *VQR*, XXVII (1951), 410-418; J. W. Beach, "How Do You Like It Now, Gentlemen?" *SR*, LIX (1951), 311-328; Harry Levin, "Observations on the Style of EH," *KR*, XIII (1951), 581-609; Isaac Rosenfeld, "A Farewell to Hemingway," *KR*, XIII (1951), 147-155; Ray B. West, Jr., "Three Methods of Modern Fiction," *CE*, XII (1951), 193-203.

Continental criticism may be sampled in: Hans Fallada, *Die Literatur*, XXIII (1931), 672-674; Klaus Mann, *Die Neue Schweitzer Rundschau*, XXIV (1931), 272-277; H. Pieritz, *Hefte für Büchereiwesen*, XVI (1933), 313-316; Jeanine Delpech, *Nouvelles Littéraires*, Apr. 3, 1937, p. 9; Artur Lundkvist, *Bonniers Litterara Magasin*, VIII (1939), 198-204; E. Cecchi, *Mercurio*, II (1945), 111-123.

Chapter XXI: Novelists of the 'Twenties

JOHN DOS PASSOS. Most of JDP's books have now been either published or republished by HM. The ML reprint of *Three Soldiers* has an introduction by JDP. Jack Potter has made *A Bibliography of JDP* (Chicago, Normandie House, 1950). There is a book-length study in German:

Werner Neuse, *Die Literarische Entwicklung von JDP* (Giessen, R. Glagow, 1931). For criticism, consult Alan Calmer, *SR,* XL (1932), 341-349; G. Hicks, *Bkm*(NY), LXXV (1932), 32-42; F. R. Leavis, *Scrutiny,* I (1932), 173-179; Michael Gold, "The Education of JDP," *EJ,* XXII (1933), 87-97; Philippe Soupault, *Europe,* No. 134, Feb. 1934, pp. 282-286; B. DeVoto, *SRL,* XIV (1936), 3+; M. Cowley, "Reviewers on Parade," *NR,* XCIII (1938), 371-372, XCIV (1938), 23-24; Mariano Lattore, "JDP y su última novela," *Atenea,* XV (1938), 216-222; Delmore Schwartz, "JDP and the Whole Truth," *SoR,* IV (1938), 351-367; Mason Wade, *NAR,* CCXIV (1938), 349-367; John Chamberlain, *SRL,* XX, June 3, 1939, p. 3+, reprinted with additions as a pamphlet, *JDP, A Biographical and Critical Essay* (HB, 1939); M. Cowley, "Disillusionment," *NR,* XCIX (1939), 163; James T. Farrell, "DP and the Critics," *AM Merc,* XLVII (1939), 489-494; Robert H. Footman, *SR,* XLVII (1939), 365-382; A. MacLeish, "Post-War Writers and Pre-War Readers," *NR,* CII (1940), 789-790; Margaret Marshall, *Nation,* CL (1940), 15-18; Milton Rugoff, *SR,* XLIX (1941), 453-468; Curtis B. Bradford, *UKCR,* VIII (1942), 267-272; Vincent McHugh, "DP Trilogy Revalued," *NYTBR,* Sept. 5, 1943, p. 8; T. K. Whipple, *Study Out the Land* (U. of Cal. Pr., 1943); J. W. Beach, *SR,* LV (1947), 406-418; Jean-Paul Sartre, *Situation,* I (1947), 14-25; M. Cowley, "Washington Wasn't Like That," *NR,* CXX, Jan. 17, 1949, pp. 23-24, and "DP and his Critics," *NR,* CXX, Feb. 28, 1949 pp. 21-23; G. Hicks, "DP and his Critics," *Am Merc,* LXVIII (1949), 623-630; Irving Howe, "JDP: The Loss of Passion," *Tomorrow,* VIII, March, 1949, pp. 54-57; G. Hicks, "Politics and JDP," *Ant R,* X (1950), 85-98; Martin Kallich, "JDP: Liberty and the Father-Image," *ibid.,* pp. 99-106; Arthur Mizener, "The Novel of Manners in America," *KR,* XII (1950), 1-19; John Lydenberg, "DP and the Ruined Words," *Pac Sp,* V (1951), 316-327; A. Mizener, "The Gullivers of DP," *SRL,* XXXIV, June 30, 1951, pp. 6-7+.

ELIZABETH MADOX ROBERTS. Except for *In the Great Steep's Garden,* all EMR's books were published by VP. The ML reprint (1935) of *The Time of Man* has an introduction by J. Donald Adams. See the following critical estimates: Glenway Wescott, "EMR, A Personal Note," *Bkm*(NY), LXXI (1930), 12-15; Mark Van Doren, "EMR: Her Mind and Style," *EJ,* XXI (1932), 521-528; J. R. Adams, *VQR,* XII (1936), 80-90; F. L. Janney, *SR,* XLV (1937), 388-410. Wescott's article was reprinted in a pamphlet, *EMR, A Personal Note,* etc., which contained also a collection of significant reviews of individual books (VP, 1930); in 1938 the reviews were augmented in another pamphlet in which Wescott was replaced by Adams' *VQR* article above and Rosamond Milner's "EMR in Kentucky," which was reprinted from the *Louisville Courier-Journal.* Mark Van Doren's article is reprinted in his *The*

Private Reader. See, also, Allen Tate, "The EMR Papers," *Lib. Cong. Q. Journal of Current Acquisitions,* I (1943), 29-31.

ELINOR WYLIE. All EW's novels may now be had in *Collected Prose of EW* (K, 1933), where see Prefaces by C. Van Vechten, C. Van Doren, S. V. Benét, W. R. Benét, and Isabel Patterson. There is a biography by her sister, Nancy Hoyt, *EW, The Portrait of an Unknown Lady* (BM, 1935). For further biographical data, see Elizabeth S. Sergeant, *Fire Under the Andes* (K, 1927); Emily Clark, *Innocence Abroad* (K, 1931); C. Van Doren, *Three Worlds* (H, 1936), pp. 215-241; Eunice Tietjens, *The World at My Shoulder* (M, 1938); H. S. Canby, *American Memoir* (HM, 1947); Mary M. Colum, *Life and the Dream* (D, 1947). Critical estimates include Herbert Gorman, "Daughter of Donne," *NAR,* CCXIX (1924), 679-686; Edmund Wilson & M. M. Colum, "In Memory of EW," *NR,* LVII (1929), 316-319; J. B. Cabell, *Some of Us* (McB, 1930); Rebecca West, *Ending in Earnest* (D, 1931); W. R. Benét, *The Prose and Poetry of EW* (Norwood, Mass.: Wheaton College Press, 1934); Osbert Burdett, *Eng. R.,* LIX (1934), 488+; Dayton Kohler, "EW's Heroic Mask," *SAQ,* XXXVI (1937), 218-228.

ROBERT NATHAN. Except for *Peter Kindred* (Duffield), *Autumn* (McB), and *The Puppet Master* (McB), all RN's novels have now been either published or republished by K. *The Barly Fields* (1938) is an omnibus, with introduction by S. V. Benét, which reprints *The Fiddler in Barly, The Woodcutter's House, The Bishop's Wife, The Orchid,* and *There Is Another Heaven.* For criticism, see Rex Smith, "A Master of Fantasy," *Overland Mo.,* Second series, LXXXVII (1929), 41-42; Roberts Tapley, "RN: Poet and Ironist," *Bkm*(NY), LXXV (1932), 607-614; Edith McE. Dorian, "While a Little Dog Dances," *SR,* XLI (1933), 129-140; Ben Ray Redman, "Expert in Depression: A Portrait of RN," *SRL,* XI (1934), 206; Joseph Mersand, *Traditions in American Literature* (Modern Chapbooks, 1939); Elliot G. Fay, "Borrowings from Anatole France by Willa Cather and RN," *MLN,* LVI (1941), 377; Leon Spitz, "RN's Jewish Types," *Am. Hebrew,* CLVIII, Nov. 2, 1948, p. 10+.

THORNTON WILDER. TW's first three novels were published by A. & C. Boni, the other two by H. The ML reprint (1929) of *The Cabala* has an introduction by Herbert Gorman. The following are critical studies: Edmund Wilson, *NR,* LV (1928), 303-305; St. John Adcock, *Bkm*(L), LXXV (1929), 316-319; Pierre Loving, "The Bridge of Casuistry," *This Quarter,* II (1929), 150-161; Henry van Dyke, *The Man Behind the Book* (S, 1929); Michael Gold, "W: Prophet of the Genteel Christ," *NR,* LXIV (1930), 266—cf. "The Economic Interpretation of W," *NR,* LXV (1930), 31-32, and Henry Hazlitt, "Communist Criticism," *Nation,* CXXXI (1930), 583-584; E. G. Twichett, *LM,* XXII (1930), 32-39;

E. Wilson, "Dahlberg, Dos Passos, and W," *NR,* LXII (1930), 156-158; Robert McNamara, "Phases of American Religion in TW and Willa Cather," *Cath. World,* CXXXV (1932), 641-649; E. K. Brown, "A Christian Humanist, TW," *UTQ,* IV (1935), 356-370; Ross Parmenter, "Novelist into Playwright," *SRL,* XVIII (1938), 10-11; Dayton Kohler, *EJ,* Coll. ed., XXVIII (1939), 1-11; Martin Gardner, "TW and the Problem of Providence," *UKCR,* VII (1940), 83-91; J. J. Firebaugh, "The Humanism of TW," *Pac Spect,* IV (1950), 426-438. European criticism is represented by the ff.: Longworth Chambrun, "Le Americanisme de TW," *Revue Anglo-Américaine,* VIII (1931), 341-344; Harry Bergholtz, *Englische Studien,* LXV (1931), 301-304; Walter Tritsch, "TW in Berlin," *LA,* CCCXLI (1931), 44-47; Gregor Heinrich, *Hochland,* 30th Year (1932), pp. 176-180, and *Deutsche Rundschau,* CCXVIII (1934), 62-63; Walther Fischer, "TW's 'The Bridge of San Luis Rey' und Prosper Mérimées 'La Carosse du Saint-Sacrement,'" *Anglia,* LX (1936), 234-240.

Chapter XXII: Novelists of the 'Thirties

THOMAS WOLFE. *Look Homeward, Angel* and *Of Time and the River* were published by S; *The Web and the Rock* and *You Can't Go Home Again* by H. The best introduction to Wolfe is *The Portable Wolfe,* ed. Maxwell Geismar (VP, 1946), which contains selections from all four novels, *The Story of a Novel* complete, and selected short stories.

George L. Preston, Jr. has written *TW, A Bibliography* (N. Y., C. S. Boesen, 1943).

For letters, see *TW's Letters to His Mother, Julia Elizabeth Wolfe* (S, 1943). There is also *A Western Journal* (U. of Pitt. Pr., 1951). Additional letters will be found in *AM,* CLXXVIII, Dec. 1946, pp. 60-66, CLXXIX, Jan. 1947, pp. 39-45, and Feb. 1947, pp. 55-61, CLXXXVI, Nov. 1950, pp. 80-83; *SRL,* XXXI, Feb. 7, 1948, pp. 6-8. Hayden Norwood, *The Marble Man's Wife* (S, 1947) deals with TW's mother.

A brief, specialized biography is Agatha Boyd Adams, *TW, Carolina Student* (UNCP, 1950). There are two brief, book-length critical studies: Herbert J. Muller, *TW* (ND, 1947) and Pamela Hansford Johnson, *Hungry Gulliver, An English Critical Appraisal* (S, 1948). See, further, Daniel L. Delakas, *TW: La France et les romanciers français* (Paris, Jouve, 1950).

A number of TW's friends and acquaintances have recorded their memories of him: Ann Preston Bridges, *SRL,* XI, Apr. 6, 1935, p. 599+; Martha Dodd, *Through Embassy Eyes* (HB, 1939); Theodore G. Ehrsam, *Book-Collector's Journal,* I, June 1936, p. 1+; LeGette Blythe, *SRL,* XXVIII, Aug. 25, 1945, pp. 18-19; Anne W. Armstrong, *Ariz. Q.,* II (1946), 5-15; Ruth Davis, *SRL,* XXIX (1946), p. 13+; L. Ruth

Middlebrook, *Am Merc*, LXIII (1946), 544-549, and LXIV (1947), 413-420; Vardis Fisher, *Tomorrow*, X, Apr. 1951, pp. 24-30. Aline Bernstein's novel, *The Journey Down* (K, 1938) is said to describe George Webber's affair with Esther Jack from the woman's point of view; cf. Claude Simpson, "TW: A Chapter in his Biography," *Southwest R.*, XXV (1940), 308-312. Other biographical articles include William Braswell, "TW Lectures and Takes a Holiday," *CE*, I (1939), 11-22; S. L. Solon, "The Ordeal of TW," *Mod. Q.*, XI, Winter 1939, pp. 45-53; Richard S. Kennedy, "TW at Harvard, 1920-1923," *Harvard Libr. Bull.*, IV (1950), 172-190, 304-319.

For TW's editor at Scribners, Maxwell Perkins, see *Editor to Author: The Letters of Maxwell E. Perkins* (S, 1950) and Perkins's article, "TW," *Harvard Libr. Bull.*, I (1947), 269-277, which is followed by "The Last Letter of TW, and the Reply To It," pp. 278-279, and "The TW Collection of William B. Wisdom," pp. 280-287. See, further: Malcolm Cowley, "Unshaken Friend," *New Yorker*, XX, Apr. 1, 1944, pp. 28-36, and Apr. 8, 1944, pp. 30-43; Harrison Smith, "Midwife to Literature," *SRL*, XXX, July 12, 1947, pp. 15-16; Struthers Burt, "Catalyst of Genius," *SRL*, XXXIV, June 9, 1951, pp. 6-8+; Vardis Fisher, "TW and Maxwell Perkins," *Tomorrow*, X, July 1951, pp. 20-25.

For TW's break with Scribners, see Roger Burlingame, *Of Making Many Books* (S, 1946). TW's Harper editor, Edward Aswell wrote of him in *A Note on TW* (H, 1941) and in *SRL*, XXXI, Nov. 27, 1948, p. 7+; see also TW's *The Hills Beyond*.

See the following critical studies: R. S. Ames, *Am. Spectator*, III, Jan. 1935, pp. 5-6; John D. Wade, *So.R.*, I (1935), 192-198; R. P. Warren, *AR*, V (1935), 191-208; Hamilton Basso, *NR*, LXXXVII (1936), 199-202; H. S. Canby, *Seven Years' Harvest* (FR, 1936); B. DeVoto, *Forays and Rebuttals* (LB, 1936); E. S. Bates, *EJ*, XXVI (1937), 519-527, and in *Mod. Q.*, XI, Autumn 1938, pp. 86-89; Jonathan Daniels, *SRL*, XVIII, Sept. 24, 1938, p. 8+; Dayton Kohler, *CE*, I (1944), 186-192; Henry T. Volkening, *VQR*, XV (1939), 196-215; Carlos Baker, "TW's Apprenticeship," *Delphian Q.*, XXIII (1940), 20-25; E. K. Brown, "TW: Realist and Symbolist," *UTQ*, X (1941), 153-166; T. L. Collins, *SR*, L (1942), 487-504; Bella Kussy, "The Vitalist Trend in TW," *SR*, L (1942), 306-324; Robert Falk, "TW and the Critics," *CE*, V (1944), 186-192; John M. Maclachlan, "Folk Concepts in the Novels of TW," *Southern Folklore Q.*, IX (1945), 28-36; Desmond Powell, *Ariz. Q.*, I (1945), 28-36; M. M. Stearns, "The Metaphysics of TW," *CE*, VI (1945), 193-199; F. I. Carpenter, *UKCR*, XII (1946), 179-187; Franz Schoenberger, *NYTBR*, Aug. 4, 1946, p. 1+; Nathan L. Rothman, "TW and James Joyce: A Study in Literary Influence," in Allen Tate, ed., *A Southern Vanguard* (Prentice-Hall, 1947); B. K. McElderry, Jr., "The Autobiographical Problem in TW's Earlier Novels," *Ariz. Q.*, IV (1948), 315-

324; W. W. Pusey III, "The Germanic Vogue of TW," *Germanic R.,* XXIII (1948), 131-148; T. W. Albrecht, "Time as Unity in TW," *NMQR,* XIX (1949), 320-329; Oscar Cargill, "Gargantua Fills His Skin," *UKCR,* XVI (1949), 20-30; M. Church, "TW: Dark Time," *PMLA,* LXIV (1949), 629-638; Richard Walser, "Some Notes on W's Reputation Abroad," *Carolina Q.,* I, Mar. 1949, pp. 37-41; John R. Heath, *The Strange Case of TW* (Chicago Literary Club, 1949); T. W. Albrecht, "The Titles of 'Look Homeward, Angel,' " etc., *MLQ,* XI (1950), 50-57; N. Cross, "TW: If I Am Not Better," *Pac Spect,* IV, Autumn 1950, pp. 488-496; Betty Thompson, "TW: Two Decades of Criticism," *SAQ,* XLIX (1950), 378-392. *The Southern Packet* issued a TW Memorial Number in April 1948.

ERSKINE CALDWELL. Most of EC's books are published by DSP. There are ML editions of *Tobacco Road* and *God's Little Acre. Cold Caravan* (World, 1946) is an omnibus with an introduction by the author. For critical comment see: Lawrence S. Kubie, " 'God's Little Acre,' An Analysis," *SRL,* XI (1934), 305+; M. E. Coindreau, *Nouvelle Revue Francaise,* XLVII (1936), 908-912; John D. Wade, "Sweet Are the Uses of Degeneracy," *So R,* I (1936), 449-466; Donald Davidson, "EC's Picture Book," *So R,* IV (1938), 15-25; P. A. Carmichael, "Jeeter Lester, Agrarian Par Excellence," *SR,* XLVIII (1940), 21-27; Kenneth Burke, *The Philosophy of Literary Form* (LSUP, 1941); M. Cowley, "The Two EC's," *NR,* CXI (1941), 599-600; J. M. Maclachlan, "Folk and Culture in the Novels of EC," *Southern Folklore Q.,* IX (1945), 93-101; "America's Most Censored Author," *Publishers' Weekly,* CLV (1949), 1960-1961.

WILLIAM FAULKNER. *Soldiers' Pay* and *Mosquitoes* were published by B & L; *Sartoris* by HB; *The Sound and the Fury, As I Lay Dying,* and *Sanctuary* by Cape & Smith; *Light in August* and *Pylon* by Smith & Haas; and everything since by RH, except for *Notes on a Horsethief* (1951), which was published in a limited, signed edition by the Levee Press, Greenville, Mississippi. The fourth through the seventh titles above are available in ML. For bibliography, see Robert W. Daniel, *A Catalogue of the Writings of WF* (YUP, 1942) and Aubrey Starke, "An American Comedy: An Introduction to a Bibliography of WF," *Col,* Part XIX (1934). There is "A Selected Bibliography of Critical Works on WF," by Bradley T. Perry, *UKCR,* XVIII (1951), 159-164. The only book-length study so far is Harry M. Campbell and Ruel E. Foster, *WF, A Critical Appraisal* (UOP, 1951), but F. J. Hoffman and Olga W. Vickery have edited an anthology, *WF: Two Decades of Criticism* (Michigan State College Press, 1951). Articles reprinted in this work are not listed separately in this note.

An excellent introduction to WF is *The Portable F,* ed. Malcolm

Cowley (VP, 1946). The selections have been well chosen to exhibit the Yoknapatawpha saga from 1820 to 1945, and the introduction is a strong statement of the case for WF. To this book and to the articles by Warren Beck my own discussion of WF is heavily indebted.

See, further, H. S. Canby, "The School of Cruelty," *SRL,* VII (1931), 673-674; G. Hicks, *Bkm*(NY), LXXIV (1931), 17-24; Marshal J. Smith, *ibid.,* pp. 411-417; A. R. Thompson, "The Cult of Cruelty," *ibid.,* pp. 477-487; Lawrence S. Kubie, "WF's 'Sanctuary,'" *SRL,* XI (1934), 218; Wyndham Lewis, *Men Without Art* (Cassell, 1934); J. W. Linn and H. W. Taylor, *A Foreword to Fiction* (ACC, 1935), which contains a detailed analysis of *Light in August;* Anthony Buttitta, *SRL,* XVIII, May 21, 1938, pp. 6-8; V. F. Calverton, *Mod. Mo.,* X, Mar. 1938, pp. 11-12; B. DeVoto, *Minority Report* (LB, 1940); Warren Beck, "F and the South," *Ant. R.,* I (1941), 82-94, and "F's Point of View," *CE,* II (1941), 736-749; Delmore Schwartz, *So. R.,* VII (1941), 145-160; Harry M. Campbell, "Experiment and Achievement: 'As I Lay Dying' and 'The Sound and the Fury,'" *SR,* LI (1943), 305-320; John M. Maclachlan, "WF and the Southern Folk," *Southern Folklore Q.,* IX (1945), 153-167; Norman Nicholson, "WF," in E. W. L. Martin, ed., *The New Spirit* (Dobson, 1946); Caroline Gordon, "Notes on F and Flaubert," *Hudson R.,* I (1948), 222, 231; Charles I. Glicksberg, "WF and the Negro Problem," *Phylon,* X (1949), 153-160; Dayton Kohler, "WF and the Social Conscience," *EJ,* XXVIII (1949), 545-553; Anon., "Two American Novelists," *LTLS,* Oct. 27, 1950, pp. 669-670; Francis Downing, *Commonweal,* LIII (1950), 255-258; L. A. Fiedler, "WF: An American Dickens," *Commentary,* IX (1950), 384-387; Tom Greet, "Toward the Light: The Thematic Unity of F's 'Cycle,'" *Carolina Q.,* III (1950), 38-44; Harvey Breit, *PR,* XVIII (1951), 88-94, and *AM,* CLXXXVIII, Oct. 1951, pp. 53-56; Cleanth Brooks, "'Absalom, Absalom': The Definition of Innocence," *SR,* LIX (1951), 543-558; Irving Howe, "WF and the Negroes," *Commentary,* XII (1951), 359-368.

Perspective has devoted two numbers to F: II (1949), 179-254, and III (1950), 179-235.

Foreign criticism may be represented by M. E. Coindreau, *Nouvelle Revue Française,* XIX (1931), 926-931; André Malraux, "Préface à 'Sanctuaire' de WF," *NRF,* XLI (1933), 744-747; Mildred Harnack-Fish, "WF: Eine Amerikanischer Dichter aus grosser Tradition," *Die Literatur,* XXXVIII, Nov. 1935, pp. 64-87; Maurice LeBreton, "Technique et Psychologie chez WF," *Etudes Anglaises,* I (1937), 418-438; J-P. Sartre. "'Sartoris' par WF," *NRF,* XXVI (1938), 323-328; A. Caraceni, *Aretusa,* II (1945), 23-28; A. Gérard, *Revue Nouvelle,* XIII (1951), 81-89; F. Guyard, *Études,* CCLXVIII (1951), 172-183; "Rabi," *Esprit,* XIX (1951), 47-65; G. Visentini, *La Fiera Letteraria,* No. 23, June 10, 1951, p. 1.

HERVEY ALLEN. HA's novels are published by R. To the items noted in the text, add Emily Clark, *SRL*, X (1933), 323.

MARGARET MITCHELL. The principal source of information concerning MM's life and personality is the Margaret Mitchell Memorial Issue of the *Atlanta Historical Bulletin*, IX, No. 34, May 1950. See also: Faith Baldwin, "The Woman Who Wrote 'Gone With the Wind,'" *Pictorial Review*, XXXVIII, May 1937, p. 4+; Edwin Granberry, "The Private Life of MM," *Collier's*, XCIX, Mar. 13, 1937, p. 22+; Duncan Aikman, "The Senseless Killing of MM," *Collier's*, CXXIV, Oct. 22, 1949, p. 20+—cf. Dec. 10, p. 6. For critical comment see: Gilbert E. Govan, "Why 'Gone With the Wind'?" *Library Journal*, LXII (1937), 690-691; Belle Rosenbaum, "Why Do They Read It?" *Scribner's*, CII, Aug. 1937, p. 23; Isabel Ehrlich, "Background for Scarlett O'Hara & Co.," *Wilson Library Bull.*, XIV (1940), 435-437; George R. Clark, *HaM*, CXCVIII, Feb. 1949, pp. 97-98.

KENNETH ROBERTS. KR's books are all published by D. *The KR Reader* (1945) contains selections from both fiction and essays. *I Wanted to Write* (1949) is a very interesting record of how the novels have been made; see, further, *For Authors Only and Other Gloomy Essays* (1935). D have published two useful composite pamphlets: *KR: A Biographical Sketch, An Informal Study, His Books and Critical Opinions* (1936) and *KR, An American Novelist* (1938). See also Ben Ames Williams, *SRL*, XVIII, June 25, 1938, pp. 8-10; Carlos Baker, "The Novel and History," *Delphian Q.*, XXIV (1941), 15-20.

ESTHER FORBES. *Paradise* and *The General's Lady* are published by HB, all the other books by HM. Miss Forbes has discussed historical fiction very ably in "Why the Past?" in Dale Warren's *What Is a Book?* (HM, 1935), and in "Historical Novels," *SRL*, XXXII, Apr. 23, 1949, pp. 7-9. See, also, D. Warren, "EF and the World She Lives In," *Publishers' Weekly*, CXLV (1944), 1844-1845.

HOWARD FAST. HF's early books were published by various publishers; from 1941 to 1947 he was published by DSP, thereafter by LB. He has expressed his own views about fiction in *Literature and Reality* (International Publishers, 1950). See G. Hicks, *CE*, VII (1945), 1-6.

AUGUST DERLETH. Most of AD's novels were originally published by S but have now been taken over by Stanton and Lee, Sauk City, Wisconsin.

CONRAD RICHTER. CR is published by K. See his "The Early American Quality," *AM*, CLXXXVI, Sept. 1950, pp. 26-30; Dayton Kohler, "CR: Early Americana," *CE*, VIII (1947), 221-227; and F. I. Carpenter, "CR's Pioneers, Reality and Myth," *CE*, XII (1950), 77-82.

JOHN P. MARQUAND. JPM is published by LB. See: Harlan Hatcher, *CE*, I (1939), 107-118; S. V. Benét and Rosemary Benét, *NYHTB*, Mar. 16, 1941, p. 5; Anon., *Newsweek*, XXXIII, Mar. 7, 1949, p. 94+; Anon., "Spencer Street Boy," *Time*, LIII, Mar. 7, 1949, p. 104+; Nathan Glick, "M's Vanishing American Aristocracy; Good Manners and the Good Life," *Commentary*, IX (1950), 435-441; G. Hicks, "M of Newburyport," *HaM*, CC (1950), 101-108.

JOHN STEINBECK. Most of JS's novels have now been either published or republished by VP. A good introduction is *The Portable S*, edited by Pascal Covici, with introduction by Lewis Gannett, enlarged edition (1946). This book contains *Of Mice and Men*, selections from other novels, short stories, etc. The ML edition of *Tortilla Flat* has an introduction by JS. Joseph Henry Jackson contributed introductions to the ML edition of *Of Mice and Men* and to the edition of *The Grapes of Wrath* illustrated by Thomas Hart Benton and published by the Limited Editions Club and the Heritage Press (1940). For bibliography see L. C. Powell, *Col*, N.S. III (1938), 558-568, and Lewis Gannett, *JS, Personal and Bibliographical Notes, a pamphlet* (VP, 1939). The pioneer study in book form is Harry T. Moore, *The Novels of JS: A First Critical Study* (Chicago, Normandie House, 1939), which contains material derived direct from JS.

   For general critical commentary, see: Ben Abramson, *Reading & Collecting*, I, Dec. 1936, pp. 4-5+; J. H. Jackson, *SRL*, XVI, Sept. 25, 1937, p. 11+; E. C. Richards, *NAR*, CCXLIII (1937), 406-413; Robert Bennett, *The Wrath of JS, or St. John Gone to Church* (Los Angeles, Albertson Pr., 1939); V. F. Calverton, "JS: Fulfilment without Promise," *Mod. Mo.*, X, June 1938, pp. 11-12+; Anon., "S of California," *Delphian Q.*, XXIII (1940), 40-45; Howard Baker, "In Praise of the Novel," *SoR*, V (1940), V (1940), 778-800; Claude E. Jones, "Proletarian Writing and JS," *SR*, XLVIII (1940), 445-456; Edmund Wilson, *The Boys in the Back Room* (San Francisco, Colt Pr., 1941); Lidia Besouchet, "Amando Fontes y S," *Nosotros*, VII (1942), 322-325; Baker Fairley, "JS and the Coming Literature," *SR*, L (1942), 145-161; Lincoln R. Gibbs, "JS, Moralist," *Ant R*, II (1942), 172-184; Stanley E. Hyman, "Some Notes on JS," *ibid.*, pp. 185-200; Carlos Baker, " 'In Dubious Battle' Revalued," *NYTBR*, July 25, 1943, p. 4+; T. K. Whipple, *Study Out the Land* (U. of Cal. Pr., 1943); S. Rosati, *La Nuova Europa*, II (1945), 31; Freeman Champney, "JS, Californian," *Ant R*, VII (1947), 345-362; Marie Forestier, *La Revue Nouvelle*, V (1947), 253-261; Donald Weeks, *Pac. Spect.*, I (1947), 447-457; Frederick Bracher, "S and the Biological View of Man," *Pac Spect*, II (1948), 14-29; Blake Nevius, "S: One Aspect," *Pac Spect*, III (1949), 302-310.

   On the special topic of the controversies inspired by *The Grapes of*

Wrath, see Marshall V. Hartranft, *Grapes of Gladness, California's Refreshing and Inspiring Answer to JS's "Grapes of Wrath"* (Los Angeles, De Vorse & Co., 1939); George T. Miron, *The Truth About JS and the Migrants* (Los Angeles, Privately printed, 1939); Frank J. Taylor, "California's 'Grapes of Wrath,'" *Forum,* CII (1939), 232-238. Consult, also, Martin S. Shockley, "The Reception of 'The Grapes of Wrath' in Oklahoma," *AL,* XV (1941), 251-261, and see JS's own earlier article on a related theme, "Dubious Battle in California," *Nation,* CXLIII (1936), 302-304. B. R. McElderry, Jr. studies the novel "In the Light of Modern Critical Theory," *CE,* V (1944), 308-313.

Chapter XXIII: A Note on the Fiction of the 1940's and After

Most of the bibliographical references for this chapter have been given in the text.

ROBERT PENN WARREN's first novel, *Night Rider,* was published by HM, the next two by HB, and *World Enough and Time* by RH. There are critical discussions of his novels by Joseph E. Baker, "Irony in Fiction: 'All the King's Men,'" *CE,* IX (1947), 122-130; Oscar Cargill, "Anatomist of Monsters," *CE,* IX (1947), 1-8; Robert B. Heilman, "Melpomene as Wallflower; or The Reading of Tragedy," *SR,* LV (1947), 154-166; Eric Bentley, "The Meaning of RPW's Novels," *KR,* X (1948), 407-424; Charles Humboldt, "The Lost Cause of RPW," *Masses & Mainstream,* I, July 1948, pp. 8-20; W. M. Frohock, "Mr. W's Albatross," *Southwest Review,* XXXVI (1951), 48-59; Peter Viereck, "RPW: The Symbolic Journey," *UKCR* XVII (1951), 279-285.

GERALD WARNER BRACE's first three novels were published by P, the others by Norton.

JOHN HERSEY is published by K. For his own literary aims, see his article, "The Novel of Contemporary History," *AM,* CLXXXIV, Nov. 1949, pp. 80+. For criticism, see Kelsey Guilfoil, *EJ,* XXXIX (1950), 355-360.

INDEX OF NAMES

Excluding characters of fiction, and, generally, critics and biographers cited in footnotes and bibliographical references. The principal reference for authors whose work is considered in this book is in italics; the symbol b, following a number, indicates bibliography.

INDEX OF TITLES

The titles of some works mentioned but not discussed in this volume are excluded from this index. The index includes only a selection from the works mentioned in the Appendix.